CRITICAL TERMS *for* RELIGIOUS STUDIES

CRITICAL TERMS *for* RELIGIOUS STUDIES

Second Edition

Edited by

SARAH HAMMERSCHLAG

Editorial Advisory Board

Alireza Doostdar, Benjamin H. Dunning,
Constance M. Furey, Amy Hollywood,
Terrence L. Johnson, James Robson, Noah Salomon

THE UNIVERSITY OF CHICAGO PRESS
Chicago and London

The University of Chicago Press, Chicago 60637
The University of Chicago Press, Ltd., London

Published 2025
Printed in the United States of America

34 33 32 31 30 29 28 27 26 25   1 2 3 4 5

ISBN-13: 978-0-226-72090-6 (cloth)
ISBN-13: 978-0-226-83985-1 (paper)
ISBN-13: 978-0-226-83986-8 (e-book)
DOI: https://doi.org/10.7208/chicago/9780226839868.001.0001

Library of Congress Cataloging-in-Publication Data

Names: Hammerschlag, Sarah, editor.
Title: Critical terms for religious studies / edited by Sarah Hammerschlag ; Alireza Doostdar [and six others]
Description: Second edition. | Chicago : The University of Chicago Press, 2025. | Includes bibliographical references and index.
Identifiers: LCCN 2024041082 | ISBN 9780226720906 (cloth) | ISBN 9780226839851 (paperback) | ISBN 9780226839868 (ebook)
Subjects: LCSH: Religion—Terminology.
Classification: LCC BL31 .C75 2025 | DDC 210.1/4—dc23/eng/20241011
LC record available at https://lccn.loc.gov/2024041082

♾ This paper meets the requirements of ANSI/NISO Z39.48-1992 (Permanence of Paper).

Contents

INTRODUCTION

Sarah Hammerschlag

Many years ago, as a graduate student, I first encountered Walter Benjamin's now famous aphorism from the *Arcades Project*: "My thinking relates to theology like blotter to ink. It is completely saturated with it. But if it were up to the blotting paper, nothing that is written would remain" (Benjamin 1999, 471). At the time, I was flummoxed by it. His thinking, I thought, is saturated by theology, but the ink remains illegible? Comparable to the blotter, rather than the ink? Thinking is figured as a passive space, absorbing leftover ink from the paper where the real writing must have occurred. And the real writing doesn't even appear in the image! Twenty years later, I must admit, I hardly ever use a pen, let alone an ink blotter, but the image seems more pertinent to me than ever, and strangely much clearer to me than it once was. Perhaps it is because I now recognize myself and those around me as more absorptive than spontaneous, shaped and formed in our beliefs and commitments by our actions and environment, rather than as purely agential actors putting our imprint upon the world. It is my career in religious studies that has allowed me to see myself as such, half a lifetime of reading. But this is not merely a vocational disposition; rather, this view of my social and cultural embeddedness reflects a set of shared commitments evident in recent scholarship in religious studies, across various methods and traditions. Indeed, if there is one common feature that unifies the field, it is this recognition of the powerful persistence of religious traditions, not as something static or transcendent, but as accruing, contingent, shape-shifting forces of authority that permeate the present as much as the past.

For this very reason, the *Critical Terms* series was made for religious studies, and religious studies for this series. This is not because, as it may appear at first glance, *Critical Terms* is a kind of handbook. If that were the case, we would have chosen terms that could provide a ready-made vocabulary for work in the field. In fact, you will find very few terms in this volume that belong to any one religious lexicon, or that claim on a meta-level to easily synthesize or organize multiple traditions. Rather, this volume is a volume of *Critical Terms* because its entries reveal how the language we so often use unthinkingly in our common parlance is itself saturated with the history of religion. Its terms, assembled in collaboration with an advisory committee, were selected to reveal key cultural sites in which that influence is crucial. To say that they are "critical terms" means both that these are terms whose force and influence in our current moment is pervasive—terms such as identity, race, sex, catastrophe, power, and money—and that the task of thinking through them can reveal the ways in which religions are embedded in and shaped by material, social, economic, and political realities.

No doubt many who maintain their tradition and pass it forward, who socialize within its boundaries, make decisions by means of it, and organize their identity around it, have known all along that religion is not merely, or even primarily, a spiritual affair. While religious studies scholars have often made the distinction between a realist approach—treating religion as something that should be taken as real or true—and an approach that suggests that one should bracket off those claims in examining how religion functions, these essays show that such a distinction does not always make sense even to the religious practitioner, because truth-claims are often not the most urgent concerns at hand. Rather, the process of adjudication, whether legal or practical, often involves multiple questions and demands. Whether we can determine the reality of an ultimate authority is only one question among others. When a glut of expired baby food is hoarded amidst a food scarcity crisis, in Noah Salomon's essay on *shari'a* in contemporary Lebanon, an economic crisis reveals "law's normative plurality" emerging from international, state, communal, and religious bodies, its sources of authority stemming from different modes of power and its influence polyvalent (Salomon, chapter 8). When the clay figure of a God has to be replaced by a Tamil Potter priest, there is the question of whether the God will agree to be reseated in a new clay vessel, but there is also the question of the quality and availability of clay given recent government environmental preservation policies in India. As Matthew Engelke writes in his chapter on matter, such "stuff is also the religion" (Engelke, chapter 10). In tension with any secularization thesis, it may even be the case that late capitalism has further increased the imbrication of economic factors and religious life, as Andrea R. Jain illustrates in her essay on "money," in which she considers the yoga industry as one particularly glaring case of this transformation.

Religion does not appear in the essays collected here as a distinct area of life. It does not take place only in megachurches and mosques, it is not easily cordoned off or self-contained. Rather, it permeates the kitchen in Elizabeth Pérez's essay on practice, the classroom in Alireza Doostdar's on reason, the computer screen in Christopher G. White's essay on (virtual) reality. This is true certainly for the anthropologists of religion represented in the volume, but it is equally true for the philosophers of religion, theologians, and historians represented here. The philosopher of religion Mary-Jane Rubenstein reminds us in her essay on nature that the very way we see a tree has already been infused by our religious history, and this in turn impacts how we see our own bodies, treat the sexes, and racialize nations. The New Testament scholar Benjamin H. Dunning, drawing on biblical sources, Greek and Roman sources, as well as more recent attempts to legislate sexual behavior in the modern courts, shows us both how biblical texts are used in the present to collapse historical distance about sex and gender and how the scholarly study of ancient texts stymies such efforts (Dunning, chapter 21). Levi McLaughlin's essay on "catastrophe" shows how this concept has itself been co-constitutive with the formation of religious responses, suggesting as well that how, when, and to what effect it gets mobilized has grave consequences for our capacity to respond (McLaughlin, chapter 1).

Terms that are deemed critical here are revealed by these essays in their persistence and malleability. It is because they have played multivalent and sometimes shifting roles in the study of religion that they require both historicization and reevaluation. What makes them critical and worthy of attention is how tracking these changes in meaning reveals the forces at work in the history of religions. This is the case with my own essay on "fetish," which attempts to restore to a term so often used uncritically its multifaceted history within the comparative study of religion (Hammerschlag, chapter 5). It is equally the case with Constance M. Furey's essay on "faith," which upends the assumption that faith is "synonymous with good religion," arguing instead for a more expansive definition that reveals its relational dynamic and its function across multiple religious traditions (Furey, chapter 3).

Despite their investments in different methods, traditions, and periods, so many of these essays involve a concern for the historical contingency of our categories and an inquiry into how that contingency impacts their subsequent transcendental potential. What does it mean to apply a term generated in the context of one tradition to talk about another? How can we engage in comparison without asking our language to transcend its original context? These are questions religion scholars must ask even about the supposedly delimiting object of their scholarship.

It has now been over twenty-five years since the coherence of the category and its complicity with colonialism and the spread of "globalatinization" emerged as major topics within the field (Fitzgerald 2003; McCutcheon 1995; Derrida 1996, 79). While the last quarter century of scholarship has not brought closure to the debate over the usefulness of the category (see Miller 2022; and Lofton, chapter 20), it has given us a host of new approaches, new questions, and new insights by which to examine this contested space. Since the publication of J. Z. Smith's landmark essay "Religion, Religions, Religious," published in the first edition of *Critical Terms for Religious Studies* (note how many authors in this volume reference this now classic essay), scholars and students alike have been asking how to respond to religion's "second-order" status, considering whether conceding the term blocks or helps foster intercultural dialogue (Josephson 2012; Batnitzky 2011; Sullivan 2018; Masuzawa 2005).

This is not to say that the study of religion is singular in asking after the culturally conditioned quality of its categories. Since the rise of the genealogical method following Michel Foucault, who was following Friedrich Nietzsche, the humanities and social sciences have traced the contingent origin and constructed nature of countless concepts once thought to be universal, whether by biological or philosophical criteria, and the consequences of such investigations have been far-reaching, altering our relationship to gender, race, and even the concept of the human (Butler [1990] 2006; Haraway 2007; Wynter 1994; Jackson 2020). While literature, art, and philosophy are no less subject to such analyses than religion, the genealogical method is particularly crucial to the study of religion, as Ryan Coyne shows in his essay on memory, because of the temptation to think of religion—as opposed to literature, art, and philosophy—as a thing of the past and to attempt to forge a space of value neutrality for the scholar in the present (Coyne, chapter 11). Unearthing these assumptions has constituted much of the crucial work of recent decades in the field but has also sometimes led to the assumption that emancipation can be achieved by looking elsewhere, to the traditions of others. Such a move risks the romantic assumption that there are traditions somehow exempt from the impulse toward domination, or even the workings of power, when in fact what Foucault argues most importantly is that power "comes from everywhere," is "multiple, productive, relational—in a word . . . polymorphous" (see Hollywood, chapter 15).

Studies of religion have nonetheless been instrumental to the task of "provincializing Europe" (Chakrabarty 2000), not only by revealing the particular intellectual and historical traditions at stake in ideas and ideals claimed to be universal but also by unearthing alternative ways to conceive of agency and action that emerge from the world's traditions and from cultural interactions between them (Keane 2007; Asad 1993). This is very much the work of Elizabeth Pérez's essay on "practice," which provides us with a detailed history of the term and its changing resonance in the field while also helping us to see how an emphasis on "salvific heroism" in the study of religion has stymied our ability "to realize the significance of everyday gendered and racialized work in theorizing religion" (Pérez, chapter 16).

If thirty years ago the field of religion was very much wrapped up in a reckoning with Christianity's long shadow, it is now in a position to redirect the angle of light, and thus to reveal how other traditions conceive of concepts such as life, mind, reason, law, and faith—to name a few treated in this volume (Taylor 1998). When examined in unexpected contexts, these terms have the power not only to reveal the otherwise invisible markings of Christian cultural influence on our thinking but to stymie it, and in the process change our very presumptions about the limits and parameters of human existence and sociality. Rafael Rachel Neis's essay on "life," for example, reveals how rabbinic texts in their multivocality can complicate dualist thinking, emphasizing the messiness of generation and persistence, even blurring the boundaries between the human and the nonhuman (Neis, chapter 9). Alireza Doostdar, drawing on the Qur'an, an Iranian textbook, and the medieval Muslim philosopher and mystic Shihabuddin Suhrawardi, as well as the philosopher Ian Hacking, reframes our conception of reason from something universal and a priori toward a conception of it as socially embedded and variable, involving a variety of styles and aimed toward world-sharing and indeed world-shaping (Doostdar, chapter 19). Dan Arnold's essay on "mind" puts in conversation first-century Buddhist texts on karma and reincarnation with contemporary arguments coming out of neuroscience, such as Pascal Boyer's *Religion Explained* (2001) and Daniel Dennett's *Brainstorms* (1981), to talk back to reductionist arguments that attempt to reduce religion to irrational forms of primitive belief, arguing instead that it is co-constitutive with the very concept of mind (Arnold, chapter 12).

It is built into the idea of cultural comparison, constitutive thus of even the earliest attempts at comparing religions, that such an endeavor could serve as a means toward self-reflection and enhance our capacity to understand others. Going as far back, perhaps, as the twelfth century, to Ibn Tufail's *Hayy Ibn Yaqqdan*, and certainly to the sixteenth- and seventeenth-century arguments that human knowledge of God represents a natural rational proclivity, the study of religion has held a pivotal position for evaluating the universality versus contingency of our philosophical categories. But the emphasis was in the opposite direction. Claims for the universality of religion were first thought to be the foundation for cultural tolerance. If all of humankind was given the capacity to know God, then this represented both a shared capacity for reason and an eternal felicity. While such claims often entail the justification of one tradition over another in its representation of divine truth, the debate itself also provided a playing field, often unlevel, for cultural negotiation between traditions. It was a game modern Jewish thinkers were invited to play in Enlightenment Europe and after, and the question remains whether it was detrimental or constructive to their cause (Mufti 2007; Arendt [1932] 2007; Asad 1993, 306). Religion could be a lever of discrimination, but it could also function as a call to conscience. Terrence L. Johnson, for example, in his essay on "race," reminds us that in the American context, African American religion, itself a fusion of traditions, has provided "new epistemic terrains" to create counter-discourses to combat anti-Blackness reaching all the way back to the early nineteenth-century activist Maria Stewart (Johnson, chapter 17).

Nonetheless, recent scholars have shown how the developmental taxonomies of human culture that resulted from early comparison between traditions served as a pretext for centuries of colonization and the development of racialized capitalism (Robinson [1983] 2021; Masuzawa 2005; Chidester 2014). This realization has encouraged a host of new studies concerning not only the complicity of the study of religion with the development of empire but also and equally its role in the invention of race (see Carter 2008; Vial 2016; Heng 2018). As Eleanor Craig shows in her essay on "identity," it was sometimes the very resistance to the defining terms of religion among cultures encountered by colonizing forces that helped sharpen the categories of race and religion in efforts to maintain and enforce clean and clear taxonomies of development (Craig, chapter 6).

It is also this process of cultural comparison that helped shape so many of the human sciences that now make up the academy. Following Hume's 1757 *Natural History of Religion*, which sought to locate religion's origins in non- or pre-rational causes, subsequent investigations to explain religion, or explain it away, were themselves instrumental to the founding of major schools of knowledge within the social sciences, including sociology. As Amy Hollywood puts it in her essay on "power," "Each theory of religion, a theory by means of which the putative object of analysis [was] displaced in favor of the central theoretical construct of the new field, [was] indispensable to justifying that field's methods of analysis" (Hollywood, chapter 15). Thus, the critical examination of the foundational texts of the discipline such as Durkheim's *Elementary Forms* and Freud's *Totem and Taboo*, as well as earlier philosophical and political sources, including Kant's *Critiques* and *Lectures on Anthropology*, Hegel's *Lectures on the Philosophy of Religion*, and Hobbes's *Leviathan*—that is to say, their reevaluation as instruments of empire and documents reflecting class and racial anxiety (Matory 2018; Slavet 2009; Morris 2017; Vial 2016)—is equally crucial to the future of religious studies and has important repercussions beyond the field.

It is the task of religious studies thus not only to reexamine the foundational texts of its own discipline but to solicit other fields of knowledge toward investigating their own religious and theological underpinnings. This reckoning with our theologically saturated present and its effacement in the guise of modern neoliberalism turns the tables on the question of whether religion is a viable category, and religious studies thus a viable field of knowledge, for it reveals the centrality of the field to so many of the major questions of our current moment—everything from race and the processes of decolonization to climate change and the Anthropocene.

Positioned in many ways between philosophy and anthropology, and in constant conversation with literary studies, art history, and cultural theory, religious studies has the capacity to historicize and contextualize philosophical debates about the nature and history of reason (Doostdar), to reframe our conception of textuality in light of its relation to biblical interpretation (Catlin), and to reorient our relation to sound (Harkness) and image (Robson). James Robson's essay on "image" and Nicholas Harkness's on "sound" treat two of the most ubiquitous of phenomena yet reveal how the intersection of religious studies with these universal human experiences isolates crucial features and allows us to see and hear differently and sometimes better, both because of and despite the fact that some religious traditions have at times treated as controversial the most basic human attempts at representation.

The position of religious studies between the humanities and social sciences entails its fruitful cross-pollination with neighboring fields. Nancy Khalek's essay on "feeling" shows, for example, how recent emphasis on the affect and embodiment in the humanities can have significant ramifications for the reexamination of religious life even when text is our primary means of study (Khalek, chapter 4). Sarah Imhoff's essay on "disability" opens with the case of the Hebrew Bible book of Leviticus, in which exclusion can indeed appear to be the name of the game. And yet she shows that the presupposition that religion is hostile to disability studies has often blocked explorations of the fields' fruitful intersections, a presumption her own essay seeks to remedy (Imhoff, chapter 2).

As is (I hope) evident from some of the brief and by no means exhaustive summaries I have offered here by way of introduction, this volume makes a claim for some features that distinguish the study of religion today: a common conviction about the persistent influence and relevance of religious traditions, a shared resistance to explaining them away, a genealogical interest in revealing the contingencies of our cultural categories and investigating their sources, and a commitment nonetheless to cross-cultural study. It reveals as well an enormous variety not only in terms of tradition and method but indeed concerning how the object of the field is constituted.

It has been nearly twenty-five years since the last edition of *Critical Terms for Religious Studies* was published. In that time some of its essays have become classics, retaining their relevance for a new millennium. It is also fair to say that in that time we have turned the page on some of the debates that were crucial a quarter of a century ago. No one is shocked any longer at the failure of the secularization thesis. We have become much better at recognizing where and how Christian assumptions clothe themselves in false claims of universality or value neutrality. Global warming is no longer an issue for theoretical debate but a reality that inflects our actions and indeed our apprehension of religious concepts such as apocalypse and catastrophe, and scholarship across the humanities and social sciences has turned a corner toward addressing the hegemonic reign of Eurocentrism, both by vastly expanding the range of texts and phenomena under examination and by bringing new critical insight to texts once treated as canonical in the traditional sense.

At the same time, there is renewed anxiety about the relevance of the humanities, as well as legitimate fear about the elimination of whole fields of humanistic study from university curricula. In these conversations, the study of religion can sometimes feel like an appendix, an easily snipped organ, whose loss would have little impact on the health of the university body. If anything, this volume exhibits, quite to the contrary, why and how the study of religion is not just relevant but foundational to the cultural questions being asked across the globe. If the publication of J. Z. Smith's essay "Religion, Religions, Religious" occasioned new conversations about whether the term itself was worthy of preservation, I hope that this volume, without resolving its complexities, clarifies the crucial nature of both the field and the term as one that encapsulates a fraught history.

As Kathryn Lofton puts it in her essay on "religion," the term itself is "a fighting term. . . . [T]he only acceptable definitions of religion are those that acknowledge the imperative of such pugilism" (Lofton, chapter 20). In her emphasis on contestation, Lofton reveals how the study of religion—at its best—can help us see even the most mundane of interactions as invested by religion's history, modes of power, and forms of relation and can teach us how to recognize them better.

If the volume, with its multiple authors, perspectives, and theoretical approaches, has one point to make, it is that attention to that history, and to the force traditions still exert on our thinking and action, can only make us better scholars, teachers, and students. The exercise of recognizing this process does not end, as Lofton reminds us, when we leave the classroom.

Suggested Readings

Asad, Talal. 1993. *Genealogies of Religion*. Baltimore, MD: Johns Hopkins University Press.

Carter, J. Kameron. 2008. *Race: A Theological Account*. Durham, NC: Duke University Press.

Chakrabarty, Dipesh. 2000. *Provincializing Europe: Postcolonial Thought and Historical Difference*. Princeton, NJ: Princeton University Press.

Chidester, David. 2014. *Empire of Religion*. Chicago: University of Chicago Press.

Derrida, Jacques. 1996. *Acts of Religion*. Edited and with an introduction by Gil Anidjar. New York: Routledge.

Furey, Constance, Sarah Hammerschlag, and Amy Hollywood. 2021. *Devotion: Three Essays on Religion, Literature, and Political Imagination*. Chicago: University of Chicago Press.

Jackson, Zakkiyah Iman. 2020. *Matter and Meaning in an Antiblack World*. New York: NYU Press.

Keane, Webb. 2006. *Christian Moderns*. Berkeley: University of California Press.

Lofton, Kathryn. 2017. *Consuming Religion*. Chicago: University of Chicago Press.

Masuzawa, Tomoko. 2005. *The Invention of World Religions*. Chicago: University of Chicago Press.

Mahmood, Saba. 2004. *Politics of Piety*. Princeton, NJ: Princeton University Press.

Mufti, Aamir. 2007. *Enlightenment in the Colony*. Princeton, NJ: Princeton University Press.

References

Arendt, Hannah. [1932] 2007. "The Enlightenment and the Jewish Question." In *The Jewish Writings*, edited by Jerome Kohn and Ron H. Feldman. New York: Schocken Books.

Asad, Talal. 1993. *Genealogies of Religion*. Baltimore, MD: Johns Hopkins University Press.

Batnitzky, Leora. 2011. *How Judaism Became a Religion*. Princeton, NJ: Princeton University Press.

Benjamin, Walter. 1999. *The Arcades Project*. Translated by Howard Eiland and Kevin McLaughlin. Cambridge, MA: The Belknap Press of Harvard University Press.

Boyer, Pascal. 2001. *Religion Explained: The Evolutionary Origins of Religious Thought*. New York: Basic Books.

Butler, Judith. [1990] 2006. *Gender Trouble*. New York: Routledge.

Carter, J. Kameron. 2008. *Race: A Theological Account*. Durham, NC: Duke University Press.

Chakrabarty, Dipesh. 2000. *Provincializing Europe: Postcolonial Thought and Historical Difference*. Princeton, NJ: Princeton University Press.

Chidester, David. 2014. *Empire of Religion*. Chicago: University of Chicago Press.

Dennett, Daniel. 1981. *Brainstorms: Philosophical Essays on Mind and Psychology*. Cambridge, MA: MIT Press.

Derrida, Jacques. 1996. *Acts of Religion*. Edited and with an introduction by Gil Anidjar. New York: Routledge.

Durkheim, Émile. 1995. *The Elementary Forms of Religious Life*. Translated by Karen E. Fields. New York: Free Press.

Fitzgerald, Timothy. 2003. *The Ideology of Religious Studies*. Oxford: Oxford University Press.

Freud, Sigmund. [1913] 1990. *Totem and Taboo*. Edited by James Stratchey. New York: Norton.

Haraway, Donna. 2007. *When Species Meet*. Minneapolis: University of Minnesota Press.

Hegel, G. W. F. 1988. *Lectures on the Philosophy of Religion: One Volume Edition—*

The Lectures of 1827. Edited by Peter C. Hodgson. Berkeley: University of California Press.

Heng, Geraldine. 2018. *The Invention of Race in the European Middle Ages*. Cambridge: Cambridge University Press.

Hobbes, Thomas. [1651] 2017. *Leviathan*. New York: Penguin.

Ibn Tufayl, Mohammed. 2009. *Hayy Ibn Yaqzan: A Philosophical Tale*. Translated and with an introduction by Lenn Evan Goodman. Chicago: University of Chicago Press.

Jackson, Zakkiyah Iman. 2020. *Matter and Meaning in an Antiblack World*. New York: NYU Press.

Josephson, Jason. 2012. *The Invention of Religion in Japan*. Chicago: University of Chicago Press.

Kant, Immanuel. [1781, 1787] 2002. *Critique of Pure Reason*. Translated by Werner S. Pluhar. London: Hackett.

Kant, Immanuel. [1788] 2002. *Critique of Practical Reason*. Translated by Werner S. Pluhar. London: Hackett.

Kant, Immanuel. [1790] 2002. *Critique of Judgment*. Translated by Werner S. Pluhar. London: Hackett.

Keane, Webb. 2007. *Christian Moderns*. Berkeley: University of California Press.

Khawaja, Noreen. 2016. *The Religion of Existence: Asceticism in Philosophy from Kierkegaard to Sartre*. Chicago: University of Chicago Press.

Latour, Bruno. 2010. *On the Modern Cult of the Factish Gods*. Durham, NC: Duke University Press.

Mahmood, Saba. 2004. *Politics of Piety*. Princeton, NJ: Princeton University Press.

Masuzawa, Tomoko. 2005. *The Invention of World Religions*. Chicago: University of Chicago Press.

Matory, J. Lorand. 2018. *The Fetish Revisited*. Durham, NC: Duke University Press.

McCutcheon, Russell. 1995. "The Category 'Religion' in Recent Publications: A Critical Survey." *Numen* 42 (3): 284–309.

Miller, Richard. 2022. *Why Study Religion?* Oxford: Oxford University Press.

Morris, Rosalind. 2017."After De Brosses: Fetishism, Translation, Comparativism, Critique." In *The Returns of Fetishism: Charles de Brosses and the Afterlives of an Idea*, edited by Rosalind C. Morris and Daniel H. Leonard. Chicago: University of Chicago Press.

Mufti, Aamir. 2007. *Enlightenment in the Colony*. Princeton, NJ: Princeton University Press.

Robinson, Cedric J. [1983] 2021. *Black Marxism*. Chapel Hill: University of North Carolina Press.

Slavet, Eliza. 2009. *Racial Fever: Freud and the Jewish Question*. New York: Fordham University Press.

Sullivan, Winnifred. [2005] 2018. *The Impossibility of Religious Freedom*. Princeton, NJ: Princeton University Press.

Taylor, Mark C., ed. 1998. *Critical Terms for Religious Studies*. Chicago: University of Chicago Press.

Vial, Theodore. 2016. *Modern Religion, Modern Race*. Oxford: Oxford University Press.

Wynter, Sylvia. 1994. "No Humans Involved: An Open Letter to My Colleagues." *Forum NHI: Knowledge of the 21st Century* 1 (1): 42–73.

1 CATASTROPHE

Levi McLaughlin

Catastrophe and Religion Are Co-constitutive

For an event to qualify as a catastrophe, people must believe it counts as a catastrophe. The same is true for religion, religions, and the religious.[1] The examples in this chapter illustrate that defining catastrophe and defining religion are analogous endeavors that connect to and depend upon one another and are formed in tandem by interconnected social and cultural forces. This assertion is inspired by the 2021 volume *Critical Disaster Studies*, which begins with the provocative declaration that "there is no such thing as a disaster" (Horowitz and Remes 2021, 1). The volume's editors, Andy Horowitz and Jacob A. C. Remes, rightly point out that it is not sufficient to state the now widely accepted truth that there is no such thing as a purely "natural" disaster, that suffering resulting from non-anthropogenic trigger events such as earthquakes and other "acts of god" is always caused, or at least exacerbated, by human ineptitude or intent. Horowitz and Remes introduce their volume with a manifesto-style assertion that a disaster is an interpretive fiction. This is not to say that there are no overwhelming circumstances in which beings suffer. Instead, "disaster" is a term that comes into usage when an event has triggered the emotions of those who have experienced it or engaged it from afar. When an event

1. Throughout this chapter, I navigate between the work of Jonathan Z. Smith, specifically his essay in the original *Critical Terms for Religious Studies* volume, to treat "religion" as ours to continually reconceive and reapply as analyses demand, and Kevin Schilbrack's (2010) emphasis on "religion" as a social fact that exceeds scholarly command.

is understood as a disaster, that understanding then shapes aid responses that require judgments about who, and what, deserves intervention.

"Catastrophe" joins a constellation that includes calamity, disaster, and many non-English words for exceptional upheaval and accompanying harm. This chapter draws accordingly on case studies and analyses that employ some of catastrophe's synonyms and adjacent terms. The title key term is a heuristic means of accessing this multitude.

Consensus that there is a difference between a recognized catastrophe, however it is expressed, and the ongoing ravage of existence is determined by management. As Horowitz and Remes put it, "consequences of 'disaster' as a belief are made real in the distribution of sympathy, material resources, and state power" (Horowitz and Remes 2021, 4). Managerial processes affirm widespread belief in some events as unambiguously catastrophic, including many profiled in this chapter. Indeed, it is difficult to imagine a pandemic, tsunami, or other event that produces widespread death and suffering as anything else. But the same managerial processes that clarify some events as catastrophes have consistently inhibited belief that global environmental crisis, misogyny, racism, and numerous other causes of mass suffering should necessarily qualify as catastrophic (Hewitt 2021).

For consensus about a catastrophe to shift, enough people must adjust their beliefs, and for a catastrophe to fully count as such, its import and ramifications require interpretation. While it is conceivable that the managed definition of a catastrophe may avoid explicit attention to religion, in many cases interpreting a catastrophe is a religion-making undertaking. The destruction of the Second Temple at Jerusalem by the Roman empire in 70 CE, to identify a canonical example of religion defined by a declared catastrophe, still serves as an epochal event for Jewish, as well as numerous Christian, subjectivities. The destruction of the Second Temple necessitated the reformulation of Judaism away from priestly authority in favor of rabbinic tradition and the rise of eschatologies centered on erecting a Third Temple where the Messiah will reign (Jones 2011).[2] In China, in the centuries leading up to and continuing past the Six Dynasties into the Tang (third to tenth centuries), worship communities formed around figures April Hughes terms "worldly saviors" who promised to quell political upheaval and the "earthquakes, floods, epidemics, and predatory demons" that accompanied it, which were understood to be evidence of

2. The extent to which the Roman conquest qualified as a catastrophe that fundamentally transformed Judaism is contested. See Schwartz and Weiss 2012.

human malfeasance (Hughes 2021, 5). Not a few of these salvific figures were identified with Maitreya, the Buddha of the next *kalpa* (aeon) whose arrival is to follow cataclysmic annihilation of a degraded world order. Exponents in these centuries also prognosticated that when "epidemics and famine [were] everywhere" and there was political upheaval in the realm, the Daoist figure Laozi would return as a messianic savior (Seidel 1969–1970, 225; see also Nattier 1988 and 1991). Religious institutions and worldviews across Asia have otherwise taken shape through mobilization in the face of identified catastrophes (Fountain and McLaughlin 2016). A smallpox (or similar) epidemic in eighth-century Japan that killed as much as one-third of the population inspired the Japanese court to sponsor a country-wide network of nation-protecting Buddhist monasteries and nunneries (Farris 1985). Some of these—most notably the temple Tōdaiji in Nara, with its famed Great Buddha—reprised their nation-preserving disease expiation roles to protect Japan from COVID-19 by enacting dedicated rituals (Lowe 2020).

Comparable co-creations are abundant across the world, and across history. I thus propose a paraphrase, and extension, of Horowitz and Remes's manifesto: the fictive, political, and temporizing processes that designate catastrophe also produce religion, and the religious understandings that are produced simultaneously influence appraisals of catastrophe. Contrasts between co-creations of catastrophe and religion across the globe challenge presuppositions about how these interpenetrating categories are understood and what both categories might include.

Let us calibrate our presumptions by starting with a brief overview of the locus classicus of defining religion with catastrophe in the modern world: the devastation of Lisbon on All Saints' Day.

Lisbon: The Trigger Event for Secularism?

At 9:45 a.m. on November 1, 1755, Lisbon's churches were full, with many of the city's approximately quarter million residents awaiting the holiday's ten o'clock High Mass (Molesky 2015; Shrady 2008). The quake that is estimated to have struck at that time wreaked overwhelming destruction in the tightly packed city (Fonseca 2020). Between ten thousand and one hundred thousand people were killed in and around Lisbon, and as many as ten thousand more perished in distant Morocco in the same seismic event. Mass attendees died in collapsing churches, thousands of others lost their lives in the ensuing fires, and many more were swept away by three successive tsunamis that reached as high as twenty meters. Portugal's global power was dealt a severe blow by the devastation of its capital, and Europe's economy went into a tailspin.

Alarming details of death and destruction in Lisbon provided ample fodder for moral condemnation by clergy and contestation by the intellectual luminaries of Europe's post-Enlightenment age (Bassnett 2006; Molesky 2015). Analyses of clerical, governmental, scholarly, and vernacular writings in the aftermath of the Lisbon disasters caution against treating them as evidence that majority sentiment shifted away from religion, given that most reactions to the compound disasters affirmed belief in God and the importance of the church (Nichols 2014). Historians, philosophers, scientists, and other thinkers nonetheless routinely treat the destruction of Lisbon as having inspired diversion from church authority in favor of rational scientific inquiry. Leading intellectuals of this period formulated approaches in response to the Lisbon cataclysm that now undergird legal discourses, scientific thinking, social conventions, and aesthetic dispositions that contrast with clerical interpretations.

Reactions were immediate, and the Lisbon catastrophe persisted as a significant area of inquiry for Europe's intellectual community. Immanuel Kant composed three treatises in the beginning of 1756 on the Lisbon disasters, which fused his concern for morality with his theories on seismology and laid a foundation for his later work on human freedom (Larsen 2006). Agonizing over how the innocent suffered in Lisbon under a creator God who was "in no wise fatherly in giving over righteous and unrighteous to destruction" informed Johann Wolfgang von Goethe's intellectual development, though he was only six years old in 1755 (Nichols 2014, 977–78). Perhaps the most famous immediate responses to Lisbon were a 1755 poem by Voltaire and a 1756 riposte by Jean-Jacques Rousseau. Voltaire's "The Lisbon Earthquake: An Inquiry into the Maxim, 'Whatever Is, Is Right'" exemplifies a European Christian fixation on theodicy by reflecting on the vexing dilemma of how an all-merciful deity can punish those seemingly least deserving of retribution. Voltaire challenged Gottfried Wilhelm Leibniz's reliance on reason, most evident in his *Theodicy*, and subsequent thinking on theodicy by Alexander Pope, as he asked in his anguished verse, "And can [one] then impute a sinful deed / to babes who on their mothers' bosoms bleed? / Was then more vice in fallen Lisbon found, / Than Paris, where voluptuous joys abound?" Rousseau's response is a sardonic rejection in straightforward prose of Voltaire's *cri du coeur*: "Should it be said then that the order of the world ought to change according to our whims, that nature ought to be subjugated to our laws, and that in order to interdict an earthquake in some place, we have only to build a city there?" (Larrimore 2001, 204–15). Kant wrote approvingly of Rousseau's discourses on theodicy, characterizing him as a second Isaac Newton for his insistence that self-knowledge alone could save us (Neiman 2015, 36–37). As Susan Neiman clarifies, Rousseau's response played an important part in his formulation of "the modern shape of the problem of evil" (2015, 55).

Complexities inherent in Rousseau's rebuke demonstrate that he was informed by concern for the divine, and his prosaic letter represents what would become a post-Lisbon standard: a perceptible distinction between public-facing scientific pursuits and privately held beliefs. Even as he dismissed Voltaire's hubristic questioning of God's intent to instead urge rational planning in advance of inevitable disasters, Rousseau confirmed theodicy as a concern as he grounded his critique in Christian faith. But he separated queries about divine intent from a rational response to calamity. This distinction was evident also in measures taken by Portugal's hereditary aristocratic power-holders, who played down charges of divine retribution in an attempt to minimize the earthquake's effects on their empire's political and economic stability. Those who ruled by the divine right of kings sought to distance their government from questions about divine judgment as they oversaw an administration that directed clergy to suppress moralistic castigations by fellow priests. The Marquis of Pombal, charged by Portugal's King José I to manage governmental relief efforts, set the Inquisition (which was seated in Lisbon) upon an Italian Jesuit priest named Gabriel Malagrida, who preached in Lisbon's ravaged streets that the disasters were God's punishment for sinfulness; the Inquisition executed Malagrida in September 1761 (Molesky 2015). Pombal otherwise exercised dictatorial powers to reconstruct Lisbon following a rationalized scheme that prioritized the bureaucrat and the merchant over the church, and even over the crown (Mullin 1992). He worked to normalize the quake as the cause of a series of problems that demanded pragmatic solutions, putting into effect what would become a pattern of normalizing state disaster responses as a responsibility insulated from fear of divine wrath.

Though distinction from the nonreligious remained ambiguous at the time of the quake, the destruction of Lisbon came to serve retrospectively as a watershed for the category "religion," the moment at which skepticism about God's role gave way to reliance on science, when deference to the church was replaced by the rise of non-clerical authorities who managed religion, conceptually and legally. J. Z. Smith surveyed ways "religion" transformed as the weight of imperial authority shifted from Iberian to northern European and British command around the time of the Lisbon cataclysm (Smith 1998). The years around the Lisbon quake saw consensus about "religion" coalesce in increasingly Protestant terms as a matter of individual belief and as a term best defined in the plural, with multiple religions and their attendant "isms" populating a racist hierarchical taxonomy tabulated by scientific inquiry. Reflections on Lisbon propelled definitions of religion that were employed by colonial powers which overran the globe in the centuries following the city's destruction, and post-Lisbon religion interpretations are now employed worldwide within corporate, legal, and political systems. The 1755 catastrophe was, in other words, a religion-making event, in the sense that it accelerated processes that delineate the contours of "religion" as a discrete sphere.

Religion Where Cataclysm Is Quotidian: Life and Death on Merapi

There is an aggregate weight to post-Lisbon narratives which advances a presumption that an epistemic shift toward an increasingly secular order became a taken-for-granted global standard. Let us consider a contrasting example closer to the historical present that demonstrates ways philosophizing by post-Enlightenment Christian figures was parochial and how the global reach of the post-Lisbon paradigm can see the persistence, but also the transmutation and marginalization, of European conceptualizations of "religion" and "catastrophe."

On October 26, 2010, the body of Mbah Maridjan was found coated in ash, prostrated in prayer toward Makkah. He died in a pyroclastic flow, a superheated blast of gas and ash, on the flanks of Gunung Merapi, the "Mountain of Fire," a highly active volcano outside the city of Yogyakarta on the island of Java, in central Indonesia. Maridjan had served for decades in the inherited post of Juru Kunci, literally "key master" and commonly "protector of the mountain," charged by the Sultan of Yogyakarta to work with the spirits within the volcano to mitigate its destructive power (Schlehe 2010). While there had been long-standing contention between the spirit-oriented views of Mbah Maridjan and rationalized approaches promoted by the Sultan, Gusti Prabuksumo, brother-in-law of the Yogyakarta king Sri Sultan Hamengkubuwono X, announced that the palace had received a premonition in dreams about Maridjan's death in advance of the 2010 eruption (Malik 2010a). Upon discovery of the volcano protector's body, competition broke out among his potential heirs to claim his rank. His son Asih was appointed the new Juru Kunci in April 2011 (Seeberg and Patmawati 2015, 30).

The Merapi protector is understood by his community to maintain a psychic connection with the Sultan as he negotiates with the volcano's spirits, beings who mirror the mountain's society of human inhabitants, to "let the volcano breathe, but not cough" (Malik 2010b). At the same time, he and his fellow community members self-identify as pious Muslims who faithfully maintain regular Islamic practices and beliefs, including the five daily prayers, and they sustain themselves through livelihoods that participate in the global market economy. The Sultanate that oversees the Special Region of Yogyakarta, and the Indonesian state, navigate between local-level regard for spirits; Islamic priorities, which depend on Javanese lineages as well as organizations and pietistic practices from outside Indonesia; and disaster management strategies predicated on scientific understandings of seismic upheavals as emergencies that require interventions by trained experts (Schlehe 2015).

The result is constant negotiation between incommensurate priorities, only some of which unambiguously articulate "catastrophe." Maridjan had survived an eruption in 2006, only to be killed in 2010, but living on Merapi means treating volcanic eruptions as routine and death by them as predictable and meaningful. The Sultan of Yogyakarta had, in 2006 and again in 2010, ordered the Juru Kunci to leave Merapi in advance of its eruptions, to no avail (Singgih 2014). Meanwhile, governmental measures are in place to install seismometers and mobilize social media use and other communications between residents to keep track of changes on the mountain and to formulate and update preset plans to implement mass evacuation orders. Residents inhabit a conflation Judith Schlehe called "spiritual cosmopolitanism" that encourages a fluid mix of categorical determinations. These include *kejawen* (the old ways), which involve careful consideration of spiritual beings called *makhluk alus* that villagers believe reside inside Merapi, food offerings to Mbok Sri (the mother goddess of rice), and spiritual warnings from Merapi offered through dreams. The "old ways" mix with modern Islamic interpretations from the Muhammadiyah organizations and others which involve concern for theodicy and characterizations of destructive events as evidence of God's judgment (Donovan 2010; Schwartz-Marin et al. 2020).[3]

3. The massive Indonesian religious and charitable group Nahdlatul Ulama accommodates local spirit reverence, while the Muhammadiyah organization, which oversees

Dispositions toward the volcano are formulated by interpenetrating traditions which are influenced by hamlet-level contingency plans coordinated by Yogyakarta's Regional Disaster Management Agency that depend on instrumental measurements. "Religion" is thus molded through interpretations of Merapi that emerge from contestations between, and within, regional and international groups. The residents who are shaped by this cosmopolitan mix produce striking conflations as they respond to eruptions. After the October 2010 eruption, for instance, some local university students who were studying clinical psychology took it upon themselves to treat the five daily prayers at refugee centers as opportunities to engage children who had lost their homes in art therapy, putting to work what they described as techniques based in Freudian concepts to reduce the effects of PTSD in young victims (Author interview, July 24, 2011). And some of those who rebuilt after the 2010 eruption regard Merapi as bestower of God's blessings, thanking the mountain for producing a new industry built around guiding visitors on "lava tours" and otherwise providing residents with revenue-producing avenues toward socioeconomic advancement.

The result of these coexisting conceptions is that, on Merapi, "catastrophe" is relativized, and it is unclear where to draw lines around the "religion" of the villagers. Eruptions cohere as catastrophes in academic and governmental assessments but are arguably other than straightforwardly catastrophic in narrations by those who live on, and with, Merapi. And while they live Muslim lives, Merapi villagers' regard for a spirit world within the volcano challenges "religion" definitions recognized by state enterprises and by those who promote contesting Islamic orthodoxies. Merapi's eruptions thus continually give rise to an unstable co-creation of the catastrophic and the religious.

Lisbon's Transmogrified Legacies? Religion after the 3/11 Disasters in Japan

Legacies of post-Enlightenment assumptions about religion and disaster response are perceptible in narrations on Merapi, in particular those prioritized by the state. These legacies also persist in Japan, another disaster-

---

the Muhammadiyah Disaster Management Center, reportedly tends to emphasize a more explicit theodicy that relies on strict adherence to interpretations of the Qur'an and Sunnah that understand the eruptions as a task or ordeal (*ujiah*) from God. See Schlehe 2010 and Rokib 2012.

prone Asian polity in which the imported category "religion" is continually reshaped under catastrophic conditions. On March 11, 2011, a date now conventionally known as 3/11, more than 22,300 people were killed or went missing in northeast Japan. Hundreds of thousands of others were temporarily or permanently displaced by a massive earthquake (the fourth-largest recorded in the world); resulting tsunamis, which reached as high as forty meters and extended ten kilometers inland; and the nuclear meltdown at the Fukushima Dai'ichi power plants. 3/11 inspired the mobilization of thousands of volunteer aid providers who distributed billions of dollars' worth of aid. A significant percentage of this aid came from religious organizations and affiliated volunteers. The disasters triggered Japan's largest dispatch of religious resources since the Pacific War, and they gave rise to distinctive post-3/11 religion-defining initiatives (Fujiyama 2020; McLaughlin 2016a).

In the co-constitution of religion and catastrophe in the wake of 3/11, there were some striking role reversals. One of the most well-publicized examples of judgments about the disasters that made use of religious language, and perhaps Japan's only well-known example of post-3/11 theodicy, came from an ostensibly secular elected official. In a press conference on March 14, 2011, Ishihara Shintarō, then governor of Tokyo, told reporters that he regarded the tsunami as *tenbatsu*, or "heavenly punishment," and a means of washing away "grime" built up on the hearts of the Japanese people (Rambelli 2014). Meanwhile, with the exception of the religion Kōfuku no Kagaku (Happy Science), which characterized the disasters as divine retribution for the Japanese people having elected the Democratic Party of Japan in 2009 (*Happiness Realization News* 2011) and remarks by the Japanese head of the Family Federation for World Peace and Unification, the Korea-based religion formerly known as the Unification Church, to the effect that all of the disaster-afflicted save those who converted to the church were doomed (*Karuto shinbun* 2012), publicized examples of condemnation or theodicy expressed by Japan's religious activists were rare. Instead, almost every Buddhist, Christian, Shinto, so-called "new religion," and other religious group suspended regular operations, and judgment about divine origins of the calamity, to mobilize aid. Within minutes of hearing about the devastation in the northeast, denominations put into effect standing plans to transform their headquarters into disaster strategy depots. They set about fundraising and gathering food, shelters, portable toilets, and other emergency supplies, and they tasked their employees with dispatching materials to the places they were most needed.

On the ground in northeast Japan, churches, temples, shrines, and other religious facilities opened their doors to house thousands of refugees, in some cases for months after the disasters (McLaughlin 2016b).

Japan's religious professionals mostly undertook a response that conscientiously observed constitutionally guaranteed divisions and made evident trepidation about religion operating in the public sphere. Careful attention to carving out an appropriate place for religious aid provision encouraged post-disaster activists to fuse their vocational specialties with attention to material needs and clinical treatments. Dealing with the enormous numbers of dead and caring for a bereaved and traumatized population required Japan's religious professionals to devise new strategies for ritual and pastoral care. Among the most prominent of their initiatives was the Counseling Room of the Heart (Kokoro no Sōdanshitsu), a collaboration founded in the city of Sendai (near the quake epicenter) between clergy from Buddhist and Christian denominations, administrators from several new religious groups, psychologists, social workers, medical staff, and other caregivers who provided counseling to survivors from their base above a crematorium. This effort expanded in the months following 3/11 to include the Café de Monk, which comprised a radio program and a mobile group of mostly Buddhist clergy who traveled to clusters of temporary housing units to engage in active listening, putting to work techniques for treating PTSD they adopted from clinical care specialists (Berman 2018; Kasai 2016).

These initiatives, which began ad hoc and served as bases for institution-building, provided people in Japan with an option to narrate "religion" through sensibilities shaped by the 3/11 catastrophe. Several of the clergy and lay affiliate caregivers who participated in the Counseling Room for the Heart cooperated on founding the Department of Practical Religious Studies at Tohoku University in Sendai; intriguingly, in spite of Japan's stringent postwar religion/state constitutional divides, religious and medical professionals were able to collaborate on establishing a new academic department in one of Japan's most prestigious public universities.[4] Training provided through this program enables clergy and lay activists to earn nationally recognized certification aimed at placing trainees in hospice care facilities, on hospital wards, in elderly care homes, and in other clinical settings. Paradoxes dominate in Japan's post-3/11 articulation of

4. For insight into sensitivities that surround religion/state divides mandated by Japan's 1947 Constitution, see Thomas 2019.

"religion," promoted at Tohoku University and in related programs. Eager to avoid transgressing boundaries between religion and the public sphere, clergy from Buddhist and Christian denominations nonetheless make use of denominational support to engage in training that encourages them to downplay their denominational identities in order to find places for themselves in clinical care teams. They train as "Interfaith Chaplains" (Rinshō Shūkyōshi, literally "clinical religious instructors") who present their teachings and rituals as relevant components of scientifically verified forms of clinic-based treatment. This reformulation of centuries-old practices allows clerical clinicians to curate a public persona that presents them and their religious resources as the offerings of individual caregivers rather than as institutional representatives serving a community of parishioners. They may offer insights from their sect's doctrine or perform rituals from their denominations if requested, but they must be equally ready to perform the rites of other faiths; a Christian priest must be ready to chant the Heart Sutra, for example, and a Buddhist priest must be willing to pray with a dying Catholic.[5]

The 3/11 disasters in Japan thus inspired a redefinition of religion that recodes the category along the lines of individuated treatment. It is an articulation that derives to some degree from post-Lisbon presumptions of ways religion should be relegated to the secularized realm of interiorized preference, while it also considers dispositions and practices that predate the importation of the category "religion" to Japan in the nineteenth century (Josephson-Storm 2012). The comparative scarcity of explicit concern for theodicy on the part of religious institutional representatives sets Japanese post-disaster articulations of religion and catastrophe apart from European genealogies. This may be partially due to an internalization of secular norms by Japan's religious professionals. But it is an attitude that is also beholden to non-European conventions. Prior to the arrival of "religion" as a discrete conceptual and legal category, there were few obvious distinctions between the "natural" and the anthropogenic in Japanese definitions of cataclysm. Military and political upset ranked alongside earthquakes and epidemics as *wazawai*, or disasters, and people's unmeritorious conduct was frequently assumed to be a primary cause for divine anger (Josephson-Storm 2012; Miura 2020). Teachings about proper ethical behavior and promises of transcendence were placed in the service of

5. For an example of an Interfaith Chaplaincy training module, see McLaughlin 2019.

pragmatic needs and tended to be articulated as consonant with contemporary sociopolitical expectations.[6] This legacy of meeting contemporary needs is apparent in the decisions made by religious professionals after 3/11, who have narrated religion as a resource for healing individuals and post-disaster national construction while conspicuously avoiding references to sectarian priorities or divine judgment.

Conclusion: Fighting for Eschatological Hegemony

To assert a catastrophe or religion is an agonistic undertaking that can become a bid for eschatological hegemony. Presumptions about what might legitimately count as either catastrophic or religious are perpetually at risk of being undermined by competing narrations. Climate catastrophe, to take a most pressing contemporary example, has coalesced belatedly as event, and catastrophic environmental conditions previously sidelined to disenfranchised temporalities now cohere as grounds for international treaties, causes for a diagnosable medical condition, inspiration for "cli-fi" genre fiction, and other means of mobilizing sentiment and material resources (Nixon 2013). But epistemological divides sharpen between those urging environmental degradation as inevitable and those who stake their authority and identities on preset end-times agendas (Alumkal 2017; Daggett 2018). Many of the same denialist forces that reject climate change opposed the validity of COVID-19 as a catastrophe. In late 2021, the World Health Organization's Coronavirus (COVID-19) Dashboard listed the global toll from the disease at just over 4.99 million deaths (WHO 2021). The pandemic earned official recognition as a disaster, to the extent that efforts to forestall contagion received funding from FEMA's Hazard Mitigation Grant Program in the United States and were otherwise enabled by emergency measures worldwide. But millions continued to imagine differently and treated pandemic mitigation measures themselves, rather than the disease, as catastrophes that affirmed cherished eschatologies (Perry, Grubbs, and Whitehead 2020).

The three case studies in this chapter demonstrate that epistemologi-

6. There were certainly those who ran counter to social or official sanction. One of the most prominent examples was Nichiren (1222–1282), the Buddhist reformer who regarded catastrophes as evidence for Japan's slander of the *Lotus Sūtra*. See Stone 1994. For examples of ascetic practices and lay devotion that subtly opposed governmental authority in Japan, see Sawada 2022.

cal contestations occasioned by calamitous circumstances propel religion-making. Lack of consensus about conjoined conceptions of catastrophe and religion characterizes conflicts between would-be definers of both terms. The examples in this chapter reveal that arbiters of these categories participate in communities that are shaped via codependent, and conflicting, articulations. And while these cases challenge easy assumptions about what either term might include, they demonstrate that co-constitutions of catastrophe and religion are historical constants.

Suggested Readings

Adams, Vincanne. 2013. *Markets of Sorrow, Labors of Faith: New Orleans in the Wake of Katrina*. Durham, NC: Duke University Press.

Barnett, Michael. 2011. *Empire of Humanity: A History of Humanitarianism*. Ithaca, NY: Cornell University Press.

Fiddian-Qasmiyeh, Elena. 2014. *The Ideal Refugees: Gender, Islam, and the Sahrawi Politics of Survival*. Syracuse, NY: Syracuse University Press.

Mauch, Christof, and Christian Pfister, eds. 2009. *Natural Disasters, Cultural Responses: Case Studies Toward a Global Environmental History*. Lanham, MD: Lexington Books.

McGinn, Bernard. 1988. *Visions of the End: Apocalyptic Traditions in the Middle Ages*. New York: Columbia University Press.

Oliver-Smith, Anthony, and Susanna M. Hoffman, eds. 1999. *The Angry Earth: Disasters in Anthropological Context*. New York: Routledge.

Samuels, Annemarie. 2019. *After the Tsunami: Disaster Narratives and the Remaking of Everyday Life in Aceh*. Honolulu: University of Hawaiʻi Press.

Simpson, Edward. 2014. *The Political Biography of an Earthquake: Aftermath and Amnesia in Gujarat, India*. New York: Oxford University Press.

References

Alumkal, Antony. 2017. *Paranoid Science: The Christian Right's War on Reality*. New York: New York University Press.

Bassnett, Susan. 2006. "Faith, Doubt, Aid and Prayer: The Lisbon Earthquake of 1755 Revisited." *European Review* 14 (3): 321–28.

Berman, Michael. 2018. "Religion Overcoming Religions: Suffering, Secularism, and the Training of Interfaith Chaplains in Japan." *American Ethnologist* 45 (2): 228–40.

Daggett, Cara. 2018. "Petro-Masculinity: Fossil Fuels and Authoritarian Desire." *Millennium: Journal of International Studies* 47 (1): 25–44.

Donovan, Katherine. 2010. "Doing Social Volcanology: Exploring Volcanic Culture in Indonesia." *Area* 42 (1): 117–26.

Farris, William Wayne. 1985. *Population, Disease, and Land in Early Japan, 645–900*. Cambridge, MA: Harvard University Press.

Fonseca, Joao F. B. D. 2020. "A Reassessment of the Magnitude of the 1755 Lisbon Earthquake." *Bulletin of the Seismological Society of America* 110: 1–17.

Fountain, Philip, and Levi McLaughlin. 2016. "Salvage and Salvation: Guest Editors' Introduction." *Asian Ethnology* 75 (1): 1–28.

Fujiyama, Midori. 2020. *Rinshō shūkyōshi: shi no bansōsha* [Interfaith Chaplains: Death's Companions]. Tokyo: Kōbunken.

Happiness Realization News, The. 2011. Tokushū [Special Issue], no. 24, June 7.

Hewitt, Kenneth. 2021. "'Acts of Men': Disasters Neglected, Preventable, and Moral." In *Critical Disaster Studies*, edited by Jacob A. C. Remes and Andy Horowitz, 184–92. Philadelphia: University of Pennsylvania Press.

Horowitz, Andy, and Jacob A. C. Remes. 2021. "Introducing Critical Disaster Studies." In *Critical Disaster Studies*, edited by Jacob A. C. Remes and Andy Horowitz, 1–8. Philadelphia: University of Pennsylvania Press.

Hughes, April D. 2021. *Worldly Saviors and Imperial Authority in Medieval Chinese Buddhism*. Honolulu: University of Hawai'i Press.

Jones, Kenneth R. 2011. *Jewish Reactions to the Destruction of Jerusalem in A.D. 70*. Leiden: Brill.

Josephson-Storm, Jason Ānanda. 2012. *The Invention of Religion in Japan*. Chicago: University of Chicago Press.

Karuto shinbun [Almost Daily Cult Newspaper]. 2012. "'Nihon Tōitsu Kyōkai' Sō sōkaichō, higashi Nihon daishinsai no tsunami higai ni kan shi 'bōgen' o renpatsu!" ["Japan Unification Church" general secretary Song (Yŏngsŏk) repeatedly hurls abuse at victims of the Great East Japan disaster tsunami!], June 21. http://dailycult.blogspot.com/2012/06/blog-post_21.html.

Kasai, Kenta. 2016. "Introducing Chaplaincy to Japanese Society: A Religious Practice in Public Space." *Journal of Religion in Japan* 5: 246–62.

Larrimore, Mark, ed. 2001. *The Problem of Evil: A Reader*. Oxford: Blackwell Publishers.

Larsen, Svend Erik. 2006. "The Lisbon Earthquake and the Scientific Turn in Kant's Philosophy." *European Review* 14 (3): 359–67.

Lowe, Bryan. 2020. "Protection without Punishment: Turning to Buddhist Gods during Covid-19." *The Immanent Frame*, June 25. https://tif.ssrc.org/2020/06/25/protection-without-punishment/.

Malik, Candra. 2010a. "Yogyakarta Palace Claims Premonition of Mbah Maridjan's Death." *Jakarta Globe*, October 27. https://web.archive.org/web/20101030073109/http://www.thejakartaglobe.com/home/yogyakarta-palace-claims-premonition-of-mbah-maridjans-death/403500.

Malik, Candra. 2010b. "My Time to Die in This Place Has Come." *Jakarta Globe*, October 28. https://web.archive.org/web/20101030082708/http://www.thejakartaglobe.com/home/my-time-to-die-in-this-place-has-come/403639.

McLaughlin, Levi. 2016a. "Religious Responses to the 2011 Tsunami in Japan." *Oxford*

Handbooks Online (April 12, 2016). https://academic.oup.com/edited-volume/41330/chapter/352333787.

McLaughlin, Levi. 2016b. "Hard Lessons Learned: Tracking Changes in Media Presentations of Religion and Religious Aid Mobilization after the 1995 and 2011 Disasters in Japan." *Asian Ethnology* 75 (1): 105–38.

McLaughlin, Levi. 2019. "Using Buddhist Resources in Post-Disaster Japan: Taniyama Yōzō's 'Vihāra Priests and Buddhist Chaplains.'" In *Buddhism and Medicine: An Anthology of Modern Sources*, edited by Pierce Salguero, 164–76. New York: Columbia University Press.

Miura, Takashi. 2020. *Agents of World Renewal: The Rise of Yonaoshi Gods in Japan*. Honolulu: University of Hawai'i Press.

Molesky, Mark. 2015. *This Gulf of Fire: The Destruction of Lisbon, or Apocalypse in the Age of Science and Reason*. New York: Alfred A. Knopf.

Mullin, John R. 1992. "The Reconstruction of Lisbon Following the Earthquake of 1755: A Study in Despotic Planning." *Planning Perspectives* 7: 157–79.

Nattier, Jan. 1988. "The Meanings of the Maitreya Myth: A Typological Analysis." In *Maitreya, the Future Buddha*, edited by Alan Sponberg and Helen Hardacre, 23–47. New York: Cambridge University Press.

Nattier, Jan. 1991. *Once Upon a Future Time: Studies in a Buddhist Prophecy of Decline*. Berkeley, CA: Asian Humanities Press.

Neiman, Susan. 2015. *Evil in Modern Thought: An Alternative History of Philosophy*. Princeton, NJ: Princeton University Press.

Nichols, Ryan. 2014. "Reevaluating the Effects of the 1755 Lisbon Earthquake on Eighteenth-Century Minds: How Cognitive Science of Religion Improves Intellectual History with Hypothesis Testing Methods." *Journal of the American Academy of Religion* 82: 970–1009.

Nixon, Rob. 2013. *Slow Violence and the Environmentalism of the Poor*. Cambridge, MA: Harvard University Press.

Perry, Samuel L., Joshua B. Grubbs, and Andrew L. Whitehead. 2020. "Culture Wars and COVID-19 Conduct: Christian Nationalism, Religiosity, and Americans' Behavior During the Coronavirus Pandemic." *Journal for the Scientific Study of Religion* 59 (3): 405–16.

Rambelli, Fabio. 2014. "Gods, Dragons, Catfish, and Godzilla: Fragments for a History of Religious Views on Natural Disasters in Japan." In *When the Tsunami Came to the Shore: Culture and Disaster in Japan*, edited by Roy Starrs, 50–69. Leiden: Brill.

Rokib, Mohammad. 2012. "The Importance of Faith-Based Organization in Shaping Disaster: Case Study of Muhammadiyah." *Jurnal Studi Masyarakat Islam* 15 (2): 321–33.

Sawada, Janine Anderson. 2022. *Faith in Mount Fuji: The Rise of Independent Religion in Early Modern Japan*. Honolulu: University of Hawai'i Press.

Schilbrack, Kevin. 2010. "Religions: Are There Any?" *Journal of the American Academy of Religion* 78 (4): 1112–38.

Schlehe, Judith. 2010. “Anthropology of Religion: Disasters and the Representations of Tradition and Modernity.” *Religions* 40: 112–20.

Schlehe, Judith. 2015. “Cosmopolitanism in the Modern Mystical World of Java.” Southeast Asian Studies at the University of Freiburg (Germany) Occasional Paper no. 24 (April).

Schwartz, Daniel R., and Zeev Weiss, eds. 2012. *Was 70 CE a Watershed in Jewish History? On Jews and Judaism Before and After the Destruction of the Second Temple*. Leiden: Brill.

Schwartz-Marin, Ernesto, Claudia Merli, Laksmi Rachmawati, Claire Horwell, and Fentiny Nugroho. 2020. “Merapi Multiple: Protection around Yogyakarta’s Celebrity Volcano through Masks, Dreams, and Seismographs.” *History and Anthropology* (August 14): 588–610.

Seeberg, Jens, and Retna Siwi Padmawati. 2015. “Between the Queen of the South Sea and the Spirit of Merapi: Political and Cosmological Dimensions of the Central Java Earthquake in 2006.” In *Past Vulnerability: Volcanic Eruptions and Human Vulnerability in Traditional Societies Past and Present*, edited by Felix Riede, 23–38. Aarhus: Aarhus University Press.

Seidel, Anna K. 1969–1970. “The Image of the Perfect Ruler in Early Taoist Messianism: Lao-tzu and Li Hung.” *History of Religions* 9 (2–3): 216–47.

Shrady, Nicholas. 2008. *The Last Day: Wrath, Ruin, and Reason in the Great Lisbon Earthquake of 1755*. New York: Viking.

Singgih, Emanuel Gerrit. 2014. “Different Views of Nature, Ecological and Disaster Mitigation Policies in South-East Asia: A Religious-Theological Perspective.” *Exchange* 43: 237–53.

Smith, Jonathan Z. 1998. “Religion, Religions, Religious.” In *Critical Terms for Religious Studies*, edited by Mark C. Taylor, 269–84. Chicago: University of Chicago Press. Reprinted in 2004 in Jonathan Z. Smith, *Relating Religion: Essays in the Study of Religion*, 179–96. Chicago: University of Chicago Press.

Stone, Jacqueline. 1994. “Rebuking the Enemies of the Lotus: Nichirenist Exclusivism in Historical Perspective.” *Japanese Journal of Religious Studies* 21 (2–3): 231–59.

Thomas, Jolyon Baraka. 2019. *Faking Liberties: Religious Freedom in American-Occupied Japan*. Chicago: University of Chicago Press.

World Health Organization (WHO). 2021. Coronavirus (COVID-19) Dashboard. Accessed July 28, 2024. https://covid19.who.int/.

2 DISABILITY

Sarah Imhoff

In Jewish and Christian textual traditions, Leviticus includes God's speech about excluding some priests from making divine offerings.

> The LORD spoke further to Moses: Speak to Aaron and say: No man of your offspring throughout the ages who has a defect shall be qualified to offer the food of his God. No one at all who has a defect shall be qualified: no man who is blind, or lame, or has a limb too short or too long; no man who has a broken leg or a broken arm; or who is a hunchback, or a dwarf, or who has a growth in his eye, or who has a boil-scar, or scurvy, or crushed testes. . . . He shall not profane these places sacred to Me, for I the LORD have sanctified them. (Lev 21:16–23, JPS translation)

Blindness, broken arms, short limbs, eye growths, scars: what is the logic of this list of exclusions? It includes both visible and invisible conditions, life-long and temporary states, and acquired and congenital conditions, while it leaves out other biblical "afflictions" such as deafness and leprosy. There is no single, identifiable, and consistent logic to the exclusions in this divine speech. This very inconsistency, however, suggests two broader truths about disability: First, it is culturally constructed, so who is disabled and what it means to be disabled differ across times and cultures, often without logical consistency. Second, disability often signifies beyond itself. Blindness, for example, is not just blindness; it appears as a sign of profanity, a sign of punishment, or even a sign of special otherworldly insight.

The question of human difference—how and why some people are physically or mentally different from others—is a perennial one. It appears in scripture, in prayer, in intimate and public settings, in conversations about everything from art to economics. In spite of this ubiquity, or perhaps because of it, the how and why of human difference remain complex and without easy explanation. Race and gender categorize two sorts of bodily difference to which cultures have attached meaning. Ability and disability are others.

Thinking about disability also necessitates thinking about its opposite: ability. There are several reasons why the category of disability has received more explicit scholarly attention than the category of ability. First, disability is the marked category—that is, ability is the assumed norm, whereas disability is the deviation from that norm. We can often see this in linguistic usage, such as the gender implications of locutions like "the doctor" and "the female doctor," or "an athlete" and "a disabled athlete." The presence of difference often triggers analysis. Disability needs explaining, whereas ability might not seem to.

Second, political activism has played a significant role in and alongside scholarship on ability and disability, especially as disability studies grew as a field in the 1980s and 1990s. At one level, the people involved overlapped: many scholars of disability identified as disabled themselves, and the voices of disabled people (whether scholars or not) became central to both scholarly writing and activism. (For brief introductions to this history, see Garland-Thomson 2013; Kent et al. 2018.) At an intellectual and political level, creating and describing the category of disability entailed the creation of a history for people with disabilities. Few able-bodied scholars or activists felt they needed to create community or argue for rights based on their shared ability, but people with disabilities saw these as crucial for fostering dignity, political power, and rights.

Here we can begin to see some of the differences—even the friction—between disability studies and religious studies. Disability studies includes activism in a way that religious studies does not, or at least not uncontroversially. Where conversations about insider and outsider perspectives in religious studies remain live debates, few in disability studies contest the idea that the voices of people with disabilities should be central.

Coming from more "insider" positions, constructive theology and scholarship speaking from within religious communities have taken up questions of disability to think about ethics or justice from those perspectives. Nancy Eiesland's 1994 book *The Disabled God*, for example, argued that Christians encounter a disabled God when they take the Eucharist, and that this kind of vision should be central, rather than peripheral, to the tradition (1994). Maysaa Bazna and Tarek Hatab (2005) argued that the Qur'an emphasizes human responsibility for alleviating the socially created disadvantage of disability. But the intersection of critical religious studies and disability studies took a little longer to get going. Now, though the analysis of disability has not become central, there is fascinating work on biblical texts, performance art, Islamic biographical works, angel-talk and afterlives, and Catholic devotionalism (Raphael 2008; Petro 2020; Walker-Cornetta 2020; Spicer n.d.; Orsi 2005).

In the field of disability studies, however, the default position has been to dismiss or denigrate religion. To take one prominent example, in spite of its investment in terms like "resurrection," the only time Robert McRuer's well-regarded 2006 book *Crip Theory* discusses religion is when it points out the damage done by Christian ex-gay movements, the "compounding threat" of Christianity in already homophobic and anti-disabled trends, and the "betrayal" of a caregiving partner's church (2006, esp. chapter 3). Even McRuer's discussion of Ricardo, who transitioned from life as the transgender Sara to life as a married member of a Christian ministry, contains no sustained discussion of religion or theology. Rosemarie Garland-Thomson's foundational book *Extraordinary Bodies* astutely analyzed Christianity in *Uncle Tom's Cabin*, but that strand of Garland-Thomson's work has not been picked up by other major theorists.

What accounts for these missed connections and dismissals? First, disability theory, especially the version that goes under the banner "crip theory," has modeled itself on queer theory. Both "queer theory" and "crip theory" reclaim a slur, and both challenge the collapse of the normal with the normative, where normal means good. Crip theory also seems to have followed queer theory in another respect: queer theory too has largely—though not completely—neglected religion or occasionally been overtly hostile to religion.[1] In the case of queer theory, neglect and hostility often reflect historical animosity. Religious communities have been sites of pain and rejection for many queer people. Religious texts have been mobilized to withhold rights and recognition. Scholars in disability studies also repeat this narrative about the relationship between queerness and sexuality, though often without depth: "Religions of all cultures

1. Harris (2014) provides a drastic example of queer theory's tendency to ignore or revile religion, including the statement that "The most important point I'm seeking to make is that, time and again, the core and impetus of homophobic rhetoric, laws, and violence facing American queers is religion" (6), and the indictment of "the power of religion to warp one's sense of ethics" (11).

have played a major part in propagating restricted views of sexuality, and historically have set strict parameters around the contexts in which sex, as a practice, should occur," explains *Keywords on Disability Studies* under the entry "Sex" (Shildrick 2015, 54). The volume presents religion as unequivocally bad for sex and for genderqueer persons.

But this narrative does not fit seamlessly with the history of the relationship of people with disabilities to religious spaces or texts. Many people with disabilities have found meaning in religious communities, including as public voices who speak for their tradition (Bejoian 2006; Walker-Cornetta 2023). Moreover, the Christians who publicly denounced gays and lesbians as hell-bound did not do something similar to people with disabilities. Christian denigration of people with disabilities has instead taken the forms of pity, charity, and exclusion from power. Interpretations of scripture have both valued *and* belittled people with disabilities. Some religious communities have marginalized or diminished the lives of disabled people in some contexts (Eiesland 1998, 200–229), while others have materially supported and politically backed people with disabilities. Garland-Thomson discusses "unlikely allies, such as scientists, religious conservatives, and disability rights groups" (2015, 78). While some might see scientists and religious conservatives as "unlikely allies," there is little warrant to assume that religious conservatives and disability rights activists are strange bedfellows at the level of political activism (Davis 2013, 98; Garland-Thomson 2015, 78). Religion's history with queerness differs from its history with disability, and therefore affords a new space for theorization.

Even before disability theories took on the mantle of "crip theory," there was little discussion of religion. The second reason for this disconnect may have to do with the ways theories of intersectionality have overlooked religion. Intersectionality, a theory that insists on analysis of the intersection of social positions such as race, gender, sex, class, and disability, rarely includes religion as one of these positions. Perhaps this is because theorists see religion as epiphenomenal, or as an effect reducible to these other social categories; but the fact is that few scholars who use intersectionality even discuss religion. And no one, to my knowledge, has theorized *why* religion is (or should be) absent. There are a few individual scholars arguing for why religion should be included as a category, but other scholars who use intersectionality do not seem to cite or engage with this material. Because intersectionality has been crucial to disability studies—and rightly so, since disability as a variable is not independent from gender, race, class, or sexuality—disability studies too seems to have often overlooked religion.

This disconnect is unfortunate because religious studies offers useful contributions to disability theory. For one, disability studies scholarship often sets out claims that privilege "insider" first-person knowledge over "outsider" knowledge—reminiscent of the familiar "insider-outsider" debates in religious studies. Most scholars share a sense that personal experience is an important part of the epistemology of the field. Most books about disability studies, for example, take some time to explain the relationship of the author to disability (see, for example, Kafer 2013; McRuer 2006; Davis 2013). This lean toward personal experience occasionally even suggests that there may be no place in the field at all for non-disabled scholars, though that view is not widely espoused.

For another, disability theory relies very heavily on personal narratives, and a great many of them discuss God or theology in one way or another. The twentieth-century Zionist Jessie Sampter reflected on the prominence of shared theological language around disability: "Jews and Christians can easily speak together of the same God, especially when one is ill," she wrote (Sampter n.d., 252). Today's memoirists have theological understandings of their bodies and speak and even argue with God. A man who is paralyzed from the chest down becomes a yoga teacher through his newly found Hindu theologies (blessed by his mother's Protestant pastor, who heard in a dream that the man would take an "alternative path"—Sanford 2006); a woman orients her own story of disability and that of her unborn child through the Jewish liturgical calendar (Cohen 2009); and a woman with schizoaffective disorder, bipolar diagnosis, and panic disorder needed to "redefine how I understood God, myself, my disorders, and the world in general" to articulate her own experiences (Coggins 2017, 200).

Many of these memoirs raise an existential question to which religious traditions have often also responded: why are some people disabled? Answers proliferate, both from within religious conversations and in wider cultural spaces. Some suggest that a disability is the fault of the person who has it—perhaps as a punishment from God or karma, or perhaps self-created, as in the case of a diabetes-related amputation. Others might be seen as someone else's fault, such as a parent who sinned or one who smoked before the child was born. Others see people with disabilities as a lesson to others—or even as a lesson for themselves, such as when people imagine that God has created a disability in a person so that they can overcome some other spiritual issue. These investments in disability—the idea that there must be a reason for it—help us see how disability can signify beyond itself as well as demonstrating the necessity for considering religious traditions in understanding these significations.

Religious studies also has much to learn from disability studies. No human is fully autonomous, and as disability theorists remind us, "no one is ever more than temporarily able-bodied" (Breckenridge and Vogler 2001, 348). Small children and the elderly exemplify the ways capacity changes over a lifetime, and even the strongest and healthiest bodies have bodily limitations. Religious studies has already moved toward critical analysis of embodiment. The last several decades in religious studies have paid particular attention to bodies—and not just in classical anthropological ways of analyzing the religion of exotic others. The rise of methodologies of lived religion, histories and theologies focused on embodiment, and theorizations about the role of pain in the construction of the self constitute just a few of those scholarly developments. (For a small set of examples, see Hall [1997] 2020; Bashir 2011; Asad 2003.)

But there can be more. Put plainly: religions are human phenomena, and humans have bodies. Those bodies have a variety of abilities and disabilities, which can change over time and fundamentally shape their practices and their theologies. Humans often turn to religious discourse to make sense of disability, even when they themselves are not religious.

Critical analysis of religion and disability together, then, constitutes a promising avenue for study—one that can contribute to conversations about such diverse topics as the materiality of bodies, the question of theodicy, and the intersections of religion and politics.

Analyzing Disability

Some disabilities are the results of the relationship between a bodily reality and natural or built environments. The disability studies theorist Susan Wendell explains that in different societies, what is normal differs, and so does what is a disability. "I, who can walk about half a mile several times a week but not more, am not significantly disabled with respect to walking in my society" because most people do not need to walk more than that. "But in some societies, in Eastern Africa for example, where women normally walk several miles twice a day to obtain water for the household, I would be much more severely disabled. It is not just that I would be considered more disabled in those societies but that I would in fact need constant assistance to carry on the most basic life activities" (Wendell 1996, 14).

The same person might be disabled in some contexts but not in others. To understand disability in our contemporary world, we must consider ideas and forces often called biopolitics—how political power seeks to affect and manage all aspects of human lives—which means that disability is created and given meaning through many of the same forces that create and give meaning to race, caste, and other systems of hierarchy.

Cultural interpretations also play a central role in defining disability. Take the examples of visual impairment and hearing impairment. In Western cultures today, many people's impaired vision is easily correctable with eyeglasses or contact lenses. Apart from associations with nerdiness, there is little stigma attached to wearing eyeglasses. Celebrities wear them to advertise for high-fashion brands. Some are brightly colored or artistic, designed to draw attention to themselves. Hearing aids, however, are generally not colorful or whimsical, and few of them are designed to look like beautiful earrings. Companies—none of which are high-fashion brands—advertise their invisibility. Many people resist getting hearing aids, and many others try to hide them because they experience the stigma that can go along with being seen as disabled. Despite the fact that both visual and hearing impairment are common, and both are in fact increasingly normal with age, the cultural ideas about them make one seem to be a disability and the other not.

Even though we recognize that the definitions of disability vary across time and space, that does not mean that the category is meaningless. In every culture, people have a variety of bodies, minds, and abilities. There will always be activities that some people can do, some have difficulty doing, others make modifications to do, and still others cannot do. So disability studies shares a sense that these differences in bodies, activities, and how cultures value them is worth attending to.

Disability studies also shares a set of methods—or perhaps it would be more accurate to say that it shares a conversation about methods. Two common ways to frame the models for thinking in disability studies are the medical model and the social model. The medical model positions disability as an abnormality within a body, and it often frames disability in terms of treatment or cure. The social model positions disability as a mismatch between people and the world they live in: the disability is not the paralysis, for example, but the lack of a fully wheelchair-accessible society. When put in oppositional terms, the vast majority of scholars in disability studies would emphasize the importance of understanding the social model. But today the field is substantially more complex than the dualism suggests. Some scholars and activists completely reject the medical model and argue that disability is entirely socially constructed. Others emphasize the importance of understanding the medical to describe historical interpretations of disability, including from people with disabilities themselves, while working with the understanding that disability is at least partially socially constructed.

These models work best to describe physical disabilities. They work less well for closely related categories such as chronic illness and chronic pain. For obvious reasons, we might be hesitant to tell people with chronic pain that the social model is wholly correct, because to do so insists that it is actually only their environment that disables them. Such a position suggests that if they could only see the situation properly, they would see that they should not seek cures or medical treatment, and they would recognize that their positionality as disabled offers political insight. The disability theorist Tobin Siebers (2001) rails against this view, saying that pain "offers few resources for resisting ideological constructions of masculinity and femininity, the erotic monopoly of the genitals, the violence of ego, or the power of capital. Pain is not a friend to humanity. It is not a secret resource for political change. It is not a well of delight for the individual." This is not to suggest that the social model has nothing to offer, but it does affirm that disability need not be seen as all about empowerment. It also points to the ways religious traditions can be complicit in valorizing or otherwise framing pain as a "friend" or a "resource." Siebers writes: "Theories that encourage these interpretations are not only unrealistic about pain; they contribute to an ideology of ability that marginalizes people with disabilities and makes their stories of suffering and victimization both politically impotent and difficult to believe" (2001, 746). Doctrinaire use of a social model can thus run counter to its purposes.

More recently, scholars have offered other models, such as Alison Kafer's political-relational model. Kafer's model takes the socially constructed nature of disability and combines it with the possibility of medicalized knowledge, while recognizing that medical knowledge too is political and constructed: "By my reckoning, the political/relational model neither opposes nor valorizes medical intervention; rather than simply taking such intervention for granted, it recognizes instead that medical representations, diagnoses, and treatments of bodily variation are imbued with ideological biases about what constitutes normalcy and deviance, and in doing so, it recognizes the possibility of simultaneously desiring to be cured of chronic pain and to be identified and allied with disabled people"

(Kafer 2013, 6). Like race or gender, disability is socially constructed and political, but that does not mean it does not also have material realities.

Two Case Studies

What all of these theorists share is historically and culturally contingent understandings of disability. Below I offer two different cultural contexts that open windows into how disability might function as an analytical category within religious studies.

Twentieth-Century Navajo Context

Even today, with the spread of Western medicine, different communities can retain diverse ways of seeing, classifying, and understanding disability. The Navajo nation in northern Arizona has a significant percentage of children and adults who were born with what doctors call "congenital hip dislocation." For some this means they walk with a limp, but pain does not necessarily accompany the condition.

Most of these Navajo live in extended family groups, spread across the plateaus, canyons, and plains. Their local economies revolve around farming, ranching, seasonal labor, government programs, and increasingly, local commercial businesses. Walking over uneven terrain and riding horses are common, especially for those who work in ranching, farming, and seasonal labor.

Starting in the late 1960s, non-Native doctors and anthropologists began to study Navajos with this "hip dislocation." They found that Western doctors had previously diagnosed and prescribed treatments for the condition, but that most Navajo did not follow their recommendations, either for themselves or for their children.

Those who draw on Navajo traditions do not reject Western medicine, but they also do not see it as the only way to approach illness, disease, or disability. In the case of hip dislocation, for example, they will see and understand X-rays, and they will listen to doctors' explanations of the physical locations of the bones. At the same time, they understand bodily difference to be the result of a set of actions and reactions in the universe. For example, when one parent was pregnant with the child, she may have cut an animal's joints while she was butchering it. The other parent may have twisted the legs of a horse in the process of immobilizing it for castration or branding (Rabin et al. 1965). These actions created disharmony in the universe (or somewhat more accurately, the intertwining of physical and spiritual worlds), which was reflected in the joints of the child. The Navajo anthropologist Jennie Joe explains that Navajo often hold both explanations together: a medical-physical explanation, such as hip dysplasia, and a spiritual explanation, such as disharmony resulting from the violation of a taboo in butchering during pregnancy (1980, 140–51).

As this example suggests, in Navajo culture "healing cannot be separated from culture, sacred narrative or religion" (Lovern and Locust 2013, 77). Health, illness, and disability are spiritual matters, not just physical conditions that can be measured with medical equipment. Jennie Joe explains that "it is the causes of illness, not the symptoms, that are most important" (1980, 146). This is not to say they deem physical symptoms irrelevant or illusory, but that Navajo thought concentrates more on spiritual causes than physical outcomes of those causes.

Medicine people have the knowledge and spiritual power to use objects, such as plants or stones, to create change in both spiritual and physical worlds. In the case of an illness or injury, a Navajo person might consult both a doctor and a medicine person: the doctor to treat the physical symptoms, and the medicine person to restore harmony within the person's body, mind, and spirit, and within the spiritual world. Navajo traditions generally link physical deformity and disharmony, so they often pursue ritual responses (Leighton and Leighton 1945). For example, the Navajo Night Chant refers to unspecified pain or difficulty in walking, and it can be used to promote harmony in cases of specific injuries or illnesses.

And yet Navajo medicine people did not suggest this ritual in cases of hip dislocation. In fact, many suggested nothing at all. Many people with the condition, or those who had children with the condition, agreed. This Navajo culture did not stigmatize walking with a limp, and few saw it as an impairment. Especially if the person did not experience pain, they saw little reason to treat it. In fact, they simply did not see it as a disability. People with this hip dislocation function normally in social and economic settings, and they have no decrease in life expectancy. They marry, raise children, and participate in all aspects of Navajo society. Other Navajos do not express repulsion or pity in response; they merely see a limp as a physical difference.

As a physical difference, the limp might have a cause (such as the butchering), but the original disharmony of the cause may have been rectified. Once the spirit world and the person's internal relationship of mind, body, and spirit have been harmonized, and if the person experiences no pain or impairment at the physical level, the situation demands no further action.

It might not be surprising, then, to learn that when doctors suggested "curing" the limp, many Navajos resisted or simply did not follow up. For adults, the recommendation is often surgery: a hip fusion procedure, which joins the bones of the joint, making it very strong, but not very flexible. From the doctors' point of view, this fixed the abnormality. The person would no longer walk with a limp. But within a Navajo community, what was a painless limp became a significant impairment. After having the surgery, which went to the doctors' satisfaction, one man could not sit on the ground with his family at meal times, ride a horse, or walk confidently over uneven ground (Rabin et al. 1965, 30).

As Jennie Joe explains: "It is implied here that Navajos do accept certain degrees or forms of disability depending to a large degree on whether the disabled person can function in society and is able to live up to his expected role. It would seem, then, the concept of health for Navajos can be fluid and flexible, making allowances for those whose state of health is assessed within the context of their ability to function" (1980, 142–43). Navajo conceptions of the body have formed through interactions with US governmental and medical establishments, but they also retain ideas about disability and stigma that exceed medicalization or even static definitions.

Judaism in Late Antiquity

If looking at ideas of biopolitics is crucial to understanding disability in modern, Western settings, how should we make sense of disability in premodern times? Many of the forces that produce or manage disability today, such as nation-states, colonialism, or racial formations, were fundamentally different or did not exist in premodern contexts. This is not to say there was less hierarchy or more inclusion; rather, it is to understand that disability in premodern contexts requires leaving behind some of our contemporary assumptions about definitions and meanings of disability.

Today, people who are deaf (or Deaf) disagree about whether or not deafness is a disability or a culture (see, for example, Leigh et al. 2020; Scott-Hill 2003; Deaf with a capital D is more often used by those who see d/Deafness as a culture or even an ethnicity). In Jewish cultures in the ancient Near East, rabbinic texts did not recognize a Deaf culture. They positioned deaf people alongside others who were not full participants in religious rituals or obligations (see Gracer 2003). The Mishnah, redacted in the second century CE, includes a series of questions about the *halakhic* (Jewish legal) requirements for appearing and participating in rituals at the Temple in Jerusalem during a pilgrimage festival: "All are obligated to appear, except a deaf person, a person with intellectual disabilities and a minor, an intersex person [*tumtum*], a hermaphrodite, women, enslaved people who have not been freed, a lame person, a blind person, a sick person, an aged person, and one who is unable to go up on foot" (Hagigah 2a).

Does this list tell the reader about disability? Yes and no. It echoes many other rabbinic lists of exclusion, such as the common triad of the deaf person, a person who is mentally or intellectually disabled, and the minor. Each of these lists suggests that the categories of people on it share an inability or lack of responsibility with respect to religious obligations. The rabbis decided that "one who is not able to go up on foot" and "lame" people would not be obligated, obviously, because of physical impairments and the Temple architecture's lack of accessibility. Culturally and religiously, then, it makes sense to say these were disabilities. The rabbis excluded blind people because they saw this particular commandment as about seeing and being seen, thus those who did not see could not fulfill the commandment. Rabbinic texts include folk etymologies for blindness, "lameness," deafness, and other embodied differences that blame the conditions on parental sins of sexuality, such as wandering eyes, oral sex, or chattiness during intercourse (b. Nedarim 20a–b). Although some disagreed with the particular norms of sexuality, the text implies a sense that these conditions were undesirable, stigmatized, and associated with someone's sinful behavior.

Yet the list also includes minors (here, very small children), who were excluded because they might be too young to understand or participate properly. Children were hardly stigmatized just for being very young. And the list also excludes everyone who is not a man: women, intersex people, and hermaphrodites did not have to participate in the pilgrimage. Should these sex differences be seen as disabilities? People with those identities certainly did experience both stigma and exclusion from important religious rituals and leadership, though the stigmas and exclusions differed from those imposed on women, intersex people, and hermaphrodites (see, for example, Strassfeld 2022). Not being a man came with significant social difficulties. But these categories of people, especially women, appear elsewhere in rabbinic literature as "normal" and able-bodied, even if they are special cases. Disability as an analytical category might help us understand some aspects of their social positions, but it is an imprecise fit.

What about deafness? Does the text construct deafness as a disability (like the person who can't go up on foot or the blind person) or as a different kind of otherness (like a woman or an intersex person)? There is nothing in the text to suggest that hearing is an essential part of this ritual, so the rabbinic reasoning must differ from the case of the blind person. The Babylonian Talmud, redacted in the fifth or sixth century CE, provides commentary on many parts of the Mishnah. In its commentary about our text on who is obligated to participate in the pilgrimage festival, it begins by quoting a part of the Mishnah's passage: "Except for a deaf person, an imbecile, and a minor." The anonymous voice in the Talmudic text explains that "a deaf person is similar to an imbecile and a minor: Just as an imbecile and a minor [are among those] who are not of sound mind, so too the deaf person is not of sound mind" (b. Hagigah 2b). The rabbis cited here (erroneously) assumed that people who could neither hear nor speak also lacked cognition and understanding.

This comparison hearkens back to another passage from the Mishnah, which clarifies what the word *heresh* means: "The *heresh*, whom the Rabbis discussed everywhere, is one who does not hear and does not speak" (Terumot 1:2). Then, the Talmudic text concludes: "One who speaks but does not hear and one who hears but does not speak are obligated" to complete the commandments (b. Hagigah 2b). In the end, then, the Talmudic text rules that if a man can hear or speak, he is included in the normal—perhaps even elite—group of men who are required to participate fully in the pilgrimage. His impairment might matter in other contexts (and it does for some, such as participating in court processes), but lack of hearing or ability to speak did not constitute a reason for exclusion from this ritual.

As my brief analysis of this passage shows, it is not always clear whether rabbinic Judaism had disability as a category. In rabbinic texts, people we would consider disabled today often appear together with people we would consider non-disabled (for another excellent example, which includes skin color and race, see Belser 2018, 161), but stigma around bodily difference also structured society and social hierarchy. Any ideas about disability would intersect with other theological-social concepts, such as purity, fertility, chosenness, or mightiness. It also raises, but does not answer, the question of whether and how contemporary categories of disability can be used to analyze historical or cross-cultural contexts where those categories do not exist or have very different contours.

Returning to the opening passage from Leviticus that grouped together blindness, broken arms, short limbs, eye growths, and scars, we should now see that different social and religious contexts map different meanings onto embodied differences. It is not that ability or disability is merely in the eye of the beholder, but that power relationships, social structures, and dominant ideas and ideals shape the very concepts. The meaning of disability—even whether something *is* a disability—depends on the worldviews and interpretations of the people living in those societies. And those worldviews and interpretations are often fundamentally shaped by religion.

Suggested Readings

Abrams, Judith. 1998. *Judaism and Disability: Portrayals in Ancient Texts from the Tanach through the Bavli*. Washington, DC: Gallaudet University Press,.

Belser, Julia Watts. 2017. *Rabbinic Tales of Destruction: Gender, Sex, and Disability in the Ruins of Jerusalem*. New York: Oxford University Press.

Ghaly, Mohammed. 2009. *Islam and Disability: Perspectives in Theology and Jurisprudence*. New York: Routledge.

Imhoff, Sarah. 2017. "Why Disability Studies Needs to Take Religion Seriously." *Religions* 8 (9): 186–98.

Petro, Anthony. 2016. "Disability Studies and Religion." In *Embodied Religion*, edited by Kent Brintnall, 359–76. Farmington Hills, MI: Macmillan.

Samuels, Ellen. 2014. *Fantasies of Identification: Disability, Gender, Race*. New York: New York University Press.

Schumm, Darla, and Michael J. Stoltzfus. 2011. *Disability in Judaism, Christianity, and Islam: Sacred Texts, Historical Traditions, and Social Analysis*. New York: Springer.

References

Asad, Talal. 2003. *Formations of the Secular: Christianity, Islam, Modernity*. Stanford, CA: Stanford University Press.

Bashir, Shahzad. 2011. *Sufi Bodies: Religion and Society in Medieval Islam*. New York: Columbia University Press.

Bazna, Maysaa S., and Tarek A. Hatab. 2005. "Disability in the Qur'an: The Islamic Alternative to Defining, Viewing, and Relating to Disability." *Journal of Religion, Disability & Health* 9 (1): 5–27.

Bejoian, Lynne M. 2006. "Nondualistic Paradigms in Disability Studies and Buddhism:

Creating Bridges for Theoretical Practice." *Disability Studies Quarterly* 26 (3). https://doi.org/10.18061/dsq.v26i3.723.

Belser, Julia Watts. 2018. "Queering the Dissident Body." In *Unsettling Science and Religion: Contributions and Questions from Queer Studies*, edited by Lisa Stenmark and Whitney Bauman, 161–81. Lanham, MD: Lexington Books.

Breckenridge, Carol Appadurai, and Candace A. Vogler. 2001. "The Critical Limits of Embodiment: Disability's Criticism." *Public Culture* 13 (3): 349–57.

Coggins, Megan L. 2017. "Fake It Until You Make It (or Until You Find Your Place)." In *Barriers and Belongings: Personal Narratives of Disability*, edited by Michelle Jarman, Leila Monaghan, and Alison Quaggin Harkin, 195–200. Philadelphia, PA: Temple University Press.

Cohen, Alice Eve. 2009. *What I Thought I Knew*. New York: Penguin Books.

Davis, Lennard. 2013. *The End of Normal: Identity in a Biocultural Era*. Ann Arbor: University of Michigan Press.

Eiesland, Nancy L. 1994. *The Disabled God: Toward a Liberatory Theology of Disability*. Nashville, TN: Abingdon Press.

Eiesland, Nancy L. 1998. "Barriers and Bridges: Relating the Disability Rights Movement and Religious Organizations." In *Human Disability and the Service of God: Reassessing Religious Practice*, edited by Nancy L. Eiesland and Don E. Saliers, 200–229. Nashville, TN: Abingdon Press.

Garland-Thomson, Rosemarie. 1997. *Extraordinary Bodies: Figuring Disability in American Culture and Literature*. New York: Columbia University Press.

Garland-Thomson, Rosemarie. 2013. "Disability Studies: A Field Emerged." *American Quarterly* 65 (4): 915–26.

Garland-Thomson, Rosemarie. 2015. "Eugenics." In *Keywords for Disability Studies*, edited by Rachel Adams, Benjamin Reiss, and David Serlin, 74–79. New York: New York University Press.

Gracer, Bonnie. 2003. "What the Rabbis Heard: Deafness in the Mishnah." *Disability Studies Quarterly* 23 (2): 192–205.

Hall, David D., ed. [1997] 2020. *Lived Religion in America: Toward a History of Practice*. Princeton, NJ: Princeton University Press.

Harris, W. C. 2014. *Slouching Toward Gaytheism: Christianity and Queer Survival in America*. Albany: SUNY Press.

Joe, Jennie. 1980. "Disabled Children in Navajo Society." PhD diss., University of California, Berkeley & San Francisco.

Kafer, Alison. 2013. *Feminist, Queer, Crip*. Bloomington: Indiana University Press.

Kent, Mike, Katie Ellis, Rachel Robertson, and Rosemarie Garland-Thomson, eds. 2018. "Introduction." In *Manifestos for the Future of Critical Disability Studies*, vol. 1. New York: Routledge.

Leigh, Irene W., Jean F. Andrews, Raychelle L. Harris, and Topher González Ávila. 2020. *Deaf Culture: Exploring Deaf Communities in the United States*. San Diego, CA: Plural Publishing.

Leighton, A. H., and D. C. Leighton. 1945. *The Navaho Door: An Introduction to Navaho Life*. Cambridge, MA: Harvard University Press.

Lovern, Lavonna, and Carol Locust. 2013. *Native American Communities on Health and Disability: A Borderland Dialogue*. New York: Springer.

McRuer, Robert. 2006. *Crip Theory: Cultural Signs of Queerness and Disability*. New York: New York University Press.

Orsi, Robert. 2005. *Between Heaven and Earth: The Religious Worlds People Make and the Scholars Who Study Them*. Princeton, NJ: Princeton University Press.

Petro, Anthony M. 2020. "Bob Flanagan's Crip Catholicism, Transgression, and Form in Lived Religion." *American Religion* 1 (2): 1–26.

Rabin, David L., Clifford R. Barnett, William E. Arnold, Robert H. Freiberger, and Gyla Brooks. 1965. "Untreated Congenital Hip Disease: A Study of the Epidemiology, Natural History, and Social Aspects of the Disease in a Navajo Population." *American Journal of Public Health* 55 (2): 1–44.

Raphael, Rebecca. 2008. *Biblical Corpora: Representations of Disability in Hebrew Biblical Literature*. London: Bloomsbury Publishing USA.

Sampter, Jessie. n.d. "Speaking Heart." Unpublished manuscript, A219, Jessie Sampter Papers, Central Zionist Archives, Jerusalem.

Sanford, Matthew. 2006. *Waking: A Memoir of Trauma and Transcendence*. Emmaus, PA: Rodale Books.

Schacht, Robert. 2001. "Engaging Anthropology in Disability Studies: American Indian Issues." *Disability Studies Quarterly* 21 (3): 17–36.

Scott-Hill, Mairian. 2003. "Deafness/Disability—Problematising Notions of Identity, Culture and Structure." In *Disability, Culture and Identity*, edited by Sheila Riddell and Nick Watson, 88–104. London: Taylor & Francis Group.

Shildrick, Margrit. 2015. "Sex." In *Keywords for Disability Studies*, edited by Rachel Adams, Benjamin Reiss, and David Serlin, 164–66. New York: New York University Press.

Siebers, Tobin. 2001. "Disability in Theory: From Social Constructionism to the New Realism of the Body." *American Literary History* 13 (4): 737–54. https://doi.org/10.1093/alh/13.4.737.

Spicer, Dale. n.d. "Disability Theologies: Notorious Bodies and Created Difference in al-Jāḥiz's *Book of the Leprous and the Lame*." PhD diss., Indiana University, in progress.

Stearns, Peter, Katie Barclay, and Sharon Crozier-DeRosa, eds. 2020. *Sources for the History of Emotions: A Guide*. New York: Routledge.

Strassfeld, Max. 2022. *Trans Talmud: Androgynes and Eunuchs in Rabbinic Literature*. Oakland: University of California Press.

Walker-Cornetta, Andrew. 2020. "Spiritual Rehabilitation: A Religious History of Intellectual Disability in Postwar America." PhD diss., Princeton University.

Walker-Cornetta, Andrew. 2023. "Without the Lord: Eliza Suggs, Religion, and the Good Disabled Subject." *American Religion* 5 (1): 66–92.

Watts Belser, Julia. 2018. "Queering the Dissident Body." In *Unsettling Science and Religion: Contributions and Questions from Queer Studies*, edited by Lisa Stenmark and Whitney Bauman. Lanham, MD: Lexington Books.

Wendell, Susan. 1996. *The Rejected Body: Feminist Philosophical Reflections on Disability*. New York: Routledge.

3 FAITH

Constance M. Furey

> You Mortals are so puzzled about this Divine Faith, and Natural Reason, that you do not know well how to distinguish them, but confound them both, which is the cause you have so many divine Philosophers make a Gallimaufry both of Reason and Faith.
> MARGARET CAVENDISH, *The Description of the New World, Called The Blazing World* ([1666] 2004)

"Faith," a poem by George Herbert (1593–1633) in *The Temple*, one of the most famous collections of devotional poems in the English language, begins with a question.

Faith

  Lord, how couldst thou so much appease
Thy wrath for sin as, when man's sight was dim,
And could see little, to regard his ease,
  And bring by Faith all things to him?

(Herbert 2007, 172)

What is it about faith that Herbert finds perplexing? In the convoluted syntax of this single sentence, spread over four lines, it is easy to get tangled up in the commas and disoriented by the line breaks. By the time the question mark appears, it feels far removed from the interrogative "how" in the first line. Faced with this confusion, the reader might throw up her hands, observe that this is a religious poem concerned with "Lord," "wrath," "sin," and "Faith," and conclude that the poem will confirm what most people already think: that faith is inward and personal, entailing trust or belief in God.

This supposition, however, closes down what Herbert's question opens up. "Lord, how couldst thou . . . bring by Faith all things to him?" From the very beginning of this eleven-stanza poem, Herbert presents faith not as inner certitude but as externalized interaction. Faith is first and foremost relational, as personified in the very first word. "Lord," the speaker says, addressing his deity with the combination of intimacy and formality that establishes the poem's persistent interest in how people are shaped by forces beyond their control. God here is wholly other but also immediately accessible, a distant sovereign and source of everything, the giver of gifts who is also the recipient of the poet's loquacious questions, testimonials, and gratitude. Indeed, the difficulty of the opening question instantiates the complexity of its topic. Faith conveys "all things." How? What indeed is faith, this interactive, relational dynamic that claims such power? From the beginning, in other words, Herbert's poem confirms that there's more to faith than most modern readers are prepared to notice and engage.

In ten subsequent stanzas, faith performs many transformative miracles. Hunger is appeased, pain is alleviated, and debts are erased:

> Hungry I was, and had no meat:
> I did conceit a most delicious feast;
> I had it straight, and did as truly eat,
> As ever did a welcome guest.
>
> There is a rare outlandish root,
> Which when I could not get, I thought it here:
> That apprehension cur'd so well my foot,
> That I can walk to heav'n well neare.
>
> I owed thousands and much more:
> I did believe that I did nothing owe,
> And liv'd accordingly; my creditor
> Believes so too, and lets me go.

Can faith alleviate hunger? Enable a mortal to amble toward paradise? Forgive debts? In each case, the answer is yes. "Hungry I was, and had no meat," the speaker laments, but with faith he was fed like a "welcome guest." Faith "cur'd so well my foot, / That I can walk to heav'n well near." And though he "owed thousands and much more," faith made it possible to live as though he had money enough. Hunger is appeased, impairment is alleviated, and debts are erased, as crushing external forces become sustaining resources for the speaker who, given what he lacked, can now claim it as his own.

Editors of an online reproduction of the 1633 edition of Herbert's poem primly advise readers to focus on the "spiritual" rather than the "literal" meaning of this stanza's miraculous claims about health and sustenance (Herbert 1633). In one sense this just echoes the Pauline injunction, "Faith [Greek *pistis*; Latin *fides*] is the assurance of things hoped for, the conviction of things not seen" (Heb 11:1). In another sense, though, it means the editors are trying to separate what Herbert himself has joined. Faith is not intangible rather than tangible, spiritual rather than material; instead it is a new relationship between them. Herbert thus emphasizes that faith brings all things and rectifies all things, including inequity, injury, and financial bondage. He *also* emphasizes faith's subjective effects by recounting how faith can alter a believer's self-perception and even change one's existential condition:

> Faith makes me any thing, or all
> That I believe is in the sacred story:
> And where sin placeth me in Adam's fall,
> Faith sets me higher in his glory.

Directly following on the previous stanza's rendition of faith's material benefits, these lines emphasize that faith's effects are also internal, engendering a sense of certainty and comfort. Human possibilities become more expansive, as people otherwise doomed to repeat the same mistakes over and over again can now imagine they might become "any thing, or all."

More subtly, faith disrupts notions of what this "all" entails. In lieu of a single, formulaic progression from sin to salvation, failure to success, or inadequacy to fulfillment, faith might humble:

> If I go lower in the book,
> What can be lower than the common manger?
> Faith puts me there with him, who sweetly took
> Our flesh and frailty, death and danger.

And equalize:

If bliss had lain in art or strength,
None but the wise or strong had gained it:
Where now by Faith all arms are of a length;
One size doth all conditions fit.

A peasant may believe as much
As a great Clerk, and reach the highest stature.
Thus dost thou make proud knowledge bend & crouch,
While grace fills up uneven nature.

While also changing perceptions of reality:

When creatures had no real light
Inherent in them, thou didst make the sun
Impute a lustre, and allow them bright;
And in this show, what Christ hath done.

George Herbert lived a relatively peaceful life as a self-described country parson, in a volatile age where claims about royal succession, monastic property, papal power, or the translation of a single biblical passage could spark wars, justify torture, or sign a death warrant. Herbert preached Christ resurrected and the salvation of all believers. Yet rather than fretfully insisting on a doctrinal definition of faith, or preaching the need for dogmatic certainty, Herbert presents faith in terms that scholars of religion should relish: as simultaneously psychological, epistemological, sociological, economic, and spiritual.

In the penultimate stanza of the poem, Herbert deemed perception as important as resurrection, depicting faith as the capacity to see differently. He paired this stanza on perspectival change with a final verse celebrating faith's ability to counter material decay.

That which before was darkn'd clean
With bushy groves, pricking the lookers eye,
Vanished away, when Faith did change the scene:
And then appear'd a glorious sky.

What though my body run to dust?
Faith cleaves unto it, counting ev'ry grain
With an exact and most particular trust,
Reserving all for flesh again.

In this work by a pious Christian poet, faith is not spiritual, if spiritual means sequestered from the world. Faith is, rather, a relational force, acting within the realm defined by everyday realities as well as salvific ideals. As it cleaves bodies, changes the scene of action, and alters tangible reality, faith troubles the distinction between receptivity and action. Faith names a heightened engagement with the relational dynamic intrinsic to being human, the experience of being undone by forces over which we have no control while also constituted in ways that enable us to destroy as well as create, to reject as well as accept, to cherish and to change.

I begin here, with this canonical Protestant poem, to demonstrate that faith deserves, and rewards, scholarly attention. Many scholars are convinced that faith is an unwelcome reminder of the field's Protestant past, a theological hangover that hinders ongoing efforts to diversify the study of religion. One rejoinder comes from George Michael's 1987 pop song, with its catchy refrain, "'Cause I gotta have faith." In Michael's song as in the George Herbert poem written nearly four hundred years earlier, faith is essential to relationships, real and imagined, limited and aspirational. Another riposte comes from Margaret Cavendish, reminding us that Protestants in the past struggled with some of the same questions about faith that afflict scholars today. Attention to faith could improve the study of religion, but only if we rid ourselves of simplistic suppositions about what faith entails. In the next section of this essay, then, I survey important critiques of how faith is perceived today, in everyday life as in scholarly discourse. This appraisal illustrates how studies that aim to challenge what people think about faith often accept the premise that faith is necessarily internal, personal, and spiritual. There are, however, exciting alternatives. These are the subject of the essay's final section: studies unafraid of faith, uninhibited by narrow, confounding definitions, and thereby able to evade modernity's attempts to capture and tame religion by equating it with a narrowly defined notion of faith.

: : :

"Scholars who study faith should have seen the Capitol riots coming," a headline from January 2021 declared (Berlinerblau 2021). Like Chief Justice Roberts, who pronounced in *Hosanna-Tabor Evangelical Lutheran Church and School v. EEOC* (565 US 171 [2012]) that the "Free Exercise Clause . . . protects a religious group's right to shape its own faith," this headline writer could assume his readers would understand faith as the inner essence of religion. Whether hailed as the source of admirable belief and trust in things unseen, or disparaged as a word that signifies opposition to science or other forms of evidence-based knowledge, faith is widely understood as religion's pulsing heart. Yet this notion that faith is a synecdoche for religion (reflected in any references to the world's "faith traditions"), or the defining feature of any religious person (evident whenever people describe adherents as the "faithful"), is demonstrably ahistorical and often dangerously exclusionary (Masuzawa 2005, 37–46). Dominant Christian groups—primarily (but not only) Protestant, and especially (but not exclusively) since the sixteenth century—have successfully promoted, and sometimes violently imposed, the idea that faith is synonymous with good religion, often in the process of condemning the rituals, beliefs, and communal commitments of other Christians (including Catholics and Orthodox) or non-Christians as fetishistic, idolatrous, or otherwise depraved.

The problem persists in secular modern societies. In fact, the impulse to prioritize faith exemplifies one of the most significant failings in the study of religion, Talal Asad observed, pointing to the work of the comparatist Wilfred Cantwell Smith—a Protestant pastor as well as a scholar of Islam—who advised scholars to shift their focus from religion to faith. Religion, according to Cantwell Smith, is a reified, structural entity. Faith, by contrast, "and by 'faith' I mean personal faith," Cantwell Smith emphasized, is an "act I make myself, naked, before God." Faith is "deeply personal, dynamic, ultimate" (Smith 1963, 79, 127). While the shift from structures to people might seem laudatory, Asad observes that in endorsing faith in this way, and this sort of faith, Cantwell Smith upheld modern liberalism's conviction that people are essentially equal, a principle that both depends on and perpetuates the premise that people's (often quite different) traditions and practices are less important than their (invisible, immaterial) beliefs (Asad 2001). This individualized notion of faith likewise informs the anthropologist Clifford Geertz's exhortation to scholars not to lose sight of inner motives and beliefs: "Religion without interiority, without some 'bathed in sentiment' sense that belief matters, and matters terribly, that faith sustains, cures, comforts redresses wrongs, improves fortune, secures rewards, explains, obligates, blesses, clarifies, reconciles, regenerates, redeems, or saves, is hardly worthy of the name" (Geertz 2000, 178). Cantwell Smith offered a relational alternative to his inner notion of faith when he argued that faith was cultivated and sustained only in the context of friendships (Smith 2013). And Geertz's anthropological studies do not privilege personal feelings over social actions and cultural meaning. Nevertheless, Smith's argument about friendship is rarely cited. And Geertz's rendition has usually been understood to affirm that a personalized spirituality is paramount. The reception of these scholars' studies confirms the need for Asad's critique. What they represent is the idea that faith is essential to the study of religion because it names the interiority that matters most.

Even works that aim to diversify our understanding of faith may fail to challenge this modern mandate, inherited from (a particular version of) Christianity. In a book with the English title *Two Types of Faith*, for example, the Jewish theologian Martin Buber (1878–1965) differentiated Jewish faith (Hebrew *emunah*) from its Christian counterpart (Greek *pistis*) by defining the former as trust and the latter as belief. Buber's study did not, however, unsettle modernity's conviction that faith is inward and spiritual (Buber 1951). Distinctions have been drawn by biblical scholars (e.g., Bultmann and Weiser 1961); classicists (e.g., Morgan 2015) and historians of Christianity, who regularly point out that before the Reformation, faith often denoted a communally oriented sense of trust and only after the Reformation became so closely aligned with belief (e.g., Shagan 2018; Taylor 2018). Reliance on these sorts of binaries—between belief and trust, for example, or communal and individual faith—hinder attempts to acknowledge the critical perspective faith provides on these and other conceptual categories.

The anthropologist Tanya Luhrmann's ethnographic study of American evangelicals similarly accepts that faith is a personal matter even as she argues that faith has been wrongly equated with belief. Luhrmann explains that for her subjects faith is not cognitive but perceptual and emotional, a way of organizing "attention and emotion." Faith, she assures her readers, should not be considered irrational, for faith is "the management of the contradiction rather than blind ignorance about the contradiction" (Luhrmann 2016, 147–49). Other studies of faith in modern contexts likewise withdraw it from generative inquiry by treating faith as mysterious in itself even as they study its effects. This is the approach taken by many studies of faith healing (Chestnut 1997; Espinosa 1999; Brown 2012). In various ways, these studies maintain faith's protected status, immunizing it against critique while preserving its central role in a modern ideology (Asad 2003, 23, 55). This ideology has insidious social as well as intellectual consequences. In the liberal order, for example, the "claim to civil immunity with regard to religious faith" reinforces "the idea of a secular state and a particular conception of religion" (Asad 2012, 36–37, 44). In modern societies, faith is increasingly tasked with redressing the problems caused by economic inequities and governmental failures. "Faith-based communities" displace social services. Faith is deemed the savior for communities denied resources and reparations. Faith is supposed to be blind to skin color and bank accounts and accents and genitalia, which in turn means that claims about faith's redemptive power often occlude or deny racism, classism, xenophobia, and other forms of structural oppression (Plaskow 2002). In many nation-states today, moreover, faith has extraordinary legal standing. "While religionists avoid talking about faith," the law and religion scholar Winnifred Sullivan observes, "judges do so with impunity" (Sullivan 2020, 38; see also Oraby and Sullivan 2020). Judicial decisions about faith determine prison conditions, workplace discrimination claims, and health care coverage. What Sullivan says of the US applies other countries as well: "the stakes are high in the US today for those who want to show 'how faith works'" (Sullivan 2020, 138). The consequences are weighty for scholars as well. Any study that perpetuates narrow Christian definitions of faith risks deepening faith's injurious social and legal standing.

No wonder many religionists—especially, but not only, those who study non-Christian sources—shun faith as a topic impossible to examine without perpetuating the conundrum it represents: that Protestant assumptions occlude, marginalize, or disparage other ways of being, knowing, and acting. And yet there are more daring possibilities, studies intrigued by faith's relational dynamic, understanding faith as enmeshed in everyday realities and attentive to limits while aspiring also to ideals and intent on change or transcendence.

Consider, for example, the way Michael Taussig's anthropological study of shamanism demonstrates the shortcomings of equating faith with narrowly cognitive or affective notions of belief or trust. Faith is essential to the work of shamans, Taussig argues, but not because faith protects shamans from the skepticism of their patients. Rather, faith is manifest in the bodied viscerality of the shamanic practice, and the way it mimicked the actions of the spirits and induced them, through mimesis, to heal the patient (Taussig 2006). In a related study, the anthropologist Anthony Shenoda opens to something beyond the axiomatic claim that faith is the opposite of doubt—an assumption he reports having previously shared with many of his Egyptian Christian interlocutors—and discovers an unexpected alternative: most expressions of faith and doubt in his field notes were not introspective reports of belief or skepticism but instead political acts, affirming solidarity among Coptic Christians and delineating differences between Copts and Muslims. All this is historically and culturally specific, Shenoda argues, reflecting a response to the perceived and real political marginalization of Coptic Christians under the presidencies of Anwar Sadat and Hosni Mubarak. Narratives of persecution and martyrdom are essential to Coptic Christians, as are the miracle stories that attest to the power of their patron saints and the persistence of Christianity despite its minority status. But in this particular political context, the miracle stories proudly narrated by pious Copts often focused specifically on reasons for skepticism about the Muslim Other and trust in the intervening acts of saintly Christians. The point is not primarily that faith may be a matter of trust rather than belief—though that is certainly true in the context Shenoda studies—but that the locus of this trust may be communal and interpersonal relationships rather than a transcendent deity.

Shenoda illustrates this with three vignettes, each detailing how miracle stories locate the Copts in their political environs. For instance, credit is given to a wonder-working nun from a popular monastery to explain how Suzanne Mubarak, the president's wife, was healed of leukemia and Copts were allowed to continue to build churches despite official prohibitions. The nun accomplished this by working in and through official and personal channels: a wealthy friend, a medical doctor, and the president's wife herself. Assured by a healthy Mubarak that she could make any request she liked, the nun asked only that the president "be well intentioned toward Christians in Egypt." At a subsequent meeting with President Mubarak, Pope Shenouda was assured that Copts could "build quietly," so long as gifts (i.e., bribes) were given and no Muslims complained (Shenoda 2012, 484). Notably, as Shenoda observes, the story demonstrates how the variables of church-state relations—the mundane and frustrating processes of obtaining or being denied building materials or offering a bribe only to find the price has increased or the official is no longer receptive—is cast in terms of faith, as distrust of the Egyptian government yields a story of how what was forbidden came to be allowed through the interactions between a politician's wife and a faithful nun.

In another of Shenoda's stories, a Christian priest, renowned as an exorcist, scoffs at a Muslim man's claim to have been healed by the priest. Certain that the man was not possessed by evil spirits, but pressured by the family to help, the priest went through the motions, offering water and proclaiming a healing which the man and his family then gratefully celebrated. The priest thereby presented himself as both clairvoyant (able to discern the absence of evil spirits) and humble (simply doing what he was asked, and not disabusing his Muslim neighbors of their foolish credulity). In these ways, the priest enacted the conviction that faith is communally identified and activated rather than objectively efficacious. This priest's story reveals that faith's ability to heal is subsumed within, and subservient to, its capacity to differentiate Muslims from Christians and to bind the latter together in communion with God. In a final vignette, Shenoda describes how a doctor's note, attesting to the miraculous status of a human arm on display in a monastery southwest of Cairo, confirms the faith that coheres the Coptic community. Faith, Shenoda concludes, has significant material and political effects and is best understood not as a personal feeling or belief but as a force of social cohesion and differentiation.

In research focused on Iran rather than Egypt, and Islam rather than Christianity, Alireza Doostdar illuminates the different ways individual, religious, and national identity can depend on faith understood as a communally cultivated dynamic. In *The Iranian Metaphysicals*, a study of middle-class people committed to occult and spiritual pursuits as rational projects in twentieth-century Iran, Doostdar draws examples from TV shows, occult writings, exorcisms, and seances to trace an evolving, interweaving series of claims about the rationality of faith, the mutuality of faith and science, and the need for the faithful to train themselves in "sciences of the heart." What emerges from these sources is faith understood as a mode of inquiry required of individuals but enacted within a community. Righteous belief is entirely dependent on "faith in the powerful God," Ruhollah Khomeini confirmed in *Unveiling of Secrets*, a 1940s book that drew on Islamic juridical, theological, and philosophical ideas as well as European science. In the same book, Khomeini insisted that "the pious are the last to believe, believe nothing without reason, and reject nothing without reason." These were compatible claims: the person who is utterly dependent on faith in the powerful God is rightly and necessarily the person who must actively test and assess his or her beliefs. Doostdar finds a similar combination of claims in the testimony of a pious police chief who believed "based on the strength of his faith" that "extraordinary powers do exist," while also insisting that his faith is and should be based on the evidence of his own eyes and careful research. Spiritists who participated in seances in order to contribute to the dawning of "spiritual science and faith" likewise understood that both should be "supported by concrete evidence" and opposed "blind faith" with "moral facts." And Sufi adherents, perceiving the heart as both fleshly and spiritual, the organ within which God works when he wants to strengthen one's faith, explained that all the faithful needed to be instructed in "sciences of the heart." The Iranian metaphysicals of Doostdar's study are those defined by this experience of faith as a mode of inquiry, inextricable from but not delimited by Islamic beliefs, sources, and communities (Doostdar 2018, 44, 116, 125, 167n3).

We might expect quite different ways of talking about faith, or even an absence of interest altogether, in non-monotheistic contexts. Practitioners and scholars of Buddhism, for example, often contend that the Sanskrit term *śraddha* should be translated as confidence or trust rather than faith. Why the reluctance to use the word faith? Because, critics argue, faith carries with it the monotheistic notion of belief or trust *in* another. Buddhist teachings, by contrast, affirm that one can realize the object of one's faith (awakening) for oneself. "Unlike a monotheistic religion, where faith centers on the power of another, and skepticism entails the rejection of that power," as people convinced of faith's inapplicability to Buddhism might argue, "faith in the Buddha's Awakening keeps pointing back to the power of your own actions" (Bhikkhu n.d.).

Those who think faith a concept that has no relevance to Buddhism are nevertheless mistaken, the modern Buddhist commentator Ṭhānissaro Bhikkhu argues, for while faith in the Buddhist context is "faith in the ability of your own actions," the aim of alleviating suffering is achieved through faith in the Buddha's teachings, and in the truth that can be revealed by testing those claims. Ṭhānissaro Bhikkhu illustrates the need for this combination of empiricism and trust by invoking the Buddha's story of a hunter searching for a bull elephant. As one commentator explains, to get to the bull elephant "you must do what the Buddha's disciple Sariputta did: he kept following the path, without drawing dishonest conclusions, until he saw the elephant within." This does not, however, mean that the process requires empiricism *rather than* faith. Faith is the conviction required to follow this particular path, but testing and confirming the rightness of the path is required to find this faith within oneself and activate its transformative power. Thus when the Buddha asked his disciple "do you take it on faith that these five strengths—faith, persistence, mindfulness, concentration, and discernment—lead to the deathless?" Sariputta could say "no, I don't take it on faith. I know." In this sense, as with science, faith is a working hypothesis subject to evaluation. But *that*, according to Ṭhānissaro Bhikkhu's commentary, is possible only through total commitment. "Only when you take apart all clinging to your inner and outer senses can you prove whether the activity of clinging is what hides the deathless." Faith, then, is not only that which needs to be tested, but the process of refining one's method of testing. Ṭhānissaro Bhikkhu's account of Buddhist faith as something cultivated by individuals who have the right sort of commitment to the tradition's teachers is thus individualized. Notably, this Buddhist definition of faith is not, however, synonymous with Cantwell Smith's definition of faith as the individual naked before God or Geertz's emphasis on the personal intensity of conviction or belief. Buddhist faith might instead be understood as a logically circuitous but experientially robust phenomenon: each follower must have faith in the path laid out by the Buddha in order to test and thereby commit to that path.

:::

To recall where this all began, Herbert's poem showcases the way faith might name an interlayering of certainties and questions, of individual and collective actions, beliefs, and emotions; of societal and perspectival change; and the interactive testing of what is known. This faith poem from the English Reformation illustrates how a term so often used uncritically might aid our efforts to make the study of religion more critically astute (and, not incidentally, how the same Protestantism that encouraged people to equate faith with inner certainty might itself reveal the limits of that version of faith). More specifically, this premodern Protestant source suggests some of what might be overlooked by those who equate faith with personal spirituality and verifies the limitations of accounts structured around the standard binaries of belief and trust; spiritual and material; solitary and social; internally felt and externally conditioned. Herbert's "Faith" conveys instead that faith could sharpen and deepen our understanding of religion's—and indeed humanity's—relationality. The interactivity intrinsic to being human should prompt us to query rather than assume boundaries between self and other, personal and communal, psychological and material, active and passive, innate and cultivated. This, I think, is the significance of a daring intervention by the anthropologists Rene Willersley and Christian Suhr, who ask in their title, "Is there a place for faith in the study of anthropology?" (Willersley and Suhr 2018). The answer? An unequivocal and surprising yes. Willersley and Suhr are not content to observe that, as respectful ethnographers, anthropologists should dutifully attribute faith to subjects who claim it for themselves. Nor are they encouraging anthropologists to "take faith seriously." Rather, they contend that there is a place for faith in the study of anthropology because faith is a methodological mandate for all anthropologists. What does this mean? Anthropology requires a leap of faith because of the radical shift of perspective required of all anthropologists—the need to observe without referring everything back to oneself, to evaluate and compare without making oneself the source and end of all comparisons. For this reason, Willersley and Suhr conclude, anthropology is better understood as a theology than a science, dependent as it is on something akin to divine revelation, a decentering insight that enables non-self-referential relationships.

> That which before was darkened clean
> With bushy groves, pricking the looker's eye,
> Vanished away, when Faith did change the scene:
> And then appear'd a glorious sky.

With Herbert, then, I conclude by inviting scholars of religion to revisit faith, to consider the possibility that when thought, lived, and assessed as it is by the sources highlighted here (as by many others, some of whom are listed in suggested readings below), faith is a critical term for religious studies because it is critical to being human. When thought, lived, and expressed in these ways, faith opens into blazing worlds of possibility—an alight, transfigurative relationship with uncontrollable forces—requiring an "exact and most particular trust."

Suggested Readings

Asad, Talal. 2001. "Reading a Modern Classic: W.C. Smith's *The Meaning and End of Religion*." *History of Religions* 40 (3): 205–22.

Doostdar, Alireza. 2018. *Iranian Metaphysicals: Explorations in Science, Islam, and the Uncanny*. Princeton, NJ: Princeton University Press.

Frederick, Marla F. 2003. *Between Sundays: Black Women and Everyday Struggles of Faith*. Berkeley: University of California Press.

Marno, David. 2016. *Death Be Not Proud: The Art of Holy Attention*. Chicago: University of Chicago Press.

Shenoda, Anthony. 2012. "The Politics of Faith: On Faith, Skepticism, and Miracles among Coptic Christians in Egypt." *Ethnos: Journal of Anthropology* 77 (4): 477–95.

Sullivan, Winnifred Fallers. 2009. *Prison Religion: Faith-Based Reform and the Constitution*. Princeton, NJ: Princeton University Press.

Van Engen, John. 1991. "Faith as Concept of Order in Medieval Christendom." In *Belief in History: Innovative Approaches to European and American Religion*. Notre Dame, IN: University of Notre Dame Press.

Willersley, Rene, and Christian Suhr. 2018. "Is There a Place for Faith in Anthropology? Religion, Reason, and the Ethnographer's Divine Revelation." *Hau* 8 (1–2): 65–78.

References

Asad, Talal. 2001. "Reading a Modern Classic: W. C. Smith's *The Meaning and End of Religion*." *History of Religions* 40 (3): 205–22.

Asad, Talal. 2003. *Formations of the Secular*. Stanford, CA: Stanford University Press.

Asad, Talal. 2012. "Thinking about Religion, Belief, and Politics." In *The Cambridge Companion to Religious Studies*, edited by Robert Orsi, 36–37. Cambridge: Cambridge University Press.

Berlinerblau, Jacques. 2021. "Bad Religion: Scholars Who Study Faith Should Have Seen the Capitol Riots Coming. They Didn't." *Chronicle of Higher Education*, January 21.

Bhikkhu, Ṭhānissaro. n.d. "Faith in Awakening." Dhammatalks.org (blog), accessed July 25, 2024. https://www.dhammatalks.org/books/PurityOfHeart/Section0005.html.

Brown, Candy Gunther. 2012. *Testing Prayer: Science and Healing*. Cambridge, MA: Harvard University Press.

Buber, Martin. 1951. *Two Kinds of Faith*. Translated by Norman Goldhawk. New York: Harper and Row.

Bultmann, Rudolff, and Artur Weiser. 1961. *Faith*. Translated by Dorothea M. Barton. London: A. & C. Black.

Cavendish, Margaret. 2004. *The Blazing World and Other Writings*. Edited by Kate Lilley. New York: Penguin Books.

Chestnut, Andrew. 1997. *Born Again in Brazil: The Pentecostal Boom and the Pathogens of Poverty*. New Brunswick, NJ: Rutgers University Press.

Doostdar, Alireza. 2018. *Iranian Metaphysicals: Explorations in Science, Islam, and the Uncanny*. Princeton, NJ: Princeton University Press.

Espinosa, Gason. 1999. "El Azteca: Francisco Olazabal and Latino Pentecostal Charisma, Power, and Faith Healing." *Journal of the American Academy of Religion* 67 (3): 597–616.

Geertz, Clifford. 2000. *Available Light: Anthropological Reflection on Philosophical Topics*. Princeton, NJ: Princeton University Press.

Herbert, George. 1633. *The Temple*. In Christian Classics Ethereal Library. https://www.ccel.org/h/herbert/temple/Faith.html.

Herbert, George. 2007. *The English Poems of George Herbert*. Edited by Helen Wilcox. Cambridge: Cambridge University Press.

Luhrmann, Tanya. 2016. "Understanding the Work of Faith." *The Cambridge Journal of Anthropology* 34 (2): 147–49.

Masuzawa, Tomoko. 2005. *The Invention of World Religions*. Chicago: University of Chicago Press.

Morgan, Teresa. 2015. *Roman Faith and Christian Faith: "Pistis" and "Fides" in the Early Roman Empire and Early Churches*. Oxford: Oxford University Press.

Oraby, Mona, and Winnifred Fallers Sullivan. 2020. "Law and Religion: Reimagining the Entanglement of Two Universals." *Annual Review of Law and Social Science* 16 (2): 257–76.

Plaskow, Judith. 2002. "Whose Initiative? Whose Faith?" *Journal of the American Academy of Religion* 70 (4).

Shagan, Ethan. 2018. *The Birth of Modern Belief: Faith and Judgment from the Middle Ages to the Enlightenment*. Princeton, NJ: Princeton University Press.

Shenoda, Anthony. 2012. "The Politics of Faith: On Faith, Skepticism, and Miracles among Coptic Christians in Egypt." *Ethnos: Journal of Anthropology* 77 (4): 477–95.

Smith, Suzanne. 2013. "Wilfred Cantwell Smith: Love, Science, and the Study of Religion." *Journal of the American Academy of Religion* 81 (3): 757–90.

Smith, Wilfred Cantwell. 1963. *The Meaning and End of Religion*. New York: Macmillan.

Sullivan, Winnifred Fallers. 2009. *Prison Religion: Faith-Based Reform and the Constitution*. Princeton, NJ: Princeton University Press.

Sullivan, Winnifred Fallers. 2020. *Church State Corporation: Construing Religion in US Law*. Chicago: University of Chicago Press.

Taussig, Michael. 2006. "Viscerality, Faith, and Skepticism: Another Theory of Magic." In *Walter Benjamin's Grave*, 121–55. Chicago: University of Chicago Press.

Taylor, Charles. 2018. *A Secular Age*. Cambridge, MA: Harvard University Press.

Willersley, Rene, and Christian Suhr. 2018. "Is There a Place for Faith in Anthropology? Religion, Reason, and the Ethnographer's Divine Revelation." *Hau* 8 (1–2): 65–78.

4 FEELING

Nancy Khalek

Introduction

Like a number of terms in the study of religion which have both colloquial and technical meanings, "feeling" is a word that seems intuitive but turns out to be extraordinarily complicated. On the one hand, everyone simply *knows* what it means to "feel something," whether we mean this in the physical sense of being affected by some object or physical state or in the sense of an inner mental or emotional experience. On the other hand, scholarly discussions of "feeling" and "emotion" are numerous and scattered across a range of subfields in religious studies and in adjacent disciplines including philosophy, anthropology, history, and political or social theory. In addition to social sciences and humanistic approaches, scientific disciplines address the physiological or cognitive dimensions of feeling, while mindfulness or contemplative studies often bridge the scientific and social-scientific or humanistic approaches to the study of religion. Any of these fields may also address different periods, explore varied literary and scholarly canons, and apply disparate methodologies. Thus, the study of feeling may include subjects as far-ranging as ancient philosophical or ethical discussions on the nature of the passions (e.g., Kastor 2007), phenomenological approaches to religious experience, the cultural politics of emotion, and affect theory (e.g., Ahmed 2004; Schaeffer 2019). There is an almost unlimited number of ways in which one might approach the study of feelings in the context of religion as well, depending on the sources and subjects in which one is interested, the examples just given representing only a subset of disciplines and methodologies available for the study of how religious feeling is generated, how religious actors experience feeling, and how feeling is connected to the constitution of religious communities, practices, or subjectivities.

Recently, religious studies has paid more attention to the explicit study of emotions as a central dimension of human experience, including religious experience. Influenced by and in conversation with the biological and social sciences (e.g., cognitive science and anthropology, to name just two examples), what used to be discussed largely in terms of philosophy of mind and within the domain of "religious experience" is now also being explored in numerous and multidisciplinary discussions on: religion and emotion (e.g., Corrigan 2000, 2004, 2017a); the nature of emotion itself (e.g., Feldman Barrett 2017; Feldman Barrett, Lewis, and Haviland-Jones 2016); and the relationship between emotions, passions, and affects (e.g., Dixon 2006, 2012; Schaeffer 2019; Ural and Berg 2019). "Feeling" approached from the perspective of the senses is also connected to emotions as varied as reverential or devotional piety, disgust, or revulsion (e.g., LeBreton 2017; Harvey 2006 and 2018; Caseau 2018). Finally, scholars of religion and emotion have tended to ask questions about emotion similar to those others have asked about religious experience, which makes sense given the good deal of overlap between these different strands of academic study. Research relevant to the study of emotion and religion appears in specialties as wide-ranging as psychology, neuroscience, philosophy, history, politics, anthropology, linguistics, media studies, art history, and literary studies.

Given the massive scope of emotions research, the overview of emotion studies presented here outlines in broad strokes some of the most salient issues in the field. I have endeavored, as much as possible, to point toward timely and comprehensive scholarship so that the reader wishing to explore different aspects of emotions research will find the references a helpful guide. In the following pages I have set out to do three things: explore some of the most common ways scholars have differentiated between emotion and affect (two terms occasionally brought together under the rubric of "feeling") and the underlying binaries or dichotomies that have dominated most of the study of religion and feeling; describe methods for getting past those enduring dichotomies as articulated by some historians and historians of religion; and conclude with a case study on the relevance of emotion for the study of medieval Islam. In that final section I suggest that insights from contemporary anthropology help us appreciate and understand how feeling is represented and constructed in the medieval, quasi-hagiographical genre of Arabic pietistic literature known as "religious merits of the Companions of Muḥammad," or *faḍā'il al-ṣaḥāba*.

Affect Theory and Emotion: Enduring Binaries

Part of the difficulty in distinguishing between affect and emotion as we attempt to assess the field of emotion studies is that terms like *emotional*, *affective*, *embodied*, and *feeling* all tend to be defined and used idiosyncratically by different scholars in their respective disciplines: occasionally subgroups of these terms appear to be synonyms; at other times scholars distinguish sharply between affect and emotion. It is not unusual to find lengthy definitions of terms in the introductions to both specific studies on emotion in a particular context and surveys that purport to present an overview of the history of emotion (Borges, Cancian, and Reeder 2021, 3; and Rosenwein and Cristiani 2018, 2). One general tendency in how some (though not all) theorists differentiate between emotions and affects is to characterize emotions as senses or feelings (which may be interpreted by a subject), and affects as biologically rooted, non-rational, and pre-cognitive. In another formulation, "emotion is treated either as a biological function akin to sensation or, more frequently, as a social expression of something that might be called a 'feeling.' Affect, in contrast, is understood to be a pre- or subconscious phenomenon that is both ephemeral and independent of conscious choices and dispositions of the individual" (Elias 2018, 40).

When it comes to the study of feeling, one outgrowth of turns to materiality and embodiment is an increasing focus on issues of religion, emotion, and the body (e.g., Mahmood 2011; Bashir 2011). This has led some scholars to emphasize the more embodied dimensions of religious, social, and political life. Underlying some engagements with affect is the occasionally uneasy relationship between the so-called hard sciences and non-science disciplines, an unease sometimes fostered by a tendency among affect theorists toward scientism and a strong emphasis on the pre-rational corporeality they deem essential to affect, which carries within it an implicit critique of traditional (and especially political) philosophy (Leys 2011). These different disciplinary approaches have manifested in enduring, sometimes overly binarized discussions that resonate throughout the history of the study of emotions. Some recent scholarship on religion and emotion, and on the history of experience, has argued for a bridging between universalist and constructivist perspectives, or between affect and emotion, claiming instead that nature and nurture or psychobiology and culture are not opposed but mutually constitutive (Boddice 2018; Dulin 2011—and even earlier, see Fuller 2006). And while some affect theorists remain adamant about distinguishing between the autonomic bodily responses of affect and emotions, others in the field have sought more productive and less abstract connections in their consideration of how emotions are the product of the interaction between bodily affects and other aspects of social life and human behavior (Elias 2018, 44; Boddice 2018, 4; Boddice and Smith 2020).

Understanding both the differences and the relationships between the physiological and social aspects of feeling has thus been a central preoccupation in the study of emotion. This has also reinforced a binary between the universal and the particular, or between the conceptualization of feelings or emotions as an unchanging and biologically consistent aspect of humanity that is accessible and analyzable regardless of time and place, and the opposing view that emotions are socially constructed, contingent, and varied. As with most paradigms in academic disciplines that are a variation on the "nature vs. nurture" binary, syntheses of these opposing assumptions have also emerged, but the underlying split has nevertheless framed a good deal of scholarship over the past few decades. The universalist view remains attractive since it offers potential access to the feelings of others, which has naturally been of interest to professional scholars of religion whose purpose is to explicate the religious subjectivity and practices of objects of study who are either closer to or further away from them in time, depending on specialization. The latter, constructivist view remains enticing but more challenging, leaning toward more ethnographic sensibilities and implying that access to the feelings and indeed to the inner lives of others is at once culturally dependent and relatively difficult to assess accurately, except in extraordinary circumstances where one has become sufficiently fluent in the language and culture of another. Anthropology has evolved its own (not uncontroversial) methodological approaches to bridging difference, and a variety of views as to how possible that bridging may be. Scholars of religion who are not engaged in ethnographic investigations or who study periods for which ethnography is impossible have had to develop alternative methodologies and philosophical and intellectual justifications for the legitimacy of their interpretation of religious feelings or emotional expression in the texts, objects, and other artefacts they study.

Undergirding the universalist/constructivist binary that permeates scholarship on religion and emotion is a central preoccupation that also drove a good deal of scholarship on "experience" which now carries over into some scholarship on "feeling." Central to the study of religious experiences and feelings has been the question of how and whether scholars of religion can possibly access the religious feelings of the objects of their study in a way that is accurate, or that arrives at some version of "truth." The notion of a scholar's ability or inability to truly know what the other is feeling or experiencing is found in the form of myriad epistemological and methodological questions: How can we know what we or other people feel? Are we to take at face value their own expression of religious feeling? How can we be sure that we are correctly interpreting the words they use to express their feelings? Should we adopt ethnographic, historical, or linguistic approaches to such dilemmas? What about premodern religious expressions of feeling—as when a pilgrim describes a sense of wonder upon arriving at the pillar of a stylite saint in the countryside of fifth-century Syria? In such a context, what exactly does the word "wonder" mean? Or, when contemporary Muslims weeping at the shrine of Ḥusayn in Cairo claim to be mourning the Prophet Muḥammad's grandson, how are we to understand the concept of grief over the death of a figure who died many centuries ago, and to whom modern pilgrims have an entirely imagined relationship? How do feelings generated by bodily practices differ when performed in community or alone, how do ritual and performance figure in the generation of religious feeling, and what of the senses and the embodied aspect of emotion? Further, how can scholars of premodern religious life avoid the obvious pitfalls of anachronism in their interpretations of, for example, medieval texts that use feeling words which are translated into modern languages in order to describe the emotional states of people from long ago? How do we differentiate between *depictions* of feelings in literary or historiographical or religious texts and *prescriptions* for how feelings ought to be experienced, managed, avoided, or cultivated in those same works or in overtly didactic materials like monastic handbooks, religious dialogues, or hagiographies? When restricted to texts and representations of feeling in varied geographical, linguistic, and chronological contexts, is it better to leave certain emotion words untranslated? Or does that fetishize language in a futile and ultimately performative attempt to disavow our own cultural biases? This list of potential questions about how to study religion and feeling is far from complete, but I offer it as a way of demonstrating how many different ways there are to begin thinking about the subject, depending on one's subfield, period, and theoretical interests.

The question of how emotions figure in religious contexts is relevant to everything from medieval saints' shrines in South Asia to modern sporting rituals to postcolonial ethno-nationalist movements.

Other foundational binaries common to the study of religion and philosophy have also shaped the study of emotion—the question of mind/body duality has made the philosophy of emotion a natural starting place for explorations of the inner religious life, particularly with respect to mysticism. In the *Handbook of Emotions*, published in 2016, in a chapter on "The Philosophy of Emotions and Its Impact on Affective Science," Andrea Scarantino outlines the history of philosophical thought on emotions from Aristotle to Descartes, through the seventeenth- to nineteenth-century period of dualist "Cartesian Orthodoxy," and then describes the Humean "rejection of the reason-passion dichotomy" (Scarantino 2016). The chapter also describes the seminal work of William James on emotion as a "revolution," beginning with his 1884 essay "What Is an Emotion?" and in the essay "The Physical Basis of Emotion," published ten years later. James tended (somewhat inconveniently) to identify emotions with feelings, and as a result he is cited as a predecessor for different (sometimes opposing) strands of emotions scholarship. As Scarantino explains, "Neo-Jamesians and Psychological constructionists have . . . found inspiration in different aspects of his work." Some "have focused on the *bodily side* of James's theory, whereas psychological constructionists . . . have focused on the *constructionist side*" (Scarantino 2016, 12). Other theories of emotion in the Jamesian vein focus on motivation, intersecting at times with evolutionary psychological approaches that branch off in several directions, including the strand of affect theory espoused by Silvan Tomkins, Paul Ekman, and others (Scarantino 2016, 18–20).

What do these long-standing iterative debates about universal phenomena and psychological constructivism have to do with how we study religion? As Scharf has described, "experience" was the resort of religious studies scholars who wished to maintain some set of universal principles governing how religion worked, but to avoid charges of cultural insensitivity or hegemony: "By appealing to non-tradition-specific notions such as the 'sacred' or 'the holy'—notions that blur the distinction between a universal human experience and the posited object of such experience—the scholar could legitimate the comparative study of religion" (Scharf 1998, 96). In Stephen Bush's 2014 work *Visions of Religion: Experience, Meaning, and Power*, the "problem" of discerning religious experience in the Jamesian tradition was put into conversation with the work of two anthropologists of religion—Talal Asad and Clifford Geertz—and then into the broader context of the discipline of religious studies as a whole. While Bush engages explicitly with the question of experience, and more implicitly with emotions per se, he nevertheless seeks to explain why universalizing models of religious experience indebted to the thought of James are salvageable tools for the study of religion. Bush does this by exploring the question of experience through the work of Geertz and Asad, and in triangulating and refining these perspectives he ultimately lands on "the social" as that which makes the experiences of others potentially intelligible to outsiders.

Social Historical Approaches to Religion and Emotion: Binaries Finally Left Behind?

In 2017, John Corrigan, arguably the leading American historian of religion and feeling (he is the author of a book titled *Feeling Religion*), delivered a lecture at the Divinity School of the University of Chicago on "Religion, Emotion and History." In his talk he presented an overview of the history of emotion and "aimed to suggest some connections between affect theory, historical inventory, phenomenology, and religion" (Corrigan 2017b, 8). In his talk he alluded to several well-known historians of emotion, including (among many others) Carole and Peter Stearns, who coined the term "emotionology" to refer to social expectations or "feeling rules" for the expression of emotion, and William Reddy, who conceptualized "emotional regimes" and "emotives" (Corrigan 2017b; see also Plamper et al. 2010).[1] In addition to Americanists like Corrigan, historians of emotion in the premodern and early modern world have long grappled with how to interpret emotions available to us only in texts or material artefacts. One of the most influential historians of premodern emotion, Barbara Rosenwein, writes in the preface to her 2006 work *Emotional Communities in the Early Middle Ages*: "I use the term emotions in this book with full knowledge that it is a convenience: a constructed term that refers to affective reactions of all sorts, intensities, and durations. We shall see that, despite its drawbacks, it is serviceable, even for the medieval world where, indeed, it had some distant ancestors—in the Latin phrase *motus animi* (motions of the soul) and in the Latin adjective *commotus* (moved). To vary my prose,

1. The reader may wish to note that these issues have all been revisited in Stearns, Barclay, and Crozier-DeRosa 2020.

I also make use of 'passions,' 'feelings,' and, to a lesser extent, 'affects' as equivalents of 'emotions'" (Rosenwein 2006, 4–5). Rosenwein's theory of emotional communities stresses "the social and relational nature of emotions; to allow room for William Reddy's very useful notion of 'emotives,' which change the discourse and the habitus by their very existence; and to emphasize some people's adaptability to different sorts of emotional conventions as they move from one group to another" (4–5).

Historians of the premodern world, while not exclusively historians of religion, have much to offer religious studies, since so much of the world they explicate is inseparable from religious themes and subjects. In general, social historians whose work is explicitly anti-universalist have been less troubled by the dichotomies and binaries outlined above. Yet they craft methodologies that allow them to argue confidently for their interpretations, and for a certain kind of political payoff. For the medieval period, for example, Rosenwein's *Emotional Communities* and Damien Boquet and Piroska Nagy's *Medieval Sensibilities: A History of Emotions in the Middle Ages* (2018) each highlight the benefits of their approaches for dispelling a false narrative that casts the medieval period as a "dark age" devoid of emotional complexity, defined by a lack of agency, and dominated by dour material constraints (Boquet and Nagy 2018). This perspective can also help counter the orientalist stereotypes that pervade representations of the Islamic world, and the two-dimensionality of much scholarship on Muslim social and intellectual life.

Emotions and Islamic Studies

When it comes to Islamic studies, scholars of the classical Islamic and later medieval period have recently begun to take emotion as seriously as their counterparts whose work centers on the European Middle Ages. Their analyses of emotions have been focused on select sources, especially the Qur'ān (e.g., Bauer 2017). The study of emotional regimes, "emotional ecologies," and "emotional habitus" (Elias 2018, 58) has also been a marked feature of scholarship on Sūfism (e.g., Moosa 2005) describing the cultivation of spiritual dispositions and the language of religious experience. Other scattered examples of emotion studies within Islamic studies include brief analyses of specific emotions such as fear or anger, as represented in a specific corpus of non-Qur'ānic texts (Melchert 2011; Ghazal 1998; Blatherwick and Bray 2019), or on piety and embodied emotionality, in the form of weeping, for example (Katz 2007 and 2013; Jones 2011).

Turns to emotion studies in the modern Islamic world have been inspired by modern provocations in which contemporary Muslims are represented as essentially—and often excessively—emotional. Starting in 1980, global controversies from the publication of Salman Rushdie's *Satanic Verses* to various "cartoon controversies" have led to a range of violent and nonviolent responses across different segments of the Muslim world, whether in Muslim-majority contexts or diasporic communities. When seemingly inevitable questions in Western media and in the academy arose as to why such seemingly harmless provocations could inspire such virulent responses, answers or explanations tended to be offered in distinctly emotional terms. Bernard Lewis penned a now infamous piece in *The Atlantic* in 1990 titled "The Roots of Muslim Rage," which set the tone for much subsequent reporting on alleged Muslim emotional immaturity, irrationality, and anger. For others who attempted to take emotion more seriously as a legitimate response to perceived cultural insult, images in satirical publications like *Charlie Hebdo* in France which openly mocked Muḥammad and Islam were seen as "injurious" or causing "hurt feelings" among Muslims, and—according to some—"shattering the very foundations of their religious identity" (Ural and Berg 2019, 208). In her 2009 article analyzing the Danish cartoon controversies of the 2000s, "Religious Reason and Secular Affect," Saba Mahmood explored the false hierarchy of secular rationalism over religious un-reason, and critiqued the view of modern Muslim political life as being animated primarily by excessive or dysregulated emotion.

There is much in Mahmood's analysis that actually resonates with critiques of a strain of premodern historical emotion studies, put forward by Rosenwein and others, that painted the *medieval* world as similarly naïve, underdeveloped, and irrational when it came to understanding emotion. Bringing these two strands together, we can see how popular media and even some scholarship tends to depict modern Muslims as if they are "acting medieval." Much as Mahmood traces the dichotomy between secular affects of detachment and religious expression of emotion to certain formulations of the modern state, Rosenwein notes that Norbert Elias's sweeping and now outdated work on emotions and history, *The Civilizing Process*, was first elaborated in the 1930s but "began to make inroads in historical circles only in the 1970s . . . [and] was interested in rationalization, bureaucratization, and the juggernaut of the modern state" (Rosenwein 2006, 7). Echoes of Elias's strikingly orientalist views about emotion resonate throughout what Mahmood characterized as "normative conceptions enfolded within . . . assessment[s] about what constitutes religion and a proper religious subjectivity in the modern world" (Mahmood 2009, 838). In light of this, it seems reasonable that if a nuanced assessment of contemporary Muslim emotional life requires more than a simplistic description of casually disdained religious feelings, and if that casual disdain itself has been predicated on a misconception about the immaturity of the "medieval," then emotion in medieval Muslim life is also probably worth a second, deeper look.

Case Study: Emotion in the "Religious Merits of the Companions of Muḥammad"

The purpose for the creation and circulation of Religious Merits traditions (short narrative vignettes—known as *ḥadīth* or *athār*—describing things Muḥammad or his early followers/the Companions said or did) was, first and foremost, "pious partisanship" in nascent Sunnī/Shī'ī struggles. The earliest narratives in this corpus constructed a hierarchy of "excellence" in which distinguishing character traits and pious deeds of exemplary early Muslim figures were enumerated and described. Here I explore a sample of reports from the earliest phase of *faḍā'il al-Ṣaḥāba*, pulled from thousands of traditions that circulated in the first centuries of Islam. Many of these narratives are well known, since they have been studied in the context of later sectarian claims about the order of caliphal succession and the relative merits of the first four caliphs—issues at the heart of what would become Sunnī/Shī'ī sectarianism.

Containing over 2,000 traditions, one of the earliest stand-alone compilations in the genre is the *Faḍā'il al-Ṣaḥāba* compiled by the famous scholar Aḥmad ibn Ḥanbal (d. 855 CE) and augmented by his son 'Abdallāh (d. 903). This compilation is one of the most extensive early works dedicated to explicating the virtues of Muḥammad's Companions. Ibn Ḥanbal, like all authors of *faḍā'il*, conceded that there were degrees of excellence among the Companions and that their ranking in terms of "merits" was a matter of both precedence in conversion to Islam (*sābiqa*) and participation in events that were momentous for the early Muslim community, as well as their personal qualities (see Afsaruddin 2002). Rather than eliding differences among the Companions, Ibn Ḥanbal was mindful of the divisions among them, and, crucially, articulated a view that aimed to harmonize competing factions within the community. Ibn Ḥanbal seemed opposed, in other words, to extreme views on either side of a burgeoning sectarian debate. He wished neither to disparage nor to unduly elevate Muḥammad's cousin and son-in-law 'Alī, who was supported by proto-Shī'īs and who received mixed reactions from some subsets of proto-Sunnīs. In general, Ibn Ḥanbal was concerned about excessive love for 'Alī, which threatened the emerging Sunnī model of caliphal legitimacy. The other controversial figure with whose reputation Ibn Ḥanbal had to contend was someone he feared would be not excessively loved, but excessively hated: the third caliph 'Uthmān, who was assassinated after having been besieged in his home. The aftermath of 'Uthmān's murder was the context (or pretext) for subsequent rebellions against 'Alī, leading to the latter's murder in turn and cementing the dichotomy between the two men ('Alī and 'Uthmān) as a paradigmatic dividing line between sectarian rivals. The characterological aspect of all this historical framing and retroactive casting of foundational stories is the heart and primary driver of the "religious merits of the Companions" genre. It is also defined in almost exclusively emotional terms.

Characterizations of 'Uthmān and 'Alī in Ibn Ḥanbal's Faḍā'il al-Ṣaḥāba

The chapter on 'Uthmān in Ibn Ḥanbal's compilation is decidedly bleak. The only "religious merit" he is said to have demonstrated was the provision of financial support for some early battles and for the expansion of the Prophet's Mosque in Medina. In a series of obviously retrospective traditions 'Uthmān is made to proclaim his innocence against charges of corruption and to lament the wrongfulness of his impending murder. He is portrayed unequivocally as a hapless victim rather than a brave martyr. The tone is tragic and confused when he laments: "On what grounds will they kill me? I heard the Prophet say a believer's blood can only be shed in three instances: adultery, murder, apostasy, and I have never in my life committed these" (*Faḍā'il* 465 and 486). In spite of this lukewarm portrayal of 'Uthmān's character, Ibn Ḥanbal's *Faḍā'il* is replete with invocations of the consensus of the community on his election, and treats his murder as a watershed for the worse. After 'Uthmān's death 'Alī is portrayed as being anxious over bad blood with 'Uthmān's supporters. In one report, the interpretation of Qur'ānic verses cements this sense of communal decline in an unwelcome realization regarding verse 39:31, "Then indeed you, on the Day of Resurrection, before your Lord, will dispute." Upon the death of 'Uthmān people recalled this verse and anticipated the end times, lamenting "This is it! This is it!" (*hādhihī hādhihī*) (*Faḍā'il* 459). What 'Uthmān lacked in life, in terms of fortitude, competence, or history as a Companion, he apparently more than made up for in death. After this excursus on the eschatological implications of his murder, we are presented with a series of ḥadīth regarding what is now to be read strictly as his martyrdom.

In sharp contrast to the portrayal of ʿUthmān, the section on *Faḍāʾil ʿAlī* begins by describing ʿAlī in terms of his merits and asceticism even before listing his connection to the Prophet, as his cousin and son-in-law. Here fairly typical ascetic tropes abound, including ʿAlī's habit of eschewing finery and wearing coarse or uncomfortable clothing. Yet the reports also reveal a complex set of emotions: in one narrative ʿAlī declares, "there will be a people who love me such that they will enter fire in their love for me, and a people who hate me so much they will enter the fire in their hatred of me" (*Faḍāʾil* 575). Similarly, one witness claims that he never met anyone who inspired as much hatred or love as ʿAlī and expresses some chagrin that in spite of his detractors, ʿAlī's knowledge of religious matters was unparalleled (*Faḍāʾil* 575). A fascinating parallel is drawn between ʿAlī and Jesus in another version of this report, in an exchange in which, when a question is posed as to whether there were any men comparable to ʿAlī, he is likened to Jesus in that one people loved him so much they lost themselves (*halakū*), while another hated him so much they too lost themselves—a reference to Christianity and Judaism (*Faḍāʾil* 576). The same comparison is put into the mouth of ʿAlī himself in another version, with the additional caveat that while those who loved or hated excessively were indeed lost, anyone who loved him and followed a "middle path or behaved moderately would be successful" (*Faḍāʾil* 600). Taken together, these narratives advocate for neither rejecting nor excessively elevating ʿAlī, an implicit criticism of the early Shīʿa for loving ʿAlī too much and of pro-ʿUthmān detractors for hating him to a similar degree. Finally, a set of reports explicitly claim that love for ʿAlī need not require hatred for ʿUthmān, since both were among "the people of Paradise." In one report by a man named ʿAbdallāh ibn Ẓālim, a man approaches another Companion named Saʿīd b. Zayd declaring, "I have loved ʿAlī more than I've ever loved anything," and is told, approvingly, that he has loved one of the people of Paradise. A bystander then says, "I have hated ʿUthmān more than I have ever hated anything," and is warned "Lo, don't you see that you have hated one of the people of Paradise?" (*Faḍāʾil* 570). Ibn Ḥanbal's assemblage of reports about ʿAlī—an obviously polarizing figure—is, in the end, a measured statement on the dangers of excessive love or hatred. A good deal of attention is paid to the uncomfortable knowledge that ʿAlī could inspire both feelings, and the reports amassed here constitute a moralizing discourse aimed at impressing upon the audience that both extremes were equally misguided.

From this brief summary, we find that even at this early stage of the genre of religious merits literature, we have a vast number of disparate traditions detailing political divides as well as personal grievances among the family and friends of Muḥammad. And while none of this is exactly surprising, given what we know about the eventual consolidation of sectarianism in a later era, what *is* revealing is the emotional and affective range in which partisan loyalty was expressed in these narratives. The predominant emotions in the chapter on ʿUthmān are shame, sorrow, and a sort of unseemly cowardice, which Ibn Ḥanbal quickly sought to mitigate by casting ʿUthmān's haplessness in the face of the opposition as a prophecy fulfilled. In the section on ʿAlī, the protagonist's merits as an ascetic and beloved Companion are constantly undercut by gossip and the burden of excessive love and hatred, the dangers of which Ibn Ḥanbal also inveighed against by amassing numerous mitigating anecdotes. What's clear is that in a work dedicated to extolling the "merits" of the Companions, a great number of traditions circulated that had implications for the *regulation of emotion*, a central theme in philosophical discussions of emotion as well as in a number of religious traditions, for the medieval audience receiving these reports—a regulation effected through commentaries on, or portrayals of, the expression of emotion by various protagonists (and antagonists) in the narratives themselves.

Conclusion

To conclude, we may bring together the various sections of this chapter to reconsider the question of the "universal and the particular" in analyzing how a genre changes over time. Appreciating the range of emotive expressions in a genre like *faḍāʾil* can shed light on how emotion itself was always central to the formation of religious communities especially in the context of encounter or conflict, since the shared stakes and communal aspects of confessional boundary-making themselves hinged on the formation of emotional communities as described by Rosenwein. Yet as Islamic sectarianism consolidated in the tenth and eleventh centuries, the emotional register of later *Faḍāʾil* compilations would shift significantly—from ambivalence and an attempt to balance between extremes, to more explicitly partisan polemics inflected with both positive and negative emotional tropes (Khalek 2020). In other words, the affective range of Religious Merits literature expanded as compilers adapted and responded to different political exigencies over time, revealing the workings of an evolving competitive discourse in which the representation of emotion was considered an instructive and persuasive narrative device. Near the end of the Introduction to *Emotional Communities in the Early Middle Ages*, Rosenwein described her book as "an invitation to others to add to the picture it sketches" (Rosenwein 2006, 29). Like their counterparts in the study of emotion in both medieval Western history and a range of contemporary religious studies, scholars of the medieval Islamic world (and in other subfields) have much to gain from emotion studies. When it comes to understanding the study of religious life and the formation of religious subjectivity in general, the analysis of religious "feeling" from the perspective of emotions research constitutes one of our generation's most exciting methodological "turns" in the study of religion.

Suggested Readings

Boddice, Rob. 2018. *The History of Emotions*. Manchester, UK: Manchester University Press.

Corrigan, John. 2004. "Emotions Research and the Academic Study of Religion." In *Religion and Emotion: Approaches and Interpretations*, edited by John Corrigan. Oxford: Oxford University Press.

Corrigan, John, ed. 2008. *The Oxford Handbook of Religion and Emotion*. Oxford: Oxford University Press.

Corrigan, John. 2017. "How Do We Study Religion and Emotion?" In *Feeling Religion*, edited by John Corrigan. North Carolina: Duke University Press.

Corrigan, John, Eric Crump, and John Kloos. 2000. *Emotion and Religion: A Critical Assessment and Annotated Bibliography*. Westport, CT: Greenwood Press.

Frevert, Ute. 2016. "The History of Emotions." In *Handbook of Emotions*, 4th ed., edited by Lisa Feldman Barrett, Michael Lewis, and Jeannette M. Haviland-Jones, 49–65. New York: The Guilford Press.

Gregg, Melissa, and Gregory J. Seigworth. 2010. *The Affect Theory Reader*. Durham, NC: Duke University Press.

Lutz, Catherine. 1988. *Unnatural Emotions: Everyday Sentiments on a Micronesian Atoll and Their Challenge to Western Theory*. Chicago: University of Chicago Press.

Rosenwein, Barbara, and Riccardo Cristiani. 2018. *What Is the History of Emotions?* Cambridge: Polity Press.

Schaeffer, Donovan O. 2019. *The Evolution of Affect Theory: The Humanities, the Sciences, and the Study of Power*. Cambridge: Cambridge University Press.

References

Abu Lughod, Lila. 1986. *Veiled Sentiments: Honor and Poetry in a Bedouin Society*. Berkeley: University of California Press.

Afsaruddin, Asma. 2002. *Excellence and Precedence: Medieval Islamic Discourse on Legitimate Leadership*. Leiden: Brill.

Ahmed, Sara. 2004. *The Cultural Politics of Emotion*. New York: Routledge.

Barclay, Katie, Sharon Crozier-De Rosa, and Peter Stearns, eds. *Sources for the History of Emotions: A Guide*. New York: Routledge Press.

Bashir, Shahzad. 2011. *Sufi Bodies: Religion and Society in Medieval Islam*. New York: Columbia University Press.

Bauer, Karen. 2017. "Emotion in the Qur'an: An Overview." *Journal of Qur'anic Studies* 19 (2): 1–30.

Blatherick, Helen, and Julia Bray, eds. 2019. "Arabic Emotions: From the Qur'an to the Popular Epic." *Cultural History* 8 (2), Special Issue.

Boddice, Rob. 2018. *The History of Emotions*. Manchester, UK: Manchester University Press.

Bonnell, V. E., and Lynn Hunt. 1999. *Beyond the Cultural Turn*. Berkeley: University of California Press.

Boquet, Damien, and Piroska Nagi. 2018. *Medieval Sensibilities: A History of Emotions in the Middle Ages*. Translated by Robert Shaw. Cambridge: Polity Press.

Borges, Marcelo J., Sonia Cancian, and Linda Reeder. 2021. *Emotional Landscapes: Love, Gender, and Migration*. Champaign: University of Illinois Press.

Bush, Stephen S. 2014. *Visions of Religion: Experience, Meaning, and Power*. New York: Oxford University Press.

Carr, David. 2014. *Experience and History: Phenomenological Perspectives on the Historical World*. Oxford: Oxford University Press.

Corrigan, John. 2004. "Emotions Research and the Academic Study of Religion." In *Religion and Emotion: Approaches and Interpretations*, edited by John Corrigan. Oxford: Oxford University Press.

Corrigan, John, ed. 2008. *The Oxford Handbook of Religion and Emotion*. Oxford: Oxford University Press.

Corrigan, John. 2017a. "How Do We Study Religion and Emotion?" In *Feeling Religion*, edited by John Corrigan. Durham, NC: Duke University Press.

Corrigan, John. 2017b. "Religion, Emotion, and History." *Criterion: A Publication of the University of Chicago Divinity School* 53 (1): 6–15.

Corrigan, John, Eric Crump, and John Kloos. 2000. *Emotion and Religion: A Critical Assessment and Annotated Bibliography*. Westport, CT: Greenwood Press.

Dixon, Robert. 2006. *From Passions to Emotions: The Creation of a Secular Psychological Category*. Cambridge: Cambridge University Press.

Dixon, Robert. 2012. "'Emotion': The History of a Keyword in Crisis." *Emotion Review* 4 (4): 338–44.

Dixon, Robert. 2020. "What Is the History of Anger a History Of?" *Emotions: History, Culture, Society* 4: 1–34.

Doyle, Cameron. 2013. "The Psychological Constructionist Model: An Approach to Understanding the Perception and Experience of Emotions." *Carolina Scientific* 5 (2): 40–41.

Dulin, John. 2011. "How Emotion Shapes Religious Cultures: A Synthesis of Cognitive Theories of Religion and Emotion Theory." *Culture and Psychology* 17 (2): 223–40.

Elias, Jamal J. 2018. *Alef Is for Allah: Childhood, Emotion, and Visual Culture in Islamic Societies*. Oakland: University of California Press.

Feldman Barrett, Lisa. 2017. *How Emotions Are Made: The Secret Life of the Brain*. Boston: Houghton Mifflin Harcourt.

Feldman Barrett, Lisa, Michael Lewis, and Jeannette M. Haviland-Jones. 2016. *Handbook of Emotions*. 4th ed. New York: The Guilford Press.

Frevert, Ute. 2016. "The History of Emotions." In *Handbook of Emotions*, 4th ed., edited by Lisa Feldman Barrett, Michael Lewis, and Jeannette M. Haviland-Jones, 49–65. New York: The Guilford Press.

Fuller, Robert. 1998. "Wonder and the Religious Sensibility: A Study in Religion and Emotion." *The Journal of Religion* 6 (83): 364–84.

Ghazal, Zouhair. 1998. "From Anger on Behalf of God to 'Forbearance' in Islamic Medieval Literature." In *Anger's Past: The Social Uses of an Emotion in the Middle Ages*, edited by Barbara H. Rosenwein, 202–30. Ithaca, NY: Cornell University Press.

Gregg, Melissa, and Gregory J. Seigworth. 2010. *The Affect Theory Reader*. Durham, NC: Duke University Press.

Hemmings, Clare. 2005. "Invoking Affect: Cultural Theory and the Ontological Turn." *Cultural Studies* 19 (5): 548–67.

Husayn, Nebil. 2021. *Opposing the Imam: The Legacy of the Nawāsib in Islamic Literature*. Cambridge: Cambridge University Press.

Ibn Ḥanbal, Aḥmad Ibn Muḥammad. 1983. *Faḍā'il al-Sahāba*. Edited by Waṣīallāh ibn Muḥammad ibn 'Abbās. Mecca: Markaz a-baḥth al-'alamī.

Jones, Linda G. 2001. "'He Cried and Made Others Cry': Crying as a Sign of Pietistic Authenticity or Deception in Medieval Islamic Preaching." In *Crying in the Middle Ages: Tears of History*, edited by Elina Gertsman, 102–35. New York: Routledge.

Kastor, Robert. 2007. *Emotion, Restraint, and Community in Ancient Rome*. Oxford: Oxford University Press.

Katz, Marion. 2007. *The Birth of The Prophet Muhammad: Devotional Piety in Sunni Islam*. London: Routledge.

Katz, Marion. 2013. *Prayer in Islamic Thought and Practice*. Cambridge: Cambridge University Press.

Khalek, Nancy. 2020. "Al-Dāraquṭnī's (d. 385 AH) Faḍā'il al-Ṣaḥāba: Mild Anger and the

History of Emotions in Religious Merits Literature." *Bulletin of the School of Oriental and African Studies* 83 (3): 415–36.

Kiernan, Frederic. 2020. "Emotion as Creative Practice: Linking Creativity and Well-being through the History and Sociology of Emotion." *International Journal of Well Being* 10 (5): 43–63.

Leys, Ruth. 2011. "The Turn to Affect, a Critique." *Critical Inquiry* 37 (3): 434–72.

Lutz, Catherine. 1988. *Unnatural Emotions: Everyday Sentiments on a Micronesian Atoll and Their Challenge to Western Theory*. Chicago: University of Chicago Press.

Mahmood, Saba. 2009. "Religious Reason and Secular Affect: An Incommensurable Divide?" *Critical Inquiry* 35 (4): 836–62.

Mahmood, Saba. 2011. *Politics of Piety: The Islamic Revival and the Feminist Subject*. Princeton, NJ: Princeton University Press.

Mahmood, Saba, with Talal Asad, Wendy Brown, and Judith Butler. 2013. *Is Critique Secular? Blasphemy, Injury, and Free Speech*. New York: Fordham University Press.

Melchert, Christopher. 2011. "Exaggerated Fear in the Early Islamic Renunciant Tradition." *Journal of the Royal Asiatic Society* 21 (3): 283–300.

Moosa, Ebrahim. 2005. *Ghazali and the Poetics of Imagination*. Chapel Hill: University of North Carolina Press.

Plamper, Jan, with William Reddy, Barbara Rosenwein, and Peter Stearns. 2010. "The History of Emotions: An Interview with William Reddy, Barbara Rosenwein, and Peter Stearns." *History and Theory* 49 (2): 237–65.

Ragab, Ahmed. 2018. *Piety and Patienthood in Medieval Islam*. New York: Routledge Press.

Rorty, Richard, ed. 1992. *The Linguistic Turn: Essays in Philosophical Method*. Chicago: University of Chicago Press.

Rosenwein, Barbara, ed. 1998. *Anger's Past: The Social Uses of an Emotion in the Middle Ages*. Ithaca, NY: Cornell University Press.

Rosenwein, Barbara. 2006. *Emotional Communities in the Early Middle Ages*. Ithaca, NY: Cornell University Press.

Rosenwein, Barbara. 2010. "Thinking Historically about Medieval Emotions." *History Compass* 8 (8): 828–42.

Rosenwein, Barbara, and Riccardo Cristiani. 2018. *What Is the History of Emotions?* Cambridge: Polity Press.

Scarantino, Andrea. 2016. "The Philosophy of Emotions and Its Impact on Affective Science." In *Handbook of Emotions*, edited by Lisa Feldman Barrett, Michael Lewis, and Jeannette M. Haviland-Jones, 3–48. New York: The Guilford Press.

Schaeffer, Donovan O. 2019. *The Evolution of Affect Theory: The Humanities, the Sciences, and the Study of Power*. Cambridge: Cambridge University Press.

Scharf, Robert H. 1998. "Experience." In *Critical Terms for Religious Studies*, edited by Mark C. Taylor, 94–116. Chicago: University of Chicago Press.

Scheer, Monique. 2012. "Are Emotions a Kind of Practice (And Is That What Makes Them

Have a History)? A Bourdieuian Approach to Understanding Emotion." *History and Theory* 51 (2): 193–220.

Smail, Daniel Lord. 2007. *On Deep History and the Brain*. Stanford, CA: Stanford University Press.

Ural, N. Yasemin, and Anna Lea Berg. 2019. "From Religious Emotions to Affects: Historical and Theoretical Reflections on Injury to Feeling, Self and Religion." *Culture and Religion* 20 (2): 207–22.

5 FETISH

Sarah Hammerschlag

> When the history of the science of religions and ethnography comes to be written, one will be astonished by the unmerited and fortuitous role the fetish has played . . . it corresponds to nothing but an immense misunderstanding between two civilizations, the African and the European.
>
> MARCEL MAUSS, *Œuvres* (1969, 244)

> Despite all the variations to which it can be submitted, the concept fetish includes an invariant predicate: it is a substitute—for the thing itself as center and source of being, the origin of presence, the thing itself par excellence, God or the principle, the archon, what occupies the center function in a system, for example the phallus in a certain phantasmatic organization. If the fetish substitutes itself for the thing itself in its manifest presence, in its truth there should no longer be any fetish as soon as there is truth, the presentation of the thing itself in its essence.
>
> JACQUES DERRIDA, *Glas* (1986, 209)

In 1927, when Sigmund Freud declared the fetish a substitute for the mother's phantasmatic penis, he was employing a term with a long and convoluted history, some of which, at least, he knew. "Such substitutes," he wrote already in 1905 of sexual fetishes, "are with some justice likened to the fetishes in which savages believe that their gods were embodied" (Freud 1953, 19). By this point, the fetish had already made its way into medical vocabulary when Alfred Binet employed it in his 1887 work *Le fétichisme dans l'amour*, but its origins lay much earlier in the cultural encounter between fifteenth-century Portuguese traders and the indigenous people of the Gold Coast. From a Portuguese designation for objects used by West Africans in ritual practice it was to become in the nineteenth century a term for the capitalist transfer of value from labor to object as well as a diagnosis for sexual perversion. In the intervening centuries, it migrated into a myriad of European languages. While current usage is marked by many facets of this history, insofar as the term "fetish" has become a noun of common parlance, it is Freud's articulation of it as a substitute object of desire that is most pervasive. Of the nearly twenty thousand deployments of the verb "fetishize" on Google Scholar, nearly all use the term to describe improper valorization. To fetishize in our common idiom—whether it is the female body, indigenous people, the past, negativity, free speech, or Mexican textiles (to name a few examples from Google Scholar)—indicates not only that one overvalues, but that one values wrongly.

To understand the fetish as a critical term is, however, to use it otherwise. It is, first and foremost to restore its history, one in which the study of religion is deeply implicated. An investigation into its past usages provides insight into debates surrounding the earliest modern attempts at cross-cultural religious taxonomy and reveals the complicity of these taxonomic projects with the concomitant activities of exploration, trade, and colonial conquest. Additionally, the history of the fetish helps us foreground the influence of religion and early attempts to study its origins on the disciplines that came to constitute the human and social sciences. More precisely, it reveals how the constitution of the colonized other's beliefs and values functioned to define in relief the parameters of the enlightened subject. As the term coalesced around certain attributes denigrated by the theological and philosophical traditions of the West, it also became a lever of critique. If Christianity was spiritual, that which pagan Africans supposedly worshipped in the fetish was material. If monotheism had the potential to be universal, the fetish was distinctly particular. If the highest truths were necessary ones, the fetish was not only contingent, but accidental. If the human being was, at its best, a free agent, the worshipper of the fetish was enthralled, subjected, and dependent. In other words, the fetish tells us far more about the cultural assumptions and values of those who employed the term than it does about those whose practices it was supposed to describe.

This is an issue, of course, that transcends this particular concept. Like the term "religion," it is "not a native category," not originally a term of self-characterization (Smith 1998, 269). More precisely, its use inevitably involves interpreting the practices of others according to concepts that arose out of a European Christian context. While this dynamic might seem to indicate a fault in the concepts themselves, awareness of it has also helped to reorient the study of religion. In the wake of J. Z. Smith's work and other parallel analyses of the history of the field, much of the scholarship of the last thirty years around the theorization of religion has sought to reveal these sites of imposition and to make that history an integral part of religious studies research (Asad 1993; Frykenberg 1993; Masuzawa 2005; Batnitzky 2011; Chidester 2014). But the concept of the fetish marks a particular sort of chapter in this history, insofar as it was explicitly rejected by the first fathers of religious studies in order to maintain the integrity of the taxonomic enterprise (Masuzawa 2000). By the 1990s, however, efforts to reexamine its significance in the field were well underway. Much of the early work done toward these ends tends toward a critical examination of its history, but in more recent years as scholars and theorists have sought out means to critique the historically dominant traditions of the West and to develop an alternative theoretical apparatus, the fetish has become one tool for reimagining modes of relation among humans as well as between humans and the world's myriad inhabitants. The fetish has become a lever to reexamine the distinction between matter and spirit, the philosophical and political usage of this distinction, and consequently our conceptualization of action and agency. Thus to treat the fetish as a critical term for religious studies means considering its history alongside the dangers and possibilities of its revalorization, beyond its common usage.

History In and Out of Religious Studies

The first and arguably most important effort to critically examine the history of the fetish was William Pietz's three-part series originally published in the journal *Res*. Pietz published his first in a series of articles on the fetish in 1985 and argued that despite its "sinister pedigree" and "discursively promiscuous" history of usage, the term provided insight into the cross-cultural encounter between "radically heterogeneous social systems" and thus into the makings of European modernity and its ideological underpinnings. Since then, various efforts by scholars in anthropology, art history, religious studies, and literary theory have sought to fill out this picture and to consider both the uses and the abuses of the term. Almost all of these efforts begin with some rehearsal of its origins and with the acknowledgment that every treatment of the term must retell this story.

To follow suit and thus to fill out the brief outline of that history offered above, we too begin here with its etymology. The term "fetish" arises from *fetisso*, itself already a pidgin word that developed out of the encounter between the Portuguese and the inhabitants of the west coast of Africa during exploration missions in the mid-fifteenth century. The Portuguese first used the term *feitico* and *feiticaria* to refer to African objects and practices (Pietz 2022, 24). While the words clearly derive from Latin, there is some disagreement concerning the root to which they are most closely tied. The root most commonly cited is the verb *facere*—to make—which points to one of the reasons fetish worship has been deemed false or problematic, as the worship of an object made by human hands (Pietz 2022, 24). However, Charles De Brosses, the eighteenth-century philosopher to whom we owe the term "fetishism" and its deployment to designate a cross-cultural type, traces the fetish to the Latin roots *fatum*, *fanum*, and *fari*. In so doing, he treats as a single "root" three terms, all associated for De Brosses with ancient religion (Morris 2017, 336). Bruno Latour has suggested that the instability in its linguistic origins is symptomatic of the concept's ambivalence, its lack of distinction between that which is enchanted and that which is fabricated or artificial (Latour 2010, 3). For Latour, it is this instability that makes the term theoretically useful, for it allows us to see within our culture the overzealous desire to maintain the distinction between agent and object.

Despite disagreements about its etymological origins, we do know that the term *fetisso* was applied to African practices and objects when Portuguese merchants in the late fifteenth century encountered the inhabitants of Africa's west coast, and was then taken up by those inhabitants themselves. It survived into the next stage of colonial history when in the seventeenth century Dutch traders ousted the Portuguese and became the dominant force in the region engaged in both the exploitation of African natural resources (gold and ivory) and the transatlantic slave trade. It is from the Dutch seventeenth- and early eighteenth-century accounts that much of the detailed description of African religion made its way into the European imagination, along with a certain lore about what the Portuguese themselves must have experienced in the initial encounter. In these accounts many things are identified as "fetissos," including animals and natural landmarks, but Pietz suggests that "the paradigmatic image tended to be an inanimate material object: a wooden figure, a leather amulet, a gold necklace, a stone, a bone, a feather—by implication, any material object at all, however useless or trivial" (Pietz 2022, 70).

Among the most influential accounts of these early modern traders is William Bosman's. Bosman began his career in Africa in 1688 at the age of sixteen as an apprentice for the Dutch West India Company, and by 1698 had risen to the position of head merchant. It is his work, translated into English as *A New and Accurate Description of the Coast of Guinea, Divided into the Gold, the Slave and the Ivory Coasts,* written after his return to the Netherlands in 1702 and published in 1704, that provided much of the source material concerning the region for the European imagination over the next century. While Bosman was no disinterested observer, but rather a businessman out to exploit both the human and the natural resources of the continent, his characterizations of the African fetish practice pointedly ridicule African priests and laypeople for the irrational self-interest he sees as evident in their practices (Pietz 2022, 89). As Pietz suggests, there is an element of frustration in Bosman's account, insofar as the Dutch understanding of the "objective" value of gold did not map onto its meaning among the coast's inhabitants. Gold was often mixed by West Africans with other metals (thus diluting its purity) and used as decoration and to mark social relations. What occurred therefore, Pietz argues, is an impasse between cultural systems. The social value of the object, determined by an alien culture, interfered with its economic and perceived "natural" value. In one famous passage cited both by De Brosses and in a myriad of other eighteenth-century accounts, which concerns not gold but the value of livestock, Bosman describes a royal decree that put to death all of one kingdom's pigs, because of anger over a "Dutch hog" having eaten a serpent deemed a fetish, or in De Brosses's words "a ridiculous divinity" (De Brosses 2017, 53). However resonant this response may be with various forms of Western prejudice, not to mention prophylactic measures around illnesses such as rabies or swine flu, in Bosman's telling and De Brosses's retelling, this is not a narrative about a conflict of values or a form of cultural resistance, but rather one that pits rationality against irrationality, natural morality against childish delusion. "Bosman's reader," Pietz writes, "is addressed in the mode of a fable as a child who can comprehend the true state of affairs by joining in the author's ironic contempt."

Additionally, the confusion portrayed on Bosman's pages is not merely attributed to the native residents—it implicates Catholicism as well (Orsi 2018, 36). Bosman, at one point, compares "the fetishes of 'negroes' with 'Italian fetishes,'" declaring finally that he likes the Italians so little that "I'd rather walk over all that the Negroes can lay for me, than have anything to do with theirs" (Iacono 2016, 17). If for the theorist Alfonso Iacono this episode represents one of the first steps in early modern cross-cultural comparison, it also reveals the fetish as marked by its lack of definition and thus its impenetrability. Bosman, it seems, knew neither how to delimit the category nor how to describe its meaning or function. However, his own lack of understanding is easily foisted off on the native practitioners themselves. Ironically, Iacono suggests, it is exactly its indeterminacy that makes the fetish ripe for the task of intercultural comparison (Iacono 2016, 17).

It is Charles De Brosses's 1760 work *On the Worship of Fetish Gods* (*Du culte des dieux fétiches*) which first brings this cross-cultural project to fruition. While not the first of its kind, and by no means the most lauded, respected, or canonical, it is nonetheless remarkable for its influence. By transforming the fetish from an unstable term for a group of objects and practices into a classificatory device, it bequeathed its terminology across the fields of anthropology, philosophy, psychology, Marxian economics, and religion, even as the term consistently resisted a stabilized definition in most of these fields.

For a contemporary reader, De Brosses's text is perhaps most notable for its transparent prejudice. The value of the term fetishism for De Brosses is its capacity to reveal a likeness between ancient Mediterranean religions in Egypt, Rome, and Greece "and a puerile worship" found all over the earth, but "maintained especially in Africa" (De Brosses 2017, 47). De Brosses wanted to show that those who read the ancient traditions as high-minded and allegorical were merely exporting their theological imagination onto the ancients. Instead, he claimed to begin with the things themselves. For the contemporary reader, there is an irony in the way De Brosses's critique reverberates back on his own text, revealing his assumptions about what is advanced and what is primitive, what is rational and what irrational, what is high-minded and what is lowly. At the same time, the text is something of a landmark in the methodological shift from a conceptual to an empiricist method within the earliest articulations of the human sciences. De Brosses concludes the text: "It is not in possibilities, but rather in man himself that one must study man; it is not a question of imagining what he could or should have done, but looking at what he does" (2017, 132). Its most prominent predecessor was David Hume's *Natural History of Religion* (1755), from which De Brosses borrowed heavily. Like Hume, De Brosses assumes that religion first arose out of hope and fear (De Brosses 2017, 110), but unlike Hume, for whom polytheism is the original religion, De Brosses argues for fetishism, characterized by literalism, irrationality, and caprice. "Fetishism belongs," he writes, "to the type of things that are so absurd that one could say that they do not even provide any purchase to the reasoning that would combat them. . . . But the impossibility of mitigating it from a reasonable point of view does nothing to diminish the certainty of the fact" (2017, 101).

By modern standards, of course, one can hardly call De Brosses's approach empirical. He cobbles together a hodgepodge of travel accounts from Africa and the Americas and then compares them to ancient accounts, claiming that the truth revealed is self-evident. That said, his commitment to combating the assumptions of Deist theories of natural religion had important consequences for Enlightenment thought. Rather than beginning with the Deist assumption that monotheism must also imply the universal ability of humanity to recognize its creator, De Brosses begins, like Hume, with the needs, wants, and fears that give rise to the desire to control an unpredictable world.

The next layer of reception appears in the late eighteenth and early nineteenth centuries in the texts of the German Idealists Immanuel Kant and G. W. F. Hegel, both of whom accept an account of fetishism as arising from the human desire to instrumentalize the divine for one's own ends. In Kant's 1793 *Religion within the Boundaries of Mere Reason* (Kant 1998), the term is first employed as a means of critique internal to Christianity, for he applies it to identify a residual primitivism in what he deems a corrupt motivation within Christian practice that he calls "priestcraft." Priestcraft is defined for Kant by its "fetish-service," which involves the prioritizing of observances and statutory rules over the principles of morality (1998, 180). For Kant, the concept of the fetish is illustrative, for it reveals that "what the Wogulite with his bear paw and the Puritan in his meeting house have in common is the desire to steer to their advantage the invisible power which presides over human destiny; they are of different minds only over how to go about it" (1998, 171).

In Hegel, too, fetishism is described as an attempt to control nature. But it appears in Hegel's 1832 *Lectures on the Philosophy of Religion* (Hegel 1988), following De Brosses, as a stage in a developmental taxonomy beginning in Africa. Hegel describes fetishes as "indeterminate, unknown powers that they [the Africans] have made themselves, and if something does not work out or some unhappiness befalls them, they throw this fetish away and get themselves another" (1988, 444). In the twenty-first century we might recognize a certain wisdom, or at least humility, in such an attitude toward a world which so often reminds us that our most steadfast efforts to control it often result in new forms of disease, storms, and wildfires. For Hegel, however, the purpose of reason is to remake the world in its image. Scientific thinking thus resembles fetishism insofar as it seeks to control nature, even if in science the means have become systematic and follow from observation and calculation. Nonetheless, for him African religion was so primitive that he described it as prehistoric, merely a precursor to the genuine development of religion within human culture. As David Chidester has pointed out, given Hegel's influence in the nineteenth century this description precipitated a lack of interest in fetishism as an African form and helped encourage its alternative function as a term to describe faulty or perverse thinking in the West (Chidester 2014, 67).

Nonetheless, over the next twenty-five years, between 1830 and 1854, back in France, the pioneer of positivism August Comte developed a detailed evolutionary theory of human sociality and religion, for which fetishism constituted an important stage indispensable both to theological thinking and to the development of scientific rationality. Following De Brosses, Comte places it at the origin of theology. Rather than dismissing it as an origin that had to be superseded, Comte described it as natural to an epoch when affective feeling had more sway over the human being. At the same time, he also saw it as instrumental to the development of social cooperation and organized procedures of transforming the world, such as the cultivation of crops and commerce (Comte 1929, 3: 108, 144). Ultimately Comte elevated fetishism to a key position in his "Religion of Humanity," advocating for its reemergence in a positivist society and lauding its superiority over Christianity, insofar as it demonstrated interest and concern for the concrete world and for the social bonds that animate it. This admiration and advocacy for the persistence of fetishism culminated in his notion of the "*Grand-Fétiche*" as an animating principle that would help humanity overcome its egotism (Pickering 1988). It is in Comte that the first inkling of an impulse toward reclaiming this concept appears. One can certainly read the contemporary French sociologist of science Bruno Latour's interest in the "factish gods" and its role in new materialism as a latter chapter in this story. In between contemporary retrievals of "thingly power" or "vibrant matter" and Comtean positivism, however, the emphasis on materiality was first associated with Karl Marx, a position the "new materialists" themselves seek to shift by restoring an emphasis on a Spinozist/Deleuzian legacy (Bennett 2010). Nonetheless, it is Marx's treatment of the fetish that catalyzed the term's role in modern theory, including in the work of Slavoj Žižek, Gilles Deleuze, Félix Guattari, and others, and whose analysis of historical forces equally contributes to the potential impact of fetish as a critical term within the study of religion (Morris 2017, 163, 176).

Marx and Marxian Reclamations

Over the same period that Comte sought to revalorize the concept of the fetish, Karl Marx too was giving the concept pride of place in his theory of capital. Like Kant before him, Marx sought to use it as a means to reveal the primitivism of modern society. However, for Marx it represented not merely a perversion of right religious motivation, but the operation at the heart of religion—the impulse to displace what belongs to the human being properly onto a foreign and ultimately imaginary entity. Besides Freud, to whom we will return shortly, it is Marx's notion of the commodity fetish that has had the most longevity in contemporary discourse. For Marx, as Sarah Kofman writes, religion is not merely exemplary of the ideological process, but is rather "constitutive of ideology as such" (Kofman 1999, 2). Marx himself wrote that "criticism of religion is the premise of all criticism" (Marx 1970, 129). Following the Left-Hegelian philosopher Ludwig Feuerbach, Marx claims that religion is a form of alienation, the projection of what belongs properly to humanity onto the divine. In constructing his notion of ideology, Marx supplements Feuerbach's take by revealing how this construct reflects society's material conditions and serves to reinforce the interests of the ruling class. Religion thus becomes the operative metaphor for Marx in explaining the alienating force of ideology. This means that Marx is dependent on religion to demonstrate illusion as such, which is evident in the passage of *Das Kapital* in which he famously introduces the concept of the commodity fetish.

> In order therefore to find an analogy [for the illusion of the commodity's value] we must take flight into the misty realm of religion. There the products of the human brain appear as autonomous figures endowed with a life of their own, which enter into relations both with each other and with the human race. So it is in the world of commodities with the product of men's hands. I call this the fetishism which attaches itself to the products of labor as soon as they are produced as commodities and is therefore inseparable from the production of commodities. (Marx 1976, 165)

So even as the concept of the commodity fetish seems to move the fetish out of the realm of philosophy of religion and into the realm of economic theory, it also smuggles religion into economics, in such a way that later theorists are easily able to reconnect the dots. The anthropologist Michael Taussig, for example, in his now classic work *The Devil and Commodity Fetishism in South America*, not only uses Marx's theory to describe how capitalism changes our relationship to things, but suggests, following Marx, that insofar as commodity fetishism is a reflection of social value and social relations, pre-capitalist society manifests a healthy fetishism as opposed to an unhealthy one: "Products appear" in such societies "to be animated or life endowed precisely because they seem to embody the social milieu from which they come." The imbuing of the objects of one's creation with life is for Taussig a sign of an "organic unity between persons and their products" (Taussig 1980, 36–37).

For other scholars, a Marxian lens provides an instrument to analyze the very process by which the fetish developed. For Pietz, it is only a historical materialist lens that can shed light on the cultural confrontation from which the concept of the fetish emerged. It was in fact the "emergent articulation of the ideology of the commodity that defined itself within and against the social values and religious ideologies of two radically different types of non-capitalist society" (Pietz 2022, 4). The fetish is thus born, he argues, out of the confrontation of commodity capitalism with African forms of tribal life refracted against the vestiges of medieval Catholicism.

In her landmark 2000 essay "Troubles with Materiality: The Ghost of Fetishism in the Nineteenth Century," Tomoko Masuzawa suggests, moreover, that the fetish comes to embody a certain nineteenth-century unease around materiality, exactly because capitalism renders things both dead and possessed. It is, furthermore, in the space of colonial conquest, and by the dehumanization of human labor, that such a transformation takes place. For Masuzawa this is an important part of a larger narrative about the field of religious studies, and the development of a hierarchical taxonomy of "world religions." It reveals an impulse within the field's history to purify the term religion itself into something scientific: to develop a univocal, ahistorical conception designating the human inclination toward the spiritual, one that could function effectively as a diagnostic. In so doing, fetishism is supposedly jettisoned from the realm of religion, relegated to the status of "mere tendency, a certain inferior disposition of weakness," a proclivity, universally present (Masuzawa 2000, 245). This move, represented most prominently in the work of Friedrich Max Müller (1823–1900), an indologist and one of the patriarchs of the field of *Religionswis-*

senschaft (religious studies, in German), solidifies its function in locating vestiges of primitivity within the civilized West, recognizable as misplaced desire. At the same time, Masuzawa argues, the term continues to haunt the field as a marker of the lowly and the material, thus inflecting each "stage" of development as a signifier of impurity. If symbolic expressions of religious devotion are marked out as idolatrous, it is their lingering dependence on materiality, their resemblance to fetishes, that places them at a lower rung of religious development. While such taxonomic efforts provided a rubric for comparison, and thus were often framed as a part of a humanist project, Masuzawa shows how they functioned to shore up an order that secured the place of Protestant Christianity at its apex (Masuzawa 2005).

From Marxian Materialism to New Materialism

In both Masuzawa's and Pietz's work we see how the fetish can operate as a critical term. For both, a rehearsal of its history provides telling insight into the forces that shaped the field, revealing the normative role of Protestantism as well as the underlying economic and colonial politics that play a part in even the most high-minded and fustiest corners of the academy. In both studies, too, the history of the fetish serves an additional function: it helps to reveal something like a counter-history, a set of possibilities for how the study of religion might have developed otherwise. Both Masuzawa's and Pietz's studies emphasize sites of cultural hybridity, reveal the historical conditions under which values get generated and how they circulate, and allow us to glimpse an alternative mode of seeing that shadows the idealist one—one where matter matters, where the differentiation between agent and object remains under negotiation, where the contingent and the serendipitous make significant appearances in our ordering of events.

Efforts to foreground these features have appeared in recent years as religious studies has made its own "material turn." The turn to new materialism—configured not in Marxist terms but to designate the underappreciated significance of thingness and assemblages—is often itself framed as an antidote to the "linguistic" and "cultural" turns of the 1970s, 1980s, and 1990s, and looks to Deleuze and Guattari and Bruno Latour as theoretical resources over Saussure, Lévi-Strauss, or Derrida. However, it is important to highlight as well how the spotlight on materiality is itself a clear outgrowth of "the linguistic turn" and remains to some extent dependent upon it (Morris 2017, 318). This, too, is a story that the history of the fetish helps us to tell.

We began our inquiry by revealing how current usages of the verb "to fetishize" evolved out of the psychological/psychoanalytic definitions of the terms in the works of both Alfred Binet and Sigmund Freud, as a substitute object of sexual desire. We have now traced out the path to this transposition from the religious sphere to the sexual. Müller's attempt to assign to the fetish the status of universal proclivity in 1888 is nearly contemporaneous with Binet's use of the term in 1887, and both followed Marx's by two decades. As both Emily Apter and Hartmut Böhme show, by the time of the late Victorian era there was already a deep interconnection between its sexual and economic appropriations, as the accoutrements of sexual performance, which are often described as examples of sexual fetishes, became tied to what Böhme calls "the dominant artificiality and theatricality of dominant culture" (Böhme 2014, 298).

At the same time, this slippage between orders—the religious, the economic, and the erotic—in the nineteenth century may also indicate something beyond that historical moment, something about the nature of these three spheres, their structural similarity, and the desire generated in and by each. This I take to be at stake in Jacques Derrida's use of the term in his 1974 text *Glas*. If Derrida's work from "Structure, Sign and Play" in 1966 forward sought to reveal how "the whole history of the concept of structure . . . must be thought of as a series of substitutions of center for center, as a linked chain of determinations of the center," thus how "the history of metaphysics, like the history of the West, is the history of these metaphors and metonymies," then the existence of a discourse concerning the fetish that roams across the sexual, economic, and religious spheres goes a long way toward making that point. What the fetish designates in all three realms, Derrida contends in *Glas*, is the site of the bad substitute. Furthermore, Derrida suggests that its persistence also reveals the elusive nature of that which constitutes the "proper" in each, the inability of that placeholder to be present. Moreover, it highlights our dependence on the opposition between the proper object and its improper other, even to *think*, to conceptualize what we take to be the founding term, the original, the center, the true locus of value. Derrida thus makes the bold claim that the work of critiquing Eurocentrism, the history of metaphysics, the dominance of Christian theology, and patriarchy all depend on rethinking our relation to the fetish. "As long as fetishism will be criticized," he asks, or perhaps demands, "for or against religion, for or against the family—will the economy of metaphysics, the philosophy of religion, have been tampered with?" (Derrida 1986, 206–7).

It is not so surprising then that as the academy, across multiple humanist disciplines, has sought to critique Eurocentrism, white supremacy, and patriarchy, the fetish would resurface as a site of revalorization. Marx, Freud, Derrida, and Deleuze have all been resources in these endeavors (Morris 2017). The philosopher of science Bruno Latour, however, has most often been cited in recent years by scholars working within the framework of the "material turn" (Houtman and Meyer 2012; Bennett 2010; Hazard 2018). In his 2010 monograph *On the Cult of the Factish Gods*, Latour raises the history of fetishism and its function as an object of critique to undermine the hard division in the West between agency and objecthood, to reveal that behind this strong distinction that charges the colonized other with "naïve belief" is a Western anxiety about the murkiness of the distinction between agent and object in our own thinking and action. The book thus seeks to show that "we have never been modern" and to recover the premodern thinking of "initiates" "for our own use" (Latour 2010, 7). The Western philosophical tradition of critique in this telling and its concomitant mission of disenchantment was an outgrowth of the reliance on a notion of autonomy and interiority, all of which falsely shored up the assumption that agents act and objects are acted upon. Releasing ourselves from this anxiety, accepting our dependencies, learning to speak in a middle voice, for Latour, opens up an era of "post-critical" thought, also itself a modality influential among recent scholars across the humanities (see Felski 2015; Anker and Felski 2017).

Certainly Latour's work extends the role the concept of the fetish can play as a critical term in religious studies, and opens up new methods and approaches to the field that have been obscured by long-reigning assumptions about objectivity and agency. Yet this 2010 work also raises the question of whether it is indeed possible to think beyond binaries. Latour's own interest in reclamation seems often to depend upon the very binaries he seeks to break down and diffuse. His attempts to recover the thinking of the "initiate" sometimes reinscribe the stereotypes he wants to overcome, for example when he describes the "transformation" of the (Black) "suburban migrant patient" during an "ethnopsychiatry" appointment to illustrate his argument about "initiates" (Latour 2010, 36–45). A careful consideration of the work thus demands that we ask the question posed by Simon Kofi Appiah of whether the fetish can be reclaimed in such a way that it successfully diffuses its history of denigration (Appiah 2022).

Recent works by Webb Keane, Patricia Spyer, J. Lorand Matory, and J. Kameron Carter have all posed this question and produced works that take a different tack. Like Latour, these writers are invested in rethinking our conceptions of both materiality and agency, but they do so with an eye to both the present and the past, aiming not to diffuse its history of denigration but to deploy it in and through an examination of the effects of the colonial and racial history of the term. As Patricia Spyer puts it in her introduction to the volume *Border Fetishisms* (1998), it is by attending to the fetish's invocation as negative and derogatory that we open up spaces for "relations between subjects and objects" to be "reassessed, redrawn and at times overturned" (1998, 3). In Webb Keane's *Christian Moderns* (2007), fetishism names the moment of encounter when representatives of one culture *think* they can see the motivations and actions of another with "a clear eye." It is the anxiety and scrutiny on both sides that disclose the concepts of autonomy and intentional agency as ideological features of "Christian modernity." It is not by forgoing its fraught history thus that we move forward, for Keane, but by deploying the term like a boomerang to unsettle the emancipatory promise of "agency," thus indicating how this progressive aim is itself tied up in Western assumptions about freedom and autonomy. J. Lorand Matory in his 2018 text *The Fetish Revisited* goes further by breaking down the distinction between theoretical texts and religious objects and analyzing both as "culturally conditioned and interested set[s] of strategies for the pursuit of well-being rather than as an ethereal cogitation transcending the cultural suppositions and material projects of its exponents." Along with the ritual altars of Yoruba practitioners, in Matory's study, Freud's and Marx's theories of the fetish appear as materially conditioned projects and expressions of embodied actors. At the same time, Matory does not abstract himself either from the ethnographic analysis, exploring how his own situated subjectivity as a Black anthropologist married to a Yoruba practitioner makes him sensitive to the history of the fetish concept and how the theories of Marx and Freud obfuscated the colonial history behind the terminology they employed. He speculates further that their own situation as Jewish men at the margins of European whiteness, seeking to conceal their own otherness, contributed to their role in forging a term that makes fetishism itself an accusation. On the flip side, Yoruba and Candoblé objects and practices yield insights into the ways in which ideas and people exist in complex networks of meaning that reference hierarchical power relations and refract past histories, both personal and political. Like these contemporary objects themselves, which are a product of a colonial history and reflect a history of (often unequal) cultural exchange, the history of the fetish is itself a resource, and a model, for reframing our relation to religious practices and objects, as well as to the theoretical inheritances that shape our thinking.

Matory's work also highlights the importance of engaging in this history for those navigating the intersection between Black studies and religion. Going back to W. E. B Du Bois's *The Negro*, the fetish has been crucial for thinking through the inheritance of African indigenous spirituality in African American practices of Christianity (Du Bois 1915, 134). In later work, Du Bois repudiates the term because of its demeaning history, but as J. Kameron Carter has argued in a reading of Charles Long, there are ways to make that history crucial to Black studies because the fetish demonstrates how Black religion in America is itself something greater and more powerful than a particular outgrowth of Christianity (Carter 2022).

The question this essay has posed is whether it is possible to escape the long history of using the fetish as a lever of valuation. Matory seeks through self-description to relativize his own standing, but the priests and practitioners he talks to are nonetheless portrayed as carrying knowledge and insight that ultimately deflects critical analysis, while Marx and Freud appear as transparently self-interested and anxious to secure their own social position. Religious studies, when not denigrating or rationalizing the primitive or esoteric, has often also contributed to its further mystification or has merely flipped the script, proclaiming the priest or shaman heroic in order to reveal the deficits of Western thought (Wasserstrom 1999). One sees similar romanticizations and mystifications in recent attempts, in the wake of the revalorization of the fetish, to speak about the power of things (Hazard 2018) or the allure of the anarchic (Carter 2022). If the terminology of the fetish developed in order to help us designate the space of the proper, and the true, is there a thinking of materiality, inspired by the history of this term, that can indeed move us beyond the language of the "bad substitute"? Can we speak critically without contrasting ourselves with those who "fetishize" this or that, whether the object is reason or the body, technology or the archaic? The fetish presents itself as a critical term for religious studies if and when it helps us recognize our own yearnings to reveal once and for all the real thing, to hold up someone (or ourselves) as the doorkeeper and possessor of the key, and the concomitant tactics by which some are deemed closer and others farther from the truth.

Suggested Readings

Böhme, Hartmut. 2014. *Fetishism and Culture: A Different Theory of Modernity*. Translated by Anna Gault. Berlin: De Gruyter.

Hammerschlag, Sarah. 2021. "A Poor Substitute for Prayer: Sarah Kofman and the Fetish of Writing." In *Devotion: Three Inquiries in Religion, Literature and Political Imagination*. Chicago: University of Chicago Press.

Iacono, Alfonso Maurizio. 2016. *The History and Theory of Fetishism*. Hampshire, UK: Palgrave.

Latour, Bruno. 2010. *On the Modern Cult of the Factish Gods*. Durham, NC: Duke University Press.

Masuzawa, Tomoko. 2000. "Troubles with Materiality: The Ghost of Fetishism in the Nineteenth Century." *Comparative Studies in Society and History* 42 (2): 242–67.

Matory, J. Lorand. 2018. *The Fetish Revisited: Marx, Freud and the Gods Black People Make*. Durham, NC: Duke University Press.

Morris, Rosalind C. 2017. "After de Brosses: Fetishism, Translation, Comparativism, Critique." In *The Returns of Fetishism*, 133–319. Chicago: University of Chicago Press.

References

Anker, Elizabeth, and Rita Felski. 2017. *Critique and Postcritique*. Durham, NC: Duke University Press.

Appiah, Simon Kofi. 2022. "Fetish Again: Southern Perspectives on the Material Approach to the Study of Religion." *Open Theology* 8 (1): 79–94.

Apter, Emily. 1991. *Feminizing the Fetish: Psychoanalysis and Narrative Obsession in Turn of the Century France*. Ithaca, NY: Cornell University Press.

Asad, Talal. 1993. *Genealogies of Religion*. Baltimore, MD: Johns Hopkins University Press.

Batnitzky, Leora. 2011. *How Judaism Became a Religion*. Princeton, NJ: Princeton University Press.

Bennett, Jane. 2010. *Vibrant Matter: A Political Ecology of Things*. Durham, NC: Duke University Press.

Binet, Alfred. 1888. "Le fétichisme dans l'amour." In *Études de psychologie expérimentale*. Paris: Octave Doin.

Böhme, Hartmut. 2014. *Fetishism and Culture: A Different Theory of Modernity*. Translated by Anna Gault. Berlin: De Gruyter.

Carter, J. Kameron. 2022. "Anarche; or, The Matter of Charles Long and Black Feminism." *American Religions* 2 (2): 103–35.

Chidester, David. 2014. *Empire of Religion: Empire and Comparative Religion*. Chicago: University of Chicago Press.

Comte, Auguste. 1929. *Système de politique positive*. 5th ed. Paris: Mathias.

De Brosses, Charles. 2017. "On the Worship of Fetish Gods." In *The Returns of Fetishism: Charles de Brosses and the Afterlives of an Idea*. Chicago: University of Chicago Press.

Derrida, Jacques. 1986. *Glas*. Translated by John P. Leavey. Lincoln: University of Nebraska Press.

Du Bois, W. E. B. 1915. *The Negro*. New York: Holt.

Felski, Rita. 2015. *The Limits of Critique*. Chicago: University of Chicago Press.

Freud, Sigmund. 1953. "Three Essays on Sexuality." In *The Standard Edition of the Complete Psychological Works of Sigmund Freud*, translated by James Strachey. London: Hogarth Press.

Frykenberg, Robert. 1993. "Constructions of Hinduism at the Nexus of History and Religion." *Journal of Interdisciplinary History* 23 (3).

Hazard, Sonia. 2018. "Thing." *Early American Studies* 16 (4): 792–800.

Hegel, G. W. F. 1988. *Lectures on the Philosophy of Religion. The Lectures of 1827*. Berkeley: University of California Press.

Houtman, Dick, and Birgit Meyer. 2012. *Things: Religion and the Question of Materiality*. New York: Fordham University Press.

Iacono, Alfonso Maurizio. 2016. *The History and Theory of Fetishism*. Hampshire, UK: Palgrave.

Kant, Immanuel. 1998. *Religion within the Boundaries of Mere Reason*. Cambridge: Cambridge University Press.

Keane, Webb. 2007. *Christian Moderns: Freedom and Fetish in the Mission Encounter*. Berkeley: University of California Press.

Kofman, Sarah. 1999. *Camera Obscura of Ideology*. Translated by Will Straw. Ithaca, NY: Cornell University Press.

Latour, Bruno. 2010. *On the Modern Cult of the Factish Gods*. Durham, NC: Duke University Press.

Long, Charles. 1999. *Significations: Signs, Symbols and Images in the Interpretation of Religion*. London: Davies Group.

Marx, Karl. 1970. *Critique of Hegel's Philosophy of Right*. Translated by Annette Jolin and Joseph O'Malley. Cambridge: Cambridge University Press.

Marx, Karl. 1976. *Capital*. Translated by Ben Fowkes. New York: Penguin.

Masuzawa, Tomoko. 2000. "Troubles with Materiality: The Ghost of Fetishism in the Nineteenth Century." *Comparative studies in Society and History* 42 (2): 242–67.

Masuzawa, Tomoko. 2005. *The Invention of World Religions; or, How European Universalism was Preserved in the Language of Pluralism*. Chicago: University of Chicago Press.

Matory, J. Lorand. 2018. *The Fetish Revisited: Marx, Freud and the Gods Black People Make*. Durham, NC: Duke University Press.

Mauss, Marcel. 1969. *Oeuvres*. Edited by V. Karady. Paris: Minuit.

Morris, Rosalind C. 2017. "After de Brosses: Fetishism, Translation, Comparativism, Critique." In *The Returns of Fetishism*, 133–319. Chicago: University of Chicago Press.

Orsi, Robert. 2018. *History and Presence*. Cambridge, MA: The Belknap Press of Harvard University Press.

Pickering, Mary. 1988. "Auguste Comte and the Return to Fetishism." *Revue Internationale de Philosophie* 52 (2): 51–77.

Pietz, William. 2022. *The Problem of the Fetish*. Chicago: University of Chicago Press.

Smith, J. Z. 1998. "Religion, Religions, Religious." In *Critical Terms for Religious Studies*, edited by Mark C. Taylor. Chicago: University of Chicago Press. Reprinted in 2004 in Jonathan Z. Smith, *Relating Religion: Essays in the Study of Religion*. Chicago: University of Chicago Press.

Spyer, Patricia. 1998. *Border Fetishisms: Material Objects in Unstable Spaces*. London: Routledge.

Taussig, Michael. 1980. *The Devil and the Commodity Fetish in South America*. Chapel Hill: University of North Carolina Press.

Wassertstrom, Steven. 1999. *Religion after Religion*. Princeton, NJ: Princeton University Press.

6 IDENTITY

Eleanor Craig

In 1523, the Spanish crown passed an edict restricting colonial migration to "New Spain" to those with *limpieza de sangre*, or purity of blood. The fantasy of a New World conquered by Old Christians, a place in which "the seeds of heresy would never sprout," excluded those labeled *moriscos* and *conversos* who converted to Christianity from Islam and Judaism, respectively (Martínez 2008, 128). The notion of blood purity in Spain had evolved from the gradual merging of notions of feudal nobility (an absence of non-noble ancestry) with those of Catholic Christian lineage uncontaminated by "Jewish, Muslim, or heretic ancestry" (79–80). Its maintenance required, among other things, intensified control and scrutiny of women's sexual relationships and behaviors. The term *raza*, or race, at first pejoratively marked Jewish and Muslim lineage and spread by the late sixteenth century to what had initially been called *casta*, or caste, targeting especially those with African ancestry (163–64).

The logic surrounding Indigenous converts "never neatly overlapped with the stain of blood impurity" (Lum 2022, 35). Spanish colonizers attributed to Indigenous people idolatry and superstition, sometimes drawing parallels between Jewish and Indigenous forms of devotion and practice to buttress claims that Indigenous converts too were "false Christians" (Martínez 2008, 210). Indigenous subjects could nonetheless, in some circumstances, evade genealogical scrutiny in applying for civic posts or religious orders because their lineage ostensibly had no religion, and was thus free from contamination (214–18).

This concentrated anxiety about true conversion and religious loyalty fused judgments about what twentieth-century "Western" discourses would later secern as "nature and culture" (Bernasconi 2023, 33). Religion was deeply imbricated with what we would now call race, class, gender, and sexuality. While these terms are all to some extent anachronistic in their present-day connotations, they signal enduring ways that religious identity takes social and political shape in dense fields of power and differentiation. The contradictions that surfaced in applying the religious categories of the Reconquista to those with no discernible Old World ancestry recall debates about those deemed to be without religion that reach back to the Crusades. In the other chronological direction, North American colonial enslavers in the seventeenth century strained theologically to distinguish the salvation of presumptively white Christians from that of baptized enslaved persons "who were not Christians in their native country" (48). The unstable determinants of religious identity in each of these contexts were embedded in wider systems of hierarchy and structures of violence.

The notion that there are discrete religious identities among which subjects choose or which they inherit—or even that there is a broader (perhaps universal) category of religion that unites and contains plural subcategories, or religions—also reflects and refracts complex historical formations. Identities are historical and contextual, and the forms of sameness they posit are likewise made relevant by contingent processes, events, and structural conditions. Identities provide means of asserting continuity and departure, requiring more and less conscious dealings with the past that conditions their present. They reflect discursive possibilities that emerge as "the differential exercise of power . . . makes some narratives possible and silences others" (Trouillot 2015, 25). The histories they invoke may not have shared the concerns they are conjured to address in the present. Identity claims may be naturalized or framed as innovations, asserting returns to the past or projections for the future, and sometimes both at once. In their calculations of sameness and difference, identities likewise project forms of otherness (that which they are *unlike*) that may be detached from and unrecognizable to the subjects they describe. Identity is a slippery term that can signal moves toward and away from coalition or solidarity, and may naturalize those moves as driven by possessive traits.

This chapter takes as its starting point that the notion of religious identity must be understood through a historical lens that tracks *the identity of religion* from colonialist classifications of non-Christian ways of being and knowing to religion's development as an academic field of study in the twentieth century and its reassessments in the twenty-first. I highlight how nineteenth-century scholars used the concept of animism to debate what was and was not religion, and to grapple with the ambiguities and inconsistencies their own modes of classification produced. Building on the work of scholars including Talal Asad, Aisha Beliso-De Jesús, Tomoko Masuzawa, and Jonathan Z. Smith, I argue that the study of religion's anxieties about disciplinary identity have largely, if unconsciously, retained epistemological hierarchies of civilization, truth, and being that attention to animism throws into sharp relief.

Religion's role in colonial rationalizations and racial formation continues to shape relationships between so-called identity politics and the academic identity of religious studies. Far from being intramural disciplinary concerns, anxieties about what in religion is compatible with reason and civilization refract these histories and associate danger, illegitimacy, and irrationality with minoritized traditions. Their domain is hardly limited to academic disputes and materializes in extralegal violence, military intervention, fearmongering speech acts, travel bans, and persecution through criminal legal systems.

The epistemological biases that underpin these phenomena are held by many who would not endorse those outcomes. They cannot, I suggest, be reworked through methods that reify religious identities, even those that eagerly affirm plurality and diversity. An alternative mode of academic engagement could attend instead to *processes of identification* as they are theorized, practiced, and experienced. This would make more visible the ripple effects of academic knowledge production, especially their implications for traditions that have been historically elevated and subordinated. It would also allow religious studies to pursue more accountable discourse about identity that holds at the forefront its perpetual and relational formation.[1]

Animism and (the Study of) Religion

In the opening to *Critique of Black Reason*, Achille Mbembe asserts that "throughout its history, European thought has tended to conceive of identity less in terms of mutual belonging (cobelonging) to a common world than in terms of relation between similar beings—of being itself emerging and manifesting itself in its own state, or its own mirror" (Mbembe 2017, 1). Animism is a revealing category for how its unfurling in studies

1. The distinction between identity and identification is inspired by texts that deploy psychoanalytic theory to analyze both (Butler 1997; Cheng 2000).

of religion tracks calculations of similarity and difference, especially related to what is perceived as reality and illusion. Real religion, a determinant of real being, disproportionately mirrors Europeanness, Christianity, whiteness, and modernity. Animism endures as a descriptive category that encompasses traditions with vastly different cosmologies and epistemologies, a problem that trails the newer label of Indigenous traditions. That both terms sit uneasily as religious classifications demonstrates that the very notion of religious identity circumscribes the kinds of differences that count, and what those differences mean. Animism has a key role in the intertwined genealogies of modern race and religion and has left a lasting imprint on what it means to study religion. As I argue below, the role the term religion itself plays in mediating assumptions about relationships between spirituality, race, and ethnicity (along with other intersections) raises the stakes of identity discourse in religious studies scholarship in ways that demand care and attention.

Talal Asad, David Chidester, Tomoko Masuzawa, and Edward Said have variously argued that depictions of religious otherness constitute, reflect, and consolidate assessments of race, culture, and modernity. Religion's co-constitution with racial categories has been rigorously pursued in works like J. Kameron Carter's *Race: A Theological Account* (2008), Geraldine Heng's *The Invention of Race in the European Middle Ages* (2018), Willie James Jennings's *The Christian Imagination: Theology and the Origins of Race* (2010), and Theodore Vial's *Modern Religion, Modern Race* (2016). As one element of these ongoing formations and calculations of racial and religious difference (beginning long before religious studies departments existed in anything like their present form), animism's challenge to the category of religion was that it could not be marked off from other aspects of social and cultural life. Sometimes deemed religion, sometimes deemed prior to or formative of it, animism enabled theorizing about group relationships to culture, history, and reason. Developmental claims about animism's place in an evolutionary narrative echoed the religious and civilizational hierarchies posited in philosophical texts of the same time period in ways that I do not elaborate here, but that connect this intellectual trajectory to the aforementioned texts on race and religion.

Cornelius Petrus Tiele's 1876 *Outline of the History of Religion to the Spread of Universal Religions* (Tiele 1905) attempts to comprehensively track religious development in human history. A theologically trained scholar and former minister, Tiele is known as an early comparativist. He was not the first to attempt a catalog of world religions—Samuel Purchas in 1613 would be a notable predecessor, and additional works that strove for comprehensiveness appeared in the eighteenth century (Bernasconi 2023, 35)—but his attempt to apply the scientific method to the study of religious diversity signals an important trajectory for racial religious reasoning. Religious differences are, for Tiele, caused and shaped by underlying racial and ethnic differences. He posits collective dispositions associated with each group's approach to subsistence, trade, and worship. Tiele asserts that "all changes and transformations in religions, whether they appear from a subjective point of view to indicate decay or progress," are *natural* according to "the character of nations and races, as well as by the influence of the circumstances surrounding them, and of special individuals" (Tiele 1905, 2). This, for him, is the unifying principle of religious history.

On the basis of this so-called natural differentiation, which is both innate and circumstantial, Tiele orders religions in a temporal and developmental hierarchy to show "the relation in which the religions of savages stand to the great historic families of religions" (1905, 15). The word "historic" indicates not prior existence, but those traditions that belong properly to a civilizational history that overcomes animism and leaves it behind.

> It is on various grounds probable that the earliest religion, which has left but faint traces behind it, was followed by a period in which Animism generally prevailed. This stage, which is still represented by the so-called Nature-religions, or rather by the polydæmonistic magic tribal religions, early developed among civilised nations into polytheistic national religions resting upon a traditional doctrine. Not until a later period did polytheism give place here and there to nomistic religions, or religious communities founded on a law or holy scripture, and subduing polytheism more or less completely beneath pantheism or monotheism. The last, again, contain the roots of the universal or world-religions, which start from principles and maxims. (3)

Tiele admits that animism can itself rise to a certain level of sophistication. Yet he calls it "a sort of primitive philosophy" distinct from religion (though it conditions or governs religion in the lives of those under its influence) and insists that it remains outside of "the proper history of religion" (5, 9). This ostensible historical deficit correlates with a presumed moral deficiency: because "rewards or punishments" depend on appeasing spirits with "sacrifices and gifts" rather than good works, Tiele concludes that animist practices involve only "selfish" motivations and values (11).

Tiele acknowledges that animism changes over time and declares it a mistake to suppose that any human group has no religion (equated here with "belief in higher beings") (1905, 6, 9). Yet he argues that nature-religions "have no history," and are the "remains" or "ruins" of "ancient prehistoric animistic religions" (6).[2] The evident contradictions in his claims—that religion is universal but not possessed by those with animism, and that animistic traditions develop in history but have no history—stand gaping and unremarked.

Tiele draws significantly from the work of Edward B. Tylor, whose *Primitive Culture* (1871) coined the term animism in its relevant usage and is the first citation in Tiele's chapter on the topic. Tylor consistently claims what Tiele only grants at particular moments—that religion's fundamental definition should be "the belief in Spiritual Beings" (Tylor 1913, 1.424). In comparison with Tiele, Tylor assigns more status to the "lower" traditions and leaves more ambiguity about the attainments of the "higher." He attributes Europeans' lack of cross-cultural understanding to hatred and arrogance and their refusal to see religion elsewhere to narrow-minded carelessness (Tylor 1913, 419–20). He argues that the transition from animism to "higher" traditions, including Christianity, is in many locations an incomplete achievement. Tylor cites, for example, Easter practices of North German peasants as showing remnants of sun worship (1913, 2.297), and notes that "the custom of opening a window or door for the departing soul when it quits the body is to this day a very familiar superstition in France, Germany, and England" (1913, 1.454). Yet Tylor's approach is decidedly supremacist, and the value for Christians of studying other religions is to understand how Christianity's "thoughts and principles" developed through religion's ostensibly less developed forms (1913, 1.421). Animist beliefs, in Tylor's framework, consist of categorically incorrect judgments owing to a lack of "scientific education" (1913, 1.445). There is an insistent disidentification at the heart of animism's elaboration

2. Jonathan Z. Smith posits that Tiele may here be indicating recognition of the impact of colonialism (Smith 1998, 278), and Tiele does in fact cite Spanish conquest as having interrupted what would have been the "independent development" of both civilizational structure and religion in Peru and Mexico (Tiele 1905, 21).

for the modern study of religion. Even when animism is cited as laying the groundwork for philosophy of religion and is admitted to be based in human reason, it is constantly measured against "the civilized world" and found wanting (1913, 1.426–27).

Émile Durkheim similarly problematizes the terms under which animism has been disparaged while upholding civilizational hierarchies. In his 1921 *Elementary Forms of Religious Life* Durkheim critiques Tylor's definition of religion, asserting that in "great religions" like Buddhism, belief in gods and spirits is not a prominent feature. He claims that, in fact, "a considerable part of religious evolution has consisted of a gradual movement away from the ideas of spiritual being and divinity" (Durkheim 1995, 29, 31). He challenges the claims by Tylor and Herbert Spencer in *Principles of Sociology* (1886) that a confusion of dreams for waking life is at the root of animist belief and generates the idea of the soul, declaring it implausible that "the primitive" would so credulously accept that whatever was perceived while dreaming was real. Any significance attributed to dreams would instead derive from a "religious system" that could give them meaning (Durkheim 1995, 53–56). Durkheim likewise refutes the notion that ancestor worship or a cult of the dead characterizes animism, claiming that some "advanced" societies deify their dead while some "lower" ones do not (59). It is unscientific, he argues, to ascribe the origins of religion to mistakes and illusion: "What sort of science is it whose principal discovery is to make the very object it treats disappear?" (67). Amid these various corrections, including an insistence that religious beliefs are not "so many hallucinatory representations, without any objective basis," the method of ordering cultures and civilizations from least to most advanced endures (65).

The scientific project of studying religion operates from an evolutionary frame that seeks to explain "higher" civilization to itself by scrutinizing those whose religion places them at an "early" stage of development. Religion's determined trajectory aims toward "the scientific explanations of the future" (Durkheim 1995, 329). Durkheim refutes frameworks that would deny all rationality or self-awareness to those he calls primitive, but keeps in place a structure of assessment that grants Western scientific epistemology a privileged claim to truth and reality. This combination of impulses—to dignify plurality while pursuing an objective scientific grasp on reality—has shaped the trajectory of religious studies, in frequent contrast with how it imagines "religion."

The Identity of Religious Studies

While it would not describe with accuracy or thoroughness the assemblage of scholars, projects, and epistemologies in present-day religious studies departments, a scientific study of religion able to hold religious identity, practice, and belief at arm's length continues to function in many contexts as the regulative ideal for the field. As religious studies began to take shape in something resembling its current form, "animism" was of less interest than religious and political formations associated with imperial competition. Yet as scholars probed the differences contained within and attributed to religious categories and identities, the previously delineated hierarchies of rationality and civilization (implicit or explicit) remained consistent.

Tomoko Masuzawa traces the beginnings of "world religions" as a common term in English-language discourse to North American and Western European concerns about geopolitical conflicts and balances of power in the 1920s and 1930s. Masuzawa connects a newly sensed instability in Europe brought on by World War I with awareness that "violent globalization in the form of colonialism and the explosive expansion of so-called free trade" had increased not only dominance, but interdependence. As purveyors of sweeping oppression and exploitation, modern nation-states aimed to control power struggles and potential rebellions. The study of world religions was partly, then, a program of surveillance aimed at gathering "global intelligence" for maintaining political dominance. Traditions considered animist or Indigenous (also called primitive, primal, tribal, or preliterate) remained lumped together, to some degree because they were not considered part of "the rising tide of modernization and increasing global competition" (Masuzawa 2005, 41–42). These traditions go from having central importance for Western self-examination to serving marginal or prefatory roles in accounts of religions "great" enough to pose a political threat.

In a similar vein, Sarah Imhoff looks at the rapid growth of religious studies that began in the mid-twentieth century and finds global political tensions to be the common undercurrent. Imhoff argues that student interest in religion, national security funding for religious studies, prioritization of existential reflection, and a determination to inculcate liberal democratic values were all related to the Cold War and anticommunism (Imhoff 2015, 490). Rather than accounting for its political entanglements, religious studies produced "a narrative of progress" that curiously resembles Durkheim's predictions for religion (2015, 492).

This progress narrative emphasizes the Supreme Court case *Abington School District v. Schempp* (374 US 203 [1963]). The case examined the constitutionality of a Philadelphia public school's routine in which students listened to a peer read ten Bible verses and were instructed to stand and repeat in unison a recitation of the Lord's prayer. Justice Clark, in delivering the main opinion of the court, noted that "our national life reflects a religious people" with widespread consensus on devotional obligations to a Supreme Being, alongside a commitment to religious freedom (*Abington v. Schempp*, 213–14). He nevertheless found that these exercises, carried out in a school which students were mandated by law to attend, violated the establishment clause of the Constitution (extended by the Fourteenth Amendment to states). He clarified that the Bible could be examined through literary, historical, or comparative study as part of a "secular program of education," but that such scenarios were distinct from the "religious exercises" in question (225).

The much-cited language from *Abington v. Schempp* distinguishing indoctrination from "teaching *about*" religion appears in concurring opinions by Justice Brennan and Justices Goldberg and Harlan (*Abington v. Schempp*, 300 and 306, italics original). Imhoff notes that many scholars of religion were already making such a distinction, and "had long considered it vital to the enterprise of teaching religion in higher education" (Imhoff 2015, 469–71). The social and political forces that grew religious studies were well underway by the time of the court's decision (474). While they may have misrepresented its centrality to the case, it is nonetheless true that advocates for religious studies frequently cited *Abington v. Schempp* for a distinction between teaching religion and teaching about religion, portraying the latter and its disavowal of theology as "the scholarly maturation" of the field (Cady 2002, 113). Disciplinary identity emerged in contexts that frequently rewarded disidentification with religion and theology (Beliso-De Jesús 2018).

These overlapping nervous projects—distinguishing between religion and religious studies, grappling with Cold War threats, and scrambling for safe distance in the fraught relationships created by global violence and its intimacies—fed controversies about emic and etic (insider and outsider) perspectives that persist today. In 1988, J. Z. Smith highlighted the terms normative and descriptive to describe the supposed contrast; more recently, Aisha Beliso-De Jesús has associated it with "academic identity-thinking" and enduring insistence on distinctions between "scholar" and "practitioner" (Smith 1988, 232; Beliso-De Jesús 2018, 312, 317). For Smith, the assumption that theology could not be critical or objective because it yielded to religious authority or canonical texts was out of touch with most current work in theology. Likewise, the notion of an objective scientific researcher had come thoroughly under scrutiny in "the current literature of human sciences" and would not fit the most up-to-date definitions of rigor (Smith 1988, 233). Beliso-De Jesús finds, however, that those who would be secure in their identities as religious studies scholars are still held to secularist expectations that proscribe the so-called practitioner's "hope for critical transformation" (Beliso-De Jesús 2018, 317). While an isolatable concept of religion in the development of religious studies might have aided departmentalization, it reinforces classificatory habits that situate the "nonsubject of science" in opposition to the unmarked (and thus dominant) race, gender, sexuality, and class of the presumed scholarly actor (2018, 319). Religion becomes an axis or category of identity but is paradoxically depoliticized because religious analyses of power are deemed overly particular.

Aligning religion with categories of identity, even historicized categories, can fall into treating minoritized religious imagination and invention as "nothing more than a cultural reflex" (Carter 2008, 126). This largely unconscious supposition essentializes a naturalized view of religion that follows a predetermined, even teleological path and identities such as race that are readily admitted to be social constructs (2008, 126–27). It elides, moreover, ongoing contestations about correct or desirable practice, historical interpretation, and spiritual and political continuity among those who might share identity labels or most aspects of social positioning. An odd effect of attributing something to religious identity is that "it spiritualizes what are material practices and turns them into expressions of something timeless and suprahistorical, which is to say, it depoliticizes them" (Masuzawa 2005, 20). In the work of Talal Asad, we see how such logic projects associations with tradition and heightened religiosity onto those who are racially and culturally imagined to be out of step with modernity and secularity (Asad 1993).

These assumptions are intensified in discourse about religion and Indigeneity. Many traditions that were formerly referred to without hesitation as animism are, in current world religions discourse, more commonly called "Indigenous traditions." This category, like animism, is largely used in contrast with world religions even when associated with that term. In contrast to world religions acknowledged to have "unique historical origins" and trajectories, so-called Indigenous religions "instead are enumerated as various transhistorical *types* defined by shared traits," such as ancestor worship or shamanism. This mode of grouping replicates, in effect if not intent, Tiele's assumption that "animistic religion is, in its nature, and even in its ideas and usages, with slight modification everywhere the same" (Tiele 1905, 15). It echoes logics that endured in explicit forms into the twentieth century that cast "savage" religion as a generalizable type within which there was little variation (Masuzawa 2005, 44).

Both animism and the general label of Indigenous mark something simultaneously transhistorical and ahistorical, because tradition is supposed to be "primordial" and inhering in culture (Wilkinson 2017, 290). Present-day continuities with modes of thought that distanced animism from modernity and development create a slippage between "Indigenous traditions" and *traditional*. They call to mind Masuzawa's observation that religion is thought to be most important in "traditional" contexts, "regardless of how much or how little we happen to know about the society in question or about its supposed tradition" (Masuzawa 2005, 1). This pattern continues, moreover, to define traditions by those features which would seem at the greatest cultural distance from European-derived empiricist views of materiality and humanity.

Coercion, Recognition, and Religious Identity

While it is true that "religion" is a colonially imposed term and that religious identity oversimplifies vast realms of human and extra-human relationships, withholding the designation of religion and refusing to recognize religious identity are racialized judgments that can carry severe consequences. In *Banning Black Gods: Law and Religions of the African Diaspora*, Danielle Boaz illustrates "the shifting boundaries of modern definitions of 'religion' and the concerning trend to exclude African diasporic faiths from this category" (Boaz 2021, 160). Some of the starkest examples Boaz documents pertain to Obeah and Santería/Lucumí, including cases in which US courts ruled these traditions to be inherently dangerous (following a religious studies scholar's characterization of Obeah) or not religion (and thus, in the case of Santería, not protected by Florida's Religious Freedom Restoration Act) (2021, 161–65). Boaz's text actively engages Brazilian, Caribbean, US, and Canadian legal systems, along with their precursors and parallels in British and African colonial history. She does not claim that African Diasporic religions exist in discrete, stable forms that are in need of more adequate recognition (Boaz writes, "What is 'Voodoo'? The answer is somewhat elusive and changes depending on the time period in question" [138]). Rather, she finds that modern legal systems restrict their definitions of religion to criminalize and stigmatize those who engage in a wide range of spiritual practices.

Legal definitions can, of course, be multivalent tools. Tisa Wenger demonstrates that under the US settler-colonial government, Native Americans' appeals to religious freedom have sometimes been instrumental for carving out domains of "cultural and political self-determination" (Wenger 2017, 103). That a claim to religious identity is made under duress does not make it disingenuous; it is rather a strategic necessity under coercive political and juridical arrangements. Additionally, the fact that such a claim sometimes succeeds does not undo the power arrangements that structure its occurrence.

Historical legal hostility to both Indigenous and African Diasporic traditions is rooted in long-standing efforts to maintain racial domination, justify colonialism, and constrain rebellion. Wenger notes that the Ghost Dance movement in Nevada "terrified many white Americans" who viewed it "as a sign of revolt against settler-colonial rule," and that this was the reason for its violent suppression (Wenger 2017, 110). Rastafarianism's anti-colonialism drove its persecution in British-controlled Jamaica. Reaching further back, eighteenth- and nineteenth-century legal bans and public denigrations of racialized spiritual practices in the Americas, from Obeah to Islam, were frequently tied to their association with slave revolts. Obeah practitioners' involvement in the 1760 uprising in Jamaica known as Tacky's Rebellion was met with a British law that "described Obeah as devil worship and suggested that the central purpose of Obeah was to try to harm others." This characterization endures in legislation against Obeah in Caribbean contexts formerly colonized by Britain, and "perceptions of this faith as fraudulent practices based on witchcraft and devil worship dominate the public forum" (Boaz 2021, 136). It reverberates in US case law, as noted above. Derogatory accounts of Vodou accelerated when the United States took New Orleans, highlighting the ostensibly superstitious practices of "newly emancipated Black populations to underscore that African Americans were supposedly unprepared for self-governance" (137).

Religion (perhaps a useful term here, even given its problematics) is in all of these instances perceived, in both accurate and fantastical ways, as a meaningful political force. The self-understandings and world-understandings cultivated across these traditions do contribute to subjective and collective action, even when the exact role of belief or practice in any given event is difficult to ascertain. At the same time, attempts to draw simple causal relationships between tradition and political praxis warrant scrutiny about the motivations and implications of such claims. They can cause us to ignore ambiguities and complexities in identity formation (including racial and ethnic identity formation) in favor of divisions that resemble those of the state and older discourses on world religions. They also downplay how identity is continually made in communities, quotidian actions, intimacies, ceremonies, and responsiveness to spirits and divinities (Nwokocha 2023).

Religious identity may, in the end, be a less helpful framework than *identification* as a process that involves interhuman struggles and affinities, human and nonhuman relationships, and dynamic navigations of human and spiritual agency. An emphasis on identification might redirect the focus on beliefs and traits that "identity" can imply and instead draw attention to processes of transformation, political negotiation, and knowledge creation. This practice could loosen naturalized notions of cause and effect without confining the power of spiritual and religious life to assumptions of voluntary or hereditary identity.

Identification Beyond Categorization

I conclude by sketching how attention to identification over identity enables a focus on epistemology through a brief engagement with studies of Hmong Diasporic spirituality. Hmong traditions, often referred to as Hmong religion, are still called animist in many scholarly and colloquial contexts. A classificatory approach to religious or ethnic identity might highlight typical "animist" convergences of ties to land/homeland, "shamanic" healing practices, and beliefs in spirits. Attention to identification would highlight instead their relational content and contextual meanings in situations ranging from personal health to the aftermath of imperial warfare. In her interviews with Hmong Americans who converted to or away from Christianity, Melissa May Borja found that their reasons were far more complex than proximity to or dependence on the missionizing activities of resettlement workers. Experiences with health, healing, and spirits often motivated their moves toward Christian *and* Hmong leaders, communities, and practices (Borja 2017). This does not suggest equivalence or even axes of comparison between Christian and Hmong cosmologies or negate the ways that people navigating both combine and relate them (Borja 2022). It also does not ignore the fact that Hmong practices (from agriculture to funerals) face significant legal obstacles in the US (DeSantiago 2020). Rather, it shows how "religious identity" embeds layers of adaptation—spiritual, personal, and collective—in the face of intertwining existential and practical concerns.

Human-spirit relationships are intellectual instigations for practitioners. Translating Hmong frameworks into terms familiar to institutional religious studies, Vincent Her explains that "the concept of the *plig* is at the core of Hmong religious philosophy. It is a theory, an emic concept, whereby Hmong Americans are able, in the words of Clifford Geertz, to suspend themselves in their own 'webs of significance'" (Her 2018, 33). Experiences of trauma and displacement can cause the dreaming *plig* (one of thirty-one *ntsuj pligs*) to wander and get lost, resulting in bodily sickness. The *plig* must be called back to the body after having been left at the site of "fright and chaos" (Vang 2021, 3–4). The same wandering *plig* rejoins the ancestors in the spirit world after death.

Plig as spirit and theory, agent and concept, traces religious identification through relationships to place, community, self, and body. In *On the Run: Secrecy, Fugitivity, and Hmong Refugee Epistemologies*, Ma Vang demonstrates how this return after death makes epistemic interventions into notions of time, space, and coloniality. Vang relates that "the plig [is] an ontology that carries Hmong knowledge. . . . While refugees may not be able to physically return to Laos as homeland, their pligs can return in death to Laos and the ancestral homeland of China. Return through death constitutes a 'political claim to Hmong sovereignty and a Hmong kingdom' such that death undoes Hmong displacement" (Vang 2021, 180). The political and spiritual implications are inseparable: They contest the notion of (re)settling as the teleology of refugee displacement and conceptions of time that exclude colonized others as "not-yet-modern." They show how fugitive forms of knowledge developed in enduring statelessness locate repair and restoration beyond anything the nation-state can offer (2021, 14, 17, 26). In calling knowledge what many scholars would call belief, Vang demonstrates that this dynamic and contextual identification is a way of knowing.

Collectively, these studies show identification to be thoroughly entangled with those supposed determinates of religion, inheritance and choice, but exceeding both in ever-unfolding ways. A pluralist, multicultural approach to religious identity glosses over conflicts as well as hierarchies.

Minoritized knowledge might be permitted, but it is simultaneously accommodated and dismissed as "personal quests, marks of belonging, or anecdotes of inclusion" (Beliso-De Jesús 2018, 328). This logic forgets disciplinary as well as geopolitical history, even when reading texts that are evidently possessed with those concerns; it periodizes works of scholarship as products of their times rather than grappling with their ongoing impact. Identity as explanation projects overdetermined forms of commonality and denies the deep, often uncomfortable connections between dominant and minoritized narratives. By shifting our lens of analysis to identification, we might become more cognizant of the challenges and possibilities that accompany genuine epistemological difference and multiplicity.

Suggested Readings

Beliso-De Jesús, Aisha. 2015. *Electric Santería: Racial and Sexual Assemblages of Transnational Religion*. New York: Columbia University Press.

Carter, J. Kameron. 2023. *The Anarchy of Black Religion: A Mystic Song*. Durham, NC: Duke University Press.

Heng, Geraldine. 2018. *The Invention of Race in the European Middle Ages*. Cambridge: Cambridge University Press.

Jennings, Willie James. 2010. *The Christian Imagination: Theology and the Origins of Race*. New Haven, CT: Yale University Press.

Lum, Kathryn Gin. 2022. *Heathen: Religion and Race in American History*. Cambridge, MA: Harvard University Press.

References

Asad, Talal. 1993. *Genealogies of Religion: Discipline and Reasons of Power in Christianity and Islam*. Baltimore, MD: Johns Hopkins University Press.

Beliso-De Jesús, Aisha. 2018. "Confounded Identities: A Meditation on Race, Feminism, and Religious Studies in Times of White Supremacy." *Journal of the American Academy of Religion* 86 (2): 307–40.

Bernasconi, Robert. 2023. *Critical Philosophy of Race: Essays*. New York: Oxford University Press.

Boaz, Danielle N. 2021. *Banning Black Gods: Law and Religions of the African Diaspora*. University Park: Pennsylvania State University Press.

Borja, Melissa May. 2017. "Speaking of Spirits: Oral History, Religious Change, and the Seen and Unseen Worlds of Hmong Americans." *The Oral History Review* 44 (1): 1–18.

Borja, Melissa May. 2022. *Follow the New Way: American Refugee Resettlement Policy and Hmong Religious Change*. Cambridge, MA: Harvard University Press.

Butler, Judith. 1997. *The Psychic Life of Power: Theories in Subjection*. Stanford, CA: Stanford University Press.

Cady, Linell E. 2002. "Territorial Disputes: Religious Studies and Theology in Transition." In *Religious Studies, Theology, and the University: Conflicting Maps, Changing Terrain*, edited by Linell E. Cady and Delwin Brown, 110–25. New York: SUNY Press.

Carter, J. Kameron. 2008. *Race: A Theological Account*. Oxford: Oxford University Press.

Cheng, Anne Anlin. 2000. *The Melancholy of Race: Psychoanalysis, Assimilation and Hidden Grief*. Oxford: Oxford University Press.

DeSantiago, Danny Vincent. 2020. "Changes, Conflict, and Culture: The Status of Social-Cultural, Environmental, and Legal Challenges for Hmong Cultural Practices in Contemporary California." *Hmong Studies Journal* 22: 1–41.

Durkheim, Émile. 1995. *The Elementary Forms of Religious Life*. Translated by Karen E. Fields. New York: The Free Press.

Heng, Geraldine. 2018. *The Invention of Race in the European Middle Ages*. Cambridge: Cambridge University Press.

Her, Vincent K. 2018. "Reframing Hmong Religion: A Reflection on Emic Meanings and Etic Labels." *Amerasia Journal* 44 (2): 23–41.

Imhoff, Sarah. 2015. "The Creation Story, or How We Learned to Stop Worrying and Love 'Schempp.'" *Journal of the American Academy of Religion* 84 (2): 466–97.Jennings, Willie James. 2010. *The Christian Imagination: Theology and the Origins of Race*. New Haven, CT: Yale University Press.

Lum, Kathryn Gin. 2022. *Heathen: Religion and Race in American History*. Cambridge, MA: Harvard University Press.

Martínez, María Elena. 2008. *Genealogical Fictions: Limpieza de Sangre, Religion, and Gender in Colonial Mexico*. Stanford, CA: Stanford University Press.

Masuzawa, Tomoko. 2005. *The Invention of World Religions; or, How European Universalism Was Preserved in the Language of Pluralism*. Chicago: University of Chicago Press.

Mbembe, Achille. 2017. *Critique of Black Reason*. Translated by Laurent Dubois. Durham, NC: Duke University Press.

Nwokocha, Eziaku Atuama. 2023. *Vodou en Vogue: Fashioning Black Divinities in Haiti and the United States*. Chapel Hill: University of North Carolina Press.

Smith, Jonathan Z. 1988. "'Religion' and 'Religious Studies': No Difference at All." *Soundings: An Interdisciplinary Journal* 71 (2–3): 231–44.

Smith, Jonathan Z. 1998. "Religion, Religions, Religious." In *Critical Terms for Religious Studies*, edited by Mark C. Taylor, 269–84. Chicago: University of Chicago Press. Reprinted in 2004 in Jonathan Z. Smith, *Relating Religion: Essays in the Study of Religion*. Chicago: University of Chicago Press.

Spencer, Herbert. 1886. *Principles of Sociology*. New York: D. Appleton and Co.

Tiele, Cornelius Petrus. 1905. *Outline of the History of Religion to the Spread of Univer-*

sal Religions. Translated by J. Estlin Carpenter. London: K. Paul, Trench, Trübner, & co., ltd.

Trouillot, Michel-Rolph. 2015. *Silencing the Past*. Boston: Beacon Press.

Tylor, Edward B. 1913. *Primitive Culture: Researches into the Development of Mythology, Philosophy, Religion, Language, Art, and Custom*. London: John Murray.

Vang, Ma. 2021. *On the Run: Secrecy, Fugitivity, and Hmong Refugee Epistemologies*. Durham, NC: Duke University Press.

Vial, Theodore. 2016. *Modern Religion, Modern Race*. New York: Oxford University Press.

Wenger, Tisa. 2017. *Religious Freedom: The Contested History of an American Ideal*. Chapel Hill: University of North Carolina Press.

Wilkinson, Darryl. 2017. "Is There Such a Thing as Animism?" *Journal of the American Academy of Religion* 85 (2): 289–311.

7 IMAGE

James Robson

Consider two well-known images created in France in the mid-eighteenth and late nineteenth centuries. The first, Jean-Léon Gérôme's (1824–1904) *Pygmalion and Galatea* (ca. 1890)—based on a story in Ovid's first-century CE *Metamorphoses*—depicts the sculptor Pygmalion in his workshop embracing the statue of Galatea that he has just completed. The naked Galatea turns and leans ever so seductively toward the sculptor as they embrace and share a kiss. The second image, Jean-Baptiste Oudry's (1686–1755) engraving *The Sculptor and the Statue of Jupiter* (before 1755), depicts a startled and frightened sculptor encountering his recently competed statue of Jupiter, which appears ready to strike him down.

Throughout history images have elicited strongly conflicting sentiments. For some, images are seductive and compel an inordinate amount of interest and attraction. Others see them as repulsive, deceptive, and dangerous objects that incite violent acts of iconoclastic destruction. It is precisely the fear and disdain of certain images that inspired iconoclasts—from the ancient Near East, France, England, and the Netherlands to China, India, Africa, Mexico, and Afghanistan—to take up hammers to smash images. That history of destruction is itself captured in images of iconomachy and iconoclasm depicted in paintings, etchings, and woodcuts. There are iconophilic "friends of interpretable objects" as well as iconophobic enemies of those objects (Tamen 2001). That tension, while often portrayed as oppositional, can reside within an individual person or a single religious tradition. The term "image," and related image practices, are, if anything else, filled with ambivalence.

There is no generally accepted definition of the term "image," and no unitary theory about images. Images have, however, generated a vast archive of philosophical and theological reflection—from Plato, Plotinus, and Augustine to Wittgenstein, Nelson Goodman, C. S. Peirce, Jean-Luc Marion, and W. J. T. Mitchell. It is a diverse field that is not amenable to synthesis. After a long period of neglect and repression, except when subjected to philosophical and theological reflection or when referred to in the negative, the term "image" and image practices have drawn increasing interest and provoked lively discussion and debate among scholars of religion. This essay will focus on the term "image" in religious studies and an assessment of image practices within a selection of religious traditions.

The English term "image" is derived from the Latin word *imāgō*, which referred to a "representation in art of a person or thing, picture, likeness" and came to have the wider sense of being an "artificial imitation or representation of something, esp. of a person or the bust of a person . . . such an imitation in solid form; a statue, effigy, sculpted figure [often a figure of a saint or divinity as an object of religious veneration]" (*Oxford English Dictionary* 1989). Related, but often conflated, terms like "icon" (positive) and "idol" (negative) are derived from the Greek. The former comes from *eikōn*, meaning "likeness," and later takes on a more restricted sense within Christianity. The latter comes from *eídōlon*, referring to a visible image or likeness lacking material form (like an image in a mirror), a phantom, or an idea. The word *eídōlon* later came to have the pejorative sense of being a "false god," a "fictitious divinity," or an illegitimate object of worship, and is the basis for the term "idolatry" (*eidōlolatreia* or the "veneration," *latreia*, of an "idol," *eídōlon*). The related English word "imagine" is derived from the Latin *imaginare*, "to form an image of." These definitions form our common understandings of the term, but they are limited and colored by Platonic and Neoplatonic notions of the image as an always imperfect representation or imitation of a prototype that lies beyond the image itself. That view had a decisive impact on later Christian theological views that held sway as the dominant discourse on religious images, but it does not serve us well in considering images in other traditions.

: : :

There is a long prehistory of cultic images before they were categorized as art, since secular modernity merely constitutes a few frames on the long reel of history. Throughout most of world history, and in most parts of the world, religious traditions have engaged with images, either in theory or in practice, positively or negatively. One cannot write the history of religions without including the history of images. "Image" is a critical term not merely due to its connection with practices related to images in temples, monasteries, shrines, homes, or the minds of religious practitioners, but also because the term and related terms—like "icon," "idol," and "fetish"—have been at the heart of lively discussions within religious traditions and in the foundation of religious studies.

Few terms have as much critical currency for the evolution of religious studies as the term "image." It has formed a fault line running through controversies about representation: immanence vs. transcendence; presence vs. absence; the iconic vs. the aniconic; the animate vs. the inanimate; and the mental vs. the material. It has been located at the crux where distinctions have been drawn between the orthodox and the heterodox, true religion and paganism, monotheism and polytheism, and religion and superstition. These distinctions become particularly apparent with the troubling drift that occurs from the use of the terms "image" or "icon" to the use of the pejorative terms "idol" or "fetish" (Pietz 1985, 1987, 1988). When the image/idol distinction is introduced, it is usually about more than mere semantics; often it signals a division between proper and improper forms of representation and proper and improper gods. The terms "idol" and "fetish" were situated on the wrong side of the line separating primitives and idolaters from the civilized. Once an image is referred to as an "idol" or "fetish," you know you have entered a battleground, shaken by charges of paganism, heathenism, and idolatry. Those charges usually precede an outburst of iconoclastic destruction. Idolatry is "an accusation, not a belief . . . there never were, nor will there ever be, idols, since these are artefacts of the iconoclast's conviction, the imaginary Other of all critical campaigns" (Koerner 2004, 98, 11). Or, in the words of Jean-Luc Marion, "the idol does not indicate, any more than the icon, a particular being or even class of beings . . . [they indicate] a manner of being for beings. . . . Indeed, a determination that would limit itself to opposing the 'true-God' (icon) to the 'false gods'" (Marion 1991, 7–8). Claims of idolatry are often nothing more than "the naïve belief in the other's naïve belief" (Latour 1997, 81). This history has cast a long and dark shadow over the study of religion. Earlier explicit acts of iconoclasm—whether those of the Byzantine or Carolingian periods, the Protestant Reformation, colonial encounters with non-European cultures, or the Cultural Revolution in China—have attracted the most attention, but one of the most critical forms of iconoclasm has been that enacted by scholars of religion themselves.

The term "image" was of central importance in the well-known evolutionary theories about religion developed by David Hume (1711–1776), Edward Burnett Tylor (1832–1917), and Lucien Lévy-Bruhl (1857–1938). Those theories downplay matter and images in favor of the immaterial, the rational, and the scientific. Within teleological narratives that envision a progression from the material to the immaterial in humanity's long march to an enlightened and rational modernity, material images did not fare well. The unfortunate consequence is that those views became naturalized within religious studies, where they have languished for a long time. One need only take a cursory glance at the *Hastings Encyclopedia of Religion and Ethics* (1908–1921), where the entry is titled "Images and Idols," to get a taste of earlier scholarly sensibilities. Not all entries are so egregious in their unpalatable statements about "primitives" or their cavalier separation of true religion from the false views of the idolatrous "other," but their negative images invariably colored twentieth-century scholarship. "Image" and "idol" became polarizing terms used to mark differences and establish boundaries. As J. Z. Smith reminds us, "difference is rarely something simply to be noted; it is, most often, something in which one has a stake" (2004, 252).

There was, indeed, a lot at stake for those religions whose images were deemed to be idols or fetishes, since the distinction served to justify claims about cultural and religious superiority that could be weaponized for colonization and conquest. That process did not begin, of course, with the cultural contacts ushered in with early modern European exploration and colonization; it is already found in the *Book of Numbers* 33:51–53: "When you pass over the Jordan into the land of Canaan, then you shall drive out all the inhabitants of the land before you, and destroy all their figured stones, and destroy all their molten images, and demolish all their high places; and you shall take possession of the land and settle in it, for I have given the land to you to possess it." In what might be described as a war of images, accusations of idolatry served as a rallying cry in battles against benighted pagans. Criticism of idolatry was "transformed into a criticism of folk religion, and the fight against idolatry into a struggle against imagination, superstition, and the masses' projection of their own world onto that of God" (Halbertal and Margalit 1992, 3).

It would have been harmful enough if such views had remained confined to the Mediterranean world, but the problem was exacerbated when that war of images was exported around the world in an era of colonial aspirations and global missionizing that brought Christians into direct confrontation with image practices in other parts of the world. Wherever missionaries went—be it Asia, Africa, or the Americas—the same story repeated itself: missionaries entered indigenous temples and desecrated, destroyed, or confiscated their so-called "idols" and "fetishes." In some cases, however, those images were sent back to missionary museums in Europe (like the London Missionary Society Museum) as proof of their successful conversions. Their work was so thorough that for many traditions little of the material record of images survives outside of those collections.

Islamic incursions into South Asia are also described as being a conquest of idols. Again, some images were destroyed, while others were captured and sent back to Baghdad, Ghazni, and Mecca as objects of wonder—including some that were housed temporarily in the Ka'ba or reused as the threshold of a mosque to be tread on—but also as evidence of territorial expansion, martial victories, and proofs of conversion (Flood 2009, 29, 277). In short, to A. M. Hocart we owe the insight that "local idols meant power dispersed," and therefore iconoclastic acts against idolaters went hand in hand with the religious and political centralization of power ([1936] 1970, 246–49).

The world opened in new ways, and studies of the world's religions evolved as travelers, missionaries, scholars, philologists, and ethnographers fanned out to distant locations and began to describe and compare the religious practices they encountered. Without denying the role of the missionaries' intolerance to the idolaters, it is also important to mention that there were some who challenged the religious assumptions of their day. Jean Frederic Bernard and Bernard Picart's *Cérémonies et coutumes religieuses de tous les peuples du monde* [The Religious Ceremonies and Customs of the Various Nations of the Known World] (1723–1743), a work of monumental importance to the development of European conceptions about the religions of the world and the comparative study of religions, includes a section on "the idolatrous nations." Rather than condemn those practices, they tried to show—notably through more than 250 pages of engraved images—how the so-called idolatrous practices of those deemed "primitives" shared features with other religions. After all, how different were the so-called idolaters' images from Catholic images of Jesus and the Virgin Mary or the rosaries they carried? Bernard and Picart's controversial book moved the needle ever so slightly away from unabashedly negative images and the long-standing fourfold division of religion into Christianity, Judaism, Islam, and Idolaters/Pagans (Hunt, Jacob, and Mijnhardt 2010). As comparisons of image practices emerged, some focused on difference and hierarchical evolution, while others gestured toward similarity and a lateral equality.

The history of the term "image" in religious studies and the place of images in the history of missionization and colonization resulted in the misrepresentation, silencing, and destruction of image practices in other parts of the world. Images, which figured prominently in earlier negative depictions of idolaters and pagans, soon became conspicuously muted in the early modern study of religion as interest shifted to philosophical and doctrinal texts. Despite that lacuna, seminal scholarship on images by art historians and historians began to appear in the early twentieth century. While scholars of religion were embroiled in debates about the theology of images and the history of iconoclasm, art historians and historians were turning away from a myopic focus on "high art" and aesthetics and toward the history of "holy images" within Christianity and the cult of images prior to the onset of iconoclasm. Edwyn Bevan's *Holy Images* was published in 1940, and it was followed by important works by Ernst Kitzinger (1954), Cyril Mango (1963), André Grabar (1968), Ilene H. Forsyth (1972), and Peter Brown (1973), among others. Scholarship on the images of other traditions, such as that by Foucher ([1917] 2020), Coomaraswamy (1926), and Paul Mus (1935) on Buddhist images; Erkes (1928) and Soper (1959) on Chinese images; and G. S. Hodgson (1964) and Oleg Grabar (1973) on Islamic images, helped to bring the image cultures of those traditions into the wider conversation.

A more profound change in the orientation to religious images came later in the twentieth century with the undeniable impact of art historians like David Freedberg (1989) and Hans Belting (1994, German original 1990). They demonstrated the limitations of depending on elite theories about religious images—aesthetic, doctrinal, or theological—and how those perspectives have caused scholars to miss a rich array of practices that challenge those theories. Freedberg primarily focused on responses to images, and Belting shifted attention to the uses of Christian images, forcefully reminding scholars that holy images were cultic images before they became art and that they "cannot be understood solely in terms of theological content" (1994, 3).

Margret Miles's essay on the term "Image" in the previous edition of *Critical Terms for Religious Studies* (1998) focused on the theology of Christian images from antiquity through the eighth-century Byzantine iconoclastic controversy, along with a brief consideration of images in twentieth-century American media. I have, therefore, felt obliged to be more capacious in my treatment of images, and at the same time compelled to strike a balance between the general and the particular. In an essay this brief I have tried to avoid a tedious cataloguing of phenomena by limiting myself to precisely those issues and themes that force us to challenge some common characterizations of images that by and large remain etched in the minds of some scholars and general readers.

Images are ubiquitous in all major religious traditions, even in those commonly depicted as rejecting them. New scholarly trajectories have challenged some widely accepted views about images in some of those traditions. Restrictive prohibitions on image-making in Judaism, Christianity, and Islam were, for example, not followed to the letter in any of them. It is not accurate to categorize complex religious traditions with overly stark (and static) distinctions between the iconophilic and the iconophobic. Freedberg summed up the ongoing efforts to resituate images within those traditions that had been described as lacking images, arguing that the earlier views were part of a "historiographic myth that certain cultures, usually monotheistic or primitively pure cultures, have no images at all, or no figurative imagery, or no images at all of the deity" (1989, 54).

The story of early Christianity had long been told as one of an absence of images, based on its rejection of pagan practices, the ban on images found in the Decalogue, and Paul's well-known stance that worship should be spiritual not material. Debates continue, but that story has been revised (supported by new archaeological evidence) to show that pre-Constantinian Christians produced images prior to the acknowledged increase in image production in the fourth century (Grabar 1968; Murray 1977; Finney 1994). Indeed, the rapid increase in image production, coupled with the ways images had come to be venerated, led to fears of idolatry and was one of the catalysts (together with social and political factors) for the onset of the Byzantine iconoclastic crisis during the sixth through the eighth centuries (Cormack 1985; Besançon [1994] 2000; Mondzain 2005; Cutler 2009). The Council of Nicaea's (787 CE) reinstatement of images, following the prohibitions instituted in the Council of Hiereia (754 CE), would itself come to be challenged in later iconoclastic movements, such as the Protestant Reformation (Eire 1986). As devastating as it was, Protestant iconoclasm did not lead to the end of image-making. Protestants surrounded themselves with new images or kept defaced ones in situ to record the destruction they had wrought. Images even circulated of Martin Luther, such as the woodcut by Hans Baldung Grien (1521) (that was defaced not by fellow Protestants, but by Catholics), the miraculous *Incombustible Luther* image, and others that were reported to sweat or bleed (Koerner 2004, 114–15, 194–96). As Joseph Koerner has perceptively observed, "image makers become image breakers, and image breakers become image makers" (2002, 167).

Alongside a long tradition of textual debates about aniconism in Judaism, images are also present—such as those discovered at Dura-Europos—despite the restrictions of the second commandment (Wolfson 1997; Gutmann 1961). Kalman Bland has, for instance, stressed that "medieval Jewish intellectuals did not act as if Judaism was aniconic" (2000, 7), and other scholars have raised the possibility that Yahweh was represented by cultic statues (Karel van der Toorn 1997). Images have also been rewritten back into Islamic history. There is no explicit rejection of image-making in the Qur'an, only warnings against usurping Allāh's role as the sole creator and about images detracting from the proper veneration of Allāh. Images were countenanced in the later Islamic tradition, including depictions of Muhammad himself (Hodgson 1964, 248; Hawting 1999; Flood 2002; Natif 2011; Elias 2012; Gruber 2019). There is also a rich Islamic amuletic tradition of figurative calligraphy that functions like an empowered image (Grabar 1973, 135; Welch 1977). The history of Islamic iconoclasm in South Asia serves as a potent example of how image-breaking led to image-making, since Hindu images, which were seen as ostentatious accumulations of precious metals, were melted down to make coins emblazoned with images that would ensure the circulation of wealth (Flood 2009, 28). While iconoclasm is part of the story, others have argued that medieval Muslims in India "appear to have been largely indifferent to the nature of idol worship . . . [and] did not see statues of Hindu gods as threatening or taboo in ways that always necessitated their destruction" (Elias 2012, 136).

Whereas some traditions were initially depicted as lacking images, the India portrayed in Islamic writing was a polytheistic land of idols and idolaters, as it was also to be described by later Europeans. Images of gods like Śiva, Gaṇeśa, and Viṣṇu are ubiquitous in modern Hinduism, but it all began rather differently. Hinduism began as an aniconic tradition. Vedic deities were initially invisible, the focus being on fire. Hinduism only admitted iconic images later, around the same time Buddhism did (first to third centuries CE, though the dates remain contested), but by the eighth century they were a fundamental part of religious practice alongside aniconic images. The story did not end there. Protracted debates expressed continuing anxiety about images (Davis 2001), underscoring how static models of the nature of images in any religious tradition are problematic.

Buddhism may also have begun as an aniconic tradition that did not produce anthropomorphic images of the Buddha until about the first century CE, even though no attested prohibitions against such images have yet been found in extant textual sources (Huntington 1990; Dehejia 1991). The Buddha was depicted by images of an empty throne, a riderless horse, a tree, a stupa, or footprints. Questions about the earliest Buddhist images remain locked in debates that have raged for over a century. Was Buddhism aniconic? Was there Greco-Roman influence (DeCaroli 2015; Karlsson 2000)? Regardless of how one might answer those questions, it is clear that images of buddhas and bodhisattvas eventually spread throughout Asia, and it was these images that Europeans encountered and classified as the idols of pagan lands—a history that would later be superseded by a textually constructed image of the Buddha that developed in Europe during the nineteenth century as philology reigned supreme (Lopez 2013). It is only recently that the pendulum has swung back in the other direction and taken Buddhist images seriously (Faure 1998; Sharf and Sharf 2001; Swearer 2004).

Chinese Buddhism has long been depicted as a (or the) "religion of images." According to the standard narrative, images were introduced to China with the arrival of Buddhism. Such claims are, however, belied by the fact that Chinese religion during the pre-Buddhist period is already shot through with images (Erkes 1928; Delahaye 1983; Greene 2018). Daoism and Confucianism, in opposition to Buddhism, are generally portrayed as image averse. It may be true that Daoism and Confucianism were initially reluctant to use material images—though mental images were important—but it did not remain that way for either tradition. The use of images was proscribed in early Daoist communities, but by the fifth or sixth century Daoism had a vast pantheon of deities represented by consecrated images (Andersen 2019). During the medieval period sacrifices to Confucius were offered to his presence in a statue or painting. It was only in the fifteenth century that anthropomorphic representations were replaced by aniconic spirit tablets. In 1530, the final blow was struck when clay images were "dissolved in water, and mud that had once given form to the sculpted bodies of Confucius" was used to paint aniconic landscapes that adorned the walls of temples (Sommer 2002).

Modern scholarship on images has been decisively impacted by the material turn in religious studies and has begun to redress Gregory Schopen's pointed remark that "scholars of religion have generally been more comfortable with ideas than with things" (Schopen 1998; cf. Kieschnick 2003;

Bynum 2011; Houtman and Meyer 2012; Morgan 1998, 2018, 2021). That development was provided further impetus by scholars outside religious studies like W. J. T. Mitchell (1986, 2005), Alfred Gell (1998), Bruno Latour (2010), Arjun Appadurai (1986), Igor Kopytoff (1986), and Bill Brown (2001). This productive cross-fertilization shaped new forms of inquiry, resulting in the publication of a prodigious amount of scholarship that has reanimated the study of religious images. Religious studies has witnessed a move away from a primary emphasis on the interiority of belief and the immaterial and toward a focus on matter and materiality. As Webb Keane has described it, "religions may not always demand beliefs, but they will always involve material forms" (Keane 2008, 124). The recent attention to images—along with relics—became an antidote to what had become overly Protestant views of religion.

: : :

Images are generally conceptualized in two ways: immanent or transcendent. This is not a rubric for making distinctions between traditions, but a tension that can run through traditions (one more Catholic and one more Protestant, for example; see Orsi 2016). The former takes images as "presentational" and the latter as "representational" or "referential."

The referential position, like a Peircian index that references something else, has been the dominant one. Referential theories point away from the material image (thereby avoiding charges of animism and idolatry). John of Damascus (ca. 675–749) provided an influential Christological defense of images, but he is clear in pointing out that the image is different in that it only refers (or leads) to the prototype, inspiring devotion. Images could also serve a didactic function, as in Pope Gregory's (ca. 540–604) famous claim that images were a *biblia pauperum* for unlettered believers. Some referential approaches emphasize the significance of "likeness." For John of Damascus, and later the Patriarch Nikephoros/Nicephoros (ca. 758–828), the likeness of an image (based on the incarnate human form of Christ) is important in effectively referring to the prototype. A later text describes in minute detail all the characteristics necessary for a portrait of Christ and cites Pseudo-Dionysios the Areopagite's claim that "the truth is shown in the likeness" (Barber 2002, 108). Yet no matter how perfect the likeness, one should not mistakenly freeze one's gaze on the image, which is the fatal error of idolaters. For others, on the contrary, referentiality did not depend on likeness. Indeed, it is precisely their non-figural form that best respects "divine invisibility by renouncing resemblance" (Mondzain 2005, 72).

Presentational theories emphasize the immanent nature of the image. The image of a deity presences the deity. This understanding of images was critiqued for smacking of animism and idolatry. One of the most significant recent shifts in scholarly orientations to images has been to take presentational views seriously and document how widespread they are.

By the mid-twentieth century, for example, the religious images of Mesopotamia, Egypt, Asia, and Africa, among other places, came back to life in scholarship, challenging entrenched Judeo-Christian theological treatments of images and the erasures they had enacted. Egyptian images were no longer dismissed as pagan idols, but viewed as more like those described in *Asclepius*: "ensouled and conscious, filled with spirit and doing great deeds, statues that foreknow the future and predict it by lots, by prophecy, by dreams and by many other means; statues, that make people ill and cure them, bringing them pain and pleasure as each deserves" (Assmann and Baumgarten 2001, xv). The living presence of Hindu and Buddhist images is now well known (Davis 1997; Sharf and Sharf 2001; Lopez 2013, 51). No longer merely critiqued as evidence of pagan idolatry or subsumed into theories of referentiality, these types of images are depicted as presentational; they are animate images that are believed to presence the deity rather than the inert stopping point or barrier that impedes passage to the referenced divine.

The presentational mode is like Hans-Georg Gadamer's description of the phenomenological immediacy of religious images. Gadamer emphasized that images are "not mere imitative illustrations, but allow what they present to be for the first time fully what it is" ([1960] 1995, 143). Images, in this view, bring something into being, they *produce* it (the word "produce" is based on the Latin verb *producere* "to bring forth"). Similarly, Bill Brown notes that an image, like a "thing," is "what is excessive in objects, as what exceeds their mere materialization as objects or their mere utilization as objects—their force as a sensuous presence or as a metaphysical presence, the magic by which objects become values, fetishes, idols, and totems" (2001, 5). When discussion is drawn in this direction, the alternative views of images that are found in the ancient Near East, Africa, Buddhism, Hinduism, and Catholicism can be better appreciated for how they foreground the immanent, what is *presenced* in matter.

Religious traditions that prioritize immanence have had to grapple with fundamental questions about how an image manufactured out of base materials by profane human hands could be a deity without diminishing or limiting it. Some traditions emphasized that the base materials were already sanctified and merely transformed, or "transubstantiated" (Gell 1992, 52). The critique that images are manufactured is also circumvented by claims that images were miraculously found—the so-called *acheiropoietic* "not made by hand" images (Belting 1994, 49–57, 208–9)—like the imprint of Christ's face on the veil of Veronica (according to folk etymologies derived from *verum icon* or "true image") that functions like a relic, or images that have fallen from the heavens or floated to shore.

Manufactured sacred images have also been described as the product of divine agency, thereby removing the artifice of the artisan. The deity, in essence, creates an image of itself. In the well-known Mesopotamian *mīs pî* "mouth-washing" ritual, for example, "the artisans held out their hands so that a priest could symbolically chop them off with a wooden sword . . . [and] chant: 'I did not make it; I swear I did not make it; I did not make it; I swear I did not make it'" (Ellenbogen and Tugendhaft 2011, 1; Dick 1999). Another approach was to claim that the carving tools acted on their own in fashioning an image (Hurowitz 2006). In texts describing the first buddha images—one a painting and the other a statue—artists are unable to capture his likeness until the Buddha projects his image onto a canvas or his shadow onto the wall of a cave for the artisan to trace.

One of the primary ways to confer, confirm, or authorize the sacrality of a manufactured image as being enlivened is through an intricate consecration ritual. The consecration process generally involves several steps that include the anointing of the image and the insertion of relics or other things, including live animals, symbolic viscera, and *materia medica*, into a cavity in the body of the image (Mango 1963, 61; MacGaffey 1988; Strickmann 1996; Gell 1998; Steiner 2001, 79–134; Swearer 2004; Brinker 2011; Robson, Lee, and Kim 2019; Arrault 2020). Tenth-century Christian images, such as the famous Saint Foy image and the so-called "Throne of Wisdom" statues (Forsyth 1972), contain relics inside them. A vast number of images found across Asia, Africa, and Polynesia also had things inserted into them. Putting things inside images created what Gell called a homunculus-effect, endowing the image with a sense of being a living being (1998, 132–33). No wonder that when missionaries encountered such images in different parts of the world, they referred to the contents as the "souls of idols."

Consecration rituals usually end by returning to the exterior of the image to ritually open the eyes or mouth, such as in the Mesopotamian *mīs pî* (mouth-washing) or *pit pî* (mouth-opening), Egyptian mouth-opening rituals (Ellenbogen and Tugendhaft 2011), and Hindu, Buddhist, and Daoist rites of dotting the eyes. These rites, focused as they are on the apertures of the body, lend a sense of interiority, and once the eyes or mouth are opened the deity is considered to be present in the image (Davis 1997; Tambiah 1984, 250, 255–57; Gombrich 1966; Swearer 2004; Lin 2015).

As important as consecration rites are, they are not always considered necessary. Inscriptions on Chinese images, for instance, do not always mention a consecration rite, and images that had not undergone a consecration were still thought to be enlivened. In one story, a woman who became sick before completing two images is nonetheless saved by their miraculous intervention (Kieschnick 2003, 63; Dudbridge 1998, 385–87).

Consecrated or not, the important point is that in the annals of religious history stories abound of images, like relics, that were enlivened and animated deities that performed miracles. Scholarly neglect of miraculous images by our predecessors was not due to a lack of evidence, which was plentiful and well documented. Such accounts are even found today, as in the case of the moving Mary image in Ballinspittle or Ganeśa images that drink milk (Davis 1998, 1). Enlivened images are widely depicted as bleeding, sweating, secreting breast milk, talking, walking around, turning their eyes and heads, and being vested with miraculous power and presence. Images are enmeshed in a network of social exchanges by being fed, dressed, and bathed. Devotees were drawn to touch, embrace, and kiss such images (Suckale 2008; Jung 2010; Bynum 2011). Some accounts suggest that some had amorous interactions with images (*agalmatophilia*) (Faure 1998, 781–82; Mylonopoulos 2010, 1), and some images were married to humans, as described for instance in numerous "Marriage to Mary" stories (Forsyth 1972, 46–47; Camille 1989, 237–41). That images were considered animate is further attested by stories about images that had to be chained down to inhibit their movement (Barasch 1992, 38–39).

Scholars have generally been reluctant to countenance images that were the locus of the divine, and serious consideration has only come lately (Freedberg 1989; Gell 1998; Morgan 2018). The reasons for the earlier silence are many and vary across traditions but were due in part to an overemphasis on theological interpretations, a Protestantism-inflected lack of interest in what people *did* with images and what sacred images *did*, and perhaps something more fundamental about the problem of imputing agency to inanimate objects. Caroline Bynum has pointed out how theological accounts of images have been misleading, "not least because it takes the words of a few theorists to describe the practice of a wide range of European Christians, who often behaved as if statues, mosaics, and wall paintings were in fact divine. . . . Nor does the traditional account adequately describe the intense presence—the 'is'-ness—of the images" (2020, 131). Animate images provoked the most criticism, inspired iconoclastic destruction, and were long dismissed as objects of scholarly inquiry since surely nobody could have ever believed such things. Yet the iconoclast's negation of images also invests them with precisely the powers they sought to deny. How we understand *why* people behave this way toward images—in the past and the present—remains an enigma; it cannot easily be dismissed as a form of irrational or pre-rational thinking (Sperber 1985; Gell 1998; Sharf 1999; Tamen 2001). Yes, the Greeks believed in their myths; yes, people believed in animated images (Veyne 1988). If Platonic conceptions of images were really so well accepted, then we would have a difficult time explaining why anyone would want to destroy icons. How would it be possible for something that is not real, and therefore has no power or agency, to be a threat? Perhaps the problem lies with the negatively charged terminology we have inherited. Could highly charged terms like animism and idolatry ever be "abstracted from the essentially pejorative context of Victorian positivistic thought" (Gell 1998, 121)?

The tension between the "presentational" and the "representational" is expressed well in Peter Galison's provocative claim about images in science: "We must have images; we cannot have images." He explains that "we *must* have scientific images because only images can teach us . . . by mimicking nature, an image, even if not in *every* respect, captures a richness of relations in a way that a logical train of propositions never can . . . and yet, we *cannot* have images because images deceive . . . truth is something wider and deeper than the pictorial imagination can ever hope to capture" (Galison 2002). This oscillation between iconoclasm and iconophilia, an iconoclash (Latour and Weibel 2002), is a tension that runs through considerations of religious images and the need to have images as the material presence of immaterial referents in order to access them and at the same time a rejection of images as unable to capture the divine or transcendent.

: : :

As important as the material turn has been to recent scholarship on images, we should not reduce everything to materiality at the expense of mental images, memory, and the imagination. Images are notoriously difficult to destroy, especially when held in someone's mind and memory. After the Chinese Cultural Revolution (1966–1976), a Western scholar visited a destroyed Buddhist temple and observed women leading children around and burning incense in front of a blank wall where "an image of the central figure had been outlined in charcoal . . . [they] were showing the young girls what to do and indicating where the images along the side walls had once been. They were also bowing to these remembered images, long since taken away" (Powell 1984, 86). In his compelling analysis of Caspar David Friedrich's *The Choir of the Ruined Cloister at Oybin* (1810), Joseph Leo Koerner too reflected on how in that painting of a ruined monastery the "trefoil lancet windows, in their elongated, anthropomorphic shapes, look like saint's effigies . . . negatively constituted, both as the shape of the openings and as the empty views through them" (2004, 443). Iconoclastic destruction leads to new forms of image production, even if the absent image is only retained in the mind or captured in another image that preserves its presence in its absence.

Debates about the use of figurative images in meditation and visualization practices reveal a discernible tension concerning the nature of images that lies at the heart of meditation and visualization practices across different religious traditions. Image-assisted meditation was integral to Western religious practices (Freedberg 1989, 161–91; Miller 2009, 82–101; Hamburger 1998). Rigorously attentive meditation on mental images in Christianity—described as painting God's image with a "spiritual imagination"—could inculcate virtues and emotions (Freedberg 1989, 167), and within Judaism "the problem of figuration or representation of God in mental images was discussed in philosophical and theological literature" (Wolfson 1994). The prioritizing of mental images is proclaimed in an inscription at the Maiestas Domini in Venice (c. 1100): "The image teaches God, but it is not itself God. You should revere this [image], but worship with your mind that which you recognize in it" (Lipton 2009, 258–59).

In some forms of Buddhist meditation and visualization practices, images are merely the starting point for a practice that culminates in formlessness (Sharf 2001b; Shinohara 2014). The practitioner begins concentrating on an image in front of them, impressing the figurative image on the mind. When they move to a different location, they should be able visualize the image clearly in their mind. Eventually the practitioner dispenses with images (both real and visualized), attains absorption, and is then in the presence of the formless Buddha.

There is, however, at least one potential danger involved with bringing a discussion of images in meditation and visualization practices back into scholarship on religion. In the wrong hands such a discourse might further serve the agenda of those who want to read into the history of images a narrow—and to them superior—teleological narrative that leads from figurative images to imageless devotion. That trajectory aims to map a misleading distinction between elite theorists and the simpleminded piety of the masses, when in fact the mental and the material usually went hand in hand (Hamburger 1998, 113–14).

Images are indispensable in making religion tangible and present in the world. We live in an image-saturated world with millions of images rebounding through the digital domain each moment (now including NFTs—Non-fungible Tokens—and AI-generated images of the Buddha, Jesus, and Saint Francis Xavier). Hume's vision of an image-free modern religion has not come to pass. Some have even called this the new age of the image, but iconoclasm also still runs rampant. The term "image" remains deeply ambivalent. Iconodules refuse to put down the hammers they use to carve images. Iconoclasts refuse to lay down the hammers they use to smash idols. Philosophers and scholars of religion may not themselves be able to forgo the hammer as they continue to interrogate the full complexity of images, but ideally, as W. J. T. Mitchell has proposed, these hammers will function rather more like Friedrich Nietzsche's (1844–1900) tuning fork used to tap an image to sound it out (Nietzsche [1889] 1990), "breaking its silence, making it speak and resonate, and transforming its hollowness into an echo chamber for human thought" (Mitchell 2005, 27).

Suggested Readings

Belting, Hans. 1994. *Likeness and Presence: A History of the Image Before the Era of Art*. Chicago: University of Chicago Press.

Camille, Michael. 1989. *The Gothic Idol: Ideology and Image-Making in Medieval Art*. Cambridge: Cambridge University Press.

DeCaroli, Robert. 2015. *Image Problems: The Origin and Development of the Buddha's Image in Early South Asia*. Seattle: University of Washington Press.

Ellenbogen, Josh, and Aaron Tugendhaft, eds. 2011. *Idol Anxiety*. Stanford, CA: Stanford University Press.

Freedberg, David. 1989. *The Power of Images: Studies in the History and Theory of Response*. Chicago: University of Chicago Press.

Gell, Alfred. 1998. *Art and Agency: An Anthropological Theory*. Oxford: Clarendon Press.

Halbertal, Moshe, and Avishai Margalit. 1992. *Idolatry*. Cambridge, MA: Harvard University Press.

Latour, Bruno, and Peter Weibel, eds. 2002. *Iconoclash: Beyond the Image Wars in Science, Religion, and Art*. Karlsruhe: Center for Art and Media.

Mitchell, W. J. T. 2005. *What Do Pictures Want? The Lives and Loves of Images*. Chicago: University of Chicago Press.

Mondzain, Marie-José. 2005. *Image, Icon, Economy: The Byzantine Origins of the Contemporary Imaginary*. Stanford, CA: Stanford University Press.

Sharf, Robert H., and Elizabeth Horton Sharf, eds. 2001. *Living Images: Japanese Buddhist Icons in Context*. Stanford, CA: Stanford University Press.

References

Andersen, Poul. 2019. *The Paradox of Being: Truth, Identity, and Images in Daoism*. Cambridge, MA: Harvard Asia Center.

Appadurai, Arjun, ed. 1986. *The Social Life of Things: Commodities in Cultural Perspective*. Cambridge: Cambridge University Press.

Arrault, Alain. 2020. *The History of Cultic Images in China: The Domestic Statuary of Hunan*. Hong Kong: The Chinese University of Hong Kong Press.

Assmann, Jan, and Albert I. Baumgarten, eds. 2001. *Representation in Religion: Studies in Honor of Moshe Barasch*. Leiden, Netherlands: Brill.

Barasch, Moshe. 1992. *Icon: Studies in the History of an Idea*. New York: New York University Press.

Barber, Charles. 2002. *Figure and Likeness: On the Limits of Representation in Byzantine Iconoclasm*. Princeton, NJ: Princeton University Press.

Belting, Hans. 1994. *Likeness and Presence: A History of the Image Before the Era of Art*. Chicago: University of Chicago Press.

Bernard, Jean Frederic, and Bernard Picart. 1723–43. *Cérémonies et coutumes religieuses de tous les peoples du monde*. Amsterdam: J. F. Bernard.

Besançon, Alain. 2000. *The Forbidden Image: An Intellectual History of Iconoclasm*. Chicago: University of Chicago Press. First French edition 1994.

Bevan, Edwyn. 1940. *Holy Images*. London: George Allen and Unwin.

Bland, Kalman P. 2000. *The Artless Jew: Medieval and Modern Affirmations and Denials of the Visual*. Princeton, NJ: Princeton University Press.

Brinker, Helmut. 2011. *Secrets of the Sacred: Empowering Buddhist Images in Clear, in Code, and Cache*. Seattle: University of Washington Press.

Brown, Bill. 2001. "Thing Theory." *Critical Inquiry* 28: 1–21.

Brown, Peter. 1973. "A Dark Age Crisis: Aspect of the Iconoclastic Controversy." *English Historical Review* 88 (346): 1–34.

Bynum, Caroline Walker. 2011. *Christian Materiality: An Essay on Religion in Late Medieval Europe*. New York: Zone Books.

Bynum, Caroline Walker. 2020. *Dissimilar Similitudes: Devotional Objects in Late Medieval Europe*. New York: Zone Books.

Camille, Michael. 1989. *The Gothic Idol: Ideology and Image-Making in Medieval Art*. Cambridge: Cambridge University Press.

Coomaraswamy, Ananda Kentish. 1926. "The Indian Origin of the Buddha Image." *Journal of the American Oriental Society* 46: 165–70.

Cormack, Robin. 1985. *Writing in Gold: Byzantine Society and Its Icons*. London: George Phillip.

Cutler, Anthony. 2009. *Image Making in Byzantium, Sasanian Persia and the Early Muslim World: Images and Culture*. Abingdon: Ashgate Publishing.

Davis, Richard H. 1997. *Lives of Indian Images*. Princeton, NJ: Princeton University Press.

Davis, Richard H., ed. 1998. *Images, Miracles, and Authority in Asian Religious Traditions*. Boulder, CO: Westview Press.

Davis, Richard H. 2001. "Indian Image-Worship and Its Discontents." In *Representation in Religion: Studies in Honor of Moshe Barasch*, edited by Jan Assmann and Albert I. Baumgarten. Leiden, Netherlands: Brill.

DeCaroli, Robert. 2015. *Image Problems: The Origin and Development of the Buddha's Image in Early South Asia*. Seattle: University of Washington Press.

Dehejia, Vidya. 1991. "Aniconism and the Multivalence of Emblems." *Ars Orientalis* 21: 45–66.

Delahaye, Hubert. 1983. "Les Antecedents magiques des statues chinoises." *Revue d'esthetique*, n.s., 5: 45–54.

Dick, Michael B., ed. 1999. *Born in Heaven, Made on Earth: The Making of the Cult Image in the Ancient Near East*. University Park, PA: Eisenbrauns.

Dudbridge, Glen. 1998. "Buddhist Images in Action: Five Stories from the Tang." *Cahiers d'Extrême-Asie* 10: 377–91.

Elias, Jamal J. 2012. *Aisha's Cushion: Religious Art, Perception, and Practice in Islam*. Cambridge, MA: Harvard University Press.

Ellenbogen, Josh, and Aaron Tugendhaft, eds. 2011. *Idol Anxiety*. Stanford, CA: Stanford University Press.

Eire, Carlos M. N. 1986. *War Against the Idols: The Reformation of Worship from Erasmus to Calvin*. Cambridge: Cambridge University Press.

Erkes, Eduard. 1928. "Idols in Pre-Buddhist China." *Artibus Asiae* 3 (1): 4–12.

Faure, Bernard. 1998. "The Buddhist Icon and the Modern Gaze." *Critical Inquiry* 24 (3): 768–813.

Finney, Paul Corby. 1994. *The Invisible God: The Earliest Christians on Art*. Oxford: Oxford University Press.

Flood, Finbarr Barry. 2002. "Between Cult and Culture: Bamiyan, Islamic Iconoclasm, and the Museum." *The Art Bulletin* 84 (4): 641–59.

Flood, Finbarr Barry. 2009. *Objects of Translation: Material Culture and Medieval "Hindu-Muslim" Encounter*. Princeton, NJ: Princeton University Press.

Forsyth, Ilene H. 1972. *Throne of Wisdom: Wood Sculptures of the Madonna in Romanesque France*. Princeton, NJ: Princeton University Press.

Foucher, Alfred Charles Auguste. 2020. *The Beginnings of Buddhist Art*. Revised and translated by Frederick William Thomas. New Delhi: Gyan Publishing House; originally published in 1917.

Freedberg, David. 1989. *The Power of Images: Studies in the History and Theory of Response*. Chicago: University of Chicago Press.

Gadamer, Hans-Georg. 1995. *Truth and Method*. New York: Continuum; original German publication 1960.

Galison, Peter. 2002. "Images Scatter into Data, Data Gathers into Images." In *Iconoclash*, edited by Bruno Latour and Peter Weibel, 300–323. Karlsruhe: ZKM Center for Art and Media.

Gell, Alfred. 1992. "The Technology of Enchantment and the Enchantment of Technology." In *Anthropology Art and Aesthetics*, edited by Jeremy Coote and Anthony Shelton. Oxford: Clarendon Press.

Gell, Alfred. 1998. *Art and Agency: An Anthropological Theory*. Oxford: Clarendon Press.

Gombrich, Richard. 1966. "The Consecration of a Buddhist Image." *Journal of Asian Studies* 26 (1): 23–26.

Grabar, André. 1968. *Christian Iconography: A Study of Its Origins*. Princeton, NJ: Princeton University Press.

Grabar, Oleg. 1973. *The Formation of Islamic Art*. New Haven, CT: Yale University Press.

Greene, Eric M. 2018. "The 'Religion of Images'? Buddhist Image Worship in the Early Medieval Chinese Imagination." *Journal of the American Oriental Society* 138 (3): 455–84.

Gruber, Christiane. 2019. *The Image Debate: Figural Representation in Islam and Across the World*. London: Ginkgo.

Gutmann, Joseph. 1961. "The Second Commandment and the Image in Judaism." *Hebrew Union College Annual* 32: 161–74.

Halbertal, Moshe, and Avishai Margalit. 1992. *Idolatry*. Cambridge, MA: Harvard University Press.

Hamburger, Jeffrey F. 1998. *The Visual and the Visionary: Art and Female Spirituality in Late Medieval Germany*. New York: Zone Books.

Hastings, James, ed. 1908–21. *Encyclopedia of Religion and Ethics*. Edinburgh: Clark.

Hawting, G. R. 1999. *The Idea of Idolatry and the Emergence of Islam from Polemic to History*. Cambridge: Cambridge University Press.

Hocart, A. M. [1936] 1970. *Kings and Councillors: An Essay in the Comparative Anatomy of Human Society*. Chicago: University of Chicago Press; originally published in 1936.

Hodgson, G. S. 1964. "Islâm and Image." *History of Religions* 3 (2): 220–60.

Houtman, Dick, and Birgit Meyer, eds. 2012. *Things: Religion and the Question of Materiality*. New York: Fordham University Press.

Hume, David. 1993. *Principal Writings on Religion: Including Dialogues Concerning*

Natural Religion and the Natural History of Religion. Edited by J. C. A. Gaskin. Oxford: Oxford University Press.

Hunt, Lynn, Margaret C. Jacob, and Wijnand Mijnhardt, eds. 2010. *Bernard Picart and the First Global Vision of Religion*. Los Angeles, CA: Getty Research Institute.

Huntington, Susan. 1990. "Early Buddhist Art and the Theory of Aniconism." *Art Journal* 49: 401–8.

Hurowitz, Victor Avigdor. 2006. "What Goes In Is What Comes Out: Materials for Creating Cult Statues." In *Text, Artifact, and Image: Revealing Ancient Israelite Religion*, edited by Gary M. Beckman and Theodore J. Lewis, 3–23. Providence, RI: Brown Judaic Studies.

Jung, Jacqueline E. 2010. "The Tactile and the Visionary: Notes on the Place of Sculpture in the Medieval Religious Imagination." In *Looking Beyond: Visions, Dreams, and Insights in Medieval Art*, edited by Colum Hourihane, 203–40. University Park: Pennsylvania State University Press.

Karlsson, Klemens. 2000. *Face to Face with the Absent Buddha: The Formation of Buddhist Aniconic Art*. Uppsala: Uppsala University.

Keane, Webb. 2008. "The Evidence of the Senses and the Materiality of Religion." *Journal of the Royal Anthropological Institute* 14 (s1): 110–27.

Kieschnick, John. 2003. *The Impact of Buddhism on Material Culture*. Princeton, NJ: Princeton University Press.

Kitzinger, Ernst. 1954. "The Cult of Images in the Age Before Iconoclasm." *Dumbarton Oaks Papers* 8: 83–150.

Koerner, Joseph Leo. 2002. "The Icon as Iconoclash." In *Iconoclash*, edited by Bruno Latour and Peter Weibel, 164–213. Karlsruhe: ZKM Center for Art and Media.

Koerner, Joseph Leo. 2004. *The Reformation of the Image*. Chicago: University of Chicago Press.

Kopytoff, Igor. 1986. "The Cultural Biography of Things: Commoditization as Process." In *The Social Life of Things: Commodities in Cultural Perspective*, edited by Arjun Appadurai, 64–94. Cambridge: Cambridge University Press.

Latour, Bruno. 1997. "A Few Steps Toward an Anthropology of the Iconoclastic Gesture." *Science in Context* 10: 63–83.

Latour, Bruno. 2010. *On the Modern Cult of the Factish Gods*. Durham, NC: Duke University Press.

Latour, Bruno, and Peter Weibel, eds. 2002. *Iconoclash: Beyond the Image Wars in Science, Religion, and Art*. Karlsruhe: ZKM Center for Art and Media.

Lévy-Bruhl, Lucien. 1985. *How Natives Think*. Princeton, NJ: Princeton University Press.

Lin, Wei-Ping. 2015. *Materializing Magic Power: Chinese Popular Religion in Villages and Cities*. Cambridge, MA: Harvard Asia Center.

Lipton, Sara. 2009. "Images and Their Uses." In *The Cambridge History of Christianity: Christianity in Western Europe c. 1100–c. 1500*, edited by Miri Rubin and Walter Simons, 254–82. Cambridge: Cambridge University Press.

Lopez, Donald S., Jr. 2013. *From Stone to Flesh: A Short History of the Buddha*. Chicago: University of Chicago Press.

MacGaffey, Wyatt. 1988. "Complexity, Astonishment and Power: The Visual Vocabulary of Kongo Minkisi." *Journal of Southern African Studies* 14 (2): 188–203.

Mango, Cyril. 1963. "Antique Statuary and the Byzantine Beholder." *Dumbarton Oaks Papers* 17: 55–75.

Marion, Jean-Luc. 1991. *God without Being*. Chicago: University of Chicago Press.

Miles, Margret R. 1998. "Image." In *Critical Terms for Religious Studies*, edited by Mark C. Taylor, 160–72. Chicago: University of Chicago Press.

Miller, Patricia Cox. 2009. *The Corporeal Imagination: Signifying the Holy in Late Ancient Christianity*. Philadelphia: University of Pennsylvania Press.

Mitchell, W. J. T. 1986. *Iconology: Image, Text, Ideology*. Chicago: University of Chicago Press.

Mitchell, W. J. T. 2005. *What Do Pictures Want? The Lives and Loves of Images*. Chicago: University of Chicago Press.

Mondzain, Marie-José. 2005. *Image, Icon, Economy: The Byzantine Origins of the Contemporary Imaginary*. Stanford, CA: Stanford University Press.

Morgan, David. 1998. *Visual Piety: A History and Theory of Popular Religious Images*. Berkeley: University of California Press.

Morgan, David. 2018. *Images at Work: The Material Culture of Enchantment*. Oxford: Oxford University Press.

Morgan, David. 2021. *The Thing about Religion: An Introduction to the Material Study of Religions*. Chapel Hill: University of North Carolina Press.

Murray, Sister Charles. 1977. "Art and the Early Church." *The Journal of Theological Studies* 28 (2): 303–45.

Mus, Paul. 1935. *Barabuḍur: Esquisse d'une histoire du bouddhisme fondée sur la critique archéologique des textes*. 2 vols. Hanoi: Imprimerie d'extrême-orient.

Mylonopoulos, Joannis, ed. 2010. *Divine Images and Human Imaginations in Ancient Greece and Rome*. Leiden: Brill.

Natif, Mika. 2011. "The Painter's Breath and Concepts of Idol Anxiety in Islamic Art." In *Idol Anxiety*, edited by Josh Ellenbogen and Aaron Tugendhaft, 41–55. Stanford, CA: Stanford University Press.

Nietzsche, Friedrich. 1990. *Twilight of the Idols*. London: Penguin Books; originally published 1889.

Orsi, Robert A. 2016. *History and Presence*. Cambridge, MA: Harvard University Press.

Peirce, C. S., and Justus Buchler, eds. 1955. *Philosophical Writings of Peirce*. New York: Dover.

Pietz, William. 1985. "The Problem of the Fetish, I." *RES: Anthropology and Aesthetics* 9: 5–17.

Pietz, William. 1987. "The Problem of the Fetish, II: The Origin of the Fetish." *RES: Anthropology and Aesthetics* 13: 23–45.

Pietz, William. 1988. "The Problem of the Fetish, IIIa: Bosman's Guinea and the Enlightenment Theory of Fetishism." *RES: Anthropology and Aesthetics* 16: 105–24.

Powell, William. 1984. "More Laughter at Tiger Creek—Impressions of Buddhism in Modern China." *Journal of Chinese Religions* 12 (1): 77–87.

Robson, James, Seunghye Lee, and Youn-mi Kim. 2019. "Introduction: The Korean Pokchang Tradition and the Placing of Objects in Buddhist Statues." *Cahiers d'Extrême-Asie* 28: 1–21.

Schopen, Gregory. 1998. "Relic." In *Critical Terms for Religious Studies*, edited by Mark C. Taylor, 256–68. Chicago: University of Chicago Press.

Sharf, Robert H. 1999. "On the Allure of Buddhist Relics." *Representations* 66: 75–99.

Sharf, Robert H. 2001a. "Introduction: Prolegomenon to the Study of Japanese Buddhist Icons." In *Living Images: Japanese Buddhist Icons in Context*, edited by Robert H. Sharf and Elizabeth Horton Sharf, 1–18. Stanford, CA: Stanford University Press.

Sharf, Robert H. 2001b. "Visualization and Mandala in Shingon Buddhism." In *Living Images: Japanese Buddhist Icons in Context*, edited by Robert H. Sharf and Elizabeth Horton Sharf, 151–97. Stanford, CA: Stanford University Press.

Sharf, Robert H., and Elizabeth Horton Sharf, eds. 2001. *Living Images: Japanese Buddhist Icons in Context*. Stanford, CA: Stanford University Press.

Shinohara, Koichi. 2014. *Spells, Images, and Maṇḍalas: Tracing the Evolution of Esoteric Buddhist Rituals*. New York: Columbia University Press.

Smith, Jonathan Z. 2004. "What a Difference a Difference Makes." In *Relating Religion: Essays in the Study of Religion*, 251–302. Chicago: University of Chicago Press.

Sommer, Deborah. 2002. "Destroying Confucius: Iconoclasm in the Confucian Temple." In *On Sacred Grounds: Culture, Society, Politics, and the Formation of the Cult of Confucius*, edited by Thomas A. Wilson, 95–133. Cambridge, MA: Harvard Asia Center.

Soper, Alexander Coburn. 1959. *Literary Evidence for Early Buddhist Art in China*. Ascona: Artibus Asiae Publishers.

Sperber, Dan. 1985. *On Anthropological Knowledge*. Cambridge: Cambridge University Press.

Steiner, Deborah Tarn. 2001. *Images in Mind: Statues in Archaic and Classical Greek Literature and Thought*. Princeton, NJ: Princeton University Press.

Strickmann, Michel. 1996. *Mantras et Mandarins: Le bouddhisme tantrique en Chine*. Paris: Gallimard.

Suckale, Robert. 2008. "An Unrecognized Statuette of the Virgin Mary by a Vienna Court Artist, ca. 1350." *RES: Anthropology and Aesthetics* 53–54: 104–20.

Swearer, Donald K. 2004. *Becoming the Buddha: The Ritual of Image Consecration in Thailand*. Princeton, NJ: Princeton University Press.

Tambiah, Stanley Jeyaraja. 1984. *The Buddhist Saints of the Forest and the Cult of Amulets: A Study in Charism, Hagiography, Sectarianism, and Millennial Buddhism*. Cambridge: Cambridge University Press.

Tamen, Miguel. 2001. *Friends of Interpretable Objects*. Cambridge, MA: Harvard University Press.

Toorn, Karel van der, ed. 1997. *The Image and the Book: Iconic Cults, Aniconism, and the Rise of Book Religion in Israel and the Ancient Near East*. Leuven: Peeters Publishers.

Tylor, Edward B. 1920. *Primitive Culture: Researches into the Development of Mythology, Philosophy, Religion, Language, Art, and Custom*. London: John Murray.

Veyne, Paul. 1988. *Did the Greeks Believe in their Myths? An Essay in Constitutive Imagination*. Chicago: University of Chicago Press.

Welch, Anthony. 1977. "Epigraphs as Icons: The Role of the Written Word in Islamic Art." In *The Image and the Word: Confrontations in Judaism, Christianity and Islam*, edited by Joseph Gutmann, 63–74. Missoula, MT: Scholars Press, 1977.

Wolfson, Elliot R. 1994. *Through a Speculum That Shines: Vision and Imagination in Medieval Jewish Mysticism*. Princeton, NJ: Princeton University Press.

8 LAW

Noah Salomon

The pictures that appeared in the press and on social media were crushing: tons and tons of expired powdered infant formula strewn across the floor of an anonymous warehouse in Karantina, on the outskirts of Beirut's recently destroyed port. While any sort of waste of this magnitude would have been distressing, this came at a time when some 55 percent of Lebanese citizens were living under the poverty line, in desperate need of products such as these.[1] The headline in the daily *an-Nahar* expressed the sentiments of many across the country: "Tons of Warehoused Children's Milk Expired . . . The Anger Is Overwhelming!"[2] And yet, it appeared to be only the tip of the iceberg: a rapid decline in the value of the Lebanese currency meant that the government had begun to subsidize basic goods (fuel, some medicines, essential food items), so as to guard against starvation and chaos. With the national financial reserve running dry, however, rumors circulated that such subsidies would soon be lifted, leading some merchants to hoard products they had bought at subsidized costs, waiting for when they could sell them at higher, non-subsidized prices or spiriting them over the border into Syria to sell at inflated rates.

The case of the expired infant formula emerged in mid-June 2021, in the midst of unprecedented financial crisis in Lebanon, described by the World Bank as one of the three worst economic collapses the world has seen since the mid-nineteenth century.[3] Limited electricity and gasoline were prob-

1. https://www.aljadeed.tv/arabic/news/local/2506202173.
2. https://www.annahar.com/arabic/section/111-15062021065256077/أحدث-الأخبار.
3. https://www.worldbank.org/en/country/lebanon/publication/lebanon-economic-monitor-spring-2021-lebanon-sinking-to-the-top-3.

lems shared across the class spectrum, while severe food shortage became a challenge even for the middle class, resulting in sporadic fights in supermarkets over basic goods.[4] "The pictures speak for themselves," exclaimed one journalist. "There is children's milk that has gone bad after its expiration in a time of scarcity and collapse. It would have been better, and preferable, had it reached those who deserve it! Who is accountable?"[5] While the reason for the milk's expiry may have been somewhat more complex than it first appeared, it sparked a major debate across Lebanon on the topic of monopolization (*al-ihtikar*): what constitutes it, how it might be combatted, what its punishment should be, as well as from what religious, moral, legal, and national standpoints it might be confronted. Living as they were, since the August 2020 port explosion, between a resigned caretaker government (*hukumat tasrif al-aʿmal*) and a *chargé* president (*ra'is mukallaf*), average citizens no longer had much confidence in law enforcement or the judiciary to handle cases like these, and social media, under the hashtag "children's milk" (*#halib al-atfal*), buzzed with creative solutions from a variety of perspectives. It is often argued that the development of modern rule of law requires the constraining of competing moral and regulatory systems to the private sphere, and yet the present inability of the state to implement an effective judicial system to guard against abuses like this began to make alternatives seem again more viable.

Thus, it did not come as a great surprise when, following the case of the expired baby formula, "monopoly" (*al-ihtikar*) was chosen as the title topic for two episodes of a popular Islamic jurisprudence call-in show, "The Lamp of *Shariʿa*," which took place in late June 2021 on the television station al-Manar.[6] "The Lamp of *Shariʿa*" aims to bring the complex *shiʿi* jurisprudential tradition to the people by applying its lessons to everyday problems. Each episode discusses one topic and, after about twenty minutes of general discussion between host and guest, delves into a series of viewer-presented call-in questions about the implications for daily life of the principles discussed therein. Al-Manar is run by the Lebanese religious militant movement Hizbullah, which in certain regions of the country, and even in neighborhoods of the capital, plays a proto-state role itself, offer-

4. https://www.lebanon24.com/news/lebanon/803275/اشكال-في-سوبرماركت-رمّالاليكم-التفاصيل-فيديو.

5. https://www.annahar.com/arabic/section/111-15062021065256077/أحدث-الأخبار.

6. https://program.almanar.com.lb/episode/173043; https://program.almanar.com.lb/episode/174000.

ing education, health care, and other social services while also providing a robust security apparatus (Deeb 2006; Marusek 2018). It is a major actor within the state and simultaneously positions itself as an outsider to it, weaving in and out of its apparati as political party, religious organization, and leader of the international resistance against US and Israeli policy in the region, inter alia (see Bou Akar 2018, 101–3). While there is much that is remarkable about this particular television station, al-Manar is not an outlier in the Lebanese media landscape, which is dominated by channels controlled by party and sectarian interests, each playing roles at the intersection of religion, law, and politics. This essay will offer a reading of the interface of law and religion through an analysis of these two episodes of "The Lamp of *Shari'a*" that took on the case of the expired powdered infant formula.

Discussions of the intersections and intertwining of law and religion in academic literature in religious studies has often focused on the blurry lines that attempt to distinguish these domains, how each has a history that is imbricated in the other, and how each comes to shape the other. Much work in the field of religious studies on "religion and law" has been preoccupied with the numerous political and religious projects that have sought (unsuccessfully) either to set up a firewall between religion and law as part of an effort at secularization (US First Amendment jurisprudence, European disestablishment), or to bring them together after episodes of forced estrangement (Islamization of the law projects of the late twentieth century, indigenous courts in the twenty-first). Yet, "The Lamp of *Shari'a*," perhaps in its ordinariness, offers something rather different upon which it seems worthwhile to focus in a chapter meant to explicate the place of "law" in religious studies: that is, an example not of a master project of secularization or religio-fication (two processes that the literature has convincingly told us are fraught with contradiction, after all—see, e.g., Sullivan 2005; Agrama 2012), but rather an illustration that we live in a legal world that is deeply polyvocal. In these instances, religion and law are not engaged as adversaries due to external imposition, as works regarding, for example, colonial efforts at codification of religious legal systems have argued (Hallaq 2009; cf. Emon 2016). Nor are they seen simply to be identical due to some kind of postcolonial redemption, as religious activists within modern states have been accused of sloppily proposing. Rather, here law and religion emerge on the same plane, overlapping and equally ordering our lives. The relationship between religion and law in these instances rests on a series of practical accommodations, a sharing of the regulatory domain between secular and religious, moral and legal, sovereign and subordinate, and even this-worldly and otherworldly courts of judgment. It is this fact that is particularly prominent in the episodes of "The Lamp of *Shari'a*" that I will analyze in this essay. Law's normative plurality—emerging as it does from international, state, communal, and religious bodies—is true across the world, as an excellent recent analysis of the literature of the field of "law and religion" makes so clear (Oraby and Sullivan 2020). Work in the field of "religion and law," spearheaded by its flagship *Journal of Law and Religion*, has come to embrace such an approach, far from its origins as a study of church-state relations and constitutional law alone (Vogel 1983). A recent appraisal of the field (Neo 2022) recognizes the importance of changing global demographics, through both migration and religious renewal, to rethinking dominant paradigms in the study of religion and law, emerging as they often do from quite circumscribed conceptions of (geographic and social) territory and its management. Other recent studies have reminded us that work in law and religion often takes place, formally, in neither, when both categories have been positioned too narrowly to capture refractions of the sacred and the sovereign throughout diverse communities across time (Jacob 2019; Yelle 2019; and, from a different angle, McNally 2020). The law and religion conversation has also begun to recognize the global purchase of legal regimes, beyond delineated jurisdiction, as analyses of efforts to promote "international religious freedom" have argued (Hurd 2015). Winnifred Fallers Sullivan reminds us that "law and religion is not so much a field as it is a sprawling interdisciplinary conversation, one which is, in part, attempting a repair of secularist and separationist assumptions in intellectual work" that preceded it, which "read law as the modern secular law of the state and religion as that which is understood to be in opposition to, defined by, and subsumed to, that law" (Sullivan 2021).

It seems that particularly at this moment of political crisis in the modern state across many national contexts, such as Lebanon, we may be in need of a new paradigm for understanding the relationship between law and religion. For far from the transcendence of the law (in terms of either chaos or pure force) that we might assume would prevail once state law becomes unstable, we encounter instead a new flourishing of legal options. That is to say, Lebanon in 2021 was not properly law-less, as it was often portrayed in media caricatures, but rather particularly law-full, even if these laws can be inconsistently implemented and sometimes in conflict with one another. In the ruins of modernity, we find disorder, we find arbitrary force, this is true, *but also markedly, we find law*. Indeed, in today's Lebanon, citizens swim in a sea of law, a rule of laws—governmental, international, voluntary/professional associational, and religious—with codified state law as just one of them, stronger in some cases, weaker in others. Lebanon is not alone here. Rule of law, if that means state sovereignty over the legal mechanisms that control people's lives, is a far-off fiction in most places, and may not even always be desirable when it empowers controversial legal systems and suppresses the sorts of legal pluralism that allow for some states with diverse populations to persevere when agreement over the identity of the nation has not been reached (Salomon 2011). What the case of Lebanon in the summer of 2021 shows us is only how unremarkable this can become.

: : :

> The subject that has presented itself in recent days to the Lebanese public square and has forced us to make an exception to the normal chain of episodes we were presenting [in this television program] . . . is the subject of monopolization. We have witnessed, and are still witnessing in Lebanon, a big wave of monopolization over goods that have had subsidies lifted on them. From here, we would love to shed the light of the lamp of shari'a on this subject so as to discover the proper rules (hudud shara'iya) for confronting it. . . .

With this introduction, turning on the "light of the lamp of shari'a" to illuminate the subject at hand, the first of the two episodes the expired milk controversy inspired commences. Immediately, several questions for the scholar of religion and law emerge: What exactly is meant by shari'a here and in what ways does a religious "law" like this exist in the context of a modern multi-confessional nation-state with its own novel definitions of both law and religion? Is shari'a reducible (or promotable) to "law" in the first place, or is it better thought of, in somewhere like Lebanon where it is restricted in the state legal code to family law alone, as, on subjects such as these (with criminal and commercial implications), a moral order, powerful but in the end unenforceable? Pinning down where law is and isn't in the context that "The Lamp of *Shari'a*" illuminates is difficult, but if we start by seeing it as a series of layers—law, upon law, upon law, each one tied into religion in some crucial and inextricable way—we might begin to get at some of the complexity of the subject at hand. Here we see that law and religion are often two terms that explain different aspects of the same phenomenon, rather than two domains that have an encounter we must untangle, as they are often imagined to be.

Throughout the two episodes of "The Lamp of *Shari'a*" on the topic of monopolization, its host, a young seminary student, the religious scholar being interviewed, and the several call-in viewers sample readily from a large bouquet of legal options, less concerned with the ontology of their source—God, the state, the political factions that be—as has been the obsession of so much contemporary debate on religion and law, and instead petitioning each equally for some measure of justice. By providing a close analysis of these two episodes in this essay, I hope to offer the reader a discussion of the topic of "law and religion" as it emerges in situ, not as a story of one canceling out the other, nor of their melding, but as a depiction of an active arena of negotiation, as along the way this particular "religious" discussion of the law threads itself through several domains of authority, epistemology, and temporality that any scholar of law and religion must confront. I will turn now somewhat systematically to a geological method to reveal and name layer after layer of the legal and religious systems that implicate this one small example of a televised discussion on monopoly from a Shi'i Islamic perspective.

1&2. Sources of Emulation (*al-maraji'*) and Islamic State Law

Following the above scene-setting introduction from the host, 'Ali Sadiq, we are introduced to the guest of the program, Shaykh Isma'il Hariri, a member of the Office of the General *Shari'a* Agent (*maktab al-wakil al-shara'i al-'am*) of the *marja'* (clerical source of emulation) Sayyid 'Ali Hosseini Khamenei, and a teacher at the Lebanese seminary, *hawzat al-rusul al-akram*. The host: "Welcome to a new episode from your program 'Lamp of *Shari'a*' in which we clarify *shari'a* judgments regarding daily challenges (*al-ahkam al-shara'iyya al-ibtila'iyya*) according to the *fatwas* of the Imam, the leader (*al-qa'id*), al-Khamenei, may his shadow always be upon us."

Immediately two distinct domains of law and religion confront us, insisting on their inseparability. On the one hand, we are dealing with the *ijtihad* (independent religious legal opinion) of a *marja' al-taqlid*, a Source of Emulation within Shi'i jurisprudence, which many in Lebanon consider Ayatollah Khamenei to be. As a *mujtahid* (one who performs *ijtihad*), Khameini is considered uniquely qualified to discern God's will for humanity, His *shari'a*, for which multiple modes of law—clerical edicts (*fatawi*), religious jurisprudence (*fiqh*), codified law (*qanun*)—might be approximated.

Other *marja*'s have significant sway in Lebanon as well, but following the Iranian revolution of 1979, Khomeini and then his successor, Khamenei, quickly became among the most visible sources of emulation in the country following the allegiance given to them by what became by the end of civil war the strongest Shi'i political force in the land, Hizbullah (Shaery-Eisenlohr 2008). Such legal judgments from Sources of Emulation, while not enforceable in the formal sense in that they normally have no sanctioning apparatus attached to them, nonetheless wield significant power, and people turn to their *marja*'s (and their representatives) often to seek guidance on matters big and small, regarding their relationship with God and society (Corbez 2015). It is Khamenei's *fatwa* on monopolization that serves as the basis of Shaykh Isma'il's words in this episode.[7]

Additionally, one immediately notices two titles the host gives to Khamenei, which suggest that we are not merely dealing with a Source of Emulation here: "al-Imam," the leader, in a spiritual sense, but also *al-qa'id*, the leader in a political sense. With both titles, it is clear that this is no average *marja'*, but rather someone who *does* hold a power of enforcement, in his case as the Supreme Leader of the Islamic Republic of Iran. While this power of enforcement is limited to Iran, despite the influence they wield over groups like Hizbullah, such *state Islamic law* is a figure that haunts the entirety of the conversation over the two episodes. As we will soon see, callers, even though they are aware of both the weakness and the non-Islamic-ness of the state in Lebanon, seem overwhelmingly preoccupied with how an Islamic government *would* regulate the problem of monopolization if one were to live in one. However, Lebanon is, of course, not Iran, but rather a multi-confessional country whose legal system is a montage of French civil law at the commercial and criminal level and a set of personal status laws that govern matters of marriage, adoption, and inheritance divided according to religious sect (Abillamah 2018). Thus, although state law is being referred to here when the conversation turns to enforceability of Islamic law, it is not the state law of Lebanon, but of another land (real or imagined), one whose specter appears at various times in this discussion, but only in its position of absence. This other land is the Islamic state that we might hypothesize in order to understand how to deal with difficult social issues such as "monopolization" in a proper way, if only we could, contemplating a legal order that will not come to pass, as

7. http://shiaonlinelibrary.com/الكتب/753_أجوبة-الاستفتاءات-السيد-علي-الخامنئي-ج-٢/الصفحة_129; (al-Khamana'i n.d., 128).

no serious argument about the Islamization of criminal and commercial law in Lebanon exists, despite common fears.

The figure of "Khamenei," which appears at the outset of the program and sits in the background throughout the rest of the two episodes, represents two distinct formations of the law and religion dynamic: (1) that of clerically produced religious legal opinion, the *fatwas* that are being consumed here by average Lebanese looking for guidance, and (2) that of an Islamized modern national state juridical apparatus that is looked up to by some in Lebanon as an ideal, however unobtainable. Here we should stress that two bodies of law that are normally separate in the modern world—clerical opinion and state law—are in this one particular case inextricably intertwined given the unique founding thesis of the Islamic Republic of Iran of *wilayat al-faqih*, guardianship of the political body by the jurist, and given that the "jurist" in question for this particular group of Lebanese Shiʿa is also the Iranian head of state who rules under this very principle.

3&4. Scripture (*al-dalil al-sharaʿi*) and Classical Juridical Opinion

Following the ceremonial beginning of the episode, in which we are introduced to the two forces that linger in the background and offer a frame to the discussion—Khamenei, the "Source of Emulation," and the Islamic state—the host and his guest attempt to offer a technical definition of monopolization as expressed in the guidance that God has given us through the Qur'an, the example of the Prophet Muhammad, and that of the twelve infallible imams that followed him, according to the Imami Shiʿi thought to which the organizers of this program subscribe. Arriving at a definition of monopolization as a Shariʿa technical term (*mafhum al-ihtikar fi-l-istilah al-sharʿi*), which we soon learn has a meaning somewhat different from, though overlapping with, the modern economic definition of monopoly, is one goal of the first part of the program, while the *sharʿi* responsibility of the Muslim toward the topic is the other (*ma huwa al-taklif al-sharʿi bi-l-nisba lahu?*). At this point in the program, which in fact mirrors many texts in *al-fiqh al-istidlali* (demonstrative jurisprudence), we are in the realm of defining our terms.

This section of the program deals in *hudud*, those rules presented unambiguously in the "texts" (*al-nusus*) and the work of the first generation of classical Imami Shiʿi jurists, who remain nameless here (there is understood to be a somewhat transparent relationship between these two bodies of literature). As many have commented, such unambiguous "law" makes up a very small portion of the scripture, where legal rules are in great measure *not* explicitly explicated, leaving them instead to be derived through complex legal interpretive method.[8] Here we have an interesting argument being waged on the basis of texts in classical Imami *fiqh*, and the source texts themselves, in which our shaykh insists that monopoly is a prime subject (*'unwan awwali*) of *fiqh*—i.e., forbidden in and of itself—and not merely a secondary subject—i.e., that which is forbidden under some larger category (that it causes harm, for example, and harm is forbidden).[9] He tells us that monopoly is expressly forbidden in the sacred sources when it comes to six products explicitly mentioned: wheat, barley, dates, and raisins (*al-ghallat al-'arba'*), and then ghee and oil. To meet the threshold of "*ihtikar*" (monopoly), it cannot be simply that a seller is hoarding these items; it is a two-way street: to be a monopoly people must be in need of the item, unable to find it elsewhere, *and* the owner must be holding onto it with a profit margin in mind. Here, with these two sources—"scripture" and classical juridical opinion—we are closest to what average people might first imagine "religious law" to be: the realm of old and dusty tomes that lay out a series of commandments. However, we will soon see that while these tomes surely have a foundational place in the discussion that follows, they are situated within a much more intricate legal and religious web, without which they cannot be understood.

5. Contemporary Jurisprudence (*al-fiqh al-mu'asir*)

The example of the sacred texts raises a dilemma. In Lebanon, it is medicines, electricity (which in 2021 was primarily provided by generator operators and not the state due to fuel shortages), infant formula, and other essential foods that are being monopolized, and that therefore are of paramount concern, and not, to say the least, raisins and dates. Must we really say that, *shari'a* speaking, only these products can be monopolized, since it is they that are frozen in the sacred texts? Here we begin to see the turn from *hudud* to *fiqh*, both sources of "religious law" but in different ways. Shaykh Isma'il tells us that the fact that these six items are mentioned does

8. In English, the best example of this method in the Shi'i tradition can be found in Roy Mottahedeh's translation of Muhammad Baqir al-Sadr's *Lessons in Islamic Jurisprudence* (al-Sadr 2003).

9. These sources are helpfully outlined in Haidar Hubb Allah's *Dirasat fi al-fiqh al-islami al-mu'asir*, part 3, *Dar al-fiqh al-islami al-mu'asir* (2011). This section of the book can also be found here: https://hobbollah.com/articles/فقه-الاحتكار-في-الشريعة-الإسلامية/.

not mean that the ruling on *ihtikar* cannot be extended to other products if the society in question has other sorts of needs: "forbidden *ihtikar* in Imami jurisprudence is particularized to specified products, but this does not forbid [the jurist] from extending [the ruling] to other products that people need, but this must be within a specific legitimate mechanism," he tells us. Here we are in the realm of *fiqh*, which is what Shaykh Isma'il himself performs throughout the remainder of the two episodes in answering the questions from callers that are specific to the Lebanese context and its needs. Though Shaykh Isma'il is throughout somewhat short on specifics, seemingly nervous to wade into potentially dicey political territory as a religious figure and not a political leader within the party, he consistently gives us a framework for how one should do so. Indeed, this makes up the bulk of the "call-in" section of the program that we will discuss below. On the one hand, Shaykh Isma'il is merely applying the fatwas of his *marja'*, Khamenei, and examining how best to self-govern *as if* he were in an Islamic state, as discussed above; but on the other hand, given the practical focus of the show on challenges facing the Lebanese public today, Shaykh Isma'il must extend and apply these opinions to new contexts. This mechanism, we might observe, is the *living component* of the religion and law dynamic, the one whose cells will continue to divide until the end of time, as new contexts and ages confront it.

6. "Secular" State and International Law

After explicating some rules and regulations around monopolization in an Islamic state, Shaykh Isma'il reminds us that "this is all in the shadow of an Islamic order (*hadha fi zull hukm islami*), yet sometimes there is no Islamic order . . . [in such an instance,] the present government, the present state, or the present system takes initiative to play this role." Here, in one of the most revealing moments of the two episodes in which, as I mentioned, Shaykh Isma'il is very cautious not to weigh in too strongly on contentious political issues, he seems to be addressing the question of secular governance and the relationship of religion to it. Indeed, at exactly this point in the program, after making the above statement, something very odd happens in the context of a program on *fiqh*, which normally limits its guests to those wearing the turbans of religious scholarly learning. Suddenly, as if on cue, the cameras cut away from the scene in front of us—a seminary student interviewing a shaykh—to a prerecorded interview with a business-suit-attired economic expert regarding the definition of monopolization in Lebanese and international law.

Why the turn to "secular law" in a program on *fiqh*, one might be tempted to ask? But this might be precisely the wrong question to ask if we understand religion and law as two ways of articulating the same processes of social regulation, as I think we should, rather than as two domains in an episode of encounter. As we see in the quote in the previous paragraph, according to the shaykh *fiqh* itself recognizes the legitimacy of a non-Islamic government to regulate monopolization in the absence of an Islamic ruler, thus secular law here is in some sense as "Islamic" as Islamic law. The program's turn to an economic expert seems to be stressing to its viewers that despite the many appeals to what an Islamic political order might look like, they must understand actual law in the country and international order in which they are situated since its jurisprudence on monopoly likely will play an outsized role in their economic lives. It is at this point in the program that suddenly the visual aesthetic shifts, from calligraphic and geometric motifs to a scholarly office, as our economic expert tells us that "the definition of *ihtikar* is every action that leads to exploitation of the economic system to create illegitimate competition."

However, while there is clearly an Islamic imperative to exist within the national legal arrangement, hence the matter-of-fact discussion of "secular law" in the context of this religious jurisprudence program, Shaykh Isma'il is also quick to point out that there is some distinction of domains here. The economic expert talks about the need for healthy competition and thus the negative repercussions of exclusive agents, but Shaykh Isma'il reminds us that this is different from the *shar'i*/Islamic meaning of monopoly, as we've seen it described above. In the *shari'a*, if we are only talking about exclusive agency (*al-wikala al-hasriyya*), but not withholding goods for economic gain, then we don't give it the title of *ihtikar*/monopoly, even if it might be legitimately regulated by the Islamic or secular state in the interest of protecting the economy.

Moral Imperative

One might think that the story ends here, with this explication of the points of commonality and difference between *shari'a* and secular state law. Yet, clearly it does not, for *shari'a* in its formal, legal sense, by which here the shaykh seems simply to mean what is permissible and impermissible, legal and illegal, *haram* and *halal*, is often supplemented in the episodes of "The Lamp of *Shari'a*" by something we might call *akhlaq*, morals. *Shari'a* is a term that bridges what in Western legal and moral theory we call law and ethics. *Shari'a* demands, understood in their formal, legal sense, are the most basic things that are required for Muslims, and much of the episodes treat *shari'a* in this way, as a kind of "law," searching for an actionable answer to Lebanon's current predicaments in its complex archive. But *shari'a* in the larger sense of its moral imperative classically includes other categories of divine indictment and encouragement, such as what is discouraged (*makruh*), what is promoted (*mustahibb*), and that for which the law is neutral (*mubah*). Indeed, the shaykh tells us this when the host insightfully pushes him about these important categories of *fiqh* (*hal hunak hatta hudud mustahabba min bab al-ihtiyat al-istihbabi*?). He replies, "yes, what is encouraged is that the Muslim should not profit from the Muslim, beyond what he needs to live." There is no problem in raising a price when you have full control over a product, from the perspective simply of the forbidden and the permissible, since, as we saw, that discussion is limited either to the six products or to others that can be derived from them by existing in an analogous situation of need. However, there is more to it, clearly, as profit is encouraged in Islam, the shaykh tells us, until it reaches what he calls the limit of unfairness "*hadd al-ijhaf*."

An example may be helpful here in order to fully explicate this final formation of the law and religion dynamic as it plays out in "The Lamp of *Shari'a*" episodes under discussion. At one point in the first episode, the shaykh takes on the subject of the phenomenon of the owners of generators (who are the main electricity suppliers to neighborhoods given the state's inability to provide this service) raising prices and saying to their customers "don't complain, you are free to buy from me or not," when there are in fact no other choices, "when it is either them or darkness." In terms of the sacred texts and classical and contemporary jurisprudence, we are not in the realm of monopolization, as it does not fit either the limited explicit mention of monopoly in "the sources" or direct analogy. But, Shaykh Isma'il continues, just because it is not properly a *shari'a* matter does not mean that the *shari'a* specialist does not also have a duty to comment on it and even pass judgment. Shaykh Isma'il tells the host, "here is where should come a feeling of social solidarity (*al-takaful al-ijtima'i*) between people, and unfortunately we see a lot of times that [this value] has been lost among these people, or a lot of them." Social solidarity is certainly not a *shari'a* category in a formal sense, and yet the moral universe of *shari'a* allows us to posit it as a social good. The moral and the legal imperatives of *shari'a* are thus inseparable here. Indeed, in a context like Lebanon where there is neither Islamic rule nor a fully functioning administrative state able to respond to rapidly changing economic conditions, the establishment of such a moral order becomes all the more urgent. In other words, when the coercive force of law does not meet the ideals of justice that the people hold, the productive force of law, for example here in creating a moral context of social solidarity, must play an outsized role in keeping society intact.

: : :

> Peace be upon you. . . . I would just like to be sure about this subject of *al-ihtikar*. The monopolizers in this country who make these prices and who waste [goods], as we saw with the milk of which children all across the country are in need . . . these kinds of people are inhumane, they have no sense of humanity (*insaniyya*)! They deserve jail! . . . That is how this country should teach these people a lesson. And without this [kind of punishment], this country will never be made right, my brothers.

This first call of the program comes from "Yusuf in Lebanon," whose tone of voice, in addition to what he says, is evidence of exhaustion and exasperation. The screen cuts to a picture of the spilled and spoiled powdered milk similar to the ones I have described above. There is not precisely a question in Yusuf's call, but rather an opinion and an appeal to humanity. The call is received in somber silence. The second question, from "Maryam," is equally exasperated, describing the inability of the average Lebanese to purchase anything in these circumstances of unimaginable inflation. "What I am supposed to do?"

After a short pause, the host intervenes to reframe these complaints into a question that a *shari'a*-explicating shaykh might answer, for otherwise there is not much more he could offer these callers other than sympathy. The host interjects, "Yusuf suggests jail for these monopolizers of the infant formula. Some perhaps might say, if they saw the scene that we just saw [on the screen], of [the expired] formula, they might say that they deserve more than that! But," turning now to Shaykh Isma'il, "what is the *shari'a* punishment (*al-'uquba al-shara'iyya*) for the monopolizer?" The question is a rather odd one, of course, for a Lebanese talk show because, as should be clear by now, Lebanese criminal law is not Islamic, nor does Shaykh Isma'il advocate a system of vigilante justice on *shari'a* basis. So, one might ask, why would one care? Although the two angry callers demand some sort of punishment, the shaykh seems to want to defuse the situation a bit, not because he is not equally outraged (though we see no indication that he is: he speaks in a calm and even-keeled voice throughout the program), but because he too is likely aware of the practical futility of discussions of earthly sanction in the current context. Thus, he quickly changes the subject from punishment in this world to the punishment inflicted on the monopolizer before God. Shaykh Isma'il answers the host's question:

> First thing is that [the monopolizer] is guilty of sin and he is responsible for it before God (SWT). . . . God will stop all people on Judgment Day to ask them about their actions. . . . He will ask them about those things that are connected to the rights of people (*huquq al-nas*). . . . So, if someone had monopolized, monopolizing in a forbidden (*muharram*) way, then naturally he is disobedient to God the most-high and he has an accounting with God.

Thus while the callers seem to demand punishment on earth for these monopolizers, which, we have learned, cannot be forthcoming either from an Islamic or a state criminal law perspective given the current state of affairs, Shaykh Isma'il turns to heavenly courts of judgment, a key domain in which religion and law play out, even if an underappreciated one in our materialist renderings.

But the callers push back. The next caller, Umm Muhammad, asks about the monopolization that is taking place in Hizbullah's stronghold neighborhood al-Dahiya, an administrative zone unto itself, under the full control of Hizbullah forces. Why, she wonders, if this is the Islamic judgment, is nothing being done about the monopolization at the very least in al-Dahiya, in particular around electricity that is in such short supply? The caller's implicit accusation is at best a subtext here: Hizbullah is performing a difficult act, both serving as an integral part of the state against which people are complaining *and* providing a forum for an expression of an alternative moral order. In the tremors of critique in the voices of all three of these callers we hear something very crucial about the religion-law dynamic that is important to highlight. Unlike the state-law dynamic, the religion-law dynamic at least opens the possibility of multiple sources of authority. If law comes from God in the end, who is to stop an educated public from offering new readings and then insisting on their implications, even on those who are supposed to be its guardians? In both the two exasperated questions and the call about al-Dahiya, Shaykh Isma'il is presented with a challenge: whose responsibility should it be to organize a world in accordance with *shari'a*? If the state is not applying it and religious parties are unable fully to protect even their own neighborhoods, then on whose shoulders does the responsibility presented by *shari'a* fall? Unlike the law of states, which, given that they can only be implemented by governments, can never truly be a fully participatory endeavor, there is something rather radical going on here with the explication of the religion-law paradigm by these callers. In a place like Lebanon where many claims to guardianship of Islamic law exist, *shari'a* is no one's law, and everyone's, and thus, as we can see in the tone of these callers' appeals, anyone is free to employ its discursive force against anyone else.

: : :

Several more questions proceed over the two episodes: loans in the context of currency fluctuation, gas lines caused by scarcity and the ethics of how to wait in them in a situation of dire need, hoarding for protection of one's family versus hoarding for profit. In each case, law is not merely being referenced, but created, bit by bit. Shaykh Isma'il pontificates on each situation the viewers present, even if he is hesitant to offer judgment, point fingers at guilty parties, or wade into politically sensitive topics. Still, and in spite of such constraints, law does emerge out of these episodes, but not the kind of law that we might assume, or on which rule of law experts might insist for countries in "the developing world." In this case, as in so many others, the legal is not a fixed domain controlled by a definable sovereign power, but rather an infinitely productive force, in whose growth multiple parties participate (Clarke 2018), here entangled in each one of the layers of the religion-law dynamic I outlined above, and not reducible to any one of them alone.

If we can begin to see law and religion in this way, as a conversation on how to regulate the communities in which we live, whose sources participate in multiple modes of authority, temporality, epistemology, and even ontology, we can begin to see them as part of a shared domain. Here the relationship between religion and law does not rely on an image of fortressed and authentic forms of each, engaged in a never-ending battle for supremacy; rather, it becomes clear that each is in fact generative of the other, as sophisticated studies of religion's law (Howe 1965) and law's religion (Hussin 2016) have so vividly shown. If we are to take this approach, gone will be the teleological myth of secularization, the victory of the judicial state over all alternate models of social order that is said to be the story of modernization. As recent studies have stressed, while alternate modes of juridical reasoning are undoubtedly transformed by the modern moment, their stories are not characterized by rupture alone, but by continuity as well (e.g., Moumtaz 2021; Richland 2008). Gone too from our discussions should be the knee-jerk fear of the uncritical collapse of religion and politics that haunts discussions on religion and law for liberals in the East and West. In its place should be a picture of the domain of law and religion as it so often exists: as an endlessly intricate complex of relations between the various forces that regulate our lives in the face of challenges that arise (in some places surely more than others). The case of the expired infant formula that inspired these episodes of "The Lamp of *Shari'a*" was never solved, and no official judgment was passed. Still, viewers used the space of these episodes to confront at least one of the seemingly never-ending challenges that plague today's Lebanon, drawing on the creative potential of the law (and religion) to imagine a world better than our own, one where justice might be served.

Suggested Readings

Chatterjee, Nandini. 2011. *The Making of Indian Secularism: Empire, Law and Christianity, 1830–1960*. New York: Palgrave Macmillan.

Dew, Spencer. 2019. *The Allites: Race and Law in the Religions of Noble Drew Ali*. Chicago: University of Chicago Press.

Emon, Anver. 2012. *Religious Pluralism and Islamic Law: Dhimmis and Others in the Empire of Law*. Oxford: Oxford University Press.

Hurd, Elizabeth Shakman, and Winnifred Fallers Sullivan. n.d. "Teaching Law and Religion Case Study Archive." Accessed July 1, 2021. https://sites.northwestern.edu/lawreligion/.

Lloyd, Vincent. 2016. *Black Natural Law*. Oxford: Oxford University Press.

Messick, Brinkley. 1993. *The Calligraphic State: Textual Domination and History in a Muslim Society*. Berkley: University of California Press.

Oraby, Mona. 2024. *Devotion to the Administrative State: Religion and Social Order in Egypt*. Princeton, NJ: Princeton University Press.

Schonthal, Ben. 2016. *Buddhism, Politics, and the Limits of Law: The Pyrrhic Constitutionalism of Sri Lanka*. Cambridge: Cambridge University Press.

Sullivan, Winnifred Fallers. 2020. *Church, State, Corporation: Construing Religion in US Law*. Chicago: University of Chicago Press.

Sullivan, Winnifred Fallers, Robert A. Yelle, and Mateo Taussig-Rubbo, eds. 2011. *After Secular Law*. Stanford, CA: Stanford University Press.

Thomas, Jolyon Baraka. 2019. *Faking Liberties: Religious Freedom in American-Occupied Japan*. Chicago: University of Chicago Press.

References

Abillamah, Raja. 2018. "Contesting Secularism: Civil Marriage and Those Who Do Not Belong to a Religious Community in Lebanon." *Polar* (*Political and Legal Anthropology Review*) 41, S1.

Agrama, Hussein Ali. 2012. *Questioning Secularism: Islam, Sovereignty, and the Rule of Law in Modern Egypt*. Chicago: University of Chicago Press.

Bou Akar, Hiba. 2018. *For the War Yet to Come: Planning Beirut's Frontiers*. Stanford, CA: Stanford University Press.

Clarke, Morgan. 2018. *Islam and Law in Lebanon: Sharia Within and Without the State*. Cambridge: Cambridge University Press.

Corbez, Elvire. 2015. *Guardians of Shiism: Sacred Authority and Transnational Family Networks*. Edinburgh: Edinburgh University Press.

Deeb, Lara. 2006. *An Enchanted Modern: Gender and Public Piety in Shiʿi Lebanon*. Princeton, NJ: Princeton University Press.

Emon, Anver. 2016. "Codification and Islamic Law: The Ideology behind a Tragic Narrative." *Middle East Law and Governance* 8.

Hallaq, Wael B. 2009. *Shariʿa: Theory, Practice, Transformations*. Cambridge: Cambridge University Press.

Howe, Mark De Wolfe. 1965. *The Garden and the Wilderness: Religion and Government in American Constitutional History*. Chicago: University of Chicago Press.

Hubb Allah, Haydar. 2011. *Dirasat fi-l-fiqh al-islami al-mu'asir*, part 3. Beirut: Dar al-fiqh al-islami al-muʿasir.

Hurd, Elizabeth Shakman. 2015. *Beyond Religious Freedom: The New Global Politics of Religion*. Princeton, NJ: Princeton University Press.

Hussin, Iza. 2016. *The Politics of Islamic Law: Local Elites, Colonial Authority, and the Making of the Muslim State*. Chicago: University of Chicago Press.

Jacob, Wilson Chacko. 2019. *For God or Empire: Sayyid Fadl and the Indian Ocean World*. Stanford, CA: Stanford University Press.

al-Khamana'i, Al-Sayyid 'Ali al-Husayni. n.d. *Answers to Requests for* Fatwas (*ajwaba al-istafta'at*). No Publisher.

Marusek, Sarah. 2018. *Faith and Resistance: The Politics of Love and War in Lebanon*. London: Pluto Press.

McNally, Michael. 2020. *Defend the Sacred: Native American Religious Freedom Beyond the First Amendment*. Princeton, NJ: Princeton University Press.

Moumtaz, Nada. 2021. *God's Property: Islam, Charity, and the Modern State*. Oakland: University of California Press.

Neo, Jaclyn L. 2022. "Law and Religion: Asia as Critical Ground for Rethinking Existing Frameworks and Dominant Paradigms." *Journal of Law and Religion* 37 (2).

Oraby, Mona, and Winnifred Fallers Sullivan. 2020. "Law and Religion: Reimagining the Entanglement of Two Universals." *Annual Review of Law and Social Science* 16.

Richland, Justin. 2008. *Arguing with Tradition: The Language of Law in Hopi Tribal Courts*. Chicago: University of Chicago Press.

Al-Sadr, Muhammad Baqir. 2003. *Lessons in Islamic Jurisprudence*. Translated by Roy Mottahedeh. Oxford: One World.

Salomon, Noah. 2011. "The Ruse of Law: Legal Equality and the Problem of Citizenship in a Multi-Religious Sudan." In *After Secular Law*, edited by Winnifred Fallers Sullivan, Robert A. Yelle, and Mateo Taussig-Rubbo. Stanford, CA: Stanford University Press.

Shaery-Eisenlohr, Roschanack. 2008. *Shi'ite Lebanon: Transnational Religion and the Making of National Identities*. New York: Columbia University Press.

Sullivan, Winnifred Fallers. 2005. *The Impossibility of Religious Freedom*. Princeton, NJ: Princeton University Press.

Sullivan, Winnifred Fallers. 2021. "Law and Religion Beyond Liberalism." *Religious Studies Review* 47 (1).

Vogel, Howard. 1983. "A Survey and Commentary on the New Literature in Law and Religion." *Journal of Law and Religion* 1 (1).

Yelle, Robert A. 2019. *Sovereignty and the Sacred: Secularism and the Political Economy of Religion*. Chicago: University of Chicago Press.

9 LIFE

Rafael Rachel Neis

Life—its generation and proliferation, its preservation and chances, its value and classification—is what stands at the center of this essay. As a quality (liveliness), an attribute that entities do or do not have, a measurable quantity (units of life, degrees of liveliness), and as divided across various life-forms (according to various criteria), it would seem to be an obvious domain of religion and hence a fundamental object of analysis in religious studies. Indeed, one could argue that life has always been a focus of religious studies—particularly in its ethical and qualitative dimensions (the good life, reward and punishment, suffering and pleasure), its relationships with temporality (death, afterlife, pre-life, multiple lives, resurrection, underworlds, heaven, ghosts, ancestors, divinity), its links with materiality (death again, decomposition, spirit or soul), and via the themes of askesis, sacrifice, and martyrdom.

In recent decades, however, one can point to a substantially different constellation of themes that ought to be subsumed under the umbrella term of "life." These are drawn from scholarship in feminist theory, queer theory, transgender studies, critical race theory, disability studies, animal studies, posthumanism, science studies, and new materialism (e.g., Barad 2007; Chen 2012; Haraway 2008; Jackson 2020). Related to these approaches, but focused on human life and usually understood as apparatuses peculiar to the modern state and governmentality, are analyses through the lenses of biopolitics, biopower, and necropolitics (Foucault 2008; Rabinow and Rose 2006; Agamben 1998; Mbembe 2019). Such scholarship across the social sciences, humanities, and even sciences, interrogates processes of value and (de)valuation, flourishing and extinction, vitality and torpidity, variation and classification of (potentially, once, or currently) living beings. Increasingly, this research is informed by a push against anthropocentrism and a critical regard for how the category of the human is variously constrained to exclude on grounds of animality, race, gender, disability, and other normate delineations (Thomson 2017; Quashie 2021; Weheliye 2014; Kimmerer 2013). Efforts to decenter and historicize the human itself pave the way for considerations of nonhuman life-forms. Whether focused on historical sources or on contemporary instantiations, such work is doubtless invigorated by modern and contemporary urgencies, including racial, gender, reproductive, disability, and environmental (in)justice and their intersections.

While aspects of these orientations and themes are being taken up disparately in religious studies (Schaefer 2015; Berkowitz 2018; Gross 2014; Raucher 2020; Watts 2013 and 2020; Tandberg 2019; Kueny 2013), there has yet to be synthetic, comparative, or programmatic reflection on the category of "life" as it joins them. What might such investigations into life, informed by the above orientations with their critical reappraisal of the human, mean for religious studies? This essay ventures an initial reflection on this question, taking ancient Jewish sources as a case study for thinking about life in religious studies. Specifically, I examine writings authored by the Palestinian rabbis of late antiquity redacted in the early third and late fourth/early fifth centuries containing traditions of Jewish sages from roughly the first to the late fourth centuries. I hazard that these works and their Babylonian counterpart (culminating in the Babylonian Talmud) offer us a prime locus for thinking through the classification of lives, the proliferations of life, and the sustainment and flourishing of lives and life-chances. I further suggest that despite easy characterizations of so-called Abrahamic, Judeo-Christian, or even more narrowly cast Jewish religious valorizations of life—particularly human life—in terms of sanctity, what we actually find in these "classical" Jewish sources defies such portrayals (cf. Haraway 1997).

To the extent that universalizing propensities of religious studies itself were once (or conceivably, remain,) coterminous with ideas that render "religion" legible in Protestant Christian terms like belief, practice, transcendence, morality, and the like, there was a concomitant assumption of the human as its most obvious subject and object. Certainly, such a characterization of religion as a fundamentally human cultural production has often, at least until quite recently, been taken for granted in, or explicitly claimed for, "Abrahamic" or "biblical" religions. Such assumptions and claims underpin and surface in the tendency to focus on humans as exemplary prime research subjects (alongside studies on material entities, divinity, spirits, angels, and demons), i.e., in the relative occlusion of nonhuman life-forms and entities in religious studies. This has been significantly challenged by the so-called material turn in religious studies, as well as the interest in animal studies. At the same time the human "in God's image" of Genesis 1 continues to loom in both academic and public religion discourse. Associated with this sacred human protagonist is the usage of *the* "Judeo-Christian tradition," which has burgeoned in American right-wing rhetoric. Uncritical uses of Judeo-Christian tradition, while less frequent, still persist in religious studies (see Gaston 2019). Furthermore, in some of the writing that has inspired the broader understandings of life above, Jewishness is hyphenated into a hegemonic Judeo-Christian West. This entity is said to authorize and originate the supremacy of human life, implicitly confirming (disapprovingly) self-identified religio-political accounts that make the same claim proudly (Haraway 1997). Assumptions that flow therefrom, e.g., about the crucial or obligatory nature of human reproduction, reverberate even in seemingly non-tendentious, more fine-grained analyses of Judaism (e.g., Boyarin 1991; Lorberbaum 2015). Without dismissing the salience of the human and its proliferation in ancient rabbinic literature, I draw on the multivocality of rabbinic textual productions to highlight significant trends that present alternative frameworks for thinking life.

The rabbis linked human and animal processes of reproduction and the classification of various life-forms. This linkage tended to deflate as much as promote human exceptionalism. Certainly, the perception that the human is elevated in Jewish traditions is not without reason. The Priestly authored strata of the Hebrew Bible—particularly Genesis 1:1–2:4 describing the creation and Leviticus 11 outlining the im/purity of animal life—embedded "species (*minim*)" and their distinctions hierarchically in a divinely created world. And the rabbis of late antiquity certainly claimed these ancient traditions as their heritage. Yet, in contrast with this oft-invoked and idealized scriptural order, the rabbis' writings plunge us into a far messier world. In their world, biblical schemata, while activated, are always partial; indeed, the creation narrative and the Levitical taxa strain to fully account for the plenitude of life. The rabbis scrutinized the various entities produced by human and animal bodies and enumerated creaturely kinds well beyond the stenographic lists in Leviticus 11, with the latter's binary distinction between pure/impure and permitted/forbidden. Even while they parsed and elaborated such distinctions, these rabbis grappled with the *unpredictability* of the generation of life, the *multiplicity* of generative modes, and the curious *resemblances* between supposedly *different* species, including nonhuman and human kinds.

In the course of their scriptural exegeses, narratives, and ritual orderings, the rabbis were intent on classifying creatureliness and exploring the contours of the human. While they may have been implicitly devoted to the notion that the human (and a particular ethno-racialized, gendered, normate human) had a special place in the order of things, they simultaneously blurred the edges of the human (Thomson 1997). This they did in the context of discussions about reproductive materials and processes, unexpectedly variant offspring, the classification of species, and sorting through the varieties of entities emitted and nested by animal and human bodies. Via these varied disquisitions, the impermeability and intelligibility of the human was, again and again, upset. The human, it turns out, was not only subject to the same kind of reproductive variability as other animals; like other animals, it seemingly produced species-variant offspring. Like other species, it was caught up in a web of resemblances that threatened its uniqueness. In the face of such phenomena, the rabbis weighed in on how the stuff of life and the making of life could confound expectations about basic questions like who is kin, who is food, and what we owe to those we designate as different.

The Priestly Making of Life

The relationship between life and death in so-called "Judeo-Christian tradition" has often been taken as one that explicitly arranges lives into a hierarchy by virtue of their origination. The Priestly authors (ca. sixth century BCE) are responsible for those biblical strata that order creaturely taxonomies and that install the human as a unique creature (Gen 1:1–2:4) who is in God's image, is blessed with proliferative properties, and is charged to dominate other kinds. This insistence on differentiation echoes through several other Priestly writings, including the birth of Seth (Genesis 5:13) and the postdiluvian divine reproductive blessings and directives to Noah (Genesis 9:1–7). It culminates in the dietary and purity rules of Leviticus 11.

Thus, concomitant to the Priestly elevation of human life is its divinely blessed proliferation along with the introduction of differential measures for the killing of human and nonhuman life-forms. Nonetheless, as a composite, multisource document, "the" Hebrew Bible evinces several taxonomies of life and its value. As just one instance, let us take Ecclesiastes 3:17–21 in which the author reflects on the human, concluding that the human and the animal are the same: "as this one dies, so does that one die, and both have the same animating breath (*ruah*), the human is not superior to the animal."

Rabbinic Life

Elevating Human Lives and Reproduction

While it is true that the rabbis, including earlier generations (the Tannaim of the Mishnah and Tannaitic Midrash), did not ignore the Priestly idea of the human as God's image, this is hardly the full picture. First, the image of God (*tselem elohim*) does not figure all that much into the valuation of *humans* or human *life* per se. It is true that a play on the paradoxical singularity of *each* human "image" trades in *tselem elohim* to secure the uniqueness and value of each human life. It is also celebrated as a mark of divine affection for the human (mAvot 3:14; Sifra Qedoshim 4) and linked to the mechanics and obligatory nature of human reproduction (per Gen 1:26–27, Gen 5, Gen 9). Indeed, what is God's blessing in the Bible becomes an affirmative obligation for humans (mYev 6:6); the omission of the blessing, on some views, is tantamount to effacing the divine image or to murder (t. Yevamot 8:7; Mekh Bahodesh 8). This elevation of the human and the commitment to its propagation the early rabbis extrapolated from the triangulation of killing, procreation, and the *tselem elohim* in Gen 9:1–7.

Humanness is inevitably made, not just through distinctions between those assigned "nonhuman" status and those considered "human," but also invariably via gradations and hierarchies among humans. In the rabbinic case, this is silently introduced by making reproduction itself a matter of commandment, and thus not only a *human* but also a *Jewish* affair inasmuch as the obligation is not universalized. While this is only implicit in early and Palestinian sources, it becomes an explicitly Jewish demographic project in the later strata of the Babylonian Talmud (bYev 62a–63b). The obligation is explicitly gendered since it is held to be limited to men (though on one minority view it is incumbent upon men and women). Further, even the gender of offspring that count is in dispute: on one view producing a boy and a girl fulfills the obligation; on another, two boys are required. These sorts of pronatalism and their gendered, ethno-racialized embodiments and afterlives are more in line with what one might expect. Yet there are also other somewhat more subversive and surprising conceptions of biopower in play. It is to these that we now turn.

Beyond Human Reproduction

If scholars focus on humans and human reproduction in the earlier rabbinic corpus (Tannaitic texts), it is no surprise that they can find the elevation of the human and its propagation as just described. However, it is possible to allow a more complex, multispecies account of life-making, or biology, to come into view. One might argue that rabbinic biology generatively (con)fuses theology, anthropology, and biology, confounding "secular" notions of a division between culture (anthropology, theology) and nature (biology, science). Moreover, even as it seeks to know other species by naming and schematizing them, rabbinic biology confronts the fuzziness of such boundaries, including those that implicate the human.

Here the term "generation" rather than "reproduction" proves salutary. From the mid-eighteenth century, Euro-Americans sought to narrow and name accounts of life's coming to be through the concept of "reproduction" (Hopwood, Flemming, and Kassell 2018). Reproduction is often narrated as a particularly human process involving dyads composed of one man and one woman engaging in very specific kinds of activity described as sex, which are then seen to result in pregnancy and culminate in the birth of offspring. "Generation," by contrast, referenced "a larger, looser framework for discussing procreation and descent" and was not human-centric, including "not just animals and plants, but minerals too" (2018, 4). Scholars often use the term "procreation" to translate the mandate to "reproduce and multiply" almost always referring to humans, even as in Genesis 1:22, God blesses nonhumans the same way. Shifting from reproduction (or procreation) to generation allows us to better grasp the more-than-human dimension of the propagation of life in ancient Judaism.

Beyond Mimesis, Beyond Monogamy

The notion of *imago dei* not only makes humans godlike; it also launches reproduction as mimesis. Thus Adam begets Seth in his image (Gen 5:2). This subscribes to the seemingly obvious, naturalized notion of "like begets like." However, Adam begets unnamed other "sons and daughters" who are not so described, and in subsequent "generations (*toledot*)" image mechanics altogether vanish. Moreover, in this chapter of generations, it is only men who "beget (*va-yoled*)," thereby effecting patrilineal generation. Even more interestingly, in Genesis 4:1 although Eve conceives and gives birth to Cain after Adam "knows" her, she declares, "I (pro)created (*kaniti*) a man with God." In this Yahwist authored narrative, instead of mimesis there is matrilineal-divine generation. Harmonizing this account of human generation with that of Genesis 1:26 and Genesis 2:21–22, and perhaps out of discomfort at the deity's supplanting Adam, the Amoraic rabbis state that while "previously, Adam was created from dust and Eve was created from Adam, from now on, it will be 'in *our* image, after *our* likeness' (Gen 1:26): neither man without woman, nor woman without man, and neither of them with the Shekhinah" (Genesis Rabbah 8:9 [Theodor-Albeck 62–63], par y. Berakhot 9:1, 12d). This entails various implications for the proliferation of human life. For one, the mechanics of ongoing generation *after* the originary genesis of the human and its intertwining with mimesis are troubled. Second, the deity becomes, as the third-century halakhic midrash puts it, one of "three partners" in the making of the human, the other two being its human parents (Sifra Qedoshim 1:4–7 [ed. Weiss 86d]). Third, nonhumans—in this case, God—are enfolded within human generative processes. For the rabbis, perhaps the significant consequence of the exceptionalism inherent in *tselem elohim* is that human generation is the effect of a ménage à trois, one that is more intricate than what modern Euro-American accounts of reproduction as dyadic cisheterosexual, same-species, sex will allow.

Generation Queerly Multiple

That this is a feature and not an exception of rabbinic generation, human and also otherwise, is apparent in the rabbis' views of the *multiple* modes and mechanisms by which life-forms come to be. In consonance with "scientific" ancient understandings, the rabbis knew of spontaneous generation: the emergence of living creatures that emerge from dissimilar beings or even inanimate matter, such as mud or liquid (Virgil *Georgics* 4.281–314; yShabb 1:2 3b; Lehoux 2017; Neis 2016 and 2023). In their midrashic commentary on the life-forms of Leviticus 11, the rabbis dubbed such creatures "those that do not reproduce and multiply," invoking the "reproduce and multiply" of Genesis. They divided life-forms into three permutations along the lines of those who do and do not reproduce sexually, and are and are not vertebrates. The Mishnah knows of small flies or gnats generated from wine or oil, which are permissible for Jewish ingestion (tYadayim 2:3, Sifra Shemini parashah 3:1 [Weiss ed., 50a]; t. Terumot 7:11). Rabbi Simon son of Gamliel refers to these as those "whose creation is from water" (mYadayim 2:2). Later sources tell of snakes arisen from spines of wicked humans, birds fertilized by the wind, snails produced by rain, and lice generated by sweat (yShabb 1:2 3b; bHull 58a; b BK 16a; cf. Pliny *Natural History* 10.86.188). The rabbis considered the matter of human generation similarly. The idea that humans emerge from a "putrid drop" (mAvot 3:1) is presented as humbling. The Mekhilta lauds God's artistic ability to fashion a son in the image of his father, out of the paternal "drop of water" (Mekh Bahodesh 8). In the latter telling, the human-only, heterosexual couple is displaced by that of God and the father, ejecting the mother completely and reconfiguring Aristotelian generation so that it is divine form that shapes passive male material (instead of Aristotle's male form molding female matter).

This idea of life itself coming into being by the mysterious activation of matter was extended to all materials by both the rabbis and other ancient thinkers. Philo of Alexandria explains how "the universe must be filled through and through with life, and each of its primary elementary divisions contains the forms of life which are akin and suited to it" (Philo *De gigantibus* 6–8). The rabbis also knew this. In its elaboration of Leviticus 11's life-forms, the Sifra introduces into the class of creeping creatures who "do not reproduce and multiply and are vertebrate" the mouse "half earth and half flesh" (Sifra Shemini Parashah 3:4 [Weiss ed 49c]; Sifra Shemini Parasha 5, 1–6 [Weiss ed. 52a–b]). In enumerating the species of *tzav* (Leviticus 11:29) as "the *arvad*, the *ben hanefilim*, and the salamander," it cites Rabbi Akiva's panegyric to creatures that grow in the sea, earth, air, and fire (Sifra Shemini, 5:6 [Weiss ed. 52b]). He emphasizes that the matter and space of generation is constitutive, even life-endowing, and conversely, that leaving it results in death. Rabbi Akiva praises God's power of multiplication (*ribuy*) on at least three levels: reproduction itself (reproduce and multiply); the sheer number and variety of different species; and the multiplicity of reproductive modes and mechanisms. All these rabbinic forays into the generation of life situate the human among a plurality of creatures and generative modes and infuse nonhuman participation and matter into the heart of human generation.

Generation between Kinds

Interspecies coupling, within what the rabbis understood as certain constraints of the possible, was also a way to generate offspring. While such interspecies life-making was technically forbidden in the Bible as "mixed kinds (*kilayim*)," a ban that was in some ways extended by the rabbis, they nonetheless used humanly instigated offspring like mules. Other sorts of interspecies unions existed for the rabbis. Genesis 6:1–4 relates how the "sons of God . . . came into the human daughters," resulting in offspring of "mighty ones." This spawned various accounts of angelic/demonic-human mating, conception, and generation. Similarly, later rabbis understood the omission of "image" language in the "generations of the human (*adam*)" to signify either that in the time of Enoch humans lost their image and were centaurs, or that their corpses knew corruption and swarmed with worms (a generative theory in and of itself), or that Adam and Eve copulated with demons and generated demonic progeny.

Another way to view the early and certainly later rabbinic midrash on the divine-human threesome that generates human life is in light of claims by early members of the Jesus movement about the generative mechanics through which Jesus came to be God's (and Mary's?) son (Rothschild 2010). Later Palestinian and Babylonian rabbis elaborated this trihybrid human generation, pointing to specific elements that each contributed (yKil 8:4 31c and bNidd 31a). Of these multiple, sometimes overlapping, sometimes contested ways of understanding generation, it is difficult, if not impossible, to isolate a singular, unified, and monolithic "Judeo-Christian tradition" grounded in what is "natural" or in cisheterosexual coupling. Perhaps even more queerly bypassing the circuits of straight human-centric reproduction, the Palestinian Talmud details the contribution of woman, man, and God in juxtaposition with the elements that horse and donkey parents, respectively, supply to their mule issue. Thus, human generation is expressed by means of analogy with interspecies generation. Of course, this is in many ways a mixed blessing, as it were, given that humans get to claim divine kinship in a way non-analogous with the dyadic making of mules. But it does demonstrate vividly how either "secularized" or "religious" narrow models of "reproduction" fail to capture the multiplicity of creaturely generation between species, among species, and across realms. An approach that fully integrates the non-human dimensions of Jewish theories of life-making, including that of the human, also allows us to better clarify the ways in which narrow reproductive models do not account for how even contemporary humans propagate, come to be, and create kin.

Variation and Resemblance

The classificatory impulse of the Priestly stratum of the Hebrew Bible is a centerpiece of rabbinic world-making as it pertains to life-forms in their variety. As I show elsewhere, the rabbis not only continue this project of classifying, naming, and enumerating life-forms into distinct and grouped kinds; they also extend it. And yet, they enfold assorted variations within the circuits of generation, including species variation (or dissemblance) and resemblance, which serves to blur the very distinctions they are simultaneously attempting. Two kinds of dissemblance and resemblance serve to illustrate this. The first concerns generative variation, in which one species gestates and delivers progeny that looks like a different species. The second pertains to the uncanny resemblances across what are taken to be distinct species—e.g., a dog and a wolf, or a human and a siren.

Thus, we learn of cases in which a pregnant human "expels something like a species of domesticated animal, wild animal, or bird" (mNidd 3:2), as well as those in which a "cow delivers something like a species of donkey" (mBekh 2:1). Other cases include humans emitting entities like red flies or fish, and cows delivering creatures like camels. With a more-than-human orientation, we read such scenarios together, taking them seriously and resisting the temptation to dismiss the human-emitted cases in contemporary rationalized, medicalized (and seemingly secularized) terms and/or by reading animality metaphorically. These scenarios thrust the human generation of life into the same sorts of variable unpredictability as nonhuman life-forms, thereby upsetting the vaunted image of God, with its exceptionalist human-divine mimetic claims. Before valorizing this, however, it is important to note that there are significant differences between human- and animal-delivered species variation. In human cases, the Mishnah specifies "one who expels"—language of miscarriage to signify that these are nonliving creatures. Not so with animals who "give birth." The difference is one of life and death. So too are the implications of the rabbis' disputes about how to classify such creatures: are they considered progeny and members of their parents' species or not? At stake lie ritual, kinship, lineage, property, and (im)purity determinations. For instance, if the animal-like delivery to a human is considered "offspring," then its nonliving body is a corpse and the parturient is considered to have undergone childbirth with attendant ritual and purity consequences; if the creature is a firstborn assigned male, there are inheritance implications, and so forth. With animals, classification of the camel-like creature delivered by the cow as offspring has consequences for ritual obligations like donation of firstborn animals to God, sacrificial rules about "blemishes," and the permissibility of the ritual slaughter and consumption of the animal by Jews (are they a camel which is impure and forbidden for consumption, or a cow?). In other words, while the details of these scenarios curtail the limits of possibility for the liveness in species' variant deliveries among human parturients, they also determine the ultimate manner of death for the nonhuman deliveries too. The cuts of species distinctions are enacted by means of life and death, viability and killability (per Haraway), and of course, by who does what to whom.

The second kind blurring of creaturely classifications across species is ostensibly driven by the rabbis' concern to parse creaturely life-forms into distinct kinds in order to avoid the prohibition of mating or working different species together (*kilayim*, Lev, Deut). The rabbis curate congeries of creatures whose resemblance—often taken to be a clue to kinship and relatedness—is misleading. For instance, "a wolf and a dog, even though they resemble one another, are forbidden to be combined (*kilayim*) with one another" (mKil 1:6). Ultimately, the rabbis theorize such resemblances, which they identify among multiple species, including the human. They posit a world of territorial doubles which distinguishes look-alike life-forms between those living in settled areas versus wild areas and those living on dry land versus the sea. On the one hand, this explains how different creatures look alike, while seemingly preserving species distinctions, but on the other hand, it troubles the singularity of kinds, including the human who confronts its own doubles of the wild and the sea. The blurry role the human—as both classifier and classified, singular yet doubled—plays in this enterprise of creaturely collection and classification exemplifies how the marking of difference fails to undo the contagion effect of resemblance. The contagion effect of likeness makes for an untamed multiplicity of life which exceeds and escapes a particular species' desire to capture the rest through classification.

Originary Genesis and Ongoing Generation

In emphasizing the queering effect of divine involvement in generation, particularly that of humans, we also hinted at the ways the originary creation serves as a kind of template for their ongoing generation and liveness. A latticework of liturgy also extends the temporality of the primal origination of various life-forms and entities into the present. The performative act of blessing in repeated, prosaic, and everyday contexts, and the very content of many blessings, make divine creation a present-tense, iterative act, converting genesis to *generation*. For example, in mBer 9:1–2, as part of a collection of sight-triggered blessings, one must say "blessed is . . . the one who makes the act of 'in the beginning' (i.e., creation, viz., Gen 1:1)" upon seeing "mountains, hills, seas, rivers, and deserts." Note that this and similar blessings are in the present tense. Many of the blessings over produce and food hail God as "the creator." When consuming produce, one blesses "the one who creates the fruit of the tree," "the one who creates the fruit of the earth," "the one who creates 'species of herb'" (mBer 6:1; par tBer 4:5), "creates species of seeds" (tBer. 4:5). When in doubt, one can bless the one "by whose word all comes to be" (mBer 6:2). Creation's temporal slip into ongoing generation is also enhanced by dubbing present-day humans with disabilities, beautiful trees, and beautiful humans *beriyot*, "creatures" or "created beings." On this register, nonhuman and human creatureliness are simply juxtaposed. Granted, this is no egalitarian creaturely landscape: the rabbis clearly set up a hierarchy of aesthetics and disability, through which "natural" phenomena from constellations to seas, and from humans to plant-life, are framed. The blessings themselves discern between variation or exception that solicits commiseration and those that engender celebration (tBer 6).

Conclusions

Ancient Jewish thought presents multiple and alternate ways of thinking generation; it hails the wondrous origins of various life-forms from unlike matter as well as the constant input of divine creativity including that expressed in different kinds of unexpectedness and variation. All these constitutive elements of life and its generation serve to interrupt a seamless world of "like begets like" and of tight distinctions between life-forms. Despite the significance of image-of-God talk, and its invocation in the proliferation of human life, humans too are part of this interrupted swarm of life and its generation. For them, like other creatures, life comes into existence in a variety of ways, sometimes unpredictably, and often not through dyadic, heterosexual, and same-species generative modes.

Many of these insights about ancient Jewish conceptions of life—and its generation—rest in readings of the evidence that take them seriously and materially, resisting the urge to metaphorize, scientize, rationalize, or "secularize" them along specific lines. It is difficult to square this proliferation of ways of coming into being with a singular, unified, or monolithic "Judeo-Christian tradition" or even "Judaism" grounded in some fixed notion of "nature" or even "creation" (which God is praised as "varied" in one blessing).

As contemporary technoscientific mechanisms for making human and nonhuman lives—from assistive reproductive technologies, cloning, and lab-grown organs and flesh to uterine transplantation—challenge narrow models of reproduction, human supremacy, and ethics of multispecies cohabitation, it is clear that the white, cishetero human dyad is far from the only game in town. A religious studies framework that homes in on life, its making, sustenance, and extinction, can enrich our understandings of generation, kin, and old-new techniques (many of which extrapolate from properties observed over centuries: the capacity of skin, organs, and tissue—human and otherwise—to heal and bind).

In juxtaposing ancient rabbinic notions of generation with contemporary reproduction, I do not mean to suggest identity or analogy between the two, nor to suggest that one set of ideas led to the other. Rather, I mean to highlight the ways in which the strangeness of the former cannot be offset or measured by an appeal to the ordinariness of the present (Chin 2017). Clearly the rabbis of ancient Palestine were not struggling with the complexities of stem cell research, creaturely extinctions, or exploitation, nor with the racialized, gendered, and material conditions that constrain our own thinking and actions. While it may seem obvious that we ought to resist explaining ancient Judaism through the present, even through contrast, it can be especially tempting, with matters related to what we think of (today) as nature, science, and religion, to succumb to narratives of progress, teleology, and triumph. But perhaps by being attuned to how we domesticate the strangeness of our lives, we can cultivate humility as we venture into religious worlds that remain secreted into a variety of material and textual residues. Concomitantly—and this is a harder and different project—by defamiliarizing the present and simultaneously studying other once-presents, now-pasts, we might even become more attuned to the multiplicity of congruities, intricacies, and potentialities nestled within our own now.

Suggested Readings

Butler, Judith. 2004. *Precarious Life: The Power of Mourning and Violence*. London: Verso.

Franklin, Sarah. 2007. *Dolly Mixtures*. Durham, NC: Duke University Press.

Keller, Catherine, and Mary-Jane Rubenstein, eds. 2017. *Entangled Worlds: Religion, Science, and New Materialisms*. New York: Fordham University Press.

Subramaniam, Banu. 2019. *Holy Science: The Biopolitics of Hindu Nationalism*. Seattle: University of Washington Press.

TallBear, Kim. 2017. "Beyond the Life/Not-Life Binary: A Feminist-Indigenous Reading of Cryopreservation, Interspecies Thinking, and the New Materialisms." In *Cryopolitics: Frozen Life in a Melting World*, edited by Joanne Radin and Emma Kowal, 179–202. Cambridge, MA: The MIT Press.

References

Agamben, Giorgio. 1998. *Homo Sacer: Sovereign Power and Bare Life*. Stanford, CA: Stanford University Press.

Barad, Karen Michelle. 2007. *Meeting the Universe Halfway: Quantum Physics and the Entanglement of Matter and Meaning*. Durham, NC: Duke University Press.

Berkowitz, Beth A. 2018. *Animals and Animality in the Babylonian Talmud*. Cambridge: Cambridge University Press.

Boyarin, Daniel. 1991. "Internal Opposition in Talmudic Literature: The Case of the Married Monk." *Representations* 36: 87–113.

Chen, Mel Y. 2012. *Animacies: Biopolitics, Racial Mattering, and Queer Affect*. Durham, NC : Duke University Press.

Chin, C. Mike. 2017. "Marvelous Things Heard: On Finding Historical Radiance." *The Massachusetts Review* 58 (3): 478–91.

Foucault, Michel. 2008. *The Birth of Biopolitics: Lectures at the Collège de France 1978–1979*. New York: Palgrave.

Gaston, K. Healan. 2019. *Imagining Judeo-Christian America: Religion, Secularism, and the Redefinition of Democracy*. Chicago: University of Chicago Press.

Gross, Aaron. 2014. *The Question of the Animal and Religion: Theoretical Stakes, Practical Implications*. New York: Columbia University Press.

Haraway, Donna Jeanne. 2008. *When Species Meet*. Minneapolis: University of Minnesota Press.

Haraway, Donna J. 1997. *Modest–Witness@Second–Millennium.FemaleMan–Meets–OncoMouse: feminism and technoscience*. With paintings by Lynn M. Randolph. New York: Routledge.

Hopwood, Nick, Rebecca Flemming, and Lauren Kassell, eds. 2018. *Reproduction: Antiquity to the Present Day*. Cambridge: Cambridge University Press.

Jackson, Zakiyyah Iman. 2020. *Becoming Human: Matter and Meaning in an Antiblack World*. New York: New York University Press.

Kimmerer, Robin Wall. 2013. *Braiding Sweetgrass*. Minneapolis, MN: Milkweed Editions.

Kueny, K. M. 2013. *Conceiving Identities: Maternity in Medieval Muslim Discourse and Practice*. Albany: SUNY Press.

Lorberbaum, Yair. 2015. *In God's Image: Myth, Theology and Law in Classical Judaism*. Cambridge: Cambridge University Press.

Mbembe, Achille. 2019. *Necropolitics*. Durham, NC: Duke University Press.

Neis, Rafael Rachel. 2023. *When a Human Gives Birth to a Raven: Rabbis and the Reproduction of Species*. Berkeley: University of California Press.

Quashie, Kevin. 2021. *Black Aliveness; or, A Poetics of Being*. Durham, NC: Duke University Press.

Rabinow, Paul, and Nikolas Rose. 2006. "Biopower Today." *BioSocieties* 1 (2): 195–217.

Schaefer, Donovan O. 2015. *Religious Affects*. Durham, NC: Duke University Press.

Raucher, Michal S. 2020. *Conceiving Agency: Reproductive Authority among Haredi Women*. Bloomington: Indiana University Press.

Roberts, Elizabeth F. S. 2012. *God's Laboratory: Assisted Reproduction in the Andes*. Berkeley: University of California Press.

Rothschild, Claire. 2010. "Embryology, Plant Biology, and Divine Generation in the Fourth Gospel." In *Women and Gender in Ancient Religions: Interdisciplinary Approaches*, edited by Stephen P. Ahearne-Kroll et al., 125–51. Tübingen: Mohr Siebeck.

TallBear, Kimberly. 2015. "An Indigenous Reflection on Working Beyond the Human/Not Human." *GLQ* 21: 230–35.

Tandberg, Håkon Naasen. 2019. *Relational Religion: Fires as Confidants in Parsi Zoroastrianism*. Göttingen: Vandenhoeck & Ruprecht.

Thomson, Rosemary Garland. 2017. *Extraordinary Bodies: Figuring Physical Disability in American Culture and Literature*. New York: Columbia University Press.

Todd, Zoe. 2016. "An Indigenous Feminist's Take on the Ontological Turn: 'Ontology' Is Just Another Word for Colonialism." *Journal of Historical Sociology* 29: 4–22.

Watts, Vanessa. 2013. "Indigenous Place-Thought and Agency amongst Humans and Non Humans (First Woman and Sky Woman Go On a European World Tour!)." *Decolonization: Indigeneity, Education & Society* 2: 20–34.

Watts, Vanessa. 2020. "Growling Ontologies: Indigeneity, Becoming-Souls and Settler Colonial Inaccessibility." In *Colonialism and Animality: Anti-colonial Perspectives in Critical Animal Studies*, edited by Kelly Struthers Montford and Chloë Taylor, 115–28. London: Routledge.

Weheliye, Alexander. 2014. *Habeus Viscus: Racializing Assemblages, Biopolitics, and Black Feminist Theories of the Human*. Durham, NC: Duke University Press.

10 MATTER

Matthew Engelke

In the first edition of *Critical Terms for Religious Studies*, there is a chapter on "Belief," by Donald S. Lopez Jr. It begins with the arresting example of Peter of Verona, who was martyred in the thirteenth century. In one painting of the martyrdom, "Martirio di San Pietro da Verona," by Giovanni Battista Moroni, the Dominican saint is on his knees, already bleeding from an axe blow to the head and about to receive another. In his last mortal moments he has managed to index his piety. For on the ground he has written, "CREDO"—I BELIEVE—in the blood pouring forth from his brow.

I believe. "That statement has a long and complicated history in Christian theology, in philosophy, and in writing about religion" (Lopez 1998, 21). In the now classic essay, Lopez charts that history by connecting the rise of religion-as-belief to the rise of Christianity, the Enlightenment, and colonialism. "Belief appears as a universal category because of the universalist claims of the tradition in which it has become most central, Christianity. Other religions have made universalist claims, but Christianity was allied with political power, which made it possible to transport its belief to all corners of the globe . . . making belief the measure of what religion is understood to be" (33). Lopez was putting the finishing touches on a broader, decades-long project seeking to provincialize belief and highlight its partiality with respect to an understanding of religion.

Times have changed. Over twenty years after the publication of Lopez's essay, what many scholars would want to begin with in a consideration of Moroni's painting is not Peter Martyr's declaration of belief, but the medium of its delivery: the *blood*, that is; the matter. Blood, which is both sacred and mundane. Blood, which signals both a presence and an absence. Blood, which is red, and liquid. Blood, which is both fleeting and indelible. Within religious studies matter has risen to the fore—even grabbing us, some might say, to secure a pride of place among rightful concerns. This chapter foregrounds the rise of matter, in part by situating it within longer-standing approaches and sensibilities, and in part by showcasing the work of three scholars whose innovative perspectives exemplify the lasting significance of an attention to matter. As with Peter Martyr's blood, there is something about matter that both grounds and unsettles (the study of) religion.

The rise of matter in religious studies is part of a broader trend within the humanities and social sciences referred to as the "material turn." It takes place against the backdrop of earlier, related trends, glossed as the "linguistic turn" and the "cultural turn." These approaches flourished from the 1960s to the 1990s. They focused intently upon discourse and meaning, often by emphasizing the instability, contingency, and situatedness of each. Power and positionality also mattered; the linguistic and cultural turns were shaped by concerns with forms of inequality, exclusion, and erasure. But increasingly over those decades, the limits of these approaches started to show (all approaches have limits) and to prompt questions. It's not that they were abandoned; it's more like they were reframed. One of the frames most commonly dismantled and then refashioned involved the subject/object distinction, especially with respect to how we understand such interests as contingency, materiality, and agency. Doing so recast some of the driving questions of work in semiotics, epistemology, and ontology. Is "meaning" or significance only ever an issue of the relationship between abstract signs? (This is a semiotic question, forcing the reconsideration of a sign's contingencies.) Must we express what we know, and relations in the world, in terms of subjects and objects, agents and artifacts? (This is an epistemological question, leading on to new understandings of materiality.) What is—or has—life, animacy, or intentionality? (This is an ontological question, prompting new approaches to the understanding of agency and being.) The gist of this material turn can be illustrated by considering actual questions posed by scholars connected to it in some way. So from the media theorist and cultural critic W. J. T. Mitchell (2005), we get: "What do pictures want?" And from the anthropologist Eduardo Kohn (2013), it is: "Can forests think?"

When we talk about a material turn then, we are talking about a fairly specific set of questions and interests. Generally speaking, it is not primarily a concern with carbon dating a relic, the chemical composition of paint chips, speculation over the vitamin intake of fasting penitents, natality rates, or an analysis of remittance practices among migrant laborers. All of these have to do with "matter," or material conditions, and they have their proponents both in academic fields (archaeology, demography) and cross-disciplinary theoretical approaches (cultural ecology, Marxism). But they are not primarily what animates the interest in "material religion." Consider rather how Caroline Walker Bynum, the historian of medieval Christianity, puts it in her collection of essays, *Christian Materiality*: "late medieval devotional objects speak or act their physicality in particularly intense ways that call attention to their per se 'stuffness' and 'thingness'" (2011, 29).

So matter is having a moment. But taking the long view, matter has often fared poorly in those realms deemed religious. This is regularly illustrated in the academic literature and historical glosses by reference to the interwoven aspects and values of the Protestant Reformation, European Enlightenment, and Western colonialism. We caught a glimpse of this earlier, via Lopez's work. His argument about the centrality of belief to our understandings of "religion" is anchored by the concern with theological and political power struggles. But another common quality of belief is its presumed immateriality: belief is what lies *within* and cannot be seen; it is what is *thought*. Belief is understood—or should be understood, in the modern era—as the message, not the medium. In contexts of colonization and reform, this often makes matter a source of trouble and anxiety in which it nearly always loses out to its ostensible other—spirit—in a hierarchical nesting.

Much of the trouble and anxiety can be understood in terms of a problem of presence (Engelke 2007). Are the gods, or God, or the divine, or this angel, or the ancestral dead *here*, and if so, how? How can the invisible, transcendent, disembodied, ethereal, otherworldly, otherwise unknowable, unquantifiable, and/or incalculable be known or sensed? For many Protestant Reformers, and the missionaries who came after them, to be properly religious—and thus properly modern or civilized—was to recognize and emphasize the contingency of things and their primarily *symbolic* function. A thing (icon, crucifix, bread, altar, vestment, amulet, tree) should always be understood as *mere*: representation at best, and not, under any circumstances, presence or identity.

The dematerialization of faith is often associated with Protestant critiques of Catholic tradition and theology. *Relics misguide our attention! Bread and wine are just symbols!* For many Protestants, an emphasis on things has often been a sign of intellectual immaturity, simplicity, or superstition. But projects of reform motivated by theological and political understandings of matter are not unique to a Protestant/Catholic divide. They are not even uniquely Christian. Iconoclasm, asceticism, antimaterialism, and world renunciation, all of which speak to an unease with matter and the body, can be found in many other religious traditions.

But to underscore the suspicion toward matter, let's stick with Christianity for now, highlighting the generality of the point by considering a Catholic case. While Protestants do on occasion and have in certain periods decried the Roman Church's devotion to things—all in favor of such "higher" and "immaterial" forms of expression as the Bible or gifts of the spirit—that doesn't mean Catholics forgo the avenue of material denigration and critique. Arguably, in fact, the most damning charge of dangerous matter comes from the sixteenth-century encounters between Catholic missionaries and merchants on one side, and West African communities on the other. For this is the crucible of colonialism and capitalism out of which that thing called the fetish emerges. "Fetish," or *feitiço* in the original Portuguese, was the term applied to certain African artifacts, such as the BaKongo *nkisi* (statuette), understood to be (in today's language) supernatural. Except they *weren't* properly supernatural (as the Europeans saw it), or just symbols standing for something else. In this nascent Catholic/colonial/capitalist imagination, what marked fetishes, and distinguished them from idols or icons, was their base and wholly immanent materiality. A fetish, in other words, is a kind of (mistaken) pure presence, like spirit and matter combined. It is an oxymoron: naturally supernatural. "The fetish is precisely not a material signifier referring beyond itself, but acts as a material space gathering an otherwise unconnected multiplicity into the unity of its enduring singularity" (Pietz 1985, 15). It is misleading, dangerous stuff, cast into the column of magic, superstition, and savage minds. So, yes: just as much as Protestantism, Catholicism allows for struggles over the propriety of things.

This is often how matter is mobilized in efforts to elevate one's understanding of semiotics and metaphysics over that of others. *You don't understand what matter is, and is not. You are confused about the difference between presence and representation.* One encapsulation of this position and project that I have always found striking comes from the Victorian anthropologist Sir Edward Burnett Tylor: "The strong craving of the human mind for a material support to the religious sentiment, has produced idols and fetishes over most parts of the world, and at most periods in its history; while the more intelligent, even among many low tribes, have often seen clearly enough that the images were mere symbols of superhuman beings, the vulgar have commonly believed that the idols themselves had life and supernatural powers" (Tylor 1865, 121).

Such imperious language is common in projects that seek to dematerialize religion. And while these projects are often driven by theological commitments, they also reflect the ways in which a secular analysis of religion has insisted on making religion something fundamentally immaterial and ideational. More famously than the claim cited above, Tylor gave us a definition of religion that, to this very day, captures much of the presumed ground and brings us full circle in this initial section: religion, for Tylor, is "the belief in Spiritual Beings" (1871, 383). This makes it *doubly* immaterial—if such a thing is possible.

A final point in this section is worth making, one which Tylor's work certainly prompts us to consider, given his emphasis on "the spiritual." This is that, although the concept of "matter" comes to the foreground of much recent work, the point is not to eclipse or outshine any ostensible opposite, such as "spirit." If anything, despite the moniker—as embraced or ascribed—the "material turn" does not usually seek to reinforce such binaries as matter/spirit, or material/immaterial; rather, it seeks to break such binaries down. We will be able to see some of how that works in practice below, as we explore what I referred to above as matter's simultaneously grounding and unsettling properties. Here I would just highlight the points made above about agency and animacy. To ask what a picture wants, after all, is to upend some key tenets of what distinguishes a subject from an object in the first place.

In the remainder of this chapter I focus on three examples of how the interest in matter provides distinctive insights into what religion "is," or can be. Their grouping here should not be taken as a suggestion that the authors would necessarily agree in every detail—or, for that matter, that they would all foreground being part of the material turn. I am using that phrase in this chapter as one of orientation. The very language of "turns" is not something all scholars embrace or find helpful. Sometimes, it can package things too neatly. But there are several shared sensibilities I want to highlight, perhaps above all the manner of seeing religion *otherwise*, of moving away from religious subjects and from their beliefs, of looking not only at what something might mean, but also what it is made of and where it is situated. Are beliefs important? Yes. Should we stop paying attention to ritual action, or the symbolism of an image, or the organization of sacred space? No. But matter points us in new directions. It prompts us both to see familiar things in a new light and to find "religion" in unexpected places.

From Belief to Blood

Let's come back to blood—not Peter Martyr's per se, but a landmark treatment of it, *Wonderful Blood: Theology and Practice in Late Medieval Northern Germany and Beyond*, by Caroline Walker Bynum, the historian so interested in what she calls per se stuffness.

In the late medieval era, a "frenzy for blood" took hold throughout much of northern Europe. In this, no place was more important than Wilsnack, in northern Germany, which became a pilgrimage center rivaling Jerusalem and Rome. In August 1383 the church at Wilsnack was burned by a marauding knight. After inspiration in a dream, a local priest sought out and found the hosts (bread consecrated for the Eucharist) in the ashes, untouched by the fire, daubed in the center by drops of blood. Miracles followed, above all miraculous healing. Pilgrims flocked to the site. For the pilgrims, and their scholastic and clerical champions, the blood miracles were holy matter: Christ's presence. Yet most figures in the Church establishment balked at the notion, and sought to quash this misapprehension—or even fraud. "It is pernicious," wrote one learned critic, ". . . and we cannot permit it without damage to God, for our catholic faith that glorified the body of Christ has glorified blood completely un-seeable in glorified veins" (in Bynum 2007, 28). Plus, he added, the local clergy were swindling "simple folk."

Despite admonishments from elites, the commitment persisted, even surging on occasion over the course of the long fifteenth century. It was not until over a decade after the Reformation took hold in Wilsnack, in the 1550s, that the blood piety subsided. At that point an evangelical pastor burned the hosts. This might be read as a kind of Protestant triumph, but the pastor was subsequently arrested and jailed for six months.

Blood symbolism is rich and complex. Throughout history and across cultures, blood is associated—often simultaneously and even paradoxically—with life and death; war and peace; purity and danger. Borrowing a popular phrase from Claude Lévi-Strauss, blood is also "good to think" with respect to notions of sex, gender, kinship, nation, and race. Throughout her work, Bynum duly notes where any such significance is or is not relevant to the context in question. She documents and acknowledges the extent to which blood obsession tells us something about ecclesiastical and secular politics and strains in the social structure. She also addresses the history and practice of antisemitic blood libel, in Sternberg, Berlin, and elsewhere (2007, 68–81). All of this is central to her interests, but does not exhaust them. In passing over the "insistent materiality" (2011, 35) of blood, Bynum argues, we dilute the strength of our understanding of just how much it reflected soteriological and ontological concerns. Blood, in other words, was not only good to think with respect to salvation, or how to understand Christ's humanity/divinity—it was *good to see*, or *good to have* in proximity. The insistence was its existence.

Bynum's point isn't to dismiss functional explanations, symbolic readings, or, say, Foucauldian analyses of biopolitics and governmentality. But by beginning with blood, rather than what blood *stands for* or tells us about *something else*, she wants to suggest that its materiality—its per se stuffness—demands recognition of those soteriological and ontological concerns. "At heart lay the question of how the unchangeable omnipotent could meet humanity . . . and the deeper question raised by the conviction that salvation came through the bloody death of the God-man who *was* that meeting point" (Bynum 2007, 253–54). How is God nowhere/now here? How does blood's liquidity, or essential role in life, *matter*, in the multiple senses of that word? Through this approach, which is both methodological and theoretical, Bynum also helps us understand medieval approaches to family, society, and politics in new ways. One she explores in great detail concerns blood in droplet form (as at Wilsnack) and spattered or sputtered bits. The droplet form matters, because through it "we begin to develop an analysis of medieval notions of fragmentation and violence, identity and representation, that may have implications for the politics of the period as well as the theology" (2007, 256). So why blood? Because it is blood.

This might smack of essentialism. It need not. Blood piety, and any other form of blood's appeal or relevance, is historically situated. Within Christianity, blood only became central over time. It is certainly important at points in Scripture, but it is not the predetermined Christian substance. Even for the signal event, Christ's death on the cross, the spilling of blood comes after the fact—and only in some accounts. It is only in John, not the Synoptic Gospels, that one of the soldiers pierces Jesus' side, and what the body emits is notably not only blood but also water (John 19: 34). As Bynum herself notes, at the very start of her lengthy book on wonderful blood, "crucifixion is not a bloody death" (2007, 1).

The emphasis on matter here is all about an attention to the ways in which material properties can help shape, or direct, any given thing's functions and significance. As such, every given thing has what many scholars call "affordances." Any given thing's affordances will depend upon the specificity of the situation, and its relation to the other things involved. So on a sunny summer day, you can find relief in the shade of a tree. Here, the affordance of shade is relief. But on a sunny winter day, you do not find relief in the shade of a tree; that comes from shifting to the sun. Any affordance depends on a set of material circumstances, yet they are relational rather than objective. An affordance is material in the sense that it is more than nothing and less than everything. This is how we might think of wonderful blood. Its material properties play a role in the affordance of presence. Blood *is* blood because it is life, yet when enough of it is spilled, it is death, too. Blood *is* blood because it can splatter, or spurt; it coagulates; it dries; it stains; it tastes like iron; it is red. And so on.

From Blood to Bodies

Let us turn now from something given, in a sense, to something made. The importance of matter comes further into view by considering the production and use of certain artifacts. We cannot get far into a discussion of "religious things" this way without coming up against the range of semiotic, epistemological, and ontological issues that matter brings to life. Here I want to consider some recent studies of Hindu gods, priests, potters, sculptors, and politicians; we can even throw mopeds, cars, and trucks into this mix. The accounts featured below, drawing from work in anthropology and art history, are thick with things.

In Soumhya Venkatesan's anthropological studies of Tamil Hindu priests, the problem of presence looks very different from what we find in late medieval Wilsnack. For the Christians, an anxiety always surrounded the propriety of matter such that even in the best of cases, "holy matter" had to be acknowledged as an oxymoron, a paradox without resolution. In many traditions of popular Hinduism, on the other hand, the "problem" with matter is not so much epistemological or ontological as one of engineering. As Venkatesan puts it, "neither divine presence nor animation is the problem. In question, rather, are the materials and techniques deployed in animation and the capacity of animated things" (2020, 455). This is because "popular Hinduism does not distinguish between divinity and the stuff of the material world. Any thing—rocks, trees, people, statues—can be made temporarily or durably divine through ritual. The ensuing relationship between divinity and thing is not one of equivalence or representation but of identity—the thing *is* the god" (448).

Statues of gods are especially common. Venkatesan worked with sculptors and priests connected to two kinds of deities: village deities and Sanskritic deities. According to a caste logic, the latter are superior because more "universal"; village deities are just connected to particular locations. Village deities are served by Potter priests and Sanskritic deities by Brahmin priests. Potter priests are just that—potters. The gods' bodies are made of clay. Sanskritic deities have stone bodies. In each case, the materials of the bodies have to be enlivened in some fashion. First they are shaped, via potter's wheel and sculptor's chisel, into the appropriate anthropomorphic form. This, though, is not the god and is not yet divine. The god in question must be installed with the help of the priests and over the course of ritual action. For Potter priests, an important consideration is the hollowness of the statue, within which the god, as *aavi* (smoke, vapor, gas), will circulate, much like blood in the body of a human. Actual blood is also important for the installation of a village deity; the sacrifice of a chicken, with its blood smeared into the statue's eyes, is what leads to the quickening. For Brahmin priests, the solidity of the stone sculpture is a quality that literally demonstrates its superiority to the stuff of gods at the village level. Stone is both more durable and not likened to a finite container; it does not hold some given quantity of *aavi*, and so cannot be seen as limited in its capacity or existence. Indeed, in both Hindu traditions, where paradox and a certain problem of presence emerges is in the recognition that any given thing at any given time might well be a god, but this fact does not exhaust or fully circumscribe the forms or modes of a divinity's presence. For the Brahmins in particular, there is no difference between god (*swami*) and embodied god (*murti*); all the same, "presence in a murti is changeable, while swami neither reduces nor increases. It just is" (2020, 454).

If clay and stone have certain affordances, each also carries risks and limitations. As Venkatesan reports, the clay that Potter priests have access to has declined in quality over the past several decades; the government has enacted environmental regulations essentially cutting off legal channels for procuring the really good clay. This can lead to uncomfortable situations, such as one, related by Venkatesan, in which an old, chipped, and dropping-stained village god image was not replaced and reseated out of the attendant priest's concern with causing offense. Although damaged, the existing body was made of an excellent clay, the quality of which could not be matched on the contemporary market. The priest had not been able to secure the deity's agreement to its reseating in a new clay body. So the priest just had to wait, anxiously. Not that quality of clay is the only solution. Other Potter priests have already made the switch to using stone, even calling upon the service of Brahmins, for whom the material and attendant rituals are well known. Here, then, matter becomes a literal medium of struggle over micro-level authority and control. For one Potter priest with whom Venkatesan worked closely, the changing times were deeply distressing. He was not happy that fellow priests had shifted their practices and views on the appropriate mediums for divine embodiment.

It's quite clear from Venkatesan's ethnography that in studying "religion," a lot of what she was observing and coming to understand were the technical and ritual processes through which matter was literally shaped. To read her work is to read about rituals, for sure—a well-worn topic in the study of "religion." But it is also to read about potters' sheds blanketed in plaster dust, the effects of government environmental preservation policies on sources and quality of clay, the affordances of a clay sculpture's hollowness versus a stone sculpture's solidity, how blood flows out of a sacrificed chicken's severed leg, the sound vibrations of a mantra, and even differences between types of granite. Her point, and a key point of the material turn more generally, is that this stuff is also the religion. It is not simply the vehicle, or the dressing, or the environmental context. What we see here is a shift in framing, an approach that reveals matter's centrality to what religion is at any given time and place. Things feed in to theologies, if you will, and vice versa; things are bound up with beliefs, with practices, with expressions and instantiations. Matter is primary not secondary.

The Matter of the Monumental

So you can be studying religion by studying clay. It—"religion"—can take such a material, sensible form. But if matter makes religion so solid, the material turn is also an excellent reminder of religion's instability. The more it is *there*, you might say, the more we realize it is *nowhere*. The work of an art historian, Kajri Jain, can help us appreciate this point. Her monograph, *Gods in the Time of Democracy*, for example, both is and is not about religion.

Something new began happening throughout India in the 1980s. The gods started coming out of the temples. They went public, and they slowly proliferated, dotting the cityscapes and even the horizons of the highways.

The gods got bigger, too—much bigger—than most of their forebears. Monumental, really. By the 2000s, these new icons were often topping 75 feet high, and sometimes even 100 feet.

Then in 2018, the gods were joined by a secular figure: India's first home minister and deputy prime minister, Sardar Vallabhbhai Patel. His statue trumped them all by a long shot, reaching a phenomenal 597 feet, or nearly twice the height of the Statue of Liberty. Patel's is known as "the Statue of Unity," though it is a version of unity put forward by a staunch Hindu nationalist, the Indian Prime Minister Narendra Modi. Jain refers to the Statue of Unity as "secular," but here that term takes on a very specific and limited meaning. It is not an icon of a god, to be sure, but it cannot be understood outside of its relations with the gods and their monumental emergence, nor the Prime Minister's Hindu chauvinism. As Jain puts it, "religious icons feed into secular power, while secular figures partake of iconic efficacy and animation" (2021, 4).

The emergence of monumental icons in India was made possible by a confluence of factors, including liberalization of the economy, wealthy patrons, the rise of Hindu nationalism, the rise of anti-caste sentiments, and India's growing sense of its place in the global world order. Bound up with these all were what we saw in Venkatesan's work concerning the shifting opinions of some Potter priests about legitimate mediums for divine embodiment. But in this larger, national-level case, the choice wasn't between clay and stone—each a canonical material in its own right. It involved a more fundamental paradigm shift to that most modern of substances: cement. Without such a material as cement, going big would have had to remain a dream. There is only so high a clay icon can be, given its infrastructural requirements and material qualities. Cement, on the other hand, is cheap, easy to mold, quick to set, and reliably sturdy. "This plasticity has made concrete available to aspirational projects of self-fashioning, social mobility, and political legitimation at a range of scales" (Jain 2021, 31). It also made cement an essential element in the gods' new form of publicity.

Several aspects of the gods' public presence speak to religious dynamics and concerns. The gods' there-ness matters; they become accessible to the pious and even just the curious in new ways, no longer attended to, and mediated by, a temple priest—or at least not in the well-worn ways. The accessibility gives critics of elitism and hierarchy a literal form of support for more direct, personal, and unmediated forms of devotion. As Jain reports, one 85-foot cement statue of Shiva, erected by an ultra-wealthy businessman next to a national highway, and just opposite Delhi's airport, has become the object of what she calls "drive-by devotion" (2021, 140). Men stop on their mopeds by the side of the road to practice *darshan*, the ritual act of "seeing and being seen" by the god. Some of these obeisances might be one-offs, but given this Shiva's prominent location, regular commuters have the opportunity to fold such practices into their work-related routines and the flow of urban life. The site itself has become something of a (theme) park, with smaller icons of other gods going up over the years and a playground for children installed. People come to this "park" to worship, but they can also pose for pictures with the gods (often prohibited within the sanctum of the temple), indulge in plane-spotting, have a picnic, or let the children frolic. So the park both is and is not a "religious" site, then, a paradox made possible by the affordances of its material makeup. "Whatever the aims with which the space was conceived, as its heterogeneous idioms came into everyday use, it turned into a mixed-use space in which people seemed intuitively to know what to do and how to be, drawing on their experiences of temples, roadside deities, pilgrimages, 'spiritual' spaces, tourist sites, historical monuments, and public parks" (144).

"Mixed use": an apt phrase. It captures something central to what is sometimes referred to as theory and method in the study of religion, and what the turn to matter can add to it. Because as Jain shows, matter relates to both theory and method. Jain situates her work in, and on, particular sites; it is very literally grounded in space and time. As such, however—through, that is, such a *concrete* focus—we get something much more fluid and unfixed. Sometimes a god is a god, but sometimes it is a statue in a park to marvel at, or—in line with an example sketched earlier—a welcome source of shade for picnickers. Hers is an approach "holding under erasure master concepts such as culture, art, nation, modernity, and—crucially in this case—religion while *also* attending to their undeniable salience." So "the object here is both theoretical and empirical, generic and singular: it is the monumental statue genre as assemblage, massive, physical, proliferating, changing, and, above all, growing" (2021, 10).

Conclusion

So we can see how Jain's work both is and is not about religion. It is about matter, really, what matter both wants and affords—what it grounds and unsettles. The present and the absent, the high and the low, the natural and the made. At one point Jain says she is interested in "what people do with icons and what icons do with people" (2021, 123). Effecting a kind of figure-ground reversal, or recalibration of the senses, all the work discussed in this chapter reconsiders what counts as the religious in religious studies. Through such a recalibration, it can make sense to say that blood is religion, clay is religion, cement is religion. The turn to matter is a turn away from the subject *as such*, her beliefs *as such*, the temple *as such*. Not, mind you, a complete turning away—but a material turning. Blood, clay, and cement can show how the qualities of things—the per se stuffness—are not incidental to theological or religious perspectives and practices. Such things are both objects *and* subjects, yet also never fully captured in binary terms. When we consider blood's elemental qualities, linger in the potter's shed, and account for the engineering potentials of cement, the sensibility and framing of the study of religion shifts in marked ways.

Suggested Readings

Bennett, Jane. 2010. *Vibrant Matter: A Political Ecology of Things*. Durham, NC: Duke University Press.

Brown, Peter. 1981. *The Cult of the Saints: Its Rise and Function in Latin Christianity*. Chicago: University of Chicago Press.

Engelke, Matthew. 2012. "Material Religion." In *The Cambridge Companion to Religious Studies*, edited by Robert A. Orsi, 209–29. Cambridge: Cambridge University Press.

Houtman, Dick, and Birgit Meyer, eds. 2012. *Things: Religion and the Question of Materiality*. New York: Fordham University Press.

Keane, Webb. 2007. *Christian Moderns: Freedom and Fetish in the Mission Encounter*. Berkeley: University of California Press.

Morgan, David. 2021. *The Thing about Religion: An Introduction to the Material Study of Religions*. Chapel Hill: University of North Carolina Press.

Rambelli, Fabio. 2007. *Buddhist Materiality: A Cultural History of Objects in Japanese Buddhism*. Palo Alto, CA: Stanford University Press.

Scheer, Monique, Nadia Fadil, and Birgitte Schepelern Johansen, eds. 2020. *Secular Bodies, Affects, and Emotions: European Configurations*. London: Bloomsbury.

References

Bynum, Caroline Walker. 2007. *Wonderful Blood: Theology and Practice in Late Medieval Northern Germany and Beyond*. Philadelphia: University of Pennsylvania Press.

Bynum, Caroline Walker. 2011. *Christian Materiality: An Essay on Religion in Late Medieval Europe*. New York: Zone Books.

Engelke, Matthew. 2007. *A Problem of Presence: Beyond Scripture in an African Church*. Berkeley: University of California Press.

Jain, Kajri. 2021. *Gods in the Time of Democracy*. Durham, NC: Duke University Press.

Kohn, Eduardo. 2013. *How Forests Think: Toward an Anthropology Beyond the Human*. Berkeley: University of California Press.

Lopez, Donald J. 1998. "Belief." In *Critical Terms for Religious Studies*, edited by Mark Taylor, 21–35. Chicago: University of Chicago Press.

Mitchell, W. J. T. 2005. *What Do Pictures Want? The Lives and Loves of Images*. Chicago: University of Chicago Press.

Pietz, William. 1985. "The Problem of the Fetish, I." *RES: Anthropology and Aesthetics* 9: 5–17.

Tylor, E. B. 1865. *Researches into the Early History of Mankind and the Development of Civilization*. London: John Murray.

Tylor, E. B. 1871. *Primitive Culture: Researches into the Development of Mythology, Philosophy, Religion, Art, and Custom*. London: John Murray.

Venkatesan, Soumhya. 2020. "Object, Subject, Thing: Tamil Hindu Priests' Material Practices and Practical Theories of Animation and Accommodation." *American Ethnologist* 47 (4): 447–60.

11 MEMORY

Ryan Coyne

Over the past few decades, the explosion of scholarly interest in memory as a "critical idiom" (Whitehead 2009) has generated a new multidisciplinary field of inquiry called "memory studies." A vast array of intellectual apparatuses now supports it: journals, book series, and professorships; university centers, international working groups, and conferences. The field's growth rate is staggering. The Memory Studies Association's website includes a non-exhaustive list of more than sixty academic centers devoted chiefly or exclusively to memory studies, the majority of which were founded during the last ten years.[1] If we factor in the proliferation of what Pierre Nora and Jay Winter, among others, call "sites of memory" (Nora 1996, 19; Winter 1995)—e.g., museums, memorials, archives—it seems that scholars are justified in underscoring the near ubiquity of memory practices in the contemporary world (Huyssen 1995 and 2003; Ricoeur 2006, 90). Practitioners of memory studies, however, are no less quick to highlight a seeming contradiction: while they insist upon the omnipresence of memory, they often claim that cultures around the globe today suffer from a deficit of it, that an inveterate presentism has taken hold of us, and that the current obsession with memory in and beyond the academy evinces a series of anxieties regarding its fragility, if not its demise. As Nora famously puts it, "memory is constantly on our lips because it no longer exists" (Nora 1996, x). Such anxieties run deep, and they are often encoded in cultural, political, and epistemological terms: large-scale displacement of peoples in a globalized world, the relentless politicization of memory practices, the investigation

1. See https://www.memorystudiesassociation.org/centers-and-projects/.

of traumas and historical catastrophes including the Holocaust, colonialism, genocide, and ongoing human rights violations are all seen as raising crucial questions about the nature of testimony, the representability of the past, and the rise of cultural amnesia. Moreover, there is the added suspicion that information technology and new media are radically transforming memory itself, or at least how we think about memory.

How do these developments bear upon the academic study of religion? Jonathan Z. Smith suggests that during the nineteenth and twentieth centuries, religious studies scholars subsumed memory into other categories such as myth, ritual, and tradition (Smith 1982, 19–36; Smith 1987, 24–46). This is arguably no longer the case: the constitution of memory as a discrete object of inquiry disentangles it from other terms of analysis. Has the field of memory studies lent its central term a new critical valence, one that is applicable in religious studies? If we start by broadly mapping applications of this idiom, several trends become evident: (1) the prevalence in religious studies of collective memory and allied concepts to demarcate the sociocultural specificity of religion; (2) definitions of religion itself as a kind of memory practice; (3) sustained reflection on questions concerning testimony and the ethics of representation; and (4) the role of mnemotechnics in religious practice. The first two trends are rooted in the social-scientific investigation of religion. The third draws heavily upon trauma studies, Holocaust studies, and psychoanalysis, whereas the fourth encompasses a wide range of work including ritual studies and the study of esotericism. The concept of collective memory exerts a strong gravitational pull on all four trends. The central question is thus to what extent it can yield new insights about the meaning and function of religion in the contemporary world.

It is well known that Enlightenment theories of religion are largely responsible for the secularization thesis, which states that modernization leads to the decline and eventual disappearance of religious belief. Widely influential until the last two decades of the last century, this thesis is currently viewed with suspicion. As Peter Berger proclaimed more than twenty years ago, "the assumption that we live in a secularized world is false. The world today . . . is as furiously religious as it ever was, and in some places more so than ever" (Berger 1999, 2). We might expect that, from the vantage point of cultural theory bent on complicating or even rejecting the secularization thesis, the proclivity for defining religion primarily in terms of memory—that religion is somehow *of the past* (as Aristotle says of memory itself)—would fall by the wayside. Yet when we look at the intersection of memory studies and religious studies, we see that the proclivity to view religion as a remnant or relic of the past is still a prominent feature of our theoretical landscape.

In part this is a function of the strategy adopted in early twentieth-century sociological theory, which emphatically rejects the notion that memory is exclusively or even primarily an individual affair. This latter assumption is prevalent throughout the modern European philosophical tradition, in the rationalist and empiricist branches alike. In common parlance, memory is deeply personal; individuals alone possess it in the proper sense. In *Matter and Memory* (1896), the French philosopher Henri Bergson offers a robust defense of this view. For Bergson, memory is the preserve of spirit, irreducible to the function of the brain or any other portion of the body. Memory in its purest sense is the activity of storing the past and bringing it to bear upon the present. As such it is the highest expression of individual freedom. The French sociological tradition rejects this defense of individual memory as hopelessly metaphysical, imbuing memory with a new critical force by rethinking it as a fundamentally collective endeavor. In "The Social Frameworks of Memory," Maurice Halbwachs, a student of Durkheim, claims that all memory, even the most private, is inextricably intertwined in social and cultural collectivities. For Halbwachs, as Paul Connerton writes, "the idea of individual memory, absolutely separate from social memory, is an abstraction almost devoid of meaning" (Connerton 1989, 37). Taking his cue from Durkheim's classic work, *The Elementary Forms of Religion*, Halbwachs argues that both the form and the content of individual memory are utterly dependent upon networks of sociocultural relations, which bestow upon individual memories the repositories of shared investments, ideas, and narratives that lend the past its meaning. For Halbwachs, collectivities themselves may be said to possess memory in the proper sense. Moreover, collective memory is living memory; Halbwachs indexes its reach to the average human lifespan, fatefully distinguishing between memory and history: whereas living memory maintains a continuity between past and present, historical inquiry posits a break between the two. The distinction, however, remains unstable: Halbwachs often extends the reach of living memory into a deep, almost unreachable past. This is particularly evident in his discussion of religion. Religion for Halbwachs is essentially a mode of collective memory, a way of organizing time in terms of truths that are "atemporal in nature" (Halbwachs 1992, 88). By this Halbwachs means not only truths relating to eternity or what surpasses the march of time. He also means truths that are linked to historical events as commemorated, memorialized, and/or ritually reenacted—a relation to the past which he describes in terms of *fixation*: "What is peculiar to the memory of religious groups is that, while the memories of other groups permeate each other mutually and tend to correspond, the memory of religious groups claims to be fixed once and for all" (Halbwachs 1992, 91–93). Halbwachs goes so far as to suggest that fixation on the past is not simply one trait of religion among others. Rather, it is religion's defining characteristic: "religion aims at preserving unchanged through the course of time the remembrance of an ancient period without any admixture of subsequent remembrances" (Halbwachs 1992, 93). If we turn to contemporary memory studies with this in mind, not only do we find endless variations on Halbwachs's theme of collective memory, but we also find endless variations on his penchant for defining religion primarily in terms of mnemic fixations.

In *Religion and Cultural Memory*, Jan Assmann echoes Halbwachs in arguing that the analysis of collectivities alone sheds light on the inner workings of individual memory, yet he also claims that Halbwachs fails to account for the ways in which memory functions as a "cultural institution made visible in signs, symbols, images, texts, and rituals" (Assmann 2006, 95). Assmann contends that, by limiting living memory to make room for history, Halbwachs obscures the genuinely diachronic character of memory in its temporal depth. Combining Nietzsche, Sigmund Freud, and Aby Warburg, while drawing upon the modern hermeneutic tradition, Assmann outlines an alternative version of the interplay between individual and collective memory that he and Aleida Assmann call "cultural memory"—namely, the retention and transmission of the past by means of cultural artifacts such as texts, monuments, and acts of commemoration including recitation and ritual observance. The theory of cultural memory aims to provide "a typological description of different cultures" (Assmann 2006, 95). Here, religion is once again depicted as a mode of memory. Thus, despite his criticisms of collective memory, there is a deep consonance between Assmann and Halbwachs, one that resonates with much of the recent work being done on religion in cultural studies. At the same time, the concept of cultural memory marks the point at which cultural theory reconnects with the metaphysical approach spurned by Halbwachs: Bergson differentiates between pure memory and what he calls habitual memory, understood as the accumulation of automatic, mechanical behaviors that are predominantly bodily in nature. The concern with habit and mnemonics, also reflected in the theory of cultural memory, plays a leading role in ritual studies. Examples of this abound. One such example is Mary Douglas's remark in *Purity and Danger*: "The mnemonic action of rites is very familiar. When we tie knots in handkerchiefs we are not magicking our memory but bringing it under the control of an external sign. So ritual focuses our attention by framing; it enlivens the memory and links the present with the relevant past. In all this it aids perception. Or rather, it changes perception because it changes the selective principle" (Douglas 1966, 65). This is precisely the kind of perspective that a concept such as cultural memory, as opposed to collective memory, is meant to furnish when it comes to religion. The task for so many theorists of culture is to show how institutionalized forms of memory, in their temporal depth, inform individual ways of perceiving the present and anticipating the future. Thus, while scholars such as Francis Yates, Mary Carruthers, and Janet Coleman have done pathbreaking work on the meaning and function of mnemonic techniques and practices, theorists of collective and cultural memory describe memory itself as the crucible in which large-scale religious imaginaries are forged and maintained.

In *Religion as a Chain of Memory* (2000), Danièle Hervieu-Léger agrees that religion may be defined by the relationship it establishes with the past, though she describes this relationship in terms of authority rather than fixation. As she writes elsewhere, "there is no religion without the explicit, semi-explicit, or entirely implicit invocation of the *authority of a tradition*, an invocation that serves as support for the act of believing. Within this perspective, one designates as 'religious' all forms of believing that justify themselves, first and foremost, upon the claim of their inscription within a *heritage of belief*" (Hervieu-Léger 2008, 256). The notion that religion essentially involved being inscribed within a heritage is paramount for Hervieu-Léger: "the religious group defines itself objectively and subjectively as a *chain of memory*, whose continuity transcends history. The existence of this chain is attested to and made manifest by the specifically religious act that consists in the remembrance (anamnesis) of the past, which gives meaning to the present and contains the future" (2008, 257). Here what binds religion to memory is not simply the activity of storing, recollecting, and retrieving a certain past, as in Halbwachs. It is rather the notion of the memory chain—evoking memory as an association of ideas—that constitutes religion in its diachronic character while assigning it a sociocultural location. One could argue that this approach to religion, no less than the typological aspiration we encountered in Assmann, belies what the French philosopher Paul Ricoeur sees as "the positivist prejudice"

(Ricoeur 2006, 124) at work in modern sociological forms of analysis: the shift to collective memory risks reifying its object of inquiry and recapitulating the metaphysical tendencies it seeks to forestall in discussions of individual memory. Even if they avoid this pitfall, applications of collective memory and its variants in religious studies tend to be functionalist in character: they explain religion in terms of its social utility. Moreover, the effort to define religion as memory runs up against a curious feature of modern historiography—namely, its close ties with secular modernity. These ties predispose scholars to associate religion not just with memory per se, but with an obsolescent past. Indeed, this predisposition is evident throughout the history of religious studies. We see it at work, for instance, in the evolutionary undertones of certain nineteenth-century and early twentieth-century thinkers such as E. B. Tylor and James Frazer. And yet, if the contemporary inheritors of the French sociological tradition are any indication, this predisposition to view religion as though it were fundamentally *of the past* continues to linger.

One of the predominant themes in religious studies over the past two generations is a case in point: the so-called "return" of religion provides the impetus to contest, if not overturn, the secularization thesis, yet it cannot avoid giving the impression that the return in question is that of a unsettled or unfinished past. In *The Writing of History*, Michel de Certeau argues that modern history "essentially begins with the differentiation between the present and the past. In this way, it is unlike tradition (religious tradition), though it never succeeds in being entirely dissociated from this archeology, maintaining with it a relation of indebtedness and rejection" (de Certeau 1992, 2). This remark explains why the tie between religion and memory is so powerful. Yet it also reinforces the perceived opposition between religion and the present. In de Certeau, for whom social-scientific and humanistic inquiry secure the intelligibility of their concepts and shore up their disciplinary boundaries by staging encounters with alterity or otherness, religiosity is often cast in the role of otherness par excellence. De Certeau's interest lies in investigating the ways in which the past acts at a distance on the present, not unlike the way the Freudian unconscious exerts a certain pressure on everyday conscious life. De Certeau maintains that the recollective gaze is not neutral. For him, the (religious) past is destined to inflect this gaze, often in uncanny ways. De Certeau thus insists that historiography is never dissociated from the religious phenomena it seeks to conjure. And he charges the historiographical operation with uncovering the lingering effects religions exert upon the putatively secular present, much along the lines of what Anne Whitehead calls "the power of the past over the present" (Whitehead 2009, 100). Such a theoretical stance cannot but reinforce the conceptual link between religion and memory.

In this sense, de Certeau's theoretical framework calls to mind the tendency among some scholars to depict Judaism, Christianity, and Islam as "memory religions." As Elie Wiesel puts it, "To be a Jew is to remember" (Wiesel 1990, 30). The centrality of memory in Judaism is arguably encapsulated by the ritual significance accorded to Deuteronomy 6:4: "Hear O Israel, the Lord our God, the Lord is One." As Harald Weinrich asserts, "the covenant stipulates that Israel must honor God's name and live in strict accordance with his law and that God in return will forever protect Israel with his mighty hand. Thus God will never forget his chosen people so long as this people does not in any way forget its God" (Weinrich 2004, 21). For Weinrich, the command never to forget infuses the entirety of Jewish life. One could offer a similar account of Christianity—as indeed Weinrich does—or of Islam. We need only consult Surah 2 (Al-Baqarah) to see the extent to which memory sustains the divine-human relationship in the Qur'an. Still, this persistent tendency only sharpens the perceived divide between religion and the modern historiographical operation as de Certeau describes it. The irresolvable tension between the two is a central concern for Yosef Yerushalmi: "Memory and modern historiography stand, by their very nature, in radically different relations to the past. The latter represents, not an attempt at a restoration of memory, but a truly new kind of recollection" (Yerushalmi 1982, 94). For Yerushalmi, while memory and history ensure that the past lives on, they carry out this task in diametrically opposed ways. Not unlike de Certeau, he notes that while memory roots the unfolding of time in a primordial historical event of unparalleled significance, the historiographical operation dissolves every devotional bond to rediscover the past in its truth. Here memory and religion are less critical tools than they are objects of critique. Accordingly, Yerushalmi contends that scholars of religion who seek to maintain their religious commitments are caught in the revolving door of an irresolvable contradiction. He thus sees religious studies as the site of a perpetual war between two antithetical impulses, as embodying "the unending competition," as Ricoeur writes, "between memory's vow of faithfulness and the search for truth in history" (Ricoeur 2006, 500). And it is precisely because religion is so radically excluded from the modern historiographical operation, as de Certeau argues, that philosophers, historians, and critical theorists so often associate it with a traumatic or unrepresentable past, transforming religion itself into a symbol of historical catastrophe.

:::

Let us forgo further examining the intersection between memory studies and religious studies—prematurely, as a fuller account would need to address topics such as the rise of post-memory as well as the impact of information technology and social media on our understanding of memory. Our brief discussion of this intersection yields a twofold hypothesis: on the one hand, attempts at defining religion as memory tend to resonate with the self-understanding of religious thinkers embedded in specific scriptural traditions (those of Judaism, Christianity, and Islam), thereby potentially skewing in their favor the application of memory as a critical term for religious studies. On the other hand, the act of defining religion in terms of memory transposes onto collectivities the powers that rationalist and empiricist thinkers often accord to memory as the guarantor of individual identity. Accounts of collective memory, in other words, are theoretically speaking no less problematic than those definitions of individual memory they seek to displace.

If we step back from the uses of memory heavily inflected by memory studies, another critical redeployment of the term comes into view, one tied to the recent proliferation of the *genealogical method*. Derived mainly from the writings of the German philosopher Friedrich Nietzsche and the French philosopher Michel Foucault, genealogy has become virtually ubiquitous in the humanities and social sciences, though it is admittedly deployed with varying degrees of rigor. In those scholarly contexts where genealogy is synonymous with historical inquiry, it is difficult to specify what is gained by its uses. In other cases, however, its practitioners suggest that it functions as a memory practice harboring the potential to volatilize entire fields of inquiry. It is worth exploring these claims in greater detail, albeit cautiously. The potential accorded to genealogy stems from several of its features that are prominent in Nietzsche's descriptions of it: first, genealogy reveals the historical origins of categories, ideas, and sentiments that we tend to think of as ahistorical, natural, or neutral; second, it rejects teleological explanations of historical contingencies; third, it insists upon the pervasiveness of power dynamics, laying bare the hidden operations of power in often unexpected ways. Since the 1993 publication of Talal Asad's *Genealogies of Religion: Discipline and Reasons of Power in Christianity and Islam*, if not before, genealogical inquiry has played an outsized role in the study of religion, where its sights have been trained mainly on the constitution of categories scholars use to ascribe meaning to sociological, anthropological, and cultural data. Following Asad, the genealogical method is often used to erode confidence in the use of analytic categories, including religion itself, as neutral or non-ideological descriptors. It does so by treating such categories as historical artifacts produced by, and productive of, certain power relations, often in the vein of post-colonialism.

Genealogy crucially fits within our discussion of memory as critical tool not only because it is so often enlisted to rethink the constitution of religion and related categories—as though recalling, and calling the entire field back to, forgotten aspects of its history—but also because memory itself plays a central role in its methodology. This is particularly clear in Foucault's reception of Nietzschean genealogy. For Foucault as for Nietzsche, genealogy is not so much a ready-made tool as it is a certain posture or attitude. Embodying what Foucault calls "the permanent critique of our historical era" (Foucault 1997, 312), the genealogical method cannot be reduced to a set of principles that are then applied to various objects of inquiry. To treat genealogy as a tool or even as a stable and timeless *method* of reasoning would be to belie the central Nietzschean insight that nothing is ahistorical. In every instance, genealogy is charged with constructing what Foucault calls "a counter-memory, i.e. a transformation of history into a totally different form of time" (Foucault 1998, 385). Foucault's appeal to counter-memory lies at the heart of what he takes to be the promise of genealogy. The question is thus how genealogy in this sense may continue to serve as a key critical resource for religious studies. This question in turn bears directly upon the distinctive contribution of religious studies to the humanistic and social-scientific inquiry broadly speaking.

Asad is just one of many scholars who argue that genealogy promises to transform the study of religion. Similar arguments may be found in the work of scholars such as Tomoko Masuzawa, Russell McCutcheon, Saba Mahmood, Daniel Boyarin, Guy Stroumsa, Azim Nanji, M. Gail Hamner, and Bernard Faure, among others, all of whom are united in their conviction that there is a pressing need to develop new analytic tools for understanding religion. In Asad's case, genealogy undermines the notion that the category of religion may be understood as a universal phenomenon. In the opening chapter of *Genealogies of Religion*, Asad famously targets Clifford Geertz's highly influential definition of religion in *The Interpretation of Cultures*. For our purposes, the details of this criticism are less important than the conclusions Asad draws from it. Asad claims, first, that every attempt to establish the universality of a category such as religion or ritual necessarily overlooks the authorizing processes by which these concepts are created; second, that such categories are ideologically encoded products of "historically distinctive disciplines and forces" (Asad 1993, 54). As such, they cannot be unproblematically applied to sociocultural data. Rather, they must be resolved into the "heterogeneous elements" (Asad 1993, 54) they comprise. The result is an unmistakable skepticism or agnosticism on Asad's part regarding the use of general and/or universal analytic categories. Indeed, Asad dwells at great length on the ways in which the theoretical search for the essence of religion simultaneously disconnects religion itself from questions concerning power and discursivity. The advantages of such an approach are readily apparent: by reinscribing the essence of religion within the context of discursive practices, Asad makes good on the Nietzschean injunction that genealogy must reveal as historical what we naively take to be ahistorical. Asad thus employs genealogy as a memory practice for the field in general, calling it back to the ways in which it remains implicated in a set of power dynamics that, he contends, must be traced back to early modernity.

But, as Asad's critics point out, the disadvantages of his genealogical approach are no less evident: on the one hand, the genealogical stance seems to exhaust itself in revealing the constructed character of analytic categories. That is, it is primarily concerned with revealing a lack of fit between construct and reality. And by purporting to let reality speak back against its ill-fitting constructs, genealogy risks falling back into inert forms of empiricism and/or representationalism. Moreover, precisely because genealogists see power as all-pervasive, they fail to provide meaningful criteria for adjudicating among competing uses of analytic categories: if all categories are historically contingent—products of discursive power—it does not follow from the revelation that a particular category is historically contingent or embedded in power that the category in question is inapplicable or unworkable. Further, if we trace the genealogical analysis of power back to its roots, we find that it is ineluctably tied to the Nietzschean critique of the will to truthfulness. Genealogy, such critics maintain, is necessarily relativistic, if not intrinsically nihilistic. If it does not show itself to be relativistic in its current usages, this is only because its inheritors fail acknowledge its true character—that is, they fail to treat the genealogical method itself genealogically.

This last criticism tempts us to revisit the three essays comprising *On the Genealogy of Morality*, where Nietzsche first elaborates the notion of genealogy at length while analyzing the concepts of good and evil; guilt and the origin of bad conscience; and the meaning of what he calls the ascetic ideal (Nietzsche 2007). In the second essay Nietzsche famously discusses memory—not, however, as though it were an innate mental faculty, but rather as a capacity that has its own history, itself as a product of power relations. The faculty of memory is not innate within us. It is historically produced. Indeed, Nietzsche surmises that it was produced during the early history of humanity primarily by practices such as torture and punishment. Here Nietzsche acknowledges that genealogy treats the history of a concept as "a continuous sign-chain of ever new interpretations and adaptations," such that its past can never dictate its strategic function in the present. Turning to Foucault, we see that the negative or critical function of genealogy foregrounded in the work of Asad and other scholars of religion has a particular orientation: it is meant to "give a new impetus to the work of freedom" (Foucault 1998, 315). In Asad's case, genealogy is not primarily destructive. Far from suppressing critical reflection on religion per se, it is meant to open spaces in which religious studies scholars reimagine anew how they constitute their own objects of study. In this sense, genealogical critique is not primarily a matter of rejecting as hopelessly inert certain analytic tools by revealing their entanglements in histories of power relation. Both Nietzsche and Foucault insist that genealogy is principally emancipatory in character, opening new spaces of discourse and even new discursive practices. This crucial point often goes unacknowledged, particularly in current discussions surrounding the so-called limits of critique. It is especially relevant for combatting the claim that genealogy is hopelessly relativistic. At its best, criticism neither stifles innovation nor exhausts itself in undermining the use of analytic categories. Rather, it must safeguard the unconditionality of free inquiry and free expression. Foucault for instance insists that the act of delimiting conceptual categories always serves the purpose of transgressing their limits.

Genealogy takes shape in Foucault's corpus at a moment when the pressing demand for political transformation leads him to revise the stakes of what he calls archeology, or the search for origins. The archeological orientation of Foucault's work through the late 1960s prioritizes two questions: how norms are established for the enunciation of truth-claims; and how mutations affecting these norms alter what counts as a truth-claim. Archeology trains its attention on *epistemes*—i.e., the totalities of discursive practices that determine which forms of thought are possible and/

or inescapable at a given time. Genealogy asks after regimes of truth. It interrogates the positivity of power, its capacity to produce social realities.

For our purposes, this shift displays two distinct methodological advantages when it comes to theorizing memory as a term of critical inquiry. First, Foucault explicitly states that the genealogical stance precludes the possibility of framing any existing sociocultural phenomenon as if it were "the reactivated remnants of an ideology" (Foucault 1977, 29). In emphasizing the productivity of power, genealogy correlates present data with technologies of power. This implies that genealogy, in principle and in fact, resists falling prey to the temptation that, as we saw above, is so deeply ingrained in modern historiography and religious studies alike—namely, the temptation to see religion itself, like memory, as being *of the past*; to interpret its present reality as the persistence or spectral return of the premodern. Second, Foucault's notion of counter-memory displaces the break between memory and history as discussed above. In "Nietzsche, Genealogy, History," he claims that genealogy rejects the continuity of tradition as well as the history as remembrance. This means that genealogy neither recovers from the past "works, actions, and creations" that offer to the present a set of stable "alternative identities," nor retrieves from the past "forgotten identities eager to be reborn" (Foucault 1997, 385f.). In so doing, it undoes, rather than shores up, the illusion that knowledge somehow "detaches itself from its empirical roots," elevating subjects of knowledge to the level of "pure speculation subject only to the demands of reason" (1997, 385f.). When Foucault contends that genealogy calls for the dissolution of the subject of knowledge (*connaissance*), he does not lapse into relativism. Far from it: he claims instead that genealogy enacts systemic changes affecting the very conditions for the possibility of knowledge (*savoir*). In so doing, he redescribes the pursuit of knowledge as a mode of self-experimentation, the purpose of which is to challenge and undo the arbitrary limits that history has placed on our knowledge in its current configuration—limits that we often represent to ourselves as set in stone.

What Foucault calls counter-memories are investigations of the past that sustain this work of experimentation. By constructing counter-memories, genealogy rejects the overly metaphysical model of memory that Foucault sees as informing both religious appeals to the continuity of tradition and the modern myth of historiographical objectivity. For Foucault, the two go hand in hand: every attempt to oppose historiography to the continuity of tradition necessarily reinscribes a naïve empiricism.

Genealogy, thus, does not eschew temporal and historical continuities by predilection. It is not that Nietzsche and Foucault simply prefer to emphasize discontinuity over continuity. The very opposition between temporal continuity grasped in terms of memory and/or tradition and temporal discontinuity grasped in terms of history exists at a level of analysis from which genealogy takes its leave. This explains why it is at best misleading to suggest that genealogy merely destroys concepts by revealing them to be the product of discursive practices, or that its critical interventions merely recover silenced or forgotten identities overshadowed by hegemonic discursive practices. For Foucault, the former tendency amounts to criticism in the pejorative sense, whereas the latter tendency lapses into antiquarianism of a sort.

So long as genealogy displays these two tendencies, it cannot fulfill its theoretical promise. And yet, by underscoring the fact that this promise is entirely bound up with the injunction to counter-memory, we can identify the advantages that genealogy offers to religious studies and that it claims *for* religious studies vis-à-vis other fields of inquiry: the investigations carried out by Asad, Masuzawa, and Stroumsa, among others, reveal the ways in which modern social-scientific and humanistic modes of inquiry obsessively define themselves over and against certain religious others. In so doing these scholars succeed in dispelling the myth of a critical perspective fully immunized against ideology. Carlo Ginzburg once suggested that historians should, like surgeons, sterilize their tools prior to using them (Ginzburg 1989, 107–8). Indeed, the conscientious scholar of religion may be tempted to call for the "conscious removal of all theological and metaphysical traditions that continue to haunt the study of religion" (Penner 2000, 66). Genealogy reveals the futility of this gesture and its underlying ideal of purity. It does so not simply by dashing any hope for theoretical neutrality, but also by revealing that this hope is sustained by the prejudice of periodization—namely, that for the true historian and theoretician alike, the religious and the theological are *of the past*. What genealogy in general and counter-memory in particular impart to humanistic and social-scientific inquiry is a mode of critical reflection that does not localize religion by figuring it primarily in terms of the past, or the past in terms of religion. And if genealogy does not exhaust itself in refutation, this is precisely because its injunction to counter-memory sustains its own kind of hope and its own kind of freedom. As Bergson (1991, 148) once wrote, "The whole of our past psychical life conditions our present state, without being its necessary determinant."

Suggested Readings

Asad, Talal. 1993. *Genealogies of Religion: Discipline and Reasons of Power in Christianity and Islam*. Baltimore, MD: Johns Hopkins University Press.

Foucault, Michel. 1998. "Nietzsche, Genealogy, History." In *The Essential Works of Foucault 1954–1984*, vol. 2, *Aesthetics, Method, and Epistemology*, edited by Paul Rabinow, translated by Robert Hurley et al. New York: New Press.

Halbwachs, Maurice. 1992. *On Collective Memory*. Translated and edited by Lewis A. Coser. Chicago: University of Chicago Press.

Masuzawa, Tomoko. 2005. *The Invention of World Religions; or, How European Universalism Was Preserved in the Language of Pluralism*. Chicago: University of Chicago Press.

Nietzsche, Friedrich. 2007. *On the Genealogy of Morality*. Edited by Keith Ansell-Pearson. Translated by Carol Diethe. Cambridge: Cambridge University Press.

Olick, Jeffrey K., Vered Vinitsky-Seroussi, and Daniel Levy, eds. 2011. *The Collective Memory Reader*. Oxford: Oxford University Press.

Ricoeur, Paul. 2006. *Memory, History, Forgetting*. Translated by Kathleen Blamey and David Pellauer. Chicago: University of Chicago Press.

Whitehead, Anne. 2009. *Memory*. New York: Routledge Press.

References

Asad, Talal. 1993. *Genealogies of Religion: Discipline and Reasons of Power in Christianity and Islam*. Baltimore, MD: Johns Hopkins University Press.

Assmann, Jan. 2006. *Religion and Cultural Memory*. Translated by Rodney Livingstone. Stanford, CA: Stanford University Press.

Berger, Peter, ed. 1999. *The Desecularization of the World: Resurgent Religion and World Politics*. Grand Rapids, MI: Eerdmans Publishing Company.

Bergson, Henri. 1991. *Matter and Memory*. Translated by N. M. Paul and W. S. Palmer. New York: Zone Books.

de Certeau, Michel. 1992. *The Writing of History*. Translated by Tom Conley. New York: Columbia University Press.

Connerton, Paul. 1989. *How Societies Remember*. Cambridge: Cambridge University Press.

Douglas, Mary. 1966. *Purity and Danger: An Analysis of the Concept of Pollution and Taboo*. New York: Routledge. Routledge Classics reprint 2002.

Foucault, Michel. 1977. *Discipline and Punish: The Birth of the Prison*. Translated by Alan Sheridan. New York: Vintage Books.

Foucault, Michel. 1997. "What Is Enlightenment?" In *The Essential Works of Foucault 1954–1984, vol. I: Ethics*, edited by Paul Rabinow, translated by Robert Hurley and others. New York: The New Press.

Foucault, Michel. 1998. "Nietzsche, Genealogy, History." In *The Essential Works of Foucault 1954–1984, vol. II: Aesthetics, Method, and Epistemology*, edited by Paul Rabinow, translated by Robert Hurley and others. New York: The New Press.

Ginzburg, Carlo. 1989. *Clues, Myths, and the Historical Method*. Baltimore, MD: Johns Hopkins University Press.

Halbwachs, Maurice. 1992. *On Collective Memory*. Translated and edited by Lewis A. Coser. Chicago: University of Chicago Press.

Hervieu-Léger, Danièle. 2000. *Religion as a Chain of Memory*. Translated by Simon Lee. New Brunswick, NJ: Rutgers University Press.

Hervieu-Léger, Danièle. 2008. "Religion as Memory: Reference to Tradition and the Constitution of a Heritage of Belief in Modern Societies." In *Religion: Beyond a Concept*, edited by Hent de Vries, 245–58. New York: Fordham University Press.

Huyssen, Andreas. 1995. *Twilight Memories: Marking Time in a Culture of Amnesia*. New York: Routledge.

Huyssen, Andreas. 2003. *Present Pasts: Urban Palimpsests and the Politics of Memory*. Stanford, CA: Stanford University Press.

Nietzsche, Friedrich. 2007. *On the Genealogy of Morality*. Edited by Keith Ansell-Pearson, translated by Carol Diethe. Cambridge, UK: Cambridge University Press.

Nora, Pierre, ed. 1996. *Realms of Memory: The Construction of the Past*. Translated by Arthur Goldhammer, English-language edition edited by Lawrence D. Kritzman. New York: Columbia University Press.

Penner, Hans. 2000. "Interpretation." In *Guide to the Study of Religion*, edited by Willi Braun and Russell T. McCutcheon, 57–74. New York: Cassell.

Ricoeur, Paul. 2006. *Memory, History, Forgetting*. Translated by Kathleen Blamey and David Pellauer. Chicago: University of Chicago Press.

Rittner, Carol, ed. 1990. *Elie Wiesel: Between Memory and Hope*. New York: NYU Press.

Smith, Jonathan Z. 1982. *Imagining Religion: From Babylon to Jonestown*. Chicago: University of Chicago Press.

Smith, Jonathan Z. 1987. *To Take Place: Toward Theory in Ritual*. Chicago: University of Chicago Press.

Weinrich, Harald. 2004. *Lethe: The Art and Critique of Forgetting*. Translated by Steven Rendall. Ithaca, NY: Cornell University Press.

Wiesel, Elie. 1990. "An Interview With Carol Rittner." In *Elie Wiesel: Between Memory and Hope*, edited by Carol Rittner, 30. New York: NYU Press.

Whitehead, Anne. 2009. *Memory*. New York: Routledge Press.

Winter, Jay. 1995. *Sites of Memory, Sites of Mourning*. Cambridge: Cambridge University Press.

Yerushalmi, Yosef. 1982. *Zakhor: Jewish History and Jewish Memory*. Seattle: University of Washington Press.

12 MIND

Dan Arnold

> As dependent upon mind, phenomena are epitomized by mind, they *consist* of mind.
> *Dhammapada*, verses 1 and 2

> Whoever controls the definition of mind controls the definition of humankind itself, and culture, and history.
> MARILYNNE ROBINSON, *Absence of Mind*

I. Critical Terms and the Reality of Mind

Critical terms, it is often supposed, are those that advance what Paul Ricoeur called the "hermeneutics of suspicion," which Ricoeur took as the stance shared by Marx, Nietzsche, and Freud. That stance, Mark C. Taylor explains, "extends Cartesian doubt by turning it back on consciousness itself," with the upshot that *consciousness* is unmasked: "Rather than being foundational, consciousness, these 'masters of suspicion' argue, is an epiphenomenon that simultaneously reflects and deflects economic, biological, and psychological forces" (Taylor 1998, 12). While "consciousness" familiarly denotes merely the condition of being awake and aware, hermeneutic suspicion particularly targets a subject of Descartes's *cogito* ("I think")—not mere awareness is targeted, but the subjectivity of *thinking*. As so conceived, critical terms would dethrone not so much consciousness as *mind*.

The Indian Buddhist Vasubandhu (fl. ca. 360 CE) extensively theorized distinctions between such mental states, and in Vasubandhu's Sanskrit terms—considered in section IV—hermeneutic suspicion thus targets *citta* ("thought") or *manas* ("mentation," "mind"), not *vijñāna* ("consciousness," "awareness"). However, despite Vasubandhu's own careful systematizing of mental functions, he contends in some contexts that all these terms are interchangeable; as noted in section IV, Vasubandhu contends that *karma* is basically *mental*, and to that extent what matters most is just that all these functions are mental. Vasubandhu's blanket term for mental functions is "representation" (*vijñapti*), which reflects the idea that these are *of* or *about* something; lest we be liable to any pitfalls of conceiving thought as "representation," I propose *mind* as better capturing what's commonly at stake for Vasubandhu and for the foregoing conception of "critical terms." For Vasubandhu, the most important thing to understand is a point on which, Roger Jackson says, "almost all Buddhists agreed"—namely, "that the mind was *the* key factor in the cosmos, and its transformation the most important single task a human being could undertake" (Jackson 2019, 428). The foregoing conception of critical terms, in contrast, aims to disclose mind as an "epiphenomenon" that merely "reflects and deflects" objective forces (economic, biological, psychological, etc.), which alone are credited as real.

Could it be right that critical terms must thus deny precisely what Vasubandhu affirms? We will see in section IV that Vasubandhu's typically Buddhist conception of mind might itself exemplify a hermeneutics of suspicion; after all, "mind," according to a Buddhist conception, is theorized consistently with the cardinal Buddhist doctrine, which has it that the *self* is finally unreal. "Mind," for Buddhists, is not an autonomous source of agency but a temporal process sustained by habituated conditions, and refutations of "self" target the very aspects of mind that Christian theists, for example, are apt to consider salient. As we will see in section III, then, the logic of theistic explanation centrally involves suppositions about mind; if a Buddhist account of mind makes sense as "hermeneutically suspicious" because it resists the intuitions that are salient for theists, perhaps it is just *theistic* ideas that are unmasked by hermeneutic suspicion, while other religious ideas escape critique. Resisting any such conclusion, I contend instead that questions about the reality and nature of mind are central not only for religious perspectives of all sorts, but also for religious studies. Indeed, the history of religious studies suggests that the very ideas of *mind* and *religion* are so closely intertwined that they may stand or fall together.

Exploring that idea, we begin (section II) with a look at ideas from William James's *Varieties of Religious Experience* (1902), considered in light of the philosophy of James's friend and contemporary Charles S. Peirce. Seminal for religious studies, James's *Varieties* is also among the works through which James popularized Peirce's "pragmatism," and it is worth appreciating what Peirce thought problematic about James's version of that: their disagreement centrally concerns whether mind is chiefly distinguished by its interiority, or whether it is best conceived as not wholly internal to a subject. A comparable divergence of opinion is evident, as well, in the works considered in the latter half of this essay. Pascal Boyer's *Religion Explained* (2001), we will see in section V, contends that "mind" consists in evolved capacities that are fully evident in individual brains, and that "religion" is an epiphenomenal by-product of these very capacities. Émile Durkheim's *Elementary Forms of Religious Life* ([1912] 1995), we will then see in section VI, would reverse what Boyer considers the obvious direction of explanation. Proposing that the conditions of the possibility of mind first came together in the performance of religious rites, Durkheim suggests that to study *religion* just is to study *mind*; in this essay, we consider the sense it makes to think so.

II. James's *Varieties* and the Problem of Interiority

Published a decade before Durkheim's *Elementary Forms*, William James's *Varieties of Religious Experience* (1902) shows that the study of religion centrally involves questions about the nature of mind; this is especially clear in the book's conclusion, which refutes the idea that a naturalistic study of religious experience entails a reductionist view of mind. At the same time, *Varieties* is among the works through which James advanced his "pragmatism," in which he took himself as following insights Charles Peirce first elaborated in the 1870s. For present purposes, it's helpful to appreciate why Peirce, although largely sympathetic to James's project, thought James had badly misrepresented his (Peirce's) pragmatism; the problem Peirce identified is perhaps nowhere more evident than in James's *Varieties*.

To understand what was at issue between them, it's important to recognize Peirce's career-long concern with formulating a coherent idea of *realism*. Peirce held that philosophers had long been misled by the presupposition that the "real" just is what lies outside of mind, such that "the absolutely external causes of perception are the only realities" (Peirce [1871] 2019, 118).[1] That presupposition is surely as prevalent now as in Peirce's

1. Peirce is here clarifying what he understands by *nominalism*, against which he staunchly advocated a conception of *realism* on which "reality belongs to what is present to us in true knowledge of any sort" (1871, 118). Cf. Forster 2011.

time; indeed, it is evident in the aforementioned idea that mind merely "reflects and deflects" objective forces (economic, biological, psychological), which forces alone count as real. To be sure, Peirce well understood why it can seem obvious that reality is external to mind; indeed, this would seem to be a straightforward way of expressing the commonsense criterion to which Peirce himself thought any conception of reality must be adequate, according to which "real" denotes what is "independent of how we think it" (Peirce [1871] 2019, 118). However, Peirce recognized that the commonsense criterion requires careful clarification, lest we foreclose debatable questions just by definition; as Robert Lane explains, "if the real is exactly that which is independent of minds, then minds themselves are not real. Realists about the mind would rightly object that defining 'real' in this way begs the question against their view" (2018, 1)

Pragmatist insights, moreover, give us particular reason for conceiving *realism* so as to avoid begging the question of mind's reality. Pragmatically speaking, the reality of mind is practically incontrovertible; after all, the explanatory "forces" disclosed by hermeneutic suspicion are themselves understood only through economic, biological, or psychological *inquiry*, and inquiry just is an activity of mind. This is among the points James pursues in the concluding lecture of his *Varieties of Religious Experience*, which argues that scientific understanding can never justify the conclusion that mind itself is unreal: "it is absurd for science to say that the egotistic elements of experience should be suppressed. The axis of reality runs solely through the egotistic places" (1902, 499–500). James's point, we might say more precisely, is that whatever is claimed for scientific understanding must be consistent with the practices that yield such understanding; that means exercises of mind cannot coherently be considered unreal. It's revealing, however, that James expresses the point in terms of the "egotistic elements" of experience; indeed, he waxes lyrical about "that unsharable feeling which each one of us has of the pinch of his individual destiny as he privately feels it rolling out on fortune's wheel" (1902, 499).

Such passages epitomize the subjectivist predilections many readers find problematic in *Varieties of Religious Experience*, richly attesting to Vincent Colapietro's observation that for James, "the most fundamental feature of personal consciousness is the irreducible fact of privacy"; for Peirce, Colapietro says, "its most basic characteristic is the ubiquitous possibility of communication" (Colapietro 1989, 78), and, notwithstanding his friendship with James, Peirce strongly criticized James's subjectivist rendering of pragmatist insights. In a 1905 essay titled "What Pragmatism Is," Peirce explained that he had since the 1870s been arguing for a realist conception of meaning, and that this aim is undermined by James's psychologism. In particular, Peirce resisted conceptions of meaning that involve reference to the psychological states of a subject and argued instead that meaning must be conceived as an *objective* element of thought. It is in virtue of *meaning*, Peirce can thus say, that "a person is not absolutely an individual," which he elaborates thus: "His thoughts are what he is 'saying to himself,' that is, saying to that other self that is just coming into life in the flow of time. When one reasons, it is that critical self that one is trying to persuade; and all thought whatsoever is a sign, and is mostly of the nature of language" (Peirce 1905, 170).

Peirce thus urged that mind, as centrally implicating meaning, is essentially *semiotic*; indeed, Peirce took mind and meaning as commonly epitomizing his metaphysical category of "Thirdness," and while it would take us too far afield to unpack that idea here, it clearly reflects Peirce's conception of mind as having little to do with individual consciousness. For Peirce, understanding *mind* means understanding *meaning*—and meaning, as Hilary Putnam famously concluded (with help from Peirce), "just ain't in the head" (Putnam 1975, 227). Émile Durkheim, we will see, travels a different route to much the same conclusion; his *Elementary Forms of Religious Life* is premised on the insight that mind is not exhaustively explicable by goings-on in a brain just because mind is an essentially *social* phenomenon. Before we get to that proposal, though, let us first entertain a couple of divergent lines of religious thought; ideas from Christian theism and Buddhist doctrines of *karma* commonly recommend acknowledging the reality of mind, but take altogether different aspects of our mental lives as salient.

III. Theistic Explanation and Philosophy of Mind

Integral to theism is the idea that God's *mind* explains all that exists; this is the basis for thinking that the causally ordered universe could not exist without cause, but that God, although uncaused, makes sense as providing that. To maintain this, theists can invoke the idea that *reasons* are irreducibly distinct from *causes*. Although disputed by many philosophers nowadays, this idea has intuitive plausibility. If asked to explain, for example, why a seated person arose and traversed a room to turn a knob on a device, it wouldn't be wrong to say neuro-electrical impulses stimulated contractions of particular muscles, causing the bodily movements in question. But no matter how detailed that kind of answer becomes, it leaves out something basic, whereas it settles the question in a different way to provide a *reason* for the action; few would think further explanation called for if the answer is that the music was too loud so this person got up to turn down the volume on the stereo. Humble as it is, this example exhibits the basic logic of theism; to the extent that reasons make sense as uniquely terminating demands for explanation, God's reasons make sense as explaining why there is a universe of causal regularities at all.

This idea, formulated by G. W. Leibniz as the "Principle of Sufficient Reason," is elaborated by Richard Swinburne's philosophical case for theism, which recasts the idea in terms of a basic difference between *personal* explanation and *scientific* explanation. This is important, Swinburne argues, because theists must explain why "the existence of God is a more satisfactory terminus for explanation than the existence of the universe with its various characteristics" (Swinburne 1991, 72). If *God* makes sense as an uncaused existent, why can it not be allowed that the universe itself is uncaused? Swinburne argues that scientific explanation gets no traction here, because scientific method cannot show "why there are any states of affairs at all; it can explain only why, given that there are such states, this state is followed by that state" (1991, 72). A complete explanation, Swinburne contends, thus requires the introduction of a *personal* perspective, which doesn't merely adduce causes but can also explain "the *reason* why the cause under the conditions of its occurrence had the effect it had" (1991, 24). The cogency of theistic explanation, on this account, thus presupposes that we can reasonably seek an answer to the question of *why there are any states of affairs at all*, and that appeal to divine reasons settles that question as no causal explanation can.

It is, however, our own experience of purposefully initiating activity that makes this idea of divine reasons intelligible. For a theist, this is of course to be expected, given the theist's contention that persons are created "in the image of God" (*imago Dei*); whatever the right direction of explanation, though, it seems the tenability of theism may depend on the adequacy with which human minds are conceived. The idea that persons are created in the divine image has traditionally been taken to recommend a dualistic account of persons; as St. Augustine says (in words approvingly quoted by Thomas Aquinas), "man's excellence consists in the fact that God made him to His own image by giving him an intellectual soul which raises him above the beasts of the field" (Augustine, *Gen. ad lit. vi, 12*, quoted in Aquinas, 1, 93, ii, ad. 4). Some kind of dualism must make sense if God's reasons are to make sense as basic. If *mind* makes sense only as instantiated in a brain, and the divine mind thus had to be embodied (as, say, the physical universe), God's *reasons* then would be the effects, as it were, of a cosmic "neurophysiology"—this, not God's "reasons," would then be doing the explaining.

Arguing that theism is thus intelligible only if a dualist account of mind is right, Charles Taliaferro's *Consciousness and the Mind of God* (1994) is largely concerned to show that physicalist accounts of mind are incoherent. Physicalism is epitomized for Taliaferro by Daniel Dennett, for whom reasons *must* be reducible to causes; "whenever we stop in our explanations at the intentional level," Dennett says—whenever, that is, the kind of *personal* explanation privileged by Swinburne is allowed as the last word—"we have left over an unexplained instance of intelligence or rationality" (Dennett 1981, 12). The task in philosophy of mind, according to Dennett, just is to explain the exercise of mental capacities, and that can only mean identifying the empirically determinate occurrences that cause these exercises. Epitomizing the presupposition that the real must lie outside of mind, Dennett thus thinks mental phenomena must be redescribed in the empirical terms of cognitive science if they are to make sense as doing anything: "Only a theory that explained conscious events in terms of unconscious events could explain consciousness at all" (Dennett 1991, 454). For Taliaferro, the question thus becomes whether it makes sense to suppose that "nonintentional explanations"—those involving only impersonal causes, without reference to reasons or aims—are "more lucid or perspicuous (more in the black, to talk in Dennett's budgetary fashion) than those which employ intentional factors" (Taliaferro 1994, 85).

At issue is whether it makes sense to think an agent's reasons could count as *real* only under a different description than could be available to the agent; could it be that our experience of ourselves as responsive to reasons is finally illusory, and that only a third-person perspective on mind identifies anything real? Recall the example of someone rising to turn down the volume on the stereo: this scenario really will admit of a wholly impersonal description (as consisting in neurophysiological events causing bodily movements), and there are contexts in which much can be gained by entertaining such descriptions. The question is whether it's reasonable to think such descriptions count as better understood than the intentional activity they are proposed as explaining. Could it make sense that the actions in our example are finally *real* only under an impersonal description, and that the experience of finding the music too loud is itself unreal? Arguing that this is incoherent, Taliaferro emphasizes that the impersonal terms of scientific understanding are themselves intelligible only as they can show up for thinking; while Dennett's conception of explanation privileges "the objective materialistic, third-person world of the physical sciences" as alone capable of yielding knowledge, Taliaferro asks: "What is it to observe things?" Scientific observation itself, he says, "seems to involve conscious episodes and sensations, and it thereby seems to rest the notion of the physical upon some notion of consciousness, a notion that is ordinarily classified as mental" (Taliaferro 1994, 95). Thus, there can be no characterization of physical reality that does not depend on *how physical things show up for us*; to claim that physical reality is more securely understood than mind, Taliaferro thus argues, is equivalent "to holding that we have a clearer conception of being tangible, visible, or witnessed than we do of touching, viewing, and witnessing" (1994, 95).

Arguments to this effect show, perhaps, that mind is inadequately conceived if considered *real* only under a scientific description. Taliaferro, though, is ostensibly concerned with *Consciousness and the Mind of God*, and to that extent it's notable that the book finally has more to do with our own minds than with the divine mind. It could hardly be otherwise; when it comes to the idea that reasons logically terminate explanation in ways that causes cannot, a theistic account gets purchase only because our experience of our *own* minds makes that idea intelligible. If theism's intelligibility depends on certain intuitions about the nature of mind, however, must the converse likewise be true? Does acknowledging the basic significance of *mind*, that is, recommend belief in God? Consideration of a Buddhist perspective suggests there may be altogether different ways for mind to make sense as religiously significant.

IV. A Buddhist Perspective: *Mind* without *Selves*

This essay's first epigraph is the refrain of the opening couplet of verses in the Pāli *Dhammapada*, among the most widely known of all Buddhist texts. The couplet concisely expresses an orienting commitment of a Buddhist account:

> As dependent upon mind, phenomena are epitomized by mind, they *consist* of mind. If one speaks or acts with a mind that is corrupt, distress thus follows him as surely as a wheel follows an ox's feet.
>
> As dependent upon mind, phenomena are epitomized by mind, they *consist*

> of mind. If one speaks or acts with a mind that is pure, ease thus follows him as surely as an ever-present shadow. (cf. Norman 2000, 1)

Mind is significant, the couplet suggests, as somehow determinative for the balance of satisfaction and suffering. The recurrent word here rendered as "mind" is the Pāli word *mano* (Sanskrit, *manas*), an Indian-European cognate with the English; it should be emphasized, however, that Buddhist philosophers classified mental states with uncommon subtlety, and that we should therefore expect to find that Buddhist conceptions of mind challenge various of the presuppositions long enshrined in Western philosophical conceptions.

The Buddhist philosopher Vasubandhu, as noted at the beginning of this essay, typically mentions *citta* ("thought") and *vijñāna* ("awareness," "consciousness") along with *manas*, and we can here elaborate on some ideas Vasubandhu thus had in mind. *Awareness*, according to a Buddhist account, is the most primitive grade of mental event, consisting, according to Vasubandhu's *Treasury of Abhidharma*, merely in the "representation" (*vijñapti*) of what is available to experience (*Abhidharmakośa* 1.16a; Pruden 1991, I.74). Mere representation of objects, however, does not by itself constitute *experience*, which requires that what is present to awareness be *taken* as somehow salient; it is "thought and concomitant mental states" which thus take up what is present. Here, "thought" (*citta*) is basically synonymous with "mind" (*manas*), and mental states "concomitant with thought" (*caitta*) include occurrences of "feeling" (*vedanā*), "intention" (*cetanā*), "attention" (*manaskāra*), and so forth. Thought and its concomitant states apprehend the particulars given to experience as exemplifying *kinds* of things, which they accomplish by *attenuating* what is present for awareness, foregrounding this or that as salient for attention. Without such constructive attenuation, experience would consist in a welter of undifferentiated sensations; owing to the constructive activity of mind, experience instead involves a world of mostly familiar things functioning in largely expected ways.

Mind's constructive attenuation of what is present for awareness is, then, indispensable. Nonetheless, Buddhists would have us recognize that operations of mind order the experienced world by imposing "constructs" (*kalpanā*), and that despite their utility these are systematically misleading. In a Buddhist account, that's because mind constructs what is present for awareness as egocentrically salient, ever reinforcing the delusional self-grasping which is, according to a Buddhist diagnosis, the root problem to be overcome. It is therefore *mind* which must be transformed if we are to be liberated from self-grasping. At the same time, the desired transformation necessarily involves efforts of mind, which, until transformed, remain apt to mislead us; no wonder Buddhist philosophers had so much to say about mind.

Indeed, despite the diversity of philosophical approaches it comprises, Buddhist tradition clearly exhibits generally idealist tendencies. These are encapsulated in the influential corpus of Vasubandhu, who, astonishingly, wrote what later Buddhist tradition would take as definitive expressions of several distinct schools of thought, beginning with works like the *Treasury of Abhidharma*, and later culminating—after Vasubandhu's adoption of a Mahāyāna perspective—in short treatises seminal for the philosophically idealist Yogācāra tradition of Mahāyāna philosophy. One of the latter treatises, humbly titled "Twenty Verses," announces at the outset that the ultimate truth of the Buddha's teachings is epitomized by the Buddha's statements, in Mahāyāna Sūtras, that "the entire threefold cosmos is merely thought" (*cittamātram*—cf. Silk 2016, 30–31). This, indeed, is among the places where Vasubandhu says the terms "thought," "mind," and "awareness" are interchangeable; while the quotation says everything is merely *thought* (*citta*), Vasubandhu says this word should here be understood as encompassing all these mental phenomena (cf. Silk 2016, 30–31).[2] What matters, he contends, is that rightly understanding the Buddha's teachings requires interpreting them as ultimately consistent with the claim that *the entire threefold cosmos somehow consists of mental functions*. While it matters for Vasubandhu's agenda that the formulation he takes as criterial for interpretation comes from a Mahāyāna Sūtra, the idealist arguments of his "Twenty Verses" leverage an idea that had always been central to Buddhist tradition—an idea, indeed, that Vasubandhu himself had elaborated in his pre-Mahāyāna *Treasury of Abhidharma*, whose fourth chapter begins by defining *karma* (literally, "action") as consisting in "intention, as well as what is done intentionally" (*Abhidharmakośa* 4.1; cf. Pruden 1991, II.551).[3]

Long prevalent in Buddhist tradition, this commitment is clearly motivated by ethical considerations; as the Madhyamaka philosopher Āry-

2. Vasubandhu also says at *Abhidharmakośa* 2.34 that these mental items are interchangeable, explaining in this context that all these are based in the senses; all take something as object; all have a qualitative feel; and all are present together in experience (Pruden 1991, I:205–6).

3. That this idea is pivotal for Vasubandhu's "Twenty Verses" is clear at verses 6–7 thereof (see Silk 2016, 56–59).

adeva (fl. ca. 200 CE) explained a couple centuries before Vasubandhu, for example, "because the merit (etc.) of actions (*moving* and all the rest) is not seen without reference to intention, *mind* therefore is what really must be explained for all actions" (*Catuḥśataka* 5.4; cf. Lang 1986, 54). This has struck some modern interpreters as the veritably Kantian idea that actions are ethically evaluable just insofar as they are, unlike involuntary occurrences such as digestion, intelligible as undertaken for a *reason* (not *caused*). However, the English word *intention* suggests considerably more autonomy than is meant by Buddhist conceptions of *cetanā*, the Sanskrit term (identical in Pāli) so translated (cf. Heim 2013). What is salient for Buddhists is that "intending" consists in mental occurrences, which means intending, like anything that occurs, is "dependently originated" (*pratītyasamutpanna*). Intentions, for a Buddhist account, are salient not as exhibiting our responsiveness to reasons but as reflecting deeply habituated dispositions; the upshot of Vasubandhu's defining *karma* as "intention," then, is that nobody is nearly as free as typically supposed.

The significance of *mind*, as conceived by Buddhists, is therefore consistent with the idea that we are not transparent to ourselves; persons act as they do largely owing to the weight of their own psychological pasts, which is not typically evident from a first-person perspective. This is the upshot of Buddhist tradition's orienting doctrine, which has it that persons are not individuated by enduring "selves" (*ātma*), which Buddhists reject as an incoherent account of agency; the continuity that distinguishes a "person" cannot be explained by an enduring locus of agency which remains, somehow, unchanged by the actions it originates. Given what was emphasized in section III's attention to the logic of theistic explanation, it's not surprising that Buddhists recognized that their critique of the idea of *self* cuts, as well, against theism. When Vasubandhu's *Treasury of Abhidharma* defines *karma* as noted above, the point has been framed as alternative to the logic of theism, the discussion having been launched by the question: "Who created the greatly wondrous diversity of the world of creatures and inanimate objects?" (cf. Pruden 1991, II.551). Vasubandhu answers: "Surely it was not deliberately created by anyone. How then? *The wondrous diversity of the world results from the karma* of sentient beings," and *karma*, Vasubandhu continues, consists (we've already seen) of "intention, as well as what is done intentionally" (cf. Pruden 1991, II.551).

The experienced world is indeed created, Vasubandhu thus says, by the mental activity of sentient beings; but insofar as sentient beings habitually construct egocentrically salient worlds, what is made objective by that activity—in language and social formations and built environments and much else besides—only reinforces the self-grasping at the root of suffering. For Buddhists as for theists, *mind* basically accounts for the experienced world; on a Buddhist view, however, the salient point is that we are ill served by this fact so long as mind remains in thrall to self-grasping. For Buddhist philosophers, then, the point in emphasizing the real significance of mind is not at all to affirm that persons typically act for the reasons they think they do; what Buddhists affirm, rather, is merely that mental events have real consequences, and that it therefore matters whether such events are liberative, or whether they reinforce the self-grasping that so misleads us.

That no autonomous *thinker* is implied by its occurrence does not mean, therefore, that *thought* is inconsequential; indeed, Buddhist philosophers invariably emphasize that the no-self doctrine is wrongly understood if taken to mean ethically evaluable actions don't matter. Denying that the no-self doctrine entails that conclusion, Buddhist philosophers argued that *mental* continuity has, as it were, a life of its own; that, indeed, is among the ideas Buddhist philosophers affirmed in arguing (as many did) for the reality of "rebirth." Of course, *rebirth* cannot, for a Buddhist account, consist in a subject's recurrently undergoing the experience of being born; that is just what the no-self doctrine denies. If the subjects of successive "rebirths" are not identical, though, that's because *identity* is not in the first place a coherent criterion of personhood; if we are to make sense of the fact that persons and minds change as they develop, we should acknowledge that it's merely *causal continuity* that individuates persons. That you remember your own childhood (not your neighbor's) is owing to the causal relatedness of mental events; causal relatedness typically takes form as *continuity*, and "persons" therefore denote relatively discrete "continua" (Sanskrit, *santāna*) of physical and mental events. "Rebirth," for a Buddhist account, thus becomes the idea that *the continuity of mind* is not interrupted by a being's death, and this because mental events are not wholly explicable by physiological occurrences.

So argues Dharmakīrti (ca. 600–660 CE), whose case for rebirth is widely taken as the Indian Buddhist tradition's definitive treatment of the subject. Focused on showing absurd consequences that result from supposing mental events reducible to bodily events, Dharmakīrti agues, for example, that if a living being consists merely in a body, there is no accounting for the body's changing at death; after all, the body has exactly the same physical constituents at death as when living (cf. Arnold 2012, 19–47). If mental occurrences (moments of thinking, feeling, intending) are not wholly intelligible with reference only to bodily causes, mental events must then include among their causes *prior mental events*; it follows, Dharmakīrti concludes, that a newborn's initial moment of awareness cannot, in fact, be the first such moment. Like the awareness experienced upon waking from deep sleep, a newborn's awareness must therefore be continuous with mental events preceding the "sleep" of death, which ends what is considered a previous lifetime.

Dharmakīrti's point is not that one enduring entity repeatedly undergoes birth, but that the ongoing efficacy of mind is indefinite; no mental continuum could make sense as the first such continuum, and the compounding effects of any particular continuum's significance extend well beyond that continuum. *Mind*, in this account, is not to be found "within" a person.

V. Is Mind "In" the Brain?

"Brainhood," Fernando Vidal observes (2009), is "the anthropological figure of modernity." This is abundantly evident in the profusion of neurocentric versions of humanistic disciplines ("neuro-ethics," "neurotheology," etc.), and it's therefore not surprising that Buddhist tradition's emphasis on mind often drops out of contemporary engagements with Buddhist thought. This is consistent, moreover, with recent neurocentric trends in religious studies, as epitomized by Pascal Boyer's *Religion Explained* (2001). Advancing a line of argument familiar from David Hume, Boyer aims to explain *why religion persists*. This is thought to require explanation because it is presupposed that a *religious* account of religion's significance could not be right; what, then, could explain the fact that such accounts nonetheless continue to be widely held? Boyer's explanation resembles that ventured by David Hume, whose *Natural History of Religion* ([1757] 1993) attributes religious phenomena to a generally human "fear of unknown causes," which inclines humans to personify impersonal forces by assigning agency to unexplained occurrences. As updated by Boyer, this becomes the point that human brains evolved "hyperactive agent detection" capacities (Boyer 2001, 144ff.); that this is best explained as an evolutionarily advantageous adaptation in brain function is evident precisely in the fact that these capacities tend to generate false positives—after all, the supposed advantage is conferred precisely by the fact that it's better to be wrong in thinking predators *present* than to be wrong in thinking them *absent*.

The point is, the brain's evolved capacities make sense, according to this picture, quite independently of whether such capacities reliably yield true beliefs. *Mind*, according to this account, thus comprises capacities best understood as evolutionary byproducts, which explains why humans tend to spin fanciful religious tales. Indeed, Boyer's accounts of *mind* and of *religion* are mutually reinforcing; it is owing to the presupposed falsity of religious belief that the explanation of religion is called for—the axiomatic falsity of religious belief is in turn taken to support the conclusion that mental capacities make more sense as conferring evolutionary advantage than as capable of disclosing anything true. Interestingly, Boyer emphasizes that an account such as his became available only once anthropologists "started taking more seriously the fact that humans are *by nature* a social species" (2001, 27).

As suggested by Boyer's emphatic italics, the point that humans are social "by nature" here has a particular sense; he means, in particular, that human sociality is wholly evident in each individual's brain, which is "so designed that it includes what evolutionary biologists call a particular form of 'social intelligence' or a 'social mind'" (2001, 27). It is axiomatic, for Boyer, that taking human sociality seriously cannot mean attending to the reality *of the social*; "the social" is an abstraction—a convenient fiction abstracted from the fact that aggregated individuals are commonly conditioned to exhibit psychological similarities. Boyer thinks this presupposition obvious enough that he finally motivates his neurocentric approach with a rhetorical question: "How could a similarity *cause* anything? There is no external force here" (2001, 36). To be *real*, in this view, is to be determinately present somewhere, and Boyer thus locates the relevant considerations in individual brains: "If people feel a conflict between their inclinations and a norm that is followed by everybody else, it is a conflict *within their heads*" (2001, 36).

This picture epitomizes what Clifford Geertz calls a *stratigraphic* conception of "relations between biological, psychological, social, and cultural factors in human life" (1973, 37). Geertz's geological metaphor captures the idea that each new "stratum" is deposited atop older strata, which are therefore completed by the new deposits; each layer is fully intelligible by itself, unchanged by anything subsequently deposited atop it. This primes the intuition that we approach what is *real* by descending to lower levels;

"motley forms of culture," furthest removed from reality, are explained by "structural and functional regularities of social organization," which in turn yield to the explanatory priority of "underlying psychological factors," below which "one is left with the biological foundations—anatomical, physiological, neurological—of the whole edifice of human life" (1973, 37). Likewise, evolutionary biology and neuroscience make sense as explaining religion, according to Boyer's account, because these sciences engage the biological foundations of mind, which alone make sense as consisting of anything real.

Insofar as *mind* thus denotes capacities that are exhaustively explicable by their conferral of evolutionary advantage, religion is easily explained as another such evolutionary epiphenomenon. Among the challenges for Boyer's account, though, is that *Boyer's proposal itself* can result only from the exercise of the same mental capacities dethroned by this account; if the most salient fact about mind is that evolutionary pressures explain its relative unreliability as advantageous, how then can Boyer be confident in the conclusions recommended by his own exercise of mind? There is another reason to resist Boyer's "stratigraphic" conception of the human, which has it that religious beliefs, however ramified, finally result from the fact that humans possess brains whose operating parameters remain as these had evolved with the emergence of Cro-Magnon man. Suppose a Cro-Magnon hominid was, owing to a lightning strike, subjected to a freakish neurochemical occurrence; does it make sense that she could, just because of such an occurrence, suddenly experience herself as, say, anxiously hoping to find an automated teller machine before her train departs (cf. Descombes 2001, 228–29)? That experience could not be available without the historical and technological developments presupposed by thoughts of trains, money-dispensing machines, and on-time departures; yet if it's supposed that whatever a person has in *mind* must be wholly explicable by what is in her *brain*, we have to acknowledge the scenario in this thought experiment as not, in fact, out of the question.

If it is acknowledged that sociohistorical and technological developments clearly expand the reach of mind, the fact that such factors cannot, like neurophysiological events, be determinately located in a brain cannot be taken as recommending the conclusion that such factors are therefore unreal. In that case, one can accept Boyer's premise that abstract sociohistorical factors basically differ from anything identifiable by fMRI brain scans, and yet draw an altogether different conclusion: if sociohistorical factors are not evident in, say, cerebral blood flow or synaptic discharging, that cannot be taken to show that such factors are not somehow constitutive of mind—the only reasonable conclusion, rather, is that *mind* does not make sense as exhaustively explicable with reference only to what is going on in a brain. That is precisely the idea behind Émile Durkheim's notion that the social science he envisaged makes sense only if distinctively *social* facts are real; his *Elementary Forms of Religious Life* shows why it makes sense to think they are.

VI. Durkheim on *Mind* as Essentially Social

Familiar to students of religion as seminally theorizing the sacred/profane distinction, Émile Durkheim's *Elementary Forms of Religious Life* ([1912] 1995) ostensibly concerns totemistic rites of Australian Indigenous peoples; Durkheim is clearly motivated, however, by questions in philosophy of mind, regarding which his presuppositions are the reverse of Boyer's. For Durkheim, "the collective ideal that religion expresses" could not result from "some vague capacity innate to the individual," and the direction of explanation must therefore be the other way around: "It is in the school of collective life that the individual has learned to form ideas" ([1912] 1995, 425).

Durkheim's orienting question concerns the availability of something like Kant's basic categories of understanding: how, that is, do we come to have the basic conceptions (causation, relation, temporal order, etc.) in virtue of which human experience involves *thought*? On this, Durkheim observes, philosophers have endlessly oscillated between two kinds of views. One is the basically Kantian notion that "the categories cannot be derived from experience" just because they are "logically prior to experience and condition it" (Durkheim [1912] 1995, 12). That is, any experience that could be adduced as advancing our understanding in the matter must itself be structured by the categories in question; these therefore cannot be explained by experience. (This is what Kant meant in characterizing such categories as *transcendental*.) Durkheim is sympathetic to this view, but worries that it means accepting the categories of understanding as simply given; he thinks there must be a natural-historical explanation of their emergence.

According to the kind of view typically opposed to the foregoing, Durkheim says, "the categories are constructed, made out of bits and pieces, and it is the individual who is the artisan of that construction" ([1912] 1995, 12).

This alternative reflects basically empiricist assumptions, starting with the idea that *perceptual* awareness is foundational for understanding; after all, if we want to explain the objective understanding of which persons are capable, it would seem a good idea to focus on our perceptual encounters with the world, in which experience is actually constrained by an environment's impinging upon a body. While it seems intuitive that the objectivity of understanding is thus secured by perception, Durkheim points out that this actually directs our focus the wrong way: "A sensation or an image is always linked to a definite object or collection of definite objects, and it expresses the momentary state of a particular consciousness. It is fundamentally individual and subjective" ([1912] 1995, 13). The upshot of the empiricist's psychologistic focus is thus to reduce "the universality and necessity that characterize reason to mere appearances, illusions that might be practically convenient but that correspond to nothing in things"—but that is "to make reason disappear" ([1912] 1995, 13). Insofar as a theory of mind must make sense of *thinking*, Durkheim thus considers the first of the foregoing views as preferable to the second; "the apriorists," he says, "are more attentive to the facts" ([1912] 1995, 13).

Thus forced back to the first horn of the dilemma, Durkheim sees a way forward by reversing the direction of the inquiry: if empiricist explanations fail because their psychologistic presuppositions direct attention inward, then "if the social origin of the categories is accepted, a new stance becomes possible" ([1912] 1995, 14). Insofar as an individual's perceptual experience is "wholly explained by the psychic nature of the individual," it must therefore be *as socialized* that human organisms become capable of thought; perceptual capacities thus differ from mind, Durkheim suggests, as "the individual from the social; one can no more derive the second from the first than one can deduce the society from the individual, the whole from the part, or the complex from the simple" ([1912] 1995, 15). Insofar as mind itself is intelligible only with reference to social facts, Durkheim contends, it cannot be right to say such facts are unreal; rather, if such facts lack the determinate spatiotemporal location of, say, neurophysiological events, the only reasonable conclusion is that *society* denotes "a reality *sui generis*" ([1912] 1995, 15).

The upshot, for Durkheim, is that mind is constitutively social, which means it cannot be adequately conceived without reference to irreducibly social facts. What has any of this to do with the "elementary forms of religious life" supposedly at issue for Durkheim? Advancing his proposal that the categories of thought are essentially social, *Elementary Forms of Religious Life* argues that their emergence can be glimpsed in supposedly primitive rites described by nineteenth-century ethnographers. While Boyer's conception of the real privileges causal explanation—his neurocentric approach epitomizes the prevalent presupposition that Peirce thought problematic, according to which (we saw in section II) "the absolutely external causes of perception are the only realities"—Durkheim turns the tables on that supposition, contending that the very idea of *causation* first became available for thought in social performances of ritual. Durkheim takes the totemistic rites described by ethnographers as salient for their producing shared feelings of "force," which is, he argues, indispensable for the abstraction of *agency* as a distinct capacity for causal efficacy: "man could not have arrived at the idea of himself as a force in charge of the body in which it resides without introducing concepts borrowed from social life" ([1912] 1995, 370).

By revealing that *agency* will admit of collective embodiment, the rites considered by Durkheim thus make categories like *causation* available; that idea is abstracted from experiencing one's own capacity for intervening in the world as capable of collective embodiment. Durkheim's thought is redolent of an idea James suggests in *Varieties of Religious Experience*: "The 'original' of the notion of causation is in our inner personal experience, and only there can causes in the old-fashioned sense be directly observed and described" (James 1902, 502n). As is his wont, James thus makes the point with an emphasis on interiority (on our "inner personal experience"). Durkheim, on the other hand, thinks the idea salient precisely for its showing individual minds to be socially constituted; the point, he explains, is that "it is in the form of the soul that man has always imagined the force that he believes he is"—and "man feels he is a soul, and thus a force, because he is a social being" (Durkheim [1912] 1995, 370).

VII. In Conclusion: Some Things Worth Keeping in Mind

Delimiting his aims in *Elementary Forms of Religious Life*, Durkheim proposes the sacred/profane dichotomy as his "first criterion of religious beliefs" ([1912] 1995, 38). Whether or not this dichotomy is reasonably taken as criterial for conceiving *religion*, it's clear why the idea matters to him: Durkheim sets out with the aim of identifying a dichotomy "elementary" enough to make sense as first arousing the idea of being indwelt by a soul, and his characterization of the sacred/profane dichotomy is clearly modeled on the duality of mind and body. Like mind, "the religious phenomenon" thus evinces "a bipartite division of the universe, known and knowable, into two genera that include all that exists but radically exclude one another" ([1912] 1995, 38). For Durkheim, however, the duality of mind and body is not to be conceived in terms of a body's *containing* a mind; religion is salient for its disclosing the real efficacy of the social, and that, Durkheim argues, is what must be acknowledged if we are to make sense of *mind* as real: "Like the ideas of religious force and divinity, the idea of the soul is not without reality. It is quite true that we are made of two distinct parts that are opposed to one another as the sacred is to the profane, and we can say that in a sense there is divinity in us. For society, that unique source of all that is sacred, is not satisfied to move us from outside and to affect us transitorily; it organizes itself lastingly within us" ([1912] 1995, 266).

Here, of course, Boyer's misgivings loom large; how could anything as indeterminate as "society" *move* anybody? Against Boyer's protest—"There is no external force here"—Durkheim can rejoin that *mind* is in the same boat: "Reason does not resist *a priori* the idea that inanimate bodies might be moved by intelligences, as human bodies are, even though present-day science does not easily accommodate this hypothesis" ([1912] 1995, 24). Durkheim thus suggests that the efficacy of *reasons*, evident in anyone's own experience of acting purposefully, suffices to disarm objections like Boyer's. Of course, one might suppose the fact that scientific understanding does not easily accommodate this idea, either, is reason to conclude that what we quaintly consider our "reasons" are finally unreal. If that's right, though, it becomes hard to see how Boyer can warrant his own conclusions; if *reasoning* is real only under a different description—if mind consists in capacities shaped by evolutionary pressures that need not have selected for truth-conduciveness—it would seem to count against his view that Boyer must nonetheless *exhibit* reasoning to support it.

If Durkheim is right, moreover, the origins of the capacities inevitably presupposed by Boyer's exercise of scientific imagination (as by all the other thinkers here considered) can be glimpsed in the social performance of religious ritual: "the idea of natural forces is very likely derived from that of religious forces," Durkheim says, "so between the one and the other there cannot be the chasm that separates the rational from the irrational" ([1912] 1995, 24). There can thus be no distinguishing a "religious" sort of rationality from any other; to that extent, no critique of religious phenomena could make sense as finally overthrowing religion—not, that is, unless such a critique could also make sense as overthrowing mind itself.

Suggested Readings

Anscombe, G. E. M. [1963] 2000. *Intention*. 2nd ed. Cambridge, MA: Harvard University Press.

Arnold, Dan. 2019. "Where in the Brain Does Buddhism Come From? Thoughts Regarding Iain McGilchrist's Reflections on Religion." *Religion, Brain & Behavior* 9 (4): 345–62.

Arnold, Dan. 2021. "Pragmatism as Transcendental Philosophy, Part I: Peirce in Light of James's Radical Empiricism." *American Journal of Theology & Philosophy* 42 (1): 50–103; "Part II: Peirce on God and Personality." *American Journal of Theology & Philosophy* 42 (2): 3–71.

Baker, Lynn Rudder. 1987. *Saving Belief: A Critique of Physicalism*. Princeton, NJ: Princeton University Press.

Barrett, Justin L., ed. 2022. *The Oxford Handbook of the Cognitive Science of Religion*. New York: Oxford University Press.

Carr, David, 1999. *The Paradox of Subjectivity: The Self in the Transcendental Tradition*. New York: Oxford University Press.

Davidson, Donald. 1963. "Actions, Reasons, and Causes." In *Essays on Actions and Events*, 3–20. Oxford: Oxford University Press, 1980.

Garfield, Jay, ed. 2019. *Wilfrid Sellars and Buddhist Philosophy*. New York: Routledge.

Godlove, Terry. 2002. "Saving Belief: On the New Materialism in Religious Studies." In *Radical Interpretation in Religion*, edited by Nancy Frankenberry, 10–24. Cambridge: Cambridge University Press.

Griffiths, Paul. 1986. *On Being Mindless: Buddhist Meditation and the Mind-Body Problem*. LaSalle, IL: Open Court.

Kachru, Sonam. 2021. *Other Lives: Mind and World in Indian Buddhism*. New York: Columbia University Press.

Ludden, David. 2020. "This Is Your Brain on Religion: The Neuroscience of Religious Belief." *Psychology Today*, February 15. https://www.psychologytoday.com/us/blog/talking-apes/202002/is-your-brain-religion.

McDowell, John. 1996. *Mind and World: With a New Introduction*. Cambridge, MA: Harvard University Press.

Newberg, Andrew. 2018. *Neurotheology: How Science Can Enlighten Us About Spirituality*. New York: Columbia University Press.

Rubenstein, Mary-Jane. 2008. *Strange Wonder: The Closure of Metaphysics and the Opening of Awe*. New York: Columbia University Press.

Schueler, G. F. 2003. *Reasons and Purposes: Human Rationality and the Teleological Explanation of Action*. Oxford: Clarendon Press.
Vasquez, Manuel. 2010. *More Than Belief: A Materialist Theory of Religion*. New York: Oxford University Press.

References

Aquinas, Thomas. 1947. *The Summa Theologica*. Translated by the Fathers of the English Dominican Province. New York: Benziger Bros.
Arnold, Daniel A. 2012. *Brains, Buddhas, and Believing: The Problem of Intentionality in Classical Buddhist and Cognitive-Scientific Philosophy of Mind*. New York: Columbia University Press.
Boyer, Pascal. 2001. *Religion Explained: The Evolutionary Origins of Religious Thought*. New York: Basic Books.
Colapietro, Vincent. 1989. *Peirce's Approach to the Self: A Semiotic Perspective on Human Subjectivity*. Albany, NY: SUNY Press.
Dennett, Daniel. 1981. *Brainstorms: Philosophical Essays on Mind and Psychology*. Cambridge, MA: MIT Press.
Dennett, Daniel. 1991. *Consciousness Explained*. Boston: Little, Brown.
Descombes, Vincent. 2001. *The Mind's Provisions: A Critique of Cognitivism*. Translated by Stephen Adam Schwartz. Princeton, NJ: Princeton University Press.
Durkheim, Émile. [1912] 1995. *The Elementary Forms of Religious Life*. Translated by Karen Fields. New York: The Free Pres.
Forster, Paul. 2011. *Peirce and the Threat of Nominalism*. New York: Cambridge University Press.
Geertz, Clifford. 1973. "The Impact of the Concept of Culture on the Concept of Man." In *The Interpretation of Cultures: Selected Essays by Clifford Geertz*, 33–54. New York: Basic Books.
Heim, Maria. 2013. *The Forerunner of All Things: Buddhaghosa on Mind, Intention, and Agency*. New York: Oxford University Press.
Hume, David. [1757] 1993. *The Natural History of Religion*. In J. C. A. Gaskin, *Principal Writings on Religion, including Dialogues Concerning Natural Religion and The Natural History of Religion*. Oxford: Oxford University Press.
Jackson, Roger. 2019. *Mind Seeing Mind: Mahāmudrā and the Geluk Tradition*. Somerville, MA: Wisdom Publications.
James, William. 1902. *Varieties of Religious Experience*. New York: Longmans, Green.
Lane, Robert. 2018. *Peirce on Realism and Idealism*. New York: Cambridge University Press.
Lang, Karen. 1986. *Āryadeva's Catuḥśataka: On the Bodhisattva's Cultivation of Merit and Knowledge*. Copenhagen: Akademisk Forlag.

Norman, K. R., trans. 2000. *The Word of the Doctrine (Dhammapada)*. Oxford: Pali Text Society.

Peirce, Charles S. [1871] 2019. [Letter to the Editor of the *Nation*, December 10, 1871]. In *The Real Metaphysical Club: The Philosophers, Their Debates, and Selected Writings from 1870 to 1885*, edited by Frank X. Ryan, Brian E. Butler, and James A. Good, 118. Albany, NY: SUNY Press.

Peirce, Charles S. 1905. "What Pragmatism Is." *The Monist* 15 (2): 161–81.

Pruden, Leo, trans. 1991. *Abhidharmakośabhāṣyam of Vasubandhu*. Vols. 1 and 2. Translated by Leo Pruden from the French translation of Louis de La Vallée Poussin. Berkeley, CA: Asian Humanities Press.

Putnam, Hilary. 1975. "The Meaning of Meaning." In *Mind, Language and Reality: Philosophical Papers*, vol. 2. Cambridge: Cambridge University Press.

Robinson, Marilynne. 2010. *Absence of Mind: The Dispelling of Inwardness from the Modern Myth of the Self*. New Haven, CT: Yale University Press.

Silk, Jonathan, ed. 2016. *Materials towards the Study of Vasubandhu's Viṃśikā*. Harvard Oriental Series, vol. 81. Cambridge, MA: Department of South Asian Studies, Harvard University.

Swinburne, Richard. 1991. *The Existence of God*. Rev. ed. Oxford: Clarendon Press.

Taliaferro, Charles. 1994. *Consciousness and the Mind of God*. New York: Cambridge University Press.

Taylor, Mark C. 1998. "Introduction." In *Critical Terms for Religious Studies*, edited by Mark C. Taylor, 1–19. Chicago: University of Chicago Press.

Vidal, Fernando. 2009. "Brainhood, Anthropological Figure of Modernity." *History of the Human Sciences* 22 (1): 5–36.

13 MONEY

Andrea R. Jain

"Elevate Your Om." This is the tagline for an athleisure wear line by Spiritual Gangster, a high-end, US-based corporation selling a variety of apparel, from T-shirts to yoga pants. Buyers and sellers of these kinds of "spiritual" products skillfully appropriate and commodify religion, hence Sanskrit words like "om" and "karma" make frequent appearances on their products and marketing materials (Jain 2014a and 2020). Products feature evocative objects, images, or ideas, resulting in commodities ranging from yoga pants with "good karma" appliqued across the butt to T-shirts featuring the expression "namaste all day." Consumers love to spend their money on these kinds of products.

Skillful cultural appropriation of "ancient" or "exotic" wisdom, however, is not always what sells. As in other areas of urban globalized culture, consumers pick and choose from a variety of religious products, practices, and worldviews to construct individualized "lifestyles."[1] That means products must suit individualized needs and identities, which might vary within a single household. Imagine a Christian household in the United States, for example, in which the bookshelf holds all of the following titles: *Every Man's Bible*; *The Woman's Study Bible*; *Teen Study Bible*; and *The Complete Illustrated Children's Bible*.

Does spending money on religion have to be as explicit as buying a

1. Mike Featherstone explains the use of the term *lifestyle* in consumer culture: "It connotes individuality, self-expression, and a stylistic self-consciousness. One's body, clothes, speech, leisure pastimes, eating and drinking preferences, home, car, choice of holidays, etc. are to be regarded as indicators of the individuality of taste and sense of style of the owner/consumer" (2007, 81).

yoga mat with "om" printed across it or a Bible suited to one's gender and stage of life? It does not. In fact, spending money is often a religious exercise even when the product being bought or sold is not explicitly tied to a particular religious tradition, institution, or worldview. In order to spend money, after all, one must ascribe a certain value, in its meanings as both prizing and assigning worth, to a certain thing. Religion too is concerned with ascribing value, and this is the case today in both of its senses. What religious adherents do—what they sing about, pray about, mourn over, eat, touch, have sex with, abstain from, and spend money on—in many cases can be said to entail a process of ascribing value to something prized, deemed better, or more pure—valuing this over that. This is true, for example, about what religious adherents allow to enter their bodies. Hence, historically, the extent of religious concern about what, when, or how a person eats is rivaled only by concerns about with whom, when, or how a person has sex. Religion is as much about what a person spends money on, another kind of consumption.

The point is that profit, status, and power may be the goals of entrepreneurs and consumers, yet the religious lives they narrate should not be separated from the social structures in which they are embedded (Jain 2020, 28); in other words, their embeddedness in economic dynamics and exchange should not be assumed to be separate or distinct from their religious lives. Religion and economy are co-produced—that is, in making one, societies make the other.

Entrepreneurs and consumers engage in religious ways of organizing, approaching, and interacting with the socioeconomic (today that means late capitalist) world in their attempts to turn a profit and in their spending behaviors. How we organize our consumer life and how consumer practices organize us are religious issues; the religion of corporate culture, for example, "is in the consumer interests they protect, the social possibilities they promote, the hierarchies they reiterate, and the commodities they sell" (Lofton 2017, xii). Religion is in everything corporations do. It is also in what consumers do (see, e.g., Lofton 2017; Jain 2014a; Jain 2020). In other words, the relationship between religious and selling or consumer practices is a dynamic and mutually constitutive one.

Put simply, a person's religious *story*, in the sense of their accepted cultural logic and processes of ascribing value, is in part told in receipts. Put more simply, *doing* religion often involves *spending* money. Hence, this chapter on *money* locates religion's disciplines, discourses, and institutions within economic frameworks, with a focus on our current and dominant late capitalist context. I theorize the relationships money has to society, politics, and culture as religious. I also ask how entrepreneurs, marketers, and consumers embody relations of religious ideas and practices to not just ethical values, but also processes of valuation through marketing, promotional, and consumer activities.

In the following discussion of *money* as a critical term in the study of religion, my concern is with late capitalism and the global market.[2] It is important at the outset to insist, however, that even though capitalism is a world system, neoliberalism is a pervasive social ethic, and there is a global market, these commonalities do not break down every barrier between human societies—spending money on religion, making money off of religion, or spending or making money in religious ways still looks different across cultures (Wesselhoeft and Moodie 2021).[3] Scholars of religion have had an "overwhelming tendency to assume that Christianity should receive prime of place in our analyses of capital" (Bartel and Hulsether 2019, 585). In fact, non-US contexts are often presented as case studies, assessed to either "verify or falsify theories developed in Euro-American and often explicitly Christian contexts" (McLaughlin et al. 2020, 704). All of this has led to a consolidation of particular versions of Christianity and Protestant secularism as the moral, political, and religious foundations of capitalism as a world system. The exact relationships between mythmaking, market dynamics, neoliberal governance, finance, and spending money, however, vary across cultural contexts (Wesselhoeft and Moodie 2021).

Furthermore, religious communities have always participated in economic production and even created financial instruments, but it is a generally unquestioned assumption that adherents of a given religion, nearly any religion, in the capitalist world system put their money toward religious ends and, in turn, adopt attitudes about money and engage in religious practices that cohere with or respond to capitalism. Indeed, what a person does (and does not) spend their money on is the pivot around which in many cases people *do* religion (from spending money on funerals and Bibles to yoga classes and mindfulness courses), which also points to the ways they organize their personal and corporate lives around shared

2. On defining *neoliberalism*, see below.

3. Wesselhoeft and Moodie (2021) provide the introduction to a roundtable published in the *Journal of the American Academy of Religion* and titled "Living Neoliberalism: Negotiating Markets and Morality Outside the West." See also the other articles in that roundtable.

values. I am suggesting, in other words, that we develop an understanding of religion in the capitalist world system in terms of what people spend their money on. In an effort to do so, after a brief survey of some of the questions surrounding the term *money* and the emergent discourse on religion and capitalism, this chapter will focus on a capitalist industry in which spending money figures prominently in *doing* religion: the multibillion-dollar global yoga industry.

Money and Religion: Situating Critical Terms

Scholars of religion have reiterated that the subject of their work is not rooted in a set of essential qualities, yet it is fair to say that the term *religion* often refers to ideas or behaviors grounded in "a shared axiology or set of values or goals" (Jain 2014a, 98). Furthermore, following Gail Hamner:

> What distinguishes each approach particularly as *religion* (and not *not* religion) has to do with modalities of valuation, that is, with how persons demarcate (acceptingly or not) an element of life as part of a larger structure of valuation and against other, competing valuations. . . . Not everything humans value gets marked or described as religion, yet whatever is claimed for religion is always marked or described in terms of values and in terms of the lived structures within which these values are embraced or rejected. Values thus refract larger social valuations, the sense, orientation, and depth of which are infinitely variable. (Hamner 2019, 1032)

As Hamner also reminds us, "the term 'value' here indicates regard, importance, worth, or usefulness, whereas the term 'valuation' indicates a process of assessment of value" (2019, 1033). Because religion concerns shared values and because social structures precede the assessment or determination of the value of things, religion is social; social structures demarcate religious behaviors and organize religious interactions. Religion is also political insofar as determining the value of things entails organizing them into hierarchies and demarcating authority and power. "Even so," as Hamner points out, "transvaluation, in the sense of resistance to structures of valuation and the production of counter-values or new values, is also an ongoing and important social process" (2019, 1033).

Identifying when ascribing value is religious and when it is not is a tricky and admittedly somewhat arbitrary process, but I suggest asking about these other things when trying to decide whether a particular act of ascribing value is a part of a larger body of religious practice: Does it involve things set apart or deemed special or particularly powerful? Is it tied to a shared worldview (even if not an all-encompassing worldview that believers think accounts for everything)? Is it grounded in a shared set of values or goals that are concerned with resolving weakness, suffering, or death? And is its value somehow reinforced through narrative or ritual? If you answered yes to any of the above, then it might be fair to describe the ascription of value as religious (Jain 2014a, 98).

The approach to religion in this chapter is a materialist one; that is, it locates religion within material conditions, religious institutions as historically contingent, and both as currently enmeshed in late capitalism—the socioeconomic system that has been in full force since about 1989, in which the cultural logic of capitalism delineates the limits of political and social life, with significant effects on education, healthcare, popular culture, life of all kinds, and even methods of resistance. In most cases religious actors and institutions are complicit with capitalist expansion, and in some cases they react against and critique it. The idea that capitalism could usurp religion and commodify it is too simple, though. Religious commodities do not replace what is otherwise authentically religious. Rather, new religious forms—within and beyond previously existing religious institutions—emerge in capitalist contexts. Monetized religion is not a takeover or replacement of "real" religion or an alternative to it, but the current dominant manifestation of religion. Another way to put this is that, although corporate and consumer practices mirror capitalist values and processes of valuation (or, again, react against them), the incidents we identify as religious have not declined; rather, what religion looks like has been transformed in (and in some cases through) commodification, marketing, and spending money.

Indeed, money has always been religious. In fact, the English term *money* is derived from the Latin *moneta*, meaning "mint" and a name of the goddess Juno in whose temple in Rome money was coined. According to the *Oxford English Dictionary*'s definition of *money*, it is "current coin; metal stamped in pieces of portable form as a medium of exchange and measure of value." Any attempt to evaluate its role in culture, therefore, solicits reflection on value. To study money, like the study of religion, is to study what has value, what value things have, and how people assess value. Nonetheless, unlike the substantive weight of discussions on ritual, myth, belief, or even the body in the study of religion, there has not been much on *money* as a critical term. That said, there is a conversation about the co-production of religion and economy and, more specifically, the entanglement of religion and capitalism.

A sample of work on the co-production of economy and religion includes studies of the following: the "fetishization of evil" in the devil among South American workers alienated from the commodities they produce (Taussig 1980); the influence of colonial economies on the production of religious ethics and salvation narratives (Comaroff and Comaroff 1991); the colonial, economic legacies of the production of the term *religion* (Asad 1993); neoliberalism as a technology of governing that takes the form of a pro-capitalist Islam (Ong 2006); the "Protestant secularism of the market" (Jakobsen and Pellegrini 2008); the Christian service ethic of the corporate culture at Wal-Mart (Moreton 2010); the "theology of money" as a dynamic social force in global capitalism (Goodchild 2009); religious formulations, Christian and non-Christian, that valorize capitalist notions of prosperity and entrepreneurship (Birla 2009; Moreton 2010; Bowler 2013; Hoesterey 2015; Frederick 2016; Shirazi 2016; Chacko 2019; Williams-Oerberg 2019; Bruntz and Schedneck 2020; Jain 2014a and 2020); the reinterpretation of Islam in service to capitalist "spiritual economies" (Rudnyckyj 2010); the "industrial religion" of factory systems and market cultures (Callahan, Lofton, and Seales 2010); religious charity initiatives that are simultaneously critical of and caught up in capitalist structures (Elisha 2011; Hackworth 2012; Atia 2013; O'Neill 2019; Watanabe 2019); the connections between economic globalization and Hindu nationalism (Nanda 2011; Jain 2020); the ways religion and economy produce one another in corporate culture (Lofton 2017); the religious asceticism of consumer culture (Jain 2014a; Logan 2017); the corporate invention of "Christian America" (Kruse 2015); the convergence of Enlightenment modernity and Christian Protestantism in the global capitalist public sphere (Vatter 2016); Christian gift-giving and finance capitalism in Colombia (Bartel 2016); the ways in which American corporate culture's success requires an emphasis on religious ideals and collaboration with churches (Porterfield 2018); the marketplace as religious archive and religious studies tools as ways of analyzing corporate structures and their projects of moral formation and meaning (Lofton 2017); examining the religious and theological sources of money's power in Christian thought and society (Singh 2018); the Christian missionary discourses and racial capitalism of Coca-Cola's multiculturalism (Hulsether 2018); the evangelical publishing industry, which is heavily influenced by Bible sales (Vaca 2019); the commodification of religious products like yoga in consumer culture (Jain 2014a and 2020); and the anti-capitalist "gestures" but underlying capitalist logic of "neoliberal spirituality" (Jain 2020).

Before I turn to an analysis of the multi-billion-dollar global yoga industry as one way of assessing *money* as a critical term in the study of religion and the co-production of religion and economy, it is important to discuss a term I have already used several times: *neoliberalism*. Scholars love arguing over the meaning of terms—hence volumes like this one—and it is fair to say that *neoliberalism* is one of the most contested terms in our contemporary lexicon.[4] I use *neoliberalism* as a diagnostic tool meant to shed light on the excesses, exploitative and extractive violence, and inequality of capitalism (Harvey 2005) as well as the ways it serves as an imperial global project that moves from the management of state power to the inner workings of the subject, normatively constructing individuals as entrepreneurial actors, forming new *neoliberal subjectivities* (Brown 2005, 37; Brown 2015). *Neoliberalism*, therefore, refers to, not just a set of capitalist, free-market economic policies, but also a governing rationality or way of thinking that disseminates market values and metrics to every sphere of life, formulating everything, everywhere, in terms of capital investment and appreciation, including and especially living beings. *Neoliberal governmentality* holds the individual fully responsible for their conditions, how much money they have, and how they spend it, and it can be seen at play in discourses of self-sufficiency, which reify the individual, construed as an automaton, ideally entrepreneurial, strong, and resilient—often illustrated in how they "make good money," make "good" consumer choices, and spend money on the "right" things.

Making and Spending Money on Yoga

We can tease out the relationship between money and religion by evaluating the ways yoga as a consumer product weds aims of material "prosperity" and "success" to the quest for liberation or "freedom," rooted in rituals of self-care and myths of ancient or exotic wisdom. "Personal growth," "self-care," and "transformation" are just some of the generative tropes we often hear in this industry as marketers attempt to convince consumers to spend their money on yoga. Huge swathes of consumers in global cities all

4. See, for example, Ganti on the debate over *neoliberalism's* utility (Ganti 2014, 99).

over the world do spend their money on yoga, hence the emergence of an over 80-billion-dollar global industry.

It would be a mistake, however, to reduce industries to the basic utility of commodities. The yoga industry, in accordance with consumer culture in general (Featherstone 1991, 112), destabilizes the basic utility of commodities and services and assigns to them new meanings. In other words, yoga brands sell products that are more than just the fulfillment of utilitarian or hedonistic needs; rather, values become contained in them. Beyond merely creating communities around a set of values or goals, yoga consumers, in fact, share many qualities with what we often imagine as traditional religions, including demarcating special and set apart spaces and times, posing solutions to the problems of suffering and death, and constructing and sharing myths and rituals (Jain 2014a, 98).

Yoga has always taken multiple forms in the many pathways of its historical development as a part of South Asian religious history, and has continued to do so through its capitalist entanglement and popularization (Jain 2014a). Since the latter half of the twentieth century, yoga has become a form of "neoliberal spirituality" whereby the consumer is called upon to exercise their personal autonomy and manifest their freedom by making careful consumer choices that reflect their compliance with and devotion to self-care, health, and success (Jain 2020). The yoga industry, therefore, is an example of how religious institutions, symbols, and behaviors remain deeply religious even in (and in some cases through) commodification and spending money, though they are religious in new and different ways than before their entry into the global market. Even though some have argued for yoga's Hindu "origins" and therefore its Hindu "essence," the yoga that is widely popularized and bought and sold around the world is closer to a religion of capitalism than to any traditional religious complex (Jain 2014a, 130–57, and 2014b).

In the latter half of the twentieth century, as late capitalism became dominant in much of the world and as consumption increasingly pivoted around individual preference, even religion often became subject to individual choice. Through mass-marketed books and other media, religious products and services were often not even tied to particular times and places, such as church on Sunday morning, but could be practiced anywhere at any time (Einstein 2008, 7). Mike Featherstone explains how, in this "time of *mass* consumption . . . changes in production techniques, market segmentation and consumer demand for a wider range of products, are often regarded as making possible greater choice (the management of which itself becomes an art form)" (2007, 81).

This period witnessed an explosion of sundry yoga brands into the global market (Jain 2014a, 73–94). Entrepreneurs, sometimes "entrepreneurial gurus" (Jain 2014a), began to brand yoga in the same ways other products and services are branded, by giving it "a name, term, design, symbol, or any other feature that identifies one seller's goods or service as distinct from those of other sellers" (American Marketing Association 2021). Brands signify different meanings by being "packaged" differently. Branding requires marketers to uniquely package their products by "mythologizing" them, a process that serves to "position" them in consumers' minds (Einstein 2008, 12). As yoga generates somatic, semantic, and symbolic fields of meaning meant to appeal to consumer desires, brands seek to signify those to millions of consumers interested in "doing yoga," as it is colloquially put. In this way, branding mythologizes yoga products and services, ranging from mats and pants to styles and teachers. Successful yoga entrepreneurs exploit popular trends by managing their brand images in ways that make them represent popular ways of conceptualizing and practicing self-care.

Most yoga entrepreneurs and organizations prescribe yoga not as an all-encompassing worldview or system of practice, but as one part of self-care that can be consumed in combination with other worldviews and practices (Jain 2014a, 78). All of this serves to make yoga attractive to large target audiences of consumers who do not want to go to an Indian ashram in order to do yoga. Instead of relying on yoga transmission through the traditional guru-disciple relationship in the isolated context of an ashram, most yoga entrepreneurs build large organizations for mass marketing the easily accessible commodities, classes, and camps or retreats associated with their yoga brands.

Today, most yoga consumers shop for conveniently located yoga classes and for other yoga products, such as yoga pants, that are immediately available in local shopping malls or through online retail sites. Constructing brands from which to choose is based on a dialectical exchange between the entrepreneurs who produce desires and needs for goods and services and consumers who buy them based on individual preferences (Holt 2002, 71–72). Yoga brands tend to offer similar ends: self-care that gets you closer to perfection through physical and psychological work. Consequently, the only way for the consumer to differentiate one set of yoga products and services from another is to interpret the idiosyncratic meanings that brands signify (Jain 2014a, 73–94). In short, buying yoga products is personal. Consequently, yoga entrepreneurs must manage their brand images in ways that make consumers feel personally connected to them.

In a capitalist world, however, a personal connection with a product is not usually enough to make it yours. Rather, getting products and services almost always requires the consumer to spend money. The amount of spending on yoga depends largely on location and brand. A consumer can purchase a pair of yoga pants at Target for $19.99, or purchase a pair from Lululemon, a Canadian high-end yoga apparel brand that at a minimum charges $98 for yoga pants. On the retail website Amazon, the consumer can choose from a variety of yoga mats with unfamiliar brands for under $20, or they can go to a specialty shop and purchase a stylish Manduka brand yoga mat, which could cost as much as $280. And all that does not include the cost of yoga classes. If a consumer is able to invest even more money in yoga, they might purchase a spot in a yoga retreat at locations throughout India, the United States, Europe, the Bahamas, or Brazil.

Some yoga products are greenwashed. There is growing concern over the images broadcast across the mainstream media of plastic waste crowding oceans and beaches. Yoga consumers might respond by buying the high-end apparel of Satva Living, which offers "mindfully designed organic fashion." The company claims to improve the health and wellness of "conscious consumers" as well as the lives of the Indian organic farmers they partner with and work with under the model of "creative capitalism," an approach that ensures that a portion of profits are invested back into the communities and agricultural programs of the farmers. Satva Living products are sold across India as well as the United States and are available, for example, at Whole Foods Market, where yoga consumers might also spend their money on organic foods and "eco-friendly" biodegradable paper plates.

There are also attempts to challenge the imperialism behind Western commodifications and appropriations of yoga, and more specifically the North American multi-billion-dollar yoga industry, by formulating yoga as a neoliberal "political ritual" and reclaiming it for India (Jain 2020, 131–56). For example, the entrepreneur, celebrity, and yoga guru Baba Ramdev runs massive yoga camps in India as well as the corporation Patanjali Ayurved, which claims to offer alternatives to the products of Western appropriations and commodifications in their natural, ayurvedic products that are made in India. Ramdev profits off of products marketed as traditional, natural foods, and ancient medicinal practices. Consumers pay for Ramdev's camps and buy Patanjali Ayurved's products because of the authority they invest in its ambassador. Ramdev consistently positions Patanjali Ayurved as a homegrown Indian company fighting foreign competitors. His company's logo and packaging use the orange, white, and green of the Indian flag, and although packaging information is written in English, it says "Made in Bharat," using the country's Hindi name, rather than "Made in India." All of Patanjali Ayurved's products are marketed as "Swadeshi" (meaning "one's own country" or indigenous to India).

Gender is central, not peripheral, to neoliberal yoga operations, especially insofar as structural transformation is not expected as the solution to inequities or discrimination; rather, resolving those challenges is a burden placed on the shoulders of the disenfranchised, that is, women and other gender and sexual minorities (Jain 2020, 101–30). Yoga, for example, is a woman's tool for breaking through the glass ceiling, not dismantling the ceiling so that all women have equal opportunity. If you are a working mom and feel exhausted all the time, take a yoga class. This is the way to achieve that envied work-life balance and increase strength, energy, productivity, and resilience, not demanding structural changes such as better parental leave policies or childcare at the workplace. Or are you seeking a cure for your socially deviant sexual desires? Baba Ramdev guarantees that he can "cure" homosexuality with yoga.

Spiritual Gangster yogawear features a variety of expressions conveying a neoliberal ethic of self-sufficiency—for example, "You're exactly where you're supposed to be," or "What you think, you become." Similarly, Baba Ramdev espouses a neoliberal ethic of "positive thinking" and "self-care," which he disseminates across India through speeches, interviews, advertisements, and other media platforms. This "self-care" spirituality is precisely the kind that informs bestselling manifestos, such as Whole Foods Market CEO John Mackey's *Conscious Capitalism*, in which the ideal person is construed as atomized, self-optimizing, and entrepreneurial (Jain 2020, 18).

We might call this the religious discourse of capitalism, for which there is a rich archive, from the expressions printed across yogawear to mindfulness manuals and health foods packaging. Spiritual Gangster and Baba Ramdev are just two articulations of this peculiar variant that has come to the forefront of global culture in the past few decades and incites its adherents to work on themselves and accept full responsibility for their own well-being, self-care, and liberation, rather than look to social resources or systemic change.

The meaning of yoga is conveyed, however, not only through what products and services consumers choose to spend their money on, but also what they choose not to spend their money on (Jain 2014a, 126–228). Although not in the majority, some practitioners in fact oppose commodification by refusing to spend money on yoga. For example, the yoga practitioner can now opt out of purchasing a yoga mat or attend donation-based yoga classes. Some choose yoga spaces that do not require a mat or payment for classes because those are believed to better signify the "true" meaning of yoga and the most "authentic" path to self-care (Jain 2014a, 126–28).

Of course, the argument that capitalism shapes self-care industries like yoga accords with the academic consensus that the present moment's dominant social systems shape the ways people are capable of thinking, even when they seek to think beyond or against them. Whichever area of contemporary religion or culture one studies, be it the so-called "spiritual but not religious" or the traditionally religiously affiliated, one will likely uncover certain capitalist assumptions: for example, that a person is entitled to as great a share of the world's resources as that person's money can buy; that the individual is fully responsible for their conditions, how much money they have, and how they spend it; that individuals should strive to be entrepreneurial—that is, to be "productive" and "make money"; and that they should be self-optimizing and self-sustaining by spending money on the "right" products (Jain 2020). The prescriptions for self-care or personal freedom that are common in the yoga industry are rarely concerned with social transformation; they more often evidence the requirements for hard workers and conforming consumers. In other words, as the demands on people to work and be productive have increased, so we have seen an increase in yoga teachers, natural dietary systems, yoga athleisure wear, and mindfulness courses, which for the most part claim to enhance productivity and conformity to rigid moral and bodily standards. A wide range of commodities are celebrated as good consumer choices, products that lead to better living outcomes. If you are unhappy, unwell, stressed, or not the proper weight, that is because you are not making the right consumer choices. You are not buying the right stuff. Where you are in life is on you—changing your conditions is your responsibility.

I do not mean to offer just one more voice bemoaning the ways corporations profit off of and consumers spend money on yoga as if its products were merely numbing devices that enable consumers to ignore the problems of capitalism or evidence of the corruption or loss of "authentic" religious forms. Many scholars have already offered referenda on the commodification of religion, suggesting these products merely serve as palliatives or coping mechanisms.[5] These commodities, in their view, function like a fetish, a fantasy that "tricks the fetish worshipper into believing that an 'inanimate object' will give up its natural character to gratify his desires" (Marx and Engels 1957, 22). In other words, they offer consumers an escape into an experience (of the present moment, of a romanticized or orientalized Other, or an idealized ancient past) that allows them to imagine themselves as separate from the busyness of everyday life, and by extension disconnected from capitalism. I do not think of yoga consumers as duped into spending money on commodities that numb them to the normalized violence and inequities of capitalism.

That said, the problem with industries like yoga is that they make promises of healing and liberation without actually addressing the structural and economic causes of our greatest threats, such as social inequality, conditions of exploitation, or climate change and planetary crisis. It is critical to examine the material and social operations of commodities, pursued with a sensitivity to subtle—and sometimes not-so-subtle—power dynamics, complicating any straightforward progress narrative about religious or spiritual democratization, increased choice, or individual autonomy among consumers. Large-scale institutions and industries, including the yoga industry, typically direct their address to the middle and upper classes, effectively erasing the problems faced by the vast majority of the population from their view. Furthermore, as much as individual consumers are not in control of their living conditions or places on the socioeconomic hierarchy, shopping or the notion of *consumer choice* gives consumers a sense of control over their lives.

All of that said, what should we make of the subversive anti-capitalist gestures of spiritual commodities that do call on adherents to think beyond the individual and even out into the environment? Spiritual Gangster's products, for example, range from yoga pants with "Good Vibes" appliqued across the butt to T-shirts that read "Peace Love Yoga," as if these three were inherently compatible and mutually reinforcing ethical

5. For example, Slavoj Žižek (2005) offers such a referendum on modern appropriations of Buddhism, and Jeremy Carrette and Richard King's *Selling Spirituality: The Silent Takeover of Religion* (2005) bemoans the co-option of spirituality by market forces, arguing that *spirituality* is a "vacuous cultural trope" that can be mixed with anything (46) and represents the "takeover" of religion.

commitments. The company also donates an unspecified percentage of every sale to provide food for those living in poverty. What about those profiting off of commodities that claim to counter the problems of unfettered capitalism with charitable giving or various forms of "conscious capitalism"? What should we make of efforts in India to challenge the imperialism behind Western commodifications and appropriations of yoga by reclaiming yoga for India? What should we make of the feminist calls for women's empowerment that are nearly ubiquitous in the yoga industry's discourses? What should we make of attempts to greenwash yoga?

I suggest we attend to these anti-capitalist gestures. Rather than a mode through which consumers ignore, escape, or are numbed to the problems of capitalism, many spending behaviors do actually acknowledge those problems and, in fact, subvert them. But they subvert them through mere gestures (Jain 2020). From provocative taglines printed across T-shirts or packaging to various forms of charitable giving, commodification serves as a strategy through which subversion itself is contained. In other words, protest against the dominant socioeconomic and cultural order is simultaneously expressed and contained when consumers spend their money on these kinds of products.

The social theorist Mark Fisher describes these kinds of anti-capitalist gestures in other areas of popular culture. He discusses, for example, Hollywood movies or television—how often is the villain the "evil corporation" (2009)? As Fisher points out, Hollywood films that villainize capitalism perform our anti-capitalism for us, allowing us to continue to consume without blame or guilt (2009, 13). In other words, the yoga industry, with its countercultural or subversive gestures, is domesticated to the dominant culture, to a capitalist logic. We are anti-capitalist in the ways we, well, spend money.

Conclusion

In the study of money and religion, we uncover how religious communities, narratives, and behaviors support the adoption of capitalist policies that put the market at the center of governance and the rise of neoliberal governmentality, both of which have had devastating consequences, including planetary crisis and extreme disparities—especially along racial, ethnic, gender, and religious lines and between species—and increased wealth for the few while the majority face greater financial and environmental uncertainties and pressures. These are unfolding across the planet where different political contexts have undergone related—if by no means identical—late capitalist structural changes, hence there are few topics as important as the co-production of religion and economy for scholars of religion.

Spending money on religion or in a religious way means participating in a capitalist world system. Whether we turn our gaze to the yoga industry (Jain 2014a, 2014b, and 2020), the evangelical publishing industry (Vaca 2019), or a thousand industries in between, we will uncover the fact that what a consumer spends money on—from a yoga mat to a Bible—is largely determined by some combination of branding, monetary issues, market pressures, class stratification, and the voice of neoliberal governance whispering, "You are what you buy."

Suggested Readings

Bowler, Kate. 2013. *Blessed: A History of the American Prosperity Gospel*. New York: Oxford University Press.

Brown, Wendy. 2015. *Undoing the Demos: Neoliberalism's Stealth Revolution*. Cambridge, MA: MIT Press.

Einstein, Mara. 2008. *Brands of Faith: Marketing Religion in a Commercial Age*. New York: Routledge.

Fisher, Mark. 2009. *Capitalist Realism: Is There No Alternative?* Hampshire, UK: Zero Books.

Harvey, David. 2005. *A Brief History of Neoliberalism*. New York: Oxford University Press.

Jain, Andrea R. 2020. *Peace Love Yoga: The Politics of Global Spirituality*. New York: Oxford University Press.

Lofton, Kathryn. 2017. *Consuming Religion*. Chicago: University of Chicago Press.

Wesselhoeft, Kirsten, and Deonnie Moodie. "Introduction" To Roundtable: Living Neoliberalism: Markets and Morality Outside the West. *Journal of the American Academy of Religion* 89 (3): 819–39.

References

American Marketing Association. 2021. "Definitions of Marketing." Accessed July 1, 2021. https://www.ama.org/the-definition-of-marketing-what-is-marketing/.

Asad, Talal. 1993. *Genealogies of Religion: Discipline and Reasons of Power in Christianity and Islam*. Baltimore, MD: Johns Hopkins University Press.

Atia, Mona. 2013. *Building a House in Heaven: Pious Neoliberalism and Islamic Charity in Egypt*. Minneapolis: University of Minnesota Press.

Bartel, Rebecca C. 2016. "Giving Is Believing: Credit and Christmas in Colombia." *Journal of the American Academy of Religion* 84 (4): 1006–28.

Bartel, Rebecca C., and Lucia Hulsether. 2019. "Introduction." *Journal of the American Academy of Religion* 87 (3): 581–95.

Birla, Ritu. 2009. *Stages of Capital: Law, Culture, and Market Governance in Late Colonial India*. Durham, NC: Duke University Press.

Bowler, Kate. 2013. *Blessed: A History of the American Prosperity Gospel*. New York: Oxford University Press.

Brown, Wendy. 2005. "Neo-liberalism and the End of Liberal Democracy." *Theory & Event* 7 (1): 37–59.

Brown, Wendy. 2015. *Undoing the Demos: Neoliberalism's Stealth Revolution*. Cambridge, MA: MIT Press.

Bruntz, Courtney, and Brook Schedneck. 2020. *Buddhist Tourism in Asia*. Honolulu: University of Hawai'i Press.

Callahan, Richard J., Jr., Kathryn Lofton, and Chad E. Seales. 2010. "Allegories of Progress: Industrial Religion in the United States." *Journal of the American Academy of Religion* 78 (1): 1–39.

Carrette, Jeremy, and Richard King. 2005. *Selling Spirituality: The Silent Takeover of Religion*. New York: Routledge.

Chacko, Priya. 2019. "Marketizing *Hindutva*: The State, Society, and Markets in Hindu Nationalism." *Modern Asian Studies* 53 (2): 377–410.

Comaroff, Jean, and John L. Comaroff, eds. 1991. *Of Revelation and Revolution: Christianity, Colonialism, and Consciousness in South Africa*. 2 vols. Chicago: University of Chicago Press.

Comaroff, Jean, and John L. Comaroff, eds. 2000. *Millennial Capitalism and the Culture of Neoliberalism*. Durham, NC: Duke University Press.

Einstein, Mara. 2008. *Brands of Faith: Marketing Religion in a Commercial Age*. New York: Routledge.

Elisha, Omri. 2011. *Moral Ambition: Mobilization and Social Outreach in Evangelical Megachurches*. Berkeley: University of California Press.

Featherstone, Mike. 1991. "The Body in Consumer Culture." In *The Body: Social Process and Cultural Theory*, edited by Mike Featherstone, Mike Hepworth, and Bryan S. Turner, 170–96. London: Sage.

Featherstone, Mike. 2007. *Consumer Culture and Postmodernism*. 2nd ed. London: Sage.

Fisher, Mark. 2009. *Capitalist Realism: Is There No Alternative?* Hampshire, UK: Zero Books.

Frederick, Marla. 2016. *Colored Television: American Religion Gone Global*. Stanford, CA: Stanford University Press.

Ganti, Tejaswini. 2014. "Neoliberalism." *Annual Review of Anthropology* 43: 89–104.

Goodchild, Philip. 2009. *Theology of Money*. Durham, NC: Duke University Press.

Hackworth, Jason. 2012. *Faith Based: Religious Neoliberalism and the Politics of Welfare in the United States*. Athens: University of Georgia Press.

Hamner, Gail M. 2019. "Theorizing Religion and the Public Sphere: Affect, Technology, Valuation." *Journal of the American Academy of Religion* 87 (4): 1008–49.

Harvey, David. 2005. *A Brief History of Neoliberalism*. New York: Oxford University Press.

Hoesterey, James. 2015. *Rebranding Islam: Piety, Prosperity, and a Self-Help Guru*. Stanford, CA: Stanford University Press.

Holt, Douglas B. 2002. "Why Do Brands Cause Trouble? A Dialectical Theory of Consumer Culture and Branding." *Journal of Consumer Research* 29 (June): 71–72.

Hulsether, Lucia. 2018. "Buying into the Dream: The Religion of Racial Capitalism in CocaCola's World." *Public Culture* 30 (3): 483–508.

Jain, Andrea R. 2014a. *Selling Yoga: From Counterculture to Pop Culture*. New York: Oxford University Press.

Jain, Andrea R. 2014b. "Who Is to Say Modern Yoga Practitioners Have It All Wrong? On Hindu Origins and Yogaphobia." *Journal of the American Academy of Religion* 82 (2): 427–71.

Jain, Andrea R. 2020. *Peace Love Yoga: The Politics of Global Spirituality*. New York: Oxford University Press.

Jakobsen, Janet R., and Ann Pellegrini, eds. 2008. *Secularisms*. Durham, NC: Duke University Press.

Kruse, Kevin. 2015. *One Nation Under God: How Corporate America Invented Christian America*. New York: Basic Books.

Lofton, Kathryn. 2017. *Consuming Religion*. Chicago: University of Chicago Press.

Logan, Dana. 2017. "The Lean Closet: Asceticism in Postindustrial Consumer Culture." *Journal of the American Academy of Religion* 85 (3): 600–628.

Marx, Karl, and Friedrich Engels. 1957. *On Religion*. Moscow: Foreign Languages Publishing House.

McLaughlin, Levi, Aike P. Rots, Jolyon Baraka Thomas, and Chika Watanabe. 2020. "Why Scholars of Religion Must Investigate the Corporate Form." *Journal of the American Academy of Religion* 88 (3): 693–725.

Moreton, Bethany. 2010. *To Serve God and Wal-Mart: The Makings of Christian Free Enterprise*. Cambridge, MA: Harvard University Press.

Nanda, Meera. 2011. *The God Market: How Globalization Is Making India More Hindu*. New York: Monthly Review Press.

O'Neill, Kevin. 2019. *Hunted: Predation and Pentecostalism in Guatemala*. Chicago: University of Chicago Press.

Ong, Aihwa. 2006. *Neoliberalism as Exception: Mutations in Citizenship and Sovereignty*. Durham, NC: Duke University Press.

Porterfield, Amanda. 2018. *Corporate Spirit: Religion and the Rise of the Modern Corporation*. New York: Oxford University Press.

Rudnyckyj, Daromir. 2010. *Spiritual Economies: Islam, Globalization, and the Afterlife of Development*. Ithaca, NY: Cornell University Press.

Shirazi, Faegheh. 2016. *Brand Islam: The Marketing and Commodification of Piety*. Austin: University of Texas Press.

Singh, Devin. 2018. *Divine Currency: The Theological Power of Money in the West*. Stanford, CA: Stanford University Press.

Taussig, Michael. 1980. *The Devil and Commodity Fetishism in South America*. Chapel Hill: University of North Carolina Press.

Vaca, Daniel. 2019. *Evangelicals Incorporated: Books and the Business of Religion in America*. Cambridge, MA: Harvard University Press.

Vatter, Miguel. 2016. *Crediting God: Sovereignty and Religion in the Age of Global Capitalism*. New York: Fordham University Press.

Watanabe, Chika. 2019. *Becoming One: Religion, Development, and Environmentalism in a Japanese NGO in Myanmar*. Honolulu: University of Hawaiʻi Press.

Wesselhoeft, Kirsten, and Deonnie Moodie. 2021. "Introduction." Roundtable: Living Neoliberalism: Markets and Morality Outside the West. *Journal of the American Academy of Religion* 89 (3): 819–39.

Williams-Oerberg, Elizabeth. 2019. "Introduction: Buddhism and Economics." *Journal of Global Buddhism* 20: 19–29.

Žižek, Slavoj. 2005. "Revenge of Global Finance." *In These Times*, May 21. http://inthesetimes.com/article/2122/revenge_of_global_finance.

14 NATURE

Mary-Jane Rubenstein

Nature Neglected

In her celebrated study of American "nature religions," Catherine Albanese writes that in the Western traditions, "religious reflection has been preoccupied with three great symbolic centers. . . . God, humanity, and nature" (1991, 7). Of these, Albanese suggests, the least considered tends to be "nature." Western philosophers, theologians, historians, anthropologists, psychologists, and homilists alike have spent far more energy decoding the nature of divinity and the nature of humanity than the nature of nature itself. Rather than the object—let alone the subject—of conceptual scrutiny, nature has traditionally served as the background, the backdrop, the stage and set against which God and God's people enact those mythic dramas of creation and law, idolatry and fidelity, estrangement and reconciliation. At once the creation of a powerful God and the passive "environment" of human history, nature in the Western religious imaginary is a *given*.

Considering this persistent inattention, one might hope to find the concept of nature more thoroughly expounded in *non*-Western traditions—especially in those Indigenous cosmologies the West has both demonized and fetishized as "nature worship" (Frazer 1926). Such hopes would be quickly dashed, however, by the realization that there is no conceptual analogue of "nature" in Indigenous traditions: no singular, impersonal, inanimate terrain standing in metaphysical opposition to culture, humanity, or divinity. As Walter Mignolo explains, the Quechuan and Aymaran *Pachamama* is at once human and more-than-human, created and divine, and natural and cultural (2011, 11–12). As Deborah Bird Rose has shown, the Aboriginal *country* names not a passive backdrop but a co-creative network of animal, mineral, and vegetable kin (2015). And as Albanese admits of the first stewards of American "nature," Indigenous Americans theorize an intra-active, multispecies, sacred-secular landscape that is "at once . . . more plural and more personal" than "the abstract 'nature' of Europe" (1991, 120).

On the one hand, then, Western religious reflection neglects the concept of nature. On the other hand, Western religious reflection is the primary source of the concept of nature. It is almost as if, as a critical term at least, "nature" were *designed* to be overlooked—or worse, instrumentalized—in the service of humanity and its God.

Although it is a limited, sometimes misleading part of a more complicated story, such a conclusion would find energetic support in Lynn White Jr.'s field-defining essay, "The Historical Roots of Our Ecologic Crisis." According to White, the West's unbridled exploitation of the natural world originated before the industrial revolution, before the birth of capitalism, and before the advent of New Science—in the late-antique and early medieval "victory of Christianity over paganism" that enabled each of these later, entangled developments (1967, 1205). How, exactly, did this Christian victory produce the exploitative ethos of techno-capitalism? By depopulating "nature." As White explains, in the pagan world of pre-Christian Europe, "every tree, every spring, every hill had its own *genius loci*, its guardian spirit. . . . Before one cut a tree, mined a mountain, or dammed a brook, it was important to placate the spirit in charge of that particular situation, and to keep it placated" (1967, 1205). In light of this terrestrial vitality, Carolyn Merchant claims that pre-modern miners offered sacrifices to the subterranean deities, "observed strict cleanliness, sexual abstinence, and fasting before violating the sacredness of the living earth," and perhaps most importantly, offered restitution to the soil they damaged and the waters they polluted (2020, 3–4).

Over against this animist metaphysic—both within Europe and beyond it—imperial Christian doctrine insisted there were no such deities and spirits: that rocks, rivers, and trees were merely inert matter, devoid of life or personhood. At the same time, this doctrine asserted humanity's exclusive claim to the "image of God" (*imago dei*) and its consequent "dominion," as Genesis promises, "over the fish of the sea and over the birds of the air and over every living thing that moves upon the earth" (Genesis 1:28). Armed with such an anthropocentric religion and anthropomorphic theology, White argues, imperial Christianity proceeded to dominate and decimate the earth. "By destroying pagan animism," he concludes, "Christianity made it possible to exploit nature in a mood of indifference to the feelings of natural objects" (White 1967, 1205).

As much of a caricature as this rendering of Christianity may be,[1] it does describe the attitude of a particularly imperial, profiteering branch of the Christian family tree—especially the one that went on to plunder the Americas. As recently as 2017, one American legislator defended Donald Trump's sudden withdrawal from the Paris Climate Accords by saying, "I worship Jesus, not Mother Earth." As Rep. Tim Walberg (R-MI) assured his constituents, Nature is the creation of an almighty God, so "if there is a real problem, he can take care of it" (Erickson 2017). However simplistic such theology might seem, its persistence in the political sphere is a function of its alignment with the interests of global empire and corporate capital. If "nature" were really a mother—or a sister, sacred temple, or network of ancestors—it would be hard to justify the violent extraction of "resources," pollution of seas and skies, and clear-cutting of forests that perpetuate what the climate activist Greta Thunberg calls our "fairy tales of eternal economic growth" (Barboza 2019). So a particularly well-funded and bellicose Christianity does, in fact, continue to provide mythic endorsement for the untrammeled industrial exploitation of an inert, passive "nature."

At the same time, it would be difficult to find a single Christian theologian who actually defends such ecocidal dominion. In the decades since White published his (in)famous essay—which concludes with a redemptive appeal to Franciscan spirituality (White 1967, 1207)—a torrent of "eco-theologies" have responded by redefining "dominion," reconceiving the *imago dei*, disaggregating "humanity" from men and rich white folks, and finding kinship with the more-than-human world.[2] No less an authority than Pope Francis (who chose his name in honor of the sainted friend to animals and steward of creation) insists that the "unbridled exploitation of nature," along with its attendant oppression of "the poor," stems from an "[in]correct interpretation of the Bible as understood by the Church" (Francis I 2015, paragraph 67). And although Francis concedes that

1. For counter-readings of early Christian sources, see Hobgood-Oster 2008; Burrus 2018; Wallace 2019.

2. The most influential of these include: Cobb 1988; Ruether 1992; McFague 1993; Adams 1993; Baker-Fletcher 1998; Gebara 1999; Crist 2004; Kearns and Keller 2007; Bauman 2009; Boff 2015; Harris 2017; Keller 2018; Jennings 2019; Carvalhaes 2021.

"Judaeo-Christian thought demythologized nature" by insisting it was not "divine," he maintains that this anti-animist, anti-pantheist metaphysic actually "emphasizes all the more our human responsibility for nature" (2015, paragraph 78). No, he insists; nature is not God. But it is a gift of God, the site of God's "continuing revelation," and the created essence of a humanity made from the "dust of the earth" (2015, paragraphs 85, 2).

Francis is hardly alone. In addition to the above-mentioned half century of eco-theological outpourings, one might cite any number of major denominational statements on the sacred mandate to care for the natural world; the exuberant liturgies for Earth Day and the Feast of St. Francis; or the 2021 "Joint Statement" of the leaders of the Orthodox, Anglican, and Roman Catholic churches that condemns the wanton misuse of "the bounty of nature" (Bartholomew, Francis, and Cantuar 2021). Of course, there are severe limitations to this nearly unanimous theo-ecclesiastical cascade, like the kinder, gentler dominionism of these institutional productions (along with their relegation of the more-than-human world to a "bounty"). But such infelicities shrink to insignificance before the larger problem that, American Christian nationalism notwithstanding, the churches wield far less influence in the contemporary world than they did during the medieval and early modern periods. In other words, the churches have much less power to fix our ecological crisis than they did to produce it. The problem is that the very doctrines the churches now condemn as bad readings of Scripture (the supremacy of humanity, the exploitation of the earth, the soullessness of animals, the inanimacy of the land) have already installed themselves at the heart of imperial politics, capitalist economics, and secular science. What began as religious teachings (tailored to support capitalist and imperial expansion) have become so commonplace that they masquerade today as secular, universal, and therefore unchangeable principles—all of which compose the seemingly neutral, seemingly self-evident concept of "nature."

Nature Denatured

The first difficulty one tends to encounter with the critical term at hand is that, to cite Bruno Latour, "nature is very big. It covers everything from the big bang to microbes. Conceptually, that makes it a complete mess" (Watts 2020). The mess multiplies as we realize that even Latour's definition of nature—that "very big" compendium of the physical world's productions—is just one of many definitions, which all edge into one another but never quite line up.

According to the *Oxford English Dictionary*, the understanding of nature as the summative "features and products of the earth" stands in opposition to "humans and human creations" (Nature, IV.11.a). Plants, animals, solar flares, rivers, and rocks compose the realm of "nature," whereas "humans and human creations" compose the realms of culture (including religion), technology, and art. Separated as it is from these anthropogenic processes of invention and change, "nature" connotes a certain inexorability, and therefore also refers to the "inherent or essential quality or constitution of a thing" (its "nature," which is often opposed to the cultural term "nurture") (III.8.a). In this particular sense, the term in question *does* include humans, whose "nature" is variously said to be self-interested, altruistic, peaceful, violent, intelligent, or idiotic. Humans also occupy the center of most of the *OED*'s "rare," "obsolete," and "euphemistic" definitions of nature, which include "excrement," "semen," "menstrual discharge," "the female genitals," "the sexual urge," and "the need of the human body to urinate and defecate" (1.2.a, I.2.b, 1.2.c, 1.3, II.4.b, II.4.d). When it does refer to humanity, then, "nature" tends to name its most bodily, nonnegotiable, embarrassing elements.

Finally, "nature" denotes not just the physical world itself, but a perceived force or source within it. In this sense, the word refers to "the creative and regulative power . . . conceived of as operating in the material world and as the immediate cause of its phenomena" (Nature, IV.10.a). This power, the *OED* continues, is usually capitalized and often "personified as a female being. Frequently as *Dame Nature* or *Mother Nature*" (IV.10.b). This gendering of "nature" courses through the European languages that regularly feminize "her," including Latin (*natura, -ae*), Greek (*physis*), German (*die Natur*), French (*la nature*), Italian (*la natura*), and Spanish (*la natura*). All told, then, "nature" in the Western imagination is singular, innate, feminine, and either opposed to (superior) humans and their productions or associated with the "lowest" parts of them.

If such a description resorts to hierarchical language, it is because, conceptually at least, "nature" *is* hierarchical (Latour 2004, 25). Precisely in its effort to gather all of existence into a single unit, the concept of "nature" arranges all beings qualitatively, in order of their reputed godliness (in one register) or complexity (in another). And whether religious or secular, nature's "Great Chain of Being" is remarkably uniform (Lovejoy 1976), beginning with allegedly inanimate things like rocks and progressing "up" the natural hierarchy to particles, microbes, fungi, plants, fish, birds, mammals, and finally human beings, who crown the "nature" they both consummate and transcend.

Given the tendency of "nature" to totalize, along with its conceptual incoherence, its preference for some beings over others, and above all its stubborn inexorability (its seeming *naturalness*), Latour insists that we have to do without it. Such conceptual renunciation is especially crucial, he says, for those of us who think we love "nature" and who seek with increasing desperation some political paradigm, spiritual discipline, or scientific practice that might clean the oceans, plant more trees, stop the fracking, slow the rising temperatures, save the bees, and do justice to the displaced. These are all *social* efforts, Latour insists, whose contingency, multiplicity, and multispecies crossings of matter and technology are not only obscured but impeded by the static hierarchy and incontestability of "nature." "*If 'nature' is what makes it possible to recapitulate the hierarchy of beings in a single ordered series*," he declares, "*political ecology is always manifested, in practice, by the destruction of the idea of nature*" (Latour 2004, 25, italics in original).

With and against Latour (and before and after him), a host of other theorists have exposed the ideological violence that "nature" both enacts and conceals—whether by policing an outdoorsy hetero-masculinity, displacing the Indigenous caretakers of the land in question, condemning queer sex and trans bodies, defending the "natural" whiteness of a family or nation, displacing toxins onto low-income neighborhoods, condoning the slaughter of animals, or opposing "unnatural" technologies like the wind turbines and solar panels that threaten to wreck a vacationer's view.[3] In the place of nature, Donna Haraway suggests we try the nonbinary and carefully pluralized "naturecultures"; Latour proposes "critical zones"; and Timothy Morton offers a "mesh of interconnectedness" (Haraway 2007; Watts 2020; Morton 2010, 38). All of these are provisional conceptual mechanisms for recalling the social constitution of the natural, the symbiotic agency of the more-than-human world, and the counter-hierarchical functioning of life itself (whose creators, sustainers, and destroyers, Lynn Margulis reminds us, are the bacteria at the bottom of the Chain [Margulis 1998, 20]).

In her *Political Theology of the Earth*, Catherine Keller concedes that "we

3. See Cronon 1996; Gaard 1997; Butler 1999, 29–30; Stryker 2006; Cone 2000; Morton 2007, 5–6; Morton 2010, 9; Mortimer-Sandilands and Erickson 2010.

must all choose which of the contaminated words in our troubled seculareligious vocabularies we will stay with" (2018, 90). As we have seen, many contemporary eco-theorists consider "nature" far too contaminated—or more precisely, not contaminated enough—to ground a constructive politics, philosophy, or theology. That having been said, this term's historical burdens and strategic limitations hardly relieve us of the critical responsibility to understand it. Conceptual incoherence and ethical undesirability notwithstanding, "nature" continues to structure the discourse of the very global-capitalized order that keeps ransacking the biosphere. The question, then, is not whether or not we should use the word, but how on earth we can account for it. How did "nature" become the object par excellence of Western neglect and longing, disavowal and ownership, invention and forgetfulness, deployment and abuse?

Nature Natured

Following the lead of Merchant, it is common to charge Western modernity with bringing about the "death" or "end" of nature (Merchant 2020).[4] Merchant begins her account just before the dawn of the scientific revolution in Europe, sketching a quasi-Edenic "Renaissance cosmology of animate spirits and ensouled beings in which everything was alive" (2020, xvii). According to this "organic" worldview, she explains, each part of nature was alive and interdependent with every other part. Nature "herself" was said to be a "nurturing mother: a kindly, beneficent female who provided for the needs of mankind" (2). As such, there were limits to what—and how—one could take from her. "One does not readily slay a mother," writes Merchant, "[or] dig into her entrails for gold or mutilate her body. . . . As long as the earth was considered to be alive and sensitive, it could be considered a breach of human ethical behavior to carry out such destructive acts against it" (3). As commercial mining loomed on the horizon, Renaissance authors cited Ovid, Seneca, and Pliny as ancient sanctions against the violent ingratitude of "penetrating" nature's "entrails" to extract her treasures (30). They warned of certain retribution in the form of earthquakes and poisoned water, and prophesied the escalation of greed, warfare, and cruelty.

Despite their impassioned delivery, such strictures could not withstand

4. See also McKibben 1989; Plumwood 1993; Worthy, Allison, and Bauman 2018.

the pressure of technological development and capitalist acceleration during the sixteenth and seventeenth centuries. Greater profits demanded increased production, which required heavier machinery, which necessitated industrial mining. Perhaps as uneasy as their ancestors with the prospect of stripping and ransacking a loving, living mother, early modernist thinkers developed a "new mercantilist philosophy" that changed the metaphor, transforming nature from organism to machine (2020, 32). Over the course of a few generations, the vibrant, generative world-mother of Renaissance philosophy gave way to the inert, passive universal-mechanism of the scientific revolution. It is this ideological overhaul, with all its materially devastating causes and effects, that Merchant calls "the death of nature" (193).

Strikingly, however, the rigorous de-animation of nature did nothing to de-gender "her." Even as Francis Bacon, Johannes Kepler, René Descartes, Robert Boyle, Isaac Newton, and a slew of other early modernists insisted that nature was a great clock, engine, or automaton, they continued to feminize it/her, likening the natural world not to a mother or goddess but to a "disorderly woman": wild, unfaithful, and in need of masculine discipline (2020, 127). Thus we find Francis Bacon calling nature a "common harlot," from whose shadowy "womb" the natural philosopher was obliged to rip out every secret (171, 169). Taking both the metaphor and the strategy from the witch trials of King James's England, Bacon called for a systemic "inquisition of nature" and assured his monarch that, just as royal interrogators should show no mercy or regret in torturing witches, "neither ought a man to make scruple of entering and penetrating into [nature's] holes and corners, when the inquisition of truth is his whole object" (cited on 168). Once these truths were finally extracted and brought into the light, nature would be tame, falling under the total control and possession of the male investigator. The point, as Bacon explained it, was to "bind [nature] to your service and make her your slave," along with "all her children" (cited on 170). In short, not only did this newly mechanized nature remain female; it became unruly, chaotic, and *dark*.

Mignolo argues that, as the industrial revolution took hold, the mechanized, feminized, racialized "nature" of early modernity morphed into "natural resources" (2011, 12). Filled as it was with lumber, minerals, oils and gases, waters, meats, and animal skins, nature became a "repository" of exploitable materials for the advancement of wealthy European men, their nations, and their families—both at home and in the burgeoning colonies overseas. Meanwhile, the people traditionally associated with such "nature"—that is, Indigenous, Black, and female-identified people—were subject to analogous regulation, exploitation, violation, and ownership in the interests of techno-imperial Europe and its light-skinned American cousins. Just as the land in the Americas was clear-cut and overfarmed, Delores Williams explains, "female slaves were beaten, overworked, and made to experience excessive childbearing in order to provide income, comfort, and leisure for slave-owning families. . . . Just as strip-mining exhausts the earth's body," she continues, "so did the practice of breeding female slaves exhaust Black women's bodies" (1993, 24–25). In this manner, "nature" and the human beings purportedly "close" to it were positioned in a circular justification of horrific abuse: just as witches could be tortured and burned, nature could be "hounded" and enslaved, and just as nature could be hounded and enslaved, so could enslaved Black bodies be tortured, bred, and burned.

Especially as Merchant tells it, this story of the death of nature leaves the reader longing for a different metaphoric register. In the face of a mechanical inertness that condones the systematic torture of animals, women, Black and Indigenous people, and the earth itself, one might find oneself longing for the organic Mother Nature of the Renaissance, or for those enspirited forests of pre-Christian Europe. As Merchant shows without always saying it, however, these ecologically gentler eras still contained the associations and hierarchies that industrialism would later go on to exploit. The nurturing mother of Renaissance "nature" could also turn demonic, causing hurricanes, droughts, and floods. In that sense, she would have to be dominated (perhaps like the ancient Babylonian goddess Tiamat, whom the warrior Marduk murders and dismembers to construct an ordered natural world [Epic of Creation 2008]). Meanwhile, in their workshops, the Renaissance alchemical magi and healers who saw themselves as "servants of nature" were still *using* nature for human improvement—and presupposing a neoplatonic Great Chain of Being in order to do so (Merchant 2020, 120). So although we might look to the Renaissance to provide what Sean McGrath calls a hermetic "alter-modernity" (McGrath 2014, 216), we should also concede with Merchant that our dominant modernity has easily assimilated this "alter"—and even found a home within it.

After all, the mechanistic model didn't last long. Less than two centuries after Robert Boyle encoded nature as a cosmic automaton of "subordinate engines," Alexander von Humboldt reframed it as a "great living organism where everything [is] connected" (Wulf 2015, 2). Meanwhile, a young

Ralph Waldo Emerson sought to recall "man" into a holistic relationship with a dynamic, enspirited "Nature," which gained further animacy and intimacy in the later works of Henry David Thoreau, John Muir, and Walt Whitman and finds reinvigoration in the "religious naturalism" of Thomas Berry, Wendell Berry, Ursula Goodenough, and Loyal Rue (Emerson 2000; Thoreau 1971; Wolfe 1979; Whitman 2005; Berry 2009; Berry 2018; Goodenough 2023; Rue 2011). Even at the height of the seventeenth century, as Isaac Newton was wrangling the natural world into the deterministic, absolute background of mechanical science, Gottfried Leibniz insisted on the vitality and relational constitution of bodies, space, and time—a counter-vision notoriously vindicated in the early twentieth century by Albert Einstein's theories of special and general relativity (Newton [1692–1693] 1756; Leibniz and Clarke 2000; Einstein 1989; Einstein 1986). And at the end of the twentieth century, James Lovelock and Lynn Margulis reimagined the planetary ecosystem as "Gaia," a symbiotic co-production of interconstituted organisms (Lovelock 1979; Margulis 1998). ("Traditional Indians are quite amused," writes Vine Deloria Jr., "to see this revival of the debate over whether the planet is alive"—Deloria 1999, 49).

In short, there is no precise moment in Western intellectual history when an originally organic conception of nature gives way to a mechanical one—or vice versa. Rather, these two strands are wound double-helix-like around one another, with periodic bonds and crossings. The mechanical strand finds its roots in biblical dominionism, Near Eastern mythic matricide, Epicurean atomism, and the Aristotelian theory of passive, feminine matter. It winds its way through the medieval Peripatetics (with Thomas Aquinas half-stretching across to the rival strand), and then on to Mersenne, Gassendi, Descartes, Bacon, Boyle, and Newton before reaching us in the form of "reductive" materialists like Richard Dawkins and Pascal Boyer. Meanwhile, the organic strand emerges from pre-Socratic naturalism, Stoic pantheism, and Neoplatonism (with Plato himself forming another horizontal rung) making its way through St. Francis, Paracelsus, Baruch Spinoza, Giordano Bruno, Leibniz, and generations of murdered witches before finally gaining respectability in the Cambridge Platonists, Vitalists, Romantics, and Transcendentalists. This organic strand now courses through our ecologies, ecopoetics, ecotheologies, pantheisms, pantheologies, religious naturalisms, ecofeminisms, animal studies, new animisms, and earth systems theories. Even in the West, then, the model of nature as animate and organic has been around all along. It has arguably even "won." Yet the ecological crisis escalates nonetheless, especially for those dark-skinned, poor, and female-gendered people persistently lauded and denigrated as "close to nature."

In this light, it might not seem to matter *how* one talks about nature, since the vitalist-organic models have not reversed or even tempered the strip-mining, industrial farming, or consumer capitalism endorsed by the seemingly moribund mechanical model. We might at this point be tempted to side with Latour, who insists that in its romantic constructions most of all, "nature" is constitutively contaminated by dominion, totality, and hierarchy. And yet as the tides rise higher and the fires burn longer and the hurricanes spin in unexpected directions, even Latour has decided to talk about Gaia—so long as he can keep "her" from becoming "a god," which is to say a transcendent, singular abstraction like "nature" (Latour 2014). So maybe models do matter, but as a product of our interactions with the world rather than a prefabricated determinant of them. If a particularly animate, counter-hierarchical, multiply agential cosmos keeps emerging in our ecologies and ecopoetics, maybe it's because "nature" is refusing to stay where "man" keeps trying to put her.

Nature Cultured

"Who can forget those moments," Amitav Ghosh writes, "when something that seems inanimate turns out to be vitally, even dangerously alive?" (Ghosh 2016, 3). Those moments when the stick becomes a snake, the dead bug jumps into your face, or—to use Ghosh's example—when the lifeless asteroid in *Star Wars* turns out to be a giant, sleeping space monster. The so-called Anthropocene is one such extended moment, as a purportedly inanimate earth asserts its dangerous vitality. In its multiplying and increasingly unpredictable storms, fires, disastrous extinctions, and floods, the natural world is not only acting, but *responding*. Far from being a lifeless backdrop to human activity, or even a counter-agent positioned against it, it turns out that the living, heaving concatenation in which we live, move, and have our being is the ongoing product of both human and more-than-human agencies.

So there goes nature—not only in Merchant's sense, but also in Latour's. The physical "death of nature" that began in sixteenth- and seventeenth-century Europe has brought about the conceptual death of "nature" in late capitalist globalism. Far from a passive, mechanical hierarchy, our Anthropocenic lifeworld announces itself as a vigorous, dynamic multiplicity of interconstituted beings, the "least" of whom are often the most influential (think not just bacteria, but bees, bats, and viruses). In its furious self-assertion—what Isabelle Stengers has called "the intrusion of Gaia" (Stengers 2015, 43)—the natural world is telling us that it is not "nature" and that "we" are not not-nature. In short, if the seventeenth-century birth of "nature" gave rise to the "death of nature," then the death of nature has provoked an uncanny rebirth. Both more and less than "nature," the biosphere now interrupting every human pretense is a natural-cultural monstrosity of which humans are a particularly dangerous product, source, and part.

Insofar as it might help to alert policy-makers to the geological gravity of our self-imposed disaster, the term "Anthropocene" can be useful for any given climate summit or cap-and-trade debate. As feminist, Black, and decolonial theorists have insisted, however, the culprits of ecological destruction are not all human beings (the *anthropos*), but rather the wealthy inhabitants of overdeveloped nations who have built their techno-industrial worlds by ravaging the worlds of others (Yussof 2019). Many scholars have therefore opted for the term "Capitalocene," which places the blame on the cultural order that bears the most responsibility for trashing the earth (Moore 2016). The problem with *this* designation is that it risks reaffirming the primarily white, wealthy agents of climate change as genuine masters of the universe, exclusively—even divinely—capable of making a whole world, however polluted and monocultural. Moreover, like the term "Anthropocene," "Capitalocene" also risks resigning the earth-lovers among us to despair. By granting this disaster the seemingly inexorable status of a geological epoch, both terms seem to announce there is nothing to be done—no way to live otherwise.

It is in pursuit of such an "otherwise" that Haraway offers her anti-defeatist, barely pronounceable "Chthulucene." If the Greek word *chthonios* means in or of the Earth, then Chthulucene names the ongoing project of irreducibly terrestrial species, trying to make different kinds of worlds together (Haraway 2016, 53). Unlike the agents of the Anthropocene or Capitalocene, Haraway's "chthonic ones" are not human—at least not in any straightforward way. After all, "humanity" is yet another conceptual mess, singling out as it does the most "rational," pale, and male among us to master and exploit that raving, dark, and feminine "nature" (Wynter 1989; Wynter 1994). "Most African-Americans owe *nothing* to the status of the human," writes Kodwo Eshun; "there's this sense of the human as being a really pointless and treacherous category" (1999, 175, 193). Moreover, as

Haraway loves to remind us, the genome of *Homo sapiens* is 90 percent "bacteria, fungi, protists, and such" (Haraway 2007, 3). So Haraway's multiracial, omni-gendered, interspecies "chthonic ones" cannot be called human in any sense other than the etymological one (they are *humus*: of the earth).

Nor are Haraway's chthonic worldmakers "sky gods," she insists—"not a foundation for the Olympiad" (2016, 53). After all, "divinity" is as instrumentalized as "nature" and as instrumentalizing as "man," hovering as it does in some otherworldly world until an otherwise self-reliant philosophy, theology, myth, or science needs it to come save the day. As Dietrich Bonhoeffer feverishly explained from his cell in a Gestapo prison, the modern West has made "God" into a *deus ex machina*, flying him on the scene to patch all the holes in our theories and answer our unanswered questions (Bonhoeffer 1997, 181–82). The culprits Bonhoeffer has in mind include Bacon, Boyle, and above all Newton, whose theory of universal gravitation needed "God" just to get the cosmic clockwork going and keep it from collapsing or exploding. If these names sound familiar, it is because the very tradition that codified "nature" by killing it off did the same thing to "God" (Rubenstein 2018). And just a few decades after Bonhoeffer, "man" would be exposed as an equally dangerous conceptual fiction (Foucault [1966] 1994; Taylor 1984, 34–51; Wynter 1989).

So much, then, for the "three great symbolic centers" of Western religion. God, humanity, and nature: all killed off in the very effort to control the things they're trying to name. But rather than trying to resurrect, reinvent, or even mourn these old characters, Haraway opts for composting. "Collect[ing] up the trash of the Anthropocene, the exterminism of the Capitalocene, and chipping and shredding like a mad gardener," Haraway's chthonic ones "make a much hotter compost pile for still possible pasts, presents, and futures" (2016, 57). Led by bacterial, vegetable, mushroomy, wormish, and even mammalian earth-others, such companion-agents are not humans, not gods, and not nature, but chimeric assemblages emerging out of their decomposition. Chthonic ones are post-apocalyptic hybrids: composting critical terms, living lives, and worlding worlds, even after the death of nature.

Suggested Readings

Adams, Carol J., and Lori Gruen, eds. 2022. *Ecofeminism: Feminist Intersections with Other Animals and the Earth*. 2nd ed. New York: Bloomsbury.

Bennett, Jane. 2010. *Vibrant Matter: A Political Ecology of Things*. Durham, NC: Duke University Press.

Berry, Evan. 2015. *Devoted to Nature: The Religious Roots of American Environmentalism*. Oakland, CA: University of California Press.

Carson, Rachel. 1962. *Silent Spring*. New York: Houghton Mifflin.

Cone, James. 2000. "Whose Earth Is It Anyway?" *Cross Currents*: 36–46.

Dillard, Annie. [1977] 1998. *Holy the Firm*. New York: Harper Perennial.

Grim, John, and Mary Evelyn Tucker. 2014. *Ecology and Religion*. Island Press.

Gruen, Lori. 2015. *Entangled Empathy: An Alternative Ethic for Our Relationship with Animals*. New York: Lantern Books.

Harvey, Graham, ed. 2013. *The Handbook of Contemporary Animism*. Durham, UK: Acumen.

Rubenstein, Mary-Jane. 2018. *Pantheologies: Gods, Worlds, Monsters*. New York: Columbia University Press.

Walker, Alice. 1989. "Everything Is a Human Being." In *Living by the Word: Selected Writings 1973–1987*, 139–52. New York: Harcourt Brace.

White, Carol Wayne. 2016. *Black Lives and Sacred Humanity: Toward an African American Religious Naturalism*. New York: Fordham University Press.

References

Adams, Carol J., ed. 1993. *Ecofeminism and the Sacred*. New York: Continuum.

Albanese, Catherine L. 1991. *Nature Religion in America: From the Algonquin Indians to the New Age*. Chicago: University of Chicago Press.

Baker-Fletcher, Karen. 1998. *Sisters of Dust, Sisters of Spirit: Womanist Wordings on God and Creation*. Minneapolis, MN: Augsburg Fortress.

Barboza, Tony. 2019. "Greta Thunberg Admonishes Leaders as U.N. Climate Summit Fails to Deliver Action." *Los Angeles Times*.

Bartholomew, Ecumenical Patriarch, Pope Francis, and Justin Cantuar. 2021. "Joint Statement on the Environment." https://www.archbishopofcanterbury.org/sites/abc/files/2021-09/Joint%20Statement%20on%20the%20Environment.pdf.

Bauman, Whitney. 2009. *Theology, Creation, and Environmental Ethics: From Creatio Ex Nihilo to Terra Nullius*. Routledge Studies in Religion. New York: Routledge.

Berry, Thomas. 2009. *The Sacred Universe: Earth, Spirituality, and Religion in the Twenty-First Century*. New York: Columbia Universitiy Press.

Berry, Wendell. 2018. *The Peace of Wild Things*. New York: Penguin.

Boff, Leonardo. 2015. *Toward an Eco-Spirituality*. Spring Valley, NY: Crossroad.

Bonhoeffer, Dietrich. 1997. *Letters and Papers from Prison*. New York: Simon and Schuster.

Burrus, Virginia. 2018. *Ancient Christian Ecopoetics: Cosmologies, Saints, Things*. Philadelphia: University of Pennsylvania Press.

Butler, Judith. 1999. *Gender Trouble: Feminism and the Subversion of Identity*. New York: Routledge.

Carvalhaes, Cláudio. 2021. *Ritual at World's End: Essays on Eco-Liturgical Liberation Theology*. York, PA: Barber's Son Press.

Cobb, John B. 1988. "Ecology, Science, and Religion: Toward a Postmodern Worldview." In *The Reenchantment of Science: Postmodern Proposals*, edited by David Ray Griffin. Albany: State University of New York Press.

Crist, Carol. 2004. *She Who Changes: Reimagining the Divine in the World*. New York: Palgrave.

Cronon, William. 1996. *Uncommon Ground: Rethinking the Human Place in Nature*. New York: W. W. Norton.

Deloria, Vine, Jr. 1999. "If You Think About It, You Will See That It Is True." In *Spirit & Reason: The Vine Deloria, Jr., Reader*, edited by Barbara Deloria, Kristen Foehner, and Sam Scinta. Golden, CO: Fulcrum.

Einstein, Albert. 1986. "Cosmological Considerations on the General Theory of Relativity (1917)." In *Cosmological Constants: Papers in Modern Cosmology*, edited by Jeremy Bernstein and Gerald Feinberg, 16–26. New York: Columbia University Press.

Einstein, Albert. 1989. "On the Electrodynamics of Moving Bodies (1905)." Translated by Anna Beck. In *The Collected Papers of Albert Einstein*, vol. 2, *The Swiss Years: Writings, 1900–1909*, 140–71. Princeton, NJ: Princeton University Press.

Emerson, Ralph Waldo. 2000. "Nature." In *The Essential Writings of Ralph Waldo Emerson*, edited by Brooks Atkinson, 1–39. New York: The Modern Library.

"The Epic of Creation (*Enuma Elish*)." 2008. Translated by Stephanie Dalley. In *Myths from Mesopotamia: Creation, the Flood, Gilgamesh, and Others*, edited by Stephanie Dalley. Oxford World's Classics, 233–77. New York: Oxford.

Erickson, Jacob J. 2017. "'I Worship Jesus, Not Mother Earth': Exceptionalism and the Paris Withdrawal." *Religion Dispatches*. http://religiondispatches.org/i-worship-jesus-not-mother-earth-american-christian-exceptionalism-and-the-paris-withdrawal/?utm_source=Religion+Dispatches+Newsletter&utm_campaign=ce0a251ec4-RD_Daily_Newsletter&utm_medium=email&utm_term=0_742d86f519-ce0a251ec4-42408801.

Eshun, Kodwo. 1999. *More Brilliant Than the Sun: Adventures in Sonic Fiction*. Interlink.

Foucault, Michel. 1994 [1966]. *The Order of Things: An Archaeology of the Human Sciences*. Translated by Alan Sheridan. New York: Vintage, Reissue Edition.

Francis I. 2015. "Laudato Si': On Care for Our Common Home." http://www.vatican.va/content/francesco/en/encyclicals/documents/papa-francesco_20150524_enciclica-laudato-si.html.

Frazer, James George. 1926. *The Worship of Nature*. New York: Macmillan.

Gaard, Greta. 1997. "Toward a Queer Ecofeminism." *Hypatia* 12 (1): 114–37.

Gebara, Ivone. 1999. *Longing for Running Water: Ecofeminism and Liberation*. Minneapolis, MN: Fortress Press.

Ghosh, Amitav. 2016. *The Great Derangement: Climate Change and the Unthinkable*. Chicago: University of Chicago Press.

Goodenough, Ursula. 2023. *The Sacred Depths of Nature: How Life Has Emerged and Evolved*. 2nd ed. New York: Oxford University Press.

Haraway, Donna. 2007. *When Species Meet*. Posthumanities. Minneapolis: University of Minnesota Press.

Haraway, Donna. 2016. *Staying with the Trouble: Making Kin in the Chthulucene*. Durham, NC: Duke University Press.

Harris, Melanie. 2017. *Ecowomanism: African American Women and Earth-Honoring Faiths*. Maryknoll, NY: Orbis.

Hobgood-Oster, Laura. 2008. *Holy Dogs and Asses: Animals in the Christian Tradition*. Champaign: University of Illinois Press.

Jennings, Willie James. 2019. "Reframing the World: Toward an Actual Christian Doctrine of Creation." *Place and Space in Systematic Theology* 21: 388–407.

Kearns, Laurel, and Catherine Keller, eds. 2007. *Ecospirit: Religions and Philosophies for the Earth*. New York: Fordham University Press.

Keller, Catherine. 2018. *Political Theology of the Earth: Our Planetary Emergency and the Struggle for a New Public*. New York: Columbia University Press.

Latour, Bruno. 2004. *Politics of Nature: How to Bring the Sciences into Philosophy*. Translated by Catherine Porter. Cambridge, MA: Harvard University Press.

Latour, Bruno. 2014. "How to Make Sure Gaia Is Not a God of Totality? With Special Attention to Toby Tyrrell's Book on Gaia." http://bruno-latour.fr/sites/default/files/138-THOUSAND-NAMES.pdf.

Leibniz, G. W., and Samuel Clarke. 2000. *Correspondence*. Indianapolis, IN: Hackett.

Lovejoy, Arthur O. 1976. *The Great Chain of Being: A Study of the History of an Idea*. Cambridge, MA: Harvard University Press.

Lovelock, James. 1979. *Gaia: A New Look at Life on Earth*. New York: Oxford University Press.

Margulis, Lynn. 1998. *Symbiotic Planet: A New Look at Evolution*. New York: Basic Books.

McFague, Sallie. 1993. *The Body of God: An Ecological Theology*. Minneapolis, MN: Fortress Press.

McGrath, Sean. 2014. "The Question Concerning Nature." In *Interpreting Nature: The Emerging Field of Environmental Hermeneutics*, edited by Forrest Clingerman, Brian Treanor, Martin Drenthen, and David Utsler, 201–24. New York: Fordham University Press.

McKibben, Bill. 1989. *The End of Nature*. New York: Random House.

Merchant, Carolyn. 2020. *The Death of Nature: Women, Ecology, and the Scientific Revolution*. 40th anniversary ed. New York: Harper One.

Mignolo, Walter. 2011. *The Darker Side of Western Modernity: Global Futures, Decolonial Options*. Durham, NC: Duke University Press.

Moore, Jason W. 2016. "Introduction." In *Anthropocene or Capitalocene? Nature, His-*

tory, and the Crisis of Capitalism, edited by Jason W. Moore, 1–11. Oakland, CA: PM Press.

Mortimer-Sandilands, Catriona, and Bruce Erickson, eds. 2010. *Queer Ecologies: Sex, Nature, Politics, Desire*. Indianapolis: Indiana University Press.

Morton, Timothy. 2010. *The Ecological Thought*. Cambridge, MA: Harvard University Press.

Morton, Timothy. 2007. *Ecology without Nature: Rethinking Environmental Aesthetics*. Cambridge, MA: Harvard University Press.

"Nature." *Oxford English Dictionary*: oed.com.

Newton, Isaac. [1692–93] 1756. *Four Letters from Sir Isaac Newton to Doctor Bentley, Containing Some Arguments in Proof of a Deity*. London: R. and J. Dodsley,.

Plumwood, Val. 1993. *Feminism and the Mastery of Nature*. New York: Routledge.

Rose, Deborah Bird. 2015. "Death and Grief in a World of Kin: Dwelling in Larger-Than-Human Communities." In *The Handbook of Contemporary Animism*, edited by Graham Harvey, 137–47. New York: Routledge.

Rubenstein, Mary-Jane. 2018. "Science." In *The Palgrave Handbook of Radical Theology*, edited by Christopher D. Rodkey and Jordan E. Miller, 747–56. New York: Palgrave Macmillan.

Rue, Loyal. 2011. *Nature Is Enough: Religious Naturalism and the Meaning of Life*. Albany, NY: SUNY Press.

Ruether, Rosemary Radford. 1992. *Gaia and God: An Ecofeminist Theology of Earth Healing*. San Francisco, CA: HarperSanFrancisco.

Stengers, Isabelle. 2015. *In Catastrophic Times: Resisting the Coming Barbarism*. Translated by Andrew Goffey. Critical Climate Change. Edited by Tom Cohen and Claire Colebrook. London: Open Humanities Press.

Stryker, Susan. 2006. "My Words to Victor Frankenstein above the Village of Chamonix: Performing Transgender Rage." In *The Transgender Studies Reader*, edited by Susan Stryker and Stephen Whittle, 244–56. New York: Routledge.

Taylor, Mark C. 1984. *Erring: A Postmodern a/Theology*. Chicago: University of Chicago Press.

Thoreau, Henry David. 1971. *Walden*. The Writings of Henry D. Thoreau. Edited by J. Lyndon Shanley. Princeton: Princeton University Press.

Wallace, Mark I. 2019. *When God Was a Bird: Christianity, Animism, and the Re-Enchantment of the World*. New York: Fordham University Press.

Watts, Jonathan. 2020. "Interview: Bruno Latour: 'This Is a Global Catastrophe That Has Come from Within.'" *The Observer*.

White, Lynn, Jr. 1967. "The Historical Roots of Our Ecologic Crisis." *Science* 155 (3767): 1203–7.

Whitman, Walt. 2005. "Song of Myself." In *The Complete Poems*, edited by Francis Murphy, 63–124. New York: Penguin Classics.

Williams, Delores S. 1993. "Sin, Nature, and Black Women's Bodies." In *Ecofeminism*, edited by Carol J. Adams, 24–29. New York: Continuum.

Wolfe, Linnie Marsh, ed. 1979. *John of the Mountains: The Unpublished Journals of John Muir*.

Worthy, Kenneth, Elizabeth Allison, and Whitney Bauman, eds. 2018. *After the Death of Nature: Carolyn Merchant and the Future of Human-Nature Relations*. New York: Routledge.

Wulf, Andrea. 2015. *The Invention of Nature: Alexander Von Humboldt's New World*. New York: Alfred A. Knopf.

Wynter, Sylvia. 1989. "Beyond the Word of Man: Glissant and the New Discourse of the Antilles." *World Literature Today* 63 (4): 637–47.

Wynter, Sylvia. 1994. "'No Humans Involved': An Open Letter to My Colleagues." *Forum N.H.I.: Knowledge for the 21st Century* 1 (1).

Yussof, Katherine. 2019. *A Billion Black Anthropocenes or None*. Minneapolis: University of Minnesota Press.

15 POWER

Amy Hollywood

> The exploitation of the marble and the exploitation of the men hired to extract it and place it in the hands of whoever had declared himself owner of the land—and how this guy managed to make the others believe that he owned the rock, this rock produced by the actions of time, to the point of making them climb rickety ladders to whack the cliff with picks, I still don't know. [. . .]
>
> Jonas takes Paula's face in his hands and asks her to imagine a time when they would be no more than myths, legends, specters in the stories of creatures that now walked the earth—who can believe in humans anymore, Paula?
>
> MAYLIS DE KERANGAL, *Painting Time*

Maylis de Kerangal's novel, *Painting Time*, is about, among other things, learning to paint exact, utterly convincing replicas of material objects—of cloth, wood, marble, and, by the end of the novel, not just the cave paintings at Lascaux, but the stone walls of the caves themselves. The novel asks, in lucid and detailed ekphrastic prose, what it means to be beholden to a tradition: does freedom come through one's immersion in technique, craft, and repetition; does it demand the refusal of these imitations; or is posing the question in this form already to misunderstand the complexity and limitations of human life, creativity, and power? De Kerangal aptly introduces my discussion of power because her questions mirror those so often encountered in the study of religion: is religion a source of constraint, suppression, and oppression from which we seek to be freed; is it the site through which liberation is achieved; or is the very dichotomy between oppression and liberation inadequate to the pulsing life of power that runs throughout human existence—and beyond it?

The questions have been in play since the beginning of the study of religion within the Western academy. The nineteenth-century European development of what the French call "the human sciences" was firmly grounded in attempts to provide theories of religion, theories meant to show that religion is, if properly understood, embedded in the structure of language, reducible to society or culture, an outgrowth of and cover for economic exploitation, or the result of the operations of the unconscious. In almost all of this literature, religion is posited as a specifically human enterprise and one from which modern scientific understanding can and must liberate us. For Max Müller, Émile Durkheim, Max Weber, Karl Marx, Sigmund Freud, and countless others, each theory of religion, a theory by means of which the putative object of analysis is displaced in favor of the central theoretical construct of the new field, is indispensable to justifying that field's methods of analysis. Philology and comparative linguistics as illuminative of the development of human thought; sociology as a method for studying human populations and societies; anthropology as the ethnographic engagement with the finely wrought patterns of culture; psychoanalysis as a set of practices through which the unconscious is glimpsed and partially if inadequately mapped—all of these methodological innovations obtain their power, at least in part, from their claim to explain what religion is, from whence it emerges, and how it might be replaced by a properly scientific understanding of the human (although it is worth noting that some are more sanguine about this possibility than others). (Each new domain also, and crucially, embeds specific articulations of putatively natural sexual difference and of race within their accounts of religion and of the discipline itself.) Religion, all of these fiercely original and ambitious scholars recognize, has enormous power, a power that they want both to explain and to tap for new, different, more putatively scientific and rational enterprises.

This all starts much earlier, of course, and philosophical attempts to reduce religion to that which reason produces or to which reason ineluctably leads might be seen as the ground from which these developments emerge. Immanuel Kant and G. F. W. Hegel, then, but before them Benedict Spinoza, David Hume, the Earl of Shaftesbury, and many others, are vital to the story. But what interests me here is the way in which the development of modern philosophy, philology, sociology, anthropology, psychology, psychoanalysis, and political science draw their power from the practices and discourses they purport to displace. This makes it all the more startling, then, that by 1966, when Michel Foucault publishes his archeology of the human sciences, the title of which is translated in English as *The Order of Things*, he can do so with very little attention to the study of religion; in other words, neither religious studies nor theology are among the human sciences whose story is told in the book (Foucault 1970). Drawing a distinction between the logic of the classical age of reason and the emergence of the human sciences in the nineteenth century, the role of religion in empowering these new explanatory frameworks is minimized, precisely as their exponents desired. Religion is displaced by language, culture, economics, and the psyche.

Of course, Foucault does write about religion, in particular Christianity, although not only Christianity, and his work has been and continues to be tremendously influential, even when he is not named directly, for attempts to bring an analysis of power into the field (see, for example, Asad 1993, 2003, 2007, and 2018; Chidester 1996 and 2014; Masuzawa 2005; Mahmood 2004 and 2015; Butler et al. 2011; and for the importance of religion to Foucault's work, see Carrette 1999 and 2000; Clements 2021; and Jordan 2014). (There are also, of course, many non-Foucauldian accounts of the role of power in religion: for example, that of Maurice Bloch and Bruce Lincoln, among many others. See Bloch 1989 and 1991; and Lincoln 2012.) Yet in providing an archeology of the grip certain discursive formations have on us, the central role explanations of religion (or perhaps better, the practice of explaining religion away) play within those discourses is often overlooked. This is important, I think, because it erases the power of religion, so readily acknowledged and seen by nineteenth- and early twentieth-century theorists, and because it enables many after Foucault to reinscribe an account of power as sovereignty within Foucault's own, much more nuanced, much more difficult, much more vital analytics of power, that first most fully presented in published form in *The History of Sexuality, Volume 1* (1978—hereafter *HS1*). (After his death it would become clear how important his lectures at the Collège de France were for his thinking on the topic.) An entire discursive stream operating under the name of political theology governs much recent work on the question of religion and power. Although purporting to bring together thinkers as different as Carl Schmitt, Georges Bataille, Hannah Arendt, and Foucault, the specificity and force of the latter's account of power is, I think, almost entirely lost in these debates (see, for example, Agamben 1998, who arguably initiates these conflations). Here I hope to show how this is the case and why it matters, both for the human sciences as a whole and for the study of religion.

: : :

Many would argue that more than enough has been said about *HS1*, but I want to return to it here in some detail, demonstrating that in it Foucault himself enacts a displacement, rewriting Freud's *Three Essays on the Theory of Sexuality*, first published in 1905 (1975): for Foucault, the central theoretical term is no longer sexuality, but power, and the primary methodological tool is not psychoanalysis, but genealogy. (A similar analysis of the relationship between Friedrich Nietzsche's *On the Genealogy of Morals* [1989] and Foucault's *Discipline and Punish* would likely yield further insight into the complexity of Foucault's thinking about power, but space constraints preclude that analysis here.) The central role of psychoanalysis as a point of continued contention throughout *HS1* no doubt underlies Foucault's insistence that he is not offering a theory of power, but rather an analytics. This is one of many instances throughout the book in which Foucault deploys crucial terms from Freud's *Three Essays*, not to describe sexuality, but instead to provide the vocabulary for a new understanding of power. In the midst of a cogent analysis and rejection of psychoanalysis as a central explanatory matrix for the modern West, Foucault makes use of its terms to provide an analytics not of sexuality, but of power itself (for Foucault's rejection of psychoanalysis, see Huffer 2009).

Yet like Nietzsche, always a crucial interlocutor for Foucault, Foucault insists that the central object of analysis cannot be addressed head on. His approach to power is always, like Nietzsche's, oblique. Hence the importance of a proper understanding of genealogy in both. Genealogy is not simply another word for history, and the history of sexuality is something more than a historical account of sexuality. Foucault makes this clear in the opening pages of *HS1* when he distinguishes between the three doubts he has about the "repressive hypothesis"—the notion that the modern West represses, silences, prohibits, and constrains sexuality. There is the "properly historical question" of whether this is in fact the case. But there is also a second doubt (and a third): "Do the workings of power, and in particular those mechanisms that are brought into play in societies such as ours, really belong properly to the category of repression? Are prohibitions, censorship, and denial truly the forms through which power is exercised in a general way, if not in every society, most certain in our own?" (Foucault 1978, 10). This, Foucault argues, is a "historico-theoretical question" (1978, 10), and it is here that his work most closely parallels Nietzsche's conception of genealogy and Freud's of analysis. (Both are also implicated in Foucault's third doubt, to which I will return and which involves how and if one can *resist*, what Foucault calls a "historico-political question.")

The particularity of genealogy as a mode of historico-theoretical and historico-political inquiry is most readily visible in Nietzsche's 1887 text, *On the Genealogy of Morals*, in which Nietzsche's immersion in the gray volumes of the archive is always driven by his concern for the present and the future (Nietzsche 1989 and 1998). Three aspects of what it means to write a genealogy rather than an intellectual history, a history of mentalities, or a history of practices are crucial for both Nietzsche and Foucault. First, although genealogy may look like a search for origins, and a certain kind of visual representation of a genealogical tree makes it seem as if everything and everyone descends from a single source—the trunk of the tree—in fact if we start from any moment in the present and go back in time, we are confronted by proliferating roots, none of which are the sole origin of anything that follows. Genealogy generates countless forebears and as such marks the refusal of the claim that there is any single origin, source, or beginning.

Second, Nietzsche insists that the past meaning of a word or term is not determinative of its current meaning. Genealogy is not, then, a record of continuity but one of rupture, change, and transformation, even as older meanings may haunt newer ones. Nietzsche pursues a genealogy of morals not to discover continuities, but instead to show that what is considered valuable *changes*, and hence that these valuations can change yet again. This brings me to my third point about genealogy: for Nietzsche, and arguably even more for Foucault, genealogy is always an account of the operations of power. Valuation is itself an effect of will, hence of force. The question underlying much of Nietzsche's writing, as much of Foucault's, is how power has its effects; in its most common and mundane articulation, Nietzsche and Foucault echo the only seemingly simplistic question posed by de Kerangal's narrator: "how this guy managed to make others believe that he owned the rock."

The extraction of natural resources and the exploitation of human labor are particularly pertinent here as Foucault opens *HS1* with a salvo against the convergence of Marx and Freud in the work of Wilhelm Reich. Foucault's argument with Reich continues throughout the book and is the note on which he ends (although by this point he has thoroughly conflated Reich with Freud). *HS1* is often taken, quite correctly, as a general critique of the ideal of sexual liberation, but the figure within that discursive terrain Foucault names is Reich, and it is Reich's assertion that sex is repressed in order to redirect its energies toward labor in the service of capitalism that is the subject of Foucault's most scathing critique. If one links sexual repression to capitalism, Foucault mockingly asserts, talking about sex can appear political, revolutionary, subversive. The sexual revolutionary, he argues, becomes a kind of secular preacher, promising their listeners that there is an outside to power and that "tomorrow sex will be good again" (Foucault 1978, 7).

> Because this repression is affirmed, one can discreetly bring into coexistence concepts which the fear of ridicule or the bitterness of history prevents most of us from putting side by side: revolution and happiness; or revolution and a different body, one that is newer and more beautiful; or indeed, revolution and pleasure. What sustains our eagerness to speak of sex in terms of repression is doubtless this opportunity to speak out against the powers that be, to utter truths and promise bliss, to link together enlightenment, liberation, and manifold pleasures; to pronounce a discourse that combines the fervor of knowledge, the determination to change the laws, and the longing for the garden of earthly delights. (Foucault 1978, 7)

The problem, for Foucault, is not simply that this historical account is wrong (although he thinks it is), but that it radically misrepresents how power works. Not primarily repressive (Freud's and Reich's position, according to Foucault), nor even simply generative of a desire it prohibits (Foucault's gloss of the work of the French psychoanalyst Jacques Lacan, whose influence was so ubiquitous when Foucault was writing *HS1* that he does not bother to name Lacan within the text), power instead constitutes and is operative throughout the very "regime of power-knowledge-pleasure" that tells us the truth of the individual and the truth of humanity lie in sexuality.

Foucault argues not that the prohibition of sex is a ruse, but that "all the negative elements—defenses, censorships, denials—which the oppressive hypothesis groups together in one great central mechanism destined to say no, are doubtless only component parts that have a local and tactical role to play in a transformation into discourse, a technology of power, and a will to knowledge that are far from being reducible to the former" (Foucault 1978, 12). The language of component parts, which echoes Freud's language in the *Three Essays*, is not in the original French, and yet I understand why the English-language translator, Robert Hurley, uses it, given how psychoanalytically laden Foucault's language is here and throughout the book. Foucault writes that "defenses, censorships, denials" are likely only local and tactical "parts" ("pièces") of a central mechanism—for Freud, repression—through which the psyche says no. The French for component parts in all of the available Freud translations, however, is "pulsions partielle." Freud insists on the singularity of the sexual drive against those who argue that there are two drives, one feminine and one masculine; yet as Hurley knows, Freud does differentiate what he calls component drives internal to that single drive, most particularly, sadism and masochism and scopophilia and exhibitionism (Freud 1975). This enables him to account for and demonstrate the malleability of the sexual drive and the multiplicity of its forms. Even though Foucault does not use the specific language of component parts, just as Freud insists that the sexual drive is in some way one and at the same time polymorphous, so too Foucault echoes Freud in insisting throughout *HS1* on the polymorphous nature of power. For both Freud and Foucault, moreover, the multiplicity of their object of analysis makes it very difficult to draw clear lines between the body and the psyche, between physical violence and psychic or cultural force.

Power as repressive, then, power as instantiated through the law or the interdict, is only one of its forms. Foucault argues that Freud misses the polymorphous quality of power even as he uses Freud's language to name it. Is this account of Freud warranted, given the centrality of the operation of repression in the formation of the psyche? Or is Foucault performing a sleight-of-hand by gradually conflating Freud and Reich, a conflation that reaches its heights in the closing pages of *HS1*? What does it mean for Foucault's account of the complex operation of power that he seems to need a theory, as general as possible, against which to posit his own accounts of sexuality and power, of bodies and pleasures? And how might returning to Freud's *Three Essays* enable us better to understand what is crucial in Foucault's analytics of power?

For far from engaging in the naturalizing and biologizing of sexuality, or claiming to speak the singular and static truth of the human subject and the human species that has been putatively cloaked in secrecy up until the appearance of his *Three Essays*, Freud, clearly and self-consciously working within the domain of the proliferating discourses around sex so aptly described by Foucault in *HS1*, is fundamentally concerned with demonstrating a particular set of difficulties posed by what he calls the sexual drive. Four points are crucial in my reading of Freud's essays, and each plays a fundamental role in Foucault's text and in his analytics of power. First and perhaps most importantly for Freud, there is no innate continuity between the sexual drive and any particular object or aim. The first of the *Three Essays* makes use of the existing nineteenth-century sexological literature to argue that inversion (purported irregularities in the object of the sexual drive) and perversion (purported irregularities in the aim of the sexual drive) are so widespread as to defeat the very idea of normative objects and aims. Nothing in the sexual drive of humans, Freud argues, renders heterosexuality or reproduction articulable as its *natural* object or aim (Freud 1975, esp. 1–38). This is related to his second key claim, noted above, that although there is one sexual drive, which he argues is the same in all human beings regardless of their biological sex, it is made up of component drives that manifest themselves in particular ways within each individual of the species (Freud 1975, esp. 32–37, 99–107).

Freud does try to organize all of this, devising stages in the sexual development of the child that correspond to three erotogenic zones (the oral, anal, and genital, all still autoerotic in the child but leading to shifts in object choice) and within each stage to specific aims (sadism and masochism, scopophilia and exhibitionism—Freud 1975, 47–50). Yet every argument for development along this putative path is stymied by the plethora of ways in which the objects and aims of sexuality multiply and proliferate. Thus, tucked into what would seem to be a compellingly and prohibitively pathologizing paragraph, Freud introduces the notion of the child's polymorphous perversity: "It is an instructive fact," Freud argues, "that under the influence of seduction children can become polymorphously perverse, and can be led into all possible kinds of sexual irregularities. This shows that an aptitude for them is innately present in their disposition. There is consequently little resistance towards carrying them out, since the mental dams against sexual excesses—shame, disgust and morality—have either not yet been constructed at all or are only in the course of construction, according to the age of the child" (Freud 1975, 57). In this respect, Freud adds, the seduced child behaves in the same way "as an average uncultivated woman in whom the same polymorphously perverse disposition persists" (Freud 1975, 57). The problem, however, is that Freud insists the sexual drive is not, in any simple sense, innate. "By a 'drive,'" he explains early in the *Essays*, "is provisionally to be understood the psychical representation of an endosomatic, continuously flowing source of stimulation, as contrasted with a 'stimulus,' which is set up by *single* excitations coming from *without*. The concept of drive is thus one of those lying on the frontier between the mental and the physical" (Freud 1975, 34, translation modified). From this perspective, any external stimulation might arouse and of necessity meet with internally derived stimuli; the sexual *drive*, however, is the psychical representation generated, Freud's later work will suggest, by conflicts internal to the subject and by those engendered through the convergence of internal and external stimuli.

It is not difficult to read Freud against the grain of his own argument and to see *every* child as polymorphously perverse and the education of the child as an education in constraining, not the sexual drive itself, but the objects and aims it finds appropriate for itself—because they are those seen as appropriate by those around them. Freud is acutely aware of how loose a grasp "culture," "civilization," or "morality" have on the sexual drive and the extent to which polymorphous perversity is everywhere around him—not just in so-called inverts and perverts, but in those who kiss, smoke cigars, take pleasure in a well-turned heel in a slim shoe, or, most dangerously, in the production of knowledge itself (on the sexual drive as the source of the desire to know, see Freud 1975, 60–63, 70–77).

Freud is clear about the challenge posed by his theory of sexuality: how, given the lack of innate ties to specific objects and aims, does heterosexual reproductive sex ever come to be the norm—or even occur at all? This brings us back directly to Foucault, for Freud makes explicit that the object and aim of the sexual drive in the individual and what he calls the demands of the species are at odds (see Davidson 2004). The former seeks pleasure anywhere and in any way it can get it; the latter depends on heterosexual reproductive sexuality in order to fulfill the evolutionary task of survival. The riddle of sexuality for Freud is how the two demands are brought into conformity with each other, and he finds himself, here and throughout his work, stumbling over the realization that they never fully are.

Foucault points to this dilemma in Freud—although without acknowledging Freud's awareness of it as a problem—when he argues that biopower, a term Foucault introduces in the final section of *HS1* to name the discursive regime of modern Western humanity, fixates on sexuality precisely because in it two distinct projects—the disciplining of the subject and the regulation of populations—come together (Foucault 1978, 145). The conjunction of these projects is crucial to the epochal shift in power's mode of operation Foucault outlines in the closing section of *HS1*. Foucault reads Freud, and Freud's repeated attempts to discipline and regulate sexuality through the theories and method of psychoanalysis, as operating with a deeply anachronistic understanding of power, one grounded in the law of "the Sovereign-Father": "to conceive the category of the sexual in terms of the law, death, blood, and sovereignty . . . is in the last analysis a historical 'retro-version.' We must conceptualize the deployment of sexuality on the basis of the techniques of power that are contemporary with it" (Foucault 1978, 150).

What is required, Foucault insists, is not a new theory of power, but a new "analytics" of power—thus not a new general account of power, but a new way of thinking its multiplicity and how we might best break it into pieces in the process of careful description leading to understanding. As for Freud, a new form of analysis requires or emerges from a new method, and it is under the title of "Method" that Foucault puts forth his most sustained articulation of the techniques of power (and of the methods for analyzing power). In explaining the objective of his enterprise in the *History of Sexuality*, at least as he conceived the multi-volume project in 1976, he describes the move toward an "analytics" of power as a move "toward a definition of the specific domain formed by relations of power, and toward a determination of the instruments that will make possible its analysis" (Foucault 1978, 82). He insists that "this analytics can be constituted only if it frees itself completely from a certain representation of power that I will term . . . 'juridico-discursive.' It is this conception that governs both the thematics of repression and the theory of the law as constitutive of desire" (1978, 82). Without naming them, Foucault targets both Freud and Lacan. For although one speaks of repression and the other of the prohibition of the father, "they both rely on a common representation of power which, depending on the use made of it and the position it is accorded with respect to desire, leads to two contrary results: either to the promise of a 'liberation,' if power is seen as having only an external hold on desire, or, if it is constitutive of desire itself, to the affirmation: you are always trapped" (1978, 83). This conception of power, moreover, is not only operative in the discussion of sexuality but is "one frequently encounter[ed] . . . in political analyses of power, and it is deeply rooted in the history of the West" (1978, 83).

To this conception of power as working through negation, rules, prohibition, and censorship, an impoverished, uniform, and unfruitful set of laws that work only to tame some already existing reality or to elicit some wan, undefined desire, Foucault opposes an understanding—he does call it a theory, as well as describing it under the heading of method—of power

> as the multiplicity of force relations immanent in the sphere in which they operate and which constitute their own organization; as the process which, through ceaseless struggles and confrontations, transforms, strengthens, or reverses them; as the support which these force relations find in one another, thus forming a chain or a system, or on the contrary, the disjunctions and contradictions which isolate them from one another; and lastly, as the strategies in which they take effect, whose general design or institutional crystallization is embodied in the state apparatus, in the formulation of the law, in the various social hegemonies. Power's condition of possibility . . . must not be sought in the primary existence of a central point, in a unique source of sovereignty from which secondary and descendent forms would emanate; it is the moving substrate of force relations which, by virtue of their inequality, constantly engender states of power, but the latter are always local and unstable. (Foucault 1978, 92–93)

Power is, however unequally, everywhere; it "comes from everywhere"; it is multiple, productive, relational—in a word Foucault uses throughout *HS1* to name it, polymorphous (Foucault 1978, 11, 32, 34, 47, 63, 106).

Foucault argues that power operates by means of "displacement, intensification, reorientation, and modification" (Foucault 1978, 23), or later "isolation, intensification, and consolidation" (1978, 48). These lists of operational terms are remarkably similar to Freud's articulation of the operations of the unconscious, particularly in the dream work. In Lacan's rereading of Freud, these modes are consolidated around metaphor (condensation—consolidation and intensification) and metonymy (displacement), but Freud's more capacious if less systematic language forcefully demonstrates reorientation, modification, displacement, and consolidation as the constitituve processes of the unconscious.

Throughout these sections of *HS1*, Foucault circles around, describes, and redescribes what he calls "propositions" and "cautionary prescriptions" about how to approach the analysis of power. (All of this warrants further comparisons with Freud and the working of the unconscious.) Certain key descriptors recur: power is mobile, relational, immanent; it comes from below and is "both intentional and nonsubjective"; subject to continual variations, power can never be full circumscribed or limited, but works in terms of varying intensities as well as varying objects and aims; there is never one single source of power and so no single causal explanation for any given phenomenon; and finally (and most controversially for many), Foucault insists that "where there is power, there is resistance, and yet, or rather consequently, this resistance is never in a position of exteriority to power" (Foucault 1978, 95). One way to understand the possibility of resistance endemic to Foucault's account of power is in terms of what he later in these handful pages on method calls the "rule of tactical polyvalence of discourses." Power *can* be consolidated, it can and does lead to situations of subjection, domination, oppression, and immiseration. But because it plays throughout all relations and moves in multiple directions, thinking in terms of dominant and dominated discourses or accepted and excluded ones is, Foucault argues, inadequate. It leads to what he fears in Lacan: a conception of power as the law, a law that is productive *and* inescapable. Foucault insists there is no outside to power, as he argues Freud and Reich posit, but he also wants to leave open, or perhaps more properly name, a space for resistance.

Foucault claims that resistance is part of how power works. It is a result of its polymorphous techniques and the polyvalent discourses it puts into play. "We must make allowance," Foucault argues,

> for the complex and unstable process whereby discourse can be both an instrument and an effect of power, but also a hindrance, a stumbling block, a point of resistance and a starting point for an opposing strategy. Discourse transmits and produces power; it reinforces it, but also undermines and exposes it, renders it fragile and makes it possible to thwart it. . . . There is not, on the one side, discourse of power, and opposite it, another discourse that runs counter to it. Discourses are tactical elements or blocks operating in the field of force relations; there can exist different and even contradictory discourses within the same strategy; they can, on the contrary, circulate without changing their form from one strategy to another, opposing strategy. (Foucault 1978, 101–2)

For these reasons, Foucault insists, we need to think of power in terms not of the law, but of power's objectives; not in terms of prohibition, but in terms of "tactical efficacy," and we must replace "the privilege of sovereignty with the analysis of a multiple and mobile field of force relations, wherein far-reaching, but never completely stable, effects of domination are produced" (1978, 102).

This account of power troubles distinctions between power-over, power-for, and empowerment, for power relations and the discursive fields with which they are entangled are too mutable, too fungible, too contradictory, and too unstable to render these terms of analysis precise (for a careful delineation of different philosophical accounts of power, see Allen 1999, 2008, and 2016). Foucault also troubles any clear differentiation between physical violence and other forms of power or force, although this does not mean no such distinction can or ought to be made (see especially Foucault 2003). (Much more needs to be said about this topic.)

Note also that in these pages of *HS1*, Foucault posits these assertions as general claims—theoretical, methodological, analytic—about how power should be understood and investigated. Only later, in part 5 of *HS1*, does he link his analysis of power to the broader historical argument about sexuality made in the earlier sections of the book. In an argument linked to that found within *Discipline and Punish* and within his lectures from 1975 to 1976, *"Society Must Be Defended,"* part 5 of *HS1* suggests that with the modern proliferation of discourse around sex, the organization of power also changes. Hence his introduction of the term biopower, the complex set of techniques and strategies through which bodies are disciplined and populations regulated. This shift goes along with a shift from a sovereign's power over life manifest solely through the right to kill to "a power to *foster* life or *disallow* it to the point of death" (Foucault 1978, 138).

Foucault recognizes that not only sexual difference and sexuality, but also religion are at issue here; the shift from power as the right to kill to power as infiltrating and shaping every aspect of life "perhaps . . . explains that disqualification of death which marks the recent wane of the rituals that accompanied it" (Foucault 1978, 138). Within a society governed by the power of the sovereign, Foucault suggests,

> in the passage from this world to the other, death was the manner in which a terrestrial sovereignty was relieved by another, singularly more powerful sovereignty; the pageantry that surrounded it was in the category of political ceremony. Now it is over life, throughout its unfolding, that power establishes its dominion; death is power's limit, the moment that escapes it; death becomes the most secret aspect of existence, the most "private." It is not a surprise that suicide—once a crime, since it was a way to usurp the power of death which the sovereign alone, whether the one below or the Lord above, had the right to exercise—became, in the course of the nineteenth century, one of the first conducts to enter the sphere of sociological analysis; it testified to the individual and private right to die, at the borders and in the interstices of power that was exercised over life. (1978, 138–39)

Suicide, Foucault writes, "was one of the first astonishments of a society in which political power had assigned itself the task of administering life" (1978, 139; almost all of the longer passage from which I draw this citation appears in *"Society Must Be Defended,"* with the crucial exception of the reference to astonishment).

A very specific Christian theological imaginary underlies this account of the logic of sovereignty and its demise, and if suicide is "an astonishment" within the realm of bio-history and biopower, it is also an escape to nowhere. Foucault claims that the religious frame within which death was putatively understood in late medieval and early modern Europe is gone. Yet if, in thinking death, we move from the world of a particular form of Christian monotheism—explicitly Protestant and explicitly modern—dependent on claims to divine sovereignty to a religious frame in which spirits, ancestors, the living, and the dead remain in relation, a world of what Aisha Beliso-De Jesús calls "copresence" and finds enacted within African Diaspora religions, we can offer an account of religion in which the polymorphous nature of power, its hold on both life and death, demonstrates, continuously, the ruse of sovereignty (Beliso-De Jesús 2014, 2015). It is crucial to recognize, moreover, that this world of copresence offers a much better account of the ontological thickness of Christianity itself.

Foucault provides a clue when he argues that power is "intentional and nonsubjective" (Foucault 1978, 94). It works tactically and strategically toward certain ends, but there is no individual subject, "no central site that presides over its rationality" (1978, 95, translation modified). This does not mean there are not those who benefit from power, who learn to deploy it toward their own ends. But power always escapes the bounds of individual agency, even that, Foucault suggests, of a putatively sovereign God—certainly those of a putatively sovereign state. For this reason I think those who insist on returning to late medieval and early modernity accounts of sovereignty and joining them to Foucault's account of biopower are fundamentally misreading the most crucial insights of *HS1*: power, in its polymorphous perversity, can never be sovereign; claims to sovereignty are always a ruse; we always stand in relation to others, human and nonhuman, whose actions ineluctably shape, even as no single relation fully determines, our fate (for a related argument against contemporary theorists of sovereignty, particularly Giorgio Agamben, see Weheliye 2014). Perhaps this is a mistake Foucault himself makes, particularly in *"Society Must Be Defended,"* but *HS1* reads to me like a critique of Agamben before Agamben (1978, 102, 137). This is where attention to the relationship between Freud and Foucault helps. For just as Freud demands, with whatever ambivalence, that his colleagues among the sexologists relinquish the dream of a determinative object and aim to the sexual drive and posits the polymorphous perversity of that drive, so too Foucault at his most insightful dethrones the sovereign, itself a modern construct, and insists on the polymorphous perversity of power.[1] To complete this move, we need to resist the lure of forms of the monotheistic imagination that insist on that singular god's sovereignty.

Most crucially, perhaps, we cannot conflate this polymorphous power with liberation, arguably the mistake made by Reich. In an oft-repeated and deeply unfortunate line, Foucault claims that the disciplining of the self endemic to modernity and to the rise of capitalism occurred "not through an enslavement of others, but through an affirmation of the self" (Foucault 1978, 123). But as he himself well knew, it occurred through *both*, and even more: the enslavement of some, the immiseration of others, the wholesale annihilation of populations seen as harmful to the population whose thriving biopower sought to enable, *and* the affirmation of the self, of the white bourgeois heterosexual unambiguously male subject, most pointedly and most particularly, although similarly situated white women were also crucial to the enterprise. Foucault sees the links between racism and biopower and names them in *HS1* and elsewhere. He is also clear that domination *does* occur, repeatedly and in sedimented, seemingly intractable ways, despite the mobility of power.

Yet the multiple ways in which power harms are not fully articulated within Foucault's corpus. Others have taken up this task, among them Achille Mbembe, Jasbir Puar, and Zakkiya Iman Jackson, with their complex arguments about necropolitics, the right to maim, and Black life as life under siege, life under the conditions of war (Mbembe 2003; Puar 2017; Jackson 2020). Whatever it might mean to resist these annihilating and destructive forms of power requires recognizing their complex and polymorphous operations, their systemic accrual within structures that cannot be dismantled through individual actions, and the simple fact that we can never know what the effects of our own actions will be. (Also here lies the endless proliferation of affect, haunting sorrows, grief, woundedness,

1. In his College de France lectures from 1975 to 1976, *"Society Must Be Defended,"* he does seem to bring sovereignty back into play under the regime of biopower. I believe that this is the ruse of sovereignty, but that is an argument for a different paper. He also there deals explicitly, if inadequately, with the issue of race and racism.

yet also delight and pleasure, engendered not only by structures or individuals, but by the complex forms of embodied sociality we live. On this see Sharpe 2016.) This does not spell defeat, acquiescence, or quietism, but instead tactical and strategic deployment of the resources available to us toward ends that we can, at least provisionally, identify as good. And throughout this enterprise, we must acknowledge that we are not alone; there are principalities and powers, entities and realities—microbial, mineral, plant, animal, and yes, perhaps even divine—that accompany us in life and death. The nineteenth-century European "human sciences" attempt to kill God and the gods in order to free humanity, but this is a ruse in which God's putative sovereignty is replaced by humans', a fantasy of absolute power that has led us to species annihilation, environmental devastation, and the brink of wholesale ecological disaster. Foucault's *HS1* continues to offer us strategies and tactics with which to name and to refuse this myth by recognizing the polymorphous nature of power and the complexity of the relations and structures to which it gives rise. Against those who insist on bringing biopower and the ruse of sovereignty back together again, I suggest we join the host of scholars asking us to slow down, to work carefully in the gray spaces of the archive, and to allow different voices to speak alongside those more familiar to the Western academy on which I focus here (see Matory 2018)—to hear the ways in which they have been speaking truth to and with power all along.

Suggested Readings

Asad, Talal. 1993. *Genealogies of Religion: Discipline and Reasons of Power in Christianity and Islam*. Baltimore: Johns Hopkins University Press.

Asad, Talal. 2003. *Formations of the Secular: Christianity, Islam, Modernity*. Palo Alto, CA: Stanford University Press.

Beliso-De Jesús, Aisha. 2014. "Santería Copresence and the Making of African Diaspora Bodies." *Cultural Anthropology* 29 (3): 503–26.

Butler, Judith, Jürgen Habermas, Charles Taylor, and Cornel West. 2011. *The Power of Religionin the Public Sphere*. New York: Columbia University Press.

Foucault, Michel. 1978. *The History of Sexuality*. Vol. 1, *An Introduction*. Translated by Robert Hurley. New York: Vintage.

Foucault, Michel. 2003. *"Society Must Be Defended": Lectures at the Collège de France 1975–76*. Translated by David Macey. New York: Picador.

Mahmood, Saba. 2004. *Politics of Piety: The Islamic Revival and the Feminist Subject*. Princeton, NJ: Princeton University Press.

Matory, J. Lorand. 2018. *The Fetish Revisited: Marx, Freud, and the Gods Black People Make*. Durham, NC: Duke University Press.

Puar, Jasbir K. 2017. *The Right to Maim: Debility, Capacity, Ability*. Durham, NC: Duke University Press.

References

Agamben, Giorgio. 1998. *Homo Sacer: Sovereign Power and Bare Life*. Translated by Daniel Heller-Roazen. Stanford, CA: Stanford University Press.

Allen, Amy. 1999. *The Power of Feminist Theory: Domination, Resistance, Solidarity*. Boulder, CO: Westview Press.

Allen, Amy. 2008. *The Politics of Ourselves: Power, Autonomy, and Gender in Contemporary Critical Theory*. New York: Columbia University Press.

Allen, Amy. 2016. "Feminist Perspectives on Power." *Stanford Encyclopedia of Philosophy*. https://plato.stanford.edu/entries/feminist-power/.

Asad, Talal. 1993. *Genealogies of Religion: Discipline and Reasons of Power in Christianity and Islam*. Baltimore: Johns Hopkins University Press.

Asad, Talal. 2003. *Formations of the Secular: Christianity, Islam, Modernity*. Palo Alto, CA: Stanford University Press.

Asad, Talal. 2007. *On Suicide Bombing*. New York: Columbia University Press.

Asad, Talal. 2018. *Secular Translations: Nation-State, Modern Self, and Calculative Reason*. New York: Columbia University Press.

Beliso-De Jesús, Aisha. 2014. "Santería Copresence and the Making of African Diaspora Bodies." *Cultural Anthropology* 29 (3): 503–26.

Beliso-De Jesús, Aisha. 2015. *Electric Santería: Racial and Sexual Assemblages of Transnational Religion*. New York: Columbia University Press.

Bloch, Maurice. 1989. *Ritual, History and Power: Selected Papers in Anthropology*. New York: Routledge.

Bloch, Maurice. 1991. *Prey into Hunter: The Politics of Religious Experience*. Cambridge: Cambridge University Press.

Butler, Judith, Jürgen Habermas, Charles Taylor, and Cornel West. 2011. *The Power of Religion in the Public Sphere*. New York: Columbia University Press.

Carrette, Jeremy, ed. 1999. *Michel Foucault: Religion and Culture*. New York: Routledge.

Carrette, Jeremy. 2000. *Foucault and Religion: Spiritual Corporeality and Political Spirituality*. New York: Routledge.

Chidester, David. 1996. *Savage Systems: Colonialism and Comparative Religion in South Africa*. Charlottesville: University of Virginia Press.

Chidester, David. 2014. *Empire of Religion: Imperialism and Comparative Religion*. Chicago: University of Chicago Press.

Clements, Niki Kasumi. 2021. "Foucault's Christianities." *JAAR* 89 (1): 1–40.

Davidson, Arnold I. 2004. *The Emergence of Sexuality: Historical Epistemology and the Formation of Concepts*. Cambridge, MA: Harvard University Press.

Foucault, Michel. 1970. *The Order of Things: An Archeology of the Human Sciences*. Translated by Alan Sheridan. New York: Vintage.

Foucault, Michel. 1977a. *Discipline and Punish: The Birth of the Prison*. Translated by Alan Sheridan. New York: Vintage.

Foucault, Michel. 1977b. "Nietzsche, Genealogy, History." In *Language, Counter-Memory, Practice: Selected Essays and Interviews*, edited by D. F. Bouchard. Ithaca: Cornell University Press.

Foucault, Michel. 1978. *The History of Sexuality*. Vol. 1, *An Introduction*. Translated by Robert Hurley. New York: Vintage.

Foucault, Michel. 2003. *"Society Must Be Defended": Lectures at the Collège de France 1975–76*. Translated by David Macey. New York: Picador.

Freud, Sigmund. 1975. *Three Essays on the Theory of Sexuality*. Translated by James Strachey. New York: Basic Books.

Huffer, Lynne. 2009. *Mad for Foucault: Rethinking the Foundations of Queer Theory*. New York: Columbia University Press.

Jackson, Zakiyyah Iman. 2020. *Becoming Human: Matter and Meaning in an Antiblack World*. New York: New York University Press.

Jordan, Mark. 2014. *Convulsing Bodies: Religion and Resistance in Foucault*. Chicago: University of Chicago Press.

Lincoln, Bruce. 2012. *Gods and Demons: Critical Explorations in the History of Religions*. Chicago: University of Chicago Press.

Mahmood, Saba. 2004. *Politics of Piety: The Islamic Revival and the Feminist Subject*. Princeton, NJ: Princeton University Press.

Mahmood, Saba. 2015. *Religious Difference in a Secular Age: A Minority Report*. Princeton, NJ: Princeton University Press.

Matory, J. Lorand. 2018. *The Fetish Revisited: Marx, Freud, and the Gods Black People Make*. Durham, NC: Duke University Press.

Masuzawa, Tomoko. 2005. *The Invention of World Religions: Or, How European Universalism Was Preserved in the Language of Pluralism*. Chicago: University of Chicago Press.

Mbembe, Achille. 2003. "Necropolitics." *Public Culture* 15 (1): 11–40.

Nietzsche, Friedrich. 1989. *On the Genealogy of Morals* and *Ecce Homo*. Translated by Walter Kauffman. New York: Vintage.

Nietzsche, Friedrich. 1998. *On the Genealogy of Morality*. Translated by Maudemarie Clark. New York: Hackett.

Puar, Jasbir K. 2017. *The Right to Maim: Debility, Capacity, Ability*. Durham, NC: Duke University Press.

Sharpe, Christina. 2016. *In the Wake: On Blackness and Being*. Durham, NC: Duke University Press.

Weheliye, Alexander G. 2014. *Habeas Viscus: Racializing Assemblages, Biopolitics, and Black Feminist Theories of the Human*. Durham, NC: Duke University Press.

16 PRACTICE

Elizabeth Pérez

> Moomintroll was already on his way out to [Little My's] rescue. Too-ticky stood looking on for awhile, and then she went inside the bathing house and put a kettle of water on the stove. "Quite, quite," she thought with a little sigh. "It's always like this in their adventures. To save and be saved. I wish somebody would write a story sometime about the people who warm up the heroes afterwards."
> TOVE JANSSON, *Moominland Midwinter*

When the coronavirus pandemic shut down much of my world in March 2020, I needed something to read. On a whim I picked up a book by the Finnish author and artist Tove Jansson. Halfway through the 1957 entry in Jansson's classic Moomin series *Moominland Midwinter*, I was struck by the passage above. My reader need not be acquainted with Moomintroll, Little My, or Too-ticky to grasp the critique articulated in it. Stories generally center protagonists and their deeds. In film and fiction, lead characters are often shown rescuing others or getting rescued; in popular history books, it is the heroic feats of adventurers that are recorded for posterity.

By 1957, scholars of religion had long been concerned with much more than saving and being saved in a theological sense, but they still tended to privilege "adventures" in the form of major rituals, rites of passage, and annual festivals. Indeed, until the turn of the twenty-first century, their "heroes" were those authoritative senior practitioners whose participation in (and explanation of) large-scale ceremonies gave anthropologists and historians something to write about. In the 1990s, Americanists challenged the notion that religious practice is exceptional rather than mundane action through the "explicit methodological mandate" of what they dubbed "lived religion" (Furey 2012, 15; Primiano 1999; Orsi 1997; Hall

1997). They were simultaneously building on and exposing a shortcoming of what had come to be called "practice theories." They paved the way for researchers to concentrate on acts that religious authorities did not consider life-changing or even remarkable, joining scholars from other fields in giving rise to what is now a varied and voluminous literature on religion as quotidian, embodied, and relationally embedded. I have taken their insights with me when gravitating toward the "micropractices" that allow for the main ritual events—the adventures—to take place: the boiling of kettles that has been left out of the story for too long.

Seeking both to situate and complicate *practice* as a key word in religious studies, I begin by tracing it to a Christian European history of ideas. After giving an overview of its conventional usages, I introduce the bodies of scholarship with the most acute influence on practice in religious studies over the last half century. I then reflect on my use of micropractices to describe religious labor like "warm[ing] up the heroes afterwards" in Black Atlantic traditions. I suggest that when dramas of salvific heroism underlie our portrayals of religious experience, we fail to realize the significance of everyday gendered and racialized work in theorizing religion. This failure stymies our ability to analyze and accurately depict practitioners' lives. Bearing in mind my interlocutors' reservations about practice, I maintain that an adequate appreciation of "the actual 'doing' of religion" requires a (re-)commitment to the minute and plural (Bell 1998, 205).

"Beliefs and . . ."

The earliest modern references to religious practice in English assume that the religion at hand is Christianity, as when the Puritan theologian William Perkins wrote in *Of the Nature and Practise of Repentance* ([1593] 1597, 37), "it is not an easy matter to practise religion: which is to live according to the Spirit, to which our naturall disposition is as contrary as fire to water." The Spanish *prácticas religiosas* appears to occur earlier than *prácticar [la] religion*, and these phrases are both predated by *práctica [e]spiritual* and the transliterated Greek and Latin *praxis ecclesiasticae*, as in Gonzalo Suárez de Paz's (1583) *Praxis ecclesiasticae et secularis, cum actionum formulis & actis processuum, hispano sermone compositis*. In a host of seventeenth-century catechisms, doctrinal teachings, and confessional manuals titled *Prácticas*, the modifier "religious" is implied. In these texts and others, European authors relied on the positive connotations of "religion" to define practice as a virtuous deed—"vera verae Religionis praxis"—not merely a neutral act (Smith 1998, 269; Bakio 1678, 392; Dufréne 1755).

When anticlerical and freethinking authors during this period derided *pratiques religieuses* as illusory, they still located spiritual exercises and imaginative "habits of mind" within the realm of phenomenal reality. They tacitly conceded the materiality of practices, even of a theoretical nature—a point obscured at times by the philosophical distinction, long predating Aristotle, between *praxis* (activity in the service of commonplace affairs) and *theoria* (excellent yet detached contemplation of eternal, unchanging matters). Contrary to stubborn misconstruals of these terms as "doing" versus "thinking," it is in Aristotelian thought that theoria and praxis converge most significantly (Adkins 1978; DeHart 1995). However, since the emergence of the "science of religion" (*Religionswissenschaft*) in the nineteenth century, scholars have tended to deem practices those tangible actions undertaken with goal-oriented ends (Aristotle's *praxeis*), in contrast to the reflective looking-at-something performed by intellectuals (Charles 1995, 305; Godzich 1994, 164).

In the first edition of *Critical Terms for Religious Studies*, practice was less frequently used in the singular than as part of the venerable dyad "beliefs and practices." The phrase may derive from the Latin *praxis fidei*, "the practice of faith," translated into *Glaubensübung*—"belief exercise"—in more than one early modern German text. According to Jonathan Z. Smith (1998, 271), "the shift to belief as the defining characteristic of religion" was "stressed in the German preference for the term Glaube over Religion, and in the increasing English usage of 'faiths' as a synonym for 'religions.'" While more than a hundred instances of "faith and practice [or 'practise']" are to be found in print before 1700, there is only one of "Beliefs and Practices"—and they are judged "false"—in a treatise whose title announces its objective: *A Collection of Texts of Scripture, with Short Notes upon Them, Against the Principal Popish Errors: Being a Summary of the Doctrine of the Church of Rome, with a Plain Refutation by Scripture* (Comber 1686, 185; Dyke 1661).

Most polemical and devotional literature from this era equates practices with repeated patterns of performances—whether solitary or collective—intended to instill mental, volitional, and physical discipline along with assent to creedal propositions (resulting in orthodoxy). These practices are normally accomplished with synchronized movement, in a certain physical space, for a specific length of time. In a short article on Pierre de Villiers's

1692 *Pensées et Reflexions sur les égaremens des Hommes dans la voye du salut* [*Thoughts and Reflections on the Wanderings of Men on the Way of Salvation*], the reviewer wrote, "We usually [*d'ordinaire*] call devotional certain religious practices, of which we make it a law to discharge on a regular basis" (Basnage de Beauval 1693, 69).

As a definition—that is, a theory of religion "in miniature"—"beliefs and practices" asserts that the cognitive operations (such as doctrinal affirmations) denoted by "belief" are not routine or primarily communal activities (Saler 1993, 85). It may be tempting to credit one of the "founding fathers" of sociology, Émile Durkheim, with the ubiquity of "beliefs and practices" in religious studies. But this terminology was well established by the time Durkheim (1897, 329) ventured to define religion in an early book review: "a set [*ensemble*] of beliefs and practices that regulate life" (Masuzawa 2005, 16). Few users of this cliché in the nascent social-scientific study of religion problematized practice as a category of human behavior, perhaps because "beliefs and practices" mapped so neatly onto the all-too-familiar binaries of mind/body, spirit/matter, interior/exterior, and substance/form.

Practice and Theory

The philologist and Old Testament scholar William Robertson Smith ([1882] 1896, 261) joined nineteenth-century theologians in referring to "religious praxis," but none insinuated any familiarity with Karl Marx's ([1845] 1945) philosophy of praxis, as either material struggle, materialist method, or creative revolutionary action (Flaxman 2017). While they declined to regard religious practice as praxis in the Marxian sense, there are such nuances in the studies of the sociologist, historian, and political economist Max Weber. Despite the erasure of Marxian thought from his oeuvre through (mis-)translation and distortion, Weber taught Marx and Engels in the classroom, critiquing them with an eye toward elaboration rather than refutation (Riesebrodt 2005, 31).

Such works as Weber's essays on the sociology of religion must be read with these inclinations in mind, especially given his preference for *Praxis* over *Praktik* as the singular of *Praktiken* (Weber 1923, 150, 168). Although he is not usually classified as a "practice theorist," Weber emphasized practice (*praxis pietatis*) over doctrine in his account of Pietism, just as he privileged "*religiösen Uebungen*" over "book knowledge" in his treatment of Zen (1920a, 96–165 et passim; 1916/1917, 739). It is "religious beliefs and the praxis of religious life"—not texts—that generate psychological drives, which in turn beget doctrines (Weber 1920a, 86). Belief is not the basis for practice or its ideological counterpart but "a '*superadditum*'" (Breuer 2019, 239). When the "moral Praxis" and consistent "ethical Praxis of ordinary [or everyday] people" become systematized into rational methods, they make history (Weber 1920a, 86; 1920b, 115).

The accent on practice as *Praxis* in Weber marks a theoretical-historical shift toward investigating the transformative power of everyday people's contribution to social process (if not progress). While we must not understate Weber's impact, the theorist of practice with the greatest claim to current influence is the ethnographer and sociologist Pierre Bourdieu. Bourdieu was indebted to both Marx and Weber in his theorization of social fields, in addition to the philosopher Immanuel Kant and the social scientist Marcel Mauss in his approach to "structuring structures," the frameworks for action produced by local histories of political and economic relations. Bourdieu examined the cumulative effects of social practice through the concept of habitus in *Esquisse d'une theorie de la pratique, précédé de trois études d'ethnologie Kabyle* (translated as *Outline of a Theory of Practice*) in 1972, followed by *La sens pratique* in 1980 (*The Logic of Practice*), and related works.

Bourdieu's theorization of religion as such has been of less consequence for historians, sociologists, and anthropologists of religions than his concept of practice, "what people do" (Dianteill 2003; Rey 2018). Its adoption has proceeded from a desire to comprehend how historical processes materialize in the world and how the proximate past shapes our bodies (including our minds) through the internalization of societal standards for action, culturally specific perceptual schemas, modes of attention, and somatic dispositions. Bourdieu distinguishes logic (as rational, conscious deliberation) from practical sense (the embodied, intuitive, and orienting experience of reality that humans draw upon to act). Religious studies scholarship predicated on the Bourdieusian theoretical toolkit gains explanatory power by extending his analyses of habitus, religious field, doxa, symbolic power, class distinction, and capital—broadened to include spiritual or sacred capital—into unexpected contexts.

Bourdieu has had his detractors. To name just one, the historian of religions Michel de Certeau weighed his insights against those of the historian of ideas Michel Foucault and found both lacking in *The Practice of Everyday Life* (1984), which centered practice in its exploration of popular culture. Published in 1980 as *L'invention du quotidien*, vol. 1, *Arts de faire*, *The Practice of Everyday Life* has proven enormously influential in its attention to walking, talking, and working as everyday activities. Among de Certeau's formulations most often incorporated into studies of religion are strategies vs. tactics; "consuming" as meaning-making; reading as poaching; and *la perruque* ("the worker's own work disguised as work for his employer"). De Certeau's elucidation of "a tactic [as] an art of the weak" acknowledges ordinary modalities of resistance—like James C. Scott's (1990) "weapons of the weak"—that are less readily observable than armed rebellions or other collective mobilizations.

In the field-defining essay "Theory in Anthropology Since the Sixties," the anthropologist Sherry B. Ortner (1984, 127, 138) branded practice "[a] new key symbol of theoretical orientation . . . in the name of which a variety of theories and methods are being developed." Ortner (1984, 144) saw practice theory as wrestling with "real people doing real things" through one "bundle of interrelated terms: practice, praxis, action, interaction, activity, experience, performance," and another "focuse[d] on the doer of all that doing: agent, actor, person, self, individual, subject." Ortner (2006, 157) later fleshed out the "practice trend" in the social-scientific study of religion as comprising a "historic turn," a "re-interpretation of culture(s)," and a "power shift" toward critical interrogation of patriarchy, white supremacy, colonialism, and capitalism. Three different formulations of practice were taken up in this trend that may be distinguished as follows: "The concept of *practice* entails that social life unfolds 'through practice,' through a myriad of everyday doings. The concept of *practical knowledge* points up the chasm between theoretical fancies and how (and why) things pan out 'in practice.' The concept of *practices* invites us to consider a range of social phenomena 'as practices,' as though they were *things* that people do" (Kustermans 2016, 195).

In over two decades of scholarship, Ortner called for agency to be underscored in investigations of whether practices sustain hierarchical systems (the sum of prevailing sociocultural, economic, and political forces) or undermine them. But Ortner's "mythical charter" reinscribed the division between anthropology's "ritual focus, or what might be called [the] focus on extraordinary practice" and "practices of ordinary living" (Gellner 2009, 8; Ortner 1984, 154). Jane F. Collier and Sylvia Yanagisako reiterated this dichotomy in "Theory in Anthropology Since Feminist Practice" (1989, 32): "It is an irony of history . . . that practice theory, which deliberately set out to analyze the 'practices of ordinary living' rather than the rituals that concerned most of Durkheim's followers, should nevertheless sometimes lead to the labelling of only some actions as symbolic, thus reproducing the sacred/profane opposition." The depiction of ritual as out of the ordinary and non-instrumental remained tenacious in a range of studies conversant with practice theory. For example, in an appraisal of Ortner's *Making Gender: The Politics and Erotics of Culture* (1996), Bonnie McElhinny (1998, 174, my italics) wrote: "The practice-based approach moves beyond a view of social behavior as ordered by rules and norms, as well as one that accords actors unlimited agency[;] it attempts to transcend distinctions between base/superstructure, and it places a greater emphasis on the practices of ordinary living (*than, say, ritual practices*)."

How is religious life to be understood if "the rituals that concerned most of Durkheim's followers" are set apart from ordinary living? Would the quotidian practice of religion mainly involve an intermittent consciousness of belief occasionally punctuated by practices "of which we make it a law to discharge on a regular basis," as in political models—I am tempted to say "fantasies"—of Euro-American secular citizenship (Basnage de Beauval 1693, 69)? The continued use of ritual as a synonym for religious practice is partly to blame for this implication. The terminological ambiguity of "practice" compels us to reckon with the aspects of ritual that are doggedly unexceptional, poised at the knife-edge between sacred and secular—if not entirely profane—yet capable of carving subjects out of infinitesimal technologies of power.

Micropractices and -Praxes

In 2003 I began conducting fieldwork in a Chicago-based, predominantly African American working-class community dedicated to the transnational West-African-inspired Afro-Cuban religion Lucumí (popularly called Santería). This house of worship has been led since 1986 by Ashabi Moseley and her son Fadesie. Since the late nineteenth century, most Lucumí practitioners have worshipped their deities in their own homes, and the micro-site of my first research project was the kitchen of Moseley's South Side bungalow. The practices I was preoccupied with happened in the wake of sacrifice, when devotees turned the organs and extremities of fowl and four-legged animals into food for the gods. In Afro-Diasporic religions, such kitchenspaces tend to be queer, women-centered sites of praxis that engender distinctive modes of storytelling. Chief among these is the initiation story, in which elders recount their initiation not as an agentive act but as an "unchosen choice," made to save themselves or loved ones from imminent death or persistent affliction.

Sacred food preparation is accompanied by other informal genres of communication, like chitchat, advice-giving, joke-cracking, and gossip. These discursive modes enter into the ethnographer's archive as chunks of dialogue or bite-sized scenes, slices of life that might shed light on underappreciated facets of embodied practice. The representation of practice presents an array of problems, which do not end with the inaccuracies that creep into fieldnotes jotted down at midnight. What configurations of action can be inscribed as emblematic of practice? For instance, what synaesthetically rich chicken-plucking session can one identify as ideal-typical enough for the purposes of exposition? What attitude to skinning goats can be isolated as so markedly representative that it might serve as the basis for a theory of butchering?

In prioritizing the domestic labor that "seasons" individuals into gendered and racialized norms in Ilé Laroye, I departed from the scholarly consensus on what Lucumí is and which practices are indispensable for the intergenerational transmission of Afro-Diasporic religions. If plucking, skinning, and eviscerating aren't rituals, though, what are they? All rituals count as practice, but not all practices are rituals. Some acts that fall in between habituate practitioners into structures of power, simultaneously securing their recognition of themselves as religious subjects. To categorize them, I drew on Foucault's concept of micropractices: routine and small-scale sequences of operations made up of yet more microscopic units of activity. Micropractices flourish at the spatiotemporal interstices of institutionalized rituals; they enskill and inculcate mastery through sensorial experience, both constraining subjects and freeing them (up). Micropractices are performed by "the people who warm up the heroes afterwards," with Cuban coffee, or with rum, or just the proverbial tea and sympathy.

I have relied on the terminology of micropractices while noting its iffy provenance (Pérez 2016).[1] Micropractices may seem like a highly technical term, yet even "practice" can sound specialized to the non-academic ear.

1. It appears that "micro-techniques," "micro-pouvoirs," and "micro-physique(s) du pouvoir" were translated into "micropractices" before Foucault ever used "micropratiques" (e.g., Jobert and Gilbert 1976, 222; Foucault 1976, 192, 197; Dreyfus 1980, 8; Fraser 1981, 272). I owe many thanks to Dr. Janet Afary for her insights on this point. The first use of "microtechniques du pouvoir" may be Manin (1979, 227). Vignau (1983, 13) cited "micro-techniques de pouvoir" in a PhD dissertation; Michel de Certeau was one of the dissertation committee's co-chairs. Also in 1983, "micropratiques" appeared in a work of urban sociology (Cazal 1983, 108); an article about current trends in anthropology (Girard 1983, 163); and an anonymous review (1983) of a sociological study.

I once used "religious practice" in a conversation with my interlocutor Arlene Stevens (personal communication, February 2005) and she corrected me, saying, "either you're in it and doing it, or not." Arlene equated practice with rehearsal, play-acting, or preparation, as in the saying, "practice makes perfect." At other moments, practice was framed as the implementation in real time of previously acquired corporeal knowledge, as when Fadesie (personal communication, May 2005) said, "you can't know without putting into practice."

In Afro-Diasporic religions, regimented and formally demarcated ceremonies might be called macropractices. Examples of these include divination sessions, rites of consecration, and drum feasts. Macropractices have clearly delineated beginnings, middles, and endings. In lending themselves to straightforward narration and explication, they correspond to the "adventures" that, in my epigraph, Too-ticky dismissed as "to save and be saved." But the preferred emic label for religious praxis of any magnitude is "work." To practice Black Atlantic traditions is to "work the spirit" or "work the religion"—whatever the religious formation in question is. Working the spirits encompasses macropractices, but it can also indicate the more modest, unglamorous efforts that make them possible, like chopping vegetables, folding laundry, and mopping sticky floors. The overlap between secular and sacred work hearkens back to the Greek etymology of "liturgy." As Joseph M. Murphy (1994, 6) and Martin Riesebrodt (personal communication, August 2009) have observed, *leitourgia* means "work of the people" or "public work" and referred to the performance of services as a civic duty in ancient Greece.

The construction of religious practice as unfree labor is thus built into the linguistic origins of liturgy, which rings particularly true for Black practitioners of Afro-Diasporic religions. Elizabeth McAlister (2002, 86) writes in the context of Vodou, "'Work' is a cultural concept with many levels of resonance in Haiti, a society that was formed in plantation slavery, where people were routinely worked to death." "Work" has the same valences in other Afro-Diasporic religions forged in the crucibles of the transatlantic slave trade, settler colonialism, racial capitalism, and unfreedom in the post-emancipation Americas. This dimension of "work" has not been reflected in genealogies of religious practice. To offer one illustration close to home, in the first *Critical Terms for Religious Studies*, "work" was used almost exclusively to refer to academic scholarship or artistic oeuvres; labor, in the sense of sacred or profane work, appeared only on a handful of pages (Aveni 1998, 366; Benavides 1998, 192, 194, 199; Lopez 1998, 25).

In retrospect, the acts I have designated micropractices may be better described as *micropraxes*, at least in the context of Black Atlantic traditions. "Micropraxes" would echo M. Jacqui Alexander's (2005) spiritual and "emancipatory praxis"; Jessica Marie Johnson's (2019) proposal of "xroads praxis" as a "black Diasporic technology" that "create[s] data without losing affect, sensation, and kinship as a framing for black life"; and N. Fadeke Castor's (2024) theorization of "sacred citational praxis." Micropraxes would also help us to think with the philosopher Sylvia Wynter, best known for her collaboration with the Black feminist theorist Katherine McKittrick. In their critical genealogy of Wynter's thought, Wynter (2015, 33) puts forward "the idea that with being human *everything is praxis*," especially when it comes to "performative enactment" of "our role allocations as, in our contemporary Western/Westernized case, in terms of . . . gender, race, class/underclass, and, across them all, sexual orientation." Their inquiries into "genre-specific praxes of being hybridly human" speak to those of us interested in religious knowledges as worked through in coloniality and other conditions of sociocultural, economic, and political domination.[2]

It's time to put the kettle on.

Suggested Readings

Alexander, M. Jacqui. 2005. *Pedagogies of Crossing: Meditations on Feminism, Sexual Politics, Memory, and the Sacred*. Durham: Duke University Press.

Asad, Talal. 1993. *Genealogies of Religion: Discipline and Reasons of Power in Christianity and Islam*. Baltimore: Johns Hopkins University Press.

Bender, Courtney. 2010. *The New Metaphysicals: Spirituality and the American Religious Imagination*. Chicago: University of Chicago.

Castor, N. Fadeke. 2017. *Spiritual Citizenship: Transnational Pathways from Black Power to Ifá in Trinidad*. Durham, NC: Duke University Press.

Gumbs, Alexis Pauline. 2019. "Being Ocean as *Praxis*: Depth Humanisms and Dark Sciences." *Qui Parle* 28 (2): 335–52.

2. The knowledges referred to here are not solely liberatory techniques passed on as factual information within communities, but also "ways of knowing," such that religious ontologies are always already epistemological (Alexander 2005, 293 et passim). In Afro-Diasporic religions, embodied procedural knowledge of how to perform efficacious actions—paradigmatically, in ritual contexts—trumps the importance of prepositional knowledge based on "neurocentric" belief (Morales 2022, 4; Pérez 2023).

Kupari, Helena. 2016. *Lifelong Religion as Habitus: Religious Practice Among Displaced Karelian Orthodox Women in Finland*. Leiden: Brill.

Mahmood, Saba. 2005. *Politics of Piety: The Islamic Revival and the Feminist Subject*. Princeton: Princeton University Press.

Martin, Joan. 2000. *More than Chains and Toil: A Christian Work Ethic of Enslaved Women*. Louisville, KY: Westminster John Knox Press.

Warnier, Jean-Pierre. 2001. "A Praxeological Approach to Subjectivation in a Material World." *Journal of Material Culture* 6 (1): 5–24.

Woodbine, Onaje X. O. 2016. *Black Gods of the Asphalt: Religion, Hip-Hop, and Street Basketball*. New York: Columbia University Press.

References

Adkins, W. H. 1978. "Theoria versus Praxis in the Nicomachean Ethics and the Republic." *Classical Philology* 73 (4): 297–313.

Alexander, M. Jacqui. 2005. *Pedagogies of Crossing: Meditations on Feminism, Sexual Politics, Memory, and the Sacred*. Durham: Duke University Press.

Anton, Paul. [1699] 1721. *Sendschreiben an einen Sächs. Theologum Die Materie von dem wahren lebendigen thätigen Glauben betreffend: und wie gefährlich solche uhralte Evangelische Lehre von einigen angegriffen werde . . .* Zeitler: Halle.

Aveni, Anthony F. 1998. "Time." In *Critical Terms for Religious Studies*, edited by Mark C. Taylor, 314–33. Chicago: University of Chicago Press.

Bakio, Theodoro. 1678. *Florilegium ethico-politicum de felicitate humana*. Frankfurt: Jobi Wilhelmi Fincelii.

Basnage de Beauval, Henri. 1693. "Review, Pierre de Villiers' 1692 *Pensées et Reflexions sur les égaremens des Hommes dans la voye du salut*." *Histoire des Ouvrages des Savans* 10 (October): 69.

Bayly, Lewis. 1613. *The Practice of Pietie: Directing a Christian how to Walke, that He May Please God*. London: John Hodgets.

Bell, Catherine. 1998. "Performance." In *Critical Terms for Religious Studies*, edited by Mark C. Taylor, 269–84. Chicago: University of Chicago Press.

Benavides, Gustavo. 1998. "Modernity." In *Critical Terms for Religious Studies*, edited by Mark C. Taylor, 186–204. Chicago: University of Chicago Press.

Bourdieu, Pierre. 1972. *Esquisse d'une theorie de la pratique, précédé de trois études d'ethnologie Kabyle*. Geneva: Droz.

Bourdieu, Pierre. 1980. *La sens pratique*. Paris: Minuit.

Breuer, Stefan. 2019. "The Relevance of Weber's Conception and Typology of Herrschaft." In *The Oxford Handbook of Max Weber*, edited by Edith Hanke, Lawrence A. Scaff, and Sam Whimster, 237–58. Oxford: Oxford University Press.

Castor, N. Fadeke. 2024. "Sacred Cites: Engaging the Spiritual in Ethnographic Knowledge (Re)production." *Studies in Religion/Sciences Religieuses* 53 (2): 247–64.

Cazal, Didier. 1983. "Lâches les flux!" *Espaces et sociétés* 43 (2): 103–10.

Charles, David. 1995. "Aristotle: Ontology and Moral Reasoning." In *Classical Philosophy: Philosophy before Socrates*, edited by Terence Irwin, 295–320. Hamden, CT: Garland Publishing.

Collier, Jane F., and Sylvia Yanagisako. 1989. "Theory in Anthropology Since Feminist Practice." *Critique of Anthropology* 9: 27–37.

Comber, Thomas. 1686. *A Collection of Texts of Scripture, with Short Notes upon Them, Against the Principal Popish Errors: Being a Summary of the Doctrine of the Church of Rome, with a Plain Refutation by Scripture*. London: Samuel Norman.

de Certeau, Michel. 1984. *The Practice of Everyday Life*. Translated by Steven Rendall. Berkeley: University of California Press.

DeHart, Scott M. 1995. "The Convergence of Praxis and Theoria in Aristotle." *Journal of the History of Philosophy* 33 (1): 7–27.

Dianteill, Erwan. 2003. "Pierre Bourdieu and the Sociology of Religion: A Central and Peripheral Concern." *Theory and Society* 32: 529–49.

Dreyfus, Hubert L. 1980. "Holism and Hermeneutics." *The Review of Metaphysics* 34 (1): 3–23.

Drelincourt, Charles. 1625. *Abbrégé [i.e., Abrégé] des controverses, ou, Sommaire des erreurs de nostre* [*sic*] *temps, avec leur réfutation par textes exprès de la Bible de Louvain*. Genève: Pierre Aubert.

Dufréne, Maximiliano. 1755. *Rudimentos Históricos ò Methodo fácil y breve para instruirse la juventud catholica en las noticias históricas*. Antwerp: Hermanos de Tournes.

Durkheim, Émile. 1897. Review of Ernest Grosse, *Die Formen der Familie und die Formen der Wirtschaft* [1896]. *L'Année sociologique* 1: 319–32.

Dyke, Jeremiah. 1661. *Praxis Fidei, oder Glaubens-Übung einer heyl durstigen Seele*. Translated by Heinrich Stockar. Bern: Georg Sonnleitner.

Flaxman, Gregory. 2017. "Introduction: Deleuze: In Practice." In *Practising with Deleuze: Design, Dance, Art, Writing, Philosophy*, edited by Suzie Attiwill, Terri Bird, Andrea Eckersley, Antonia Pont, Jon Roffe, and Philipa Rothfield, 1–15. Edinburgh: Edinburgh University Press.

Foucault, Michel. 1976. *La volonté de savoir (Histoire de la sexualité, I)*. Paris: Gallimard.

Fraser, Nancy. 1981. "Foucault on Modern Power: Empirical Insights and Normative Confusions." *Praxis International* 1 (3): 272–87.

Furey, Constance. 2012. "Body, Society and Subjectivity in Religious Studies." *Journal of the American Academy of Religion* 80 (1): 7–33.

Girard, Christian. 1983. "Profession: africaniste." *Autrement* 49: 162–71.

Gellner, David N. 2009. "The Uses of Max Weber: Legitimation and Amnesia in Buddhology, South Asian History, and Anthropological Practice Theory." In *The Oxford Handbook of the Sociology of Religion*, edited by Peter Clarke, 48–62. Oxford: Oxford University Press.

Godzich, Wlad. 1994. "The Tiger on the Paper Mat." In *The Culture of Literacy*, 159–70. Cambridge: Harvard University Press.

Hall, David D., ed. 1997. *Lived Religion in America: Toward a History of Practice*. Princeton: Princeton University Press.

Hussain, Azfar. 2000. "Joy Harjo and Her Poetics as Praxis: A 'Postcolonial' Political Economy of the Body, Land, Labor, and Language." *Wicazo Sa Review* 15 (2): 27–61.

Jansson, Tove. 1958. *Moominland Midwinter*. Translated by Thomas Warburton. New York: Walck [Trollvinter 1957].

Jobert, Bruno, and Claude Gilbert. 1976. *Système scientifique et développement urbain: villes et reproduction des différences sociales, l'organisation scientifique de l'espace*. Grenoble: Institut d'Etudes politiques.

Johnson, Jessica Marie. 2019. "Xroads Praxis: Black Diasporic Technologies for Remaking the New World." *sx:archipelagos* 3 (July 9): 1–21.

Kustermans, Jorg. 2016. "Parsing the Practice Turn: Practice, Practical Knowledge, Practices." *Millennium* 44 (2): 175–96.

Lopez, Donald. 1998. "Belief." In *Critical Terms for Religious Studies*, edited by Mark C. Taylor, 21–35. Chicago: University of Chicago Press.

Manin, Bernard. 1979. "Saint-Just, la logique de la terreur." *Libre: politique, anthropologie, philosophie* 6: 165–231.

Marx, Karl. [1845] 1994. "Theses on Feuerbach." In *Selected Writings*, edited by Lawrence H. Simon, 98–102. Indianapolis: Hackett Publishing.

Masuzawa, Tomoko. 2005. *The Invention of World Religions*. Chicago: University of Chicago Press.

McAlister, Elizabeth. 2002. *Rara! Vodou, Power, and Performance in Haiti and Its Diaspora*. Berkeley: University of California Press.

McElhinny, Bonnie. 1998. "Genealogies of Gender Theory: Practice Theory and Feminism in Sociocultural and Linguistic Anthropology." *Social Analysis* 42 (3): 164–89.

Morales, Juan. 2022. "The Ecology of Religious Knowledges." *Religions* 13 (1): 1–13. https://doi.org/10.3390/rel13010011.

Murphy, Joseph M. 1994. *Working the Spirit: Ceremonies of the African Diaspora*. Boston: Beacon Press.

Orsi, Robert. 1997. "Everyday Miracles: The Study of Lived Religion." In *Lived Religion: Toward a History of Practice*, edited by David D. Hall, 3–21. Princeton, NJ: Princeton University Press.

Ortner, Sherry. 1984. "Theory in Anthropology since the Sixties." *Comparative Studies in Society and History* 26 (1): 126–66.

Ortner, Sherry. 2006. *Anthropology and Social Theory: Culture, Power, and the Acting Subject*. Durham, NC: Duke University Press.

Pérez, Elizabeth. 2016. *Religion in the Kitchen: Cooking, Talking, and the Making of Black Atlantic Traditions*. New York: New York University Press.

Pérez, Elizabeth. 2023. *The Gut: A Black Atlantic Alimentary Tract*. Cambridge: Cambridge University Press.

Perkins, William. [1593] 1597. *Two Treatises: I. Of the Nature and Practise of Repentance. II. Of the Combat of the Flesh and Spirit*. Cambridge: John Legate.

Primiano, Leonard Norman. 1999. "Postmodern Sites of Catholic Sacred Materiality." In *Perspectives on American Religion and Culture*, edited by Peter W. Williams, 187–202. Oxford: Blackwell.

Review, *Paradigmes sociologiques et pratiques sociales*. 1983. *Bulletin signalétique: Histoire et science de la littérature* 523: 2.

Rey, Terry. 2018. "Pierre Bourdieu and the Study of Religion: Recent Developments, Directions and Departures." In *The Oxford Handbook of Pierre Bourdieu*, edited by Jeffrey J. Sallaz and Thomas Medvetz, 529–30. Oxford: Oxford University Press.

Riesebrodt, Martin. 2005. "Dimensions of the *Protestant Ethic*." In *The Protestant Ethic Turns 100: Essays on the Centenary of the Weber Thesis*, edited by William H. Swatos and Lutz Kaelber, 23–52. Boulder: Paradigm.

Robertson Smith, William. [1882] 1896. *The Prophets of Israel and Their Place in History to the Close of the Eighth Century B.C.* London: Black.

Saler, Benson. 1993. *Conceptualizing Religion: Immanent Anthropologists, Transcendent Natives, and Unbounded Categories*. Leiden: Brill.

Scott, James C. 1990. *Domination and the Arts of Resistance: Hidden Transcripts*. New Haven: Yale University Press.

Smith, Jonathan Z. 1998. "Religion, Religions, Religious." In *Critical Terms for Religious Studies*, edited by Mark C. Taylor, 269–84. Chicago: University of Chicago Press. Reprinted in 2004 in Jonathan Z. Smith, *Relating Religion: Essays in the Study of Religion*. Chicago: University of Chicago Press.

Suárez de Paz, Gonzalo. 1583. *Praxis ecclesiasticae et secularis, cum actionum formulis & actis processuum, hispano sermone compositis*. Salmanticae: apud Petrum Lassum Typographum.

Vignau, Sylvaine. 1983. "Sémiotique littéraire et sémiotique architecturale: Butor, Pérec, Soleri." PhD diss., University of California, San Diego.

Weber, Max. 1916/1917. "Die Wirtschaftsethik der Weltreligionen: Hinduismus und Buddhismus II." *Archiv für Sozialwissenschaft und Sozialpolitik* 42 (3): 687–814.

Weber, Max. 1920a. "Die protestantische Ethik und der Geist des Kapitalismus II: Die Berufsethik des asketischen Protestantismus." *Gesammelte Aufsätze zur Religionssoziologie*, vol. 1. Tübingen: Mohr.

Weber, Max. 1920b. "Die religiösen Grundlagen der innerweltlichen Askese." In *Gesammelte Aufsätze zur Religionssoziologie I*. Tübingen: Mohr.

Weber, Max. 1923. "Die orthodoxen und heterodoxen Heilslehren der indischen Intellektuellen." In *Gesammelte Aufsätze zur Religionssoziologie II, Hinduismus und Buddhismus*. Tübingen: Mohr.

Wynter, Sylvia. 2015. *Sylvia Wynter: On Being Human as Praxis*. Edited by Katherine McKittrick. Durham: Duke University Press.

17 RACE

Terrence L. Johnson

The History of Race and Religion in the United States

Scholars of political theory and religious studies have written widely on nineteenth-century appropriations of religion both to endorse and to erase racial domination and racial hierarchies in the aftermath of the transatlantic slave trade. Fewer have written on the political implications of religion's enduring role in sustaining race and racism during the nascent era of political liberalism and global universal rights. The tension between religious freedom and toleration, as noted by Ronald F. Thiemann in *Religion in Public Life: A Dilemma for Democracy*, dates to the early discussions of the theoretical wall separating church doctrine from state politics and policies, leaving generations to scavenge the archives to discern and decipher the constitutional framers' understanding of the complex role of religion and race in a democracy committed to pluralism. To this end, debates on religion's role in public life have been circumscribed by a razor-sharp focus on the religious clauses in the First Amendment without adequate attention to religion's role in denying those same liberties and more to enslaved Africans and their descendants. To understand the complexities of religion in the United States, race is a necessary conversation starter in any deliberation on rights, liberty, and equality.

Dating back to the eighteenth century, race was a category of classification in the natural sciences used to describe human variation. The category increasingly shifted in the nineteenth century to define race based on visual representation, crude science, and insidious misinterpretations of the Bible during a period of increasing debates on the theological and political justifications of African enslavement (West 1982, 55). This essay will define race as a political category sustained by religion (principally Christianity) to normalize racial difference in relation to the white/Black binary, a racial model of hierarchies distinguishing moral/rational humans (Whites) from immoral/inferior nonhumans (Blacks).

From the Hebrew Bible's narratives of Cain and Abel (Genesis 4:1–16) and the curse of Ham (Genesis 9:18–27) to accounts of slavery in the New Testament (1 Peter 2:18, Ephesians 6:5–8, and Colossians 3:22–24), theologians, enslavers, and politicians obscured a very real history. As noted in Ivan Hannaford's *Race: The History of an Idea in the West*, the efforts among the Christian hierarchy to differentiate barbarians from the civilized and evil from good can be traced back to the inquisitions and the history of colonization, when religious leaders turned to violence, oppression, and exploitation to convert or violently subdue religious minorities. The existing binary categories of the Jew and Gentile and Canaanite and Hebrew established a theoretical framework for privileging one group over another and subsequently condemning and justifying the radical *otherness* of non-Christians. "The badge that distinguished people who could not be set apart by their physical appearance in later times became the mark of Cain and then absorbed by logic and associations of ideas into the mark of race" (Hannaford 1996, 126).

During the thirteenth-century Spanish Inquisition, for instance, the Catholic Church relied on torture, violence, and property confiscation to combat heresy and dissent, when the expansion of empire created the conditions for the abuse and misuse of Christianity. Protestants and Muslims were targeted, as well as individuals who questioned Church authority and doctrine. Jews paid a unique price during this period when Catholic leaders "openly advocated that Latin Christendom rid itself of its Jewish population, whether through missionizing, forced expulsions, or physical harassment that would induce conversion or flight" (Cohen 1982, 14).

These biblical narratives animated political doctrines of racial difference. Indeed, the racial misapplication of the curse of Ham is legendary and substantial in both Judaism and Christianity. The story in Genesis goes like this: after the great flood, Noah planted a vineyard and subsequently became drunk from its wine. Noah's son Ham stumbled upon his father's nakedness and shared the encounter with his brothers. When Noah awoke and ascertained his own humiliating actions, he cursed Ham and his offspring for gazing at his nakedness, while blessing his son Shem and his descendants for covering him. It is worth pointing out that Ham has been a shifting metaphor for a people rejected by God because of their disobedience. Ham was Jewish in the thirteenth century and morphed into a Black character in the nineteenth century (Braude 2005, 81) as colonizers searched for ways to justify beliefs in the inferiority of Blacks and solidify *Blackness* as a metaphor for unredeemable difference. Linking Blacks to the cursed Ham narrative was a "national, and not merely Southern, concern" (Johnson 2004, 32). The enduring narrative "between skin color and slavery" grew "increasingly explicit, thus serving to maintain—by divine mandate—the social order" (Goldenberg 2005, 170).

In Jon Butler's noted book *Awash in a Sea of Faith: Christianizing the American People*, the historian extended the claim that Christianity was rebirthed in the New World. He argued that both African enslavement and Christianity in colonial America shaped each other in spiritual and material ways that were guided by an unmitigated principle oriented by a "planter ethic of absolute slave obedience that ran thoroughly counter to contemporary English political and social theory and became a principal foundation of American slavery's distinctive paternalism, violence, and sentimentalism in late colonial and antebellum society" (Butler 1990, 129). Just as Christianity empowered the planter class and indentured people alike, it offered renewal through salvation in the present as well as in the afterlife. But to sustain a national economy fueled by African enslavement, Christian ministers depended on biblical interpretations that, on the one hand, relied on Pauline epistles to justify slavery, and on the other hand, cultivated a Christianity that decried human exploitation, oppression, and violence. In this sense, Butler asserts, the Christianization of Africans established ongoing theological contradictions that subsequently led to slave revolts and simultaneously established an Anglo-Christianity that was often both complicit and at odds with its slave legacy.

Abolitionists have been exemplary models of individuals retrieving religion *appropriately* to affirm political liberalism's core principles of liberty and equality. Consider Maria W. Stewart, the renowned early nineteenth-century Bostonian and feminist activist who, speaking in response to the 1832 Second Annual Convention for the Improvement of the Free People of Color in These United States, implored her audience of freed Blacks, abolitionists, and a handful of whites to remain steadfast in their fight to abolish slavery. Born free in Connecticut in 1803, Stewart exposed the religious and moral roots of public law, slavery, patriarchy, and gender bias. The first "American-born woman" to deliver a political address to both women and men, Stewart threaded biblical imagery alongside liberal principles of equality and liberty throughout her political speeches and writings—

as was customary of New England's jeremiad tradition—to reject ontological claims of Black inferiority. "This is the land of freedom. The press is at liberty. Every man has a right to express his opinion. Many think, because your skins are tinged with a sable hue, that you are an inferior race of beings; but God does not consider you as such. He hath formed and fashioned you in his own glorious image, and hath bestowed upon you reason and strong powers of intellect" (Stewart and Richardson 1987, 28).

Transgressing the acceptable boundaries of Enlightenment's racial reasoning, Stewart wove Black bodies into the tapestry of the Psalms, particularly descriptions of David's affirmation of God's hand in human creation, Psalm 8:5, and God's inescapable presence in human existence. Stewart also appealed to the Constitution to justify her claims, noting that "according to the Constitution of these United States, he hath made all men free and equal." However, unlike many of her male peers, such as Richard Allen and William Lloyd Garrison, this "unlettered" seamstress took an unexpected hermeneutical turn in her analysis in two critical ways. First, she claimed that Blacks were made in the image of God, defying long-standing beliefs in Black inferiority predicated on the Genesis account of the curse of Ham. Second, Stewart appealed to what she believed to be the spirit of equality embedded within the United States Constitution, contradicting Garrison's vehement rejection of the legal text as fundamentally evil and racist (Barnett 2011, 165). Stewart's corrective disclosed an often overlooked contribution by the abolitionist: religion's role in normalizing race and racial difference in the United States. Unlike the philosophers who framed religion as a possible tool for bolstering the liberal social contract, Stewart implicitly recognized religion as the source of the ideological deployment of race as a totalizing and immutable category of social difference. "Oh, America, America, foul and indelible is thy stain! Dark and dismal is the cloud that hangs over thee, for thy cruel wrongs and injuries to the fallen sons of Africa" (Stewart and Richardson 1987, 33). To be sure, she captured the nadir of race and racial reasoning shortly after the nation's founding, when scripture, science, and Christian morality coalesced to manufacture race into a constant but shifting social construction utilized to maintain racial hierarchy and racial oppression. Her abolitionist and feminist critique is unique for two reasons: first, she reads the Constitution as a living text through a dialogical exchange; second, her interpretive appeal to the Bible both condemns the nation and affirms Black humanity, as well as animating Black political action.

The turbulent and tedious history of race in the United States established an enduring political maze of racial difference and domination through which the nation has been meandering without an immediate exit plan. What makes this history disconcerting is its fetishization of Blackness: the multilayered course of actions, discourses, and normative beliefs that both elide and overshadow the irrationality of race and racial differences. Abolitionists have long pointed to the obtuseness of the "one drop" rule, which categorized one as Black or racially mixed if one's family lineage had been "spoiled" by "nonwhite" persons. Scholars have pointed to a similar claim raised by Frederick Douglass in his first autobiography, *Narrative of the Life of Frederick Douglass*, where he challenged African enslavement premised on political constructions of race and racial difference. If embodied Blackness is the erasure of humanity, how then might one characterize biracial and multiracial persons far removed from Africa? "Multiracial" or "biracial" persons "will do away [with] the force of argument, that God cursed Ham, and therefore American slavery, is right. If the lineal descendants of Ham are alone to be scripturally enslaved, it is certain that slavery at the south [*sic*] must soon become unscriptural; for thousands are ushered into the world, annually, who, like myself, owe their existence to white fathers, and those fathers most frequently their own masters" (Douglass 2016, 15).

Christian slaveholders fundamentally shifted the role of the Bible in slaveholding contexts. Scripture was no longer used for the singular purpose of proselytizing and conversion; it was also seized on to normalize race, asserts Ariela Gross, as a signifier of social and epistemic difference (Gross 2008, 4). Whites possessed freedom and reason, while Blacks symbolized unfreedom, the absence of humanness without reason or a soul. "On the one hand, race was supposed to be immutable and clear; on the other hand, it was shifting and hard to define; either way, it was central to people's identities and a crucial factor in determining their social lives, their economic opportunities, and the way they were perceived by others" (Gross 2008, 17). Race, then, demarcated political, economic, and social markers of hierarchy. On the one hand, race translated into a signifier of ontological Blackness. On the other hand, the category of "white" remained a non-racialized category that increasingly extended itself beyond Christian white male landowners to include Italians and Jews. Model minority groups, including Asians and Asian Indians, complicated the developing white/Black binary. Should model minorities be included in racial categories? In the earliest legal cases on United States citizenship, Asians often claimed either that they were descendants of the Aryan race or that they deserved to be defined as white because they owned businesses and achieved educational success—characteristics that were more aligned with middle-class whites than with Blacks (Ngai 2014). In fact, the invention of "ethnicity" as a demarcation of "unique" social and cultural norms further compromised the already significant incoherency of race and racial difference. It accentuated the liminality of culture within an otherwise hermetically sealed paradigm dependent on racial difference. "The invention of ethnicity furthermore suggests an active participation by the immigrants in defining their group identities and solidarities. . . . In inventing its ethnicity, the group sought to determine the terms, modes, and outcomes of its accommodation to 'others'" (Conzen et al. 1992, 5). It is important to note that the so-called *invention of ethnicity* happened within the social ontology of race and racial difference in contrast to the non-racial and universal category of *whiteness* as ideal, pristine, and normative.

This racial hierarchy became the justification for racial domination and oppression predicated largely on the white/Black binary. The political use of race and racial hierarchies uprooted existing historical methods of identifying groups with their land, tribe, or language, rather than religiously generated constructions of race and racial difference. This framework established the context for envisioning the white/Black racial binary as normative, natural, and necessary in the industrial New World. Whereas many architects of political liberalism viewed race as a fleeting metaphor or flimsy social marker reaching its nadir after the abolition of slavery, abolitionists like Stewart saw something else: the interplay of religion and politics as enabling race and racial difference, to the detriment of democracy.

W. E. B. Du Bois and the "Conservation of Races"

Late nineteenth-century Black intellectuals inherited a theoretical discussion of race immersed in the vestiges of the Enlightenment. Race was generally characterized in biological and anthropological terms, embodying the material iteration of nature, bloodline, or culture. In most instances, the "studies" of places in Africa, Asia, and South America, for instance, explained social, political, and cultural traditions and habits in contrast to the normative practices and beliefs in Western civilization. W. E. B. Du Bois's 1897 essay, "The Conservation of Races," is emblematic of this inheritance, both for its polished dispensation of modern discourses on race and its inventive taxonomy of human beings. Without fully refuting the

Enlightenment's Victorian moralizing and biological determinism, Du Bois attempted to transgress those boundaries by redefining race as a group of human beings singularly bound by common "blood" but distinguished by "deeper spiritual and psychical differences" who were designed to fulfill in the world the "unique" vision of the race (Du Bois and Sundquist 1996, 41). K. Anthony Appiah is noted for his fierce pushback against Du Bois's major argument, charging Du Bois with replacing biological determinism with the slippery notion of a "common history" that collapsed into a "sign of racial essence" (Appiah 1985, 30). Nevertheless, Appiah's insightful analysis overlooks Du Bois's conscientious efforts to expose the varying ways human beings disrupt and reinvent existing structures and paradigms through language, tradition, and culture. What Appiah and others did not immediately acknowledge was Du Bois's effort to weaken the political uses of race and racial difference in the American context. Indeed, the entanglement between Christianity and African slavery fundamentally altered the direction of American democracy in general and sustained religion's role in shaping it. To secure the nation's slaveholding economy and subsequent industrialization, African slaves and their descendants needed to remain inferior, nonhuman laborers in the American project. Without this political move, the racialization of democracy would lose its grip on the American people.

Writing in 1898, Du Bois characterized the socioeconomic dilemma facing the nation as the "Negro problem," the fundamental belief in Black people, according to Lewis R. Gordon, as *the* problem. A problem people did not face social, political, economic, and moral impediments; if they did, their political agency would demonstrate their will to survive and to dismantle structural barriers. Instead, Blacks became the *problem* that white racists had to subdue to maintain racial (and economic) dominance. One might extend Gordon's argument by suggesting that the Negro problem sustains itself in and through the collision between religion and politics in debates on justice, the fragments retrieved to explain the moral reasons vis-à-vis individual and group apathy toward ongoing systemic political and economic inequalities in Black communities.

Another way to frame Du Bois's insight is to consider Evelyn Brooks Higginbotham's metalanguage of race. She notes: "When we talk about the concept of race, most people believe that they know it when they see it but arrive at nothing short of confusion when pressed to define it" (Higginbotham 1992, 253). The ambiguity surrounding race-talk has everything to do with an unexamined historical contempt for racial difference that is informed and shaped by a legacy of denial, one in which racial discrimination is ignored, buried, and forgotten. Racial contempt manifests itself in the white normative gaze—what Cornel West construes in *Prophesy Deliverance!* as the comparative and hierarchical ordering of values and norms that reinscribe Black inferiority. Du Bois anticipated the effects of racial contempt in his analysis of the psychic violence of race and racialization within this theory of double consciousness. "It is a peculiar sensation, this double-consciousness, this sense of always looking at one's self through the eyes of others, of measuring one's soul by the tape of a world that looks on in amused contempt and pity" (Du Bois and Sundquist 1996, 8). Contempt for race, and for Blackness, in particular, surfaces whenever the haunting racial past is discussed. It is a contempt well characterized in US Supreme Court Chief Justice Roger Taney's defense of Black inferiority. Whether enslaved or not, Taney argued in *Dred Scott v. Sandford* (60 US 393 [1856]) that citizenship was off-limits to Blacks, an inferior race by birth and moral orientation.

> They had for more than a century before been regarded as beings of an inferior order, and altogether unfit to associate with the white race either in social or political relations, and so far inferior that they had no rights which the white man was bound to respect, and that the negro might justly and lawfully be reduced to slavery for his benefit. . . . This opinion was at that time fixed and universal in the civilized portion of the white race. It was regarded as an axiom in morals as well as in politics which no one thought of disputing or supposed to be open to dispute, and men in every grade and position in society daily and habitually acted upon it in their private pursuits, as well as in matters of public concern, without doubting for a moment the correctness of this opinion. (60 US 407 [1856])

Blacks would remain subjugated to and dominated by whites, the superior class. Taney appealed to the Western world's long history of anti-Black and anti-African racism to defend his decision to deny citizenship to Mr. Scott.

Nearly four decades after *Dred Scott v. Sandford*, Du Bois grappled with the spirit of Taney's racial hierarchy in the existing political, cultural, and social normative values. Applying his sociological interpretive lens to *the Negro problem*, Du Bois discovered both the material and the moral reasons for racial contempt. Whites, and poor whites in particular, feared the looming economic consequences of the expansion of the workforce that would come with the elimination of enslavement and legalized segregation. Just as importantly, the contempt for Blackness was also fueled by a moral indignation about the *possibility* of Black freedom and economic equity. Herein sat the Du Boisian challenge to American democracy: the Negro problem. No matter the reach of American democracy's grand achievements in freeing women and democratizing citizenship laws, or its noble vision of equality and inalienable rights, the near absence of race and slavery from the primary documents undergirding the nation's Constitution is a perennial reminder of its irrevocable fallibility. As Du Bois noted: "Merely a concrete test of the underlying principles of the great republic is the Negro Problem, and the spiritual striving of the freedmen's sons is the travail of souls whose burden is almost beyond the measure of their strength, but who bear it in the name of an historic race, in the name of this the land of their fathers' fathers, and in the name of human opportunity" (Du Bois and Sundquist 1996, 13). Even as the nation failed to live up to its ideals in legislation and culture, many African American abolitionists, civil rights advocates, and religious leaders consistently invoked the ideals of the US Constitution and the Declaration of Independence, for instance, to legitimate their political struggle for freedom, justice, and equality under the law.

Double consciousness transgresses the racialization of Blackness and intersects with religion in several ways. Muslim scholars have incorporated the theoretical framework to explicate Islamophobia and the racialization of Islam in the United States. "Racial meanings of Otherness, nationalism, boundary making, denial of citizenship, and a denial of belonging are all inscribed onto the Veil, thereby shaping the relations of the racializing with Muslim Americans, dominant society's perceptions of Muslim Americans, and the internalization of these perceptions by the racialized" (Islam 2020, 436). According to Inaash Islam, double consciousness helps to explicate "self-formation" in a racialized society, explore the role of religion in defining a Muslim consciousness in non-Muslim societies, and engage the "multiple subjectivities" of Muslim identity. "The Muslim ban, in particular, communicates to Muslims that they will not be accepted as part of the nation, due to the racialized meanings attributed to their Muslim identity" (2020, 437).

In Tension with the White-Black Binary: Jews and Racialized Others

Racialization, the performative structural practices that inscribe a racial category onto groups otherwise self-defined by religion, language, and tribal affiliation, is uniquely American, as illustrated by the nation's history of citizenship laws. Since the nation's founding, Native Americans, Jews, and Chinese immigrant laborers, among others, faced legalized racial discrimination. For instance, the Chinese Exclusion Act of 1882 prohibited the immigration of Chinese laborers to the United States for reasons largely predicated on racial discrimination that in turn were based on the perceived radical *otherness* of Chinese people. Unlike African Americans, however, Jewish and Asian immigrants in particular engineered different strategies for overcoming racial oppression. Many relied on cultural assimilation and legal claims of their non-Black status as the safest and most expedient tactics to achieve full citizenship and equal protection under the law. The early twentieth-century case *Ozawa v. The United States* (260 US 178 [1922]) is a clear example of the legal strategy adopted by many immigrant groups. Ozawa was born in Japan but lived in the US for twenty years as culturally white and insisted in his court case that he should therefore be treated as "free white persons" had been. The Court ruled against him, asserting that Japanese people were not members of the "Caucasian" race. The case further reinforced a legal logic of racial constructions as teetering on scientific racism and Anglo-Saxon cultural norms. What emerged in subsequent legal cases on race and citizenship anchored racial difference and hierarchy grounded in a white/Black racial binary.

As the nation and its Christian slaveholders reified anti-Black normative beliefs in both private and public spheres, the legal definition of its antithesis—*whiteness* or the white race—remained largely ambiguous and amorphous. The legal historian Ariela Gross notes that whiteness in the nineteenth century was primarily construed performatively, mostly represented in and through civic rituals of voting, land ownership, and obtaining higher education. Even as class created a vast and towering hierarchy between white aristocrats and landless white men, the economic need to maintain white domination over enslaved Blacks significantly weakened intra-racial class lines: "Southern gentlemen were expected to adhere to a code of conduct that prescribed unique ways of interacting with social inferiors, peers, and superiors—customs meant to distinguish them from the vast majority of common folk. Yet, Southern politics depended on a belief that all white men were equals, that only blacks constituted the 'mudsill' class" (Gross 2008, 48–49). Through such civic actions as voting, sitting on juries, and participating in militias, citizenship "democratized" white men and emerged as ritual acts that perpetuated white dominance (2008, 49). The Georgia State Supreme Court could therefore deny citizenship to "free people of color" as it did in *Bryan v. Walton* (14 Ga 185 [1853]) because they did not have a history of civic engagement through voting and land ownership—both of which symbolized the privileged status of whiteness (Gross 2008, 49). For that reason alone, immigrants who successfully performed whiteness through higher education, entrepreneurship, and land ownership did not experience the same kind of social and racial exclusion and discrimination. And within this framework, the next logical step in the "performance of whiteness" would have been the attainment of voting rights. To be sure, performing whiteness amplified a buried racial doctrine: whiteness as moral *and* exemplifying social and economic capital, signs of the *moral* fitness of the group. The groundbreaking application of Protestant moral doctrines to explain religion's (necessary) role in shaping capitalism in Max Weber's *The Protestant Ethic and the Spirit of Capitalism* (1904) inspired a growing industrial nation with slaveholding origins to extend the moral necessity of racial hierarchy. Indeed, evangelical Christians, argues Anthea Butler, launched a political revival fueled by Weber's work. "Evangelicals' use of morality in the nineteenth century forged the pathway by which racism and white supremacy became part and parcel of evangelical history, how they constructed a public and nationalistic vision for America, and how they used morality to both convert and oppress African Americans in slavery and in freedom" (Butler 2020, 14).

Saving Religion from White Supremacy and the Racial Contract

Following the late political philosopher John Rawls, philosophical debates on religion have largely focused on the appropriate (or improper) role of religion in politics and public life. According to this logic, the question of whether religious doctrines affirmed political justice would determine religion's applicability and appropriateness in a liberal democracy. This is particularly true of the "racial contract," a theory within the philosophy of race that underscores or makes plain the philosophical commitments buried within the nation's unfortunate racist legal history. Charles Mills rightly asserts in *The Racial Contract* (1997) that natural laws, the backdrop from which equal rights, liberty, and equality emerge, oriented themselves in what Mills called a "moral flaw" that mapped "Blackness" as a social marker of the innate absence of morality, intelligence, and beauty due to a "blindness to Christian light, which necessarily results in moral blackness, superstition, devil worship" (Mills 1997, 46). The "state of nature" within the "Dark Continent" "is thus *actual*, a wild and racialized place that was originally characterized as cursed with a theological blight as well, an unholy land" (1997, 46). The moral and political differentiation between "whites" and enslaved Africans produced the racial contract, according to Mills, and the agreed-upon norms, laws, and economic structures sustained by enslaved Black labor and justified by beliefs in the subhuman and inferior nature of Blacks. All whites benefit from the racial contract by virtue of not being Black.

Respectability politics and racial uplift, the political and ideological cornerstones of historic institutional Black churches, implicitly understood the broad implications of the racial contract. However, while the racial contract excluded Blacks from benefiting from public rights, Blacks appealing to racial uplift ideology nevertheless modeled themselves and their institutional Black churches in accordance with liberal norms. As such, Higginbotham characterized the Black church as a counter-public sphere, "a public distinct from and in conflict with the dominant white society and its racist institutional structures" (Higginbotham 1993, 11). Barbara Savage implicitly expanded the notion of counter-publics in *Your Spirits Walk Beside Us: The Politics of Black Religion* to include Black religion more broadly, as ideological expressions of Black Nationalism, Black feminist and Womanist thought, and Black internationalism increasingly influenced the direction of Black politics during and after the civil rights movement.

The chief architect of Black theology of liberation, James Cone, ushered into the academic study of religion in the late 1960s race and Blackness as theological categories to extend and expand application to society. His influential works, *Black Theology & Black Power* (1969); *A Black Theology of Liberation* (1970); and *God of the Oppressed* (1975), informed how religious historians as well as ethicists and theologians defined and delimited religious responses to anti-Black racism and racialized gender discrimination. As he noted in *A Black Theology of Liberation*: "The task of black theology, then, is to analyze the nature of the gospel of Jesus Christ in the light of oppressed blacks so they will see the gospel as inseparable from their humiliated condition, and as bestowing on them the necessary power to break the chains of oppression. This means that it is a theology of and for the black community, seeking to interpret the religious dimensions of the forces of liberation in that community" (Cone 1990, 28). He would later critique the deployment in the United States of the most sacred Christian image: the cross. Writing in *The Cross and the Lynching Tree*, Cone deconstructed historic interpretations of Jesus's death. "The crucifixion was clearly a first-century lynching," wrote Cone. "Both are symbols of the death of the innocent, mob hysteria, humiliation, and terror. They both also reveal a thirst for life that refuses to let the worst determine our final meaning and demonstrate that God can transform ugliness into beauty, into God's liberating presence" (2013, 30).

Cone's theoretical framing of liberation faced fierce criticism. Delores Williams in *Sisters in the Wilderness* exposed the limits of liberation theology drowning in masculinity, and its towering desire to wield political and economic power within Black publics on par with white men. Williams eviscerates the false belief in liberation that originally undergirded this Black theology of liberation. Building a Womanist interpretation of the "Egyptian slave-girl called Hagar," Williams re-narrates the slave girl's abandonment by her "owner," Sarah, who exiled Hagar and her infant son from her home and forced her into the wilderness without any resources. "Hagar was brutalized by her slave owner, the Hebrew woman Sarah. The slave narratives of African-American women and some of the narratives of contemporary day-workers tell of the brutal or cruel treatment black women have received from the wives of slave masters and from contemporary white female employers" (Williams 1993, 3).

Victor Anderson's *Beyond Ontological Blackness: An Essay on African American Religious and Cultural Criticism*, for example, untangles historical uses of "Blackness" to expose its misuses and abuses in analyzing African American political, cultural, and religious expressions. He pointedly calls out Black liberation theology and Womanist thought for essentializing Blackness for the sake of reproducing a triumphalist narrative of Black life from enslavement to life after segregation. He also exposes the limits of liberation as a generative category given its failure to account for the lived reality of Black life. Anderson interrogates the "cultic devotion" to "utopian" ideals of African American traditions and culture. This hermeneutical move introduced an unexamined logic of racial apologetics within African American philosophical examinations of "categorical racism." He wrote: "As a counter-discourse to categorical racism, black racial apologetics reinscribed the black presence in American culture as aesthetically heroic and creative and morally masculine and self-determined. Black leaders did not see these qualities as imaginative of white genius; rather, they regarded them as essential qualities of black genius. Black heroic genius constituted authentic black presence" (Anderson 1995, 79).

Whether or not Anderson's criticisms ushered in a new paradigm within African American religions will be determined by historians in the years to come; however, shortly after the publication of his highly contested book, increasing numbers of books on aesthetics, political philosophy, and African-derived religious traditions surfaced in the academic study of African American religions. Alongside Anthony Pinn's decided shift away from Christian theology emerged a cohort of scholars who inherited a scholarly tradition of African American religions that was deeply informed by James Cone's tradition of liberation theology and Albert J. Raboteau's Exodus-informed account of African American religious history. These scholars include Dianne Stewart, Eddie Glaude Jr., Yvonne P. Chireau, Tracey Hucks, Anthea Butler, William Hart, and Rachel Harding. They interrogated race, religion, and anti-Black racism through interdisciplinary conceptual schemes produced in material culture, aesthetics, political theory, and critical race theory, establishing paradigm shifts that moved away from immediate concerns and claims of God's role in liberating the enslaved to examine instead lived expressions of religion in culture, politics, the arts, and African-derived religious traditions and practices. J. Kameron Carter in *Race: A Theological Account* asserted that the epistemic problem facing theology is not "race in general but whiteness in particular" (Carter 2008, 372). In fact, he argues, it is the racialization of Jesus as Western and ostensibly "white" that transforms Christianity into an epistemic tool of the "West" for racial and gender domination.

Transgressing Ontological Blackness

As the academic study of religion expanded beyond Afro-Christianity, African American religions, including Black Islam, Humanism, and African Diasporic religions, introduced new epistemic terrains through which to investigate race and religion. Scholars of Asian American and Latino/a religions developed overlapping paradigms in the academic study of religion. David Yoo, for instance, in *Contentious Spirits: Religion in Korean American History, 1903–1945*, argues that race as a conceptual category is critically important to the study of religion, one aimed at dismantling the stark lines between religion and race, migration and exile, religion and politics, and colonialism and independence (Yoo 2010, 5). He writes, "For many Korean Americans, religion informed the dilemma of their racial status in the United States. Some wondered how a supposed Christian nation could harbor racism toward fellow believers" (2010, 5). Ada María Isasi-Díaz's *Mujerista Theology: A Theology for the Twenty-First Century* views theology and religious expression through a hermeneutical lens based on "our condition as racially and culturally mixed people" (Isasi-Díaz 1996, 64). Miguel

De La Torre goes even further, calling for a radical repudiation of "Eurochristianity." This is especially cogent for persons "who find themselves situated in the in-between space, residing in the contradiction of competing cultures, embracing Jesus's teachings while rejecting Eurochristianity may be possible, even healing. Latinx thinkers—specifically Chicanos—have referred to this 'in between,'" where liminality resists rigid racialization and religious nationalism (De La Torre 2023, 30).

The 2008 election of Barack Obama to the US presidency ushered in a monumental paradigm shift in national conversations on race and anti-Black racism, one framed in the contexts of a post-racial America, the new Jim Crow, and Black pessimism. The wrenching and perpetual backlash against Obama by the white Republican establishment and a small but surprising number of middle-class African Americans, mostly Black men, accelerated religiously motivated conspiracy theories against Obama during his two-term presidency. From claiming Obama was a secret Muslim planning to overtake America to false assumptions that he was born outside the United States, leaders from the Republican party exploited racist stereotypes to capitalize on a political culture already boiling in hatred from the election of the nation's first Black president, the establishment of a constitutional right to same-sex marriage, and increasing numbers of racial minorities in the US (Du Mez 2020, 253). Donald Trump's racist, sexist, and xenophobic presidential campaign rhetoric was a divine sign to the religious Right.

Donald Trump's stunning victory over Hillary Clinton in the 2016 US presidential race lifted the veil to reveal the ugly face of racism that many white elites had ignored, or wrongly assumed only found refuge in rural or southern America among non-college degree holders. Trump's victory exposed an unacknowledged, though deeply historical, Christian commitment to racism among many evangelicals, Protestants, and Catholics (Jones 2020, 135–37). "Trump's own racism allowed him to do what other candidates couldn't: solidify the support of the majority of white Christians, not despite, but *through* appeals to white supremacy" (Jones 2020, 20). Nationwide racial and religiously motivated hate crimes skyrocketed during his presidency (Jones 2020, 19–20, 215). And as the nation reckoned with the Black Lives Matter movement, increased attention to police shootings of mostly unarmed African American men and women, and a worldwide COVID-19 pandemic, Asian American theologians found a way to squeeze into the otherwise tight-knit conversation on race. In a 2018 essay "The Spirit of God Was Hovering Over the Waters," Jonathan Tran envisions the ongoing racialization as a call for Christians—and Asian Christians in particular—to engage race and religion from the standpoint of "missional people, people who believe that the Spirit is ushering in a new future to which Christian lives bear witness" (Tran 2018, 230). In his essay, Tran, like a growing number of scholars, returns to theological resources to construct new possibilities for (re)imagining race, religion, and democracy. But Tran later questioned in *Asian Americans and the Spirit of Racial Capitalism* (2022) the theoretical usefulness of the white/Black binary, as he claimed it reveals the "circumstance" of race and racial difference without fully explicating the structural origins of the binary. If scholars understood the historical conditions fueling the binary, Tran argues, they would have a clearer sense of its limits. "Committing to race talk entails committing to binary talk. The work of including other races requires fitting them into (or, more precisely, onto) the binary" (Tran 2022, 122).

The amorphous but enduring white/Black category returns the debate to questions of the nature of the human, power, domination, and racial violence. Of concern is the eventual eradication of the political usefulness of race as distinguishing who possesses power (Whites?) and who does not (Blacks?), as well as determining who is human (Whites?) and who is not (Blacks?). Along with these epistemic frameworks, Black critical theorists find themselves grappling with new questions interrogating, if not outright rejecting, political liberal categories of democracy, rights, self, and freedom; and instead exploring social death, fugitive, death-bound, and dispossession. Sylvia Wynter, Fred Wilderson, and Fred Moten prefigure the all-star lineup of Black critical theorists cultivating new theoretical discussions on race in the post-Obama political era.

Sylvia Wynter posits that the search for the "human" is cultivated through the "decoding" and unmasking of "complex differences" as ways of understanding "expressing and mapping an ongoing human geography" through "space, place, and poetics" (McKittrick 2006, 122). Wynter investigates the reinvention of the "human" as "Man" starting from ancient Christianity's "Church fathers" and the Enlightenment period to the rise of the transatlantic slave trade and the civil rights movement. She "refuses to embrace the entity of the Human independently of the epistemic categories and concepts that created it by suggesting instead that our conceptualizations of the Human are produced within an autopoietic system" (Mignolo 2015, 108). That is to say, the varying modes of existence create the possibility to incite systemic reinventions and upheavals. In her essay "1492: A New World View," Wynter argues for reimagining Christopher

Columbus's "discovery" beyond the terror and triumph interpretive modes to encapsulate a third perspective, possibly a new and ecumenically human view of history contingent on culture-specificity and the "interrelatedness" of all "species." The species inherited a European, Christocentric, patriarchal, and sexist structural means of delimiting and manufacturing domination through new technologies and economies. Columbus's voyage turned the world upside down, representing for Wynter "an intellectual revolution of humanism" (Wynter 1995, 13). The epoch shift could be duplicated or manipulated for the political and social advantage of the formerly enslaved. Indeed, as Wynter suggests, species are not unconditionally circumscribed by their inheritance. The epistemic revolts and social uprisings of the civil rights and Black Power movements emerged from a newer "revolution of humanism," an indication of Wynter's indebtedness to the psychiatrist and political philosopher Frantz Fanon. According to Wynter, "the general upheaval of the 1960s made possible a new opening—that of the collective challenge made to the symbolic representational systems and their 'stereotyped images' by which we have hitherto nonconsciously woven our innumerable modes of the Self and their innumerable Others" (1995, 50). Frantz Fanon's new humanism emerges, Wynter noted, from this revolution as a "new contestatory image of the human" (1995, 50).

In contrast, Frank B. Wilderson III's *Afropessimism* explores how Blackness produced and sustains the social-political economy of the world shaped by the transatlantic slave trade. Afropessimism is a "metatheory" deployed to interrogate existing disciplinary modes of discourse that delimit Blacks and define the terrains of their knowledge, traditions, and culture. Afropessimists pay particular attention to those theoretical frameworks claiming the possibility of liberation and emancipation. As Wilderson asserts, Afropessimism "is pessimistic about the claims theories of liberation make when these theories try to explain Black suffering or when they analogize Black suffering with the suffering of other oppressed beings. It does this by unearthing and exposing the meta-aporias, strewn like land mines in what these theories of so-called universal liberation hold to be true" (Wilderson 2020, 14). Liberation assumes the possibility of emancipation from structures, persons, nations, or tribes, all of which operate under norms or laws designed to protect sentient creatures or humans. The ontology of Blackness prevents the possibility of manumission for Black people. Wilderson orients Afropessimism on one piercing claim: "that Blackness is coterminous with Slaveness: Blackness 'is' social death: which is to say that there was never a prior metamoment of plenitude, never equilibrium: never a moment of social life" (2020, 102). Put differently: all non-Blacks are human, and all Blacks are nonhumans created through white violence and existing in the perennial state of social death for the sadistic and "sadomasochistic pleasures" of non-Blacks (2020, 15). Unlike non-Black immigrants, who are extended a "transformative promise of a narrative arc" and are identified as the "junior partners of White men in civil society," Blacks remain slaves without the possibility of transformation, liberation, or emancipation. Scholars of African American religions have retrieved Afropessimism as a framework for exploring the political economy of race in religion—the varying ways racial categories, racial violence, and oppression invent and inform religious traditions and religious practices of resistance and endurance.

Fred Moten disrupts and displaces prima facie accounts of liberal and neoliberal evaluations of race, racial difference, and racial capitalism. Indeed, Blackness is nothingness, as opposed to Blackness as an extension of the white/Black binary, and it destabilizes the epistemic terrain inherited from respectability and racial uplift ideologies. What Moten calls the "mobility of place" appears to be the recognition of the nothingness of Blackness: the "fugitive field of unowning, in and from which we [Black people] ask" (Moten 2013, 742) and interrogate the undeniable enmity and bitterness constitutive of Blackness. Engaging the world on its antagonistic terms, without fear of embodying hope or pessimism, Moten suggests, creates the possibility of toppling thought and existence as we know it in exchange for "life" and a contingency-based "optimism." Moten's writings, and his turn to mysticism, underscore the ongoing tension in Black studies between hope and pessimism, subjectivity and negation. The tension brings the conversation back to the origins of race and religion's role in transforming race into a violent political category to sustain racial difference, domination, and oppression.

Suggested Readings

Alba, Richard D., Albert J. Raboteau, and Josh DeWind. 2009. *Immigration and Religion in America: Comparative and Historical Perspectives*. New York University Press.

Fields, Karen E., and Barbara Jeanne Fields. 2012. *Racecraft The Soul of Inequality in American Life*. London: Verso.

Goldschmidt, Henry, and Elizabeth A. McAlister. 2004. *Race, Nation, and Religion in the Americas*. Oxford University Press.

Higginbotham, A. Leon. 1998. *Shades of Freedom: Racial Politics and Presumptions of the American Legal Process Race and the American Legal Process*. Vol. 2. New York: Oxford University Press.
Long, Charles H. 1986. *Significations: Signs, Symbols, and Images in the Interpretation of Religion*. Philadelphia: Fortress Press.
Pinn, Anthony B. 2003. *Terror and Triumph: The Nature of Black Religion*. Fortress Press.
Sharpe, Christina. 2016. *In the Wake: On Blackness and Being*. Durham: Duke University Press.
Wenger, Tisa Joy. 2017. *Religious Freedom: The Contested History of an American Ideal*. The University of North Carolina Press.
Wynter, Sylvia. 2003. "Unsettling the Coloniality of Being/Power/Truth/Freedom: Towards the Human, After Man, Its Overrepresentation—An Argument." *CR: The New Centennial Review* 3 (3): 257–337.
Yountae, An, and Eleanor Craig. 2021. *Beyond Man: Race, Coloniality, and Philosophy of Religion*. Duke University Press.

References

Anderson, Victor. 1995. *Beyond Ontological Blackness: An Essay on African American Religious and Cultural Criticism*. New York: Continuum.
Appiah, Anthony, K. (1985). "The Uncompleted Argument: Du Bois and the Illusion of Race." *Critical Inquiry* 12 (1): 30.
Barnett, Randy E. 2011. "Whence Comes Section One? The Abolitionist Origins of the Fourteenth Amendment." *The Journal of Legal Analysis* 3 (1): 165–263.
Braude, Benjamin. 2005. "Michelangelo and the Curse of Ham: From a Typology of Jew-Hatred to a Genealogy of Racism." In *Writing Race Across the Atlantic World*. London: Palgrave Macmillan.
Butler, Anthea D. 2020. *White Evangelical Racism: The Politics of Morality in America*. The University of North Carolina Press.
Butler, Jon. 1990. *Awash in a Sea of Faith: Christianizing the American People*. Harvard University Press.
Carter, J. Kameron. 2008. *Race: A Theological Account*. New York: Oxford University Press.
Cohen, Jeremy. 1982. *The Friars and the Jews: The Evolution of Medieval Anti-Judaism*. Ithaca, NY: Cornell University Press.
Cone, James H. 1990. *A Black Theology of Liberation*. Maryknoll, NY: Orbis Books.
Cone, James H. 2013. *The Cross and the Lynching Tree*. Maryknoll, NY: Orbis Books.
Conzen, Kathleen Neils, David A. Gerber, Ewa Morawska, George E. Pozzetta, and Rudolph J. Vecoli. 1992. "The Invention of Ethnicity: A Perspective from the USA." *Journal of American Ethnic History* 12 (1): 3.

Cooper, Anna J. 1990. *A Voice from the South*. New York: Oxford University Press.

De La Torre, Miguel A. 2023. *Resisting Apartheid America: Living the Badass Gospel*. William B. Eerdmans Publishing Company.

Douglass, Frederick. 2016. *Narrative of the Life of Frederick Douglass, an American Slave: Written by Himself*. New Haven, CT: Yale University Press.

Du Bois, W. E. B. 2009. *The Souls of Black Folk*. Oxford: Oxford University Press USA.

Du Bois, W. E. B., and Eric J. Sundquist. 1996. *The Oxford W. E. B. Du Bois Reader*. New York: New York: Oxford University Press.

Du Mez, Kristin Kobes. 2020. *Jesus and John Wayne: How White Evangelicals Corrupted a Faith and Fractured a Nation*. Liveright Publishing Corporation.

Goldenberg, David M. 2005. *The Curse of Ham Race and Slavery in Early Judaism, Christianity, and Islam*. Princeton, NJ: Princeton University Press.

Gordon, Lewis R. 2000. *Existentia Africana Understanding Africana Existential Thought*. New York: Routledge.

Gross, Ariela Julie. 2008. *What Blood Won't Tell: A History of Race on Trial in America*. Cambridge, MA: Harvard University Press.

Hannaford, Ivan. 1996. *Race: The History of an Idea in the West*. Baltimore, MD: Johns Hopkins University Press.

Higginbotham, Evelyn Brooks. 1992. "African American Women's History and the Metalanguage of Race." *Signs: Journal of Women in Culture and Society* 17 (2).

Higginbotham, Evelyn Brooks. 1993. *Righteous Discontent: The Women's Movement in the Black Baptist Church, 1880–1920*. Cambridge, MA: Harvard University Press.

Higginbotham, Evelyn Brooks. 2017. "'The Metalanguage of Race,' Then and Now." *Signs: Journal of Women in Culture and Society* 42 (3): 628–42.

Isasi-Díaz, Ada María. 1996. *Mujerista Theology: A Theology for the Twenty-First Century*. Maryknoll, NY: Orbis Books.

Islam, Inaash. 2020. "Muslim American Double Consciousness." *Du Bois Review* 17 (2).

Jones, Robert P. 2020. *White Too Long : The Legacy of White Supremacy in American Christianity*. New York: Simon & Schuster.

Johnson, Sylvester. 2004. *The Myth of Ham in Nineteenth-Century American Christianity: Race, Heathens, and the People of God*. Palgrave Macmillan.

McKittrick, Katherine. 2006. *Demonic Grounds: Black Women and the Cartographies of Struggle*. Minneapolis: University of Minnesota Press.

Mignolo, Walter D. 2015. "Sylvia Wynter: what does it mean to be human?" In *Sylvia Wynter: On Being Human as Praxis*, edited by Katherine McKittrick. Durham, NC: Duke University Press.

Mills, Charles W. 1997. *The Racial Contract*. Ithaca, NY: Cornell University Press.

Moten, Fred. 2013. "Blackness and Nothingness (Mysticism in the Flesh)." *The South Atlantic Quarterly* 112 (4).

Ngai, Mae M. 2014. *Impossible Subjects: Illegal Aliens and the Making of Modern America*. Princeton, NJ: Princeton University Press.

Stewart, Maria W., and Marilyn Richardson. 1987. *America's First Black Woman Political Writer: Essays and Speeches*. Bloomington: Indiana University Press.

Tran, Jonathan L. 2018. "'The Spirit of God Was Hovering over the Waters': Pressing Past Racialization in the Decolonial Missionary Context; or, Why Asian American Christians Should Give Up Their Spots at Harvard." In *Can "White" People Be Saved? Triangulating Race, Theology, and Mission*, edited by Love L. Secrest, Johnny Ramírez-Johnson, and Amos Yong. Downers Grove, IL: InterVarsity Press.

Tran, Jonathan. 2022. *Asian Americans and the Spirit of Racial Capitalism*. Oxford University Press.

West, Cornel. 1982. *Prophesy Deliverance! An Afro-American Revolutionary Christianity*. Philadelphia: Westminster Press.

Wilderson, Frank B. 2020. *Afropessimism*. New York: Liveright Publishing Corporation.

Williams, Delores. 1993. *Sisters in the Wilderness*. Maryknoll, NY: Orbis Books.

Wynter, Sylvia. 1995. "1492: A New World View." In *Race, Discourse, and the Origin of the Americas: A New World View*, edited by Vera Lawrence Hyatt and Rex Nettleford. Washington, DC: Smithsonian Institution Press.

Yoo, David. 2010. *Contentious Spirits: Religion in Korean American History, 1903–1945*. Stanford University Press.

18 (VIRTUAL) REALITY

Christopher G. White

It is possible to recount the history of electronic media in the last century as a history of naïve viewers mistaking televisual worlds for reality. Films and TV shows themselves have often dramatized this issue. The 1902 silent film *Uncle Josh at the Moving Picture Show*, a paradigmatic example, depicts a man who thinks that what he sees on the screen is real. In the film's first scene, a dancing woman does the can-can and Uncle Josh jumps out of his seat to join her on the stage. He dances next to the projection screen. In the second scene a train approaches and Uncle Josh panics, leaping from the stage to avoid it. (This scene is clearly indebted to the Lumiere brothers' 1895 *L'Arrivée d'un train en gare de La Ciotat*, which evidently aroused panic in audience members.) In the third and final scene, a couple pumps water at a local well while the pump handle repeatedly hits the man in the head, something Uncle Josh finds hilarious. He watches and laughs. Then the couple embrace and kiss, however, and Uncle Josh becomes agitated. Out of jealousy or anger—it is hard to tell—he attempts to grab the man but ends up instead with the projection screen in his arms. Everything had been a projection, an illusion. The film is comedy because audience members see a country rube who has mistaken a novel technology for something real. Audience members laugh because only a simpleminded naïf would get worked up over a moving picture show.

The trope of the naïve viewer may be funny, but today we are all naïve viewers. Though we have certainly adjusted to the initial shock of moving pictures, new media technologies, from television to video games and virtual reality, have forced upon us ongoing perceptual and cognitive adjustments. It is not just that these technologies produce representations that look and feel real, though this is important. It is also that they have insinuated themselves into our social world and personal space in new ways—and have therefore shifted the boundaries of our embodied experience. So we might discern a progression from seeing and hearing a television, to seeing, hearing and touching a computer, to seeing, hearing, touching, and wearing a more or less permanently pocketed phone or strapped-on augmented reality (or virtual reality) apparatus. As media technologies have changed during the last century, they have delivered higher and higher levels of what I am calling *sensational credibility*—that is, they have produced increasingly believable and realistic representations and incorporated more and more of our senses.

They therefore generate what we might call (following Walter Benjamin) "shock effects" that recalibrate our sensational apparatus and open us up to new experiences and imaginative world-building. In 1935 Benjamin pointed out that films replaced contemplative viewing (of, for example, a painting) with an uninterrupted sequence of moving images that shocked audience members and generated a kind of absent-minded viewership (1969, 238). Benjamin was not the only one to discuss these and other shock effects (*Chockwirkung*) of technological media on our sensibilities. Marshall McLuhan, Friedrich Kittler, and others have commented at length on the media, reality, and ontology, examining how media have reorganized our ways of thinking about and sensing things. The philosopher and phenomenologist Alfred Schutz, who was a contemporary of Benjamin, offered a detailed analysis of what it felt like to move into and out of imaginative experiences, including those generated by electronic media. "The epoché of the natural attitude which suspends doubt in its existence is replaced by other epochés which suspend belief in more and more layers of the reality of daily life, putting them in brackets," Schutz wrote (1972, 233). I want to suggest that media-generated shock experiences do not just transport us temporarily into different bracketed experiences, however, but rather trouble our understanding of what is real and expand the range of things that seem real. This has important implications for how we think about things that used to seem imaginary and impossible—entities such as ghosts, gods, guardian angels, and holy spirits. It also has important implications for how we might reassess religious practices in lived contexts that are electronic and mediated.

I

Commentators have already documented the ontological confusion and existential shock that telegraphy, radio, and then television induced. TV in particular generated some arresting examples. As Leo Bogart has written, people generally were aware of how films and even books were edited, reworked, and revised, but televisual stories and events had a liveness and immediacy to them that made them seem real. But it was not just that broadcast television seemed to be happening now or that it seemed more (a)live; it was also that television brought things that were remote and difficult to see into the intimate spaces of the home (Bogart 1958, 28, 30–31). For these reasons, the invention of the TV was accompanied by new conversations about the nature of real versus electrical space. Genre television in the 1950s and 1960s pointed to this issue with characters who moved magically between television studios and "real" life, as for example in *The Twilight Zone*'s "World of Difference" and *Lights Out*'s "Something in the Wind." In "Something in the Wind," for example, a director who cuts characters from a script is confronted by these characters when they come to life and demand their lines back. In other genre TV from this era, characters see future events, spectral presences, or their own thoughts miraculously appear on the screen. Sometimes they try to get into (or out of) the screens they watch. Films during the last fifty years have also pondered the reality of the diegetic worlds on the small screen. Films have featured TVs coming alive (*The Twonky*) or controlling, kidnapping (*Poltergeist*), and killing people (*The Ring*). An anxious psychological literature has accompanied these self-reflexive fictional narratives, probing why TV seemed to create confusion and psychopathology. The American activist and writer Jerry Mander rehearsed these concerns in his *Four Arguments for the Elimination of Television* (1978), in which he commented on cases in the psychological literature where patients felt lost in the television or controlled and confused by it (Mander 1978, 86–87, 108–12).[1]

Philosophers and media theorists also have examined how televisions have generated perceptual shocks and ontological confusion. "It has long struck me," Samuel Weber once argued, that "the self-evident quality of this experience of visual perception is increasingly being shaken, but also exploited, by a medium such as television" (in De Vries and Weber 2001, 94). We have always trusted our experience of audiovisual perception, but with the television we can no longer believe unquestioningly what we see and hear. What is the status of the things we see and hear on television? Are they real? What is the real? "As a visual medium," Jenny Slatman has

1. See also White 2018, 255–58.

written, touching upon the same problems, "television asks us to believe in something that we have not seen with our own eyes. Thus, it obscures the apparently clear-cut distinction between faith and seeing, a distinction that has thoroughly dominated our tradition." Slatman also argued that tele-vision was structurally similar to seeing the transcendent, for everything on TV always existed in a location that was *beyond*—in other words, it was always "tele" (remote) vision. "The tele-visible is the transcendent being" (Slatman 2001, 216, 221). Maurice Merleau-Ponty put this in a slightly different way, saying that on television there was a "crystallization of the impossible" (Slatman 2001, 218). There is therefore a kind of perceptual play that television creates, because it forces viewers to doubt whether they see things truly and causes us to wonder about the possibility of seeing transcendently.

Those pondering this latter possibility, that televisions could help us see transcendent things, produced shows and other narratives that framed televisions as portals to a realm of the really real. One of the first television broadcast shows ever produced, the New York-based broadcast *The Television Ghost* (1931–33), used fifteen-minute episodes that featured the departed spirits of murder victims who materialized on-screen to describe how they were killed. In other cases, families reported ghosts that materialized in TV static and would not be tuned out. In December 1953 the *New York Times* reported the case of Jerome Travers, who was watching *Ding Dong School* with his three children when a woman's face appeared on the screen and would not go away—even after the set was turned off. (The only solution was to turn the TV toward the wall.) In another case, it was the image of an Indianapolis housewife's dead grandfather that appeared on the screen—not a metaphorical ghost lost in static but a literal one haunting the set. After two days of trying to get rid of the image, Mrs. Mackey worried she was "going crazy" and took the TV to the police. At the police station the set was activated and Mackey's grandfather again appeared in the suit he was buried in months before (Sconce 2000, 1–2, 124). Were TVs somehow able to tune in to the really real? These events point to ways that the American public, a group mostly ignorant about how electromagnetic waves and cathode tubes worked, wondered about the reality of the things they saw on TV (figure 19.1). Televisions mysteriously received invisible transmissions from far-off places; could they also detect spiritual transmissions from heavenly places?

It is important to point out that this kind of thinking is common today

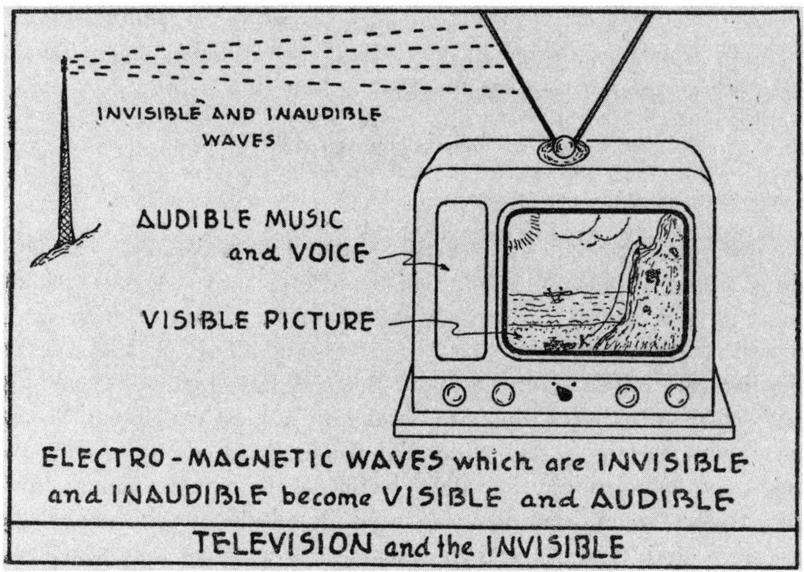

FIGURE 19.1 Televisions fired the imagination with new metaphors of transmission and reception. Reminding us that modern physicists have proved that reality is not solid but closer to "thoughts" or energies, the theosophical writer E. Norman Pearson wrote that the human mind is a lot like a "receiving set" for these energies (Pearson 1957, 22–23).

around the world. Religious studies scholars and media anthropologists working in different contexts have revealed what would have seemed an unlikely reality fifty years ago—that gods and other supernatural things commonly appear on electronic devices (see for example Apolito 2005; Beliso-De Jesús 2015; Meyer 2009; Van de Port 2006; Pype 2012; De Witte 2005, 314–35). This fact presents challenges and opportunities. How do we find ways of understanding the aesthetics and the materiality of electronic media? How do we think about mediation as a set of practices and actions? How do we think about how media devices are restructuring religious and spiritual experiences around the world? When people use personal computers or mobile phones every day, how are their relationships with angels, gods, or ancestors reimagined, how are rhythms of their daily devotional practices altered? As Kim Knibbe and Helena Kupari have written, we need to consider anew "how the ubiquitous presence of (social) media in people's daily lives influences their lived experience of religion and spirituality" (2020, 168). The result would be not only new ways of understanding what religious people are thinking and doing today, but also new theoretical insights about mediation, representation, embodiment, and technology.

II

Theorists working in different fields have already begun considering these questions. For instance, probably the most influential thinker examining the culture of moving images and how they trouble the real was the French social theorist Jean Baudrillard, who staged Western history in terms of epochs of media representations. He wrote that in the pre-modern period, people understood that images were clear counterfeits or placeholders for real things. Representations pointed to their referents. This epoch gave way to representation in the industrial revolution, during which the distinction between image and reality began to break down because of the mass production of copies. Mass-produced objects threatened to occlude underlying reality by imitating it so well. The postmodern order of representation, finally, has confronted us with an endlessly proliferating set of media-generated images that entirely obfuscate the real.

Baudrillard provided different examples of how the postmodern media environment worked. He often focused on consumer culture and advertising: we no longer purchase things because of real needs, he said, but because commercialized images stimulate desires in us. These commercialized images keep us "one step removed from the reality of our bodies or of the world around us" (Felluga 2003, 80). The rise of the Internet in the 1990s accelerated this process. Thus we have the emergence of what he called the hyperreal, defined as "the generation by models of a real without origin or reality," a dystopian situation in which consumer society and media images colonize all of life. Our hypermediated world was a new lived reality that had no clear origin point in what we used to call the "real world." "The great event of this period, the great trauma, is this decline of strong referentials, these death pangs of the real and of the rational that open onto an age of simulation" (Baudrillard 1994, 1, 31). Media representations seemed so real that the real was abolished.

While Baudrillard worried that this new separation from the real generated confusion, melancholy, and a kind of unfulfilled longing for authenticity, it is possible to argue that our moving-image culture did not destroy the real but rather refigured it, revealing the "objective" world of matter and facts to be *more mediatic* in nature—more dynamic, imaginative, illusory, elastic, and even what we might call "spiritual." Could our ongoing participation in the simulated worlds of electronic media point the way to a revised notion of the real?

Reflections on the nature of cyberspace and the simulated worlds of video games have led in precisely this direction. "When my family got an Atari video game console," the game designer and entrepreneur Rizwan Virk recalled in the introduction to his book *The Simulation Hypothesis*, "I became intrigued not just by the gameplay itself but by the 'illusion' that there was a self-contained world 'in there.'" "What happened when no one was playing the video game? Did the characters and the buildings still exist, or did they simply cease to exist?" In the 1990s and 2000s, as Virk designed and sold games that were more and more realistic and were played by many people simultaneously, his questions lingered. "If multiple users were playing the same game online, did it mean they were part of a shared world that existed independent of their computers? If so, where was it—was it on a server, or was it in some other metaphysical landscape in 'cyberspace'? Or did the world only exist when it was rendered on someone's local computer?" Moreover, was the world "in there" similar in certain ways to the world "out here" (Virk 2019, 2–4)? Could reality either be similar to the simulated world of video games or, more radically, have been constituted as some kind of simulated world by another form of intelligence? Virk came to believe the latter—that reality was a simulation being run on a cosmic supercomputer.

III

Of course, Virk was not the only one who found that electronic media led to novel metaphysical reflections on the real. In a truly remarkable development, the widespread adoption and use of personal computers has made many things seem computational—theological ideas, the human mind, even the deep structures of the cosmos. Some theologians have reimagined concepts such as *God*, *incarnation*, and *the Church* in response to a universe that suddenly seems networked, (hyper)linked, informational, and dynamic (Campbell and Garner 2016; Davies and Gregersen 2010; Friesen 2009; Han 2016; Hutchings 2017; Spadaro 2014). Other religious folks, such as the many metaphysical and "spiritual but not religious" practitioners in America, also have reshaped beliefs and practices using terms and categories such as networks, frequencies, transmissions, and the virtual. If we cast our net still wider, we see how the culture of ubiquitous computing has influenced aesthetic trends in art, music, and architecture. James Bridle has offered examples of the irruption of the computational in the material world—pointing to consumer products with blocky, digital patterns, art or music structured around technical glitches (e.g., "glitch art" and "glitch music"), pixilated stained glass church windows, and advertising campaigns that render real-world objects as something one might see in Minecraft (Bridle n.d.). Regarding theories of mind, there likewise has been an explosion of computational theories and models. Psychology textbooks and pop psychology trade books commonly talk about the mind as a layered set of computer programs running on the hardware of the brain, as Daniel Dennett does in his 1991 bestseller *Consciousness Explained*. The idea that the mind is a computational system has become an important idea in cognitive science, computer science, AI, and other fields.[2]

Finally, computational and virtual theories of the cosmos have not only fired the imagination of designers like Rizwan Virk, but also appear in cosmological debates staged by sober-minded scientists who used to eschew this kind of speculation. In the last twenty years, physicists and cosmologists have asserted that the universe resembles a mathematical code and that it might be a simulation of some kind. Max Tegmark at MIT and James Gates at the University of Maryland, for example, have argued that the laws that govern quarks, electrons, and other particles resemble error-correcting codes that make browsers work (Moskowitz 2016). Neil deGrasse Tyson has argued that it is "very likely" that we are living in a simulation akin to the simulations we run on computers; the Nobel Prize-winning physicist George Smoot gave a popular TED Talk with the playful title "You Are a Simulation and Physics Can Prove It."[3] (He did not actually prove it.) "Anyone who's seen *The Matrix* has contemplated the possibility that the world around us might be an illusion," the Columbia

2. See Michael Rescorla, "The Computational Theory of Mind," *Stanford Encyclopedia of Philosophy*, Stanford University, February 21, 2020, https://plato.stanford.edu/entries/computational-mind/. "Today's embrace of the computational metaphor in the cognitive and neural sciences is so widespread and automatic that it begins to appear less like an innovative leap than like a bandwagon phenomenon" (Daugman 2001, 32).

3. Smoot argues that "human beings are not good at figuring out if they are real." He displays optical illusions and other images to show that we do not perceive things properly. The reason, he says, is that we "lack computing power" and have to rely on "compromise algorithms" (see Smoot 2014).

University physicist Brian Greene pointed out in 2017. "What might be going on is we're just some elaborate computer simulation. All our thoughts are nothing but electrons flowing through very sophisticated circuitry." Increasingly powerful computers had led to these new speculations. "As we look at the capacity of computers—VR, AR—to recreate with ever greater reality the world around us," Greene thought, "you can at least imagine the possibility that we will be able to create consciousness inside of a simulated world." In fact, he thought, there was a "high probability" that we were a simulation (Greene 2017).

Thinking about the cosmos as computational and simulated has led some scientists to metaphysical reflections on the real that sound—well—religious. Could we be a simulation created by some kind of physicist-hacker God? "We have, as a species, for a very long time, struggled with deep questions. . . . Did some divine being bring us into existence?" Brian Greene said. "If indeed we are a simulation, we would have a creator and that creator would not stand outside the laws of science. So, strangely, from this point of view, you can be led to admit the possibility of a creator, but one that is not supernatural. So it's a weird situation where individuals like me, who never really considered the realistic possibility that there's a divine being behind it all, all of a sudden were led to the same set of thoughts and ideas that have been around for thousands of years of human civilization" (Greene 2017). "If the simulation hypothesis is valid," the physicist James Gates argued, echoing Greene, "then we open the door to eternal life and resurrection and things that formally have been discussed in the realm of religion." The reason was quite simple: "If we're programs in the computer, then as long as I have a computer that's not damaged, I can always re-run the program" (Moskowitz 2016). The Stanford physicist Andrei Linde has gone as far as to wonder why this "physicist hacker" God would create a universe and how he might have communicated with his simulation via revelatory messages coded into nature. If he had, who would be able to read such revelations? Physicists, of course (Linde n.d.).

The important point here is that this kind of novel metaphysical thinking was generated in the shocking encounter with computers and computer-generated realities, an encounter that is still ongoing. It is worth underscoring an obvious point: if computers and video games had never been invented, the cosmos and the mind would not today look like computers or computer simulations. These models of reality, these ways of thinking, have been entirely created by new technologies.

IV

Computers may provide a particularly dramatic example of the kind of technological shock and cognitive readjustment I am identifying, for they bring with them a remarkable level of *sensational credibility*. I use this term to point to two things: (1) computer-generated virtual worlds seem more and more realistic and believable; and (2) our encounters with computers and their virtual worlds incorporate more and more of our senses. On the latter point, computers and digital devices are different from film and television because they have insinuated themselves into our social world and everyday perceptions: We touch, hold, carry, and speak into laptops and mobile phones all day long. So there is a kind of progression in the sensational credibility of media during the last century, from seeing and hearing a television, to seeing, hearing, and touching a computer, to seeing, hearing, touching, and wearing or carrying a phone or strapped-on VR or AR apparatus.[4]

How should we think about the sensational and perceptual aspects of our encounters with technology—the ways we see, hear, touch, and interact with these devices? When discussing computers, other digital devices, and our understanding of the real, we certainly have to think about *touch*. How do these devices put us "in touch" with reality in new ways? The sociologist Mark Paterson has argued in an influential book on technology and touch that we associate touching with sensations of "feeling-with," a bringing near of distant things, and contact and proximity (Paterson 2007, 147). Touch brings distant things near and creates both a physical point of contact and an empathetic link to things in our environment. We recognize the power of touch to create emotional and epistemological points of contact in metaphorical phrases such as "her words touched me"; "let's stay in touch"; and "he lost touch with reality." "When I see a stone, it is 'out there' and does not see me, but when I touch that stone, it is 'right here' and touches me," the media theorist Mika Elo has written. "This sense of concreteness and immediacy lends the sense of touch certain credibility. A seen stone can be made of plastic even if it looks just like a stone, but when I touch it I can feel the material. It is due to this fullness of touching that the tactile metaphor of 'grasping' can stand for 'fully understanding

4. McLuhan focused on how media technologies extended the human sensorium, calling this "discarnation" and discussing how our faculties were extruded into a pervasive electronic environment.

something'" (Elo 2012b). *Touching is grasping and knowing something.* The point is as old as the Bible's doubting Thomas, who did not trust his senses until he had touched the risen Jesus. Seeing was not enough. "Thus reality," Elo has averred in another essay, "has been understood as being in touch with something real" (Elo 2012a).

The question then becomes how being constantly in touch with computers and other digital devices is changing how we register things as real. How do we in-corporate into experience new kinds of touching that are now quite routine—touching keyboards, mice, touchscreens, app icons, joysticks, and other technological interfaces? The philosopher Hubert Dreyfus has pointed out that the engaged body and its ability to interact with and alter things is crucial to our understanding of the real—"what gives our sense of being in direct touch with reality is that we bring about changes in the world and get perceptual feedback concerning what we have done" (Dreyfus 2000, 57). There are differences, of course, between virtual handshakes (mediated by haptic interfaces), joystick-controlled computer game interactions, and using a mouse to stop and start YouTube videos, but in each situation a novel experience of touch changes our relationship to the world. We might consider one example—our interaction with ghost videos online. We point at, click on, grasp, start and stop, move and control them. We do not touch ghosts directly, but we touch the thing that touches the ghost—and we do this in our lived space all day long. So daily computing leads to a recalibrated sensorium that is attuned to keys, trackpads, buttons, and interactive screens, all of which somehow deliver (among other things) ghosts that we can see, hear, (sort of) touch, and therefore "grasp." Our multisensory interactions with computers mean that the realities they reveal to us seem closer because they literally come within our grasp. Thus, if we have reformatted media devices to be touched, media devices have reformatted us so that we touch and thus grasp/know things in new ways.[5]

The reorientation forced upon us by shocking technological devices, then, goes beyond the realm of new ideas and beliefs. These changes encourage us to consider mediation as practice, embodiment, and action. They require bringing new approaches to our lived religious lives that examine how religious subjectivities are constituted by new media. And they

5. Elo has a nice phrase for how our new haptic environment alters our sense of the real, saying that "these taps, pushes and sweeps challenge the familiar concretia of the world" (see Elo 2012b).

require that we understand how our relationships with other souls and supernatural gods are now structured by electronic devices.

Conclusion

Some technology entrepreneurs are embracing all of these changes, pressing ahead with media devices that generate shock experiences, metaphysical insights, and electronic practices. In 2016 the American spiritual icon Deepak Chopra teamed up with Wevr, a California VR firm, to create a meditation virtual reality app called "Finding Your True Self." Chopra's son, Gotham, a filmmaker in Los Angeles, came upon the idea after listening to his dad talk about the illusory nature of reality for many years. Could VR be harnessed to teach this lesson in a particularly immersive way? "I'm a big fan of how technology can shift consciousness," Chopra has written. "I have also been focused on the idea of shifting people's experience of life through deeper meditation or visualization or experiences in nature or through music. And when they have a life altering experience, their biology changes. When VR came around I thought it was a perfect way to amplify and make more powerful what I have been doing for the last thirty years" (Chopra n.d.). The father-son team developed a beta version with Wevr, and one day Chopra arrived at Wevr's headquarters to test the system. He had his own shock experience. "I'll never forget Deepak's response when he first tried on the goggles," Anthony Batt, Wevr's cofounder, said. "He said, 'This is going to change the world, and it's going to help me explain to everybody what I've been saying for the last 30 years: We're all living in a simulation" (in Dean 2016).

What did this new technology reveal? The app is a guided meditation that begins gameplay on an open plain underneath the wide-spreading branches of a Bodhi tree. To the right is the Bodhi tree's gnarled trunk, which at times pulses with light energy. Deepak narrates the experience, calling attention to the breath in the style of a typical mindfulness meditation. As he does, luminous objects appear on the horizon, including Hindu gods surrounded by garlands and light. "Mentally ask yourself, who am I?" he says about four minutes into the meditation, signaling that this technology might help uncover an unknown truth about the self. He then asks players to focus either on his voice or on aspects of the gameplay environment as it changes, pointing out that regardless of one's momentary sensations and thoughts, there is always an "I am" behind the perception of these things. That enduring "I am" is an eternal self—it senses different things, experiences different memories or emotions, or withdraws into silence, but it exists independent of these states of awareness.[6] As the eighteen-minute meditation ends, the tree and the open plain disappear, replaced by a dark screen that foregrounds a giant floating Buddha, with beams of light radiating from his third eye.

Though commentators often question the realness and authenticity of virtual experiences, including online religious experiences, the fascinating aspect of this VR meditation is that it claims to reveal the really real: it is the shock experience that uncovers the true self. "When you don a virtual reality (VR) headset," Chopra wrote in his 2019 book *Metahuman*, "the simulation you are plunged into is like a wrap-around, three-dimensional movie of such vividness that it overwhelms the senses and causes a dislocation from what we deem as everyday reality" (2019, 36–37). This odd experience of another reality does not fool us into thinking that the virtual environment is real; it helps us realize that the real environment is virtual. We realize our everyday world is one that we also experience via a headset—that is, via a set of limited and sometimes unreliable senses that cannot in any event yield the whole truth. "Getting real is a process that begins by confronting your misplaced trust in illusions every day," Chopra writes in the same book (2019, 36–37). VR forces us to confront this truth.

Thus Chopra's VR represents a different kind of shock experience from that felt by naïve audience members watching early films such as *Uncle Josh at the Moving Picture Show*. Uncle Josh was fooled into thinking the virtual was the real, but more sophisticated onlookers knew the truth. Chopra's "Finding Your True Self," however, points the way to a new mediated practice. This media technology neither obscures the real nor introduces a counterfeit real; by bringing a high level of sensational credibility to an electronically mediated experience, it shows us that experiences that seem real can be faked and that we might therefore trust our everyday perceptions of the real a bit less. Though religious people might embrace the illusory nature of material things with alacrity, all people immersed in electronic media are forced to confront not just a set of unexpected sensations and perceptions but an additional possibility once understood only by mystics: that all things we perceive are merely projections in a world that is fundamentally mediatic and simulated.

6. Gameplay video is here: https://www.youtube.com/watch?v=ItCYA8I32B8.

Suggested Readings

Campbell, Heidi, ed. 2013. *Digital Religion: Understanding Religious Practice in New Media Worlds*. London: Routledge.

De Vries, Hent, and Samuel Weber, eds. 2001. *Religion and Media*. Palo Alto: Stanford University Press.

Meyer, Birgit. 2009. *Aesthetic Formations: Religion, Media and the Senses*. New York: Palgrave.

Paterson, Mark. 2007. *The Senses of Touch: Haptics, Affects and Technologies*. Oxford: Berg.

Sconce, Jeffrey. 2000. *Haunted Media: Electronic Presence from Telegraphy to Television*. Durham, NC: Duke University Press.

White, Christopher. 2018. *Other Worlds: Spirituality and the Search for Invisible Dimensions*. Cambridge: Harvard University Press.

References

Apolito, Paolo. 2005. *The Internet and the Madonna: Religious Visionary Experience on the Web*. Chicago: University of Chicago Press.

Baudrillard, Jean. 1994. *Simulacra and Simulation*. Translated by Sheila Glaser. Ann Arbor, MI: University of Michigan Press. Retrieved from https://web.archive.org/web/20120309115319/https://www9.georgetown.edu/faculty/irvinem/theory/baudrillard-simulacra_and_simulation.pdf.

Beliso-De Jesús, Aisha. 2015. *Electric Santeria: Racial and Sexual Assemblages of Transnational Religion*. New York: Columbia University Press.

Benjamin, Walter. 1969. "The Work of Art in the Age of Mechanical Reproduction." In *Illuminations: Essays and Reflections*. New York: Schocken Books.

Bogart, Leo. 1958. *The Age of the Television: A Study of Viewing Habits and the Impact of Television on American Life*. New York: F. Ungar Publishing.

Bridle, James. n.d. "Booktwo.org—The Blog of James Bridle: Art, Literature and the Network, Since 2006." booktwoorg. Accessed February 16, 2021. http://booktwo.org/.

Campbell, Heidi, and Stephen Garner. 2016. *Networked Theology: Negotiating Faith in Digital Culture*. Grand Rapids MI: Baker Academic.

Chopra, Deepak. n.d. "Finding Your True Self: Deepak Chopra Meditation Simulation." Wevr Transport (website). Accessed May 4, 2022. https://transport.wevr.com/chopra.

Chopra, Deepak. 2019. *Metahuman: Unleashing your Infinite Potential*. New York: Harmony Books.

Daugman, John. 2001. "Brain Metaphor and Brain Theory." In *Philosophy and the Neu-*

rosciences: A Reader, edited by William P. Bechtel, Pete Mandik, Jennifer Mundale, and Robert S. Stufflebeam. London: Blackwell.

Davies, Paul, and Niels Henrik Gregersen, eds. 2010. *Information and the Nature of Reality: From Physics to Metaphysics*. Cambridge: Cambridge University Press.

De Vries, Hent, and Samuel Weber, eds. 2001. *Religion and Media*. Palo Alto: Stanford University Press.

De Witte, Marlene. 2005. "The Spectacular and the Spirits: Charismatics and Neo-Traditionalists on Ghanaian Television." *Material Religion* 1:3.

Dean, Sam. 2016. "Is Virtual Reality the Medium That Buddhism Has Been Waiting For?" *Medium*. September 21. https://medium.com/mel-magazine/is-virtual-reality-the-medium-that-buddhism-has-been-waiting-for-7a0f9c2a5169.

Dreyfus, Hubert. 2000. "Telepistemology." In *The Robot in the Garden: Telerobotics and Telepistemology in the Age of the Internet*, edited by Ken Goldberg. Cambridge: MIT Press.

Elo, Mika. 2012a. "Digital Finger: Beyond Phenomenological Figures of Touch." In *Journal of Aesthetics and Culture* 4:1. https://www.tandfonline.com/doi/full/10.3402/jac.v4i0.14982.

Elo, Mika. 2012b. "Formatting the Senses of Touch." In *Transformations: Journal of Media and Culture* 22. http://www.transformationsjournal.org/wp-content/uploads/2016/12/Elo_Trans22.pdf.

Felluga, Dino. 2003. "The Matrix: A Paradigm of Post-Modernism or an Intellectual Poseur?" In *Taking the Red Pill: Science, Philosophy, and Religion in* The Matrix, edited by Glenn Yeffeth. Dallas: BenBella Books.

"Finding Your True Self." n.d. Wevr. https://transport.wevr.com/chopra.

Friesen, Dwight. 2009. *Thy Kingdom Connected: What the Church can Learn from Facebook, the Internet and Other Networks*. Grand Rapids, MI: Baker Academic.

Greene, Brian. 2017. "Are We Living in a Simulation?" January 6. http://www.briangreene.org/2016/01/06/are-we-living-in-a-simulation/.

Han, Sam. 2016. *Technologies of Religion: Spheres of the Sacred in a Post-Secular Modernity*. London: Routledge.

Hutchings, Tim. 2017. *Creating Church Online: Ritual, Community and New Media*. New York: Taylor & Francis.

Knibbe, Kim, and Helena Kupari. 2020. "Theorizing Lived Religion: An Introduction." *Journal of Contemporary Religion* 35:2.

Linde, Andre. n.d. Interview: "Are We Living in a Simulation?" *Closer to Truth*. Accessed March 5, 2021. https://www.closertotruth.com/series/are-we-living-simulation.

Mander, Jerry. 1978. *Four Arguments for the Elimination of Television*. New York: HarperCollins.

Meyer, Birgit. 2009. *Aesthetic Formations: Religion, Media and the Senses*. New York: Palgrave.

Moskowitz, Clara. 2016. "Are We Living in a Computer Simulation?" *Scientific American*.

April 7. https://www.scientificamerican.com/article/are-we-living-in-a-computer-simulation/.

Paterson, Mark. 2007. *The Senses of Touch: Haptics, Affects and Technologies*. Oxford: Berg.

Pearson, E. Norman. 1957. *Space, Time and Self*. Wheaton, IL: Theosophical Publishing House.

Pype, Katrien. 2012. *The Making of the Pentecostal Melodrama: Religion, Media and Gender in Kinshasa*. New York: Berghahn Books.

Rescorla, Michael. 2020. "The Computational Theory of Mind." *Stanford Encyclopedia of Philosophy*. February 21. Stanford University. https://plato.stanford.edu/entries/computational-mind/.

Schutz, Alfred. 1972. "On Multiple Realities." In *Schutz, The Problem of Social Reality: Collected Papers I*. Netherlands: Springer.

Sconce, Jeffrey. 2000. *Haunted Media: Electronic Presence from Telegraphy to Television*. Durham, NC: Duke University Press.

Slatman, Jenny. 2001. "Tele-Vision: Between Blind Trust and Perceptual Faith." In *Religion and Media*, edited by Hent de Vries and Samuel Weber. Palo Alto: Stanford University Press.

Smoot, George. 2014. "You are a Simulation & Physics Can Prove It: George Smoot at TEDxSalford." February 12. Salford, England. TEDx video, 19:26. https://www.youtube.com/watch?v=Chfoo9NBEow.

Spadaro, Anthony. 2014. *Cybertheology: Thinking Christianity in the Age of the Internet*. New York: Fordham University Press.

Van de Port, Mattijs. 2006. "Visualizing the Sacred: Video Technology, 'Televisual Style' and the Religious Imagination in Bahian Candomble." *American Ethnologist* 33:3.

Virk, Rizwan. 2019. *The Simulation Hypothesis: An MIT Computer Scientist Shows Why AI, Quantum Physics and Eastern Mystics Agree We Are in a Video Game*. San Francisco: Bayview Books.

White, Christopher. 2018. *Other Worlds: Spirituality and the Search for Invisible Dimensions*. Cambridge, MA: Harvard University Press.

19 REASON

Alireza Doostdar

> And so, the parable of those who are bent on denying the truth is that of the beast which hears the shepherd's cry, and hears in it nothing but the sound of a voice and a call. Deaf are they, and dumb, and blind: for they do not use their reason.
> THE NOBLE QUR'AN (2:171), translated by Muhammad Asad

Consider these two questions from an Iranian high school textbook:

1. We pour some sand, iron filings, and fragments of wood and glass in a box. We close the box and ask someone to insert a magnet and tell us what material is inside. What is the most correct answer they can give? What reason can they offer to justify their answer?
2. Imagine a person who has gone fishing and casts a net into the sea to catch fish. When they retrieve the net, they find some fish inside. If someone were to ask this person what exists in the sea, what is the most correct answer they can give? What explanation can they provide to justify their answer?

What are we to make of these questions? We might answer the first by saying that there are iron filings inside the box, and also air, but that we would need more data to say anything further because magnets attract iron and little else. To the second question, we might respond that the sea has fish, water, and much else besides. But also, is it not a bit odd to ask a fisherman about the contents of the sea? What sorts of questions are these, and what kind of reasoning do they elicit? Are they lessons in the scientific method? In philosophical reasoning? Or something else entirely?[1]

The mystery evaporates as soon as we place the questions within the context of the lesson in which they appear—an extended theological argument against scientistic atheism in an eleventh-grade religion textbook. Titled "Can God Be Denied?," the lesson's reasoning proceeds as follows: Our five senses are analogous to the magnet and fishing net in the questions. We cast these instruments into the "sea of being" to understand the realities of the universe. But we catch only those beings that can fit "the net of our senses"—i.e., material existence. It follows that because our senses cannot grasp everything, we cannot deny immaterial reality based on sense experience. The textbook goes on to argue that the empirical sciences are unable to discount the existence of God or immaterial beings, because these sciences only have material experience at their disposal. "The stance of the empirical sciences toward immaterial beings," therefore, "is the stance of 'I don't know.'"

Seen within this extended argument, the two questions form a fragment of what Western philosophers call natural theology, that is, a case for the existence of God (or, as here, against the denial of God) that draws only on common sense and ordinary experience. The common sense presumed here includes basic familiarity with modern empirical sciences, which any high school student should ostensibly be able to muster. Nowhere in the lesson do the authors enlist the help of divine revelation or prophetic tradition, those sources considered authoritative by Muslim theologians.

The high school lesson in natural theology is one among numerous instances in which Iranian students are taught to engage in religious reasoning. Learning to reason religiously is a fundamental part of what it means to grow up Muslim in Iran, as it is in many other parts of the world. But for the Islamic Republic and the Ministry of Instruction and Cultivation that publishes all school textbooks, religious reasoning also forms a cornerstone of state power: not only for the justification of ruling ideas, but also for the formation of citizens and the bureaucratic processes by which populations are governed. A core assumption at the heart of these attempts is that humans are, by God-given nature, rational beings who can be taught to reason correctly to attain happiness both in this world and in the hereafter.

1. I am grateful to Sawyer French, Sarah Hammerschlag, Nick Lorenz, Nada Moumtaz, Noah Salomon, and Yunus Doğan Telliel for comments on an earlier draft.

What can this theology lesson teach us about reason in a comparative perspective? To answer this question, we need first to decide our starting point: Do we begin our inquiry by thinking of reason as a noun, or as a verb? That is, do we approach reason as a faculty, capacity, or entity with specific qualities? Or do we instead examine reason as an activity—not so much something humans possess as something they do? I have opted in this essay to take the second path for two reasons (and here, of course, we run into another nounal sense of reason that permeates my essay: statements offered to justify or explain something). First, conceptions of reason as an entity, faculty, or capacity vary within and among religious traditions. There is no single undisputed Islamic idea of "reason," nor is there consensus over how to situate human intellectual powers in relation to revelation and the divine intellect. Looking beyond Islam, conceptions of reason and ideas of what counts as reasonable multiply still further. Second, if we were to define the faculty of reason not by beginning with any specific religious tradition but instead by leaning on a second-order concept developed in the humanities and social sciences (including those traditions of inquiry that make up religious studies), we would still face the problem of having to choose from a wide range of conflicting options, each of which would present challenges in capturing how reason is imagined from within religious traditions.

Faced with the bewildering multiplicity of reason, I have adopted an empirical approach to *reasoning* as a social activity encompassing aspects that seem to be universally human and those that are historically specific. I propose that we think of reasoning as (1) a discursive activity in which people reflect on something (2) of theoretical or practical interest (3) to form, justify, or explore some opinion, understanding, or practice, (4) in accordance with one or more styles, (5) in the course of building and inhabiting a valued form of life. From this approach there emerges a nounal sense of reason as a universal human capacity to engage in the social activity of reasoning, while leaving space for additional tradition-specific senses that may integrate with or sit alongside (comfortably or not) the empirical sense.

A Discursive Activity

When the Qur'an criticizes unbelievers for their lack of reason, it sometimes, as in the epigraph above, calls them "deaf, dumb, and blind." The idea seems to be that the failure to reason or understand is like an inability to discern (deafness and blindness), but more intriguingly, also to speak. There is a clear resonance here with the ancient Greek equation of reason with speech through *logos*, a notion that medieval Muslim theologians and philosophers took to heart, as did their Jewish and Christian counterparts. Just what the relationship between reason and speech should be concerns me here primarily in the most basic way: that language lies at the center of reasoning and that people distinguish between correct and incorrect reasoning, reason and unreason, by evaluating discursive data, most clearly but not only in the form of reasons offered to justify statements and actions (even when people judge an action to be reasonable or unreasonable in the absence of the actor's expressly articulated reasons, there is a presumption that the action is *intentional under a description* in the sense elaborated by G. E. M. Anscombe and Donald Davidson). How precisely reasoning should be conceptualized, how its proper scope should be delineated, and what should count as good reasons will vary widely across social groups, geography, and history. But it seems to be universally the case that human groups assume themselves capable of reasoning (even if they do not always grant that capacity to their others, or indeed, to some of their own members), and that this capacity lies at the heart of their ability to communicate with one another, even across linguistic and cultural difference.

Among anthropologists, the assumption that all humans are capable of reasoning has long formed the bedrock of the discipline. Known as the "psychic unity of mankind," this doctrine was once arrayed against scientists who differentiated human cognitive abilities on the basis of biological descent ("race"). Anthropologists who subscribed to psychic unity argued that every human had the same cognitive machinery, but this belief did not in itself spell the end of racial hierarchies. Instead, European ideas about inborn intellectual differences gave way to ideas about cultural variation distributed on an evolutionary ladder of progress, preserving much of the older structure but with the biological foundation pushed to the background. What this meant was that rather than denying the capacity of so-called "primitive" or "savage" humans to reason, some evolutionist anthropologists granted them reasoning powers much like their own, while still maintaining that their reasoning led them to the wrong inferences. "Savage" reasoning supposedly produced the illusions of magic and religion, while civilized reasoning produced scientific knowledge.

While anthropologists shed this evolutionary framework in the early twentieth century, the doctrine that humans everywhere had the same cognitive capacities stuck. One challenge to this idea came from the French philosopher Lucien Lévy-Bruhl, who argued that "primitive mentality" was radically different from the mentality of Europeans—so different that Europeans would find it hard, if not impossible, to grasp what it would be to think like a "savage" at all. For Lévy-Bruhl, the radical alterity of primitive thought was not a product of variations in cognitive machinery, but a result of differences in living conditions and the collective representations that emerged from them. While primitives did reason, he argued, they mostly did so in concrete ways attuned to the sensuous details of everyday life. They did not, that is, reason conceptually, abstractly, or according to logical principles. Lévy-Bruhl was largely dismissed in his own time and has appeared to later generations as little more than a historical curiosity. Even so, shorn of baseless speculations about primitives, the notion of nonconceptual reasoning is less controversial than it may at first appear. We find a parallel, for example, in studies of intuitive decision-making, the process that occurs in practical situations, as when a driver decides on the quickest route through rush-hour traffic, or a firefighter or clinician makes choices in an emergency. We find it as well in work on "imagistic" (Brewer 2001), "physical," or "domain-specific" reasoning (Bermúdez and Cahen 2020), like what is involved in the mental assessment of whether a piece of furniture will fit in a particular spot in a room (see also Roberts 2008), and perhaps in complex scientific reasoning as well (Yip, Zhao, and Sacks 1995). Beyond adult cognition and decision-making, researchers have investigated nonconceptual reasoning among agents who are not, or not yet, capable of language, as for example human infants, chimpanzees, chicks, and computer models.

It is important to keep in mind that wherever reasoning is said to proceed nonconceptually, the agent would have to perform some extra work to provide an intelligible account for their decision (even if this is merely a matter of articulating the intuitive character of their reasoning, as when someone says "I acted in this way because it felt right to me"). In some cases (as with chimps, infants, and software), this extra work may not be possible at all. Nonconceptual decision-making may therefore be excluded from the act of reasoning in the more restricted sense I am considering here. Such a distinction would be in line with a dominant psychological approach that conceptualizes human reasoning as a dual system that consists of separate analytic and intuitive processes, where only the first is guided by conscious deliberation. But this does not mean that the two are entirely independent kinds of activity. Intuitions lend support to reasoned deliberations, including in religious matters (see for example Luhrmann 2020). Indeed, it may be that no reasoning is possible at all without intuition and other feelings (Schaefer 2022). Conversely, making intuitive decisions in specific contexts often depends on prior acts of discursive reasoning. Anthropologists of ethical action have focused on precisely this connection where they speak of the habituation of the body and the cultivation of virtues, a topic to which I will turn later.

We should also remember that while the capacity for discursive reasoning may seem to distinguish humans from animals and machines, some religious traditions grant it a lesser value than certain forms of nonconceptual knowledge. In Sufi Islam, for example, the most profound secrets of the cosmos are not available to discursive reason at all and must be approached through a supersensory experience known as "unveiling" or the mode of apprehension known as "tasting" (*dhawq*). While discursive reason can help spiritual aspirants train themselves for achieving such nonconceptual apprehension, it is also a serious obstacle if left untamed. Likewise, in some strands of Buddhism, conceptual reasoning can help achieve a kind of nonconceptual consciousness that is alone able to realize emptiness. That is, emptiness is an ultimate truth that transcends what discursive reasoning can ever comprehend by itself (Lopez 1987). Examples can be found in other traditions as well (for an influential comparative account that privileges Christianity, see Otto 1923).

Of Theoretical or Practical Interest

The object of reasoning in the Iranian high school lesson is theoretical. It reflects on questions about the existence of God and the epistemic merits of different modes of inquiry into such questions. In the Islamic tradition, there are domains of inquiry besides theology that are similarly guided by theoretical interest: speculative mysticism and a good deal of qur'anic exegesis, for example. On the practical side, we have ethics, political science, law, practical mysticism, and some forms of Qur'an commentary. If in the first set reasoning is directed toward knowledge of whether, what, how, and why things *are*, in the latter the relevant questions are about how one must *act*. Of course, the distinction is not so simple. Practical reasoning will always depend on ideas that may themselves be the outcome of theoretical reflection. On the side of theoretical reason, too, reasoning often proceeds with the practical dimension of knowledge in sight. Speculative mysticism is a good example of this, where the author's audience is almost never a disinterested academic reader (as are, say, most modern scholars of Islamic studies in American universities), but aspirants on the path of self-purification.

There is another way to link theoretical and practical reasoning. Every form of reasoning relies on specific dispositions whose cultivation will itself be subject to practical reflection. The high school theology lesson is imparted in the context of formal schooling, a long process of intellectual, emotional, and bodily education, the goals of which are encoded into the very title of the governmental body that oversees this training: the Ministry of Instruction and Cultivation. The idea here is that a person can only reason correctly and reach the correct conclusions if she is correctly disposed, which means not only that her intellective faculty will be sharpened but also that her moral temperament will be trained to help her attain the right spiritual qualifications. Doing so requires the cultivation of a range of affective dispositions, modes of attention, and intuitive sensibilities according to specific ethical models whose purview extends far beyond instructing students in specific rational arguments (Wainwright 1995 and 2016; Hirschkind 2006; Lempert 2012).

To Form, Justify, or Explore Some Opinion, Understanding, or Practice

When scholars discuss religious reasoning, they often focus on apologetic arguments that justify some theological dogma. The example in the Iranian religious textbook fits this same pattern. Given that we are dealing with an already existing doctrine, the task of religious reasoning is to provide good arguments for believing it. Dogma-justifying reasoning might take on very different forms. Some marshal deductive arguments from one or more premises presumed to be universally valid. Some, like our textbook example, combine deduction with reasoning by analogy. Others build their arguments on top of statements given in an authoritative text, make recourse to the demonstrative force of mystical experience, or recruit the evidentiary power of scientific facts.

But not all reasoning justifies preexisting dogma. In legal and ethical reasoning, for example, believers seek to resolve practical dilemmas or find solutions to theoretical problems that permit a wide field of exploration and disagreement. Ask a group of contemporary Muslim theologians if the material body is resurrected in the afterlife, and you are unlikely to hear much disagreement. Ask a group of jurists if sex-change through surgery and hormonal therapy is permissible, and disputes are sure to arise. The breadth of disagreement is not only due to doctrinal presuppositions (these often do play a role), but rooted in differences in legal methodology, which is to say, the modes of reasoning by which jurists arrive at their rulings. Even identical methods can lead two jurists to arrive at different rulings because they may draw on contrasting sets of legal principles or disagree over the probative force of specific pieces of evidence. The point is that religious reasoning is not limited to the defense of belief, but just as often is focused on the formation of new opinions or prescriptions.

Even those statements we tend to think of as theological dogmas are seldom unchanging mantras. Like any other kind of knowledge, doctrines are shaped by inquiry and are subject to disagreement. What this means is that we need to attend not only to the forms of reasoning by which a doctrine is formed and justified, but also to the questions it attempts to answer. What kind of puzzle is a theological statement meant to resolve? In what "scene of inquiry" (Jardine 2000) was it possible to come to grips with this puzzle? How have changes in the intellectual, social, and political environment led to shifts in how people understand its meaning and import?

In seeking to understand religious reasoning as inquiry, it may be fruitful to make a distinction between what philosophers of science have called the context of discovery and the context of justification. In this thinking, asking how a religious idea was conceived is different from asking how people subsequently defend it. In the philosophy of science, the context distinction was used for much of the twentieth century to argue that insofar as philosophy is engaged in a normative endeavor, it can only properly speak about justification, as in evaluating and testing hypotheses. Reasoning, the proponents of the distinction held, is not applicable in the discovery or origination of scientific ideas because these are unpredictable, creative, and impervious to systematic rational analysis. Critics of this distinction have argued that discovery can also incorporate procedures of reasoning amenable to philosophical examination. Some scholars have pointed to abductive inference as a generative mode of reasoning distinct from induction and deduction. Others have emphasized methods of discovery involving analogy and the construction and manipulation of mental models. Still others have pointed to the importance of the articulation and development of ideas, as distinct from both the creative flash of discovery and the rigorous evaluation and verification of hypotheses (see Schickore 2018).

Is it possible to locate religious reasoning in the context of discovery? The medieval Muslim philosopher and mystic Shihabuddin Suhrawardi claimed that he arrived at the knowledge contained in his *Hikmat al-Ishraq* (Philosophy of Illumination) not through "cogitation," but rather "through something else," by which he meant direct, unmediated intuition and unveiling. Even so, he wrote that he subsequently sought discursive proof for this knowledge, so that "should I cease contemplating the proof, nothing would make me fall into doubt" (Suhrawardi 1999, 2). In this example, discovery and justification seem to be quite distinct, the former achieved through mystical intuition and the latter through logical reasoning. However, for Suhrawardi it seems that *justification* could also be the result of mystical experience: a true experience of unveiling will be so powerful as to be self-confirming. Here, discursive reasoning seems to play no role in discovery at all, and perhaps only a secondary role in justification (to protect against doubt).

And yet it may be possible to conceive a role for reasoning even in extreme cases like the formation of Suhrawardi's mystical intuitions. While Suhrawardi claimed that he received the "science of lights" through mystical unveiling, he developed this science in part through the construction of a theory of vision that he contrasted with prevalent "intromissive" and "extramissive" theories. What Suhrawardi called "knowledge-by-presence" (unmediated knowledge, contrasted with mediated "acquired knowledge") was an expansion and elaboration of this theory. Perhaps the idea for knowledge-by-presence really did come to him through mystical unveiling. But on the other hand, it could be that engaging in analogical modeling—vision as a model for supersensory perception and for unmediated knowing—primed his mystical intuitions. Analogical reasoning would then be an activity that does not merely interpret and make sense of a past mystical vision, but also gives shape to subsequent intuitions.

Suhrawardi's example is important for another reason particular to our own time, when scientific concepts, models, and methods have become central to how many believers understand the realm of the immaterial and the supernatural. In my study of New Age spirituality and the occult in contemporary Iran, I found that concepts and models from physics—thermodynamics, electromagnetism, quantum mechanics—often guided how people conceived of such things as the soul and the afterlife. What is important in these examples is not only how people deploy scientific ideas to justify religious belief, but how they come to form these religious ideas by analogy and in relation to models they acquire from science. The role modeling plays in religious knowledge requires sustained exploration, for there is more than one way to think about the relationship between the two. For example, while Suhrawardi thought of vision as a kind of knowledge-by-presence, such that his analogizing of knowledge with vision paved the way for articulating a theory of vision *as* knowledge, some of my interlocutors thought of scientific modeling as only tentative experimental attempts to make a religious statement *plausible*. What was important for them was less a decisive statement of fact than a suggestion that something could make sense within their given conceptual universe. Their reasoning took on an exploratory character whose primary goal was not to convince an opponent but instead to probe and examine various possibilities, which meant that it could also generate unpredictable insights.

In Accordance with One or More Styles

Some acts of religious reasoning appear to be idiosyncratic and ad hoc. I knew a wealthy middle-aged Iranian woman who argued for the truth of her spiritual path by referring to such diverse justifications as Baird T. Spalding's *Life and Teaching of the Masters of the Far East* and a marijuana-induced mystical vision (see Doostdar 2018, 105–11). Others are like the religion textbook example in that they cohere into distinct styles of thinking that have been elaborated over generations and have become integrated into established traditions of inquiry. Wherever reasoning is *taught*, we should expect to find patterns, norms, and perhaps meta-reflection on the act of reasoning itself.

We can understand "styles" of religious reasoning in at least two ways. One would be to draw attention to discursive form, in the sense of rhetoric, poetics, or speech genre. Storytelling and allegorical reasoning are good examples of the kind of reasoning amenable to such analysis. Their role in religious thought and practice is immense and well documented. In the Islamic tradition, allegory and storytelling have long played a crucial part in ethical instruction among the Sufis and among popular preachers to this day. They have also been taken up by some philosophers as supplements to rational proof that open imaginative paths toward spiritual insight (Zargar 2017). Style as genre can also be deployed in examining religious reasoning in such modern expressive forms as novels, TV serials, and film. We might also ask how conventions from one medium might be translated into another, as in the adoption of filmic visuality in religious sermons (Hirschkind 2006, 153–56).

A second way to understand style would be through the concept of "styles of reasoning" developed most systematically by the philosopher of science Ian Hacking (1985 and 1992). His concern has been scientific inquiry, but we can extend his framework to religious reasoning as well. Hacking says that styles are those models or standards by which we have come to understand what it is to reason correctly about particular topics. For most scientific statements and certainly for the most interesting, he argues, a statement can only be a candidate for truth-or-falsity once we learn to argue in its appropriate style. Such are, for example, laboratory-based and statistical styles of reasoning. It is not that arguments from laboratory experiments make a particular scientific statement true, but that we cannot make a true-or-false judgment about a lab-experiment-based argument at all unless we engage in lab-experimental arguments. New styles of reasoning bring novel true-or-false sentences into existence, and they bring with them new objects, evidentiary considerations, modalities of argument, and debates about how such reasoning should proceed. Styles can also help us see that reasoning is not just a linguistic activity, but one that mobilizes materials, instruments, technologies, and infrastructures, including the human body.

It would be tempting to establish one-to-one relationships between styles and disciplines of inquiry (or "sciences")—hence a theological style, a jurisprudential style, an exegetical style, and so on. But Hacking's framework is more fine-grained than this: a style is a model that may be taken up by more than one discipline, and any one discipline is made up of more than one style. Laboratory reasoning, for example, is joined in many modern sciences by statistical thinking. In the Islamic tradition, grammatical and analogical styles of reasoning have been established in jurisprudence as well as speculative theology, qur'anic exegesis, and others. The experiential style of Sufi unveiling can be found in various philosophical traditions including the illuminationist and the Akbarian, but also in occult practices like geomancy and bibliomancy.

The incorporation of new styles of reasoning into established disciplines of inquiry offers one window onto transformations in a religious tradition (see for example Doostdar 2018 and Moumtaz 2018). But even without direct incorporation, once a specific style of reasoning brings a new object or evidentiary consideration into existence, these may find their way into other modalities of argument. We may think, for example, of how new economic concepts, medical phenomena, or psychological taxonomies have been taken up by Islamic jurists as they respond to novel social arrangements.

Do the ad hoc idiosyncratic forms of argument scholars often encounter among ordinary practitioners have any relationship with the more stabilized styles of religious scholarship? Sometimes we may be able to identify echoes of reasoning learned in school, encountered in texts, or heard in religious settings, even if they are adapted and combined in unexpected ways. But it would be a mistake to draw a hard distinction between popular and elite reasoning on this basis. Just as ordinary practitioners may learn to reason expertly (as much of the literature on pious self-cultivation has shown—e.g., Deeb 2006 and Mahmood 2005), scholars too sometimes resort to idiosyncratic mixtures that may give rise to stable forms over time (Doostdar 2018). Any new style of reasoning is likely to look idiosyncratic to its critics (see Shapin and Shaeffer 1989 for a now classic treatment of the laboratory style).

In the Course of Inhabiting a Valued Form of Life

Earlier I said that religious reasoning can be theoretical or practical, but that it would be difficult to find any instance where it is purely one or the other. In a larger sense, all religious reasoning can be thought of as practical insofar as it is integrated with the practices necessary for living a life that aspires to virtue, proximity to God, or any other telos imagined within reasoning's guiding tradition. It is rarely just an abstract intellectual exercise; most often it is an activity in the service of contemplation, exhortation, teaching, moral advice, worship, critique, and so on. While apologetic and justificatory ends may play an important part in these practices, they are often oriented toward other goals like the expression of devotion (on which see Clayton 2006) and the deepening of faith (for example, see Telliel 2019; for a nuanced fictional exploration, see Chiang 2019). In all these ways, reasoning can be an ongoing activity that people do together while constructing a mutual life (Asad 2020; Laden 2012; MacIntyre 2012). It is both rooted in the forms of life that people share with one another, and integral to the task of building, critiquing, and refining those forms of life. Reasoning, then, can be an activity of "sharing the world, of attuning ourselves to others within reciprocal relationships" (Laden 2012, 46). This world-sharing dimension of religious reasoning is an important feature that sets it apart from modern scientific thought (the question is different for the pre-modern world, where science and religion did not carve up distinct territories in the ways that have become familiar for the past few centuries; see Harrison 2015) and brings it into a sphere that might also encompass ethics and politics (although see Asad 2020, 411–13).

As an activity of world-making and world-remaking, religious reasoning is also a conduit for power. Power suffuses every aspect of reasoning I have discussed here: it sets the parameters of discourse; defines the scope and boundaries of reflection; determines the norms of discovery, justification, evidence, and argument; brings forth possibilities for truthmaking; makes some things thinkable and others unthinkable. We can see power in the intimate relationships through which ethical subjects are formed, but also in the imperial modes of intellection and argument that justify social hierarchies, sustain rulership, and rationalize the domination of some groups over others. Sometimes it is difficult to disentangle the intimate workings of power from the imperial (for example, see Ayubi 2019). In other instances, they may work at cross purposes with one another. Nowhere is this more obvious than in the context of secular states that have made it ever more difficult to sustain the forms of life in which religious reasoning can thrive (see, for example, Asad 1993). But such conflicts can also be seen in self-defined religious states like the Islamic Republic of Iran where the ends of pious community often do not line up with the determinations of state power.

With the rise of modern states and momentous transformations in the distribution and circulation of power, we also need to attend to how power works through governmental logics (legal, educational, hygienic, economic, and others) that manage and care for populations. This brings us once again to the theology lesson with which I opened the essay. As it turns out, the lesson is not addressed to Muslim students at all, but appears in the eleventh-grade religion textbook published for Iran's recognized religious minorities (Zoroastrian, Jewish, and Christian). This is the "common" textbook for these communities, the presumption being that each community will also have separate religious lessons specific to their own traditions and produced by their own institutions. The common element in this textbook looks a lot like what is sometimes called "rationalist" Islamic theology, but it is stripped of the most overt Islamic referents such as any mention of the Qur'an or the Prophet Muhammad (although a well-known prayer for the Prophet and his household does appear on the title page). A cynical reader might see the book as a thinly veiled attempt at proselytization.

Whether or not this is the case, the textbook is a component of larger processes by which access to university education is distributed. A good grade on the religion exam means a higher likelihood of admission to the university and major of the student's choice. That is, the theological reasoning imparted in this lesson is not just a tool for fashioning virtuous subjects but also an instrument for managing the care of a population by aiding governmental decisions on how to allocate the limited resource of free higher education.

Ultimately, while religious reasoning is critical for the creation and sharing of a social world with other people, the textbook theology lesson shows how such reasoning may be vulnerable to instrumentalization in ways that can undo that same world or bring it under pressures that warp it beyond recognition. These are the risks that religious reason faces when it is disembedded from the forms of life that once sustained it, and reoriented toward a secular horizon.

Suggested Readings

Clayton, John. 2006. *Religions, Reasons and Gods: Essays in Cross-Cultural Philosophy of Religion*. Cambridge: Cambridge University Press.

Daston, Lorraine, and Peter Galison. 2007. *Objectivity*. New York: Zone Books.

Harrison, Peter. 2015. *The Territories of Science and Religion*. Chicago: University of Chicago Press.

Laden, Anthony Simon. 2012. *Reasoning: A Social Picture*. Oxford: Oxford University Press.

Luhrmann, T. M. 1991. *Persuasions of the Witch's Craft: Ritual Magic in Contemporary England*. Cambridge: Harvard University Press.

Schaefer, Donovan O. 2022. *Wild Experiment: Feeling Science and Secularism after Darwin*. Durham, NC: Duke University Press.

Verran, Helen. 2001. *Science and an African Logic*. Chicago: University of Chicago Press.

Wainwright, William J. 2016. *Reason, Revelation, and Devotion: Inference and Argument in Religion*. New York: Cambridge University Press.

References

Asad, Talal. 1993. "The Limits of Religious Criticism in the Middle East: Notes on Islamic Public Argument." In *Genealogies of Religion: Discipline and Reasons of Power in Christianity and Islam*, 200–36. Baltimore: Johns Hopkins University Press.

Asad, Talal. 2020. "Thinking about Religion through Wittgenstein." *Critical Times* 3 (3): 403–42.

Ayubi, Zahra. 2019. *Gendered Morality: Classical Islamic Ethics of the Self, Family, and Society*. New York: Columbia University Press.

Bermúdez, José, and Arnon Cahen. 2020. "Nonconceptual Mental Content." In *The Stanford Encyclopedia of Philosophy* (Summer 2020 Edition), edited by Edward N. Zalta. https://plato.stanford.edu/archives/sum2020/entries/content-nonconceptual/.

Brewer, Bill. 2001. "Précis of Perception and Reason." *Philosophy and Phenomenological Research* 63 (2): 405–16. https://doi.org/10.1111/j.1933-1592.2001.tb00113.x.

Chiang, Ted. 2019. "Omphalos." In *Exhalation: Stories*, 237–69. New York: Alfred A. Knopf.

Clayton, John. 2006. *Religions, Reasons and Gods: Essays in Cross-Cultural Philosophy of Religion*. Cambridge: Cambridge University Press.

Deeb, Lara. 2006. *An Enchanted Modern: Gender and Public Piety in Shiʿi Lebanon*. Princeton: Princeton University Press.

Doostdar, Alireza. 2018. *The Iranian Metaphysicals: Explorations in Science, Islam, and the Uncanny*. Princeton: Princeton University Press.

Hacking, Ian. 1985. "Styles of Scientific Reasoning." In *Post-Analytic Philosophy*, edited by John Rajchman and Cornel West. New York: Columbia University Press.

Hacking, Ian. 1992. "'Style' for Historians and Philosophers." *Studies in History and Philosophy of Science* 23 (1): 1–20.

Harrison, Peter. 2015. *The Territories of Science and Religion*. Chicago: University of Chicago Press.

Hirschkind, Charles. 2006. *The Ethical Soundscape: Cassette Sermons and Islamic Counterpublics*. New York: Columbia University Press.

Jardine, Nicholas. 2000. *The Scenes of Inquiry: On the Reality of Questions in the Sciences*. 2nd ed. Oxford: Oxford University Press.

Laden, Anthony Simon. 2012. *Reasoning: A Social Picture*. Oxford: Oxford University Press.

Lempert, Michael. 2012. *Discipline and Debate: The Language of Violence in a Tibetan Buddhist Monastery*. Berkeley, CA: University of California Press.

Lopez, Donald S., Jr. 1987. *A Study of Svātantrika*. Boulder, CO: Snow Lion.

Luhrmann, T. M. 2020. *How God Becomes Real: Kindling the Presence of Invisible Others*. Princeton, NJ: Princeton University Press.

MacIntyre, Alasdair. 2012. *After Virtue: A Study in Moral Theory*. 3rd ed. Notre Dame: University of Notre Dame Press.

Mahmood, Saba. 2005. *Politics of Piety: The Islamic Revival and the Feminist Subject*. Princeton: Princeton University Press.

Moumtaz, Nada. 2018. "'Is the Family *Waqf* a Religious Institution?' Charity, Religion, and Economy in French Mandate Lebanon." *Islamic Law and Society* 25: 37–77.

Otto, Rudolf. 1923. *The Idea of the Holy*. Translated by John W. Harvey. London: Oxford University Press.

Roberts, Tom. 2008. "Action and Experience." PhD diss., University of Edinburgh.

Schaefer, Donovan O. 2022. *Wild Experiment: Feeling Science and Secularism after Darwin*. Durham, NC: Duke University Press.

Schickore, Jutta. 2018. "Scientific Discovery." In *The Stanford Encyclopedia of Philosophy* (Summer 2018 Edition), edited by Edward N. Zalta. https://plato.stanford.edu/archives/sum2018/entries/scientific-discovery/.

Shapin, Steven, and Simon Schaeffer. 1989. *Leviathan and the Air-Pump: Hobbes, Boyle, and the Experimental Life*. Princeton: Princeton University Press.

Suhrawardi, Yaḥya ibn Ḥabash, 1999. *The Philosophy of Illumination: A New Critical Edition of the Text of Hikmat al-Ishraq*. Edited, translated, and with an introduction by John Walbridge & Hossein Ziai. Provo, UT: Brigham Young University Press.

Telliel, Yunus Doğan. 2019. "Miraculous Evidence: Scientific Wonders and Religious Reasons." *Comparative Studies of South Asia, Africa and the Middle East* 39 (3): 528–42.

Wainwright, William J. 1995. *Reason and the Heart: A Prolegomenon to a Critique of Passional Reason*. Ithaca, NY: Cornell University Press.

Wainwright, William J. 2016. *Reason, Revelation, and Devotion: Inference and Argument in Religion*. New York: Cambridge University Press.

Yip, Kenneth, Feng Zhao, and Elisha Sacks. 1995. "Imagistic Reasoning." *ACM Comput. Surv.* 27 (3) (September): 363–65. https://doi.org/10.1145/212094.212130.

Zargar, Cyrus. 2017. *The Polished Mirror: Storytelling and the Pursuit of Virtue in Islamic Philosophy and Sufism*. London: Oneworld.

20 RELIGION

Kathryn Lofton

An 1890 biography of US President Abraham Lincoln reports he liked to quote someone named Glenn from Indiana: "When I do good I feel good, when I do bad I feel bad, and that's my religion." In his 1936 autobiography, the first prime minister of India, Jawahral Nehru, writes: "The spectacle of what is called religion, or at any rate organized religion, in India and elsewhere, has filled me with horror and I have frequently condemned it and wished to make a clean sweep of it. Almost always it seemed to stand for blind belief and reaction, dogma and bigotry, superstition, exploitation and the preservation of vested interests." In a 2005 interview, the novelist Octavia Butler says, "religion is everywhere. There are no human societies without it, whether they acknowledge it as a religion." In 1902, the psychologist William James published a series of lectures in which he argues, "religion, therefore, as I now ask you arbitrarily to take it, shall mean for us the feelings, acts, and experiences of individual men in their solitude, so far as they apprehend themselves to stand in relation to whatever they may consider the divine." In 1999, the comedian George Carlin says, "religion easily has the greatest bullshit story ever told." In that same year, I am riding a bus while reading the first edition of *Critical Terms for Religious Studies*. A man sees its cover, and says, "I think my brother goes to mosque too much."

Every idea of religion is a reaction to it. Lincoln's anecdotal Glenn rejects complicated theology; Nehru rejects the Hindu nationalism that murdered Mahatma Gandhi; Octavia Butler rejects secularization; William James rejects the idea of religion requiring collectivity; George Carlin rejects nonsense; my bus seatmate rejects devotional excess. Or maybe Glenn did not like pastors, and Octavia Butler did not like churches, and my bus conversation partner did not like his brother. Knowing the terms of their rejection is a difficult telepathy. What is apparent is that religion's definition names and rejects in equal measure. To define religion is to comment on religion, and this comment is rarely mild. Do not mistake Glenn's position for chill.

These reactions are individual acts of criticism. Criticism conveys not only what an individual thinks but also the systems that contributed to their understanding. Capitalism is a system; so is liberalism. Within those systems are many smaller systems, like educational or banking or voting systems. Criticisms usually reflect the critic's vantage in those systems. Scholarship is a system that ritualizes critique. And the disputative attribute of religion's definition propels scholarship. "Can Religion Be Defined?" is a question posed in academic articles. "What Is Religion?" titles many academic books. Works emerging under such questions offer histories of the category's differing use. These works also often include linguistic comparisons to demonstrate that the English word *religion* has no precise analogy in Arabic (*dīn*), Chinese (*jiao*), or Sanskrit (*dharma*), underlining that religion is a term with a Latin root, a Mediterranean origin, and a Christian advantage. If you are interested in understanding the history of religion's meaning, there are strong rehearsals of this point (Feil 2000; Miles 2014; Nongbri 2013). If you want to see what elementary aspects of religion scholars have emphasized in their interpretations of religion, there are compendiums of those discussions (Bloesch and Minister 2018; Hughes and McCutcheon 2021; Kunin 2006; Olson 2003; Pals 2021). If you want to read argument for a specific definition of religion, emphasizing one or another aspect and criticizing others, many theories are available for your perusal (e.g., Jensen 2014; Long 1986; Nemec 2020; Tweed 2008). If you are interested to learn how religion is a category used to serve largely European Christian persuasive interests, there are works that make that case (Dubuisson 1998; Masuzawa 2005; Yelle 2012). In summary, there is a significant amount of work on religion's definition that exhibits how significant a critical subject it is.

This work suggests the difficulty—even, to borrow from Winnifred Sullivan's work, the impossibility—of defining religion (Sullivan 2005 and 2020). Standing before this wall of historiography might suggest that more definitional words on the subject are unhelpful, even problematic. There is a bloody history in most scholarly pursuits, but especially in the study of religion, whose record of hierarchizing sects and dividing modern from nonmodern made its terming a tool of power. Scholars of religion practice this power when they perform learnedness about the category's challenge. Someone offers a definition of religion (such as, "religion is belief in God"), and I, the scholar, nod supportively. Before long, though, a "but . . ." will creep forward. This is the start of my incursion. *But* that does not account for traditions without gods; *but* that does not recognize the importance of ritual, law, or doctrine; *but* that does not acknowledge the scholar's role; *but* that does not explain Daoism. I reiterate power by butting my way through, heaving into religion's disputative dialectic the bibliography I shape into the throne of scholarly authority.

Perhaps it is best to decide religion is an irresolvable word defined, if anything, by its multiple interpretive prospects. This is not the tack of this essay. Instead, it reviews dictionary definitions of the term and finds repeatedly two kinds of definition: those that refer to religion's transcendence ("belief in god") and those that refer to its immanence ("system of worship"). These pages commit to the second definition, the one that focuses on the form religion takes. I am interested in the social life religion as a form of criticism begets. This commitment is disputable. You could prefer your definition of religion to mention god and to mention belief. I do not prefer that because I want to spotlight how groups of people are made groups, and how then those groups establish and shift systems. Here, I am seeking to broaden the subjects that scholars of religion examine to include banking and capitalism as much in the systems that religious studies study as catechism and Catholicism. The moral legacy, though, of such pattern-recording is decidedly mixed. To define is an act of control.

Religion is a system of worship. A system is a set of connected things that operate together. Worship means to show reverence for something. You can worship alone but you can't worship without a relationship to something else—something your behaviors show you treat more highly than other things. To describe religion as a system of worship is to demand that anything called religion organizes more than one thing to be held above other things. Perceiving the persistence of this definition in vernacular discourse comprises part one of this essay. Part two discusses why such a definition prods scholars to do the critical work on religion that needs scholarly doing. To seek definition is to seek conclusion, and many readers may not prefer the conclusion drawn here. If "system of worship" dissatisfies, then argue forward an alternative. Part two suggests that the central work ahead for students of religion is to understand systems of political, economic, epistemic, and social power. In the absence of such work, the study of religion—as an undergraduate curriculum, as a space of graduate learning and research, and as a space of academic debate and publishing—has little vitality. "Whatever else religion might be," Richard Callahan, a historian of religion in the US, writes, "it is also a system of expressing, navigating, and managing power—political, economic, and even ontological power" (Callahan 2022, 352). Power is the ability to act or produce an effect, and worship ritualizes power's relation. Glenn and Nehru and Butler do not agree on what religion is, but they agree it is a fighting term. I argue that the only acceptable definitions of religion are those that acknowledge the imperative of such pugilism to religion's past and future.

I

The earliest uses of the Latin root *religio* find it applied to forces understood as malevolent and revered. Epicureans used it to index excessive concern about the gods. Early Christians applied it to boundaries of legitimate veneration. These are not light descriptions of religion. Rather, they imply that the word "religion" refers to something that moderates, systematizes, and structures relations to overwhelming potencies. Scholars of the ancient world argue also that religion is not a word used by most groups. Only one group showed it significant categorical interest. That group was the diverse gathering of persons who identified as Christian. Other cultures in the eastern Mediterranean basin did not distinguish between the worship of gods, priestly rules, and other cultural forms, between religion and "eating, sleeping, defecating, having sexual intercourse, making revolts and wars, cursing, blessing, exalting, degrading, judging, punishing, buying, selling, raiding and revolting, building bridges, collecting rents and taxes" (Barton and Boyarin 2016, 4). It is not that religion was everything as much as that prior to Christianity there was, according to the historians of religion Carlin A. Barton and Daniel Boyarin, no meaningful distinction for religion (Barton and Boyarin 2016; Boyarin 2018). There was religion if that describes worship and reverential obedience. But societies before Christianity did not categorically distinguish those worshipful behaviors from everything else. Worship was social life as social life emerged from circuitries of worship. The very oldest thing scholars observe when they observe religion is worship.

The arrival on the conversational scene of "religion" as a category increased other kinds of speech. New categories introduce new ways of talking. Religion metastasized talk parsing between behaviors, between what is religion and what is not, between what is true and what is false worshipful action (Rice 2023). Christianity instigated and instituted this comparative work with gusto, and nearby groups inevitably picked up the language game. For instance, medieval Christians used religion to indicate whether someone submitted to a monastic rule and to delineate right and wrong worship (Nongbri 2013, 28–33). Christianity emerged as a sifting procedure, one defined by insistently hierarchal observations about what religion really was. Historians of religion repeat that this aspect of Christian practice indicates its specific missionary character (Jennings 2010; Johnson 2019). And this capacity is how Christianity aligned itself so easily with the dominion of settler colonies. Christianity reframed colonial inequality as a spiritual hierarchy, offering the latter as an alibi for the former (Chidester 1996).

As Christianity carved a set of distinctions in the West between religious and not religious, including eventually an opposition between religion and the secular state, Robert Campany, a historian of Chinese religions, explains how no such analogous distinction existed in China since "the state was itself a (what we would call) religious institution founded on sacrificial rituals and a legitimating theology of the 'mandate of heaven'" (2018, 369). Campany has worked assiduously to demonstrate how religion, and analogies for religion, operate in a non-Western geographic context (2003, 2012, 2018). Other scholars of religion addressing topics related to traditions of India, China, Japan, and Tibet wrestle too with the challenge of thinking inside traditions for which religion's terminological analogy is imperfect even as there are abundant documents recording deity worship and rule systems for that reverence (Geslani 2018; Lopez 1998b; Sun 2013). One of Campany's most powerful points is to observe how in medieval China the subject of religious interest was not "gods, ghosts, demons, or the afterlife," since those were "normal elements of the cosmological furniture" in that place and time. Rather, the textual tradition he examines emphasizes how human beings grapple with encountering such figures. "What was strange was that this person, in an otherwise ordinary situation, should have 'suddenly,' as the texts very often say, encountered such a being" (Campany 2018, 361). The striking thing to record is the ability of people to recognize and name when they encountered anomalous beings. Campany suggests that for a definition of religion to include this social world it needs to reckon with not just the gods and their worship, but the relations manifest between humans and nonhuman beings.

I turn to Campany's work to raise an example of a context where "belief in god" is an inadequate definition of what religiously transpires. Returning to use of the category in Europe and the Anglophone world: John Kersey's *Dictionarium Anglo-Britannicum; or, A General English Dictionary* (1708) is one of the earliest dictionaries of the English language. In the preface, Kersey wrote that he intended the volume for the public, and, to that end, used as few words as possible to convey definitions.

> **Religion**, the Worship of a Deity, Piety, Godliness
> **Religionist**, one that professes a Religion
> **Religious**, belonging to Religion, or to a Regular Order; Devout, Godly

Two hundred years later, James Henry Murray's *A Companion Dictionary of the English Language* (1903) sought also to be a portable version of the longer *Oxford English Dictionary* (Winchester 1998). Note what remains the same and what is new.

> **re-lig'-ion** (-llj'-un), n. belief in, love of, and obedience and service to, God; any system of faith in, and worship of, some divine (or supposed divine) ruling power.
> **re-lig'-ion-ist**, n. one attached to, and a strong upholder of, a certain religious belief.
> **re-lig'-ious** (-llj'-us), adj. pious; godly; devout; god-fearing: n. a person bound by religious (esp. monastic) vows (as a monk, friar, or nun).

Comparing these two sets of definitions is something that could occupy many scholarly paragraphs and academic volumes. That work would consider whether piety and godliness are rightly defined as "belief in, love of" God; what the meaning and importance of belief is; to what extent "belonging" and "bound" are synonyms; why "system of" becomes important. Let us bracket those intriguing sidebars and say what is consistent. What remains is worship of a deity, and the possibility that strong vows connected to that worship put human beings in some order. There is a relationship between humans and gods; how that relationship is manifest can be described as "worship" or as "system," or both.

Are dictionaries the right tool for asking questions about a word's usage? I turn to dictionaries because this genre offers an index for the vernacular and, not unrelatedly, is among the essential implements of validating and democratizing knowledge. The subtitle of one 1735 dictionary is "for the Use and Improvement of Such As Are Unacquainted with Learned Languages." This draws the distinction between the learned and the unlearned, marking the unlearned as needful of improvement. Their authors write from specific historically conditioned perspectives, and authored dictionaries as pedagogical instruments meant to instruct audiences. Such instruction assumed correct and incorrect usage. The earliest English-language dictionaries also assumed a sermonic purpose for right knowledge. Thomas Dyche and William Pardon defined religion in *A New General English Dictionary* (1735) as "that awful Reverence and pure Worship that is due to the Supreme Author of all Beings called God, tho' tis very often abused and applied to the superstitious Adorations too commonly paid to Saints, Angels, &c. among the Christians and to Idols and false Gods among the Heathens, &c." John Ash defined religion in *The New and Complete Dictionary of the English Language* (1775) as "the true fear of God in the heart, a particular system of divine faith and worship." This thickening of judgmental affect in their definitions reflects their authors' Christianity: John Ash was a Baptist minister and Thomas Dyche an Anglican priest.

Again, though, buried within the Christian missiological need for comparative religions, the notion of "worship" persists, as does some idea of deity as its object. These definitions do not alter significantly in the wake of the Enlightenment, the time of purported secularization of knowledge and the emergence of human sciences. In her research on early English dictionaries, Carey McIntosh explains that dictionary authors did try to winnow the "superstitious adorations" inlaid in many English words. She gives the example of Kersey's definition of "gossamer" in 1708 as "a kind of thin Cobweb-like Vapour that hovers in the Air, and is suppos'd to rot Sheep,"' whereas Ash defines gossamer in 1775 as "the down of plants, the long white cobwebs which unusually float in the air about the time of harvest" (McIntosh 1998, 4–5). McIntosh marks Samuel Johnson's *A Dictionary of the English Language* (1755) as the apex of this Enlightenment revision, describing how his dictionary saw the total eschewal of chiromancy and magic in the definition of terms (1998, 17). However, turning to Johnson's definition of "religion" explains why McIntosh does not include this specific word in her argument. This is because religion, unlike gossamer and so many other terms the natural sciences deracinated, cannot be so easily culturally evacuated of its polemical purpose. Johnson describes religion as, first, "virtue, as founded upon reverence of God, and expectation of future rewards and punishments," and second, as "a system of divine faith and worship as opposite to others." If Johnson offered the peak effort to remove magic from the English language, he did so from the vantage of an Enlightenment organized as much by biblical Christianity as it was by any form of secular reason (Sheehan 2005). Samuel Johnson understood that gossamer did not rot the sheep, but he still expected future rewards and punishments for his virtue. Secularization has always been such a halfway covenant, representing more the addition of scientific language than the diminution of religion's power.

Tripping into discussions of the secular is an appealing if distracting sidebar. Note again that, even in Johnson's virtue-promoting definition, worship and system persist as signal constancies in the English-language defining of religion. Mark Valeri teaches how eighteenth-century Protestant observers criticized wrong connections between worship and power in the wake of global missionary experiences that allowed them to use religious criticism as a weapon in political battles against Jacobites and French Catholics (Valeri 2023). Naming what is the superior religious way appears in most definitions of religion. Consider how *Webster's Complete English Dictionary* (1886) offers a right recognition in its first definition, namely "the recognition of God as an object of worship, love, and obedience; right feelings toward God as rightly apprehended; piety." An assessment of properly right feelings will be a part of the policing ahead. Of interest here is the second definition, which takes a bit of a step back from deciding on rightness and instead says any system, *any*: "Any system of faith and worship; as, the religion of the Turks, of Hindoos, of Christians; true and false religion." Even when definitions try neutrality (*any* system), still a hierarchization appears (*true* and *false* religion). Designating who practices false religion invariably creates a population targeted for conversion to right religion (Lum 2022). It is hard to find someone defining religion in the eighteenth or nineteenth century who is not also trying to make clear whose worship is righter.

Interestingly, "system" sticks across several centuries of definitions, only to get diminished in the twentieth century when belief snuffs it out. Beginning with Murray's 1903 definition of religion as "belief in, love of, and obedience and service to, God," the language of belief is not only present, but determining in subsequent dictionary generations. Here from the 2020 edition of *The American Heritage Dictionary*, it is clear how central belief is to religion's definition (also, too, how system still makes a sidebar appearance):

a. The belief in and reverence for a supernatural power or powers, regarded as creating and governing the universe: *respect for religion*.
b. A particular variety of such belief, especially when organized into a system of doctrine and practice: *the world's many religions*.
c. A set of beliefs, values, and practices based on the teachings of a spiritual leader.

Belief strings this set of definitions. A belief in supernatural power; a variety of such belief organized into systems; a set of beliefs based on teachings. Religion is not only system but also *trust in* the system. Which is something not everybody has, or else it wouldn't need to be flagged. To have belief is special because it is not what everybody has. Trust is hard, especially so in systems of worship.

The preponderance of belief in twentieth- and twenty-first-century American definitions of religion is a subject of significant scholarly interest (Ahmed 2020; Lopez 1998a; McCrary 2021; Sullivan 2005). This work resolves with the rejection of belief as determining of religion's definition because it involves naming an individual state of mind that can only be known through the believer's utterance. Such an utterance requires the speaker's testimony to be known. Yet many systems including worship of deities make no such demand of their supplicants. Indeed, many systems include no use of the first person at all. What is the system most committed to first-person testimony? The forms of Christianity that developed in fifteenth-century Europe and were distributed, ardently and under many sectarian banners, in the missiological project of European empires. Uses of "belief" in definitions of religion indicate the powerful hold of post-Reformation theologies on contemporary religious studies. In 1995, the historian of religion Jonathan Z. Smith authored "religion, definition of," an entry in *The HarperCollins Dictionary of Religion*. For that entry, he defined religion as "a system of beliefs and practices that are relative to superhuman beings" (1995, 893). Using the word "system" with "belief," Smith here offers a definition that is half externally observable—scholars can evidence a practice—and half harder to record. Archiving belief is something scholars repeatedly seek to do through reading doctrine or diary entries, but scholarship on non-Christian systems suggest its emphasis in any definition biases efforts to catalog and compare practices of worship, since many people who participate in worship practices leave no recorded claims of conviction about that participation. They do it as a form of social participation for which the first person is precisely rendered inconsequential.

In the wake of belief's debunking as the literal Easter egg—namely, the sign of Christianity—in religion's Anglophone definition, scholars have turned to seeing how worshipful systems emerge around other subjects, including power, profit, and whiteness. Reflecting on Disney, a multinational mass media and entertainment conglomerate, as an instantiation of religion, the Marxist critic of religion and scholar of ancient Christianity William Arnal writes: "'Religion' is an artificial agglomeration of specific social behaviors, whose basis of distinction from other social behaviors is a function of the specific characteristics of modernity" (Arnal 2001, 4). This "artificial agglomeration" does not just include but is dominated by politics and economics, producing rafts of scholarship addressing how religion's "agglomeration" is one and the same as that of capitalism and the state (Arnal and McCutcheon 2012; Martin 2014; Slezkine 2017) as well as colonialism and empire (Carey 2010; Foster 2013; Hurd and Sullivan 2021; Johnson 2015; Thomas 2019). Recent work underlines how complicity with capitalism requires seeing religion's central role in the formation of race, and the resultant ideology of white supremacy (Carter 2008; Heng 2018; Hulsether 2018; Jennings 2010; Nye 2019). Arnal's laudable contribution to the study of religion is to diminish its sense of uniqueness from the social worlds it occupies, and instead to press the scholar of religion to see their job as a critic of systems that distribute and organize superhuman powers. Superhuman powers may be gods, or gods may be the systems that organize the attentions and labors of human beings.

II

Although only scholars appear in the foregoing citations, it is not only scholars who enter the disputative parry and thrust of religion's definition. It is easy to find people arguing over religion: about whether it is a Western category or a cognitive projection or social problem; whether it is individualizing or socializing; instigating of madness or enlightenment; whether it is isomorphic with colonialism, capitalism, or race; whether it is coextensive with culture, politics, or economy. The anthropologist of religion Cody Musselman calls these exchanges instances of "colloquial religion" (Musselman 2022). "If Religion is insanity, then that means more than half of the People in the World are Insane," Tweets @BesapLilly in March

2021. "Religion and spirituality is not the same," @asteriasaura replies a few minutes later. "Humans are flawed, just because the majority believe in something supernatural, doesn't make it true," @TheTweetOfRhea responds to that. "Religion is the illusion of agency, I wouldn't call it insane," someone else replies. To talk about religion is to debate it. People inside the university are no more combative than those outside its bounds. The surfeit of academic bibliography addressing religion's definitional problem becomes then another illustration of religion: whatever it does, it makes us continue to argue with one another.

Given popular interest in debating religion's meaning, it is peculiar how repeated is Jonathan Z. Smith's comment that "'religion' is not a native term; it is a term created by scholars for their intellectual purposes and therefore is theirs to define" (Smith 1998, 281). This narrowed casting for religion's definition runs at odds with the findings of the cultural history of religion that the university-appointed scholar is but one figure of many in the story of religion's naming. In the oft-cited essay where this statement appeared, Smith records how a profusion of imperialistic data about religion provided by "missionaries, colonial officials, and travelers" contributed to the production of encyclopedias, lexica, and handbooks about what religion is (1998, 275). The concluding comment ("'religion' is not a native term; it is a term created by scholars") restricted the broad territory of religion's definitional argument to a campus map. Historians, some of them inspired by Smith's research, have shown how land surveyors, shopkeepers, legislators, settlers, soldiers, enslaved persons, lawyers, doctors, protesters, and pundits are engaged in the project of naming religion in society (e.g., Burris 2002; Chidester 2014; Evans 2008; Johnson 2015; Sullivan 2014; Walker 2019; Wenger 2009 and 2017). These scholars demonstrate that the only way one could imagine that religion was invented by scholars is if that term, "scholar," means something significantly more populist than its common usage.

Religious studies enshrined Smith's expression of the scholar's determining role in the definition of religion as a shibboleth. This suggests religious studies needed this claim to power, in part to manage the din inclusion makes, in part to shore up their role as scholars relative to the broader world. Letting all definers into the kingdom of knowledge makes it harder to figure out who is expert and inexpert, teacher and student, not to mention who is religious and who a student of religion. One way to clean up the confusion is to name who is in charge and suggest that the crevasse between scholarly power and others who are not scholars is difficult to traverse. Bibliography is a sacralizing barrier: between me and the comedian George Carlin there are many differences, but the one that shores up my domain is that I convert Carlin to a data point on a definitional scatter plot. He does stand-up comedy and gets laughs; I lecture in a college classroom and, whether the students snooze or smile, I have won the ritual plot of my own reiteration as the controlling hand in whether he is in or out of that speech.

Scholars of religion cannot pretend to claim primacy over the subject of religion. More than some of their peers in the university, the student of religion exists in a social world rife with competing claims for their subject. This ardency of popular investment in religion is an opportunity and not only a problem. @BesapLilly confronts institutionalized divides between theology and religion, spirituality and religion, being religious and studying religion. The reiteration of those distinctions in the study of religion reflects a desire to create a classroom in which the work can be focused on controllable data points and delimited subjects discussing them. How, then, to do this? To think about a room where Glenn, Nehru, James, and Butler struggle alongside one another, building something together? Doing so will require, as philosopher Nancy Levene writes, a richer recognition of other people:

> I therefore agree that the attempt to pick out some special dimension of human experience and thought that is uniquely religious is doomed to fail. But I do not agree with the ordinary drift of such thinking, which holds religion to be a "second-order term" used by scholars to analyze pieces of human data, whether or not they call themselves religious. The difference could not be sharper. If the position that religion is a scholar's category holds that religion cannot be found in the world because there is nothing there to correspond to it, I hold that religion can name "everything" and thereby the fundamental challenge of human existence—to contend with or, as [Edward] Said would say, to survive distinction. Religion is inseparable from art, politics, and ethics insofar as it expresses the principle of inclusion, of the neighbor—the other that human beings struggle to recognize, stabilize, interrogate, or obfuscate. (2017, 50)

Levene presses scholars to observe critically how they hear and mishear the subjects they interpret. "Teaching religion," she writes elsewhere, "is the consciousness of confrontation and the responsibility to understand" (Levene 2020, 137). Developing such consciousness requires recognizing that interpretation necessitates struggle in its very enactment. Scholars cannot place themselves outside any subject and claim they understand. Their work, the work of understanding, places them in the fray, joining the fight and explaining what they are doing there, and listening to what replies accede and resist their findings.

I am talking to a friend, and he reports that many of his teaching evaluations for his "Introduction to the Study of Religion" say the same thing. "I like the teacher," they repeat, "but I didn't learn anything about religion." We discuss what is we agree a mixed pedagogical result. We hypothesize that the students imagined they would get more analysis of worship in the class and less discussion of secularism. They imagined more gods and less systems. The students and the teacher entered the classroom as equal inheritors of a definitional regime in which religion is understood to be available in a variety pack and in which the way religion is received is as a form of systematic life. The problem is not that students and faculty disagree about what religion is, but that they cannot see the other through the systems that brought them to their role: the forms of discipline that produce "student" and "teacher" as figures of purported voluntary copresence in a single room. Nothing in that room, including their roles, is simply voluntary, or neatly free.

Although it seemed the teacher pressed more into systems while the students desired more about worship, they are inextricable from one another. Students and teachers exist, too, in systems that hierarchize value and make difficult, but not impossible, a shared responsibility to recognize the other in their difference. The challenge of studying religion is not its definition, but the evaluation of the forms of relation it propounds. It is difficult to stand in hierarchy and see its operation. Students, comedians, poets, presidents, and peddlers are in this work, evaluating whether the systems they occupy rightly serve their preferred highest powers. Understanding what systematic networks of relation, obligation, and power emerge from worshipful attention is something every disputation of religion—that is, its definition—does. Debates about religion exist in scholarly footnotes; they also flood the streets. Repeatedly and loudly, the world clamors for answers: What is that thing, the thing people call religion? And what is it good for, if not the social good? Some scholars understand their role-specific obligation as requiring them to answer the first question and stand as observers to how others answer the second. Yet defining a religion involves naming what is worshipped, which is, for those worshipping, something treated as if it is a higher good than something else. Let us get to work, understanding both questions and subjects as immanent for the study of religion and the societies that are subject to its critique.

Suggested Readings

Arnal, William. 2001. “The Segregation of Social Desire: ‘Religion’ and Disney World.” *Journal of the American Academy of Religion* 69 (1).

Chidester, David. 1996. “The Church of Baseball, the Fetish of Coca-Cola, and the Potlatch of Rock ’n’ Roll: Theoretical Models for the Study of Religion in American Popular Culture.” *Journal of the American Academy of Religion* 64 (4).

Curts, Kati. 2015. “Temples and Turnpikes in ‘The World of Tomorrow’: Religious Assemblage and Automobility at the 1939 New York World’s Fair.” *Journal of the American Academy of Religion* 83 (3).

Greene-Hayes, Ahmad. 2023. “Hair, Roots, and Crystal Balls: Archival Viscerality, Black Conjuring Traditions, and the Study of American Religions.” *Journal of the American Academy of Religion* 91 (4).

Levene, Nancy. 2020. “The Religion of Confrontation: Concepts, Violence, and Scholarship.” *Harvard Theological Review*.

Weisenfeld, Judith. 2020. “The House We Live In: Religio-Racial Theories and the Study of Religion.” *Journal of the American Academy of Religion* 88 (2).

References

Ahmed, Arif. 2020. “Belief and Religious ‘Belief.’” *Religious Studies* 56 (1).

Arnal, William. 2001. “The Segregation of Social Desire: ‘Religion’ and Disney World.” *Journal of the American Academy of Religion* 69 (1).

Arnal, William, and Russell T. McCutcheon. 2012. *The Sacred Is the Profane: The Political Nature of “Religion.”* New York: Oxford University Press.

Barton, Carlin A., and Daniel Boyarin. 2016. *Imagine No Religion: How Modern Abstractions Hide Ancient Realities*. Bronx, NY: Fordham University Press.

Bloesch, Sarah, and Meredith Minister, eds. 2018. *Cultural Approaches to Studying Religion: An Introduction to Theories and Methods*. London: Bloomsbury Academic.

Boyarin, Daniel. 2018. *Judaism: The Genealogy of a Modern Notion*. New Brunswick: Rutgers University Press.

Burris, John P. 2002. *Exhibiting Religion: Colonialism and Spectacle at International Expositions, 1851–1893*. Charlottesville: University of Virginia Press.

Callahan, Richard J. 2022. “Wobbly Religion: Tactical Formations of Religious Idioms and Space in the Industrial Capitalist City.” *Journal of the American Academy of Religion* 90 (2).

Campany, Robert Ford. 2003. "On the Very Idea of Religions (In the Modern West and in Early Medieval China)." *History of Religions* 42 (4).

Campany, Robert Ford. 2012. "Religious Repertoires and Contestation: A Case Study Based on Buddhist Miracle Tales." *History of Religions* 52 (2).

Campany, Robert Ford. 2018. "'Religious' as a Category: A Comparative Case Study." *Numen* 65.

Carey, Hilary. 2010. *God's Empire: Religion and Colonialism in the British World, c. 1801–1908*. Cambridge: Cambridge University Press.

Carter, J. Kameron. 2008. *Race: A Theological Account*. New York: Oxford University Press.

Chidester, David. 1996. *Savage Systems: Colonialism and Comparative Religion in Southern Africa*. Charlottesville: University Press of Virginia.

Chidester, David. 2014. *Empire of Religion: Imperialism and Comparative Religion*. Chicago: University of Chicago Press.

Dubuisson, Daniel. 1998. *The Western Construction of Religion: Myths, Knowledge, and Ideology*. Baltimore: Johns Hopkins University Press.

Evans, Curtis J. 2008. *The Burden of Black Religion*. New York: Oxford University Press.

Feil, Ernst, ed. 2000. *On the Concept of Religion*. Albany: State University of New York.

Foster, Elizabeth A. 2013. *Faith in Empire: Religion, Politics, and Colonial Rule in French Senegal, 1880–1940*. Palo Alto: Stanford University Press.

Geslani, Marko. 2018. *Rites of the God-King: Santi and Ritual Change in Early Hinduism*. New York: Oxford University Press.

Heng, Geraldine. 2018. *The Invention of Race in the European Middle Ages*. Cambridge, MA: Cambridge University Press.

Hughes, Aaron W., and Russell T. McCutcheon, eds. 2021. *What Is Religion? Debating the Academic Study of Religion*. New York: Oxford University Press.

Hulsether, Lucia. 2018. "The Grammar of Racism: Religious Pluralism and the Birth of the Interdisciplines." *Journal of the American Academy of Religion* 86 (10).

Hurd, Elizabeth Shakman, and Winnifred Faller Sullivan, eds. 2021. *At Home and Abroad: The Politics of American Religion*. New York: Columbia University Press.

Jennings, Willie. 2010. *The Christian Imagination: Theology and the Origins of Race*. New Haven: Yale University Press.

Jensen, Jeppe Sinding. 2014. *What Is Religion?* Oxford: Routledge.

Johnson, Sylvester. 2015. *African American Religions, 1500–2000: Colonialism, Democracy, and Freedom*. Cambridge: Cambridge University Press.

Johnson, Sylvester. 2019. "Religions in All Ages and Places: Discerning Colonialism with Jonathan Z. Smith." *Journal of the American Academy of Religion* 87 (1).

Kunin, Seth D. 2006. *Theories of Religion: A Reader*. New Brunswick: Rutgers University Press.

Levene, Nancy. 2017. *Powers of Distinction: On Religion and Modernity*. Chicago: University of Chicago Press.

Levene, Nancy. 2020. "The Religion of Confrontation: Concepts, Violence, and Scholarship." *Harvard Theological Review* 113 (1).

Long, Charles H. 1986. *Significations: Signs, Symbols, and Images in the Interpretation of Religion*. Philadelphia: Fortress Press.

Lopez, Donald S., Jr. 1998a. "Belief." In *Critical Terms for Religious Studies*. Chicago: University of Chicago Press.

Lopez, Donald S., Jr. 1998b. *Prisoners of Shangri-La: Tibetan Buddhism and the West*. Chicago: University of Chicago Press.

Lum, Kathryn Gin. 2022. *Heathen: Religion and Race in American History*. Cambridge: Harvard University Press.

Martin, Craig. 2014. *Capitalizing Religion: Ideology and the Opiate of the Bourgeoisie*. New York: Bloomsbury.

Masuzawa, Tomoko. 2005. *The Invention of World Religions: Or, How European Universalism Was Preserved in the Language of Pluralism*. Chicago: University of Chicago Press.

McCrary, Charlie. 2021. *Sincerely Held: American Religion, Secularism, and Belief*. Chicago: University of Chicago Press.

McIntosh, Carey. 1998. "Eighteenth-Century English Dictionaries and the Enlightenment." *The Yearbook of English Studies* 28.

Miles, Jack. 2014. "General Introduction." In *The Norton Anthology of World Religions*, vol. 1. New York: W.W. Norton.

Musselman, Cody. 2022. "Embodying the Brand: Fitness and Colloquial Religion in the United States." PhD diss., Yale University.

Nemec, John. 2020. "Toward a Volitional Definition of Religion." *Journal of the American Academy of Religion* 88 (3).

Nongbri, Brent. 2013. *Before Religion: A History of a Modern Concept*. New Haven: Yale University Press.

Nye, Malory. 2019. "Race and Religion: Postcolonial Formations of Power and Whiteness." *Method & Theory in the Study of Religion* 31 (3).

Olson, Carl. 2003. *Theory and Method in the Study of Religion: A Selection of Critical Readings*. Belmont, CA: Thomson/Wadsworth.

Pals, Daniel. 2021. *Ten Theories of Religion*. New York: Oxford University Press.

Rice, Carl Ross. 2023. "*Religio Licita*: Empire, Religion, and Civic Subjects, 250–450 CE." PhD diss., Yale University.

Rubenstein, Mary-Jane. 2012. "The Twilight of the 'Doxai': Or, How to Philosophize with a Whac-A-Mole™ Mallet." *Method & Theory in the Study of Religion* 24 (1).

Sheehan, Jonathan. 2005. *The Enlightenment Bible: Translation, Scholarship, Culture*. Princeton: Princeton University Press.

Slezkine, Yuri. 2017. *The House of Government: A Saga of the Russian Revolution*. Princeton: Princeton University Press.

Smith, Jonathan Z., ed. 1995. *The HarperCollins Dictionary of Religion*. New York: HarperCollins.

Smith, Jonathan Z. 1998. "Religion, Religions, Religious." In *Critical Terms for Religious Studies*, edited by Mark C. Taylor. Chicago: University of Chicago Press. Reprinted in 2004 in Jonathan Z. Smith, *Relating Religion: Essays in the Study of Religion*. Chicago: University of Chicago Press. Chicago: University of Chicago Press.

Sullivan, Winnifred Fallers. 2005. *The Impossibility of Religious Freedom*. Princeton: Princeton University Press.

Sullivan, Winnifred Fallers. 2014. *A Ministry of Presence: Chaplaincy, Spiritual Care, and the Law*. Chicago: University of Chicago Press.

Sullivan, Winnifred Fallers. 2020. *Church State Corporation: Construing Religion in US Law*. Chicago: University of Chicago Press.

Sun, Anna. 2013. *Confucianism as a World Religion: Contested Histories and Contemporary Realities*. Princeton: Princeton University Press.

Thomas, Jolyon. 2019. *Faking Liberties: Religious Freedom in American-Occupied Japan*. Chicago; University of Chicago Press.

Tweed, Thomas A. 2008. *Crossing and Dwelling: A Theory of Religion*. Cambridge: Harvard University Press.

Valeri, Mark. 2023. *The Opening of the Protestant Mind: How English-Speaking Protestants Embraced Religious Liberty*. New York: Oxford University Press.

Walker, David. 2019. *Railroading Religion: Mormons, Tourists, and the Corporate Spirit of the West*. Chapel Hill: University of North Carolina Press.

Wenger, Tisa. 2009. *We Have a Religion: The 1920s Pueblo Indian Dance Controversy and American Religious Freedom*. Chapel Hill: University of North Carolina Press.

Wenger, Tisa. 2017. *Religious Freedom: The Contested History of an American Ideal*. Chapel Hill: University of North Carolina Press.

Winchester, Simon. 1998. *The Professor and the Madman: A Tale of Murder, Insanity, and the Making of the Oxford English Dictionary*. New York: HarperCollins Publishers.

Yelle, Robert A. 2012. *The Language of Disenchantment: Protestant Literalism and Colonial Discourse in British India*. New York: Oxford University Press.

21 SEX

Benjamin H. Dunning

In the Book of Romans in the Christian New Testament, the Apostle Paul famously offers the following diagnosis of sexual degeneracy: "For this reason God gave them up to degrading passions. Their women exchanged natural intercourse for unnatural, and in the same way also the men, giving up natural intercourse with women, were consumed with passion for one another. Men committed shameless acts with men and received in their own persons the due penalty for their error" (Romans 1:26–27, NRSV). While this text has functioned in modern intra-Christian debate as the locus classicus for the problem of "the Bible and homosexuality," biblical scholars have compellingly cast the issue in a different light. Summarizing some of the best scholarship on the passage, Stephen Moore offers a particularly incisive (if seemingly confounding) appraisal: "the Paul of Romans 1:26–27 is neither *anti-gay* nor *pro-gay*—nor is he *neutral*—on the issue of homosexual sex." How can this be? The point, as Moore goes on to elaborate, is not simply to offer an infuriating paradox. Rather, he explains, "the logics of sexuality that underpin Romans 1:26–27, on the one hand, and modern logics of sexuality, on the other, are so drastically different as to preclude any paraphrase of this incalculably influential passage that would assimilate it to the modern concept of homosexuality" (2001, 134–35, emphasis original, with reference to Martin 1995b).

In this way, the passage—while clearly about sex in multiple senses of the term—serves up more questions than answers. To specify just a few: What kind of God is this who is giving people over to degrading passions? What does that mean? And what responsibility does God bear, if any, for what unfolds? What exactly are degrading passions? What do "natural" and "unnatural" mean here? Do the unnatural actions that the women engage in necessarily have anything to do with homoeroticism? (Note that the passage never actually specifies this; one has to reason backward by way of analogy with the discussion of men that follows.) And what is the precise purview of "the shameless acts" that men commit with other men? Is Paul talking about the entire range of possible erotic acts that two or more male bodies could engage in together? Or are there particular acts in view? Even more fundamentally, what defines a "man" and/or a "woman" in this specific context? Can we assume that these specifiers of "sex" are simply transhistorical givens, each an uncomplicated marker of bodily anatomy? Or, similar to other formulations in the passage that are more immediately opaque, do these seemingly self-evident categories also need to be thoroughly historicized in terms of both the culturally specific ideological codes of the Roman imperial world in which Paul wrote and the distinctive theological/religious logics that he advanced?

On the one hand, as Moore and numerous other scholars have shown, ancient Roman ideas about "sex" (whether the sense in view is that of bodily anatomy or erotic acts) were substantially different from modern Western ones, the former predicated on concerns about status, gender, penetration, and active versus passive roles, with "adult male citizens, defined as impenetrable, [standing] atop a pyramid of 'potentially penetrable' bodies of lower status" (Dunning 2019c, 574, citing Walters 1997, 41). Thus, drawing direct lines of unbroken continuity to the present proves problematic; and sex in Roman antiquity emerges as a question to be probed rather than a given to be assumed. On the other hand, these ancient ways of thinking never disappear entirely; and they remain, in some complicated way, an irreducible part of our inheritance in Western modernity. Furthermore, religion has been a pivotal player in the story of how this legacy was passed down, transformed, and/or contested through time.

In her magisterial *Love Between Women: Early Christian Responses to Female Homoeroticism* (1996), Bernadette Brooten offers a telling historical anecdote that vividly illustrates this latter point. In 1811 in Edinburgh, Scotland, two British schoolteachers named Miss Marianne Woods and Miss Jane Pirie were accused of engaging in a sexual relationship. The accusation was based on the testimony of a schoolgirl named Jane Cumming who claimed to have seen the teachers having sex. Miss Woods and Miss Pirie vehemently denied the accusation and sued for libel. And one of their lawyer's principal arguments was to question whether "sexual relations between women *are even possible*" (Brooten 1996, 189, emphasis added). As the case unfolded along these lines, Romans 1:26 figured prominently:

"women exchanged natural intercourse for unnatural." This text was offered by the opposing side, along with other ancient texts from Greece and Rome referencing female-female erotic relations, as evidence that women could indeed have sex with one another. But the schoolteachers' lawyer pointed out that, while many ancient texts do make such references, "these always included the use of a penetrating object. Since the schoolgirl had never alleged the use of an artificial instrument, then no sexual act could have taken place" (1996, 189). At play in this argument is the modern inheritance of a fundamental—and highly patriarchal—ancient assumption, witnessed throughout elite Greek and Roman literary sources, that sex acts are basically all about men, penetration, and penises (or a stand-in for the latter). Once such an assumption is operative, the idea of female-female sex without an artificial penetrating object becomes a bit of a quandary. As Brooten notes, "the focus on an artificial instrument is both ancient and modern. Male lawyers, judges, poets, and theologians wonder again and again: 'What could women ever possibly do together without one?'" (190). And what about Romans 1:26? The lawyer for Woods and Pirie argued that, since no artificial object is mentioned, the verse must refer not to sex acts between two women but to "unnatural intercourse" (i.e., anal sex) between *a man* and a woman. The House of Lords concurred, and "the schoolteachers won their case on the grounds that sexual contact between two women . . . was impossible" (189).[1]

I begin with this example of a contentious biblical passage and its fraught afterlife precisely because of the difficult yet generative questions, both historical and theoretical, that it raises (even as exploring answers to these questions with respect to this specific example falls beyond the scope of my purposes here; for further discussion, see Dunning 2019c). What we encounter in these verses from Romans is neither the absolute alterity of another time or culture nor a "consoling play of recognitions" from the standpoint of the present (Foucault 1984, 88), but rather an interplay of resemblance and difference, continuity and rupture. And yet, their status as authoritative Christian scripture—admittedly, an authority that functions variably across different branches and periods of Christianity—also works to efface or obscure this interplay, putatively collapsing historical

1. This argument also included specifically racialized and colonialist dimensions that I am not able to take up here (the primary witness in the case was a native of South Asia, a fact upon which the lawyer for Woods and Pirie elaborated to polemical ends); see discussion and references in Brooten 1996, 189–90.

distance. They thus stand as a case in point for how the study of religion complicates the periodization of sex, gender, and sexuality in ways that require fine-grained historical analysis. Furthermore, the case of Miss Woods and Miss Pirie epitomizes the dynamic role that religious logics can play in the sphere of practice (whether the practice in view is interpreting a sacred text or engaging in an erotic act) and in the constitution of sexed bodies. In this way, Romans 1:26–27 encapsulates and showcases a set of ambiguities and possibilities that are entailed in the larger topic of this essay: the intersection of sex and religion.

Terminology, Concepts, Categories

Any critical study of the term "sex" must contend not only with the term itself but with an entire complex of related terms, concepts, and categories, including "gender," "sexuality," and "sexual difference" (all of which have some bearing, whether implicit or explicit, on the example just discussed). In his 1998 essay, "Gender," in the first edition of *Critical Terms in Religious Studies*, Daniel Boyarin invokes the term "sex," first and foremost, in the sense of a biological dimorphism that characterizes bodies, female and male. Toril Moi summarizes the qualities that have been attributed to this anatomical/physiological sense of binary sex in much discussion of the twentieth century: "Considered as an essence, sex becomes immobile, stable, coherent, fixed, prediscursive, natural, and ahistorical: the mere surface on which the script of gender is written" (2005, 4). Here Moi references the sex/gender distinction, wherein "gender" serves to designate the social and cultural norms that shape interpretations of biology (i.e., "sex"), assigning meaning to binary differences between bodies in historically specific ways. This distinction was a powerful conceptual tool mobilized by second-wave feminists in the 1970s and following. As Moi notes, "the feminists who first appropriated the sex/gender distinction for their own political purposes were looking for a strong defense against biological determinism, and in many cases the sex/gender distinction delivered precisely that" (5). What the distinction attempted to do was to pry apart that which was putatively fixed and natural about the body (its biology) from that which was cultural (the meanings ascribed to that biology) so that the latter could then ostensibly be changed. (For the classic articulation of the sex/gender distinction, see Rubin 1975; for a concise overview of the complex history of the term "gender" and its uptake within feminist theory, see Dunning 2019a.)

In the present volume's previous edition, Boyarin's essay assumes this background but then enters the discussion at a moment when the theoretical viability of the sex/gender distinction had fallen into crisis. Referencing with tongue-in-cheek nostalgia a time when the distinction was still tenable, he observes that "the task of writing [this] entry would have been much simpler in those halcyon days, as religion is clearly for many if not most cultures one of the primary systems for the construction of gendered roles as well as for the interpellation of sexed subjects into those gendered roles. Things are not quite as simple anymore, however, and the distinction between 'sex' and 'gender' is no longer as clear" (1998, 117). Here Boyarin has in view the interventions of feminist theorists such as Monique Wittig and Judith Butler—and most especially Butler's now well-known argument that bodily sex is not an essence or natural given but is instead established and secured through the apparatus of gender, a process of historical sedimentation whereby the repeated performance of gendered norms in everyday life works to produce the effect of a prediscursive sexed body (Butler 1990, 11). In this way, Butler argues, bodily sex should be seen as "an ideal construct which is forcibly materialized through time. It is not a simple fact or static condition of a body, but a process whereby regulatory norms materialize 'sex' and achieve this materialization through a forcible reiteration of those norms" (1993, 2). Boyarin builds on this argument to pose the question, "has there ever been in history a culture within which gender did not operate in this way to produce so-called natural sex?" He then proceeds to argue that "early Christianity is just such a culture," staging a comparative conversation between early Christianity's pursuit of gender transcendence and rabbinic Judaism's commitment to "a completely naturalized 'sex'" (1998, 118).[2] Contending that each of these positions seems inevitably to end up in a problematic place (transcendence relies on denigration of the body and leads to an androgynous "neutral" that is always already masculine; valuing sexual particularity results in the trap of biological determinism for women), Boyarin ultimately argues that we need to maintain "[both] poles of this dialectic [i.e., the possibilities afforded by the transcendence of gender and the commitment to the importance of embodiment as sexed] . . . in tension and in suspension such that neither of them can overwhelm the other. . . . Even in the absence of the

2. For my appreciative critique of Boyarin's position with respect to the Christian half of this equation—and especially the complexity of early Christian theologies of sexual difference—see Dunning 2011.

synthesis, the thesis and antithesis can perhaps protect us each from the excesses of the other" (133). As for the term "sex," it would seem to be subsumed under the hierarchical dictates of gender, whether that sex is the site of bodily difference to be overcome eschatologically (but at the price of reinstating masculinism via the gendered valuation of mind over body) or the site of an irreducible truth about the human subject (but at the price of ontologizing gender hierarchy). In this way, to follow Butler's famous formulation, "perhaps [sex] was always already gender" (1990, 10–11).

But matters are more complicated still. In a 1994 article, Butler tracks the shifting senses of the term "sex" and the irreducible interrelation of those senses as they operate to police the disciplinary boundary between feminism and lesbian and gay studies—and to demarcate the object of study "proper" to each. One of these senses is that which has already been discussed above—sex as "identity and attribute," i.e., female or male; and sex in this sense has sometimes been treated as the proper object of feminist inquiry (one of multiple proprietary claims that Butler critiques). Another sense of the term is that of "sex" as erotic desire and action, this one putatively belonging to lesbian and gay studies (1994, 2). Within the latter domain, often referred to by the shorthand of "sex and sexuality," one must consider the well-established claim, as argued by Michel Foucault, that sex in this sense does in fact have a history. Along these lines—and most pointedly—Foucault queries the very unity of sex (here understood as sex acts) as a category: "the notion of 'sex' made it possible to group together, in an artificial unity, anatomical elements, biological functions, conducts, sensations, and pleasures, and it enabled one to make use of this fictitious unity as a causal principle, an omnipresent meaning, a secret to be discovered everywhere: sex was thus able to function as a unique signifier and as a universal signified" (Foucault 1978, 154). Throwing the givenness of "sex" qua sex acts into question, then, is a crucial piece in producing a third (and overarching) sense of the term, what Butler calls "the Foucaultian sense of 'sex' as a regime of identity or a fictional ideal by which sex as anatomy, sensation, acts, and practice are arbitrarily unified" (Butler 1994, 2). And while deeply appreciative of and indebted to Foucault's insights, Butler also articulates numerous concerns with respect to the ways in which this broad Foucauldian notion of sex can be used to take up and include "sex" as identity and attribute (that is, sex as conflated with gender) yet simultaneously elide its distinctive significance, thereby underwriting, whether unwittingly or not, the supersession of feminism by lesbian and gay studies.

While Butler's expressed concern is a relatively focused one (namely, the disciplinary politics and boundaries of feminism/women's studies and lesbian and gay studies), the substantive issues that she raises on this score are decidedly interdisciplinary in their scope and reach—and thus deeply relevant to a critical interrogation of the term "sex" in the study of religion. One of these is the tendency of "sex" in the broad Foucauldian sense—i.e., sex as a comprehensive unity or coherent ideal—to cover over the distinctive differences of sexed embodiment in its multiple forms. Returning to my opening example, it is precisely this tendency that underwrites readings of Romans 1:26–27 that treat the text as being simply "about sex" in a seemingly self-evident way (and then leave it at that) rather than interrogating the many complex and culturally particular specificities that come together to prop up the appearance of a coherent, unified, and taken-for-granted domain.

On the theoretical level, one way that Butler responds to this tendency is to invoke an alternative concept drawn from psychoanalytic theory—sexual difference—as a way of refusing or throwing into question the terms of the sex/gender distinction described above (Butler 1994, 3). Julia Kristeva offers the following definition of the term: "Sexual difference—which is at once biological, physiological, and relative to reproduction—is translated by and translates a difference in the relationship of subjects to the symbolic contract: a difference, then, in the relationship to power, language, and meaning" (1981, 21). What is at stake here is a theoretical frame that allows for the interplay between the differences of bodies, the psychic representation of those differences, and the meanings assigned to them within diverse cultural imaginaries in ways that exceed or simply do not fit the dualistic and somewhat inflexible parameters of the sex/gender distinction (see further discussion of psychoanalysis and the study of religion below). Butler points out that "a feminist analysis that takes sexual difference as a point of departure tends to ask how it is that masculine and feminine are constituted differentially . . . [whereas] the analysis of gender, on the other hand, tends toward a sociologism [i.e., taking masculine and feminine as simply given, sociologically speaking], neglecting the symbolic or psychoanalytic account by which masculine and feminine are established in language prior to any given social configuration" (1994, 18). But this does not mean that we ought simply to retire the terminology of sex and gender and replace it with that of sexual difference. On this point, Amy Hollywood offers the important caveat that to understand the full complexity of the interplay in question, we continue to need an analytic vocabulary for verbalizing the inevitable gaps between anatomically distinct bodies (even if those distinctions are always mediated through cultural frames) and the ideologies that bear upon those bodies (2002, 284n42). Thus, the methodological significance of these terminological debates in feminist theory for subsequent work in the humanities and social sciences is twofold: (1) it is important to resist the seductive pull of "sex" in the broad Foucauldian sense as a unifying and all-encompassing category, at least insofar as it works to assimilate, erase, or refuse the questions sexual difference poses—that is, as Butler argues in a later essay, "the permanent difficulty of determining where the biological, the psychic, the discursive, the social begin and end" (2004, 185); (2) our inquiries into the constitution of sexed bodies, erotic desires, and gendered and sexualized practices in various cultural contexts, be they present or past, should never ignore the complex and historically specific ways these formations take place in relation to signification/language and the field of power (see, e.g., the interpretive intricacies of the British schoolteachers anecdote as a case in point).

A second issue is the degree to which disciplinary formations that artificially separate "sex" as gender from "sex" as sexuality have the effect of minimizing or sidelining the consideration of race and class as constitutive aspects of sex in all of its senses. Butler asserts unequivocally that "the analysis of racialization and class is at least equally important in the thinking of sexuality as either gender or homosexuality, and these last two are not separable from more complex and complicitous formations of power" (1994, 21). This assertion tracks along lines similar to numerous other interventions that have led to an increased focus on intersectionality in both feminist and queer studies (for classic formulations, see Combahee River Collective 1982; Crenshaw 1991; Collins 2000; for important critical perspectives, see Puar 2007 and 2012; Nash 2019). Yet with respect specifically to the complexities of the term "sex," we might put a finer point on the need to attend to what Sharon Patricia Holland calls "the *everyday* system of terror and pleasure that in varying proportions makes race so useful a category of difference" and especially the sexed, gendered, and eroticized dimensions of "the psychic life of racism" as it has operated historically in a range of cultural contexts and continues to operate today (2012, 6–7, emphasis original).

Third, there is a question about which groups of "erotic dissidents" (Rubin 2003, 156) count as sexual minorities, and whether the purview of the term "queer" can or should be limited in this respect. Here, what Butler calls "the constitutive ambiguity of 'sex'" comes into play (1994, 6; see also Sedgwick 1990, 27–35), insofar as transgender, nonbinary, and intersex identities—none of which could be considered "sexualities," strictly speaking, even if they are often grouped this way in colloquial usage—certainly fall within the parameters in question (Halberstam 2018; Fausto-Sterling 2020). Less clear, as Cathy Cohen has argued in an important critique, is how far such coalitional thinking might expand to interrogate nonnormative varieties of *heterosexuality* and thus include, for example, "women—in particular women of color—on welfare, who may fit into the category of heterosexual, but whose sexual choices are not perceived as normal, moral, or worthy of state support" (1997, 442). The question of whether, how, and/or to what degree the term "queer"—which has come to signify "an open mesh of possibilities, gaps, overlaps, dissonances and resonances, lapses and excesses of meaning" (Sedgwick 1993, 8) but in a sometimes fraught and not entirely straightforward relationship to "sex"—might be mobilized here for both analytic and political purposes remains an open one (Butler 1994, 11).

Sex and the Study of Religion

So where does the study of religion intersect with this conversation and what might it bring to the table? First, and as noted previously, the study of religious history complicates the periodizations that inform modern genealogies of sex and thus can contribute to a more nuanced and historically accurate account of how we have gotten to where we are. Modern Western modes of knowing, classifying, and disciplining sexed and desiring bodies (an apparatus that terms like "sex," "gender," "sexuality," and "sexual difference" attempt to capture) come from somewhere; and the history of that somewhere predates Foucault's nineteenth century or the Enlightenment or other benchmarks typically used to delineate the distinctiveness of sex and the sexual in modernity. Within the Western intellectual tradition, this is a history that is tied up with religion—in particular Christianity, Judaism, and (to a lesser degree) Islam. More specifically, from antiquity to the Middle Ages, theological articulations of sex drew on a common set of resources, growing out of diverse Greco-Roman medical and philosophical traditions. Important representatives of these traditions include the medical literature of Galen, Soranus, and the Hippocratic corpus, as well as the natural philosophies of Aristotle, Plato, and the Stoics. Here pre-modern thinkers discovered ancient debates about the human condition, ranging from the basic mechanics of the body to the relationship of the body and the soul, that proved useful for their own projects in what we could call religious or theological anthropology. Selective reading of these materials together with key scriptural texts (such as the creation narrative in Genesis or, in a Christian context, the Apostle Paul's comments on marriage and sexual continence in 1 Corinthians—and, of course, his scathing denunciations in Romans 1 already discussed) served as a platform upon which to make arguments concerning sexual practices or to articulate various constructions of sex, gender, and sexual desire. In short, along with scripture (however defined), ancient medical and philosophical discourses were the tools with which pre-modern religious thinkers formulated, promoted, and contested different conceptions of sex and their attendant implications. To restate the point of this essay's opening example in broader perspective: scholars of pre-modern Christianity and Judaism have done essential work—even as more remains to be done—in illuminating both the remarkable amount of diversity that characterized these projects and the sheer extent of their historical distance from the contemporary world, thereby rendering problematic any easy conflation between ancient configurations of the sexual and our own (see, as representative, Brown 1988; Boyarin 1993; Martin 1995a; Brooten 1996; Martin 2006). But equally important to the work of genealogy is the question of inheritance, a complex interplay of both historical difference and continuity—here carried largely, but not entirely, by way of Christian theology—that continues to haunt our received sexual categories in the present (see Jordan 1997; Dunning 2011; Marchal 2011).

Second, there is a need to take seriously in this discussion the *practices* of religion—not only formal rituals but also the work, both individual and communal, of interpreting sacred texts and forming everyday ways of being—in their role as constitutive of sexed identities broadly conceived, that is, embodied subjectivities that are religiously inflected. What I have in view here is the kind of historical sensitivity, cross-cultural awareness, and de-centering conceptual leverage that careful comparative work in the study of religion can provide. Indeed, it is worth pausing over the force and challenge of Eve Sedgwick's seemingly obvious first axiom in *Epistemology of the Closet*, "people are different from each other"; thus, "identical genital acts mean very different things to different people" and some "experience their sexuality as deeply embedded in a matrix of gender meanings and gender differentials," while others do not (1990, 22, 25–26). Sedgwick points out that the standard critical toolkit available for probing these differentials consists of "a tiny number of inconceivably coarse axes of categorization" such that "even people who share all or most of our own positionings along these crude axes may still be different enough from us, and from each other, to seem like all but different species" (22). And this remains basically as true today as it was when Sedgwick wrote in 1990. Here specifically religious logics (of practice, self-formation, communal understanding, etc.) that undergird and animate sexed, gendered, and sexualized ways of being in the world are a crucial factor that requires painstaking critical analysis, yet all too often can remain more or less illegible within the standard parameters of categorization to which Sedgwick points. Exemplary for the way in which it takes up this project is Saba Mahmood's *Politics of Piety* (2005), a now classic ethnography of the women's mosque movement within the context of the Islamic Revival in Cairo, Egypt. Seeking to denaturalize Western liberal presuppositions about sex, gender, and agency in order to make sense of "modes of actions indebted to other reasons and histories," Mahmood explores the question "how do we analyze operations of power that construct different kinds of bodies, knowledges, and subjectivities whose trajectories do not follow the entelechy of liberatory politics?" (14). In this context, then, the study of religion works to parochialize assumptions about the question of "sex"—and, to put a finer point on it, "about the constitutive relationship between action and embodiment, resistance and agency, self and authority" (38)—in ways that push back on easily presumed certainties of much Western scholarship.

Third, religious studies (and also theology) may have much to contribute to the project of complicating and opening up the category of the "queer"—that is, in Sedgwick's apt phrase, "to pluralize and specify it" (1993, 25). This means, first of all, as Melissa Wilcox describes, "paying close attention to the dynamics of gender and sexuality that religions hide in plain sight, and . . . examining the roles of religion in both inscribing and challenging heteronormativity and dualistic conceptions of gender" (2006, 93; for a current appraisal of the state of the field in this respect, see Wilcox 2021; for a range of suggestive examples, see Lofton 2008; Beliso-De Jesús 2015; Fuhrmann 2016; Tonstad 2016; Watts Belser 2016; Crawley 2017; Strongman 2019). But it also means pushing the boundaries of what constitutes the queer, as in Carolyn Dinshaw's work on medieval Christian writers, in which queerness functions by way of "contiguity and displacement; like metonymy as distinct from metaphor, queerness knocks signifiers loose, ungrounding bodies, making them strange" (1999, 151). Hollywood notes that this strategy both sidesteps the fraught historical question of whether it is possible to do lesbian and gay history prior to modernity and also allows Dinshaw "to include within the category of the queer a woman like Margery Kempe, whose sexual imagery remained resolutely heteronormative, even as her actions often worked against the norm" (Hollywood 2016, 164). As noted above, deploying the category of queer in ways that exceed the explicitly sexual is a contested move (see, e.g., Bersani 1995, 2). But this is a debate in which the study of religious subjectivities ought to play an important role.

Sex, Religion, and Psychoanalysis

Throughout the foregoing discussion, psychoanalytic concepts, questions, and modes of argument have been consistently in the background (or occasionally the foreground), whether the topic in question has been terminology, intersectionality, genealogy and inheritance, bodily practices, or the boundaries of the queer. In conclusion, then, I want to reflect briefly on the place of sex (in all of its interrelated definitions) at the intersection of psychoanalysis and religion. The study of religion has historically had an ambivalent and often conflicted relationship with psychoanalysis and the multifaceted claims, perspectives, and tools of psychoanalytic theory. Clayton Crockett observes that while "psychoanalytic theory is not marginalized in literary or cultural theory . . . it has not had as much influence on religious theorists, including those who study philosophers strongly influenced by Freud and Lacan" (2007, 18)—so, for example, appropriations of Butler or Derrida within religious studies that pass over these thinkers' deep critical engagement with psychoanalytic thought. In a 2013 article discussing queer studies and religion, Kent Brintnall notes a queer theoretical trajectory in which psychoanalytic arguments are central and then concludes that this variety of queer theory is "virtually absent from religious studies and theology" (2013, 54). And while this may not have been entirely the case even in 2013 (and certainly is not so now), Brintnall nonetheless points to a dynamic that remains operative in the field. Indeed, more often than not, the insights and challenges of psychoanalytic theory are simply sidelined or ignored, even in sophisticated studies that are heavily engaged with theoretical questions in the study of religion (see, e.g., Clark 2004, 193n1).

Objections to the psychoanalytic tradition from religionists can include its reductionism, as Crockett discusses, or its attempts to speak in universalizing, transcultural, and ahistoricizing ways. And while not coming out of the discipline of religious studies, Lynne Huffer's critique of the prominence of psychoanalysis in queer theory is worthy of note, laden as it is with the figurative language of religious authority. Huffer cites the following passage from Foucault's *History of Madness*: "But, on the other hand, [Freud] exploited the structure that enveloped the medical character: he amplified his virtues as worker of miracles, preparing an almost divine status for his omnipotence" (Foucault 2006, 510). She then goes on to conclude, "I can think of no critique of psychoanalysis—feminist or otherwise—more devastating than this one. In investing the psychoanalyst with the patriarchal powers of the doctor, Freud both creates new techniques of moral control and exploits the ancient power of priests and magicians" (Huffer 2010, 159). Later she refers to her "previously unreflective use of psychoanalysis as a master code for deciphering the mysteries of the world" (187)—and it is precisely this putative drive toward mastery, I suggest, that can provoke opposition and irritation among some scholars of religion, especially those whose objects of study entail competing discourses of mastery.

Yet I would argue that the mode of Foucauldianism for which Huffer advocates (not, I should note, the only way to read Foucault in relationship to psychoanalysis) can only take us so far and is not able to engage very effectively with the multiplicity of ways that bodies can actually matter (Butler 1993). Thus, facility and engagement with psychoanalytic categories and arguments, in addition to being necessary to a careful, thorough reading of some of the philosophers and critical theorists with whom religionists engage, may offer additional critical insights to the study of sex and religion. For one, there is a need for analytical structures that can help us think through the mediation of culture *and* bodies rather than reducing the discussion to a single pole—and Freudian concepts such as the psyche and the unconscious, while deeply implicated in their own problematic colonialist histories that need further excavation (see Hollywood 2021), nevertheless remain a potent starting point for posing these questions. Second, as numerous thinkers in queer theory have repeatedly emphasized, Freud had radical insights into the primary variability of human desires; and although he, for the most part, did not develop the implications of those insights in his own work, there are potential avenues here that are worth pursuing (Bersani 1986; Davidson 1987; de Lauretis 1994, 3–28). This leads to two further points: (1) certain uptakes of Freud in later Continental thought (and especially those influenced by Jacques Lacan) emphasize not Freud's outdated scientific presuppositions but rather the relationship between desire and sexual difference on the one hand and language and signification on the other, an intersection that invites and indeed demands attention to historical particularity; and (2) psychoanalysis continually reminds us that the structures of desire we call sexuality are always on some level inseparable from kinship formations, however mutable and contingent those formations may be. Butler argues that the attempt to sever sexuality from kinship in the interest of studying the former as a standalone object—effectively a "turn from psychoanalysis to Foucault" (1994, 13)—will always fail, in the sense of substantially impoverishing the analysis in question. Further, insofar as this move presents desire as putatively free of the kinship-laden history that constitutes the psyche, it may have the added effect of (wishfully?) casting the former as more coherent, self-sufficient, and internally harmonious than it ever in fact is (14–15). This points to one final challenge posed by the psychoanalytic tradition that I want to highlight: the need to wrestle with what Jacqueline Rose calls the "irreducible discontinuity of psychic life," the disavowal of which allows the ongoing presence of psychic conflict—"that divided and disordered subjectivity . . . *in us all*"—to be construed as "either an accident or an obstacle on the path to psychic and sexual continuity" (1986, 99, 101, emphasis added). Whether or not one chooses to call this irreducible discontinuity "the unconscious" in a directly Freudian sense (less important, to my mind), its outright dismissal is, following Rose, always a kind of mythmaking.

Overall, then, what I have in view with respect to the study of religion is not a wooden or rigid application of psychoanalytic tenets to religious texts and phenomena, ancient or modern, but rather a theoretical orientation that is more supple and dynamic—as in, for example, Amy Hollywood's work, which thinks both with and against psychoanalysis to illuminate medieval Christian thinkers and contemporary theorists alike, as well as the complex relations between the two (Hollywood 2002 and 2016; for additional recent examples from a range of subfields and a variety of approaches within religious studies, see Jacobs 2012; Roberts 2013, 173–99; Seitz 2013; Kotrosits 2020). Is there a universalizing impulse in this methodological platform? Perhaps of a sort (here Hollywood helpfully notes her terminological preference for the language of "generalizable"—see Hollywood 2021, 271)—but if so, I would argue, it is primarily a call to careful attentiveness to "the formative and consequential markings of *culturally specific* familial organizations, powerful and shaping experiences of sexual prohibition, degradation, excitation, and betrayal" (Butler 1994, 15, emphasis added), grounded in the fact that human beings everywhere are sexed, engage in a range of erotic practices that we might call sex, and negotiate both of these senses of the term and the slippage between them in complex and variable ways.

And it is precisely here that the study of religion has something vital to offer within the broader study of sex and sexuality in the humanities. That is to say, the analysis of religious cultures, discourses, and subjects need not render the psychoanalytic irrelevant via standard historicist critiques. Rather, the study of religion may offer a kind of pushback against a certain singular, myopically modern, Euro-American-centered *reading* of psychoanalytic theory, thereby opening up critical space for recognizing and engaging with modes of embodied subjectivity that might otherwise be rendered invisible by whatever normative discourse one finds oneself within. Here, in addition to some of the work referenced above, potential examples in religious studies run the gamut. Stepping outside of modernity—and returning full circle to the starting point of this essay—the orientation I have in view might allow us to read Romans 1:26–27 in light of the way in which normative and stable sexual subject positions in Paul's thought inevitably unravel on terms internal to his system itself, thereby calling into question the epistemological confidence on which this difficult text's judgments on "sex" rest (Dunning 2019b). But additional possibilities abound, such as, for example, exploring the relationship between desire and the undoing of the self in Sufi tradition (Ewing 1997) or highlighting the analogues, resonances, and overlaps between South Asian Kālī traditions and psychoanalytic discourse (Kripal 2003). In methodological terms, then, this ought not to be a one-way relationship in which authoritative "theory" is applied to religion as the inert object of study. Rather, the point, when it comes to the complicated terrain demarcated by the term "sex," is about the way in which a conversation between multiple critical discourses might untangle and illuminate exceedingly opaque specificities, with respect to not only what we can and do know but also what we cannot know and/or refuse to know within the worlds, religious or otherwise, that human beings make.

Suggested Readings

Brooten, Bernadette J. 1996. *Love Between Women: Early Christian Responses to Female Homoeroticism*. Chicago: University of Chicago Press.

Butler, Judith. 1990. *Gender Trouble: Feminism and the Subversion of Identity*. New York: Routledge.

Butler, Judith. 1994. "Against Proper Objects." *differences: A Journal of Feminist Cultural Studies* 6: 1–26.

Dinshaw, Carolyn. 1999. *Getting Medieval: Sexualities and Communities, Pre- and Postmodern*. Durham, NC: Duke University Press.

Foucault, Michel. 1978. *The History of Sexuality*. Vol. 1, *An Introduction*. Translated by Robert Hurley. New York: Vintage Books. French original 1976.

Hollywood, Amy. 2016. *Acute Melancholia and Other Essays: Mysticism, History, and the Study of Religion*. New York: Columbia University Press.

Mahmood, Saba. 2005. *Politics of Piety: The Islamic Revival and the Feminist Subject*. Princeton, NJ: Princeton University Press.

Wilcox, Melissa M. 2021. *Queer Religiosities: An Introduction to Queer and Transgender Studies in Religion*. Lanham, MD: Rowman & Littlefield.

References

Beliso-De Jesús, Aisha M. 2015. *Electric Santería: Racial and Sexual Assemblages of Transnational Religion*. New York: Columbia University Press.

Bersani, Leo. 1986. *The Freudian Body: Psychoanalysis and Art*. New York: Columbia University Press.

Bersani, Leo. 1995. *Homos*. Cambridge, MA: Harvard University Press.

Boyarin, Daniel. 1993. *Carnal Israel: Reading Sex in Talmudic Culture*. Berkeley: University of California Press.

Boyarin, Daniel. 1998. "Gender." In *Critical Terms for Religious Studies*, edited by Mark C. Taylor, 117–35. Chicago: University of Chicago Press.

Brintnall, Kent L. 2013. "Queer Studies and Religion." *Critical Research on Religion* 1: 51–61.

Brooten, Bernadette J. 1996. *Love Between Women: Early Christian Responses to Female Homoeroticism*. Chicago: University of Chicago Press.

Brown, Peter. 1988. *The Body and Society: Men, Women, and Sexual Renunciation in Early Christianity*. New York: Columbia University Press.

Butler, Judith. 1990. *Gender Trouble: Feminism and the Subversion of Identity*. New York: Routledge.

Butler, Judith. 1993. *Bodies That Matter: On the Discursive Limits of "Sex."* New York: Routledge.

Butler, Judith. 1994. "Against Proper Objects." *differences: A Journal of Feminist Cultural Studies* 6: 1–26.

Butler, Judith. 2004. *Undoing Gender*. New York: Routledge.

Clark, Elizabeth A. 2004. *History, Theory, Text: Historians and the Linguistic Turn*. Cambridge, MA: Harvard University Press.

Cohen, Cathy J. 1997. "Punks, Bulldaggers, and Welfare Queens: The Radical Potential of Queer Politics?" *GLQ* 3: 437–65.

Collins, Patricia Hill. 2000. *Black Feminist Thought: Knowledge, Consciousness, and the Politics of Empowerment*. 2nd ed. New York: Routledge.

Combahee River Collective. 1982. "A Black Feminist Statement." In *All the Women Are White, All the Blacks Are Men, But Some of Us Are Brave: Black Women's Studies*, edited by Gloria T. Hull, Patricia Bell Scott, and Barbara Smith, 13–22. New York: Feminist Press.

Crawley, Ashon T. 2017. *Blackpentecostal Breath: The Aesthetics of Possibility*. New York: Fordham University Press.

Crenshaw, Kimberlé. 1991. "Mapping the Margins: Intersectionality, Identity Politics, and Violence against Women of Color." *Stanford Law Review* 43: 1241–99.

Crockett, Clayton. 2007. *Interstices of the Sublime: Theology and Psychoanalytic Theory*. New York: Fordham University Press.

Davidson, Arnold I. 1987. "How to Do the History of Psychoanalysis: A Reading of Freud's *Three Essays on the Theory of Sexuality*." *Critical Inquiry* 13: 252–77.

de Lauretis, Teresa. 1994. *The Practice of Love: Lesbian Sexuality and Perverse Desire*. Bloomington: Indiana University Press.

Dinshaw, Carolyn. 1999. *Getting Medieval: Sexualities and Communities, Pre- and Postmodern*. Durham, NC: Duke University Press.

Dunning, Benjamin H. 2011. *Specters of Paul: Sexual Difference in Early Christian Thought*. Philadelphia: University of Pennsylvania Press.

Dunning, Benjamin H. 2019a. "The New Testament and Early Christian Literature in the History of Gender and Sexuality." In *The Oxford Handbook of New Testament, Gender, and Sexuality*, edited by Benjamin H. Dunning, 1–15. New York: Oxford University Press.

Dunning, Benjamin H. 2019b. "Pauline Anthropology as System and the Problem of Romans 1." In *Bodies on the Verge: Queering Pauline Epistles*, edited by Joseph A. Marchal, 239–65. Atlanta: Society of Biblical Literature.

Dunning, Benjamin H. 2019c. "Same-Sex Relations." In *The Oxford Handbook of New Testament, Gender, and Sexuality*, edited by Benjamin H. Dunning, 573–91. New York: Oxford University Press.

Ewing, Katherine Pratt. 1997. *Arguing Sainthood: Modernity, Psychoanalysis, and Islam*. Durham, NC: Duke University Press.

Fausto-Sterling, Anne. 2020. *Sexing the Body: Gender Politics and the Construction of Sexuality*. 2nd ed. New York: Basic Books.

Foucault, Michel. 1978. *The History of Sexuality*. Vol. 1, *An Introduction*. Translated by Robert Hurley. New York: Vintage Books. French original 1976.

Foucault, Michel. 1984. "Nietzsche, Genealogy, History." In *The Foucault Reader*, edited by Paul Rabinow, 76–100. New York: Pantheon Books. French original 1971.

Foucault, Michel. 2006. *History of Madness*. Translated by Jonathan Murphy and Jean Khalfa. London: Routledge. French original 1961.

Fuhrmann, Arnika. 2016. *Ghostly Desires: Queer Sexuality and Vernacular Buddhism in Contemporary Thai Cinema*. Durham, NC: Duke University Press.

Halberstam, Jack. 2018. *Trans*: A Quick and Quirky Account of Gender Variability*. Oakland: University of California Press.

Holland, Sharon Patricia. 2012. *The Erotic Life of Racism*. Durham, NC: Duke University Press.

Hollywood, Amy. 2002. *Sensible Ecstasy: Mysticism, Sexual Difference, and the Demands of History*. Chicago: University of Chicago Press.

Hollywood, Amy. 2016. *Acute Melancholia and Other Essays: Mysticism, History, and the Study of Religion*. New York: Columbia University Press.

Hollywood, Amy. 2021. "Response—On Impassioned Claims: The Possibility of Doing Philosophy of Religion Otherwise." In *Beyond Man: Race, Coloniality, and Philosophy of Religion*, edited by An Yountae and Eleanor Craig, 269–85. Durham, NC: Duke University Press.

Huffer, Lynne. 2010. *Mad for Foucault: Rethinking the Foundations of Queer Theory*. New York: Columbia University Press.

Jacobs, Andrew S. 2012. *Christ Circumcised: A Study in Early Christian History and Difference*. Philadelphia: University of Pennsylvania Press.

Jordan, Mark D. 1997. *The Invention of Sodomy in Christian Theology*. Chicago: University of Chicago Press.

Kotrosits, Maia. 2020. *The Lives of Objects: Material Culture, Experience, and the Real in the History of Early Christianity*. Chicago: University of Chicago Press.

Kripal, Jeffrey J. 2003. "Why the Tāntrika Is a Hero: Kālī in the Psychoanalytic Tradition." In *Encountering Kālī: In the Margins, at the Center, in the West*, edited by Rachel Fell McDermott and Jeffrey J. Kripal, 196–222. Berkeley: University of California Press.

Kristeva, Julia. 1981. "Women's Time." *Signs: A Journal of Women in Culture and Society* 7: 13–35.

Lofton, Kathryn. 2008. "Queering Fundamentalism: John Balcom Shaw and the Sexuality of Protestant Orthodoxy." *Journal of the History of Sexuality* 17: 439–68.

Mahmood, Saba. 2005. *Politics of Piety: The Islamic Revival and the Feminist Subject*. Princeton, NJ: Princeton University Press.

Marchal, Joseph A. 2011. "'Making History' Queerly: Touches across Time through a Biblical Behind." *Biblical Interpretation* 19: 373–95.

Martin, Dale B. 1995a. *The Corinthian Body*. New Haven, CT: Yale University Press.

Martin, Dale B. 1995b. "Heterosexism and the Interpretation of Romans 1:18–32." *Biblical Interpretation* 3: 332–55.

Martin, Dale B. 2006. *Sex and the Single Savior: Gender and Sexuality in Biblical Interpretation*. Louisville, KY: Westminster John Knox.

Moi, Toril. 2005. *Sex, Gender, and the Body*. Oxford: Oxford University Press.

Moore, Stephen D. 2001. *God's Beauty Parlor: And Other Queer Spaces in and around the Bible*. Stanford, CA: Stanford University Press.

Nash, Jennifer C. 2019. *Black Feminism Reimagined: After Intersectionality*. Durham, NC: Duke University Press.

Puar, Jasbir K. 2007. *Terrorist Assemblages: Homonationalism in Queer Times*. Durham, NC: Duke University Press.

Puar, Jasbir K. 2012. "'I Would Rather Be a Cyborg Than a Goddess': Intersectionality, Assemblage, and Affective Politics." *philoSOPHIA: A Journal of Transcontinental Feminism* 2: 49–66.

Roberts, Tyler. 2013. *Encountering Religion: Responsibility and Criticism After Secularism*. New York: Columbia University Press.

Rose, Jacqueline. 1986. *Sexuality in the Field of Vision*. London: Verso.

Rubin, Gayle. 1975. "The Traffic in Women: Notes on the 'Political Economy' of Sex." In *Toward an Anthropology of Women*, edited by Rayna R. Reiter, 157–210. New York: Monthly Review Press.

Rubin, Gayle. 2003. "Thinking Sex." In *Culture, Society and Sexuality: A Reader*, edited by Richard Parker and Peter Aggleton, 143–78. New York: Routledge.

Sedgwick, Eve Kosofsky. 1990. *Epistemology of the Closet*. Berkeley: University of California Press.

Sedgwick, Eve Kosofsky. 1993. *Tendencies*. Durham, NC: Duke University Press.

Seitz, John C. 2013. "Keep Research Weird: Psychoanalytic Techniques and Fieldwork in the Study of Religion." *Method & Theory in the Study of Religion* 25: 26–52.

Strongman, Roberto. 2019. *Queering Black Atlantic Religions: Transcorporeality in Candomblé, Santería, and Vodou*. Durham, NC: Duke University Press.

Tonstad, Linn Marie. 2016. *God and Difference: The Trinity, Sexuality, and the Transformation of Finitude*. New York: Routledge.

Walters, Jonathan. 1997. "Invading the Roman Body: Manliness and Impenetrability in Roman Thought." In *Roman Sexualities*, edited by Judith P. Hallett and Marilyn B. Skinner, 29–43. Princeton, NJ: Princeton University Press.

Watts Belser, Julia. 2016. "Brides and Blemishes: Queering Women's Disability in Rabbinic Marriage Law." *Journal of the American Academy of Religion* 84: 401–29.

Wilcox, Melissa M. 2006. "Outlaws or In-Laws?: Queer Theory, LGBT Studies, and Religious Studies." *Journal of Homosexuality* 52: 73–100.

Wilcox, Melissa M. 2021. *Queer Religiosities: An Introduction to Queer and Transgender Studies in Religion*. Lanham, MD: Rowman & Littlefield.

22 SOUND

Nicholas Harkness

Sound is born agnostic, and everywhere it is made religious. A topical survey of the critical role of sound in religious studies would include, most obviously, silence and noise, speech and song, recitation and audition, music and movement, and various sonic dimensions of ritual. It would also probably include sound as ethics, pedagogy, or politics; as bearing a message or exceeding linguistic representation; as communal and interactive or as private, individuated, and interior; as inclusive or exclusive; as disposition or dispensation; as affective and emotional; as awareness-raising and figurative; as atmospheric and vibrational; as instrument, medium, or infrastructure; as ephemeral and fleeting; as materializing and corporeal; as historical or futurological; as spatial and territorial; as generating presence or signaling absence; as producing social fusion or institutional fission; as poetically ordered, cacophonous, or disorienting; as identitarian and nostalgic; as gendered, raced, ethnicized, or classed; as multimodal or monomodal; as immanent or transcendent; as world-affirming or world-denying.

As interesting as this sonic diversity of religious life is, this list presents no clear path toward specifying what is specifically religious about any of it. The list of sonic attributes and effects in the preceding paragraph could apply just as well to expressly nonreligious domains of social life. J. Z. Smith, in the conclusion to his entry for the first *Critical Terms* edition, wrote, "'Religion' is not a native term; it is a term created by scholars for their intellectual purposes and therefore is theirs to define. It is a second-order generic concept that plays the same role in establishing a disciplinary horizon that a concept such as 'language' plays in linguistics or 'culture' plays in anthropology" (Smith 1998, 281–82). Smith's point was that "there can be no disciplined study of religion without such a horizon."

What then is the horizon by which sound can be deemed relevant to religious studies? What would make "sound" a *critical* term for the study of religion? In specifying the religious, we have learned not to chart a disciplinary horizon according to the concepts of one tradition (e.g., the divine, belief, the sacred, the afterlife, or the supernatural). Likewise, we have learned that specific sonic phenomenologies—whether justified as traditional musicology, professional philosophy, or counterhegemonic epistemology—are methodologically dubious starting points for theoretical generalization. Where, then, might be a good starting point for the question of sound in religion? What approach would neither produce a mere catalog of difference nor reproduce cultural dominance?

By way of example, consider the following sounds. Which ones are necessarily relevant to religious studies?

the sound of light mid-morning traffic in an Asian megacity as I exit the subway to attend a Wednesday morning service at the Yoido Full Gospel Church in Seoul

the sound of the rain that washes over me as I run to the church in the summer monsoon season with a uselessly small umbrella

the sound of a mosquito buzzing near my ear as the rain stops and I approach the church building

the sound of my hand swatting my neck in an attempt to kill the mosquito

the sound of a magpie, just after I swat the mosquito, squawking from the concrete steps leading up to the front doors of the church

the sound of low-frequency vibrations passing through the massive concrete church building, caused by the music, prayers, and bodies of more than 10,000 Christians, and perceptible to me as I open the door to the lobby and ascend the stairs

the sound of the higher frequencies that suddenly seem to tear through the air, as the doors of the main sanctuary open and I pass into the central resonating chamber

the sound of amplified Christian praise music rhythmically segmenting the cacophony of the group prayer

the sound of a male preacher alternating between oratorical Korean and glossolalia, audible over the music and prayer through an amplified microphone

the sound of various languages, and glossolalia, all around me as I am ushered directly to the international section of the church the sound of some of these languages being spoken by simultaneous interpreters, men and women, who transduce the verbal force of the male preacher's Korean speech, including his pacing and prosody, into various linguistic codes, which I hear through the headphones I pick up from the back of the pew in front of me

the sound of my own vocalization, barely audible but proprioceptively present to me in my throat and face as more than 10,000 congregants and I collectively sing the hymn that follows the cacophonous prayer

the sound of the traffic, the rain, the mosquito's buzzing, and the magpie's squawking in my memory after the preacher tells us that we have just heard the voice of God, and after he instructs us to ask ourselves when and where else we had listened to God that day

My aim in this chapter is to move from the problem of sound as born agnostic to a set of sonic relationships that can be diagnostic of the kinds of things that will probably be deemed most relevant to—indeed *critical* for—religious studies. That is, I will try to identify and develop not so much principles as pressure points that I think might direct our attention to sound's least agnostic moments when it comes to religion as a disciplinary horizon. And I will do so by returning to the examples above. But first, let us widen the scope and recite some scriptural fragments from different religious traditions.

I laud Agni, the chosen Priest, God, minister of sacrifice.

Rigveda, Agni, Hymn 1, line 1 (Griffeth 1889)

Thus I have heard. At one time the Buddha was in the country of Magadha, in a state of purity, at the site of enlightenment, having just realized true awareness.

Flower Ornament Scripture, The Wonderous Adornments of the Leaders of the Worlds, line 1 (Cleary 1984)

Then God said, Let there be light; and there was light.

The Pentateuch, Genesis 1:3 (Coogan et al. 2010)

In the beginning was the Word, and the Word was with God, and the Word was God.

The Gospels of the New Testament, John 1:1 (Coogan et al. 2010)

> In the name of God, the Lord of Mercy, the Giver of Mercy!
> Praise belongs to God, Lord of the World.
>
> Qur'an 1:1–2 (Haleem 2004)

Each of these scriptural fragments introduces an agent and situates a narrating voice in relation to this agent. The voicing structures of source fragments like these lay out an uneven distribution of representational agency. These arrangements place a represented world of possible agents in dynamic relation with a smaller number of privileged representing agents. Not all represented agents can represent, and of those that can, not all are legitimate in doing so. The narrated worlds of such text artifacts provide a guide—selectively, unevenly, incompletely, conditionally, politically—for choosing and authorizing narrators, as well as for shaping and constraining acts of narration. And the narrated speech within such texts—i.e., that which is reported to have been said or done verbally ("laud," "hear," "say," "Word," "name," "praise")—anchors narrating speech beyond such texts, forming some of the crucial semiotic foundations of religious practices and institutions. Insofar as source fragments like these continue to be uttered vocally, speech sounds—understood in terms of phonology, prosody, tone, timbre, and voice more generally—form a point of articulation among possible agents, representational forms, and sound as such. I take this point of articulation as a point of departure for considering the specific problem of sound within religious studies more generally.

I will begin with possible agents and representational forms. A crucial element of Webb Keane's influential study of Christian modernity on the Indonesian island of Sumba was his elaboration of the concept of semiotic ideology (Keane 2007). This concept in a general sense "refers to people's underlying assumptions about what signs are, what functions signs serve, and what consequences they might produce" (Keane 2018, 64). The problem of "what signs are" leads directly to assumptions about possible agents, linking "the ways people make sense of their experiences to their fundamental presuppositions about what kinds of beings animate the world (spirits? witches? gods? or, as in the case of indigenous Australia, geological formations?)" (Keane 2018, 66). Keane's formulation contains within it a pointed critique of disciplinary legacies that continue to treat (and disregard) complex, multidimensional sign processes in terms that are narrowly, reductively, and often dismissively linguistic. Instead, Keane expands the terms and methods of the semiotics of religion well beyond the usual distinction of "words and things."

At the same time, this formulation of semiotic ideology is fundamentally an extension, via the anthropology of religion, of many decades of research and theorization on the problem of *linguistic* ideology. To parallel Keane's definition above, linguistic ideology refers to people's underlying assumptions about what language is, what functions language serves, and what it might produce. Here, the word "language" refers to a specific semiotic domain, seemingly set apart by its most unique function: denotation, or the way linguistic forms predictably stand for classes of things (and, as above, are often ideologically reduced to "words for things"). And yet, language does not merely represent; it is pragmatically continuous with broader sociocultural processes via its other semiotic, especially indexical, functions (see Silverstein 2023). Insofar as language is unique in its systematic capacity both to represent denotationally and to participate practically in a broader host of processes recognizable to analysts of the social, then the broader problem of semiotic ideology is necessarily connected to, anchored by, and dependent upon the more focused problem of linguistic ideology. A reckoning with the latter is unavoidable for a thorough analysis of the former.

The five scriptural fragments above provide glimpses into the complexities of this connection between language and a broader semiotics, with consequences for our understanding of sound in relation to the disciplinary horizon of religious studies. In their very composition, these fragments constitute shifting pivot points between the broad universe of entities and actions reported by scripture, and the particular social location of the utterer, the act of uttering, and the form of utterance within this universe. In this sense, the scriptural utterer is a highly specified kind of semiotically enabled being within the world being represented: of all possible agents, a representing one; of all representing ones, a speaking one; of all speaking ones, an authorized speaker. This is the case whether we focus on the biographical figure invoked by the original composition, or the historical subjects animated and thereby generated by its repeated utterance. For the former, we can think of some obvious examples: the Prophet Muhammad, the Archangel Gabriel, or one of the Christian apostles. For the latter, we might compare two powerful accounts of the phonic, sonorous modes of action that connect religious self-expression, personal cultivation, and social institutions. Akin to my treatment of privileged speakers in relation to the scriptural fragments above, Anna Gade (2004), a scholar of Islam, explains how ongoing, escalating, and affectively motivating Qur'an recitation in Makassar, Sulawesi constitutes a far-reaching and effective system for the acoustic and embodied production of pious Muslim persons and publics in the overtly religious context of Indonesia. By contrast, shifting the focus from speech to song, Hyun Kyong Hannah Chang (2020), a musicologist and historian of trans-Pacific Korea, excavated the micropolitics and personal pleasures of Korean colonial life under Japanese rule to demonstrate how a genre of sentimental songs, written and sung in Korean and created in the intimate missionary contexts of new Christian communities, formed the basis of a secular vernacular in twentieth-century Korea. The historical biography of these religious texts was, in effect, a transformation from what she calls a "fugitive Christian public" operating musically under sentimental cover into a modern public of post-liberation sonic sentiment. Situated in different sociohistorical contexts and emphasizing different semiotic media, both cases depict the narrowing and specifying of a scripturally described agent to a privileged point of utterance, and the effects of this utterance on a whole range of effects, from the obviously sonic to the broadly social. The relative distribution or restriction of this kind of narrative capacity is a central ingredient of the institution of religion. Who can speak? And about what?

Each religious tradition's way of distinguishing agents according to their possible and justified kinds of agencies—sonic and otherwise—resembles the tendency of linguistic systems to do something similar. Although linguistic codes and sociocultural systems are not predictive of one another, cross-linguistic regularities are helpful for thinking through some of the sociocultural problematics that seem to recur across radically different settings. Like the narrowing scope of religious agency, with more and more specification of the kinds of agents related to the specification of possible kinds of agency, linguistic systems deal with possible agents through a system of formal "markedness," or absorptive asymmetries between more general and more specific categories. These more specific categories add additional information to the more general category, thereby standing both within and apart from it. This linguistic formulation of markedness treats the marked category not as necessarily being "out of the ordinary," but rather as being distinctive within the larger category to which it belongs by bearing a "mark" of more information.

Cross-linguistic comparison reveals that agents tend to be linguistically marked (albeit in different ways) among the possible representable things in the world. This should not be surprising, if we accept that human social groups everywhere have probably had to deal with the problem of representing and differentiating among types of agents (and agencies) in their speech practices. As Michael Silverstein (1985, 225–27) explained, but in a very different thematic discussion (regarding language and gender), this kind of markedness regularity in language can be viewed as a relationship across three analytical planes: a formal plane of grammar, a notional plane of the "sense" or "idea" associated with the form; and a referential plane of the stereotypical exemplar that anchors the category (i.e., the things a speaker might point to as a good example of the category). On their own, the exemplary items listed in the referential plane and the corresponding ideas of the notional plane might seem like a random, even inscrutable collection of things in the world: states-of-being or ideas as abstractions; segmentables or wholes that can be enumerated; food or artifacts that can be eaten or used; inanimate shapes or physical characteristics that can be manipulated; small creatures qua simple "things"; spirit or weather with potency and volitional force; relatively large beings such as beasts (i.e., not merely "things"); and humans with various sociological attributes, such as status or role. However, when we view this list from the formal plane of noun phrases, this heterotopy of disordered particulars gives way to some semblance of order, even lucid illumination. This is because of the system of markedness through which languages signal classificatory relations and distinctions (*n.b.*, not all languages make all of the distinctions in the same way).

Most relevant for the present discussion is the way the formal model of possible noun types highlights and situates a typical zone of religious inquiry: the relation between non-agent and agent. Among all things in a given world, only some will be treated as agents. Linguistically, there is a formal shift from abstractions, to stuff that can be counted or segmented, to things that can be used or consumed, to the shapes or physical characteristics of such things, to a very fuzzy category exemplified by small creatures (figuratively "fuzzy" at least, but also sometimes literally fuzzy), the status of which might differ dramatically across societies (rules about killing and/or eating are helpful guides here). At each step, a given category of noun types both belongs to the one preceding it and also stands apart from it by exhibiting some special or new or distinctive information, manifesting as increasing specialization—the markedness of one category with respect to another. In this cross-linguistic model, each category is "marked" as constrained relative to the more absorptive categories adjacent to it, and each category is anchored by an exemplary referent or set of referents, while the boundaries between categories remain ambiguous and problematic.

A religiously consequential transition occurs when we ascend to the class of agents, conceptualized as potent or volitional, with referential exemplars being the weather or—this is important—a spirit. These exemplary agents are known by, indeed defined by, their effects. The distinction between non-agents and agents will be drawn, blurred, and crossed differently in different sociohistorical contexts.

Among possible agents, moreover, there is another religiously important category: some agents will be considered "animate"—i.e., they will seem to exhibit a property roughly corresponding to "alive" or, perhaps better, "sentient." By mentioning animacy, I am not resurrecting or even reanimating the old social evolutionary typology of E. B. Tylor, in which animism is the "essential source" of all religion, leading, through a civilizing process, to polytheism and ending in absolute moral monotheism. Rather, I indicate that the relative animacy of agents is everywhere probably a problem to be conceptualized and represented, and that linguistic systems manifest this fact.

Among animate agents, furthermore, there will be an even more restricted class of those that can (or should) be personified, with a social status or role that resembles and is exemplified by sociologically recognized humans. The intersecting problems of relative agency, animacy, and personification extend from religious doctrine that asserts the body of a personified deity to have materialized in something edible, to political movements that assert that medium- and small-sized beasts should be treated as family members (having ascended from the social category of "man's best friend"), to political tragedies in which some humans are deemed less personifiable than others (e.g., slavery), to theoretical trends that assert that various inanimate objects have considerable volitional agency.

For religious traditions in particular, foundational text artifacts, such as those we recited above, are often centrally concerned with two sets of relationships among these classes: the first is between agents broadly and animate agents specifically; and the second concerns how the first animate-agent relation bears upon a more restricted class of personifiable animate agents. That is, the lens of religious studies tends to focus on social groups that labor to establish, formalize, and organize themselves in terms of this animate-agent nexus as a general existential issue with consequences for a very specific type of personified animate agent: humans.

I am now able to make my argument about sound. For religious studies, I propose that a crucial diagnostic for sound in its least agnostic mode is the way the increasingly (and markedly) nested "pressure points" of agency, animacy, and personification described above relate to a roughly parallel nesting structure of markedness involving the sonic, the phonic, and the interdiscursively voiced. Let us now turn to sound.

Working again from the general category to the more specialized or marked one, we begin, like contemporary scholars of "sound studies," with the broad conceptualization of sound as "mechanical radiant energy that is transmitted by longitudinal pressure waves in a material medium (such as air) and is the objective cause of the sensation of hearing" (Merriam-Webster 2005–). An important narrowing of this definition of "sound as such" comes when sound waves become a perceptible object of sensory attention. Such attention may focus on vibrations visibly perceived in water, haptically felt through solid or semi-solid materials, proprioceptively felt in the body, or, in its most typical channel, audibly heard through the medium of air. From here, sound-as-heard can be segmented and enumerated: e.g., we feel an obligation in English grammar to signal with a plural *-s* suffix the experience of identifying more than one sound (not all languages require this). And then we can attempt to describe what we experience as the different sounds' features and characteristics, and their effects on us—affective, emotional, or otherwise.

Central to the significance of sound for human social life is not merely the fact of perception but *apperception*, or the assimilation of signals to landmarks of perception that shape and bias our classificatory abilities (Boas 1889). And through the apperception of types of sound, we move closer to sound as *sourced*: i.e., not merely "sound as such" or even "a type of sound," but sounds heard as being distinctively produced by some other class of things. Such sounds signal a relation not only to other sounds (as similarity or difference), but also to something non-sonic. At each step—from "sound" to "sounds" to "features of sound" to "sounds of"—there is, as above, a shift in markedness to a category that provides more information than, and thus stands apart from, what precedes it. And in this shift from the abstract "sound as such" to the more specific "sounds of"—i.e., in the shift toward heard sounds that direct attention to their source—we enter a zone of sound production corresponding roughly to the problem of agency. The English phrase structure "the sound of X" and its approximate equivalents in other languages beg three questions: (1) whether X is an agent or some agentive activity, (2) whether the sound directly relates to X's distinctive form of agency, and (3) whether the sound itself is agentively produced by X.

We encounter a further categorial transition when the production of sound is attributed—via hearing—not only to an agentive source, but to a specifically animate one. Animate agents, in particular, seem to engage in *phonic* acts that are both continuous with and markedly distinct from a broader *sonic* domain of possibly agentive sound production. Animate agents seem not merely to produce sound (e.g., as a kind of passive or accidental emission), but also to participate in and contribute to sonic systems of value through which sounds are apperceived. That is, animate agents seem—variously, at different levels and scales, with different degrees of reflexivity and modes of uptake, through different media, instruments, and prosthetics—to *communicate*.

The sounds of speech, song, and various other types of human vocality serve as a referential anchor point for the shift from the broadly sonic to the more markedly phonic. This shift is reflected in various technical terms derived from Greek, e.g., for vibrating, adducting vocal cords (phonation), the cross-linguistic inventory of documented speech sounds organized by manner and place of articulation (phonetics), the structured system of contrastive sound categories in language (phonology), or compositional techniques of music (polyphony, homophony, monophony). However, the phonic, as I introduce it here, refers broadly to any act of sound production that is oriented to and participates in a sonic system of value. As a marked category of the sonic, the phonic remains relatively expansive, pertaining to a range of acts, media, and sensuous features of sound production oriented to sonic values—bodies and their anatomy, instruments and their materials, individuals and groups, various nonhumans more generally.

The human voice, broadly conceived, is an exemplary reference point for the contribution of phonic activities to various, often intersecting sonic systems of value. That is, the human voice is a generative *phonosonic nexus* (Harkness 2014), with widespread, if variable, use across human populations. Conceptualizing the human voice as a phonosonic nexus helps us begin to sort through the sonic elements in and around the ritual space of the Pentecostal sanctuary described at the start of this essay. The repeated phrase "the sound of" in my list above might provoke the feeling that all of these sounds are comparable existential arrangements. Indeed, we can represent the production of very different classes of sound in largely the same formal linguistic way. And yet both the sensuous forms and the various sources of these sounds may ultimately be heard, conceptualized, represented, and treated very differently. It is the work of the religious context to make some of them "sound" more alike than others and, moreover, to direct listeners to an agentive source: if glossolalia could sound like speech, could prayerful cacophony sound like a chorus, the mosquito like the magpie, or the traffic like the rain?

There, the preacher's speech in Korean (and its interpretation into multiple other languages) becomes a phonosonic reference point for speech-like sounds that are not readily intelligible, such as glossolalia. The musical accompaniment during worship anchors and organizes the cacophonous prayer of the crowd. When the pastor asked the congregants when and where they had listened to God that day, the pastor was also projecting these overtly and more markedly phonosonic aspects of human vocality beyond the human voice proper. Was the deity also speaking through the magpie, the mosquito, the rain, or the traffic? In this example, the broader sonic world itself has the potential to be become a massive resonating phonosonic nexus—one that *communicates*. The whole world can resonate like the ritual sanctuary, which envelops humans in sound, and through which they navigate a dynamic semiotics of animate agency (this potential, in fact, is continuous with longer traditions of shamanic, Buddhist, and Confucian practices in Korean religious life). And in this way, the specific phonosonic nexus of vocality participates in and affects sonic apperception and activity well beyond the throat, conditioning not only what can be uttered or sung, but also, and fundamentally, what can be heard and how to hear it.

We now arrive at a final step. Just as the marked category within animacy is that of relative personification—animate agents that can participate as social beings, with the related notional concept being that of the human—the marked category within the phonic is interdiscursive "voicing." We draw on this term—stemming from a phonosonic concept of musical composition, adapted by Mikhail Bakhtin to literary analysis, and returned in this case again to sound—to refer to the way biographical individuals, characterological figures, and generic social perspectives break through into, stand apart from, blend with, or otherwise seem to materialize through semiotic form. This can happen in stylistic inventions like "free indirect discourse" or full-blown genres such as religious oratory, in the denotational opacity of glossolalia or the musicality of song (for an analysis of the empirical intersection of all of these possibilities, see Harkness 2021). Braxton Shelley, for example, has recently demonstrated, with vivid technical detail, how in Black gospel performance "an invisible but audible force seems to be at work" (Shelley 2021, 6) for persons who expect "the infinite to be made immanent in the everyday" (294). From the phonosonic nexus to interdiscursive voicing, we transition from asking *what* animate agent is audibly at work to asking *who* is audibly at work and for *whom* (for a related analysis of the raced, gendered, sexualized "who," see Jones 2020). If the voice as phonosonic nexus sits close to the throat, anchored materially to the way the human functional anatomy of the oral cavity is mobilized sensuously, structurally, and socially to engage in sonic frameworks of value, interdiscursive voicing has an inherently expansive constitution, drawing contextually from across communicative events to invoke a minimally recognizable social figure who stands out from a wide range of possible animate agents and a narrower range of personified animates (see, e.g., Wirtz 2018).

And lest we too quickly assume silence to be merely the passive absence of sound, and thus the ontological negative of all that I have discussed, we can consult the vast record of religious inquiry into the concerted creation, and often fragile maintenance, of silence itself. We find documentation of such observations covering the historical and ethnographic archive, from the works of Émile Durkheim and William James to Richard Bauman's (1983) landmark study of speaking and silence among seventeenth-century Quakers, where silence itself is the collaborative result of multiple human agencies which are animated and focused toward producing the state necessary for the "small still" voice of the deity to be heard.

This relation between the phonosonic nexus and interdiscursive voicing allows us to return, via the sounds associated with Korean Pentecostal worship, to the scriptural examples that initiated this essay. In these examples, our concern is not the linguistic representations as such. Rather, we are attuned to how the narrators' utterances actively situate these narrators in a narrated world of *possible agents*, *animate agents*, and *personified animates*. Each of these is connected in different ways, at different times, with different arrangements of the *sonic*, the *phonic*, and the *interdiscursively voiced*. The "who" that recites these scriptural passages—inhabiting the role of narrator, invoking the figure of an authorized speaker, narrating a world of other figures—reconstitutes the point of articulation between sound and religion *viva voce*, with consequences for the experience and production of both sound and agency well beyond the utterance.

Consider the heartbeat. A biomechanical emission of sonic waves, barely audible, the heartbeat can be felt through haptic sensations, amplified through aural prosthesis, or made visible through sonographic representation. From one perspective, the alternating systolic-diastolic pulsation of the cardiac cycle is a binary sign of life, where the minimal conditions of animacy are either present or absent. From a professional medical perspective, the heart's rhythm indicates something about the health and condition of that life. A more overtly religious frame expands the facts of animacy in the direction of both agency and personhood. By one influential view, the heartbeat is a sign not just of life but of *individuated* life—"a life," perhaps at its end or at its very beginning. So ideologically powerful is the phonic force of the sound shape of embryonic humanity that it can rise to the overtly political level of voice, consubstantiating agency, animacy, and personhood in a pulse. And so politically powerful is the apperceptive commitment to "hear" a heartbeat among the earliest sign shapes of human animacy that the patterned electrical activity of cells, transduced into an audible signal manufactured by an ultrasound machine, becomes—in some cases by law—the "sound" of the heart even prior to the development of the four ventricular chambers that are necessary to generate a "beat."

In this essay I have tried to develop a diagnostic of sound in religion by pursuing the generative engagement between two nested structures of markedness. The pressure points within these dynamic structures highlight a parallel between some things that regularly appear under the lens of religious studies and some things that tend to organize apperceptions of sound. For religious studies, it is the way social groups labor to establish, formalize, and organize themselves in terms of an animate-agent nexus as a general existential issue with consequences for a very specific, problematic, personifiable type of animate agent: humans. For sound studies, it is the way markedly phonic participation in broadly sonic domains shapes and is shaped by interdiscursive voicing—with the full range of sensuous and sociological complexity this entails. For the present essay, the problem lies at their intersection, where sound seems to be least agnostic, and where we can expect some markedly religious aspects of life to make themselves heard.

Suggested Readings

Adams, Margarethe, and August Sheehy, eds. 2020. "Sound and Secularity." Special Issue of *Yale Journal of Music & Religion* 6 (2).

Agawu, Kofi. 2016. "Tonality as a Colonizing Force in Africa." In *Audible Empire: Music, Global Politics, Critique*, edited by Ronald Radano and Tejumola Olaniyan. Duke University Press.

Bohlman, Philip, and Jeffers Engelhardt. 2016. *Resounding Transcendence: Transitions in Music, Religion, and Ritual*. Oxford University Press.

Eidsheim, Nina Sun, and Katherine Meizel. 2019. *The Oxford Handbook of Voice Studies*. Oxford University Press.

Eisenlohr, Patrick. 2018. *Sounding Islam: Voice, Media, and Sonic Atmospheres in an Indian Ocean World*. Berkeley: University of California Press.

Feld, Steven. 1996. "Waterfalls of Song: An Acoustemology of Place Resounding in Bosavi, Papua New Guinea." In *Senses of Place*, edited by Steven Feld and Keith Basso, 91–135. Santa Fe, NM: School of American Research Press.

Hirschkind, Charles. 2006. *The Ethical Soundscape: Cassette Sermons and Islamic Counterpublics*. New York: Columbia University Press.

Ochoa Gautier, Ana María. 2014. *Aurality: Listening and Knowledge in Nineteenth-Century Colombia*. Durham, NC: Duke University Press.

Schmidt, Leigh Eric. 2002. *Hearing Things: Religion, Illusion, and the American Enlightenment*. Harvard University Press.

Weiner, Isaac. 2014. *Religion Out Loud: Religious Sound, Public Space, and American Pluralism*. New York University Press.

References

Bauman, Richard. 1983. *Let Your Words Be Few: Symbolism of Speaking and Silence among Seventeenth-Century Quakers*. Cambridge: Cambridge University Press.

Boas, Franz. 1889. "On Alternating Sounds." *American Anthropologist* 2 (1): 47–54.

Chang, Hyun Kyong Hannah. 2020. "A Fugitive Christian Public: Singing, Sentiment, and Socialization in Colonial Korea." *Journal of Korean Studies* 25 (2): 291–323.

Cleary, Thomas. 1984. *The Flower Ornament Scripture: A Translation of the Avatamsaka Sutra*. Translated by Thomas Cleary. Boulder: Shambhala Publications; distributed in the US by Random House.

Coogan, Michael D., Marc Z. Brettler, Carol Newsom, and Pheme Perkin. 2010. *The New Oxford Annotated Bible: New Revised Standard Version: with the Apocrypha: an Ecumenical Study Bible*. Fully revised 4th ed. Oxford: Oxford University Press.

Gade, Anna. 2004. *Perfection Makes Practice: Learning, Emotion, and the Recited Quran in Indonesia*. Honolulu: University of Hawaiʻi Press.

Griffeth, Ralph. 1889. *The Hymns of the Rigveda*. Translated by Ralph Griffeth. Benares: E. J. Lazarus.

Haleem, M. A. S. Abdel. 2004. *The Qur'an*. Translated by M. A. S. Abdel Haleem. Oxford: Oxford University Press.

Harkness, Nicholas. 2014. *Songs of Seoul: An Ethnography of Voice and Voicing in Christian South Korea*. Berkeley: University of California Press.

Harkness, Nicholas. 2021. *Glossolalia and the Problem of Language*. Chicago: University of Chicago Press.

Jones, Alisha Lola. 2020. *Flaming? The Peculiar Theopolitics of Fire and Desire in Black Male Gospel Performance*: Oxford University Press.

Keane, Webb. 2007. *Christian Moderns: Freedom and Fetish in the Mission Encounter*. Berkeley: University of California Press.

Keane, Webb. 2018. "On Semiotic Ideology." *Signs and Society* 6 (1): 64–87.

Merriam-Webster. 2005–. *Merriam-Webster Unabridged Dictionary*. Springfield, MA: Merriam-Webster.

Shelley, Braxton. 2021. *Healing for the Soul: Richard Smallwood, the Vamp, and the Gospel Imagination*: Oxford University Press.

Silverstein, Michael. 1985. "Language and the Culture of Gender: At the Intersection of Structure, Usage, and Ideology." In *Semiotic Mediation: Sociocultural and Psychological Perspectives*, edited by Elizabeth Mertz and Richard Parmentier, 219–59. Orlando: Academic Press.

Silverstein, Michael. 2023. *Language in Culture: Lectures on the Social Semiotics of Language*. Cambridge: Cambridge University Press.

Smith, Jonathan Z. 1998. "Religion, Religions, Religious." In *Critical Terms for Religious Studies*, edited by Mark C. Taylor, 269–84. Chicago: University of Chicago Press. Reprinted in 2004 in Jonathan Z. Smith, *Relating Religion: Essays in the Study of Religion*. Chicago: University of Chicago Press.

Wirtz, Kristina. 2018. "Materializations of Oricha Voice through Divinations in Cuban Santería." *Journal de la Société des Américanistes* 104 (1): 149–77.

23 TEXT

Samuel P. Catlin

> I call this the *deficiency of philology* [*den* Mangel an Philologie]; to be able to read off a text *as text* [*einen Text* als Text *ablesen*], without intermingling an interpretation, is the last form of "inner experience,"—perhaps one hardly possible. . . .
> FRIEDRICH NIETZSCHE, *Nachgelassene Fragmente*, spring 1888

The Philological Text: The Wrench and the Screw

For the academic study of religion, which has one of its historical sources in the faculty of theology, the very word "text" is inextricably bound up with one of its disciplinary birth pangs—namely, the emergence of critical biblical scholarship in the seventeenth and eighteenth centuries. As the biblical scholar Hermann Gunkel wrote in 1914: "To the scientific study of the Old Testament [*alttestamentliche Wissenschaft*] the Bible is primarily a book produced by human means in human ways. Science has brought it down from heaven and set it in the midst of the earth" (Gunkel 1928, 18–19).

However, modern biblical criticism did not spring forth from Spinoza's head fully formed as a methodologically self-contained enterprise. In fact, it came about only via what the anthropologist Clifford Geertz later described as "a thoroughgoing conceptual wrench" (Geertz 1983, 30). Gunkel continues: "[*Alttestamentliche Wissenschaft*] treats the Old Testament and the people of Israel with the same methods as would be applied to any other book and any other people" (1928, 19). This statement implies a temporality: before *alttestamentliche Wissenschaft*, there already existed a discipline that had developed methods for the study of "any other book" by "any other people"—namely, the discipline of philology, the study of texts. The "thoroughgoing conceptual wrench" consists, per Gunkel's slant-allusion to Deuteronomy 30:12, of bringing scripture down from heaven, or, put differently, of making a new claim concerning its proper disciplinary situation. Biblical criticism brought scripture down from the faculty of theology, still into the nineteenth century considered the "queen of the sciences" in European universities, and set it amidst the philologists alongside other books by other peoples. What made this wrench possible was, precisely, "text." As a philological subdiscipline, modern biblical criticism proceeds from the premise—itself the product of many years of theological, philosophical, exegetical, and yes, philological investigation—that the Bible is a text, meaning an object written by human beings and therefore just as subject to the vicissitudes of history as any other human work.

On the one hand, this familiar episode in the genealogy of religious studies seems to affirm banally the commonsense definition of "text": a written thing. A little reductively, this is more or less what philologists mean when they speak of a "text." On the other hand, though, the same episode exemplifies how "text" overflows and undercuts that definition. "Text" names not one but two different, albeit interrelated, phenomena. For if "text" names the category of objects which are proper to philology, we see in the emergence of modern biblical criticism how recourse is made to "text" in order to wrench or, less violently put, to *translate* an object, in this case the Hebrew Bible, *between* different discourses, different disciplines. In this case, "text" is not just a category of objects but also an interface and an event: a translation, an appropriation, "invasion, struggle, plundering" (Foucault [1971] 1998, 369).

This is why we speak here, quite deliberately, not only of "text" in the *history* of religious studies but also of disciplinary *genealogy*, in the sense given the latter term by Friedrich Nietzsche and Michel Foucault, and then taken up in religious studies by scholars such as Talal Asad, to whom we shall return later on. In fact, Foucault—following Nietzsche in staging a methodological translation of his own (from "positive history" to "genealogy")—plunders history itself right out from under the noses of the "positive historians" by making recourse to a certain idea of "text": the genealogist not only interprets an archive of textual evidence in the philological sense, but *interprets the past itself as a text*. "Genealogy . . . operates on a field of entangled and confused parchments, on documents that have been scratched over and recopied many times" (Foucault [1971] 1998, 369). It is demonstrably not the case that every archival document Foucault treats in his genealogical studies is a palimpsest; "scratched over and recopied many times" refers here not to the material practice of scraping and reinscribing a parchment, but to the layers of interpretation, contestation, and resignification of the world and the human that, laminated together, make history. Asad adds: "When a project is translated from one site to another, from one agent to another, versions of power are produced. As with translations of a text, one does not simply get a reproduction of identity" (Asad 1993, 13). Like modern biblical criticism, then, the Foucauldian intervention in historical scholarship is made possible by the translatability that "text" affords.

However, there is a significant and obvious difference between the textualization of the Hebrew Bible by philologists—who indeed took the Bible, as it has come to us, to be a divergent compendium of "entangled and confused parchments . . . scratched over and recopied many times," an imperfect product of human history riddled with errors, lacunae, and redactorial interventions—and Foucault's textualization of history: the textualization of scripture proceeds from the empirical observation that the Hebrew Bible *is* manifestly a written thing, in addition to whatever else one believes it to be. This fact gives the conceptual wrench its torque. By contrast, Asad's diction ("*as with* translations of a text") suggests that "text" is for the Foucauldian genealogist a type of analogy, a means of enabling a relation of two objects through the heuristic suspension of their essential difference. Yet this is not quite the whole story, for Foucault or, in practice, for Asad. In the discourse of genealogy, "text" is meant literally—but what "text" *literally means* underwent a radical reconceptualization around the time Foucault wrote those words in 1971. Thus, to call the past a text is no mere figure of speech; it is a metaphysical and methodological reconfiguration. How was this possible?

The answer, once again, has everything to do with that conceptual wrench called "text." The difference between Gunkel's "Bible" and Foucault's "history" is that in the latter case the translation is not necessarily underwritten by a philological object such as a document or a book. "Text," in the sense of a translational event that happens where discourses and disciplines intersect, has here become detached from parchments, scrolls, and codices. Texts in the philological sense are still texts, but so too are a good many other things (the past, for instance). It is *this* conceptual wrench whose history and consequences for the academic study of religion—unlike the very well-trammeled history of modern biblical criticism (on which see, e.g., Legaspi 2010)—need to be accounted for. And it is this wrench's methodological turns of the screw which we will be following out in the present essay. These turns must be observed at the juncture of religious studies and literary criticism, for as we have already suggested, "text" is definitionally never a matter of just one discipline.

The Semiotic Text: Signs without Wonders

In the *Course on General Linguistics* (1916), compiled from the notes of lectures delivered at the University of Geneva in 1907–1911, Ferdinand de Saussure writes that the linguistic sign is not a *motivated* "link between a thing and a name," but instead an *arbitrary* connection of a "concept," which Saussure calls the "signified," and a "sound-pattern," which he refers to as the "signifier" (Saussure [1916] 1986, 67). The sound-pattern "book," for example, is connected, for no natural or essentially necessary reason, to the concept of a book. Among the manifold consequences of Saussure's structuralist definition of the sign, three are salient here. The first is that even the simplest meaning is constituted by an internal difference from itself: there is no case in which the signifier and the signified are synthetically unified and identical. The second is that the system of language and cognition consists of signifiers and signifieds, not of things-in-themselves. And the third, following from the first two, is that not only are signs internally differentiated from themselves, but the difference proper to each sign is itself produced only through differentiation from every other sign. Since there is no sign whose articulating difference—the linking of signifier and signified—is proper, essential, natural, or motivated, every sign is in turn produced by differentiation from all the other differential articulations of signifier-signified connections. Thus, for example, the sign "book" means what it means only and precisely because other signs do *not* mean what "book" means.

Saussure's semiotic linguistics was taken up by postwar French literary critics as part of a Marxist critique of the romantic theory of capital-L *Literature* (see Barthes [1984] 1986, 3–75; Jameson [1988] 2008, 20–76; Mowitt 1992; Culler 2007, 99–116), but the impact of the triple consequence of his argument in the *Course* reached far beyond literary criticism proper, touching on the very notion of communication and the foundations of subjectivity itself. If communication is signifying to the other, and signs are arbitrary constructions within a differential system, no communication is *absolutely* the conveyance of the speaking subject's pure, unmediated intention; rather, communication involves "representation" and "expression" of that intention, and then the interpretation of the expressed representation by the other (see Derrida [1971] 1988, 5). In various writings of the 1960s and 1970s, the philosopher Jacques Derrida staged a critique of philosophical reason, especially in phenomenology, via a radicalization of this problem. Derrida argues that the sign must be repeatable in order to be a sign: after all, it is not a *sound* which indexes a concept, but rather a sound-*pattern*; only where there is repetition and repeatability can there be a pattern which can then be taken, by two different speaking subjects, as the index of a concept. Derrida's key philosophical claim in these early works is that this differential repeatability, or "iterability" (Derrida [1971] 1988, 7), is "writing [*l'écriture*]" in an inflated, generalized sense. With this move, Derrida reconfigures the matrix of differences, which had for Saussure constituted language, and projects it onto the model of writing—thus performing a superimposition of terms, therefore of "text" (see Mowitt 1992, 90), or rather, of "textuality." "Textuality" means "text" in this general sense: not the written object of the philologists, but the material infrastructure of iterability as such, an infinite, diffuse chain or tissue—the word "tissue," not coincidentally, sharing an etymology with "text"—of "supplements" and "traces," as Derrida writes in *Of Grammatology* (see Derrida [1967] 1997). To combine Saussure's and Derrida's insights, not even a direct spoken communication between subjects could not partake of textuality. Even when one thinks, Derrida suggests, that thought comprises signs. If it were possible to telepathically beam one's thoughts directly into the mind of another person, the message would still not consist of one's pure intention, but rather of representative signs; the intention itself would already be semiotic. Wherever there is signification, there is textuality, and so neither communication nor cognition can exist without text. In short, as Derrida infamously stated in a pronouncement still submitted, today, to regular misinterpretation: "There is no outside-the-text [*Il n'y a pas de hors-texte*]" (Derrida [1967] 1997, 158).

If the philological text enables, for example, the appropriation of the Bible from the theologians, the semiotic text (the text-in-general, or textuality) effects a far more radical shift. It is not that an object which was once the "property" of one discipline now belonged to another discipline. Rather, it is that disciplinarity itself, the parceling-up of the field of human culture and knowledge, was annulled by the notion of textuality. Initially, the turn to linguistics in French literary criticism was born of an attempt to specify the quality that made literature *literature*. If the name "literature" indexed a coherent and discrete class of signifying objects and practices, this would have to be differentiated essentially from other signifying objects and practices, and so the science of semiotics, inaugurated by Saussure, was marshaled to analytically isolate this essential difference: the specific quality of "literariness." "Yet once language was identified as that which supported and defined the specificity of literature," writes John Mowitt, "it was difficult to continue attributing to literature the prestige that separated it from other language practices" (Mowitt 1992, 86). As Roland Barthes commented in 1971: "We might say, as a matter of fact, that *interdisciplinary* activity, today so highly valued in research, cannot be achieved by the simple confrontation of specialized branches of knowledge; the interdisciplinary is not a comfortable affair: it begins *effectively* (and not by the simple utterance of a pious hope) when the solidarity of the old disciplines breaks down . . . to the advantage of a new object" (Barthes [1971] 1986, 56, emphases in original). That object was textuality. By the 1970s, religious studies too would be caught up in the interdisciplinary web of text.

However, semiotic theory itself was still *located* largely within the institutionalized discipline of literary criticism. This gets at a contradiction—especially in the American academy, where the European thinkers producing and reflecting on textuality were absorbed primarily (in some cases exclusively) by scholars housed in departments of English, French, and comparative literature (see Jones-Katz 2021). Textuality effectively brought under the aegis of the academic study of literature a host of objects and discourses previously foreign to it: from the past (as in Foucauldian genealogy) to the psyche (via, e.g., Jacques Lacan's dictum that "the unconscious is structured like a language"), from buildings to symphonies, and beyond (see Johnson 1995). Ironically, then, a semiotically informed literary studies became a master-discipline of sorts for the humanities and interpretive social sciences—not unlike how theology had once claimed to be the sovereign essence of the university—despite and indeed *because of* the thoroughgoing critique of disciplinarity mounted by literary critics.

One object that the wave of textuality washed up onto the shores of literary studies in the 1970s was the Hebrew Bible. Literary critics at American and Israeli universities operating with the new interdisciplinary idea of text gave the early modern philologists' methodological screw another turn: the Bible was one written product of human culture among others, yes, but, *as such*, it therefore partook of textuality in the general sense. Hence it could be argued that there was nothing intrinsically different about how textuality in the Bible operated from how it worked in other texts to which it might be compared, and even if there were such a difference, it would still have to be demonstrated—if only negatively—using the tools of semiotic analysis. This meant a more radical leveling of the hierarchical distinctions cordoning off the biblical text than the philologists had managed. In 1982, retelling Gunkel's genealogical story from 1914, the biblical critic Adele Berlin declared: "The Bible is fair game for everyone. Once the treasured possession of the religious establishment, it has, in modern times, been wrested from their exclusive grasp by secularists of various persuasions. In the vanguard of these secularists stand the literary critics" (Berlin 1982, 323). Gunkel had narrated the relocation of the Hebrew Bible from heaven to earth, but he still maintained the authority of a specific academic discipline (*alttestamentliche Wissenschaft*) to produce knowledge about the biblical text. For Berlin, by contrast, "the literary critics" do not so much take over custody of the biblical text as liquidate the notion of disciplinary custody altogether, making the biblical text "fair game for everyone."

Meir Sternberg, whose 1985 monograph *The Poetics of Biblical Narrative: Ideological Literature and the Drama of Reading* is the high-water mark of the "Bible-as-literature" trend, ratchets the stakes of the semiotic intervention up even higher. "What kind of text is the Bible, and what roles does it perform in context?" Sternberg asks at the outset of his book (Sternberg 1985, 1). Acknowledging that the Hebrew Bible is a disciplinarily—not to mention religiously—contested text, he warns that "laissez-faire gestures ('You go your way and I'll go mine' or, more belligerently, 'You keep off my grass and I'll keep off yours') . . . only confuse the issue. They speak as if there were one Bible for the historian, another for the theologian, another for the linguist, another for the geneticist, still another for the literary critic. But there are not enough Bibles to go round, and even Solomon's wisdom cannot divide the only one we do possess among the various claimants" (17). Making his case for biblical literariness, Sternberg elaborates an argument first ventured by the philologist Erich Auerbach: Hebrew biblical narrative, he writes, is "ideological literature," meaning a literary text in which the narrator and the reader exist in a dramatically asymmetrical epistemological relationship. This asymmetry, along with the narrator's strategic divulgence of just enough information to adumbrate a sublime—and subliminal—"background [*Hintergrund*]" whose full depths are withheld from the reader, creates the rhetorical effect of narratorial omniscience and authority (see Auerbach [1946] 2003, 3–23).

The divine authorship of the Hebrew Bible—the very thing the philologists threw into doubt—is thus restored to the biblical text, not as a theological essence but as an effect of textuality. In Daniel Boyarin's summation: "It does not matter . . . if the inscribing of God as the author of the Torah is a product of human work and therefore a fiction or an effect of actual divine authority," because "God is the implied author of the Torah"—implied, that is, by the peculiar but not undeterminable fashion in which the biblical text signifies. "This is not a theological or a dogmatic claim but a semiotic one" (Boyarin 1990, 40). The "literary critics" of whom Berlin writes thus do not reverse the philologists' conceptual wrenching; in a study like Sternberg's *Poetics of Biblical Narrative*, the biblical text is decidedly not re-scripturalized, re-situated "in heaven" beyond the reach of human interrogation or analysis. Rather, textuality allows these scholars to analyze dynamics like authority and mystery as rhetorical effects of Hebrew biblical narrative's mode of signification—without reinvesting the Bible with these qualities as transcendental essences.

This move has applications well beyond the study of "the Bible as literature." For example, "symbol" is the crucial term in Mircea Eliade's massively influential version of the comparative history of religions. As Jonathan Z. Smith and others have pointed out, for Eliade symbols function as a kind of transcendental backstop, a limit beyond which inquiry cannot progress (see Gill 1998, 304–6). The intellectual edifice Eliade erected on the foundation of the symbol does not survive a semiotic critique, since such a critique would pry apart the signifier and the signified and insist on their arbitrariness. Textuality, even when it is not named as such, facilitates an interdisciplinary translation allowing comparative historians of religions like Smith to get traction on the same phenomena catalogued by Eliade as "human methods of constructing reality, of engaging the world *meaningfully*" (Gill 1998, 305, emphasis mine). In the context of twentieth-century religious studies, so profoundly shaped by Eliade's project, the emergence of "text" could mean an end of taking signs for wonders.

The Genealogical Text: Textualizing "Religion"

Fields like the comparative history of religions and the anthropology of religions are good places to look if we wish to assess how textuality has been registered in religious studies—a far better place, in fact, than biblical criticism (which is ambivalently affiliated with religious studies anyway). To lend biblical criticism exemplary status would be a mistake, both because it could suggest that the interpretation or historicization of sacred scriptures are the major scenes of academic study of religion (they aren't) and because it would still leave us in the domain of the philological text, the written object, even if the methods brought to bear on this text are no longer philological but semiotic. Textuality, as Derrida reminds us, is not only a property of "empirical writing." Even the "language of action" is "written" in Derrida's sense of *l'écriture* (Derrida [1971] 1988, 7). Actions are texts, composed of signs: they are constructed and interpreted, they produce meaning. If we forget this, we miss the point of Derrida's statement that there is no outside-the-text, and thus we fail as well to grasp the stakes of textuality for religious studies. Textuality does not denote, or at least does not only denote, "text-centered" studies in a philological sense: "the study of . . . liturgical, theological, poetic, or narrative words and concepts," as the editors of *Material Religion* characterized it in their journal's inaugural issue ("Editorial Statement" 2005, 5). Rather, it is precisely when we leave behind, or at any rate try to leave behind, the philological text and shift our attention to what the philological text *excludes* that the conceptual wrench of "text" begins its next turn.

The figuring of text as "a thoroughgoing conceptual wrench" is, we recall, Clifford Geertz's. While Saussure's ideas made their way into anthropology via the pivotal work of Claude Lévi-Strauss, it was Geertz who, in the essay "Thick Description: Toward an Interpretive Theory of Culture" ([1973] 2000), spelled out most explicitly the stakes for ethnographic scholarship. In "Thick Description," Geertz draws on the philosopher Gilbert Ryle's distinction between "thin description" and "thick description." "Thin" descriptions of a wink and a twitch, Ryle argued, will be identical: both consist of "rapidly contracting the eyelids" of one eye. But they are not the same: one is an involuntary spasm, the other an intentional signification. To this basic confusion, Ryle adds a series of increasingly unsettling wrinkles: how could a "thin" description tell apart, for example, not just the winker and the twitcher, but also a third person who, "to give malicious amusement to his cronies," parodies the winker's wink? This parodist would need to execute the action in such a fashion as to be understood as burlesquing the wink rather than actually winking—or, for that matter, twitching. Perhaps, Ryle continues, in order to ensure her success, she "may practice at home before the mirror," in which case she "is not twitching, winking, or parodying, but rehearsing"—although, again, the "thin" description of all these actions would be identical (Geertz [1973] 2000, 6–7). "Thick description," then, would be a description that allows the observer to *interpret* an action, utterance, or other material object by locating it within a semiotic matrix—that is to say, by textualizing it.

Between thin and thick description, Geertz writes, "lies the object of ethnography: a stratified hierarchy of meaningful structures in terms of which twitches, winks, fake-winks, parodies, rehearsals of parodies are produced, perceived, and interpreted, and without which they would not . . . in fact exist." When Geertz adds that this is true even of the involuntary twitch of the eyelids, "which, *as a cultural category*, are as much nonwinks as winks are nontwitches," he translates Saussure's idea of the linguistic system as constituted by differences into the domain of what Derrida calls the "language of action" (Geertz [1973] 2000, 7, emphasis in original). Like that system, what we have here is naught but "winks upon winks upon winks" (9). "There is an Indian story," Geertz adds, "about an Englishman who, having been told that the world rested on a platform which rested on the back of an elephant which rested in turn on the back of a turtle, asked (perhaps he was an ethnographer; it is the way they behave), what did the turtle rest on? Another turtle. And that turtle? 'Ah, Sahib, after that it is turtles all the way down.' Such is the condition of things" (28–29). Winks all the way down, then. Or twitches. Or. . . .

Moving from Ryle's contrived fiction about twitches and winks to a passage from his own field journal, Geertz uses his ethnographic notes to argue that the anthropologist's "data" are in fact always already texts, "our own constructions of other people's [the native informants'] constructions of what they and their compatriots are up to." In "ethnographic description of even the most elemental sort," the sheer thickness—the extent to which ethnographies consist of signs (the "finished anthropological writing") representing interpretations of other signs representing interpretations of still other signs, and so on—is "obscured because most of what we need to comprehend a particular event, ritual, custom, idea, or whatever is insinuated as background information before the thing itself is directly examined. . . . Right down at the factual base, we are already explicating; and worse, explicating explications." The anthropological analysis of culture "is sorting out the structures of signification . . . and determining their social ground and import." The phrase "structures of signification" already tags Geertz's text as a product of the semiotic turn. Ryle, Geertz adds, would describe these structures of signification as "established codes," but this is "a somewhat misleading expression, for it makes the enterprise sound too much like that of the cipher clerk *when it is much more like that of the literary critic*" (Geertz [1973] 2000, 9, emphasis mine). The upshot of the comparison between the literary critic and the ethnographer is a rigorous clarification of the status of anthropological knowledge as interpretative, and "second- and third-order . . . to boot" (19). Geertz has harsh words for those who would forget or elide the interpretative essence of anthropology: "To set forth symmetrical crystals of significance, purified of the material complexity in which they were located, and then attribute their existence to autogenous principles of order, universal properties of the human mind, or vast, a priori *weltanschauungen*, is to pretend a science that does not exist and imagine a reality that cannot be found" (20).

Despite his evident alertness to textuality and the critical difference it draws between "the object of study" and "the study of it" (Geertz [1973] 2000, 15), Geertz's own 1966 landmark essay on religion, "Religion as a Cultural System," becomes the target of Talal Asad's critique in "The Construction of Religion as an Anthropological Category" (originally published in 1983, and subsequently included in Asad's 1993 book *Genealogies of Religion*). In the 1966 text, Geertz had defined "religion" as "(1) a system of symbols which acts to (2) establish powerful, pervasive, and long-lasting moods and motivations in men by (3) formulating conceptions of a general order of existence and (4) clothing these conceptions with such an aura of factuality that (5) the moods and motivations seem uniquely realistic" (Geertz [1973] 2000, 90). Working through each step of this definition, Asad argues that Geertz reifies the "symbols" of religion, and the category of "religion" itself, by dehistoricizing them: "What appears to anthropologists today to be self-evident, namely that religion is essentially a matter of symbolic meanings linked to ideas of social order . . . that it has generic functions/features, and that it must not be confused with any of its particular historical or cultural forms, is in fact a view that has a specific Christian history" (Asad 1993, 42). Asad charges that Geertz's admirably thoroughgoing notion of "winks upon winks upon winks" nevertheless elides "the occurrence of events and the authorizing processes that give those events meaning and embody that meaning in concrete institutions" (43). In short, Geertz forecloses the question of *power*—that is, of how a given sign becomes a "religious symbol" as a result of historical acts of production, construction, and discipline. Even if we were to concede that Geertz's attribution of features and functions to the religious symbol is correct within a particular historical frame—and Asad certainly does *not* concede this—it would still be the case that the very idea of "religion" as a category with a transhistorical essence, an idea without which Geertz's argument in "Religion as a Cultural System" cannot get up and running in the first place, is produced historically through the operations of political force. Furthermore, it is just this historicity, this notion of "heterogeneous life (acting and being acted upon)," which the recourse to a synchronic idea of textuality erases (Asad 1993, 79; see also Ryan Coyne's chapter on "Memory" in this volume).

Importantly, though, Asad's critique of Geertz consists not in the jettisoning of textuality, but in historicizing the *use* of signs. He would have us account not just for the codes that allow the interpreting subject to tell winks from twitches, signs from wonders, literature from scripture, but also for how such distinctions discharge power across a social field. On this argument, the semiotic text is not inert, but rather dynamic, effective, material; it is something fashioned by the interpreter, who is enmeshed in the power relations constitutive of social life no less than the signs she interprets. Interpretation is a performative act of making and deploying knowledge in history—including the (second-order) category of "religion" itself. Still, this very insight is one afforded by semiotics; it would not have been possible without the concept of textuality. With Asad's contributions to the academic study of religion, we return to genealogy as Foucault theorized it: "operat[ing] . . . on a field of entangled and confused parchments, on documents that have been scratched over and recopied many times." As Foucault's imagery suggests, the genealogical approach does not mark the closure of textuality. It is a product of the textual epoch. It attends to the material traces of what had been minimized or invisible in semiotic readings, but it does not afford us access to historical things-in-themselves.

Conclusion: The Outside-the-Text

It was the immense achievement of scholars working in the wake of the semiotic and the genealogical texts, including Asad, to have recognized that reified concepts of *sui generis* "religion," "religious symbol," and "religious experience" could, and often did, function in scholarship as ideological lures holding out specious promises of presence, immediacy, and transcendence. In the first edition of *Critical Terms for Religious Studies*, Jonathan Z. Smith demonstrated that "'religion' is not a native term; it is a term created by scholars for their intellectual purposes and therefore is theirs to define. It is a second-order, generic concept that plays the same role in establishing a disciplinary horizon that a concept such as 'language' plays in linguistics or 'culture' plays in anthropology" (Smith 1998, 281–82). No religionist since has ever been allowed to forget Smith's lesson, but there is a concomitant risk of forgetting that Smith presents it via comparison; religion is not unique in this regard. This is an insight Smith would appear to have absorbed from the rise of "text" in the humanities and social sciences in the second half of the twentieth century: the objects we study never appear to us unmediated or uninterpreted.

The past two decades have witnessed a growing dissatisfaction with the limitations textuality imposes on intellectual inquiry. Such dissatisfaction, stirred in part by the excesses and the disciplinary hegemony of semiotic and genealogical modes of analysis, motivates various neo-pragmatist and post-humanist theories across the humanities and social sciences, as well as the increased interest, among scholars of religion, in lived religions and material culture. Yet this does not quite mean textuality has been disposed of or overcome. The salutary shift of attention to enchantment, materiality, and alterity—to phenomena and agencies that exceed the machinal grid of textuality—is still insistently textual inasmuch as such attention requires the interpretation of objects and the communication of interpretations. Furthermore, just as Asad notes that the anthropological category "religion" itself presumes a Christian history, so too does that Christian background register in recent polemical claims that scholarly discourse and/or its objects exist beyond textuality. In their valorization of presence and transcendence and their denigration of the modes of critique enabled by textuality, such claims potentially cast textuality as the killing letter, so that a methodological turn replays the Christian theological narrative of the supersession of Judaism.

Yet the rediscovery of all that the hegemony of the text has prevented us from recognizing need not be accompanied by a repetition of supersessionist theology. This will in fact be a task of religious studies in the coming years: vigilantly recalling, with Asad, their own discipline's genealogical imbrication in Christianity and/as coloniality, scholars of religion could instead hold their colleagues in the humanities and social sciences accountable for such relapses. Conceptual wrench in hand, religious studies in this sense would help to keep the academy's methodological screws from coming loose by returning to us the knowledge that even as we strive to apprehend the outside-the-text, the very notion of an outside-the-text is itself a product of the textual epoch we are still living out. "Text" names an ineluctable mediation constitutive of our objects, our discourse, and our selves; its implications are often frustrating or outright disturbing, but they are not, for all that, easily dismissed. The desire to be finished with textuality only reveals the extent to which textuality is not finished with us. And if remembering this in Derrida's terms (*il n'y a pas de hors-texte*) now seems too restrictive, too flattening, or too quietist, then we might instead adopt as our maxim a paraphrase of Franz Kafka: there is an outside-the-text—but not for us.

Suggested Readings

Asad, Talal. 1993. *Genealogies of Religion: Discipline and Reasons of Power in Christianity and Islam*. Baltimore, MD: The Johns Hopkins University Press.

Barthes, Roland. 1986 [1984]. *The Rustle of Language*. Translated by Richard Howard. New York: Hill & Wang.

Barton, John. 1996 [1984]. *Reading the Old Testament: Method in Biblical Study*. 2nd ed. Philadelphia, PA: Westminster John Knox Press.

Culler, Jonathan. 2007. "Text: Its Vicissitudes." In *The Literary in Theory*, 99–116. Stanford, CA: Stanford University Press.

De Man, Paul. 1983 [1970]. "Literary History and Literary Modernity." In *Blindness and Insight: Essays in the Rhetoric of Contemporary Criticism*, 2nd ed., 142–65. Minneapolis: University of Minnesota Press.

De Man, Paul. [1976] 1979. "Promises (*Social Contract*)." In *Allegories of Reading: Figural Language in Rousseau, Nietzsche, Rilke, Proust*, 246–277. New Haven, CT: Yale University Press.

Derrida, Jacques. [1971] 1988. "Signature Event Context." In *Limited Inc*, translated by Jeffrey Mehlman and Samuel Weber, edited by Gerald Graff. Evanston, IL: Northwestern University Press.

Derrida, Jacques. [1967] 1997. *Of Grammatology*. Translated by Gayatri Chakravorty Spivak. 2nd ed. Baltimore, MD: The Johns Hopkins University Press.

Foucault, Michel. 1998. *Aesthetics, Method, and Epistemology*. Edited by James D. Faubion. New York: The New Press.

Geertz, Clifford. [1973] 2000. *The Interpretation of Cultures*. New York: Basic Books.

Geoghegan, Bernard Dionysius. 2023. *Code: From Information Theory to French Theory*. Durham, NC: Duke University Press.

Gumbrecht, Hans Ulrich. 2003. *The Powers of Philology: Dynamics of Textual Scholarship*. Champaign: University of Illinois Press.

Jameson, Fredric. [1988] 2008. "The Ideology of the Text." In *The Ideologies of Theory*, 20–76. London: Verso Books.

Kristeva, Julia. 1980. *Desire in Language: A Semiotic Approach to Literature and Art*. Translated by Thomas Gora, Alice Jardine, and Leon S. Roudiez. Edited by Leon S. Roudiez. New York: Columbia University Press.

McGann, Jerome J. 1991. *The Textual Condition*. Princeton, NJ: Princeton University Press.

Mowitt, John. 1992. *Text: The Genealogy of an Antidisciplinary Object*. Durham, NC: Duke University Press.

Said, Edward W. [1975] 1983. "The World, the Text, and the Critic." In *The World, the Text, and the Critic*, 31–53. Cambridge, MA: Harvard University Press.

Turner, James. 2014. *Philology: The Forgotten Origins of the Modern Humanities*. Princeton, NJ: Princeton University Press.

References

Asad, Talal. 1993. *Genealogies of Religion: Discipline and Reasons of Power in Christianity and Islam*. Baltimore, MD: The Johns Hopkins University Press.

Auerbach, Erich. [1946] 2003. *Mimesis: The Representation of Reality in Western Literature*. Translated by Willard R. Trask. 50th anniversary ed. Princeton, NJ: Princeton University Press.

Barthes, Roland. [1984] 1986. *The Rustle of Language*. Translated by Richard Howard. New York: Hill & Wang.

Berlin, Adele. 1982. "On the Bible as Literature." *Prooftexts* 2 (3): 323–327.

Boyarin, Daniel. 1990. *Intertextuality and the Reading of Midrash*. Bloomington: Indiana University Press.

Brod, Max. 1954. *Franz Kafka: eine Biographie*. Berlin: S. Fischer Verlag.

Culler, Jonathan. 2007. *The Literary in Theory*. Stanford, CA: Stanford University Press.

Derrida, Jacques. [1971] 1988. "Signature Event Context." In *Limited Inc*, translated by Jeffrey Mehlman and Samuel Weber, edited by Gerald Graff, 1–24. Evanston, IL: Northwestern University Press.

Derrida, Jacques. [1967] 1997. *Of Grammatology*. Translated by Gayatri Chakravorty Spivak. 2nd ed. Baltimore, MD: The Johns Hopkins University Press.

"Editorial Statement." 2005. *Material Religion* 1 (1): 4–8.

Foucault, Michel. [1971] 1998. "Nietzsche, Genealogy, History." Translated by Donald F. Brouchard and Sherry Simon. In Michel Foucault, *Aesthetics, Method, and Epistemology*, edited by James D. Faubion, 369–391. New York: The New Press.

Geertz, Clifford. 1983. *Local Knowledge: Further Essays in Interpretive Anthropology*. New York: Basic Books.

Geertz, Clifford. [1973] 2000. *The Interpretation of Cultures*. 2nd ed. New York: Basic Books.

Gill, Sam. 1998. "Territory." In *Critical Terms for Religious Studies*, edited by Mark C. Taylor, 298–313. Chicago: University of Chicago Press.

Gunkel, Hermann. 1928. *What Remains of the Old Testament and Other Essays*. Translated by A. K. Dallas. New York: Macmillan.

Jameson, Fredric. [1988] 2008. *The Ideologies of Theory*. 2nd ed. London: Verso Books.

Johnson, Barbara. 1995. "Writing." In *Critical Terms for Literary Study*, edited by Frank Lentricchia and Thomas McLaughlin, 2nd ed., 39–49. Chicago: University of Chicago Press.

Jones-Katz, Gregory. 2021. *Deconstruction: An American Institution*. Chicago: University of Chicago Press.

Legaspi, Michael C. 2010. *The Death of Scripture and the Rise of Biblical Studies*. Oxford: Oxford University Press.

Mowitt, John. 1992. *Text: The Genealogy of an Antidisciplinary Object*. Durham, NC: Duke University Press.

Nietzsche, Friedrich. 1967 ff. *Digitale Kritische Gesamtausgabe Werke und Briefe*. Based on the critical text by Giorgio Colli and Mazzino Montinari, edited by Paolo d'Iorio. *Nietzsche Source*, accessed August 5, 2022. http://www.nietzschesource.org/#eKGWB.

Saussure, Ferdinand de. [1916] 1986. *Course in General Linguistics*. Translated by Roy Harris. Chicago: Open Court Press.

Smith, Jonathan Z. 1998. "Religion, Religions, Religious." In *Critical Terms for Religious Studies*, edited by Mark C. Taylor, 269–84. Chicago: University of Chicago Press. Reprinted in 2004 in Jonathan Z. Smith, *Relating Religion: Essays in the Study of Religion*. Chicago: University of Chicago Press.

Sternberg, Meir. 1985. *The Poetics of Biblical Narrative: Ideological Literature and the Drama of Reading*. Bloomington: Indiana University Press.

Acknowledgments

It has been a long road, but in the seven years it has taken to bring this volume from possibility to reality, Kyle Wagner has been an ideal editor, advocate, and advisor from start to finish. He believed I was the right person to lead it even when I was somewhat incredulous. Without his faith, encouragement, and insight, it would not have come to fruition. I am grateful to the readers of the proposal and manuscript for their invaluable reports. They approached the project with seriousness and insight and gave feedback that influenced the shape and vision of the book. The production editor, Elizabeth Ellingboe, made the editing process painless, and the copyeditor, Evan Young, was patient and meticulous in clearing up an array of oversights. Working with the writers whose essays appear here was its own reward. I feel lucky to have such brilliant colleagues in the field. Thanks go to my two research assistants: Livia Bokor and Mukti Patel. Livia was indispensable. Not only did she keep me on top of the process, her incisiveness, clarity, and generosity made it a better book. Mukti contributed in the final stages of submission, and I counted on her attention to detail and organizational acumen. I am grateful to everyone who served at one time on the advisory board, including Cassie Adcock and Aisha Beliso-De Jesús (who had to withdraw from the project because of other commitments), for their time, insight, support, and feedback. I owe an additional shout-out to Amy Hollywood and Constance Furey, my dear friends, role models, and advisors, who talked me through every up and down of the book's progress over the years. Thanks go to my students and teaching assistants who read the volume's introduction and who sat through my lectures on the fetish. My daughter, the wise Lila Coyne, was a patient listener and source of advice on both intellectual and political matters related to the book. Finally, Ryan, the extraordinary gift of having you as a companion in life *and* thought is never lost on me.

Contributors

DAN ARNOLD is professor at the University of Chicago Divinity School. He is the author of *Buddhists, Brahmins, and Belief: Epistemology in South Asian Philosophy of Religion* (Columbia University Press, 2005), and of *Brains, Buddhas, and Believing: The Problem of Intentionality in Classical Buddhist and Cognitive-Scientific Philosophy of Mind* (Columbia, 2012).

SAMUEL P. CATLIN is the Irving M. and Marilyn C. Shuman Visiting Assistant Professor of Jewish Thought at the University at Buffalo, SUNY. His writing on topics including religious hermeneutics and literary theory, secularism, and the history of American higher education has appeared or is forthcoming in *Prooftexts*, *Naharaim*, *Oxford Bibliographies in Jewish Studies*, *Parapraxis*, and elsewhere.

RYAN COYNE is associate professor of the philosophy of religions and theology at the University of Chicago Divinity School. He is the author of *Heidegger's Confessions: The Remains of Saint Augustine in* Being and Time *and Beyond* (University of Chicago Press, 2015). He studies modern European philosophy and the history of Christian thought, with special attention to phenomenology, hermeneutics, psychoanalysis, and deconstruction.

ELEANOR CRAIG is a provost's postdoctoral fellow at Emory University in East Asian studies and women's, gender, and sexuality studies. They write about race, gender, coloniality, and religion through literary and philosophical methods. They are co-editor of *Beyond Man: Race, Coloniality, and*

Philosophy of Religion (Duke University Press, 2021) and special issues of *Political Theology* and *Representations*.

ALIREZA DOOSTDAR is associate professor of Islamic studies and the anthropology of religion at the University of Chicago Divinity School. He is the author of *The Iranian Metaphysicals: Explorations in Science, Islam, and the Uncanny* (Princeton University Press, 2018) and articles on Islam, politics, and popular culture. He is also co-creator of a YouTube video series titled *Gaming Islam*.

BENJAMIN H. DUNNING is Florence Corliss Lamont Professor of Divinity and professor of New Testament and early Christianity at Harvard Divinity School. He is the author of *Aliens and Sojourners: Self as Other in Early Christianity* (University of Pennsylvania Press, 2009), *Specters of Paul: Sexual Difference in Early Christian Thought* (UPenn Press, 2011), and *Christ without Adam: Subjectivity and Sexual Difference in the Philosophers' Paul* (Columbia University Press, 2014) and editor of *The Oxford Handbook of New Testament, Gender, and Sexuality* (Oxford University Press, 2019).

MATTHEW ENGELKE is professor and chair of the Department of Religion at Columbia University. He is the author of three books: *A Problem of Presence: Beyond Scripture in an African Church* (University of California Press, 2007), which won the 2008 Clifford Geertz Prize and the 2009 Victor Turner Prize; *God's Agents: Biblical Publicity in Contemporary England* (California, 2013); and, most recently, *How to Think Like an Anthropologist* (Princeton University Press, 2018).

CONSTANCE M. FUREY is Ruth N. Halls Professor of Religious Studies at Indiana University Bloomington. She is the author of *Erasmus, Contarini, and the Religious Republic of Letters* (Cambridge University Press, 2006) and *Poetic Relations: Intimacy and Faith in the English Reformation* (University of Chicago Press, 2016); co-author of *Devotion: Three Inquiries in Religion, Literature, and Political Imagination* (Chicago, 2022); and co-founder of the Center for Religion and the Human as well as the Teaching Religion in Public project.

SARAH HAMMERSCHLAG is the John Nuveen Professor at the University of Chicago Divinity School. She is the author of *The Figural Jew: Politics and Identity in Postwar French Thought* (University of Chicago Press, 2010) and

Broken Tablets: Levinas, Derrida and the Literary Afterlife of Religion (Columbia University Press, 2016), co-author of *Devotion: Three Inquiries in Religion, Literature, and Political Imagination* (Chicago, 2022), and editor of *Modern French Jewish Thought: Writings on Religion and Politics* (Brandeis University Press, 2018).

NICHOLAS HARKNESS is the Modern Korean Economy and Society Professor of Anthropology and director of the Korea Institute at Harvard University. He is the author of *Songs of Seoul: An Ethnography of Voice and Voicing in Christian South Korea* (University of California Press, 2014) and *Glossolalia and the Problem of Language* (University of Chicago Press, 2021), as well as numerous papers in linguistic and semiotic anthropology.

AMY HOLLYWOOD is the Elizabeth H. Monrad Professor of Christian Studies at Harvard Divinity School. She is the author of *The Soul as Virgin Wife: Mechthild of Magdeburg, Marguerite Porete, and Meister Eckhart* (University of Notre Dame Press, 1995); *Sensible Ecstasy: Mysticism, Sexual Difference, and the Demands of History* (University of Chicago Press, 2002); and *Acute Melancholia and Other Essays* (Columbia University Press, 2016). She is also the co-editor, with Patricia Beckman, of *The Cambridge Companion to Christian Mysticism* (Cambridge University Press, 2012) and, with Eleanor Craig, Niklaus Largier, and Kris Trujillo, of a special issue of *Representations*, "The Poetics of Prayer and Devotion to Literature" (2021). She is also the co-author of *Devotion: Three Inquiries on Religion, Literature, and Political Imagination* (Chicago, 2022).

SARAH IMHOFF is Jay and Jeanie Schottenstein Chair in Jewish Studies and professor in the Department of Religious Studies and the Borns Jewish Studies Program at Indiana University Bloomington. She is author of *Masculinity and the Making of American Judaism* (Indiana University Press, 2017) and *The Lives of Jessie Sampter: Queer, Disabled, Zionist* (Duke University Press, 2022). She is also the founding co-editor of the journal *American Religion*.

ANDREA R. JAIN is professor of religious studies at Indiana University Indianapolis, editor of the *Journal of the American Academy of Religion*, and author of *Selling Yoga: From Counterculture to Pop Culture* (Oxford University Press, 2014) and *Peace Love Yoga: The Politics of Global Spirituality* (Oxford, 2020). She writes about capitalism, religion, sex, and society in our contemporary world.

TERRENCE L. JOHNSON is the Charles G. Adams Professor of African American Religious Studies at Harvard Divinity School. He is a faculty associate of the Edmond & Lily Safra Center for Ethics and affiliate faculty of the Program in American Studies. He is the author of *Blacks and Jews in America: An Invitation to Dialogue* (Georgetown University Press, 2022, with Jacques Berlinerblau), winner in 2023 of the Association for Ethnic Studies Outstanding Book Award; *We Testify with Our Lives: How Religion Transformed Radical Thought from Black Power to Black Lives Matter* (Columbia University Press, 2021); and *Tragic Soul-Life: W. E. B. Du Bois and the Moral Crisis Facing American Democracy* (Oxford University Press, 2012).

NANCY KHALEK is associate professor of religious studies and history at Brown University in Providence, Rhode Island. She has researched and written about medieval Islamic history and historiography, late antiquity and early Islam, material culture in the medieval Islamic world, and most recently, on the history of emotion and medieval Muslim piety. She is the author of *Damascus After the Muslim Conquest: Text and Image in Early Islam* (Oxford University Press, 2011).

KATHRYN LOFTON is Lex Hixon Professor of Religious Studies and American Studies and professor of history and divinity at Yale University. She is the author of *Oprah: The Gospel of an Icon* (University of California Press, 2011), *Consuming Religion* (University of Chicago Press, 2017), and with Laurie Maffly-Kipp, *Women's Work: An Anthology of African-American Women's Historical Writings from Antebellum America to the Harlem Renaissance* (Oxford University Press, 2010).

LEVI MCLAUGHLIN is professor in the Department of Philosophy and Religious Studies at North Carolina State University. He is co-author of *Kōmeitō: Politics and Religion in Japan* (IEAS Berkeley, 2014) and author of *Soka Gakkai's Human Revolution: The Rise of a Mimetic Nation in Modern Japan* (University of Hawai'i Press, 2019; in Japanese from Kodansha, 2024), as well as numerous book chapters and articles on disaster, religion, politics, and other topics.

RAFAEL RACHEL NEIS is professor of history and Judaic studies at the University of Michigan. They are the author of *The Sense of Sight in Rabbinic Culture: Jewish Ways of Seeing in Late Antiquity* (Cambridge University Press, 2013), which won the Salo Baron prize for the best first book in Jewish Studies; and *When a Human Gives Birth to a Raven: Rabbis and the Reproduction of Species* (University of California Press, 2023).

ELIZABETH PÉREZ is associate professor of religious studies at the University of California, Santa Barbara. Her first book, *Religion in the Kitchen: Cooking, Talking, and the Making of Black Atlantic Traditions* (New York University Press, 2016), was awarded the 2017 Clifford Geertz Prize in the Anthropology of Religion. Her second book, *The Gut: A Black Atlantic Alimentary Tract* (Cambridge University Press, 2023), received the 2024 Leonard Norman Primiano Book Prize on Vernacular Catholicism.

JAMES ROBSON is the James C. Kralik and Yunli Lou Professor of East Asian Languages and Civilizations at Harvard University and the Victor and William Fung Director of the Harvard University Asia Center. He is the author of the *Power of Place: The Religious Landscape of the Southern Sacred Peak [Nanyue 南嶽] in Medieval China* (Harvard University Press, 2009), which was awarded the Stanislas Julien Prize by the Académie des Inscriptions et Belles-Lettres and the Toshihide Numata Prize in Buddhist Studies. He is the editor of the *Norton Anthology of World Religions: Daoism* (W. W. Norton & Company, 2015) and author of the forthcoming *The Daodejing: A Biography*. He is the co-editor of *Images, Relics and Legends–The Formation and Transformation of Buddhist Sacred Sites* and *Buddhist Monasticism in East Asia: Places of Practice* (Mosaic Press, 2012).

MARY-JANE RUBENSTEIN is dean of the social sciences and professor of religion and science and technology studies at Wesleyan University. She is author of numerous books on the intersections of science and religion, including *Worlds Without End: The Many Lives of the Multiverse* (Columbia University Press, 2015), *Pantheologies: Gods, Worlds, and Monsters* (Columbia, 2018), and *Astrotopia: The Dangerous Religion of the Corporate Space Race* (University of Chicago Press, 2022).

NOAH SALOMON is Irfan and Noreen Galaria Research Chair and associate professor in Islamic studies in the Department of Religious Studies at the

University of Virginia. He is the author of *For Love of the Prophet: An Ethnography of Sudan's Islamic State* (Princeton University Press, 2016) as well as numerous articles on the intersections of religious criticism, political aesthetics, and Islamic practice in contemporary Africa and the Middle East. From 2018 to 2023, Salomon was a Mellon Foundation New Directions Fellow, circulating between Beirut, Khartoum, and Muscat, exploring Islamic modes of performing, managing, and negotiating difference, particularly at inflection points of social and political change.

CHRISTOPHER G. WHITE is professor of religion at Vassar College. He is the author of *Unsettled Minds: Psychology and the American Search for Spiritual Assurance* (University of California Press, 2008) and *Other Worlds: Spirituality and the Search for Invisible Dimensions* (Harvard University Press, 2018), which won a "best book" prize from the International Society for Science and Religion. He teaches and writes about science, spirituality, media, and popular culture.

Index

GOD'S HOMECOMING

The Forgotten Promise of Future Renewal

N. T. WRIGHT

HarperCollins books may be purchased for educational, business, or sales promotional use. For information, please email the Special Markets Department at SPsales@harpercollins.com.

harpercollins.com

FIRST EDITION

Designed by Michele Cameron

Library of Congress Cataloging-in-Publication Data has been applied for.

ISBN 978-0-06-256417-7

Printed in the United States of America

26 27 28 29 30 LBC 6 5 4 3 2